ETHICS
in CRIMINAL JUSTICE

In Search of the Truth

Sam S. Souryal

Sam Houston State University

5 FIFTH EDITION

AMSTERDAM • BOSTON • HEIDELBERG • LONDON
NEW YORK • OXFORD • PARIS • SAN DIEGO
SAN FRANCISCO • SINGAPORE • SYDNEY • TOKYO

Anderson Publishing is an imprint of Elsevier

ELSEVIER

Anderson Publishing is an imprint of Elsevier
30 Corporate Drive, Suite 400, Burlington, MA 01803, USA

Library of Congress Cataloging-in-Publication Data
Application submitted

British Library Cataloguing-in-Publication Data
A catalogue record for this book is available from the British Library.

ISBN: 978-1-4377-5590-9

Printed in the United States of America
11 12 13 14 15 10 9 8 7 6 5 4 3 2 1

For information on all Anderson publications
visit our website at www.elsevierdirect.com

In memory of Dr. T. Henry Souryal, my mentor, my friend, and my brother. He was not ours and he was not mine. He was a gift from God who succeeded a little bit in making the world a little better and when he was finished, he silently yet gallantly went Home.

FOREWORD

At the heart of every social institution is at least one paradox. The paradox of the criminal justice system is the working assumption that good will result from punishment. This idea, a perversion of the philosophic utilitarianism of Mill and Bentham that shaped Anglo American criminal law, substitutes ex post facto retribution for prevention, policy for reasoning, and organizational culture for human concern. To conceal such paradoxes, mystifying ideologies are produced and reproduced. Thus, in the American criminal justice system a deep and pervasive common belief obtains that pragmatism and diverse forms of expediency are the only principles available. This argument appears in many guises: from the cynical view that "nothing works," to the intellectually flawed presumption that IQ and/or some pattern of genes create "criminals" or "career criminals." Perhaps the most irresponsible guise is the argument urging still more of the same; that is, more prisons, more police, more courts, and more lawyers. Such arguments strongly suggest that our goals are obscured and our purposes lost.

Not only is there a paradox at the heart of the system, but the system also manifests patterned anarchy. Martha Feldman (1989) aptly calls this "order without design." This means simply that a system with no overall design can work. The idea that a criminal justice system exists by design, and that it is held together by laws, flowcharts, algorithms, dispositions, and outcomes, is a relatively recent conceit. It is yet to be proven what common values and purposes, other than communicating itself (Luhmann, 1985), bind together this notional system. Perhaps the subsystems are articulated around negotiations over particular cases, shaped by dramaturgical principles of "looking good" and "maintaining respect," and governed by a self-sustaining wish to produce and reproduce uncertainty in "outposts." These "rules of thumb" reflect expediency, pragmatism, and sensitivity to a local political order. This state of affairs, according to Souryal, can and should be altered if one takes ethical principles seriously.

The arguments found in this book, presented in an admirably clear prose style, are courageous and refreshing principles. Souryal urges readers to consider basic ideas and their applications. A humanist, he sees most laws as good, yet people as flawed. They are not "flawed" in the intrinsic sense of lacking redemption, but rather are ignorant of their own potential and of the essential entailments of humanity. He argues that the humanistic and philosophic bases for decisions be taught explicitly. Although I am sympathetic with this notion, I despair at times. I once asked a criminology class of nearly 200 how many had read Albert Camus, *The Stranger* (3); *Crime and Punishment* (5); and how many knew (anything) about the theater of the absurd or surrealism (2). In this vacuous context, how does one critically discuss issues of punishment, of rationality, of the kinds of evil best punished by criminal laws? Unfortunately, I do not consider this ignorance anomalous on modern campuses. If one assumes, as Souryal does, that the humanistic mandate of the social sciences, reflected in the field of criminal justice, is an essential grounding of all serious moral argumentation and enterprise, then the systematic teaching of ethics and ethical questions should have a primary role in any criminal justice curriculum.

Souryal pleads for a humanity entailing a measure of goodness, tolerance, and compassion. He is sensitive to the paradox previously noted, and argues that the way in which the state treats the evil and ignoble is essentially revealing. He urges noble treatment of the ignoble. This may be stated in yet another fashion that builds on the relationship between the self and the other. The criminal, the sick, the ignorant, the mad and sad, and the omnipresent other are essential, for they provide the mirror of ourselves. The others are, metaphorically speaking, the screen upon which dances our selves, dances our often denied and suppressed passions, pain, and failures. The other, at best, represents our choices and our negations. When the United States government wages war to "liberate Afghanistan" and causes thousands of Afghan deaths as a result of "collateral damage," while denying the crying needs of the inner cities of this country, it is making a choice, displaying a value, and casting a vote. Who is the relevant other? What other is denied?

This book advances a thematic perspective with area-specific guidance for ethical decisions in criminal justice. The quest is surely an ambitious one: shaping a "collective conscience" or "soul" for the discipline of criminal justice. This concept of a soul—a powerful metaphor that combines action, thought, and feelings—if developed, will facilitate balancing: sustaining basic values, while enabling change; encouraging technological innovations, while resisting dehumanization; seeking policy changes and rewarding critical self-renewal and reflection. One inference from Souryal's work is that the core idea essential to "soul-building" is self-reflexivity and critical self-evaluation. Drawn from Souryal's review of ethics from the early Greeks to John Rawls, this idea is consistent with the notion that the criminal justice system sustains an "ambivalent reality." Souryal believes that fundamental ethical clarity will reduce the salience of the "root sins" of lying, prejudice, and abuse of authority.

In this and in other ways, this is a courageous book. In arguing for the utility of ethics, Souryal also implies the failure of the policy sciences and public administration approaches that have long shaped criminal justice. These approaches have failed for a variety of reasons, not the least of which is the inability of combining a public administration approach appropriate for some reformist (largely western American) cities with the political organizing approach needed in other developing cities (in the South and Southwest) and the aging and politicized cities along the eastern seaboard. The politics of policing differ in these environments, and therefore policing differs. Nor can vague democratic values alone guide the criminal justice system (nor criminal justice practice). History shows that these values have been used to rationalize fighting wars in several continents since World War II, sending troops to South America to enforce U.S. drug laws, sustaining slavery and segregated education, justifying capital punishment as not cruel and inhumane, and rationalizing governmental terrorism in inner cities in the name of a "war on drugs." Although the "sciences of justice" possess scientific methods and techniques, science—and even criminology, the study of the logic of crime—remains a small but important aspect of criminal justice. Finally, very little effort has been given to clarifying the meaning of justice itself. There is more interest in the criminal than in justice in American criminal justice research.

In the last 25 years, criminal justice education has been increasingly scientific, methods driven, technologically preoccupied, and pragmatic in focus. Think of some of the recent research questions that have surfaced: "Can we control police shootings?" "Can we create a minimum sentencing grid?" "How can we increase the amount of available medical care in prisons?" "How can we better educate the police?" "How can one reduce calls to the police?" "How can we increase the arrests of drug users?" "Can electronic surveillance reduce the costs of parole supervision?" These are short-term questions, shaped by federal research agendas and the local political order. They obscure the questions of the purpose of such research, the intent in "solving" them, and the intended direction of social change. Tactical thinking is characteristic of emerging organizations just developing their sense of purpose and philosophic rationale.

What options remain? Clearly, most practitioners in the system believe that they can do little else than "fight fires" and "keep the ship afloat." Externally sponsored reform without a clear ethical position and a principled purpose is often self-serving and self-deceptive. It rarely takes into account the unanticipated consequences of short-term and expedient actions. It begs questions of justice, the sought-for quality of life, and the political and moral foci of such efforts. Perhaps long-term goals are inconsistent with such short-term tactical efforts, for they require a paradigm within which to consider the consequences of one's actions. This does not presently exist. For example, good evidence suggests that contact with the criminal justice system in any form tends to amplify "deviance." How can the arrest of teenagers for school absences, spouses for violence against a spouse, DARE programs in schools, criminalizing drinking and driving, and longer and more severe sentences reduce crime? Are crime-control blitzes in inner cities mere expediency, or do they predict a rising use of the criminal sanction against lifestyles and minority preferences?

Such observations, my own reflections on the ambivalent reality of the American criminal justice system, lead me to advancing an idea consistent with Souryal's suggestions. If the purpose of crime control is increased justice and an enhanced sense of justice, then justice-seeking ought be governed by ethical principles. Something like "Do unto others ..." seems a reasonable idea. It is at least possible that the "others" typically conceived of in public policy statements are not the others found in us, deeply embedded parts of us, but are a denied and projected, strange and inhuman other who can be brutalized with impunity in the name of law, the state, or authority of some kind. This raises again the paradox: how to combine the application of force and striving toward doing good.

The book is based upon philosophic humanism, ethical analysis, and the study of history. Souryal raises many questions, perhaps more than he can answer. Unfortunately, I would like to conclude by raising a further query. Perhaps the idea of deterrence should be reconsidered. Our current notions of deterrence and incapacitation are based on eighteenth- and nineteenth-century philosophies about motivation and choice, such as (a) people are guided in the present by anticipation of the future consequences of their actions; (b) people have a stake in conformity to the current social order; (c) people are willing to carefully reflect upon and weigh their choices; (d) a governing philosophic calculus guides these choices; (e) a limited pool of lawbreakers exists. Those caught are deterred, and those who are not caught will be deterred by awareness of the punishment of lawbreakers.

There are serious difficulties in this position. In the first instance, Jack Gibbs's (1975) review of the problems associated with the concept of deterrence and its conceptual vagaries is devastating. Unfortunately, the concept is still used in research in an ad hoc fashion. Furthermore, ethnographies, biographies, and autobiographies suggest that it is unlikely that these tenets apply to our financial leaders on Wall Street or people on the streets of Detroit, Boston, or Miami. Do they explain the actions of lawyers and judges weighing decisions? Do these ideas explain the actions of the executives of Exxon, General Motors, environmental activist groups, McDonald's, and those running the savings and loans? Perhaps

John Braithwaite (1989) is correct when he argues that fear of being shamed and making public restitution are more powerful forces shaping behavior than imagined punishment.

The paradox remains: Can violence be applied ethically? Can one be educated in such principles? Today we are educating tomorrow's leaders. Will these students reflect, develop principles and ethical standards, and evaluate themselves against ideas presented here? Can they analyze an ethical argument to spot the flaws and self-deceptions built into it? Will ethics shape the criminal justice professions? A tentative first step toward considering these questions in the depth Souryal urges is to read this rather challenging and, at times, passionate book.

P.K. Manning
Boston
2010

PREFACE

Despite advances in the legal and technological aspects of criminal justice, practitioners continue to face difficult moral choices. These include whether to arrest, use deadly force, prosecute, offer plea bargaining, impose punishment, and from an organizational standpoint, whether to comply with policy, cooperate with supervisors, or treat the public equitably. As in other public service sectors where discretion is essential, individual and institutional ethics become major vectors. Surprisingly, while the consequences of such choices continue to cause great public anguish, the moral grounds for these choices have seldom been examined.

In a free society, issues of crime and punishment are perhaps the most deserving of the moral imperative of justice—a quality the state must extend freely to the guilty and the innocent alike. Moral behaviors need no validation by the state, because they constitute justice unto themselves. It is in responding to immoral behaviors that civilized governments cannot rightfully employ immoral means. Succinctly stated, the more civilized the state, the more willing it is to address the "worst in us" by the "noble means" available.

The purpose of this book is not to question the value of the law as the primary instrument of criminal justice, but to present ethics as an "umbrella of civility" under which the law can be more meaningful, rational, and obeyable. By way of analogy, if the law is compared to the Old Testament, ethics is comparable to the New Testament. They complement each other, making Christianity blissful and tolerable. This view of ethics may not impress hardened practitioners who believe that we only "live by the law" but forget that we also "die by the law." By the same token, this view may not enthuse students who are so enamored with the trimmings of criminal justice so as to overlook its noble substance. To both of these groups, there is one rational reply: "No one is free until we can see the truth of what we are seeking." Without capturing the truths of criminal justice, we are left with images that may be not only irrational, but also disgraceful.

This book rejects the cynical view that ethical knowledge and moral character are peripheral to the administration of justice. Indeed, every conduct in the administration of justice is directed either by the moral of a rule or policy, or by the moral judgment of the practitioner who implements it. Furthermore, the obligation to "establishing justice and insuring domestic tranquility" continues to be the central force behind any act of criminal justice. Therefore, without a fresh look at our weaknesses, biases, and prejudices, the young discipline of criminal justice will grow into a degenerative field; more like a temple without a god, a body without a soul, and a theory without a meaning.

In this book students and practitioners will be introduced to the fundamentals of ethical theory, doctrines, and controversies, and the rules of moral judgment. They will be exposed to the ways and means of making moral judgment—but not in specific situations. That is beyond the capacity of any book, and must be left to the minds and hearts of the well-informed practitioner. Knowledge will be presented in two forms: (1) a thematic perspective, which will examine ethical principles common to all components of the discipline, such as wisdom, goodness, morality, and justice, as well as the common vices of deception, racial prejudice, and egoism; and (2) an area-specific perspective, which will address the state of ethics in policing, corrections, and probation and parole.

Every academic discipline or professional field is born an infant and slowly grows into maturity. In the process, practitioners test its limits, establish its boundaries, and legitimize its claims. During the maturation process serious excesses and failures appear that create contradiction between the goals of the field and the means by which objectives are to be met. In attempting to reason away contradiction, an introspection usually emerges urging caution, denouncing falsity, and searching for the truth. This introspection gradually hardens, constituting the collective conscience of the discipline—its soul. Eventually, the soul becomes instrumental in halting intellectual ostentation, in exposing fallacies, and in reaffirming basic values. This collective conscience keeps a vigilant eye whenever new technology is introduced or a major policy shift is inaugurated. In time, the membership of the discipline or field comes to recognize that collective conscience and call it by its true name: professional ethics.

The field of criminal justice is certainly young, but not too distant from maturity. It lacks a unifying philosophy that can give it autonomy and inner strength. Primary issues of crime and justice still beg for clarification. Secondary issues continue to frustrate rationality; for instance, the role of the police in maintaining order, the role of prosecutors in controlling entry into the system, the role of judges in dominating the sentencing process, the role of victims in reclaiming the central court of justice, and the role of lawbreakers in sabotaging the system by ingenious means. All such claims compete in an environment of ambiguity, egoism, and fear. The resulting picture is a mosaic of incoherence and lack of scruples. Consequently, the field has not proven successful beyond mere survival. Its efficacy has been questioned both from within, by its officials, and from without, by its users. Few artificial reforms have been introduced in the area of criminal justice management, the field's most logical instrument of reform. Top management is often controlled by a syndicate of lobbying bureaucrats who lack integrative thinking and, at times, the tenacity to reason away simple problems. Middle managers are unwitting brokers who "dance on the stairway"; they are as hesitant to face those at the top as they are reluctant to confront those at the bottom. Frontline workers operate as an army of "apparatchiks," or functionaries. They suffer from bureaucratic fatigue, a disturbing subculture, and a confused view of reality.

The introspective voice of ethics in criminal justice is yet to be heard louder and louder as the comforting shriek of a first-born infant heralds the coming of age of his parents. Until it is, criminal justice will continue to be perceived with uneasiness and suspicion.

With these well-intended thoughts, this work is dedicated to the better understanding of ethics—the indestructible soul of criminal justice.

Sam S. Souryal
Huntsville, Texas
2010

ACKNOWLEDGMENTS

Inspiration for this book came from my students. Precisely, it came from undergraduates who were dedicated to the ideals of criminal justice, yet were dismayed by its image. They could not comprehend the "schizophrenic ballad" of criminal justice: How could it be that criminal justice practitioners serve such a "noble cause," yet many of them are accused—and, worse still, found guilty—of so much injustice, cruelty, and acts of corruption?

In my early years of teaching, I responded to my students' skepticism by naively suggesting that the problem was inadequate control. So I wrote about discipline, supervision, and other administrative tools. In later years, I also naively thought that the problem was lack of guidance. So, I wrote about motivation, leadership, job enrichment, and similar managerial tools. In recent years it became apparent to me that while administration and management have a major role to play, the "schizophrenic ballad" of criminal justice is the product of the ethical indifference of practitioners, especially those who claim to be administrators and managers. While many of these may appear to be efficient, effective, eloquent, and polished, in reality many may still be dishonest and immoral.

Criminal justice is essentially a moral function, and professional criminal justice agencies must operate in an environment of moral values. When these values are internalized in the soul of practitioners, agencies flourish in professionalism and decency, and when they are not, they sink in the toxicity of corruption and decay. In the latter case, the situation can be reversed only through a Herculean effort by conscientious practitioners and administrators who possess the moral fortitude to stem the tide and restore institutional morality.

The intellectual guidance offered by the works of John Kleinig, Sissela Bok, Peter Manning, Samuel Walker, Herman Goldstein, Charles Friel, and Michael Braswell was instrumental in treating this difficult subject. I quoted them frequently and liberally. I wish I were able to read their minds, to penetrate their reasoning, and to engage them in the dialectics of crime, justice, and ethical values. If I erred, however, in responding to their challenges, only my passion for justice is to blame.

My thanks are due to all those who assisted in this project, especially Gerald Jones (the constant skeptic), George Eisenberg (the interpreter of history), Adam Trahan (the silent enhancer), and Dennis Potts (the outspoken critic, the kind every doctoral program should have—and keep!). They painstakingly read several drafts of this manuscript and provided me with invaluable insights into the workings of many criminal justice agencies with which I was barely familiar. Dennis Potts, in particular, was concerned about making this book "more friendly." I am glad I did not take his advice, because too many friendly books remain on the shelf. Perhaps that is also a reason why Mr. Potts—who had left academe when the first edition appeared—has recently returned! I owe a very special thanks to Elisabeth Roszmann Ebben, my editor at Elsevier/Anderson Publishing. She has been helpful, patient, and always a joy to work with.

CONTENTS

Chapter 2
Familiarizing Yourself with Ethics
Nature, Definitions, and Categories   45

Chapter 3
Understanding Criminal Justice Ethics
Sources and Sanctions   81

Chapter 4
Meeting the Masters
Ethical Theories, Concepts, and Issues   **117**

Chapter 5
The Ambivalent Reality
Major Unethical Themes in Criminal Justice Management 193

Chapter 6
Lying and Deception in Criminal Justice   217

Chapter 7
Racial Prejudice and Racial Discrimination   235

Chapter 8
Egoism and the Abuse of Authority
269

Chapter 10
Ethics of Criminal Justice Today
What Is Being Done and What Can Be Done?   333

Chapter 11
Ethics and Police   345

Chapter 15
What Can Be Done to Restore Ethics?
Concluding Comments   **481**

Name Index   **485**

Subject Index   **493**

On the Virtues of Man

Three monkeys sat in a coconut tree
Discussing things as they are said to be.
Said one to the others, "Now listen you two,
There's a certain rumor that can't be true.
That man descended from our noble race,
The very idea is a dire disgrace.
No monkey ever deserted his wife.
Starved his babies and ruined their life.
And you never heard of a mother monk
Leaving her babies with others to bunk;
Or passing them on from one to another
'Til they hardly know who is their mother.
And another thing, you will never see
A monk build a fence around a coconut tree
And let all the coconuts go to waste.
Forbidding all other monks to taste.
Why, if I built a fence around this tree,
Starvation would force you to steal from me.
And here's another thing a monk won't do,
Go out at night and go on a stew
And use a club or a gun or a knife
To take some other monkey's life.
Yes, man descended, the ornery cuss,
But brother, he didn't descend from us."

Author Unknown

1

Acquainting Yourself with Ethics
A Tour of the Ethics Hall of Fame

They honestly consider they are doing the right thing.
E.W. Elkington, 1907, on New Guinea Cannibals

Or are you a clear thinker examining what is good and useful for society and spending your life in building what is useful and destroying what is harmful?

Kahlil Gibran, *Mirrors of the Soul*

Good laws lead to the making of better ones; bad laws bring about worse. As soon as any man says of the affairs of the State, "What does it matter to me?" the State may be given up for lost.

Rousseau

The present moral crisis is due among other things to the demand for a moral code which is intellectually respectable.

R. Niebuhr

What You Will Learn from This Chapter

To understand the foundation of ethics, you should learn the virtue of knowledge and reasoning, the sources of intellect, the nature of truth, the nature of reality, the nature of morality, the nature of goodness, the relationship between actions and consequences, determinism and intentionalism, and the image of the ethical person.

You will also learn the reasoning process, Plato's divided line, the definition of morality and ethics, the grammar of goodness, the principle of *summum bonum*, and the utilitarianism measure.

Key Terms and Definitions

Reasoning is a pure method of thinking by which proper conclusions are reached through abstract thought processes.

The Divided Line is Plato's theory of knowledge. It characterizes four levels of knowledge. The lowest of these is *conjecture* and *imagination*, because they are based on impressions or suppositions; the next is *belief*, because it is constructed on the basis of faith, images, or superstition; the third is *scientific knowledge*, because it is supported by empirical evidence, experimentation, or mathematical equations; and the highest level is *reasoning*.

Theory of Realism is Aristotle's explanation of reality. It includes three concepts: *rationality*, the ability to use abstract reasoning; *potentiality* and *actuality*, the "capacity to become" and the "state of being"; and the *golden mean*, the middle point between two extreme qualities.

Ethics is a philosophy that examines the principles of right and wrong, good and bad.

Morality is the practice of applying ethical principles on a regular basis.

Intrinsic Goods are objects, actions, or qualities that are valuable in themselves.

Non-intrinsic Goods are objects, actions, or qualities that are good only for developing or serving an intrinsic good.

Summum Bonum is the principle of the highest good that cannot be subordinated to any other.

$E = PJ^2$ is the guiding formula for making moral judgment. E (the ethical decision) equals P (the principle) times J (the justification of the situation).

Utilitarianism is the theory that identifies ethical actions as those that maximize happiness and minimize pain.

Determinism is the theory that all thoughts, attitudes, and actions result from external forces that are beyond human control. They are fixed causal laws that control all events as well as the consequences that follow.

Intentionalism is the theory that all rational beings possess an innate freedom of will and must be held responsible for their actions. It is the opposite of determinism.

Overview

Compared to other disciplines, criminal justice is an infant discipline. This is probably one reason it is far more concerned with crime rather than with justice, and with process rather than with philosophy. As a result, most criminal justice students and practitioners today have not been adequately exposed to the philosophy of justice or, for that matter, to any serious philosophical studies. Courses in ethics and justice are not usually required for a criminal justice degree, nor are they included in programs of professional training. A study in the ethics of criminal justice may therefore be an alien topic and can understandably cause a degree of apprehension. In order to reduce your anxiety and to better acquaint you with the topic, this chapter is designed to take you on a tour of the world of ethics. I will take you, if you will, on a journey into the "Ethics Hall of Fame," introduce you to key concepts, and familiarize you with the works of leading philosophers. Knowledge gained from this chapter will serve as the foundation for the remainder of this book. Figure 1.1 illustrates the layout of the Ethics Hall of Fame.

Exhibit 1—Knowledge and Reasoning

Our first stop on this tour is at a pedestal carrying the bust of Socrates. The sculpture symbolizes the *virtue of knowledge*, because Socrates was considered the wisest man in ancient Greece.

Born in Athens—at the time, the greatest democracy of all—Socrates spent his entire life in search of the truth. Not surprisingly, he was later hailed as the patron saint of Western philosophy. We are more certain of the facts of his death than of the circumstances of his life, because Socrates left no record of his own. The information about his accomplishments was gathered from the accounts of his disciples, particularly

Figure 1.1
The Ethics Hall of Fame

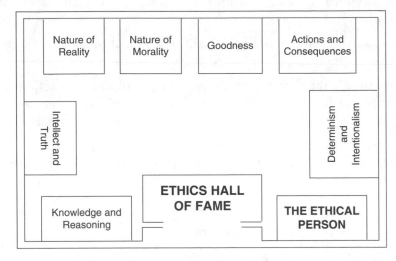

Plato, who was his most prominent student. According to these accounts, Socrates was an outstanding philosopher who served Athens well during times of war and peace.

A Life Unexamined Is Not Worth Living

Socrates (469–399 B.C.) was central to the enlightenment of the world. He taught in the marketplaces of Athens, free of charge. Appearing uninterested in physical speculation, he went about engaging people in conversations and asking them familiar but important-to-everyday-life questions. He raised difficult questions about the meaning of life and, in particular, the natures of knowledge and virtue. He challenged his audiences to rethink and reason their lives rationally. In arguing his views, he demonstrated the power of "counterargument" and stung his opponents by exposing their unexamined beliefs. His famous credo was the memorable exhortation "a life unexamined is not worth living." By the same token, we should think today that "a belief unexamined is not worth following," "a policy unexamined is not worth executing," and "a practice unexamined is not worth adhering to." Every subject, topic, or issue in life must be open to intellectual scrutiny regardless of its nature or origin. The "beginning of wisdom" is allowing the human intellect to think freely and to emancipate the mind from the clutches of ignorance and the fetters of cultural, social, or religious bias.

Consistent with this Socratic dictum, students and instructors of criminal justice should be encouraged—rather than discouraged—to examine every policy, practice, or controversy in criminal justice without shyness, discomfort, or guilt. For instance, questions about crime and justice, the limits of punishment, the authority of the state, the role of prisons, fairness in the workplace, and other controversial practices in criminal justice should all be openly discussed. The reasoning behind such a commitment is dualistic: (1) as citizens of a nation dedicated to "liberty and justice for all," it is our obligation to enable everyone to experience the full measures of "liberty" and "justice" in our daily life that would make us better citizens; and (2) as criminal justice professionals, it is our obligation to call attention to system failures and short-comings in order to correct them. Failure to do so would make us responsible before the future generations of Americans who may point to their ancestors and ask, "If they kept doing it the same way, how did they expect it to come out differently?" (Friel, 1998).

Exploring Virtue

Socrates's typical method of exploring virtue was through arguing popular but erroneous beliefs in what was known as the *dialectic method*. Such arguments were conducted in a dialogue form in which the parties involved would engage in an exchange of questions and answers. The direction of questions and the validity of answers would point out the presence of contradiction or fallacy. By continuing this process, the truth of the disputed question would either be established or denied. The dialectic method, which was the trademark of ancient Greek philosophy, was later labeled the *Socratic method* in honor of its most skillful master.

In his philosophical teachings, Socrates addressed general questions such as knowledge, wisdom, and character, and also discussed specific topics of a moral nature, such as goodness, courage, and temperance. Regardless of the topic of inquiry that Socrates pursued, there is no doubt that his overall aim was to reeducate the people of Athens in the nature of *arete*, or virtue.

Knowledge and Virtue

Socrates argued that *virtue is knowledge and knowledge is virtue*. Both are one and the same. He taught that a person who *knows* what is right will, by virtue of such knowledge, do what is right. Conversely, committing a wrong act results from ignorance, because evildoing can only be involuntary. At this point, it has been reported that the students of Socrates interrupted him skeptically, suggesting that many Athenian leaders and politicians had frequently been in prison, thus proving Socrates to be wrong in his central assertion. To that, Socrates reportedly answered that those Athenians were certainly not knowledgeable enough; if they had been, they would have been able to anticipate the consequences of their intentions and abstain from doing wrong.

Socrates taught that genuine knowledge amounted to *moral insight*, which he considered prerequisite to success and happiness in life. Hence, Socrates's classical exhortation to his students: "Know thyself." By that dictum, Socrates referred to the obligation of all individuals to be knowledgeable of themselves, their talents and goals, as well as their limitations. Socrates emphasized that success can be assured only through living an intelligent life in accordance with knowledge. It is interesting to note, at this point, that while Socrates was obviously most knowledgeable among his peers, he always pretended to be limited in his intellect; hence the term *Socratic irony*.

To be a "philosopher" and to "study virtue" meant the same thing to Socrates. This is basically because the study of virtue requires a high level of diverse knowledge that can be possessed only by students of philosophy. In arguing philosophical matters in general, and ethical issues in particular, one quickly discovers the imperative of being well versed in other fields of knowledge. A worthy judgment of good and evil, Socrates pointed out, must depend on "whether it is made under the guidance of knowledge." The Socratic quest for virtue was thus a fierce search for the truth that "every man can only find for himself." Perhaps the central theme in the Socratic theory of knowledge can be restated in the rule that philosophers (as you should now start considering yourselves) are not free to make judgments about issues of which they have limited knowledge. Furthermore, proper ethical judgment cannot be based on whether one likes or dislikes an act or approves or disapproves of a policy, but on whether the act or the policy is consistent with *reasoning*, the highest level of intellectual capacity.

The Reasoning Process

Reasoning is a capacity that differentiates the human race from animals, birds, trees, and rocks. It is especially critical to the study of ethics because it is the only legitimate method of reaching the truths of life and living. Any other means is suspect. Reasoning is *a pure method of thinking by which proper conclusions are reached through abstract thought processes*. Based on the universal assumption that understanding is an exercise in duality—life and death, good and evil, light and darkness, happiness and misery—reasoning has developed as *an exchange between a point and a counterpoint*. Such an exchange can take place between two or more persons or within one's own mind. The initial point in any such exchange is known as *thesis* and its response as *antithesis*. As a result, an intellectual compromise can be reached. This is known as *synthesis*. Every synthesis in turn becomes a new thesis that warrants a new antithesis, which in turn produces a new synthesis, and so on. The reasoning process can thus continue indefinitely until the debaters reach a point at which no further point can be made. At that point, the knowledge produced would be accepted as *truth,* as far as human beings are capable of discerning. When truths are recognized over a long period, or are universally accepted, they become *self-evident truths*.

Pure reason emanates from the human intellect and functions independently of other faculties of consciousness such as will or desire. As such, pure reasoning can be defined as *an intellectual talent that proceeds rationally and logically without reliance on sense perception or individual experience*.

The goal of reasoning is to determine the true nature of life and to investigate the intricacies of human choice—questions that are always present, right under our noses, but elude our knowledge. The independence of reasoning is what makes it superior to all other thought patterns. It keeps the thinking process immune to the noises of history and the distractions of cultural and social surroundings. As such, thoughts of pure reason are capable of transcending the walls of opinion, the myths of tradition, the fallacies of dogma, and the darkness of ignorance. Through this transcending power, reasoning can capture the truth and refute hostile and stray ideas. Without the reasoning process, the unaided truth will have very little chance to triumph in the marketplace of conflicting ideas.

Most people today live in a thoughtless world that is dominated by political ideology, public opinion, and changing social and economic interests. The absence of reasoning has turned the world into a disheartening environment of ignorance, impenetrable by the forces of intellect. Reasoning, therefore, may be the only rational tool left for recapturing the truth. Only through the reasoning process can philosophical issues be rationally debated. Philosophers systematically proceed from examining the premises, to inferring facts and values, to reaching conclusions, without having to rely on social, cultural, or personal prejudices. Consequently, a debate that does not allow for reasoning is doomed to missing the truth.

Socratic Reasoning

The Socratic method of reasoning incorporates two interrelated functions: first, establishing the *purpose* of the phenomenon in question, which is considered the beginning of wisdom; and second, demonstrating the goodness of the phenomenon by fulfilling its purpose. In this tradition, Aristotle (384–322 B.C.) always asked his students to answer three basic questions: (1) *What is it?* This is the question that the scientists of nature are supposed to be able to answer. (2) *What good is it for?* This is the question that ethicists are supposed to be able to answer. (3) *How do we know?* This is the question that logicians and epistemologists are supposed to be able to answer (Jowett & Butcher, 1979).

The reasoning process should flow methodically and without contradiction. It moves from establishing the purpose of the idea, to confirming its goodness, to the fulfillment of its purpose. Consider, for example, the issue of gun control: If it can be shown that the main purpose of bearing arms is to ensure self-defense, then for goodness to be confirmed, it must also be shown that bearing arms would not hinder the purpose by being used as tools for crime. Probably because of the influence of Socrates, Western philosophers have consistently formulated their theories about truths, moral values, and human behavior by pursuing the Socratic method of reasoning—systematically arguing the idea from purpose to goodness while maintaining an open, intelligent, and methodical mind.

The Death of Socrates

The teachings of Socrates were not well received by the citizens of Athens, who resented his acrimonious criticism of their hypocrisy. In 399 B.C. he was accused of seditious teachings and was indicted by the Athenian Senate. After a historic trial in which he provided his own defense, Socrates was sentenced to die for being "an evil-doer and a curious person, searching into things under the earth and above the heavens, making the worse appear the better cause, and teaching all this to others" (Albert et al., 1988:9). Socrates could have avoided death by leaving Athens before the trial began, as was customary when acquittal was in doubt, but he refused. Even after his conviction, his supporters assured him that the state of Athens was not seriously keen on carrying out the death sentence against its most prominent teacher. His friend Crito offered him a way out by suggesting that he escape to an adjacent state. Nevertheless, Socrates rejected all offers, accepting instead the death sentence. He based his stand on three moral principles; he proudly proclaimed: (1) it is morally wrong for anyone to break the law by fleeing; (2) it is morally wrong to value one's life any higher than one's honor and reputation (thus, accepting Crito's offer would have been an act of cowardice); and (3) it is morally wrong for the state that represents "one's parent and teacher" to violate the principles of justice by setting a "criminal" free, even if that criminal was Socrates. Socrates chose what he perceived to be the moral path. He ended his life by drinking poison hemlock in prison in the company of his friends, neighbors, and students. As later described in Plato's *Apology,* when Socrates accepted the death sentence, he made his final and immortal stand on the virtue of ethics for generations to follow.

> The lesson to be learned from this stop is to appreciate the importance of reasoning in making ethical judgment. One should open every issue for debate, hold every bias in abeyance, and pursue the objective criteria of first establishing the purpose of the phenomenon and then demonstrating its goodness or its lack of goodness.

Exhibit 2—Intellect and Truth

Our second stop is by a *shining ray of light* that brightens a spot on the floor. The light symbolizes human intellect, and the spot represents the *truth*. Both are paramount for mastering the reasoning process.

Human intellect is a mysterious force that is unique to mankind. It sets human beings apart from the rest of nature—animals, birds, trees, and rocks. It originates in the mind and is nurtured by rigorous thinking. Given proper training, the mind develops into a marvelous thinking center, able to observe, compare, distinguish, abstract, and conclude. Some important questions, however, must first be asked: "What is the source of intellect?" and "Why do some people seem to have more of it than others?" There have been several views in response to these questions. The most popular among them are the *divine view*, which ascertains that intellect is a gift from God, and the *naturalistic view*, which considers intellect a natural property in the evolution of man.

Sources of Intellect

Thinkers who support the *divine view* believe that intellect is a God-given gift offered to man in order to communicate with God and fellow human beings. Conversely, how well one utilizes intellect is man's gift back to God. Most Greek philosophers (and, of course, religious theorists) subscribed to this view, advocating that the purpose of intellect is to better achieve the good life. On the other hand, thinkers who subscribe to the *naturalistic view* of human existence regard intellect as a physiological process that continues to be perfected by the evolutionary process. As such, it naturally emerged to coordinate human activity and to assist man in his struggle for self-preservation. Hobbes, Darwin, and Nietzsche supported one version or another of these naturalistic theories. They considered intellect as primarily an autonomic activity that stimulates one's sense of survival and enriches his pursuit of social harmony. Both groups of thinkers, however, seem to agree that when people cease to use intellect, they lose their control over the unexplained phenomenon of existence.

Nature of the Truth

The Greeks considered *veritas* (the truth) the focal point of philosophy—*the reason for being, the essence, and the intellectual explanation of all human existence.* Without knowing the truth, the human race would be like children living in a world of fantasy, or worse still, as a herd of animals in an open pasture. The truth is the central point of reference around which all intelligible forms revolve. Without establishing this point, living would be random and reasoning would be meaningless, because neither the *purpose of life* nor the *goodness of society* would make any distinguishable difference.

But what is the nature of the truth? Is it eternal and absolute, as most religious and classical philosophers claim, or is it subject to interpretation and extrapolation? What, for instance, is the relationship between truth, science, and beliefs? Can a statement be considered true or false because our senses tell us so? There are three main views.

First, the *religious view* identifies the truth with God's testaments and revelations to man. God's word is the eternal truth "yesterday, today, and tomorrow," and God's truth is the truth even if it contradicts every scientific theory. Dogmatic religious thinkers argue that if it were not so, God would have had to explain. But because He did not, no other truth can, or should, exist.

Second, the *scientific view* is substantively critical of the divine view of the truth. Scientific thinkers argue that all truths exist within the realm of empirical science and substance. The truth must be tangible, repeatable, and clinically testable. Anything that falls short of these properties must be a product of faith, opinion, misinformation, or fabrication.

Third, the *sociological view*, while not negating the powerful word of God, allows for liberal interpretations of the truth. Many social scientists formulate "reasonable" statements that may conflict with the divine truth yet do not strictly adhere to the empirical nature of science. For example, on the origin of man, they may accept an accommodation between the divine theory of creation and the scientific theory of evolution. They support such a position on the basis that God, in His ultimate wisdom, may have created the right environment that allowed for the natural evolution of man.

It is noteworthy, however, that while religionists and social scientists frequently find themselves attacked by physical scientists, they often end up attacking each other. For example, controversies about the morality of abortion and euthanasia best illustrate the disagreement between the religionists, who view them as acts of killing, and the social scientists, who justify them as issues of privacy and choice.

Plato's Divided Line

Studies in the nature of truth are found in the field of *epistemology*, or the theory of knowledge, because only through knowledge can the truth be ascertained. Plato has been acknowledged as a pioneer in this field through his theory of the *divided line*. He explained that knowledge of the truth can be attained through a hierarchy of four levels. The lowest level of knowledge consists of *conjecture and imagination*, because they are based solely on impressions or suppositions. A good illustration of this is when one bases his or her views of what causes crime on personal experiences and contacts with others, and nothing else.

The next level of knowledge in Plato's hierarchy is *belief*. At that level, truth is constructed on the basis of one's faith in real objects, images of reality, or superstition. Belief is a *state of mind* that takes over a person due to strong forces of religion, custom, tradition, indoctrination, or any popular view of the time. Religious beliefs are especially difficult to question, because cognitive knowledge is usually subjected to the forces of metaphysics, deity, and ritualism. One's belief in the Christian doctrine of the Holy Ghost, the Islamic duty of *Jihad*, or the existence of heaven and hell are good illustrations of knowledge at this level.

The third level in Plato's hierarchy is *scientific knowledge*. It is supported by empirical evidence, experimentation, and mathematical equations. Examples include rules of gravity, flying, and buoyancy; medical sciences; and, to some extent, criminal behavior. The highest level of knowledge on Plato's hierarchy is *reasoning*, the intelligible integration and balancing of all knowledge—physical and metaphysical—in a rational manner. Figure 1.2 illustrates Plato's divided line theory.

Figure 1.2
Plato's Divided Line Theory

Plato assigned a lower degree of credence to the first two levels of knowledge, equating them with ignorance and superstition, respectively. Both fall within the realm of primitive knowledge. He valued scientific knowledge because it is objective, universal, repeatable, and subject to scrutiny. He nevertheless acknowledged the limitations of scientific inquiry in terms of three serious weaknesses: (1) it rests upon unexamined first principles (for example, we know about the force of gravity on earth and between planets without understanding its cause or origin); (2) it is tied to matters particularly connected to the visible world (for example, we know how the human body functions, but we cannot determine whether superior creatures exist, let alone how they function); and (3) it is piecemeal and fragmentary (for example, we have only recently learned that the atom is divisible and that HIV exists, although those truths were certainly there long before they were discovered).

Plato considered science to be an imperfect discipline and argued that "what is imperfect cannot serve as a valid measure." While science can answer the question of "what can be done," Plato argued, it is incapable of answering the question of "what should be done." Even if science were capable of explaining how people behave, it cannot prescribe how they "ought to behave," or for that matter, what "ethical" behavior should be like.

Plato placed his highest trust in reasoning, which he considered supreme knowledge. While he appreciated the value of science as an experimental tool, he credited reasoning with the ability to explain the phenomena of life and living. *Reasoning transcends science and overrides its investigatory value.* As such, it can direct scientific inquiry, evaluate its practical goodness, and devise the time and place for its application. As a case in point, while nuclear scientists today can easily build all sorts of atomic bombs, they certainly cannot make a value judgment as to where or when to use them. By the same token, medical science today can practically keep a "corpse" alive, but only by reasoning can it be determined when life support should be discontinued. Plato, and most philosophers since his time, continued to view reasoning as supreme knowledge because it enables the trained mind to navigate the limitations of lower levels of knowledge.

Plato's Dual Truths: Physical and Metaphysical

Building upon the Socratic search for the truth, Plato directed his attention to investigating both the *physical* and the *metaphysical* worlds. His insistence on examining both worlds is of special significance. Knowledge of the truth, he argued, depends not only upon physical objects experienced by the human senses, but also upon metaphysical ideals, forms, and essences that emanate from higher sources beyond the comprehension of man.

To illustrate this dualist theory of knowledge, Plato used his famous *allegory of the cave*. In the allegory, mankind is symbolized by a group of people imprisoned in a cave that has only one entrance. Deep inside, the prisoners are chained to the ground, facing the inner wall of the cave. They have never seen the light of day or experienced any activities outside the cave. The prisoners live their entire lives watching only shadows of reality, and the voices they hear are only echoes from the wall they face. They naturally cling to their familiar shadows and to the passions and prejudices to which they are accustomed, because those are all they know. If these people were unshackled and allowed to turn around and see the light that produces the shadows, they would be blinded by the sunlight. Furthermore, they would become agitated and would want to turn back to watching their shadow world. But if they were dragged out of the cave, they would see the marvels of the outside world and experience the light and warmth of the sun (Lavine, 1984:27). Plato's allegory illustrates two basic principles: the ignorance of all men who are shackled in the darkness of untruths, and the eternal truths that, like the rays of light, shine from above and provide the virtues of goodness, wisdom, and justice.

Plato's dualist theory of inquiry obligates the philosophers to investigate the intelligible world of metaphysics without losing sight of the physical world around them. He proposed, for example, that philosophers should be able to move from studying the love of the human body, to the love of beauty in general, to the love of the beautiful mind, and finally to the "science of beauty everywhere." As to how people can learn metaphysical reasoning, Plato would reply, "through one's love of the truth." He emphasized that such love can propel one's imagination, transcendent thinking, and moral understanding into a fusion of both worlds. This kind of heightened intellect would culminate in achieving the "supreme aim of the soul," or what Maslow calls "the particular attainment from a height" (Maslow, 1971:xix).

> The lesson to be learned from this stop is to seek the truth for its own value, to capture both its physical and metaphysical attributes, and to utilize such knowledge in mastering the reasoning process.

Exhibit 3—The Nature of Reality

Our third stop is by an *empty hole* in the ground. The hole symbolizes the philosopher's concern for reality. For ethical theory to be practical, philosophers must keep their attention focused on the reality of what is and the sum total of what exists. This is probably one of the most difficult challenges to ethical theory.

Ethical statements regarding what actions *should* be taken and *why* must be based on an objective reality of the situation under consideration. To add to the challenge, any attempt to determine reality must be made independent of human perception, passion, bias, or cultural experience. This is clearly a commitment that is easier made by gods than by men. To complicate matters even further, phenomenological literature is replete with views that deny the existence of reality altogether; "things are not what they appear to be." Furthermore, the nature of reality constantly changes. Even if we assume that there is a "reality" of some sort, by the time observers get to studying it, it may have already changed. The Greek philosopher Heraclitus declared that the fundamental character of reality is change. Everything is in process, in flux, and is no longer the same. "One cannot step into the same river twice," Heraclitus wrote, because it is endlessly flowing and changing (Lavine, 1984:24).

Discovering Reality

Ethicists grapple with the question of how people should behave. This will be meaningless, however, unless behavior is viewed in real situations. Ethicists must therefore determine what is real and what is not. Is the real only what is physical, material, or tangible, or can it also be found in the human mind, in eternal truths, or in the wisdom of the gods? Indeed, the study of ethics begins with such fundamental questions about reality: "Why should one be moral in the first place?"; "What is justice, and why should people be committed to justice?"; "What sentiments should one have toward another, and what values should guide one's actions?" These questions are obviously raised against few known facts about life, living, and dimly perceived guidelines concerning reality.

A more certain view of reality is the scientific view. Science recognizes only physical properties such as matter, energy, mass, and movement. Scientific reality is *empirical*—it can be sensed, validated, and measured by sensory means. Supporters of this view maintain that aside from scientifically measurable "realities," all phenomena are products of human perception. In accordance with this view, all social or moral values, such as kindness, sincerity, honor, fidelity, honesty, and so forth, are products of social fabrication. They are "unreal," because *if they exist at all*, they are subjective values that can be judged differently by different individuals and in different contexts.

Aristotle's Ethical Realism

A leader in the field of *ethical realism* was Aristotle. He was Plato's most talented student and friend, but by no means his most devoted disciple. Disillusioned by his master's idealism and attachment to

metaphysical forms and ideas, Aristotle objected to Plato's sense of realism, exclaiming, *Magnus amicus Plato Maior amica veritas*, or "Dear is
Plato, but dearer still is truth." This is a particularly powerful dictum
because it demonstrates that even among the best of friends, one should,
out of conviction, still courageously disagree and argue one's point of
reasoning. Furthermore, the dictum implies that *personal* loyalty to a
superior or a boss is not that important when the resolution of the issue
at hand must be based on truths rather than sentiments. Unquestionable
loyalty to an individual, rather than to a principle or to an ideal, may
be harmful—if not outright dangerous. It can, as in Watergate, Iran-
Contra, and many other lesser cases, compel well-trained professionals
to overlook the truth.

Aristotle was a philosopher, a scientist, and a gentleman. He harbored
a well-balanced view of realism. While he accepted the idea of metaphysical realities, he insisted that they cannot be detached from objects in
the sensible world. Both are interrelated because there can be "no form
without matter, and no matter without form." Aristotle subsequently
produced a more comprehensive *theory of realism*, which was grounded
in three principles: (1) the principle of *rationality*, (2) the connection
between *potentiality* and *actuality*, and (3) the *golden mean*.

Reality as Rationality: Aristotle defined rationality as the ability to use
abstract reasoning as the primary source of knowledge. Only through
rationality can realistic truths be found. Such truths must possess the
attributes of self-sufficiency, finality, and attainability. Consequently,
what is rational is real, and what is real is rational. Among the qualities
of the rational person, Aristotle signified thoughtfulness, intellectual
tenacity, courage, and temperance. He nevertheless warned against
expecting a high degree of precision in determining ethical realism,
because human diversity makes it difficult to reach universal consensus. The uncertainty of human reasoning, he added, may make it
difficult for rationality to be applied objectively.

Reality as the Actualization of Potential: Aristotle argued that what has
the ability to grow must be real. And because human beings are born
with the potential to become full-grown individuals, actualization
must be real. Aristotle's concept of potentiality and actuality relates to
Heraclitus's idea of change and the imperative of human development.
Aristotle defined *potentiality* as the "capacity to become," and *actuality*
as the "state of being." To explain this connection, he used the analogy of
the acorn: As the acorn can actualize its potential by becoming an oak
tree, so people can actualize their potential by achieving a life of reason
and civility. He further explained that the natural tendencies of youthful
persons to be erratic, aggressive, and impatient can, through the practice
of reasoning, be channeled into a life of maturity, modesty, and wisdom.

Reality as the Golden Mean: According to this principle, the reality of
a given value lies in the middle ground between two extreme qualities.

For example, the reality of *courage* is the middle ground between cowardice and foolhardiness; the reality of *magnificence* is the middle ground between meanness and vulgarity; and the reality of *gentleness* is the middle ground between indifference and irascibility. Aristotle recommended that ethical realism always reflect moderation between two extreme behaviors.

A radically different view of realism exists, however. It has been reflected in the philosophy of the modern *existentialist school*. Exponents of this school are mainly European philosophers, including Soren Kierkegaard, Martin Heidegger, Jean-Paul Sartre, and Simone de Beauvoir. Their view of reality is based on either denying its existence altogether or reducing its significance dramatically. These philosophers argued that *all knowledge relates to human existence rather than to human essence*. All doctrines of philosophy or theology, therefore, are "absurd." These views have been supported by the premises that the human condition is ambiguous; that human beings come from "nothingness," and that upon death they return to "nothingness"; that religious teachings have no real value; that universal morality is a myth; and that existence is the sole reality of mankind. While this view has its supporters, it is not the most popular among moral philosophers, especially among those who espouse a conservative view of reality.

> The lesson to be learned from this stop is to remove ethics from the realm of mysticism, to apply it to real situations, and to treat ethical judgment as a rational science applicable to everyday human conduct.

At this point in the tour, I suggest that we pause for a moment to consider what we have learned so far. You may have already realized how confusing ethical terms can be. If so, you are correct and you are not alone. One of the main challenges in the study of ethics is the *jungle of semantics* with which one is confronted at every turn. On the other hand, this jungle is what gives philosophy its fecundity and gives the study of ethics its profoundness and beauty.

Exhibit 4—The Nature of Morality

Our fourth stop is at a huge painting depicting the Garden of Eden with Adam, Eve, and the apple tree in its midst. The painting symbolizes concern for *morality* and *proper behavior*. Morality is an integral part of the study of ethics, because it represents its operational side and provides the ground rules for its application.

Part of the difficulty of understanding morality is the manner in which the term is used. It has seldom been used without qualification. We refer to "American morality," "Greek morality," or "Christian morality," but seldom to morality itself. This is partly due to the widespread belief that there is no *universal morality,* a code of conduct that can be adopted by all mankind. Although nations and communities have moral differences, this belief is arguably inaccurate (Gert, 1973:3). The problem may be that most people are unable to adequately distinguish between moral principles and cultural and social habits. Furthermore, most people tend to believe that they either have no moral problems, or that they know all there is to know about morality. Moreover, given the diversity of political, social, and economic systems in the world, few people may be willing to accept a universal code of conduct.

More than 2,000 years ago, however, Plato knew that there were differences in the conduct of various societies. Yet that did not discourage him from formulating a code of conduct that everyone would accept. He believed that a thorough analysis of human nature could provide a foundation upon which to build a universal core of morality (Gert, 1973:5). Of course, all rational men may not always agree, but ethical philosophers continue to identify moral values that all, or most rational persons, would accept.

Morality and Ethics

The terms *morality* and *ethics* have been used interchangeably. This is an inaccurate use of the terms, although the terms are clearly interrelated. Ethics is *a philosophy that examines the principles of right and wrong, good and bad.* Morality, on the other hand, is *the practice of these principles on a regular basis, culminating in a moral life.* As such, morality is conduct that is much akin to integrity. Consequently, while most people may technically be viewed as ethical (by virtue of knowing the principles of right and wrong), only those who internalize these principles and faithfully apply them in their relationships with others should be considered moral.

Morality Defined

The term *moral* has two connotations: First, the *capacity to make value judgments*—one's ability to discern right from wrong. In this sense, the term may be contrasted with *amoral, nonmoral,* or *unmoral.* These denote a person who is either unable to judge rightness or wrongness (as in the case of a young child or an insane person) or is disinterested in the moral point of view. Second, *a behavior that is consistent with ethical principles.* Here, the term can be contrasted with *immoral*—an adjective that describes wrongful or evil behaviors

(Sahakian, 1974:2). In this sense, the term *moral* is used to characterize virtuous qualities such as love, charity, or compassion, or to describe the goodness of an action, an institution, or an entire society. This definition is more common in moral philosophy and is the definition that will be used throughout this book.

Moral Principles

Moral principles arguably exist before individuals are born (indeed, generations before) and continue long after they depart. People learn moral principles through their association with the social system in which they live. Social systems dictate certain rules of conduct to be followed. Of course, while not all individuals conform to the same rules, those who choose not to conform cannot escape the moral sanctions of their choice. When a person conforms to society's rules of conduct, he or she is said to behave morally, and when a person deviates from them, he or she is said to behave amorally or immorally.

While moral principles should not be absolutized, they signify general patterns of behavior rather than a preference or a freak behavior on the part of an individual or a group. Also, like learning language, religion, and citizenship, morality is usually learned by practicing moral principles such as "honor one's father and mother," "don't tell a lie," and "don't betray your friends." Indeed, Aristotle always taught that people become just by learning to do just things.

It should also be noted that when moral standards are applied, they can overlap with the standards of *law* and *etiquette* (Frankena, 1963:6). Yet, the concept of morality is distinguishable from both. It is different from law in at least two ways: (1) the standards of morality are not formulated by a legislative act, nor are moral standards subject to review by a court of law; (2) while immoral acts are sanctioned by words or gestures of social disfavor, disapproval, or ostracism, illegal actions are punishable by legal sanctions, including fines, jail sentences, corporal punishment, or death. As to the rules of etiquette, these are generally associated with the appearance of sophistication regardless of whether the person is moral or immoral. Moral standards, on the other hand, represent a conscientious concern for moral behavior even at the risk of being mistaken as unsophisticated or crude.

Relativist Views of Morality

Among the most notorious advocates of relativist morality were the *Sophists of Greece*, who have so far evaded us on the tour. The Sophists lived during the age of Socrates, and their views may have prompted his emergence to the philosophical pinnacle of Athens. They are said to have taught for a fee, which in the opinion of Socrates was an evil practice. They appeared to be eloquent debaters, yet their arguments were rather petty and their reasoning fallacious. Under the tutorship of Thrasymachus, the Sophists argued that no absolute truth existed, and furthermore: (1) all things are the creation of one's consciousness at the moment; (2) the individual is the measure of all morals; (3) things are not what one says they are; and (4) all truths are relative to the social, cultural, and personal predisposition of the individual. In essence, the Sophists advocated what has recently become known as *situational morality.*

Relativist morality is based on the assumption that standards of conduct are neither sacred nor etched in stone—different folks need different strokes. While this view is less controversial than the radical view, it too denies the presence of universal truths. According to relativists, any behavior can be both right and wrong, depending on the cultural scenario one manufactures. Moral relativity has indeed been instrumental in disguising human prejudices that may justify privileges to certain people while denying them to others. Examples include slavery and the detention of Japanese Americans during World War II. By the same token, relativists can deny equal rights to certain groups under certain conditions (for example, prison inmates and patients in psychiatric hospitals). In all of these examples, the relativist response to moral principles is, invariably, "it all depends." As Allan Bloom critiques, the point of relativism is "not to correct the mistakes and really be right, rather it is not to think you are right at all" (Bloom, 1987:17).

Although the characterization of morality as relativist is not uncommon, it is generally considered deceptive. Gert, in his criticism of relativism, attributed why it may be so popular to four reasons: (1) no moral philosopher has yet presented a universally definitive account of what moral conduct "ought to be"; (2) despite the powerful role of social morals over the centuries, it has been stymied by the forces of social change, political lobbyists, and commercialized media; (3) the absence of formal ethical education allows most individuals to think that they know what morality is without truly knowing; and (4) the failure of contemporary morality to distinguish between a "code of conduct" (that could conceivably include amoral and frivolous standards such as dress codes, hair codes, and the like) and a substantive code that has at its core "distinctive moral doctrines," such as the values of freedom, equality, and justice. Gert's chief concern was with the last reason, which, in his view, dilutes the essence of morality to cheap ritualistic appearances (Gert, 1973).

Situational Morality

Situational morality is another view of relativism. It emphasizes *contrast perception* and *double standards* in the formulation of ethical principles (for example, what is good for one society is not good for another; what is good for a white person is not necessarily good for an African American or Hispanic; and that the ends of liberty and justice that justify action in one situation may not justify it in another).

Among the more common assumptions in situational morality are that (1) the values of goodness, truth, and humanity are all neutral; (2) one person's moral judgment is as good as another's; (3) morality depends on who one is, where one is, and the point at which a decision is made; and (4) spiritual and philosophical doctrines are nonbinding and therefore of no particular significance. Not surprisingly, support for situational morality seemed to increase in popularity in the recent decades, which have been characterized by such phrases as "What's in it for me?" and the "me society." The philosophy of situational morality seems to be consistently invoked by the young against the old, the non-conformists against the traditional, and the semi-educated against both the educated and the ignorant.

Allan Bloom is a critic of situational morality. In his compelling work *The Closing of the American Mind* (1987), he presents a powerful indictment of relativist morality in the United States. While the book is directed primarily to college students, Bloom clearly sends a message of moral awakening to the entire society. He emphasizes that contrary to everything we experience in today's world, universal moral truths exist. In an admonishing manner similar to Socrates's style, Bloom "screams" through his moral gauntlet, "You have forgotten how to look and how to think." He declares that questions of wisdom must be answered by a "Hegel" and not a "Joyce Brothers."

Bloom grieves for the youthful minds of America that have ignored their cultural resources, neglected to study the "great minds" of history, and forgotten how to challenge conventional wisdom. He nevertheless reserves his harshest moral indignation for the values of materialism and personal convenience. He points out that the fundamental human concern for goodness seems to have been reduced, under the selfish and irrational practice of situational morality, to ignorance, mindless commitment, and trashy sentimentality (Bloom, 1987).

The Jimmy Carter Story

Jimmy Carter was not only a critic of situational morality, he also exposed it by his behavior. Throughout his distinguished career in public service, including four years as President of the United States (1976–1980), he has shown extraordinary commitment to moral prin-ciples and moral duties. As a former president, he continues to be America's foremost advocate of human rights and has worked with civic and religious organizations to enhance the quality of life in the world. As a result, he has been sought out by foreign countries such as Russia,

North Korea, Somalia, and the Sudan to assist in rebuilding their democratic infrastructures.

In 1994 the United States was about to invade the island of Haiti to restore the former democratic president to power. To avoid unnecessary bloodshed, President Clinton dispatched a high-level delegation to the island to negotiate its peaceful return to democracy. The delegation consisted of Jimmy Carter, Senator Sam Nunn, and General Colin Powell. The charge to the delegation was to secure agreements by which (1) members of the military junta would step down, and (2) they would leave the island into exile.

The delegation began its negotiations and in a week's time reported progress. Carter reported to President Clinton that the first charge had been accomplished. As to the second, Carter stated that he chose not to do it. He argued that sending anyone into exile—including citizens of foreign countries—is an act of banishment that is unconstitutional in the United States. And because the United States is the champion of human rights in the world, it would be a serious human rights violation if he (Carter) would carry it out in Haiti. On the other hand, Carter argued that if members of the junta were to be accused of criminal acts, he would be willing to charge them and try them in a court of law.

Carter's position is an excellent example of commitment to ethical principles and the denunciation of situational morality. He certainly could have applied pressure on members of the junta and prevailed, without any significant criticism. He instead chose not to do so, because it would be immoral, especially by a great nation that champions human rights principles around the world. The surprising response to Carter's position was that no one criticized it. His decision was accepted by all concerned as a "self-evident truth." Carter did the right thing on the basis of moral authority alone.

> The lesson to be learned from this stop is to seek and exercise moral judgment, to abide with universal rules of moral behavior, and to attempt at all times not to delude universal morality by succumbing to the temptations of radical and relativist ethics.

Exhibit 5—Nature of Goodness

Our fifth stop is at a *fountain* that gushes pristine water several feet high. The fountain is shapely, and the water is aesthetically pleasing. The fountain symbolizes the concept of goodness that lies at the core of morality and forms its raison d'être. Without goodness, morality cannot exist.

The adjective *good* comes from the root *god*, the only characterization human beings know of completeness or perfection. The idea of goodness represents the essence of being godlike, and morality signifies its true embodiment. Thus, the idea of goodness is central to the study of ethics.

Specifically, the term *good* refers to an object, a value, a trait, or a desire that enriches the human life. It is naturally conducive to happiness and pleasure and is opposed to misery and pain. The idea of goodness also implies an evolutionary value; without a core of goodness, societies cannot survive. Furthermore, the term *goodness* conveys laudatory qualities such as approval, excellence, admiration, and appropriateness. In the philosophy of criminal justice, it should be understood that while all societies experience crime, only "good societies" can naturally minimize its occurrence.

The Good Life

Greek philosophers were mystified by the idea of goodness, which they associated with pursuing *the good life*: a state denoting the ultimate in human character. In moral philosophy, however, the good life was interpreted in different terms. For instance, Plato, the fundamentalist, identified it with the "achievement of an intelligent and rational order of thinking"; Aristotle, the scientist, associated it with the "self-realization of one's potential"; Aristippus, the hedonist, used it to mean the "achievement of physical pleasure"; and Bentham, the utilitarianist, defined it as "felicity," or happiness.

On the other hand, there are philosophers who were much less definitive. For instance, G.E. Moore (Lavine, 1984) maintained that "the good life" is a natural quality that can be grasped only by intuition; a state of happiness that is independent of desires, aversions, pleasures, and pains. As such, it is indefinable. Thus, when one says that "personal affection is good," the statement should be considered true.

In practical terms, however, all rational individuals and groups pursue some sort of good life in all their endeavors. Explicitly or implicitly, they identify with certain cultural values that represent goodness (for example, the Jewish view of "fear of the Lord," the Islamic doctrine of "submission to God," the Christian doctrine of "salvation," the Hindu identification with "dharma," or the Chinese principle of "Jen"). As such, achieving "the good life" should be a continuing endeavor, and the practice of goodness is its foundational tool.

The Grammar of Goodness

Despite its native simplicity, goodness remains a perplexing concept. People continue to ask questions such as "Is all goodness equal?" and "How can choices be made between two or more principles of goodness?" For example, between one's obligation to enforce all the laws faithfully and one's counterobligation to ignore minor law violations by work partners, or between one's duty to keep classified information confidential and the duty to be loyal to a supervisor who wants the information released.

Associated with this line of questions are some of the most notorious controversies that students in every ethics class never miss an opportunity to raise; for instance: (1) the perceived right of police officers to accept "free coffee and half-price meals" from eateries at any time in their districts—especially under the guise that those eateries offer that perk for no other reason than pure hospitality; (2) the perceived right of police officers to enjoy the "professional courtesy" of not ticketing fellow officers when they violate the speed limit on public roads—especially under the guise that it is conducive to police professionalism; and (3) the perceived right of correctional officers to use brutality against inmates who fail to show respect to the officer—especially under the guise that it is good for the inmate's rehabilitation.

Answers to these questions can be very complicated, especially if one argues from biased perspectives. In such a case, determining moral judgment would simply be reduced to an exercise in opinion and conjecture. The following section will present three substantive rules and a formula that if used in good faith can make it easier to determine moral judgment. Each of these rules will be presented in a premise, a discussion, and a rule statement.

First Premise: There are two categories of goodness—intrinsic and non-intrinsic

Intrinsic goods are objects, actions, or qualities that are valuable in themselves, rather than for accomplishing something else. Consequently, intrinsic goods are known as *end values or goods of the first order*. Examples include life, justice, liberty, and happiness. These do not serve as instruments to any other goodness. They are simply good in themselves. Therefore, they should be universally upheld by all reasonable persons. Intrinsic goods cannot be downgraded or seconded to any instrumental goodness.

Non-intrinsic goods, on the other hand, are objects, actions, or qualities, the value of which depends upon serving as a means for bringing about or maintaining an intrinsic good. Consequently, non-intrinsic goods are known as *instrumental values or goods of the second order*. Examples include money, food, discipline, and personal loyalty. These are presumed to be valuable, not for their own sake, but for what they can accomplish. Money, for instance, is only good for what it can buy. When money cannot be exchanged for goods, or if the desired commodity is not offered for sale, it becomes worthless. Likewise, food is good only for its nutritional value. If one eats (or overeats) just for the sake of eating, one may become ill. By the same token, discipline and loyalty are good only for instilling a sense of duty among employees and for promoting a high standard of performance. Taken in its own right, enforcing discipline for its own rigor can be tedious, boring, and certainly a costly endeavor. Consequently, money, food, and discipline cannot be considered intrinsically good.

Based on this dichotomy, when one is faced with two (or more) kinds of goodness, moral judgment requires that one first select the principle that supports an intrinsic good. Principles that support a non-intrinsic value would be secondary, therefore immoral in this case.

This establishes the first rule of ethical choice:

Rule Statement 1: Intrinsic good supersedes non-intrinsic good.

As an example of this rule, consider the choice between being personally loyal to your supervisor (not the agency itself) and your obligation to be honest. According to the previous rule, personal loyalty is a non-intrinsic value that serves only the need to maintain discipline. At times it might even be dysfunctional, because it can promote the practice of "sucking up" to superiors. Honesty, on the other hand, is an intrinsic value that is good in itself. If honesty were to be sacrificed or seconded to the instrumental value of personal loyalty, it would be detrimental to the integrity of the agency. Therefore, dishonest behavior cannot be justified for the sake of personal loyalty. History indicates that failure to distinguish between these two values has caused disastrous consequences. A brief review of the recent history of the United States (for example, the Vietnam War, the Watergate scandal, the Iran-Contra affair, and so on) should make this reasoning much more enlightening and interesting.

Second Premise: There are two categories of evil—intrinsic and non-intrinsic.

Intrinsic evil refers to objects, actions, or qualities that are evil or harmful in their own right. Examples include death, slavery, injustice, and brutality. All of these should be avoided, if possible, or replaced with a lesser evil. Non-intrinsic evils, on the other hand, are objects, actions, and qualities that serve as a means for bringing about or maintaining evil. For example, poisons, lethal weapons, and nondemocratic government are non-intrinsic evils. Although they are not evil "in themselves" (in the hands of an ethical person, they could be), they are potentially evil. A good example of accepting non-intrinsic evil in lieu of an intrinsic evil is the slogan by Eastern European societies after World War II of "better Red than dead." When people in these societies were faced with a choice between annihilation and communism, they chose the latter, because it was a lesser evil. While having a communist government is bad in itself, it is less evil than mass destruction. Based on this reasoning, non-intrinsic evil is less harmful than intrinsic evil and should replace it whenever possible.

This establishes the second rule of ethical choice:

Rule Statement 2: Non-intrinsic evil supersedes intrinsic evil.

Based on these two rules, moral judgment (unless complicated by other factors that will be examined later) should favor intrinsic good over non-intrinsic good, and non-intrinsic evil over intrinsic evil.

Third Premise: Levels of goodness (or evil) are hierarchically ranked, culminating in summum bonum.

Goodness (intrinsic or non-intrinsic) is of different grades; some are higher than others. As such, they can be rank-ordered in an ascending manner culminating in the highest good, or *summum bonum.*

Based on this premise, if there is a conflict between two or more goods, a lower-grade good cannot be justified in the presence of a higher-grade good. For example, in judging the grades of happiness, there is the physical level, the emotional level, and the intellectual level, with the last being the highest. By the same token, in judging the evil of killing, there is killing by lethal injection, by shooting, by starvation, or by torture, with the last being the most evil. Therefore, it is necessary for the ethical reasoner to pursue the highest level of goodness attainable and to steer away from the lower grades of evil as much as they can be avoided. As to the exact criterion for distinguishing between higher and lower levels of goodness or evil, we will learn that later in the book.

The Principle of *Summum Bonum*

Summum bonum is the principle of the highest good. The term is Latin and means the *ultimate good,* one that cannot be subordinated to any other. The principle obligates the ethical reasoner to examine all levels of goodness that bear on the issue, to rank them in ascending order, and to choose the highest among them as the "master good." Such ranking can be based on the quality of goodness, the number of beneficiaries, and the utility of goodness, among other factors. As such, the concept of *summum bonum* characterizes the "moral of all morals" and the "ethic of all ethics."

In the classic tradition of ethics, philosophers have reduced *summum bonum* to either a single "master" goodness or a set of related values, and argued their viewpoint from that perspective. For Socrates, for instance, the master goodness was *knowledge*; for Plato it was *justice* (a just state, a just society, a just city, or a just agency); and for Aristotle it was *moral character* (an activity of the soul when in accordance with virtue). By contrast, hedonist philosophers identified *summum bonum* with the quality of pleasure (both physical and mental), and Christian philosophers identified it with degrees of piety. Saint Augustine, in the fifth century, for example, identified *summum bonum* with faith, hope, and salvation, while Saint Thomas Aquinas, in the thirteenth century, identified it with the ability to see God as "He is." This, Saint Thomas Aquinas taught, comes about through a long life of obedience to Christian principles.

The function of *summum bonum* is analogous to that of a "lighthouse" that guides ethical behavior on the stormy sea of uncertainty. It is also comparable to the point of "true north" on the moral compass. To better understand the concept, imagine that all the values that bear on the issue are stacked on a totem pole representing the hierarchy of values. In this sense, *summum bonum* would be the pinnacle of the pole that caps all lower values and gives them sequence, rank, and relative worth.

This establishes the third rule of ethical choice:

Rule Statement 3: When selecting between grades of goodness (or evil), seek the summum bonum. *Toward that goal, any grade of goodness can be ignored or violated in favor of a higher grade.*

A Guiding Formula for Moral Judgment

An author once stood before an ethics class, lecturing on the value of discretion in criminal justice and the imperative of moral judgment. As he emphasized the process of moral judgment in qualitative terms, he was interrupted by a young, obviously upset student who shouted, "All of you professors tell us to use judgment, but none of you show us how. I was born in Vietnam! What am I supposed to fall back on?" (Souryal, 1993). At that moment, everything around the instructor fell silent, except for the echoing question, "What am I supposed to fall back on?" The instructor did not have a convincing answer at the time. Several years later, he developed one guiding formula that is *simple* and *memorable*.

The formula consists of four steps:

1. Select the moral principle that best defines the problem in question (for example, is it a matter of honesty, fairness, equity, loyalty, and so on).

2. Justify the situation at hand by examining whether it conforms to the selected principle. If it does not, determine the accentuating or mitigating factors that could make it more or less fitting.

3. If the situation fits the principle (exactly), the judgment should be made in accordance with the principle (exactly).

4. If the situation does not fit the principle exactly, judgment should be made by determining a high likelihood or a low likelihood that the situation fits the principle. Accentuating factors support a high likelihood, and mitigating factors, a low likelihood.

While this formula is certainly not meant to be a precise mathematical configuration, it is presented to illuminate the way we can make better moral judgments. More quantitative formulas in the future may be able to assign numbers to each principle and to each level of justification.

$$E = PJ^2$$

In this simple formula, E (the ethical decision) equals P (the principle) times J (the justification of the situation).

From a mathematical standpoint, P is a linear dimension and J is quadratic. The square value of J is proposed here to allow for justification to be ratcheted up or down depending on the power of accentuating or mitigating factors. And because the power of P is always constant (unless we are comparing the power of one principle to another), the *morality of judgment should be a function of justification*. Does the situation justify the principle? If not, how close is it to an exact justification?

Take, for example, Aristotle's principle of debt paying. While as a principle, people should always repay their debts, Aristotle recognized situations in which compliance with that principle could be unethical. He cited the example of a person who borrows a knife from another who, in the meantime, has become insane or suicidal. In this case, the disturbed state of the knife owner is an accentuating factor, because returning the knife may make it easier for him (the knife owner) to hurt himself or threaten the life of another. In a sense, the debt-paying principle may not be exactly justifiable, and compliance with the principle may be unethical. Keeping the knife until the owner recovered would therefore be perfectly justified.

Let us take another example: the sanctity of life. Throughout the literature of history, ethics, theology, and law, life has been considered sacred, and killing, an intrinsic evil. The principle is based on the assumption that life was created by God and that if (hypothetically) all people resorted to killing, society would self-destruct. Thus, killing is evil, unless it is justified.

Justifications for killing have been recognized since the beginning of history. For example, in Greece, it was justified to appease the gods, thus dissuading them from destroying the world. In war it was justified to protect society from being vanquished. Yet, consistent with this justification, the crusaders were praised for liberating Jerusalem, despite the fact that they killed thousands of innocent people. In recent history, killing in war has been less justifiable. Nowadays, it is no longer justified unless the war itself is just and as long as the armies involved comply with the universal rules of warfare. If neither condition prevails, those responsible are held accountable. Furthermore, if the forces kill noncombatant persons, those responsible are considered barbarians. Moreover, if the forces single out innocent people for extermination, those responsible are tried as war criminals.

Let us take another scenario that justifies killing: the case of self-defense. The practice has been universally justified as consistent with the principle of survival, although Saint Augustine condemned it on the basis that a good Christian should rather die than kill. Yet killing in the case of euthanasia or abortion has been controversial. While some ethicists justify euthanasia because of the painful suffering experienced by terminally ill individuals, most disapprove in the case of those who are simply tired of living. In the case of abortion, justification has been even more difficult. While most ethicists would justify it when the life of the mother is threatened, fewer would allow it otherwise.

When similar situations are examined under the rigor of principle, one can discern (and at the same time appreciate) the complexity of the justification process involved in $E = PJ^2$. As in the previous examples, one should realize that killing under certain justifications can be an act of nonintrinsic good, or even of mercy. The utilitarian theory of ethics that will be examined later in the book will provide additional knowledge that might make it easier to apply $E = PJ^2$.

$E = PJ^2$ in Practice

In 1996, the New Haven Police Department issued an Order Maintenance Training Bulletin in which the department proposed a new policy for order maintenance that closely resembles the philosophy of $E = PJ^2$. While the bulletin preceded the formula expressed in this chapter, it seemed to confirm and legitimize it.

The New Haven Training Bulletin defined *order maintenance* as "working with neighborhood residents and others who use public spaces to maintain order legally, humanely, respectfully, and equitably." The purpose of the new policy was "to prevent crime and reduce citizen fear, to facilitate public discourse and activities, to create an atmosphere of diversity, and to improve and restore the quality of life in neighborhoods." The problems referred to in the bulletin included abandoned cars, prostitution, noise, graffiti, public drinking, and disorderly conduct, such as aggressive panhandling.

The New Haven Police Department recognized that its order maintenance activities are discretionary at all levels of the department, from police chief through all personnel. Discretion, the bulletin emphasized, does not imply personal inclination, but the application of officers' professional knowledge, values, and skills to particular problems and incidents. The starting point of all professionalism, the bulletin stated, is the law. Nevertheless, the New Haven Police Department required that the officers always use the least forceful means possible to achieve its purposes. While officers should not hesitate to cite or arrest offenders, their approach, at all levels of the organization, will be to attempt to get citizens to obey the laws and ordinances as unintrusively as possible. The department proposed *three levels* of intervention:

1. The first level of intervention, whether by managers, supervisors, or police officers, will be to educate the public about civility, the consequences of incivility, and the laws that oblige citizens to behave in particular ways. This can be done in neighborhood meetings, in schools, or in interactions with citizens. The bulletin stated that some citizens do not fully understand their obligations, and if those obligations—for example, regarding a noisy car or public drinking in parks—are patiently explained, citizens will adhere to the law.

2. The second level of intervention will be to remind citizens of their responsibilities if they were disorderly—that they were breaking the law and will be subject to penalties if they persist. This, too, can be done in a variety of ways. It can be done by visiting a problem location and warning people that if their behavior continues, they will be subject to penalties. Similarly, owners of locations that have chronic problems can be so warned by individual officers.

3. The final level of intervention will be law enforcement—the use of citation and arrest.

According to the New Haven Training Bulletin, the criteria for police discretion further articulates the "square" as in the $E = PJ^2$

formula by emphasizing five factors that can help the officers make more ethical discretionary decisions:

1. Time disorder: Time disorder has important chronological aspects. Society acknowledges this culturally through the observation of holidays (for example, the Fourth of July, Thanksgiving Day, St. Patrick's Day) and other periods when society is more tolerant of behavior and entertainment (for example, Friday and Saturday nights, New Year's Eve).

2. Location: Different neighborhoods have different thresholds for various kinds of activities. Certainly, the bulletin stated, one can be more tolerant of noise levels in downtown New Haven than in residential areas. Likewise, some forms of disorderly behavior are absolutely inappropriate around schools (public urination by adults, for example) and would be the basis not for education or warning, but for strong legal condemnation.

3. Condition of the offender: The bulletin stated that the officers would be concerned about whether a person is intoxicated or under the influence of drugs, or behaving in a variety of inappropriate or disturbed ways. Illness, and behavior associated with illness, would be another variable affecting the police response (seizures and post-seizure, for example). The New Haven Police Department emphasized that it is not concerned about matters of social class, race, homelessness, and so on when it refers to the condition of the offender. The department emphasized that the focus of police discretion is behavior. For example, the officers would be less concerned about a person who urinated in public if the person attempted to find a solitary location and maintained a sense of modesty than someone who flagrantly exposed him- or herself in a highly visible location.

4. Condition of the victim/witness: The officers of the New Haven Police Department would be more concerned about aggressive panhandling, for example, that targeted vulnerable persons—children, the elderly, people with disabilities—than about similar approaches to sturdy youths. Similarly, the officers, as a matter of policy, would always be more concerned about the impact of disorderly behavior on children.

5. Numbers, volume, or aggregation: The New Haven Police Department emphasized that one panhandler is one type of problem, but 10 panhandlers is another. Similarly, every form of disorder would have a different meaning depending on the number and concentration of the people committing the act or acts.

Finally, the New Haven Police Department insisted that these factors and others would be primary in determining police response to disorder whether on a departmental, substation, or individual officer level. Yet all the officers are expected to use their discretion wisely and proudly.

Summary

The three principles and the formula discussed here form the rules of moral judgment:

1. Intrinsic evils are the lowest levels of morality and should always be avoided.

2. Intrinsic goodness is the highest level of goodness and should be actively sought.

3. *Summum bonum* is the highest moral choice and should always be sought.

But:

4. If intrinsic goodness cannot be achieved, the highest level of non-intrinsic goodness should be sought as the next justifiable ethic.

And:

5. Whenever intrinsic evil can be avoided, the highest level of non-intrinsic evil should be sought as the next justifiable ethic.

Furthermore:

6. When in doubt, apply $E = PJ^2$.

Figure 1.3 illustrates this rank order of moral judgment.

Figure 1.3
Rank Order of Moral Reasoning

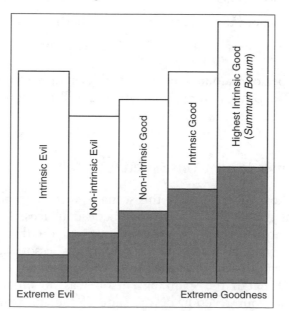

The lesson to be learned from this stop is to differentiate between intrinsic and non-intrinsic values, to evaluate each on a scale from the least valuable to the most valuable, and to make moral judgments by seeking the highest attainable good—the *summum bonum* of all available virtues.

Exhibit 6—Actions and Consequences

Our next stop is by *a young woman spanking her child* for wandering about, at risk of being lost in the crowd. The mother is inflicting pain on the child, who is crying uncontrollably, inviting pity and sympathy from the surrounding people.

What is your reaction to this scene? Could you justify the action of the concerned mother, or would you consider her behavior cruel and unethical? This scenario symbolizes a central issue in ethical theory: the dilemma of human *actions and consequences* (also known as the *ethics of means and ends*). The issue, if you will recall, was previously raised when we stopped at Exhibit 4 to view the depiction of the Garden of Eden.

Ethical judgment should always be made in relation to human actions. Sentiments, feelings, and intentions are improper to judge, because they cannot be ascertained objectively. But when actions occur, we are faced with four possible configurations:

1. "Good" actions that lead to "good" consequences

2. "Bad" actions that lead to "bad" consequences

3. "Bad" actions that lead to "good" consequences

4. "Good" actions that lead to "bad" consequences

Rational persons should have no difficulty judging the first two configurations. The other two are complex and will therefore be discussed in detail.

Bad Actions/Good Consequences

The spanking of the child in this scenario represents the dilemma of "bad" actions that could lead to "good" consequences. The infliction of pain (a bad action), however, can be justified on the basis that the mother was trying to teach the child a useful lesson (a good consequence). But would you have the same reaction if the woman was not the mother? What if the spanking person was an older brother or a cousin? Would your reaction be the same if the spanking turned into an ugly beating? Obviously, moral judgment in these cases should depend upon examining the nature of the action, the "utility" of the consequence expected, and, certainly, the relationship between the actor and the recipient.

The nature of the relationship is of particular significance because it may be considered rooted in cultural and social terms. For instance, it is acceptable (indeed an obligation) in some European cultures for an uncle or a cousin to discipline a disobedient child. In Moslem culture it is acceptable even for a perfect stranger to do the same. What must be emphasized here, however, is that while judgment in these instances cannot be universalized, the ethical principle upon which judgment is made can be universalized. The utilitarian theory of actions and consequences examines these relationships and establishes useful rules for their practice.

In order to better understand the relationship between bad actions and good consequences, magnifying the situation to a much greater scale can be of great assistance. Let us consider some classic situations from recent history. For instance, dropping the atomic bomb on Hiroshima in 1945 was widely justified by the consequences of shortening the war in the Pacific and saving American lives. The detention of Japanese Americans during World War II was justified by the consequence of reducing potential collaboration with the enemy. The trial and subsequent execution of top Nazi generals after the war was justified by the consequence of deterring war crimes. Even on a smaller scale, in many states the use of capital punishment has been justified on the grounds of deterring crime, and the practice of disciplining employees in the workplace is justified by reinforcing compliance with work standards, therefore increasing productivity and improving the quality of work.

Good Actions/Bad Consequences

Examples of this category include the cases of a friend who helps another by lending him a car and the friend later causing a traffic accident; a father who increases the weekly allowance to his adolescent child, who uses the money to buy alcohol or drugs; and a professor who helps a student secure a job at a department store, where the student is arrested for shoplifting. Obviously, the motives behind these actions are "good," and the behaviors of the friend, the father, and the professor should be considered morally worthy. But what about their disastrous consequences? Who is to blame? The answer depends on the amount of knowledge each of these "Samaritans" was *expected* to have about the probability of these consequences happening—at the time the decision was made. One's capacity to assess the value of an action against the potential risk that may ensue distinguishes the knowledge level of the actor and establishes his or her responsibility for the outcome. Those who are more knowledgeable are considered more blameworthy when they commit an unethical act than those who are less knowledgeable. Indeed, Aristotle argued that if two individuals commit the same crime, the one who is more knowledgeable should be punished more severely.

The Utilitarian Measure

The theory of *utilitarianism* is perhaps the most suitable for studying the relationship between actions and consequences. The theory identifies ethical actions as those that tend to maximize happiness and minimize pain; the greater the happiness, the greater the moral value of the act. Furthermore, the more persons benefiting from an action, the more praiseworthy the act. The theory also distinguishes between two main utilitarian principles: *act-utilitarianism* and *rule-utilitarianism*. In the scenario of the mother spanking her child, an act-utilitarianist would disapprove of the act, while a rule-utilitarianist approves. The rationale is as follows:

> *Act-utilitarianists* are rather rigid. They judge the morality of an act only on the basis of its propensity to produce happiness or pain. And because in the scenario of the mother and the child, spanking would inflict pain, it would be morally unacceptable, regardless of the noble consequences that might ensue. As to the need to teach the child not to wander off, act-utilitarianists would advise the mother to speak with the child, try to persuade him or her, and find an acceptable alternative to the infliction of pain.

> *Rule-utilitarianists* are more flexible. They would overlook the act and focus on the rule behind it; if the rule is conducive to good consequences, then the act is justifiable. If the rule is not, the act is unjustifiable. A rule-utilitarianist would most likely agree with the spanking, because it is consistent with the policy of "spare the rod, spoil the child." He or she would probably reason that if the rule is not carried out, we will end up with a community of spoiled children. Therefore, it is permissible to spank children as long as no serious damage is done. Furthermore, if as a society we follow the rule of spanking children in an appropriate manner and in appropriate circumstances, we would be a better-functioning society. Rule-utilitarianists insist that what distinguishes the goodness or evil of an act is simply the rule that prompts it.

Pioneers of Utilitarianism

Among the champions of the utilitarian theory were Jeremy Bentham and John Stuart Mill. Bentham was the acclaimed originator of the *principle of utility* (hence, the theory of utilitarianism). Bentham established a rule for judging the rightness or wrongness of actions by evaluating their tendency to augment or diminish the happiness of the parties whose interests are in question. In a later version of his theory, Bentham developed a more objective instrument for measuring the morality of actions by computing the "amount" of happiness they can produce. Bentham's instrument established a quantitative scale, or matrix, consisting of seven elements:

1. Intensity of happiness

2. Duration of happiness

3. Certainty of happiness

4. Purity of happiness

5. Extent of happiness

6. Propinquity of happiness

7. Fecundity of happiness

Influenced by the success of the scientific method in other fields, Bentham tried to apply the same method to ethics in a quasi-mathematical formula.

John Stuart Mill was a utilitarian who disagreed with Bentham's scientific method, calling it a "pig philosophy." He was more concerned with the *quality* of happiness than with its *quantity*. As to how such quality can be measured, Mill deferred to a "jury of experts" who are acquainted with the kind of happiness in question. He called these people "hedonistic experts," or judges who would be knowledgeable in the appreciation of different pleasures. These experts, Mill proposed, would be governed in their judgment by *internal* and *external* sanctions or forces. Internal sanctions, he thought, had far greater impact because they include the attributes of reason, sensitivity, and fairness. External sanctions are of lesser significance and include one's fear of God and readiness to face adverse public opinion (Sahakian, 1974:35). Mill tended to favor the qualitative approach as long as the judgment of consequences was determined on the basis of "prudence and foresight."

> The lesson to be learned from this stop is to carefully examine actions and their consequences before making ethical judgment, and to consider utilitarianism as a reasonable criterion for choice.

Exhibit 7—Determinism and Intentionalism

Our next stop is *beside a young man sitting on a bench*. He appears to be a student from a Middle Eastern country. He holds some note-books on his lap while he stares with disbelief at an examination paper in his hand. He is wailing and lamenting his "bad luck." He has just flunked a crucial college exam and will not be allowed to graduate. When asked about his problem, he pitifully cries that he was "doomed to failure," he "knew it all along," and there was nothing he could do "to change his destiny."

The foreign student's behavior symbolizes the issue of human *determinism*. This is a particularly critical issue to the study of ethics, because it can cast serious doubt on the validity of human choice. Unquestionably, if human beings are not free to choose between possible courses of action, then studying moral judgment is contradictory and teaching ethics is deceptive.

Determinism

The concept of determinism means that all thoughts, attitudes, and actions result from external forces that are *beyond human control*. All things in the universe are "governed" by, or operated in accordance with, fixed causal laws that determine all events as well as the consequences that follow.

Determinist philosophers argue that what appear to be independent decisions in favor of certain dispositions (to act or not to act) are not decisions at all, because no real choices are involved. Human actions are inevitable events that follow a grand design that dictates when, where, and how everything will happen. Therefore, it would be illogical, and certainly unfair, to hold someone responsible for such actions. Subsequently, it would be a fallacy to preach or to recommend certain values when people are incapable of making independent choices.

Literature of determinism also refers to a more chronic form of determinism known as *predestination*. This view is more closely associated with the idea of *fatalism*. While the concept is often linked to a dogmatic interpretation of God's will, it is sometimes associated with astrological forces that control the movement of stars in the heavens. According to the theory of predestination, every happening is attributable to a cosmic power that predetermines its occurrence. Human beings are simply supposed to accept such inevitable events, to cope with them the best way they can, and to go on with their lives. Examples of this concept are the practice of reading one's horoscope every day before leaving the house, or consulting a fortune-teller before making an important decision. In many cultures, predestination is accepted as a way of life; for instance, in Arab culture it is called the *maktuub* (written), in the Greek culture it is called *moira* (meant to be), and in the Roman culture it was incorporated in the philosophy of Stoicism.

In the scenario of the young foreign student, he most likely subscribes to predestination. He blames his failure on bad luck and considers his inability to graduate from college as "written" in his destiny. Furthermore, he believes he is incapable of reversing his predestined fate. He may be unwilling to make a choice to repeat the course he failed, to select another area of study, or to possibly move to another college where he could do better. Most knowledgeable people today have abandoned the predestination view and regard it as merely an interesting historical curiosity (Porter, 1980:54).

Scientific Determinism

Modern-day determinism is supported by a scientific view. A scientific determinist would maintain that a person's character, conduct, and choices are products of either hereditary or environmental factors. Together they form *operative elements* that control one's ability to think and judge. Basically, operative elements are the following:

1. Genetic conditions that make up the chemical, anatomical, and physiological characteristics we inherit through the medium of genes and chromosomes

2. Climate and geography that influence our personality and temperament (for instance, in countries with cool climates, people are generally perceived to be more active, industrious, and efficient)

3. Society and culture that provide us with most of our ingrained traditions, beliefs, desires, and tendencies to do or not do certain actions

4. Education and socialization that provide the necessary knowledge base we need in the fields of sciences and the arts, as well as in the areas of critical thinking and reasoning

The fact that most inmates in state penitentiaries today characteristically combine a low IQ score with a low level of formal education might help explain the last element even more clearly.

Still, in the literature of determinism there is a distinction between two forms of determinism: *hard* and *soft*. While both forms accept determinism as a set of operative elements, each views human choices differently. *Hard determinists* maintain that operative elements eliminate free will. They argue that to speak of freedom of choice and personal responsibility for actions, when actions follow a strictly causal chain, makes no sense. *Soft determinists*, on the other hand, hold that although actions can be strongly influenced by the operative elements, the individual is still relatively free to shape and reshape the causal chain. After all, it is the individual's nature and the circumstances that surround it that cause these factors to develop and take hold. In the case of the foreign student we met, he certainly lived long enough in the United States to be able to learn the American way of coping with difficult odds. However, the distinction between hard and soft determinism—while important in certain contexts—is not crucial to the broader sense of this discussion.

Intentionalism

The opposite view of determinism is the *libertarian view*, also known as *intentionalism* or *free will*. This view affirms that all rational beings possess an innate freedom of will and, as such, must be held responsible for their actions. The theory maintains that people are in control of their actions by virtue of their ability to think and to choose their actions freely. Yet while no one is "absolutely free" or can "always" be free (because people could at times be forced to act against their will), people can still make choices, given the free will they possess. For example, while prison inmates are physically behind bars, many continue to make intelligent decisions regarding their adaptation to prison life, education, rehabilitation, and plans for early parole.

Arguments in favor of the libertarian theory can be summed up as follows:

1. External forces of heredity and environment are merely *influences*, rather than determinants. Once we become aware of their forces upon our ability to decide, they lose their power. Consequently, we should be able to rationally accept, reject, or alter all options available to us.

2. Talk about causes of actions can be misleading, because it indicates that people are controlled by a strict system of cause–effect instinctive response. But by virtue of human intellect, people are still capable of reasoning their way out of the grip of the "elements" and making good choices. Even if a cause–effect relationship exists, the libertarians question the narrow interpretation used by the determinists, whereby a preceding event is assumed to cause the action that follows. For example, they argue that although millions of Americans drive their automobiles to and from work each day and thousands of them are involved in traffic accidents, it would be illogical to assume that work causes traffic accidents.

3. Arguments in favor of the determinist position are in themselves incoherent, because the determinists base their position on the belief that all ideas are, in essence, determined in advance. But because the concept of determinism is itself an idea, those who advocate determinism must be admitting a belief that they did not freely examine or choose to advocate.

> The lesson to be learned from this stop is to consider ethical judgment as a product of intentionally and freely made choices, unless there is evidence to the contrary. In this case, the impact of operative elements must be considered.

Exhibit 8—The Ethical Person

Now we come to the end of the tour, by *a shiny, late-model red automobile* displayed on a revolving platform. There are powerful floodlights aimed at it from overhead and it looks good. The automobile is the product of the latest scientific, technological, and artistic accomplishments in the automobile industry. The car symbolizes an object that is beautiful, valuable, functional, and pleasurable to drive and own.

The image of that car represents the profile of the ethical person, the ultimate portrait of the civilized person, the admirable person, the good person. The following description by Abraham Maslow is one of the most comprehensive and accurate profiles in the literature. It best illustrates the type of person we, as criminal justice professionals, should strive to be. The profile presents values that can enrich the quality of our lives and make our careers in criminal justice much more worthwhile. Read Maslow's profile carefully, reflect on the values it embodies, and discuss its applicability with your classmates, coworkers, and acquaintances. Note where discrepancies exist, and reflect on the reasoning behind these discrepancies. Are they products of individual indifference, of the nature of criminal justice in particular, of bureaucracy in general, or of the culture in which we live?

> The lesson to be learned from this stop is to grasp and admire the attributes of the ethical person and to try to emulate them in both your public and your private life.

Profile of the Ethical Person

Delight in bringing about justice.

Delight in stopping cruelty and exploitation.

Fight lies and untruths.

They love virtue to be rewarded.

They seem to like happy endings, good completions.

They hate sin and evil to be rewarded, and they hate people to get away with it.

They are good punishers of evil.

They try to set things right, to clean up bad situations.

They enjoy doing good.

They like to reward and praise promise, talent, virtue, etc.

They avoid publicity, fame, glory, honors, popularity, celebrity, or at least do not seek it. It seems to be not awfully important one way or another.

They do not need to be loved by everyone.

They generally pick out their own causes, which are apt to be few in number, rather than responding to advertising or to campaigns or to other people's exhortations.

They tend to enjoy peace, quiet, pleasantness, etc., and they tend not to like turmoil, fighting, war, etc. (they are not general-fighters on every front), and they can enjoy themselves in the middle of a "war."

They also seem practical and shrewd and realistic about it, more often than impractical. They like to be effective and dislike being ineffectual.

Their fighting is not an excuse for hostility, paranoia, grandiosity, authority, rebellion, etc., but is for the sake of setting things right. It is problem-centered.

They manage somehow simultaneously to love the world as it is and to try to improve it.

In all cases there is some hope that people and nature and society can be improved.

In all cases it is as if they can see both good and evil realistically.

They respond to the challenge in a job.

A chance to improve the situation or the operation is a big reward. They enjoy improving things.

Observations generally indicate great pleasure in their children and in helping them grow into good adults.

They do not need or seek, or even enjoy very much, flattery, applause, popularity, status, prestige, money, honors, etc.

Expressions of gratitude, or at least of awareness of their good fortune, are common.

They have a sense of noblesse oblige. It is the duty of the superior, of the one who sees and knows, to be patient and tolerant, as with children.

They tend to be attracted by mystery, unsolved problems, by the unknown and the challenging, rather than to be frightened by them.

They enjoy bringing about law and order in the chaotic situation, in the messy or confused situation, or in the dirty and unclean situation.

They hate (and fight) corruption, cruelty, malice, dishonesty, pompousness, phoniness, and faking.

They try to free themselves from illusions, to look at the facts courageously, to take away the blindfold.

They feel it is a pity for talent to be wasted.

They do not do mean things, and they respond with anger when other people do mean things.

They tend to feel that every person should have an opportunity to develop to his highest potential, to have a fair chance, to have equal opportunity.

They like doing things well, "doing a good job," "to do well what needs doing." Many such phrases add up to "bringing about good workmanship." One advantage of being a boss is the right to give away the corporation's money, to choose which good causes to help. They enjoy giving their own money away to causes they consider important, good, worthwhile, etc. [They take] pleasure in philanthropy.

They enjoy watching and helping the self-actualization of others, especially of the young.

They enjoy watching happiness and helping to bring it about.

They get great pleasure from knowing admirable people (courageous, honest, effective, "straight," "big," creative, saintly, etc.). "My work brings me in contact with many fine people."

They enjoy taking on responsibilities (that they can handle well), and certainly don't fear or evade their responsibilities. They respond to responsibility.

They uniformly consider their work to be worthwhile, important, even essential.

They enjoy greater efficiency, making an operation more neater, more compact, simpler, faster, less expensive, turning out a better product, doing with fewer parts, a smaller number of operations, less clumsiness, less effort, more foolproof, safer, more "elegant," less laborious.

Review Questions

1. Socrates taught that virtue is knowledge and knowledge is virtue. How can college education in the field of criminal justice improve the quality of justice on the street?

2. Of the four sources of the truth (opinion, belief, science, and reasoning), which is the most necessary for the criminal justice professional, and why? Give examples.

3. Plato used the allegory of the cave to illustrate the resistance of unprofessional people to face the truth. How does this relate to the behavior of criminal justice practitioners who insist on using unjustified labels and clichés? Discuss three such clichés and explain the reasons behind the resistance.

4. Aristotle's theory of realism was grounded in the concepts of potentiality and actuality, and the mean. What from this philosophy can professional police officers use when dealing with juvenile delinquents?

5. What is the relationship between the ethics of corrections and the obligation of correctional officers to be moral at the workplace? Give three examples.

6. Define relativist morality and discuss its origins. How does relativist morality influence the behavior of police officers, especially those who patrol areas where minority groups reside?

7. Explain the hierarchy of values, beginning with the lowest intrinsic evil and ending with the highest intrinsic good. How can adherence to this hierarchy enhance the performance of probation and parole officers?

8. Should a criminal justice practitioner adhere to the act-utilitarian philosophy, the rule-utilitarian philosophy, or both? Give examples from the field of policing.

9. Do you agree or disagree with the statement that ethical judgments are "a product of intentionally and freely made choices, unless there is strong evidence to the contrary"? Why or why not?

10. Examine your actions at the workplace as well as the actions of your colleagues. How closely do such actions fit Maslow's profile of the ethical person?

References

Albert, E. M., Denise, T. C., & Peterfreund, S. P. (1988). *Great Traditions in Ethics* (6th ed). Belmont, CA: Wadsworth Publishing.

Bloom, A. (1987). *The Closing of the American Mind*. New York: Touchstone.

Frankena, W. K. (1963). *Ethics*. Englewood Cliffs, NJ: Prentice-Hall.

Friel, C. M. (1998). *Personal Interview*. Huntsville, TX: Sam Houston State University.

Gert, B. (1973). *The Moral Rules: A New Rational Foundation for Morality*. New York: Harper & Row Publishers.

Jowctt, B., & Butcher, S. H. (1979). (Trans.) *Aristotle: Politics and Poetics*. Norwalk, CT: The Eastern Press.

Lavine, T. Z. (1984). *From Socrates to Sartre: The Philosophic Quest*. Toronto: Bantam Books.

Maslow, A. H. (1971). *The Farther Reaches of Human Nature*. New York: Viking Press.

Porter, B. F. (1980). *The Good Life: Alternatives in Ethics*. New York: Macmillan Publishing.

Sahakian, W. S. (1974). *Ethics: An Introduction to Theories and Problems*. New York: Barnes and Noble Books.

Souryal, S. (1993). What Am I Supposed to Fall Back On? Culture Literacy in Criminal Justice Ethics. *Journal of Criminal Justice Education*, 4(1) Spring.

2

Familiarizing Yourself with Ethics
Nature, Definitions, and Categories

I never did or encountered in public life a single act inconsistent with the strictest good faith; having never believed there was one code of morality for a public and another for a private man.

Thomas Jefferson, 1809
Letter to Don Valentine de Feronda

Genuine goodness threatens those on the opposite end of the moral spectrum.

Charles, Earl Spencer

All men's appetites have a tendency to promote both the private and the public good.

Bishop Butler

Right and wrong is originally a concept connected with power and having to do with the motivation of those who are not bound to obedience.
Bertrand Russell

The difference between good and evil is the difference between order and disorder.

Plato

What You Will Learn from This Chapter

You will learn the philosophy of ethics. It includes understanding the concept of wisdom, the nature of ethics, the scope of ethics, and the essence of ethical theory. You will also learn the credibility of ethics and the way arguments are made from both deontological and teleological perspectives.

You will also learn the role of moral judgment in criminal justice, the deceptive nature of occupational subculture, the distortion of fallacious reasoning, the rule of reasonableness, and the historical origins of ethics.

Key Terms and Definitions

Philosophy of Wisdom is the only legitimate method of determining moral issues. It is the "superconductor" of all disciplines.

A Prior *Knowledge* is knowledge that is derived from pure reasoning without reference to sensory experience.

A Posteriori *Knowledge* is knowledge derived from sensory experience.

Knowledge by Acquaintance is knowledge derived from people, places, and things based on hearsay.

Fallacy is an incorrect way of reasoning. It is an attempt to persuade others emotionally or psychologically, but not logically.

Formal Fallacy is an error of logic in which the conclusion is not derived from the premise.

Naturalistic Fallacy is an invalid argument. It is an error in deductive logic that attempts to derive evaluative conclusions from descriptive premises.

Genetic Fallacy is an invalid argument based on the mistake of evaluating a theory, a statement, or conduct on the basis of the person who created such.

Normative Ethics is the category of ethical theory that formulates moral standards of conduct and articulates the principles and sanctions that govern such conduct.

Metaethics Theory is a complex category of ethical theory that investigates the meaning of ethical terms and critiques how ethical statements are verified.

> *Deontological Theory* is a subcategory of normative ethics that judges the rightness or wrongness of behavior on the basis of the act itself.
>
> *Teleological Theory* is a subcategory of normative ethics that determines the moral worth of an act on the basis of its consequence or intention.

Overview

As in government everywhere, criminal justice practitioners often face moral dilemmas that require making unusual judgments. In routine situations, moral judgment can be made with greater ease because the criteria for choice are fairly constant—following the rules and regulations and adhering to the voice of tradition. In unusual situations, however, making moral judgments can be agonizing, because the criteria for choice often involve conflicting values—cultural, legal, religious, or personal. While public practitioners are invariably capable of making right choices, it is not uncommon that bad decisions are made. When they are, they could cause substantial embarrassment to the parties involved, to the agency itself, and to society at large.

In order to fully appreciate the complexity of moral judgment, the following two cases—of Captain Balian and Lieutenant Lotem—will be discussed. While they represent diametrically opposed views of what constitutes moral judgment, by contrast they provide a profoundly enlightening lesson regarding the quality and grade of moral judgment.

Captain Balian's Story

Several years ago, the USS *Dubuque* was sailing the South China Sea near the borders of Vietnam under the command of Captain Alex Balian. The midsize navy ship was on a routine peacetime mission. The United States was not at war with any of the surrounding countries, and no hostile action was anticipated. One afternoon, over the calm sea, the sailors on deck spotted a small wooden sailboat that appeared to be in distress. Upon approaching the boat, the sailors discovered it to be overcrowded with Vietnamese people who were seeking refuge in the Philippine Islands. Several refugees jumped the boat, swam to the *Dubuque*, and held tightly to safety ropes dropped for them by the sailors. They were screaming and begging to be taken aboard, complaining that their group had been out of food and water for several days. Captain Balian negotiated with the men on the ropes but denied the refugees' plea to be taken aboard. He instead decided to provide them with provisions of food and water sufficient for one week. When the men on the ropes intensified their plea to be taken aboard and refused to return to the boat, the captain allegedly ordered them shrugged off. Three of them drowned in view of the sailors on deck. Shortly afterward, the *Dubuque* left the scene with many of its sailors disappointed in their captain's decision.

Several weeks later, some of the boat people reached the Philippines. They reported to the authorities that the provisions they had received from the *Dubuque* lasted for only three days, causing 72 refugees to starve to death. They also reported that during the final days, violence erupted because the starving refugees had resorted to cannibalism. Three men were forcibly drowned and their bodies were consumed.

The Department of the Navy held Captain Balian accountable for the disaster, and he was tried before a navy court-martial. Faced with charges ranging from murder by omission to failure to aid fellow human beings, the captain defended his decision by invoking the navy code of rules and regulations. "I went strictly by the book!" the captain exclaimed. After a brief trial, the captain was found guilty of lesser charges and was relieved of his command.

Was the Captain Right?

The case of Captain Balian represents, in an anecdotal way, the failure of moral judgment to transcend conventional values. Some questions related to this case, however, may illuminate the captain's dilemma: On what grounds did he base his judgment not to take the refugees aboard his ship? Did he take into consideration the full range of practical, humanitarian, and American values? Was his judgment based on knowledge and reason? Did he consider the potential consequences of leaving the refugees unaided on the high seas? Did he exhaust all reasonable means for ensuring the safety of the imperiled refugees? Did the nationality of the refugees have any prejudicial influence on his decision? Would his judgment have been different if they were, for instance, American, British, French, German, or Israeli?

Captain Balian's decision was certainly grounded in the ethics of duty and strict compliance with navy rules. He was probably concerned about the logistical problems of taking in a large number of refugees, of disturbing the well-being of his crew by requiring them to share rations and lodging space, and of the potential havoc these strangers would cause on board his ship. He obviously decided to follow what he believed was his professional duty. But despite his dedication to the rules and regulations of the navy, the tribunal found the captain's decision lacking in other fundamental areas: his higher responsibility as a sea captain for the life and safety of those stranded on the high seas; his responsibility as an American captain for turning away refugees fleeing an oppressive state; and his responsibility as a human being for causing—albeit to a small measure—the human tragedy of compelling the survivors to resort to cannibalism.

In other words, what was on trial was not only the ethics of professional duty, but also the captain's *failure to transcend lower-level values.* The captain undoubtedly had ample time to consider a wide variety of options ranging from natural law values (rescuing fellow human beings in distress), to criminal law values (avoiding murder by omission), to Christian values (aiding one's neighbor, especially when in need), to compliance with navy duties (calling in assistance to rescue the survivors), to concern for the welfare of his crew (avoiding unnecessary hardship on board his ship). The court-martial clearly determined that the skipper failed to make the proper decision as a U.S. Navy captain.

Lieutenant Lotem's Story

In 1997 Yuval Lotem was a lieutenant in the Special Forces of the Israeli army reserve. However, he was jailed for 26 days for resisting service at the military prison of Megiddo to protest the detention of Palestinians detained there without trial. Lotem's act of resistance was a rare phenomenon in the history of the Israeli Armed Forces (*Houston Chronicle*, August 25, 1997).

What signified the case of Lieutenant Lotem was that while he was serving time in the army stockade, two Palestinian suicide bombers struck in a Jerusalem market, killing 14 people and themselves. The Israeli army responded with a series of punitive measures and a wave of arrests of suspected Palestinian militants. At least 140 of them were jailed without trial in what is known as administrative detention, bringing the total of detainees to 380. Such detainees are held for periods of 6 months, which could be extended. Many have been jailed for more than 1 year, and human rights lawyers say that more than 50 have been held for 2 or more years (*Houston Chronicle*, August 25, 1997).

Israeli officials defend the detention of suspected Palestinians as imperative security measures taken to ward off serious threats. Suspects are jailed without charges because, the officials contend, bringing them to trial would disclose vital intelligence sources, and their reports would be inadmissible in court anyway under the standard rules of evidence.

Lieutenant Lotem, who had refused reserve duty in the West Bank, Gaza Strip, and Lebanon during the previous 15 years on the ground that he would have nothing to do with the military occupation, recalled the scene he saw when he was first called for duty at the Megiddo prison. He saw "two young Palestinian prisoners taking out the garbage, ringed by military police officers and a platoon of reservists carrying tear-gas canisters, helmets, and clubs." Lotem reported to the newspaper that when he saw that scene, "He immediately sensed how right he was when he refused to be a part of it" (*Houston Chronicle*, August 25, 1997).

Lieutenant Lotem completed his prison sentence in July 1997. Upon his release, he reported in an interview that "In this case the people are denied the basic right to defend themselves, and the principle of innocent until proven guilty is turned completely upside down ... these (Palestinians) are political prisoners held because of their opinions, not because of anything they've done. If they had done anything they would have been indicted" (*Houston Chronicle*, August 25, 1997). The lieutenant further added, "In school we were brought up on justice, as a people who have suffered so much from anti-Semitism, persecution and discrimination. In Russia people were jailed without trial for years, and now at home we're doing exactly the same thing." The lieutenant concluded by saying, "There is no enlightened occupation, and there is no good jailer when the prisoner is jailed without justification" (*Houston Chronicle*, August 25, 1997).

Was the Lieutenant Right?

The case of Lieutenant Lotem represents an opposite view to that of Captain Balian. In the lieutenant's case, he was in the service of his country in a time of war. He was facing a hostile population, because a state of war existed between the State of Israel and the Palestinians. He was certainly aware of the danger to his people from the brutal attacks by Palestinian terrorists. Under these conditions, he would have been justified in supporting his country's policies to arrest and detain enemy groups. He must have also known that had he followed his commanders' orders, he would have stood a better chance of being recognized as a good, loyal soldier and probably would have been decorated for valor. By the same token, the lieutenant must have also known that by not supporting his country's war effort, he would be shunned by his family and friends, disciplined by the army, and most likely convicted of treason.

Nevertheless, Lieutenant Lotem was concerned about much higher values than those with which common soldiers are usually concerned. Reminiscent of President Carter's decision on Haiti, Lotem's moral judgment reflected a higher level of transcendence—human rights.

Obviously, the lieutenant could have taken the "low road" by acquiescing to army orders, yet he chose the "high road." As a soldier in a nation that prides itself on surviving one of the worst tragedies in the history of the human race, he probably thought that to put up a "good fight," he had to put up a *principled fight*—one that ensures justice even to the enemy.

In the final analysis, while the lieutenant may have suffered during his imprisonment for 26 days, he proudly reasserted the principles of justice, regardless of who gives it and who receives it.

Moral Judgment in Criminal Justice

With the cases of Captain Balian and Lieutenant Lotem in mind, let us turn to some situations with which criminal justice professionals are routinely faced. You should be forewarned, however, that answers to these questions will not be explicitly given to you in the pages of this book. You will have to "know thyself" and find the answers on your own. By the time you finish reading this book, your enlightened mind will have provided you with a menu of ethical solutions, and your enriched soul will have guided you in making the right decisions. Moral choices, after all, are found in the "brewing of the human experience" and can be reached only through the integration of sharpened intellect, moral reasoning, and a heightened conscience.

Consider the following situations:

1. Should a police officer enforce traffic laws equally on all violators, or is he or she justified under a twisted interpretation of police discretion to apply selective enforcement in accordance with his or her personal values relating to the race, sex, or status of the violator?

2. Should a subordinate in a probation department be recommended for promotion, or otherwise denied, on the basis of loyalty to the "person" of the boss or being a member of an active "good old boys" clique?

3. Should a parole supervisor "cover up" information pertinent to an upcoming budgetary decision if the release of such information would be financially injurious to the division or unit the supervisor served?

4. Should a correctional official in charge of scheduling assignments at a prison unit "give a break" to a popular worker and arrange her schedule in such a way that she can attend classes at a nearby university while declining the same "break" to others?

5. Should an instructor at a training academy waive certain academic requirements to a "buddy" who served with her in a prior capacity or shared in a private enterprise they operated while off duty?

6. Should inmate "snitches" or police informants who provide crucial testimony to assist prosecutors in putting others behind bars receive lenient treatment, and perhaps even money, as a quid pro quo for their dubious contribution?

7. Should police officers be forced to submit to random drug testing whenever the supervisor deems necessary, even if the supervisor is known to be a drug user?

8. Should officials in a drug enforcement unit lie in their reports or falsify the numbers they submit to higher authorities or to the media to gain the upper hand in their effort to win the war on drugs in the community they serve?

9. Should governmental rules against nepotism be continued in such a manner that when two highly productive employees in the same department decide to marry each other, one of them must quit the job?

10. Should professors in criminal justice departments be allowed to do consulting work at the price of neglecting their classes and ignoring the needs of the students at the academic institutions they serve?

These are real situations that have been gleaned from many years of experience in the field of criminal justice. They happen every day, but as a matter of ignorance, convenience, self-interest, or corruption, they go unexamined—if recognized at all. Most practitioners prefer not to discuss these questions, nor do they want them discussed by outsiders. Furthermore, as long as the legal and administrative rituals of the job are met, most practitioners would prefer not to be bothered by the moral implications of such practices, especially if they have no impact on their own careers.

Warning: The Deception of Occupational Subculture

Criminal justice agencies are bureaucratic organizations. As such, they are pyramidal, formal, impersonal, and to a large extent, frustrating. In a bureaucracy it is not uncommon that authority is abused by unethical supervisors, power is yielded by a group of "good old boys," rules are bent to accommodate a cohort of "benefactors," and discipline is applied in a vindictive manner. As a result, the work environment may be dissatisfying, stifling, and at times hostile. As in other public agencies, criminal justice practitioners perceive such practices as hypocritical. In response, they develop informal ways and means for coping with an unhealthy work environment and, perhaps, getting even with uncouth managers. Thus, an *occupational subculture* emerges. While some subcultures can be informative and useful, in the vast majority of agencies, they are negative and harmful. These normally consist of a set of counter-beliefs, counter-values, and counter-methods that can ensure *what workers have to do to survive.*

Occupational Subculture

Occupational subcultures invariably represent a negative reaction to the way the department is governed. They often operate in an underground network that may be best described as "locker room philosophy," "survival mentality," or the agency's "unspoken values." In a typical subculture, the ideals of professionalism, devotion to duty, and self-denial are either ignored altogether or replaced by a pragmatic ideology that allows more freedom and less accountability for the workers. Moral concerns are usually considered esoteric, impractical, or unnecessary, and practitioners concerned for moral principles are often ostracized for being too naive, romantic, or sentimental. In such subcultures, the image of pragmatism is held as the *super value*, loyalty to one's work group as an *absolute*, the use of deception as a *utilitarian procedure*, and manipulation as a *trademark* of effectiveness.

While the existence of unhealthy work environments cannot be justified, the consequences of occupational subculture in criminal justice have been deplorable. They have been widely discussed in the literature of *occupational deviance and corruption*. Frequently they lead to criminal or unprofessional acts committed under the guise of legitimate work procedures. In the field of policing, for instance, they may include blatant lying to suspects and victims; misuse of authority; brutality; perjury in defense of one's partner; and the use of derogatory language in dealing with nonconformists and minorities (Barker, 1978; Carter, 1984; Manning, 1971; Skolnick, 1985). In the fields of corrections and probation and parole, subcultural attitudes function in the same way and produce similar consequences (Crouch & Marquart, 1980; Toch, 1990). Large-scale participation in subcultural behaviors has long undermined the ethical fabric of criminal justice in a free society.

From an occupational point of view, subcultural values have been applauded as "essential for survival." At times, they have even been justified as conducive to workers' unity (the "one for all and all for one" cliché), to safeguarding agency interests (the "us against them" cliché), and to projecting an image of operational effectiveness (the "macho syndrome").

From an ethical point of view, however, occupational subcultures should be considered dangerous and their impact immoral. The main objections to these negative subcultural practices include the following:

1. They violate the ethics of public service and cast serious doubt on the society's commitment to upholding justice.

2. They undermine the essential bond between justice practitioners and the clients they serve—without which the goals of justice cannot be effectively achieved.

3. They are conducive to corruption, which, if allowed to take hold, can destroy the integrity of the agency altogether.

4. They usually are based on ignorance, bias, and psychological egoism, traits neither supported by reason nor justified by goodness.

Consequently, the counter-ethics of occupational subculture should be considered immoral, and enlightened practitioners should always shun them. Submission to these pseudo-ethics can demolish the essence of the criminal justice profession, tarnish the image of dedicated agencies, and demoralize honest practitioners devoted to the ideals of professionalism and justice.

The Philosophy of Wisdom

Having been warned of the dangers of occupational subculture, we must now turn our attention to the previous set of questions and ponder how they can be ethically addressed. These are clearly problematic questions that cannot be answered by a simple yes or no, if a satisfactory answer is possible at this stage. They require a high level of knowledge, objectivity, and, above all, reasoning. If the truth is to be discerned, these questions must be treated in a truly philosophical fashion.

Emotional debates, as we have learned, can be dysfunctional because they are based on opinions, beliefs, and the absence of reasoning (remember Plato's divided line theory). In order to avoid intellectual embarrassment, an environment of *wisdom* should prevail. In this regard, Vincent Barry suggested a set of rules he called "The Three Don'ts of Moral Reasoning." Because they are self-evident, they will be stated here without further elaboration: (1) don't rely on emotionalism, (2) don't rely on popular feelings, and (3) don't support immoral principles (Barry, 1982:22).

The main difficulty in debating ethical questions lies in the multiplicity of intellectual disciplines that bear on the subject and are too difficult for any one person to master. Therefore, the proper resolution of these questions cannot be made on the basis of one's knowledge of legal, religious, sociological, psychological, or economic literature alone. Ethical choices are high-powered decisions reached only through an elevated level of intellectual awareness. For example, the issue of abortion can hardly be viewed as a medical problem only; the issue of crime cannot be characterized as a legal problem only; and the issue of prejudice should be seen as far broader than bad psychology. In that sense, philosophical inquiries must rely on a wider range of knowledge best known as the *philosophy of wisdom*.

Short of divine revelation (which may or may not be valid), the philosophy of wisdom is the only legitimate method of determining moral issues, because it is the "superconductor" of all disciplines. Indeed, it is the receptacle of all human knowledge, and as such, all human problems become its subject matter.

The philosophy of wisdom is the only legitimate means for examining ethical issues. Its goal is to discover *moral truths*, its obligation is to pursue *goodness*, and its primary tool is *pure reasoning*. It cannot be in conflict with scientific knowledge, because it concerns itself not with the nature of scientific data, but with the moral implications such data may have on human behavior. For that reason, the philosophy of wisdom often is referred to as a *metasubject*—a subject above all subjects. It searches into the foundations of virtue—what it consists of, what it flows from, and what it rests upon. In making an ethical judgment, the philosophy of wisdom provides the most rational method—one that transcends intuition, emotion, sentiments, perceptions and, above all, popular experience.

In philosophical wisdom, the facts and values of any issue, along with its past and present, are all fused into one. The practitioner engages in a dialectic (point–counterpoint) discourse with others—or with himself—concerning the goals to be pursued and the means that can best accomplish them. Consequently, all available knowledge is harnessed and directed toward the discovery of the truth. Only when the ethical researcher is able to muster such an intellectual skill can one be considered a philosopher of sorts. Here lies the significance of Plato's doctrine of the *philosopher king*—either philosophers rule society, or the rulers of society become philosophers.

Wisdom and Knowledge

Human wisdom is the product of two main intellectual activities: *epistemology*, the allocation of available knowledge; and *philosophy*, the kneading of information into usable knowledge. The first activity relates to the quality of methods used in collecting knowledge; the second relates to the talents of the knower. In the field of epistemology, there are three kinds of knowledge:

1. *A priori knowledge* is derived from pure reasoning without reference to sense experience. *A priori* truths are truths of pure reason. They are universal, transcendental to experience, and applicable to all inquiries. They relate to the kinds of knowledge that, if denied, must lead to contradiction. *A priori* knowledge cannot be invalidated; it is considered true under all conditions and at all times and places. Examples of this kind of knowledge include "all triangles have 180 degrees" and "uncaused events cannot exist."

2. *A posteriori knowledge* is derived from sensory experience. These are truths of fact. Because sense experience is relative, inconsistent, and not always reliable, this kind of knowledge is also known as *probable knowledge*. It cannot be certain. It is true only under specific conditions of existence and can be denied under other conditions without being accused of contradiction. Examples of this kind include "rape is always a crime of violence" and "prisons are schools of crime." The truth or falsity of *a posteriori* knowledge can be checked against a stronger argument derived from a stronger sense experience, or better still, against *a priori* truth.

3. *Knowledge by acquaintance* is the knowledge of people, places, and things. This kind of knowledge is fairly simple because it is based on hearsay. For instance, one may have knowledge of a person without ever meeting him or her; of a place without ever being there; or of certain assumptions without facts that can support either truth or falsehood.

In *philosophy of the mind*, one is considered knowledgeable only if one achieves a reasoning capacity—a product of the first two types of knowledge. Only such persons can legitimately argue philosophical issues and present their views in a rational manner. They are usually intelligent persons, capable of abstract thinking, and of mastering the art of logic and systematic inference. Such individuals have also been described as wise, gifted, and learned. While such talent is usually obtained through arduous learning at a center of higher education (for example, university, institute, or academy), that is not always a requirement. Many people do reach that level through extraordinary, thoughtful experiences; association with "significant others"; or living a well-directed, soul-searching life.

Fallacious Reasoning

Integral to the philosophy of wisdom is the *absence of fallacious reasoning*. Broadly defined, a fallacy is "an incorrect way of reasoning or an attempt to persuade others emotionally or psychologically, but not logically" (Barry, 1982:14). The term *fallacy* comes from the Latin *fallax*, which means "deceitful." While fallacious reasoning has existed since the beginning of human history, serious condemnation of that kind of reasoning has been noted since the time of the Sophists of Athens. These individuals relied on elegant and sophisticated premises and initially were held in great respect. But soon after they were publicly exposed by Socrates and his disciples, they began to fall into ill repute. Indeed, the word *Sophist* later came to mean "a cheat," "a quibble," or both. In the vernacular of Greek philosophy, the term *sophistic argument* became synonymous with a statement that is subtle or clever but intended to mislead. Fallacies are classified into two categories: *formal* and *informal* (sometimes referred to as *semi-formal* or *quasi-formal*):

Formal fallacies are errors of logic in which the conclusion does not follow from the premise. Such errors are misleading because, while contradictory, they are used to give the appearance of correctness. They have a deceptive effect on how people are expected to think, reason, or decide. Two major formal fallacies are particularly significant to understanding the wisdom of ethics:

1. **Naturalistic Fallacy** is an invalid argument or an error in deductive logic that attempts to derive evaluative conclusions from descriptive or quantitative premises. The fallacy was principally associated with the British philosopher David Hume (1711–1776). According to its standard version, a naturalistic fallacy is committed when an argument asserts that because certain facts exist concerning human behavior or the physical world, certain values must follow as a consequence. It is labeled as naturalistic because values are claimed to flow from natural premises (Porter, 1980:13).

   Consider, for example, this statement: "Because Americans eat 500 billion hamburgers every year, then hamburgers are good for Americans!" Obviously, the fallacy is assuming that when people desire something, that (something) must be *worth desiring*—which is not always true. Many people desire bad things. Furthermore, if the statement were true, then it should follow that when statistics indicate that "2 million Americans commit crime each year," it would mean that "crime is good for America"! Succinctly, the fallacy assumes that "what a person likes is good by virtue of being liked," or simply, "what is, is what ought to be."

2. **Genetic Fallacy** is an invalid argument based on the mistake of evaluating a theory, a statement, or conduct on the basis of its source. More specifically, it is the error of judging the validity of an idea or action on the basis of the *person* behind it (Porter, 1980:15). Also known as the *biographical fallacy*, it represents a major confusion of fact and value. Examples of this fallacy include dismissing Islamic virtues because Mohammed is not considered a

prophet in Western culture, or ignoring Martin Luther King Jr.'s contribution to civil rights because he was an African American leader. By the same token, a genetic fallacy can be committed when people approve of certain actions or ideas because they admire the person or persons behind them. Examples include accepting vegetarian food because it was advocated by Gandhi or justifying the slapping of soldiers by their commanding officers because we admire General George Patton, who was accused of so doing.

Informal fallacies are errors of reasoning that lead to incorrect conclusions. They are numerous and in some sources exceed 40 fallacies. A listing of the more significant fallacies includes: (1) the fallacy of black and white; (2) the fallacy of arguing from power or force; (3) the fallacy of discrediting the integrity of the opposite arguer; (4) the fallacy of arguing from ignorance; (5) the fallacy of arguing by appeal to pity; (6) the fallacy of arguing by appeal to personal interest; (7) the fallacy of arguing by appeal to what is popular at the time; (8) the fallacy of arguing by appeal to authority; (9) the fallacy of arguing in order to create ambiguity; (10) the fallacy of begging the question; (11) the fallacy of slanting by deliberately omitting or overemphasizing certain points in the argument; and (12) the fallacy of equivocation, in which a word is used with one meaning in one part of the argument and another meaning in another part. A classic example of this is the statement "nothing beats a good doctor, but a bad doctor is better than nothing." The fallacious implication must be that "a bad doctor is better than a good doctor" (Angeles, 1981:95).

The Nature of Ethics

The term *ethics* originated from the Greek root *ethikos*, which means "character." The term is synonymous with *moral philosophy*, which is more prevalent in European universities and literature.

Ethics Defined

Ethics can be defined as a branch of philosophy that is concerned with the study of what is morally right and wrong, good and bad. Right and wrong are qualities usually assigned to actions, conduct, and behavior. Ethicists inquire into the correctness of such acts as promise keeping, truth telling, integrity, deception, and compassion. Good and bad, on the other hand, are qualities that characterize ends and consequences. Ethicists inquire into the events of living and working—the results that should be pursued and the worthiness of what people accomplish in their lives (Porter, 1980).

A more practical definition of ethics is *a rule of principle*. Consistent with this definition, any action, statement, or behavior that is not anchored in a principle is questionable and more likely immoral. The reasoning behind this definition is that principles are *recognized reiterations of values*. They tend to be (1) well thought out, (2) approved on a universal scale, and (3) able to pass the test of time. Examples of ethical principles include honesty, fairness, fidelity, modesty, duty, obligation, loyalty, patriotism, and mercy.

The term *ethics* has also been used to signify specific connotations. These include the following:

1. The theory that explains the worth or propriety of an act on the basis of the values inherent in such an act

2. The analysis of statements or arguments used in support of a virtuous behavior or, conversely, in denouncing an immoral one

3. The inquiry into the nature of morality and the search for the good life

4. The characterization of an identifiable group that shares moral values or traits, such as "professional ethics," "utilitarian ethics," "work ethics," or "unethical behavior"

A Definitional Caveat

With the increasing use of the term *ethics*, especially in political and journalistic contexts, there has been a proliferation of inaccurate definitions. Many such definitions are motivated by the failure to capture the essence of ethics; by the popular desire to split what is organically whole; or simply by a desire to undermine the legitimate role of ethics. For instance, we keep referring to "white ethics," "African American ethics," and "feminist ethics," as well as "Christian ethics," "Islamic ethics," or "Jewish ethics." While these terms call attention to the concerns of some moral agents—thus enriching moral discourse—their use can indirectly blur the true focus on the "humanness of ethics," its most legitimate character. By creating schisms, special groups only call attention to the special interests they represent and advocate.

At the core of all ethics are *moral senses* that enrich the human race and nurture civilization. Physical differences, religious differences, and socioeconomic differences, while meaningful, cannot alter the fact that people have *human interests* that transcend their local interests. These include survival, justice, peace, honesty, kindness, and a sense of decency. If this were not the case, the evolutionary value of the world community would have diminished over the years. Consider, for instance, the notion that white people, African American people, and Hispanics cannot live peacefully together; that Christian countries cannot enter into peace agreements with Muslim countries; that male students cannot get along with female students; or that the Universal Declaration of Human Rights is ineffectual because it fails to take into account the interests of local groups or populations.

Wilson, in *The Moral Sense* (1993), makes a powerful argument that moral senses are natural: "they are formed out of the interaction of their innate dispositions with their earliest familial experiences." Wilson adds that to some important degree, in almost all people, "moral senses shape human behavior and the judgments people make of the behavior of others" (Wilson, 1993:2). As such, they precede all civilizationary divisions by race, gender, color, or religion. Subsequently, the study of ethics, while recognizing local differences among social groups, should be perceived as humanist in nature rather than as individually defined.

The Scope of Ethics

The discipline of ethics encompasses a wide range of human behaviors, actions, and statements, as well as the evaluation of their consequences. Whenever the rightness or wrongness of a behavior is examined, we search for the principle upon which it is based and the reasons that may support its justification. In this sense, ethical studies maintain a close association with physical and humanistic sciences because they also inquire into the intricacies of human conduct. Yet while ethical studies recognize that each of these sciences possesses a useful body of knowledge, the discipline of ethics does not extract its moral principles from these sciences. It relies on knowledge provided by these sciences only to construct an independent "science" of ethics.

Also, while other humanistic disciplines may concern themselves with moral issues, only ethics can make value judgments concerning the "goodness" or "badness" of such issues. Compare, for example, the study of ethics with anthropology, psychology, and logic. Anthropology investigates moral aspects in terms of the origin of beliefs, customs, and practices of past and present cultures. Psychology explores the causation and motivation of behavior and examines the factors that characterize the psychological makeup of individuals. Logic is concerned with the rational argumentation of a theory or an idea. But this is where the comparison ends.

Only ethical inquiry can ask value questions such as, when one culture condones a certain practice, such as the killing of infants, and another culture condemns it, which culture is right and which is wrong? What values influence judgment of what is right and wrong? What principles are being reasoned, and are they worth reasoning about? By pursuing this line of inquiry, the ethicist is led to appreciate the moral principles of justice, decency, and goodness. As such, ethics must be considered a bona fide science of valuation.

The overriding concern of ethics is formalizing true statements about what moral behaviors "ought to be." This concern for the *shoulds* and *oughts* rather than the *is's* and *are's* is what distinguishes the true nature of ethical theory. It must also be emphasized that, as a science of valuation, ethical studies establish moral theories regardless of whether the individuals concerned approve or disprove or whether public opinion agrees or disagrees. In this sense, ethical philosophers and physical scientists are similar; they are not concerned with what is *believed* to be "the shape of the earth" but rather with what *is* its "actual shape."

Ethical Theory

In uncomplicated language, a *theory* is a hypothesis or a proposition, assumed to be valid, that is used to explain or predict a broader topic or problem. All intellectual disciplines produce theories about their universal concerns. In the same manner, ethical philosophers—individually or in groups—produce theories about ethical matters. Such theories are usually stated in general, abstract, or ideal terms. The following features characterize the essence of ethical theory.

First, ethical theories reduce complexity by introducing general principles that can explain a wide variety of cases. For instance, Socrates explained all human evil in terms of ignorance. Bentham, Carlyle, and Mill measured the morality of any act in terms of its utilitarian contribution to happiness or pain. Saint Augustine, Saint Thomas Aquinas, and other Christian theorists explained evil in terms of the absence of God. Today we measure democracy by the principles of majority rule; due process of law; one person, one vote; and freedom of speech.

Second, ethical theories determine the validity (truthfulness) of moral principles by checking their internal consistency and ensuring the absence of contradiction in their premises and conclusions. For instance, Aristotle proposed an elaborate theory of inductive logic, or categorical syllogism, by which the forms and contents of a statement can be recognized through the method of "squares of contradictories." Francis Bacon and Immanuel Kant basically followed in Aristotle's footsteps.

Third, ethical theorists, in their clamor to justify moral principles, often end up furthering knowledge in other disciplines. For example, Plato's ethical theory of *polis* continues to influence modern political theory by asserting the unignorable moral responsibility of modern states. Mill's theory of liberalism continues to shape the fields of government, economics, and public service, particularly in the area of social policies. By the same token, John Rawls's theory of social justice has been instrumental in legitimizing equal opportunity and civil rights movements in America and other societies with multiple racial or ethnic populations.

Credibility of Ethics

Critics accuse ethics of being a soft discipline, one based on broad subjective statements. They argue that ethical statements cannot be considered true by all people and in all situations. They further maintain that society cannot rely on ethical theories, because unlike legal principles, ethical theories are difficult to prove "beyond a reasonable doubt," and unlike physical sciences, ethical theories are not supported by empirical data.

This criticism may be valid, but only to a point. It is certainly true that ethical problems cannot be resolved by rules of evidence or empirical observation in the laboratory. Nevertheless, when people claim that ethical theories are beyond justification, they basically mean that they are baffled as to how to validate them. Not knowing how to validate a value is not the same as declaring it to be nonexistent or unjustifiable. Furthermore, even among scientific theories, there has always been a credibility problem. Some scientific theories are less credible than others. Einstein's theory of relativity has not been tested empirically, and the validity of evolution theory has been conditional at best. Credibility depends on whether certain objections can be answered adequately; whether there are good reasons (independent of the theory itself) that support the premises; and whether the theory explains (better than competing theories) the broader phenomenon of life.

On the other hand, stringent criteria for validating ethical theory do exist, although scientific empiricism is not one of them. The standards most often employed in justifying sociological theory are also applicable in validating ethical theory. Basic among these is the *rule of reasonableness*: that the principle that most conforms to the dictates of reason is judged to be true. In ethical studies, this criterion is applied even more vigorously.

The Rule of Reasonableness

For an ethical principle to be valid, it must meet three basic standards: (1) consistency within itself and the absence of contradiction; (2) inclusion of all relevant facts into consideration; and (3) fitting the human experience (Porter, 1980:3).

1. *Consistency and the absence of contradiction.* This standard requires that an acceptable theory must conform to its major premise or hypothesis and proceed without any contradiction. For instance, it would be contradictory, and therefore invalid, to claim that all events are controlled by divine providence, while

maintaining that people are individually responsible for their lives. Such a proposition is inconsistent because it is based on the premise that all events are preordained, and because human actions are also events, they also must be preordained. As such, it would be unreasonable to hold people accountable for actions that are clearly beyond their control. Such a position has been taken at various times by theologians such as Saint Augustine, Martin Luther, and Kierkegaard, who tried to explain away the inconsistency by calling it a divine mystery. This explanation invalidates the theory of free will and illustrates the type of muddled thinking that should be avoided if we are to arrive at a sound philosophical position (Porter, 1980:3).

2. *Inclusion of all relevant facts.* This standard requires that all relevant facts be taken into consideration at the time the ethical judgment is made. For instance, the outdated premises that the earth is the center of the universe and that the heart is the repository of knowledge (for example, knowing something by heart) must be discarded in favor of modern knowledge as to the earth's location in the solar system and the brain as the sole generator of thought. By the same token, Socrates theorized that all wrong acts must be products of ignorance. Following this line of thought, one must conclude that no one who knows what is good would deliberately commit wrong. Modern psychological knowledge, especially in the post-Freudian era, has clearly exposed Socrates's error. Mentally challenged people and hypocrites can act in irrational and destructive ways, fully aware of the wrongfulness of their actions. Evidence of that includes the fact that many knowledgeable people commit crimes, use harmful drugs, drink excessively, indulge in overeating, and continue to pollute the earth.

3. *Fitting the human experience.* This standard requires that the principle under investigation offer the most plausible interpretation of human actions or explain them "better" than other competing theories. For example, the doctrine of a retributive universe (also known as the *Job principle*) has long been used to explain why certain people are afflicted with disease or suffer natural catastrophes. According to the doctrine, unfortunate occurrences happen to people because of some transgression they committed or because the gods have chosen to test them at certain stages in their lives. The doctrine becomes even more unreasonable when upright and God-fearing people are the victims of similar disasters, while bad people enjoy good health and prosperity.

A more probable interpretation as to why certain people become victims of a catastrophe is simply because they happen to be at a certain place when the event occurs, regardless of the nature of the catastrophe. Similarly, the reason people develop cancer or suffer heart attacks has to do with microscopic forms of life present in their bodies, regardless of the moral or immoral character of the person (Porter, 1980:6).

Categories of Ethical Theory: Normative and Metaethics

Ethical theories are divided into two major categories: *normative ethics* and *metaethics*. Normative theory constitutes the larger and more substantive category. It involves formulating moral standards of conduct and articulating the principles and sanctions that govern such conduct. Metaethics theory, on the other hand, is a more complex category that investigates the meaning of ethical terms and critiques how ethical statements are verified. It is a secondary category whereby normative theories are reviewed and commented upon. In this capacity, metaethicists serve as a behind-the-scenes intellectual force that offers criticism when normative ethicists go too far, or when they fail to explain moral principles. In light of this relationship, normative ethics can be compared to a court of primary jurisdiction, whereas metaethics can be compared to an appellate court. Each level benefits from the contribution of the other. But also, as in the judicial field, normative ethics theory and metaethics theory can be so closely interconnected that at times it becomes difficult to distinguish where one ends and the other begins.

The categories and subcategories of ethics are illustrated in Figure 2.1.

Figure 2.1
Categories of Ethics

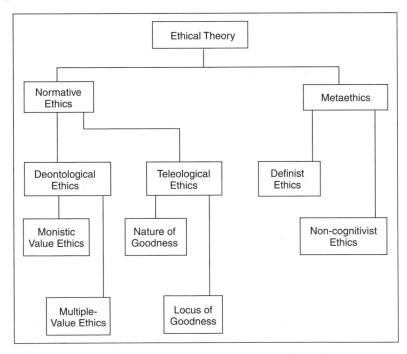

Normative Ethics

Theories of normative ethics *determine which moral standards to follow and which actions are considered morally right or wrong.* They do so by (1) setting forth moral norms as guidelines for moral behavior, (2) proposing and evaluating moral conduct, and (3) establishing moral duties.

Normative ethics theory is directly concerned with studying what people ought to do (or refrain from doing), what kind of relations they ought to pursue, and what behaviors are considered worthwhile. For example, most people believe that ethical action springs from moral standards such as "Do unto others as you would have them do unto you," "Act in such a way that you bring about the greatest good for the greatest number," and "Always seek your own best interest." But some of these principles may be contradictory. Which standards, then, should we adopt, and under which circumstances? These concerns are basically what normative ethics theory attempts to discover (Barry, 1982:6).

In the language of normative ethics theory, terms like *good, bad, right,* and *wrong* are used to express a favorable judgment of an action or, conversely, a denunciation of the same. As such, normative theory addresses such questions as the following:

1. What should I do?

2. What characteristics make people morally good or bad?

3. How should society be organized, and what specific policies should various agencies pursue?

4. What is a good life, and what experiences are considered worthwhile or desirable?

5. How can people choose among a hierarchy of values, especially conflicting ones?

6. What is the profile of the ethical person?

Normative ethics has been as popular and pervasive as it has been influential. Historically, most prophets, reformers, and philosophers fell into this category of normative thinkers.

Metaethics

The term *meta* means "after" or "beyond" and was common among Greek philosophers who were accustomed to making philosophical commentaries about all aspects of knowledge. The term *metaethics* was used by A.J. Ayer in 1949 in his famous work "On the Analysis of Moral Judgment."

Metaethics can be defined as *the study of methods, language, logical structure, and reasoning used in arriving at, or in justifying moral judgment.* Its role is to make evaluative commentaries regarding how a principle is justified. Metaethicists are more directly concerned with analyzing the meaning of terms such as *good* and *bad* than with judging the conduct itself.

Metaethicists avoid any attempt to define moral standards of conduct. Their main concern is with evaluating the quality and validity of claims made by normative theorists and examining the way such claims are substantiated. As such, metaethicists point out if a certain claim is acceptable or unacceptable.

In contrast to the *first-level thinking* of normative theorists, metaethicists provide a *second level.* As such, the relationship between normative ethics and metaethics is akin to that between a district court and an appellate court in the judicial system. Consider, for example, the Christian philosopher who advocates doing good on the ground that such an action pleases God or conforms to one's Christian conscience. Stated in these terms, people are supposed to do good because otherwise God will punish them, or their conscience will make them remorseful. A metaethicist would most likely find these answers suspect and far too simple to be universally accepted. He or she would most likely argue that it is all too common a fault to invent a purely emotive explanation by naming a divine entity that, if it existed, would solve all problems. The same philosopher may even question the basic theories of God or conscience, arguing that no real evidence supports their existence.

Metaethics theories are in turn divided into two subcategories, based on whether one believes that moral judgments do or do not exist as realities. Those who believe in the existence of moral reality are known as *definists* or *cognitivists*, because in their commentaries they refer to tangible properties, objects, or actions of direct moral concern. The Darwinist school best represents this subcategory, because it is based on the scientific explanation of evolution. On the other hand, those who disagree with the view of moral reality are known as *noncognitivists*, or *nondescriptivists*. They assert that value judgment neither confirms nor denies moral properties; it simply constitutes evocations or expressions of opinion (Sahakian, 1974:6).

Finally, it should be emphasized that the fields of normative ethics and metaethics are closely interdependent, because each contributes to the development of the other. Consequently, most ethics philosophers today seem to pursue a double-track philosophy, combining both approaches in a variety of ways, with emphasis on one approach or the other.

Normative Ethics: Deontological and Teleological

The field of normative ethics is divided into two fairly distinguishable subcategories. The division is based on whether the emphasis of moral valuation is put on the front end, *the action itself*; or at the back end, the *consequences* of the action. The former is known as *deontological* theory and the latter as *teleological* theory.

Deontological Theory

This subcategory is also known as *obligation theory*, because *deontos* in Greek means duty, or obligation. Deontological theorists judge the rightness or wrongness of an act on the basis of its obligatory nature. If the act is right, neither the intent behind it nor its consequence matters—the act is right.

To deontologists, the act is all that matters and all other factors are irrelevant. That is why deontological theories are also known as *inconsequential*, unconcerned with the consequences. For instance, assisting others is considered ethically right and no other consideration makes it wrong. The fact that assistance may later prove to be harmful makes no difference in the moral equation. A correct action is correct even if it turns out badly or if it was committed for the wrong reason. Accordingly, telling the truth is considered good in itself regardless of the injurious consequences to which it might lead (for example, an employee being ostracized for reporting corrupt coworkers). Furthermore, acts that are considered right must be universally right—everywhere and at all times (Porter, 1980:40).

Deontological theorists consider actions to be moral or immoral on the basis of two standards: (1) *what they are* (for example, telling the truth, serving one's country), or (2) *what principle they conform to* (for example, concern for discipline, patriotism, or a legal obligation). As such, spanking a child, fighting a war, or incarcerating a criminal would all be good despite the cruelty or misery they may involve. As mentioned earlier, deontological theorists would not give much thought to the consequences of actions. Thus, in the previous examples, they would not be concerned with whether the child grew up to be an irresponsible person, the war ended in defeat, or the incarceration failed to deter would-be criminals.

Deontological theories are in turn divided into two subcategories: *monistic* or *multiple*. In the first subcategory, consideration of morality is based on a singular value of goodness. Examples of this category include the theory of *hedonism*, which holds that pleasure is the only good and the total good, and Kant's theory of duty as the only obligation in life. In the second subcategory, deontological theories can be either *dualistic* or *pluralistic*, in which case they are based on two or more values of goodness. Examples include the combination of wealth and beauty, as in the case of a person marrying a rich, good-looking spouse; or the threesome of wealth, beauty, and knowledge, as in the case of a person marrying a wealthy, good-looking, and highly educated spouse.

By way of summary, deontological theories judge moral value strictly on the basis of the act itself, regardless of what the consequences of that act might turn out to be. As such, they constitute sanctions that are firm, material, and universal, or at least have a determining effect on human choices.

Teleological Theory

The Greek term *teleios* means "consequence," or "bringing the matter to its end or purpose." Teleological theory determines the moral worth of an action by the extent to which that action accomplishes a purpose or an end. Therefore, the consequences of the act determine the act's correctness—if the result is good, then the act is right, if the result is bad, then the act is wrong. Thus, in the previous examples, the correctness of spanking a child is in reforming her behavior, the rightness of fighting a war is in restoring peace, and the goodness of incarcerating a criminal is in deterring others from committing crimes.

Among the two best-known teleological theories are *utilitarianism* and *social justice*. According to utilitarian theory, an action or policy may be moral or immoral only in terms of its capacity to achieve the greatest good for the greatest number of people. Therefore, a policy that raises the minimum wage or increases Social Security benefits is of great utilitarian worth, because it can benefit a larger segment of the population. By the same token, the theory of social justice affirms that ultimate morality exists when society is able to maximize liberty for all citizens without sacrificing the needs of the poor and the underprivileged.

Teleological theories are also divided into two subcategories: *quality of goodness* and *locus of goodness*. In the first subcategory, teleologists rank the levels of goodness in terms of a hierarchy based on their quality. For example, as we observed during the tour of the Ethics Hall of Fame, the goodness of justice is of a higher quality than the goodness of pleasure. By the same token, the intrinsic goodness of pleasure is of a higher quality than the non-intrinsic goodness of wealth. Thus, actions that enhance the values of justice and happiness are morally superior to those that maximize economic gain.

In the second subcategory, the *locus of goodness*, teleologists determine the goodness of an action in terms of its location—where it benefits the most. For instance, while the theories of egoism and utilitarianism are both teleological, they differ in terms of the number of beneficiaries. An egoist would value an act in terms of the amount of happiness that would accrue to him or her. By contrast, a utilitarianist would value the same act in terms of the number of people who would benefit from it.

By way of summary, teleological theories hold that the morality of an action is based on the morality of its consequences. Therefore, a great deed that produces unhappy consequences is "immoral," and a medio-cre deed that produces happy consequences is "moral." Furthermore, teleological theories stress that moral considerations must be interpreted in terms of the interests of society as a whole, because morality is an agent of universal happiness.

Historical Origins of Ethics

The concept of good is the distinguishing feature of any act we call moral, because morality means being guided by goodness. We continu-ously ask ourselves, our children, our friends, our neighbors, and our colleagues to be good, to behave decently, and to avoid evil. We expect our government, our courts, and our police to act justly and to treat people fairly. Some fundamental questions, however, must be asked here: Why is there such an attachment to (if not an obsession with) goodness? Why should rational people be moral in the first place? Why shouldn't anyone be free to lie, cheat, and steal at will? In other words, what is so bad about evil, and why shouldn't people pursue evil if they so desire? Whose commands are these, after all, and why should we comply with them?

These questions are not easy to answer, because most people are incapable of understanding the intricate mysteries of life and living. Delving into the "point of origin" should therefore make us better able to respond to these complicated questions. Consider, for a moment, being asked the previous questions by your younger brother at home or by a subordinate at work. There are, of course, many replies you could give. You could point out that we ought to be moral because the "ideal man" among us is an extension of a perfect universe and, as such, we should reflect the perfection of that universe. This answer may not be very convincing, especially if you are responding to your brother at the dinner table. You might then point out another answer: that we must be moral because we are religious people and God wants us to be good. But this answer may not be convincing either, especially to an atheist subordinate at work. You might then point out a third answer: that we ought to be moral because it is in our best interest as members of a civilized society. Moral people are generally happier people—they care for each other's needs and feelings. Finally, if none of these answers is satisfactorily accepted and you become frustrated with the other party's lack of understanding, you may respond angrily, "because I said so!" If you chose the first answer, you would be subscribing to the *metaphysical/eternal law* view of ethics. If you chose the second answer, you would be subscribing to the *religious* view of ethics. If you chose any of the latter replies, your view of ethics would most likely correspond with the *social/legalistic* school.

In virtually all societies—ancient, medieval, or contemporary—people followed certain rules of conduct. In a society such as that of ancient Greece, which had no concept of religion as we know it, metaphysical and eternal laws were considered the main source of ethical thought. In traditional societies, such as those in medieval Europe and Islamic countries, where ethics and religion are closely intertwined, divine law is considered the basic source of ethical thought. In Western communities, especially the United States, social and legal views are considered the chief source of ethical thought.

With that in mind, the following discussion will focus on (1) the *metaphysical/eternal law* view, (2) the *religious* view, and (3) the *social/legalistic* view.

Metaphysical/Eternal Law View

This view represents a belief in the supernatural and the function of the "soul" as its human seat. It originated in pagan societies prior to the emergence of religion as a spiritual institution. Ancient Egyptian mythology reflected this view. The pharaoh was considered a god to be worshipped, and his life on earth was the first reign of several to follow in the hereafter. By the same token, the concepts of metaphysics constituted the body of eternal law during the Hellenistic period, around the third and fourth centuries B.C.

Metaphysics is the realm of the universe beyond this world. The universe is an outpouring of the One (the Creator) and depends upon Him for its existence and order. However, "If you take away the One," metaphysical philosophers would say, "you take away the universe," and the further away from the One a creature is, the less spirituality and perfection it possesses. The universe, however, is not identical to the One. The concept of emanation was presented to explain this complex relationship. According to metaphysical doctrine, the universe, as well as all creatures, come forth from Him. ("Creation" is a close meaning of *coming forth*, but not quite.) For example, consider the relationship between light and shadow: Light emanates from the sun and is dependent upon it but is not identical to it. Shadow, by the same token, is a product of light and is dependent upon it, but shadow neither looks nor acts like light.

Through the concepts of metaphysics and emanation, philosophers were able to explain the phenomenon of life and living. The Greek philosophers mastered this logic and used it as a cornerstone of their philosophical thought. While other philosophies, such as those practiced in Islamic, Buddhist, and Hindu societies, adhere to the metaphysical view (with some variation), the Greek philosophy remains the most notable. Plato's work immortalized that view to the extent that it became synonymous with the *Platonic theory of forms*.

The metaphysical view was further developed in Aristotle's *Theologia*. The historical value of this work is immense because it illuminates the origin of Greek ethical thought. In *Theologia* the perfection of the One and the manner in which He generates the entire order of being was presented. The One, the God, the Supreme, was portrayed as "motionless, timeless, above and beyond everything else, both intelligible and sensible, all things emanate from Him, and tend toward Him." The One is none of the things that emanate from Him, while everything comes forth from Him. He is above all beings. He is *perfect* and lacks nothing (Fakhry, 1970:37).

In *Theologia* emanation furnished man with the gift of the soul that links the intelligible world of the One and the sensible world of man. The soul, which is the *seat of reason*, is the intermediary between the world of forms and the world of senses. It maintains a link with the One by obeying His universal rules, while accommodating the rules of the world where it temporarily resides. It can direct its gaze upward toward the One and acquire "guidance and light," or downward and lose itself in the absurdity of the world of senses. Consequently, one's morality is judged by whether the soul is preoccupied with the "ignoble" objects of sense or with the "noble" objects of reason.

In *Theologia* Aristotle describes the perfection, beauty, and excellence of the intelligible world as rising above the sensible world and imparting to it the perfection with which it is endowed. The intelligible world is the locus of all forms of virtue, such as honesty, decency, justice, kindness, and mercy. These forms are *eternal truths*—spiritual, universal, immutable, and everlasting. As such, they are prototypes of objects, actions, and relations in the natural world, and the soul is their moral agent. The human body, Plato asserted, is only a dungeon to which the soul is temporarily consigned. Upon its release from the body, the soul rejoins the One in His metaphysical abode.

Religious View

No one knows exactly when ethical sentiments began. Those who subscribe to the *evolutionary theory* of the human race argue that it began when *homo erectus*, the monkey on two legs with an 800 cc brain, began sharing food with others of his species. That sharing of food and work was probably the beginning of human morality. It was this willingness to share that constituted the basis of all human sympathy. This in turn made human beings the world's dominant species (Thomson, 1993:59).

On the other hand, those who subscribe to the *creation theory* argue that ethical sentiments began with the creation of Adam. He was made in the image of God, and because God is perfect the human race must be good. This view has been strongly supported by early Jewish and Christian philosophers, who, being well versed in Greek metaphysics, continued to apply it in their versions of religious faiths. While pagan philosophy located the origin of ethics in the soul, which through reason can mirror the perfection of the universe, Jewish theologians located the origin of ethics in Mosaic law, which is to be served through *obedience* to God. By the same token, Christian theologians located the origins of ethics in the teachings of Christ, which are to be fulfilled through *salvation*.

Also, while Christianity rejected specific provisions of the Mosaic code, it retained the idea of a code of ethical conduct inspired by God. The *summum bonum* of Christian theology remained the idea of sanctification or perfection of the soul. This sublime quality can be attained only by emulating the life of Jesus Christ and abiding with His commandments. Foremost among these commandments is the doctrine of love, epitomized in the verse "Love God above all and love your neighbor as yourself." To equate virtue with love of our fellow human beings may not have been the most rational view in moral theory, especially at a time when people were indoctrinated in the practice of "an eye for an eye, and a tooth for a tooth." Yet Christian ethics, especially according to the teachings of Saint Augustine and Saint Thomas Aquinas, is not necessarily doing what is rational or what is popular, but what is *commanded by God*.

Saint Augustine was the first true Christian thinker. Following biblical teachings, he equated evil with distance from God. He taught that mankind was divided into two opposite camps: the *city of Jerusalem* or God (the saved), and the *city of Babylon* or the devil (the damned). To distinguish between these two camps, Saint Augustine taught that because Adam freely chose to disobey God, mankind has since become sinful and all of Adam's descendants have become residents of the city of the devil. Like the apostle Paul, Saint Augustine stressed that only through salvation can man redeem himself from the original sin and be selected as a resident of the city of God. In the philosophy of Saint Augustine, the origin of ethics is the bliss of salvation that provides man with the virtues of faith, hope, and love, with temperance as the chief virtue.

Saint Thomas Aquinas merged Aristotelian philosophy and science with Christianity. In his *Summa Theologica* he demonstrated that philosophy and Christianity were compatible. Like Aristotle, he believed that every free action is directed toward some end, ultimately the final good of man. His theological theory of obligation was even constructed along the same lines as Aristotle's famous *Nicomachean Ethics*. But Aquinas's definition of the final good obviously differed. While Aristotle identified the final good as natural happiness in the form of a life of contemplation, Aquinas identified it as the supernatural unity with God in the afterlife. He located the origin of ethics in the virtues of character, good actions, and devotion to God, which can be attained only through a holy existence with God.

In Islam, elements of Plato's metaphysical theory are also apparent. The One is *Allah*. He is characterized with 99 universal names or virtues that he communicated to believers through the prophet Mohammed in the holy *Quran*. The origin of ethics in Islamic theology is *submission to the will of God*, because human beings are considered incapable of distinguishing right from wrong on their own. It was for this reason that guidance was sent to them by the prophets. In the Quran, God also decreed an all-embracing code of conduct called *Shariah*, or the pathway. Under Shariah rules, all human activities receive a transcendent dimension: They become purposeful and sacred, earthly and heavenly, for this day and for the hereafter. When human beings do good deeds, they earn righteousness with God, and when they do bad deeds, they lose proportionally in the same way.

According to *Shariah law*, human conduct is classified as (1) obligatory, (2) meritorious, (3) reprehensible, (4) disapproved, and (5) forbidden. Believers are required to do what is good (classes 1 and 2) and to abstain from what is blameworthy (classes 3, 4, and 5). As in Christian philosophy, Islamic rules of moral conduct are not subordinated to rational theory or judged by a standard of human reason. Only through submission to God's will and compliance with the commandments of *Shariah* can God's plan be revealed to man and his rewards be received on earth, as well as in heaven.

Social and Legalistic Views

This view holds that human intellect is not an autonomous activity independent of determinate social and cultural conditions. The origin of ethics in this view is found in the social and cultural environment that envelops man's existence. Even Plato and Aristotle, who subscribed to the primacy of metaphysical thought, never quite overlooked the impact of social conditioning on human conduct. They viewed society as fundamentally an "exchange of services" or a "social division of labor," in which all people benefit from the performance of diversified functions. Aristotle, in particular, considered human beings "social animals" who become individuals only insofar as they are able to absorb a social way of life. To quote Aristotle's famous phrase, "A person able to exist by himself is either a beast or a God" (Rossides, 1978:35). However, one reason Plato and Aristotle favored the metaphysical view (over social custom and religion) was their dissatisfaction with the social environment of Athens. Throughout their lives they continued to endorse the primary ideas of metaphysics and rationality and relegated custom and religion to an inferior level.

The Medieval View

The medieval view of ethics was strongly influenced by Christian doctrine. Medieval people lived in a *gemeinschaft* society—a German term that means one that is characterized by heavy dependence on custom, family traditions, and religious dogma. Due to their lack of enlightenment and the strong yoke of feudalism, communities of the Middle Ages accepted, without reservation, the moral values they inherited through codes of custom. Morality was based on generations of tradition and was considered sacrosanct either because it was of a divine origin, or because it had successfully withstood the test of time. Custom not only regulated moral behavior, but along with religion, also gave individuals their basic identity. Social class, prestige, and prosperity were seen as predestined by birth. The family, graded into "noble" or "ignoble," was the basis for assigning relatively complex religious, political, and economic status.

During the Middle Ages, the concepts of state, government, and legislation did not exist as we know them today. Civil administration was maintained on a personal customary basis. There were no legal codes for settling disputes, because, theoretically, disputes were not supposed to arise when human behavior and custom coincided perfectly. As a result, feudal communities were unable to distinguish among religion, custom, and morality. To them, custom was the essence of being, and tampering with its canons of conduct was considered sacrilegious (Rossides, 1978:17).

Throughout the decades, however, mistrust of human nature began to develop, giving rise to the Enlightenment. Aside from the economic and physical hardships of living at that time, the supporting role of religion gradually began to erode, giving way to an anti-church sentiment. Church leaders had struck alliances with local rulers, and clergymen became supporters of reigning emperors. As Kroptkin (1968) describes, the church "forgot the forgiveness of injuries, church representatives became owners of serfs equally with the nobility, and gradually acquired the same power as the counts, the dukes, and the kings" (Kroptkin, 1968:122). In using their power, leaders of the church proved to be just as vengeful and greedy as lay rulers.

Beginning with the tenth century, cities in feudal Europe sank into social turmoil as the citizens became more enlightened. Due to increased contact with the Eastern nations and flourishing commercial activity by sea and land, European citizens developed new trades, crafts, arts, and, above all, a spirit of freedom. As a result, cities began to overthrow both their secular rulers and their bishops. Citizens of the revolting cities drew up "charters" and "statutes" to protect their collective and individual rights. Towns created armed militias and entered into alliances with other free cities. Gradually, the liberation of cities and the formation of free communities spread throughout Europe, and the era of the Renaissance began ushering in the theory of social contract and the institution of government.

The Social Contract View

The *social contract* theory emerged in response to human enlightenment and civic awareness. It is based on the belief that natural existence without a binding agreement among those who live together can create danger for all concerned. People would not be secure in their property, rights, or claims; feuds would ensue in which the stronger would subdue the weaker; and human freedom from dependence on the will of others would be destroyed.

The social contract theory provided relief from social and religious injustice by proposing that (1) all human beings are individuals who possess an independent identity that predated society; (2) humankind is composed of people who are all relatively equal and entitled to happiness in their own right; (3) individuals, rather than being society's creatures, create society; and (4) society is to be maintained as a congregation of "free and equal individuals" who relate to each other by virtue of mutual interest and on the basis of what they have acquired through their exercise of humanity. The new society was termed *gesellschaft* and was largely characterized by functionalism, rationalism, and personal achievement. Among the most notable champions of the social contract theory were Hobbes, Locke, and Montesquieu.

Thomas Hobbes (1588–1679) was an English philosopher and a staunch champion of the social contract theory. He advocated that individuals would be best served by entering into a collective agreement that could ensure their individual security and prosperity. He also advocated the imperative need for a central governing authority able to arbitrate conflicts and settle disputes. Without such an authority, the safety of the people and the preservation of their property would be in question. Only through a contract, Hobbes argued, can man be transformed from his "natural state" to that of a civil society.

Hobbes despised the idea of natural law because he thought man already had a "pretty dismal nature." He equated human nature with a life of egoistic emotions, a continual struggle for self-preservation, and perpetual war. He thought that society under natural law was bereft of reason and was sustained solely by bloody competition among its members. Based on such a reductionist view of mankind, he articulated (probably better than anyone else) the concept of social contract: "Everyone gives up his right of governing himself and authorizes a designated person or assembly of men to govern his actions on the condition that every other citizen does the same and abides with the authority of the said person or assembly" (Albert et al., 1988:141). Only on these terms can individuals be transformed from their natural presocial state into the state of social civility within a commonwealth that is to be ruled by a sovereign ruler or an absolute king. When the commonwealth is so ruled, Hobbes argued, peace would be maintained, justice would be preserved, and collective happiness would be achieved.

John Locke (1632–1704) built on Hobbes's theory of social contract, but turned it into a greater essay on freedom. He merged the concepts of freedom and government in the larger doctrine of *liberalism*. He advocated individual freedom as the supreme end of government. While he was sympathetic to the institution of commonwealth as advocated by Hobbes, he favored a more liberal form of government than Hobbes's absolute monarchy. He disliked any complicated political system that might hinder individual and group economic prosperity. He saw the role of political authority as limited only to the necessary means of settling exceptional disputes that arise between individuals or groups.

Unlike Hobbes, Locke had great respect for man's moral judgment. He believed that people were basically "pleasant chaps" who brought into society a fairly advanced sense of natural decency. His views of natural law were also different from those of Hobbes. While Hobbes looked at the natural state of man with the eye of a physical scientist and saw in it conflict and disarray, Locke looked at it with the eye of an economist and saw in it the roots of a dynamic capitalist mentality. Locke viewed natural law as a state of perfect freedom, conducive to a market economy, an extensive commerce, and an unlimited opportunity for the pursuit of happiness. When he was later asked how such a liberal society could function in an orderly fashion, he reportedly replied, "by leaving it in every man's hands." Locke eventually qualified his view by proposing the doctrine of separation of powers and the establishment of a system of checks and balances.

Given the complex world of today, Locke's views on liberalism could easily be criticized for being too idealistic, if not outright naive. On the other hand, it was Locke's advocacy of liberalism in its idealistic form that first introduced the concepts of liberty and free enterprise to the Western world. Building on Locke's concept of liberalism, many of his lofty principles were incorporated in the Declaration of Independence, and as a result the United States became the free and prosperous nation it is today.

The French philosopher Montesquieu (1689–1755) was an equally impressive thinker. He introduced the world to the social idea of laws in his 1748 masterpiece *The Spirit of the Laws*. His work has been regarded as the charter of sociology and the beginning of modern-day legal systems. Montesquieu was a behavioral philosopher who harbored suspicion of religious beliefs and unsubstantiated philosophical dogma. He was more inclined to trust social institutions that worked moderately well. He devoted the opening part of his work to the study of natural law, which, like Locke, he thought provided adequate standards of justice, happiness, and morality.

Montesquieu's *theory of law* provided a legitimate foundation for the institution of government that he strongly supported. He nevertheless distinguished between the *nature of government* and the *principle of government*. The *nature of government* referred to the number of people that possessed supreme power in a given society. On the basis of this number, governments can be republics, monarchies, or dictatorships. The republican forms of government, which can be either democratic or aristocratic, are motivated by civic virtue; monarchies are motivated by honor; and dictatorships by fear. Each of these forms, Montesquieu suggested, signifies the unique relationship between the people, their level of civilization, and their attachment to reason. By *principle of government* Montesquieu referred to the tendency of government to uphold moral and spiritual standards, as opposed to practicing crude control and intimidation. Montesquieu clearly located the origin of ethics in the presence of laws that are to be obeyed because they are good in themselves. Montesquieu's views of social legalism have been remarkably influential in the United States, where ethical judgment continues to be based on the principles of rule of law, constitutionalism, and rational-legal values.

Review Questions

1. If you were in Captain Balian's place, what could you have done to save the lives of the Vietnamese refugees without violating the rules of the navy?

2. Do you think occupational subculture can be changed? What does it take to effectively change the subculture of a prison unit?

3. What are the three types of knowledge? Which type is most conducive to the philosophy of wisdom?

4. Assume that you have been promoted to the position of training sergeant in a small police department. How can you teach wisdom to your subordinates?

5. Define *naturalistic fallacy*. Give two examples of such a fallacy derived from your work environment.

6. What is the criterion of reasonableness in the study of ethics? How can you measure the degree of reasonableness in a report written by one of your workers?

7. Differentiate between normative ethics and metaethics. Is the police code of ethics considered normative or meta? Why?

8. Define deontological and teleological theories of ethics. Should probation officers be more concerned with the former or the latter in their treatment of parolees? Why?

9. What are the historical origins of ethics? Define the central element of each view.

10. Define *social contract* and explain the different views of Hobbes and Locke.

References

Angeles, P. A. (1981). *Dictionary of Philosophy*. New York: Barnes and Noble Books.

Ayer, A. J. (1949). On the Analysis of Moral Judgments. *Horizon, 20.*

Barker, T. (1978). Peer Group Support for Police Occupational Deviance. *Criminology, 15*, 3.

Barry, V. (1982). *Applying Ethics: A Text with Readings*. Belmont, CA: Wadsworth Publishing.

Carter, D. L. (1984). Theoretical Dimensions in the Abuse of Authority by Police Officers. *Police Studies, 7*(4), 224–236.

Crouch, B. M., & Marquart, J. W. (1980). *The Keepers*. Springfield, IL: Charles C. Thomas.

Fakhry, M. (1970). *A History of Islamic Philosophy*. New York: Columbia University Press.

Israeli Lieutenant Makes Stand in Defense of Jailed Palestinians. (1997, August 25) *Houston Chronicle.*

Kroptkin, P. (1968). *Ethics: Origin and Development*. New York: Benjamin Blom.

Manning, P. K. (1971). The Police: Mandate, Strategies, and Appearances. In J. D. Douglas (Ed.), *Crime and Justice in American Society*. Indianapolis, IN: Bobbs-Merrill.

Porter, B. F. (1980). *The Good Life: Alternatives in Ethics*. New York: Macmillan Publishing.

Rossides, D. W. (1978). *The History and Nature of Sociological Theory*. Boston: Houghton Mifflin Company.

Sahakian, W. S. (1974). *Ethics: An Introduction to Theories and Problems*. New York: Barnes and Noble Books.

Skolnick, J. H. (1985). A Sketch of the Policeman's Working Personality. In A. S. Blumberg & F. Neiderhoffer (Eds.), *The Ambivalent Force: Perspectives on the Police* (3rd ed). New York: Holt, Rinehart and Winston.

Thomson, O. (1993). *A History of Sin*. New York: Barnes and Noble Books.

Toch, H. (1990). Is a 'Correctional Officer,' by Any Other Name, a 'Screw?' In S. Stojkovic, J. Klofas & D. Kalinch (Eds.), *The Administration and Management of Criminal Justice Organizations*. Prospect Heights, IL: Waveland Press, Inc.

Wilson, J. Q. (1993). *The Moral Sense*. New York: The Free Press.

3

Understanding Criminal Justice Ethics

Sources and Sanctions

Nails are not made out of good iron, nor soldiers out of good men.
A Chinese Saying

The true joy of man is to be kind to them that are of the same kind as he is himself.

Marcus Aurelius

A good man is one who gives bread to the hungry, water to the thirsty, raiment to the naked, a boat to one who has none.
The Egyptian Book of the Dead

The Khmer Rouge are not criminals, they are true patriots.
Prince Norodom Sihanouk

What You Will Learn from This Chapter

You will learn the major sources of criminal justice ethics. These are natural law, religious testaments, constitutional and legal provisions, professional codes of ethics, and philosophical theories. You will learn their characteristics and their moral implications in the exercise of criminal justice.

You will first learn the hierarchical order of virtues, the role of religion in society, the idea of legitimacy, incorruptibility, and the concept of positive law. All of these should be examined as they relate to issues of religiosity, constitutionalism, public service, and professionalism.

Key Terms and Definitions

Natural Law is a set of principles that regulate the behavior of individuals and groups on the basis of their universal characteristics and common experiences.

Religiocentrism is one's tendency to take for granted the superiority of his or her religion above all others.

Law is a formal ordinance of reason that is directed toward a common good.

Positive Laws are sanctions approved either directly by the citizens or indirectly through political representation. Positive laws form a country's legal foundation.

Incorruptibility is a form of behavior that directs one to live in accordance with the highest standards of excellence.

Codes of Ethics are institutional guidelines designed to reinforce ethical conduct by practitioners.

Professionalism is a behavior that strives for excellence in whatever the practitioner does.

Overview

Particularly when *ethics* is defined as the "rule of principles," students are quick to ask, "But whose principles are they?" The implication, of course, is that the study of ethics is "all subjective," after all. This interpretation is inaccurate, especially because ethical studies in criminal justice have been increasingly quantitative in nature. Nonetheless, in response to the original question of "whose principles these are," I usually advise students to make a short trip to the library and perform a computer search on the words *ethics*, *morals*, or *principles* and to watch the huge number of references appearing on the screen. It is likely to be in the thousands, depending on the size of the library. In criminal justice ethics alone, there are at least 250 recent books and articles (Smith & Kleinig, 1996). Regardless of the numbers, however, the origins of criminal justice ethics can be found in an amalgam of the following sources:

- Natural law
- Religious testaments
- Constitutional provisions
- Professional codes of ethics
- Philosophical theories

Ethics of Natural Law

To appreciate the role of natural law, in general and in criminal justice ethics in particular, we should once again recall the cases of Jimmy Carter in Haiti, Captain Balian in the North China Sea, and Lieutenant Lotem in Jerusalem. All of these dealt directly with issues of natural law and natural rights.

When I ask my students to define natural law, and its role in criminal justice, they usually respond with one or more of these replies: "We are not sure what natural law is"; "Of course, Professor, we know; but hasn't natural law been dead for centuries?"; or "Isn't natural law part of political science? What has it got to do with criminal justice?"

In response to these answers, I present the idea of natural law as analogous to the musical scale. Throughout the centuries, the scale has been the same in the ever-changing world of music. Despite the radical changes in musical composition—from classical music, to dance music, to jazz, to rock-and-roll, to heavy metal music—the original pitches remain unviolated and unchanged. Of course, composers do improvise as much as their talents allow, but they cannot add to, or delete from, the original pitches of the musical scale. Likewise, the essence of natural law remains unchanged; its unchanging moral foundation is as much the basis of modern laws as the pitches of the musical scale are to modern music.

Natural Law Defined

The term *natural* stems from the Latin *natura*, which means "born," "a universal phenomenon," "a creation of God," or conduct that is based on "basic conditions." The idea of natural law stems from the notion that the universe is a rational whole and that all things (including human beings) are parts of a higher entity. As such, natural laws are crucial to the survival of all creatures. They include *scientific rules*, such as those of gravity, motion, and physics, and *societal rules*, such as those of sympathy, rearing children, and grieving for the dead.

In the latter sense, *natural law* can be defined as "sanctions that regulate the behavior of individuals and groups on the basis of universal traits and common experiences." In this sense it can be contrasted with common law, civil law, statutory law, and even religious law.

Recognizing natural law as a set of rules that govern human morality began with the Romans, who were strongly influenced by the Stoic philosophy of the Greeks. They distinguished between laws that govern the rights and privileges of Roman citizens, *jus naturale*, and those that regulate the affairs of all others, *jus gentium*. Christian philosophers later advocated that natural law applies to everyone, because in a sense it represents the dictums of God under a secular guise. They pointed out that natural laws emanated from God before theological testaments were revealed. Other jurists viewed natural law as the law of custom that evolved throughout human history, representing the triumph of good over evil. Still others simply view it as the law of reason that evolved as a product of civilization.

Because the concept of natural law frequently overlaps the concept of natural rights, a brief clarification is in order. *Natural rights* are "undisputed entitlements that people possess by virtue of being human beings." These are patrimonies that are inalienable and irreducible. Examples include life, freedom, and the pursuit of happiness. Natural rights also signify the dignity of man, because they underscore human individuality and one's right to be treated equally and fairly, independent of any social class, economic status, or political allegiance.

Natural law is therefore the legitimate steward of natural rights. As such, it takes on an eminent value with respect to four distinctive characteristics:

- *Its origin*: Natural law goes back to the beginning of mankind.
- *Its domain*: It applies to all people regardless of nationality, race, sex, religion, or socioeconomic status.
- *Its worth*: It is the ultimate standard of human morality that supersedes all other laws without exception.
- *Its rigor*: Its elements are hardly mutable or changing.

Natural Law as the Law of Humanity

For the purposes of this discussion, natural law should be conceived as the law of humanity. It is based on human reason and transcends the legislative or legal provisions of government. Natural law provides the moral compass that specifies the fundamental rights all individuals should possess. People and governments can of course legislate positive laws, amend them, and rescind them, but they cannot change natural law.

As an example of the durability of natural law (vis-à-vis positive laws), consider the practice of allowing extra credence to statements made by dying suspects or witnesses; of offering a special meal to the condemned person before execution; and, of course, of mourning the dead. Consider in particular the continuing practice of allowing funeral processions to proceed slowly on public roads unimpeded by changing traffic lights, despite the complications such processions can cause to the flow of traffic. The moral of this practice is showing respect for the dead and honoring a person's final journey to the grave.

In modern times, principles of natural law have been incorporated in the American Declaration of Independence, the French Declaration of the Rights of Man, and the constitutions of most democratic states. In 1948 the fundamentals of natural law were incorporated in the United Nations *Declaration of Human Rights* (1948) and have since been invoked whenever issues of human rights are raised. Among the general rights specified in the declaration are the following:

- All human beings are born free and equal in dignity and rights.

- Everyone has the right to life, liberty, and security of person.

- No one shall be subjected to slavery or servitude.

- No one shall be subjected to torture or to inhuman or degrading treatment or punishment.

- Everyone is equal before the law.

- Everyone has the right to freedom of thought, conscience, and religion.

- Everyone is entitled to all of the rights and freedoms set forth in the Declaration.

Among the natural law principles that restrict state power are the following:

- Governments shall not deprive anyone of liberty or citizenship.

- Governments shall not banish individuals.

- Governments shall not disallow habeas corpus.

- Governments shall not arbitrarily deprive anyone of property.

The fact that these principles may not be fully incorporated in the constitutions of all countries does not undermine their effect or make them less binding. Theoretically, the principles of natural law need not be codified to be enforced, because their power stems from the universal human bond.

At present, natural law is advocated around the world as the law of civil rights, the law of democracy, and the law of civilization. Failure to abide by these laws can deny a country its membership in the world community. The chief influence of natural law, however, continues to be its moral imprint on legislation and rule making. With the spread of democracy in the world, the footprints of natural law are becoming more and more visible in the social, legal, and economic laws of individual governments. This is evidenced by the increasing demands to end discrimination by gender, race, color, age, or religion; to protect the unborn; to protect privacy rights; and to enforce the preservation of endangered species.

The moral implications of natural law in criminal justice are plentiful. These include principles that every criminal justice professional should honor. Some of these are as follows:

- People are to be treated with dignity by virtue of being people.

- Man as a rational being must be governed only by rules of reason.

- Equality of mankind is an unimpeachable doctrine.

- Actions by government officials are to be guided by moral standards conducive to the happiness of the governed.

- Maintaining peace and meting out justice are the chief goals of a civilized community.

- In the absence of more definitive rules, one must resort to the principles of natural law.

Relevance of Natural Law

The ethical implications of natural law in criminal justice focus, before anything else perhaps, on the fundamental obligation to preserve human dignity. Criminal justice is a special field of justice. As such, the community of criminal justice (officials, clients, offenders, or inmates) should be seen as endowed with inalienable rights that cannot be violated without a legitimate justification. It is regrettable, however, that because of personal, social, or ideological biases, some practitioners tend to ignore this emphasis and at times deny it altogether. Such behaviors should be considered *moral aversions* that can pass neither the test of reasoning nor the measure of civility. If you take the Socratic view, for instance, these behaviors are manifestations of ignorance; if you take the Aristotelian view, they are irrational; and if you take the Christian view, they are transgressions against God.

Furthermore, natural truths of criminal justice are not to be judged by whether practitioners like them or dislike them. They are eternal and universal values that must be applied equally to the entire commonwealth of mankind. More specifically, in a free society, the discriminatory treatment of people on the basis of who are the governors and who are the governed is unacceptable, because the governors are not always powerful and the governed are not always powerless. In a civilized community, each individual dignifies the humanity of the other.

The Hierarchical Order of Virtues

Understanding natural law theory serves a fundamental function: It establishes a clear and distinct *hierarchical order* of virtues. Practitioners of criminal justice, whether they are police officers, court workers, or correctional officers, should appreciate this rule and honor its ranking order: professional virtues, American virtues, and human virtues.

> *Professional virtues*: Despite their unquestionable worth, professional virtues are the *lowest values* on the hierarchy of virtues. Contrary to popular views, professionalism characterizes the practitioner as an expert only in his or her field or occupation. Professionalism alone, however, is hardly sufficient for making an ethical person or organization. While individual practitioners can be efficient, effective, punctual, and obedient, they still can be morally indifferent, or even immoral. It should be remembered that even the high level of professionalism among military and police groups has not prevented thefts on army bases or the fabrication of evidence by police. By the same token, history reveals the German SS troops during World War II were perhaps among the most professional military organizations ever assembled since the Praetorian Guard of Rome. They were all Aryans, tall, handsome, well educated, well disciplined, and well supervised. Yet their morality was demonstratively lacking. Their professionalism was perhaps best suited to the arts of killing and destruction.

> *American virtues*: These form the *second highest level* on the hierarchy of virtues. They represent a commitment to the constitutional and democratic doctrines of the United States. These include liberty, justice, equality, due process, equal protection, rationality, and accountability, among a large inventory of values. These values set the American criminal justice practitioner apart from his or her counterparts in other countries. In accordance with these virtues, practitioners of criminal justice should avoid violating people's rights, torturing suspects of crime, detaining prisoners without charges, or depriving inmates of humane treatment. It should be emphasized that the true "moral" of criminal justice is shunning such behaviors, even if they may be the most effective. The practical test of this moral, therefore, is to accept options that are considered "American—but less effective" and to resent those that are "un-American—but more effective." It is precisely this choice that distinguishes criminal justice practitioners in the United States from those in developing countries.

Human virtues: These constitute the *highest level* of the hierarchy of virtues. They are characterized by total (almost chivalrous) dedication to the truths of natural law. According to these values, rendering justice is the *summum bonum* of all values; its practice is as holy as worship, and its delivery as dutiful as patriotism. Consistent with human virtues, justice should be served in the interests of society, even if it antagonizes government; fairness should be exercised even if it violates procedure; and goodness should be pursued in situations normally handled by villainy and deception.

Moral Implications

In accordance with the *hierarchical order of virtues*, professional rules and regulations can be modified, or even ignored, if they are inconsistent with American values. A good example of this is the ever-increasing practice of discharging hard-working practitioners who are convicted of seemingly "insignificant" civil rights violations. By the same token, American values can be suspended if they are found to be inconsistent with human values. Examples include the conviction of Captain Balian (with whom we are already familiar) and Lieutenant William Calley for his responsibility in the My Lai massacre during the Vietnam War. The lieutenant was convicted of murder and sentenced to a prison term for killing unarmed, innocent Vietnamese men, women, and children, even when it was shown in court that he was simply obeying orders from his superiors.

Human values, on the other hand, *cannot* be sacrificed for any reason, except perhaps for the sake of God—and only if one is a true believer. Accepting the legitimacy of the hierarchy of virtues is the beginning of wisdom. Failure to follow its dictates indicates the absence of ethical commitment on the part of the practitioner and, indirectly, on the part of the supervisors and leaders.

Finally, it should be emphasized that the theory of natural law, sublime as it may be, has not been equally received by all jurists. Communist and fundamentalist jurists continue to reject it because it curtails the powers of government or undermines God's law, respectively. Jurists from Fascist governments criticize it for being too uncertain, ambiguous, and difficult to enforce. Still others find it too idealistic. Nevertheless, most governments have incorporated the main principles of natural law in their constitutions, setting aside the rest simply as moral guidelines.

Ethics of Religious Testaments

It must be stated at the outset that delving into any study of religion can cause unnecessary emotional agony. Individuals hold deep religious convictions that can strongly influence their perception of reality.

Religious values, regardless of how they are addressed, are first and fore-most matters of faith, and the essence of faith is accepting given assump-tions without questioning. As a result, individuals who hold religious convictions are not usually interested in philosophical argument or sci-entific scrutiny.

Nevertheless, the intellectual pursuit of religious issues is what gives religion its unique utility and independence from the fields of sociology, psychology, or even philosophy. Furthermore, fearing to discuss religious issues may give the impression of spiritual indifference, as Martin Luther charged in his famous indictment of the church in 1517, or a sense of disinterest in the truth. The following discussion should not, therefore, be construed as a ruling on the truth or falsity of religion in general, or a judgment of the correctness of one faith or another.

The Role of Religion in Society

Religion has always played a significant role in the development of individuals and the stability of society. To some degree, the pilgrims who first journeyed to the New World took an enormous risk for religious purposes. Indeed, nearly all of the first 13 colonies were formed around particular interpretations of the Christian faith. When the colonies were finally united, religious principles were an integral part of the comp-romises that resulted in the doctrine of separation of church and state. Ironically, the doctrine was supported by leaders who had considerable doubts as to the role of God in the conduct of human affairs. Washington, Jefferson, Franklin, and many other founding fathers espoused *deism*, a theological stance that holds that the world was created by a Divine Creator who is no longer involved with it (Chalfant et al., 1987:4).

One of the fullest and most productive attempts to explore the role of religion in modern society was made by Emile Durkheim. Durkheim defined religion as a "unified system of beliefs relative to sacred things, that is to say things set apart and forbidden" (Durkheim, 1933:61). He further added that such beliefs unite believers into a moral community called *church*, or *congregation*. Through the instrument of church, organized religion emerged as an independent realm of awareness iden-tifiable with three basic characteristics:

- It is concerned with things considered sacred by virtue of being apart from mundane daily activities.

- It involves beliefs and practices directed primarily by faith.

- It is the property of the group of believers, rather than the individ-ual (Chalfant et al., 1987:13).

In explaining the function of religion in society, numerous authors offered their views on the subject. Among the prominent scholars who represented a mainstream thought were O'Dea and Aviada (1983). They viewed the chief function of religion as providing church adherents with a general sense of morality and responsibility. The authors suggested that religion in society serves six essential functions:

1. Providing society with a point of reference that transcends the everyday world

2. Promoting among believers a feeling of security and a sense of worth

3. Giving an added emphasis to the norms and values of society

4. Presenting believers with a sense of prophecy

5. Assisting the individual in establishing a group identity

6. Facilitating the growth and maturation of members of the church group

Radical Views of Religion

While O'Dea and Aviada's views are fairly moderate and popular, they are not uniformly shared by all philosophers and scientists. There were those who disagreed and instead expressed radically different views. Freud, for instance, was one of those theorists. As a psychiatrist, he championed the psychoanalytical method that explains religion in terms of a myth that had been lingering since the primitive age of man. He associated religion with a universal neurosis—the Oedipus complex. That complex is an allegory based on the myth of a primal father slain by his sons in order to gain control of the woman he kept for himself (their mother). Freud used the complex to describe a strong feeling that combines love and dependence, respect and fear, obedience and hostility. Nevertheless, Freud defended religion as a useful therapeutic technique that can protect the individual from social neuroses.

Marx was another radical critic of religion. As an economist and a revolutionist, he harbored hostility toward the capitalist system. Critical of religion as a tool of the rich, he labeled it the "opiate of the people." That opiate, he believed, was offered by the *bourgeoisie* (the economically dominant class) to the *proletariat* (the working class) as a sedative representing the will of God. Marx explained that the exploited classes needed such a sedative to enable them to cope with the state of helplessness they lived in and accept the economic and social inequalities inflicted upon them. Marx added that members of the working class, alienated and dehumanized by the severe economic conditions imposed on them, created their own gods and worshipped them as a means of alleviating their frustration.

Dysfunctions of Religion

Religion may still have a dysfunctional effect on individuals and groups. The term sociologists often use to describe that effect is *religiocentrism*: one's tendency to take for granted the superiority of his religion above all others. Religiocentric views can seriously undermine social cohesiveness in the world we share. Throughout the centuries, religious squabbles, splits, and schisms have caused painful consequences to those involved in wars of religion. Consider, for example, the bloodshed and warfare prompted by religiocentrism during the Crusades and the Inquisition. In modern times we witness the devastating conflict between Jews and Muslims in the Middle East, Protestants and Catholics in Northern Ireland, and Hindus and Sikhs in India, among other tragedies. Ironically, while all these religions emphatically prohibit killing, the irrational fervor of their adherents remains out of control.

Examples of religiocentrism in the United States may include the justification of slavery in terms of the "white man's burden" and the negative sentiments toward Jews, Jehovah's Witnesses, and Black Muslims. Religion, in these examples, has been irrationally used to justify and perhaps exacerbate human prejudice. Instead of serving as an instrument of social unity, signifying love and compassion among men, religion became an instrument of social divisiveness and, in the case of slavery, economic exploitation. Even at the individual level, religiocentrism may also be dysfunctional. Many sociologists argue that being "overcome by religion" can, in a psychological sense, cause emotional instability, frustration, and even biological harm to the well-being of the individual (Chesen, 1972; Gerard, 1968; Richardsen, 1975).

Religion and Ethics

People make the erroneous assumption that ethical positions are based on religious convictions and that religion is the foundation of all ethics. This was probably the prevailing thought in the past, but not anymore. One should be reminded that ethics was already a hotly debated subject before Moses, Jesus, or Mohammed. Nevertheless, philosophy in the Middle Ages was considered the "handmaid of theology." Its function was to reinforce the biblical truths and refute heresies. When conflicts between scriptures and philosophy eventually developed, human reasoning had to give way to God's word, which was considered the only source of knowledge. As Porter states, "Athens must not take precedence over Jerusalem" (Porter, 1980:16).

With the passing of the Middle Ages, philosophy gained independence from theology and began serving both religious and nonreligious causes. While it continued to clarify competing theological interpretations, it favored only whichever position was closest to the truth. At times, it attacked church dogma, as when Bishop Martin Luther in the sixteenth century "made his stand," declaring himself "Luther the free." Luther questioned the church position of being above critical examination. If the church failed to meet the critical test, he pronounced, perhaps it was *faith*, and not philosophy, that should be called into question. With the liberation of philosophy from religion, ethics was fully liberated.

But regardless of how liberated ethics has been, religious beliefs continue to be deeply intertwined with ethical behavior. One's sense of religiosity is strongly related to one's sense of morality, fairness, and sociability. For example, our attitudes toward minority groups, women, homosexuals, and drug addicts have been consistently associated with religious beliefs (National Opinion Research Center, 1985). Furthermore, in a broader sense, religious beliefs may affect one's work attitude, desire to succeed, cooperation with colleagues, respect for authority, compassion to subordinates, and other perceptions of work activities. For example, the famous sociologist Max Weber proposed that capitalism could not have developed in the West without the religious ethos of Calvinism, which emphasized work as a "calling from God." By the same token, one can easily trace many negative attitudes toward the poor, criminals, and the homeless to a secularized version of a religious belief.

Ethics in Christianity

There are many organized religions in the world today. Among the more traditional are, of course, Christianity, Judaism, Islam, Hinduism, and Buddhism. In a broader sense, they all advocate goodness, piety, decency, and moral behavior. In fact, aside from a few specific, albeit significant, differences, they all advocate "Peace among men on earth and glory to God in the heavens." For the purposes of our discussion, only ethics of Christianity will be presented, because it is almost impossible to discuss all the others' scriptures, although you may wish to pursue them on your own.

Christianity has its roots in Hebrew teachings, but its moral philosophy goes far beyond, due to the central figure of Christ and the works of the apostles who followed him. Christian philosophy established four major doctrines that came to characterize ethics in the Bible:

1. Religion and ethics are indissolubly united. God's relationship with man is predicated not only upon obeying God's law, but also upon loving his fellow man.

2. Man's kindness toward his fellow man is part of worship.

3. God's forgiveness of sin requires that people forgive those who transgress against them. People no longer need to shed blood in the resolution of conflicts (which may be the strongest argument today against the practice of capital punishment).

4. Man should expect God's rewards for righteous behavior—if not on earth, then in heaven.

The ministry of Christ presented the most crucial difference between Judaism and Christianity. Christ's teachings changed the direction of religion from worthiness through obedience to worthiness through salvation. In Christ's teachings, the *summum bonum* of all values was essentially the goodness of *love, justice,* and *charity.* For example, on the morals of love we read that we are to love God with all our hearts; that we are to love our neighbor as ourselves; that we are to love not only our friends, but our enemies; that we are to forsake hatred because it stirs strife; and that he who loves life shall lose it.

On the morals of *justice* we read that he who rules over men must be just; that the path of the just is as the shining light; that the mouth of the just brings forth wisdom; that the tongue of the just is as choice silver; that through knowledge justice shall be delivered; that no evil will happen to those who are just; that it is joy to do justice; and that the just shall increase in faith.

On the morals of *charity* we read that all things should be done with charity; that we must follow righteousness with charity; that the greatest tiding of our faith is charity; and that above all things charity shall never fail.

Yet the main body of ethics in Christianity is certainly to be found in the Sermon on the Mount. The sermon authoritatively reconstructed the law of Torah into a Christian science of love. From the sermon we are taught the following:

Blessed are the poor in spirit: for theirs is the kingdom of heaven.

Blessed are they that mourn: for they shall be comforted.

Blessed are the meek: for they shall inherit the earth.

Blessed are they which do hunger and thirst after righteousness: for they shall be filled.

Blessed are the merciful: for they shall obtain mercy.

Blessed are the pure in heart: for they shall see God.

Blessed are the peacemakers: for they shall be called the children of God.

Blessed are they which are persecuted for righteousness' sake: for theirs is the kingdom of heaven.

Blessed are ye, when men shall revile you, and persecute you, and shall say all manner of evil against you falsely, for my sake.

Rejoice, and be exceeding glad: for great is your reward in heaven: for so persecuted they the prophets which were before you.

Ye are the salt of the earth: but if the salt have lost his savour, wherewith shall it be salted? It is thenceforth good for nothing, but to be cast out, and to be trodden under foot of men.

Moral Implications

Based on what has been said, the ethical reasoner should ponder why religious principles are not commonly adhered to in the practice of criminal justice. To those who claim they are religious, these principles are intrinsic goods and should not be violated, except for a higher value. What secular values can be more worthy than these? Can religious values be subjected to secular values? Is this consistent with ethical theory as we now understand it?

These are difficult questions because they touch on the essence of faith and the cultural and social mores one has learned since childhood. Our analysis, therefore, must be considered subjective and interpretive in nature. Chalfant, Beckley, and Palmer, in *Religion in Contemporary Society*, attempted to respond to these questions, suggesting that Christian values are more likely to be ignored due to the following:

- Ignorance on the part of the believer who fails to capture the true spirit of the values required in the teachings of her faith.

- One's inability to distinguish between the purpose of religion and the process of religion. The purpose is, of course, piety to God and goodwill to man. Process, on the other hand, can be a flurry of religious-like activities to be performed as frequently as required by some religious ritual.

- Absence of commitment to religious values, which may provide for an allowance to be made in advance for sacred values to be subjected to more convenient secular ones. The Greeks used the concept of *akrasia* to describe such allowance by which, while aware of what he ought to do, one would reserve (in his mind) the right to do otherwise. Examples include one's presupposed justification of marital infidelity, of accepting bribes, or of practicing discrimination.

- An unhealthy work environment that popularizes the view that mixing work decisions with religious principles is a professional weakness. Ironically, supporters of that attitude often find it necessary to use religious phrases such as "render unto Caesar that which is Caesar's and unto God that which is God's" to support their misguided attitude.

- Human weakness that causes one to falter in faith without predisposed reservations—"the spirit is willing but the flesh is weak."

While religion remains a powerful source of moral values, ethical principles are certainly not limited to religious values. Socrates indeed advocated virtue 400 years before Christ. He debated Euthyphro about whether "piety and holiness are good because they are loved by the gods," or whether "they are loved by the gods because they are pious and holy." While the distinction may appear trivial and pedantic, it has an enormous impact on the autonomy of the field of ethics today. For if one accepts the first part of Socrates's quandary, then God is the creator of all morals and aside from Him no morals can exist. Human conduct becomes right or wrong only insofar as it is valued by God. On the other hand, if one accepts the second part of Socrates's quandary, then morality is independent of religion, and questions of rightness and wrongness do not depend upon God's approval or disapproval.

It seems more reasonable to believe that God can condone only actions that are right and prohibit actions that are wrong. While believers would agree that within traditional Western thought, God is omnipotent, it is also assumed that He is not a self-contradictory God. He would not make cruelty right and compassion wrong, would not forgive some sinners and refuse to forgive others, would not perform some miracles and fail to perform others—although He certainly is capable of doing so. As a point of interesting trivia, logicians for centuries have asked questions relating to God's power. A typical question is, "Can God create a rock so large that He cannot lift it?" Obviously, "yes" or "no" replies are equally unsatisfactory; if He cannot create such a rock, then He is not a creator. On the other hand, if He cannot lift it, then He is no God. One must realize, however, that God would not choose to be self-contradictory even if He is clearly capable of being so (Porter, 1980:18–20).

In summary, while religion should be considered a *powerful* source of ethics, it is by no means the only source of ethical principles.

Ethics of Constitutional Provisions

This source of ethics is much more concrete and easier to comprehend. A constitution represents the highest law of the land. It establishes a social contract between the governors and the governed by establishing sanctions against the abuse of power by those empowered to rule. Practically all nations today have a written constitution, except for the United Kingdom, which continues to maintain an unwritten constitution based partly on statutes and partly on common law and practice. British political history seems to send a clear message about the durability of ethics to the rest of the world. As a consensual society, Britain continues to be governed by an ancient set of historic acts and customary rules. Based on the belief that "the king never dies," the crown, government, and people share a common interest and see no reason for a written constitution or having to worry about amending it when times change. The governors as well as the governed in Britain trust that the political accommodation they forged in 1688 concerning the functions and limits of government will continue by virtue of tradition, ethical consensus, and the participants' pledge of support.

Ethics of the U.S. Constitution

The United States Constitution is brief, simple, and logical. It presents not only a set of sanctions, but an implied moral order as well. Over the years, the Constitution became the most revered expression of unity, continuity, and purpose of the American nation. It serves as both a *symbol* and an *instrument*. As a symbol, the Constitution is an oracle that epitomizes the truths of the social contract that unites the citizens and their government and sets the fundamental values of political order. In that sense, it is above politics and beyond criticism. As an instrument, the Constitution outlines the institutions by which the American people are to be governed. It articulates their powers, sets up their limitations, and prescribes the procedures through which these institutions may function.

Chief among the constitutional provisions in the United States is the *Bill of Rights* (the first 10 amendments), which specifies individual immunities from possible oppression by government. The Bill of Rights provides three categories of guarantees that ensure individual freedom in a democratic society. The first consists of those seemingly abstract freedoms that protect the individual's integrity and independence. Freedom of religion, press, speech, assembly, and petition form the core of these rights. The second category relates to the protection of the individual from governmental arbitrariness. This category includes provisions that protect persons and property against unreasonable searches and seizures, as well as specific procedural guarantees related to indictment, fair trial, and punishment. The third category consists of provisions designed to protect property. Although guarantees preventing unreasonable searches and seizures and quartering of troops may be included under this heading, the most important clauses related to property rights are those that prohibit confiscation without due process of law and the appropriation of property for public use without just compensation (Havard, 1965:25).

Constitutional provisions in the United States, especially those stated in the Bill of Rights, are central to the ethics of criminal justice because they define what is "just" and what is "unjust." But if one takes the position that what is just (or unjust) depends solely upon the government's interpretation of the Constitution, one will be taking too narrow a view and may be considered an *ethical definist* or a *constitutional absolutist*.

There are obviously more moral issues than are mentioned in the Constitution. These include abortion, the right to die, and the right to privacy, among other contemporary issues. Furthermore, the morality of government cannot be superior to the morality of its officials. There have been many governments in history that made evil interpretations of noble ideals, and many still do. We are familiar with the atrocities committed by the Nazi government "to sustain the purity of the Aryan race," by the Stalinist regime "to promote a classless society," and by the apartheid regime in South Africa "to protect the rights of all people."

Even in the United States it can be safely argued that constitutional provisions have not always been successful in preserving the principles of justice and goodness. Examples include the practice of slavery, the internment of Japanese Americans in the 1940s, the notorious investigations during the McCarthy era of the 1950s, and the Iran–Contra scandal in the 1980s. But while the Constitution was insufficient during these episodes of national stress, the moral fortitude of the American people was not lacking. Through public demonstrations, open debates, and media condemnations, citizens—acting as the moral judges of society—were able to rectify injustices and restore the normalcy of democratic ethics.

On the other hand, if one takes the position that what is just or unjust can also be determined by principles independent of, and antecedent to, the institution of government (a position I strongly recommend), one will certainly be expressing a higher level of ethical awareness and manifesting unfettered intellectual judgment. Such a position can be supported on the basis of the following assumptions:

- Man does not live by laws alone, because the human "heart" can hold superior convictions to those required by the dictates of the law.

- Constitutions are only products of human intellect. Even in their most advanced versions they still can stand the risk of being wrong. A good example of that is the Eighteenth Amendment (Prohibition) (1919). It was later repealed by the Twenty-first Amendment (1933).

- Constitutional governments, even democracies, do not necessarily mean good government, because legitimacy (and goodness) can be ensured only by public recognition of how well government officials abide with constitutional provisions.

- Moral governments cannot be guaranteed to always remain moral. It is possible that under misguided leadership or during periods of national stress, they may turn immoral, even wicked.

- Citizens in a free society are morally obliged to prevent the perversion of government by not aiding in its hegemony or contributing to its perpetuity.

At this juncture it might be pertinent to remind ourselves of the ethical storehouse we have in the U.S. Constitution. It is certainly beautiful—and ethically healthy—to review the words of the preamble:

> We the People of the United States, in order to form a more perfect union, establish *justice*, insure domestic *tranquillity*, provide for the common defense, promote the *general welfare*, and secure the *Blessings of Liberty* and *Prosperity*, do ordain and establish this Constitution for the United States [italics added by author for emphasis].

The preamble is the executive summary of the moral contract between the governors and the governed. In the preamble, *justice* is mentioned second only to the formation of the Union, making it the leading constitutional virtue. Next to justice, the preamble exalts the ideals of domestic tranquility, general welfare, and the blessings of liberty and prosperity. This rank order is of paramount significance to all practitioners of criminal justice. It should be taught and retaught at each and every criminal justice training seminar as a reaffirmation of ethics.

Ethics of Law

Laws are necessary sanctions for the continued existence of society. They should be properly enacted and wisely enforced. Citizens, on the other hand, are obligated to abide by the dictates of the law and support its appropriate enforcement.

Legal theorists define *law* as a "formal ordinance of reason that is directed toward a common good." This definition is excellent. No reasonable person can argue with it. But a definition is not reality. We are certainly familiar with the existence of good laws and bad laws. As a case in point, Prohibition laws were enacted in 1919 on the assumption that they would improve social conditions, yet they were repealed in 1933 because they failed. Ethical questions arise when we are confronted with laws that are "unreasonable" or are not "directed toward a common good." In other words, should laws be obeyed simply because they are the will of government, or only when they are reasonable and embody a common good? This is a crucial question that has existed since the inception of the Republic and continued during the national controversies about Vietnam, civil rights, affirmative action, and abortion, to mention just a few. Resolving this question is crucial to making moral choices. Answers, however, can be highly complex.

Here are the main assumptions: If one takes the view that "the law is the law and that is all that concerns me," one can be accused of being narrow-minded, insensitive to the broader needs of society, and ethically indifferent. On the other hand, if one takes the extreme opposite view, scrutinizing every law and obeying only those with which one agrees, one can be accused of being radical, unsociable, insubordinate, and perhaps unpatriotic. The proper judgment must depend on one's knowledge, understanding of reality, and steadfastness of moral courage. In the following section, this will be clarified through a brief discussion of some fundamental issues—the ideas of legitimacy, law and ethics, ethical discretion, and incorruptibility.

The Idea of Legitimacy

Positive law is a relatively recent concept, because it was not fully articulated in Western thought until approximately the seventeenth century. Prior to that period, laws solely represented the command of the sovereign and had to be obeyed regardless of their content. Jeremy Bentham (1748–1832) was one absolutist philosopher who defended that view, declaring that "the existence of the law is one thing, its merit or demerit is another." This perception later stimulated great debates in Europe and led to radical political reforms that ensured that laws reflect clear reasoning and produce a verifiable common good. The reformers advocated that obedience to the law must be based on its legitimacy rather than on its pedigree.

The idea of legitimacy may be deceptively simple: It is *unnatural* for free people to obey unreasonable laws. Furthermore, if people were forced into obedience, they would be neither free nor brave. Not surprisingly, Greek philosophers supported that view, and when confronted with untenable laws, they either left the state, refused to comply, or shunned the particular area the law attempted to regulate. We know of at least one person—Socrates—who chose death over accepting state censorship. In the early Christian era, Saint Augustine declared that *lex injusta non est lex*—"an unjust law is no law at all." In the modern age, numerous reaffirmations were made in support of the legitimacy view by great thinkers who championed the cause of democracy. Thomas Jefferson and Abraham Lincoln were among those thinkers. Jefferson exhorted citizens to resist unjust laws and, if necessary, sacrifice life and liberty in rescinding them. His memorable words still resound in the conscience of all free people: "The tree of freedom must be watered by the blood of martyrs." Lincoln poignantly stressed the same doctrine, stating that "those who deny freedom to others, deserve it not for themselves, and under a just God, cannot retain it."

From an ethical perspective, the prevailing view of democratic philosophers is that a law that does not qualify as an instrument of reason, or is not conducive to common good, should be rescinded, amended, or simply disregarded. The United States was born on that liberal assumption, the abolition of slavery affirmed it, and the civil rights movement cemented it. The traditional theory of obeying the law regardless of its legitimacy makes no ethical sense; it is contradictory, and what is based on contradiction is unethical.

Ethics of Positive Law

All civilized societies have constitutions. Most are written, some are not. Constitutions are social contracts forged by representatives of society regarding the relations between the governors and the governed. Constitutions establish broad principles regarding the limits of government, the rights of citizens, and the methods by which conflicts can be resolved. One of these methods is the government's power to regulate public safety, civil matters, the economy, common defense, and the general welfare. Positive laws form the core of a country's legal foundation. They are approved either directly by the citizens or through some political representation designated in advance. In the United States, positive laws include federal laws, state laws, and local laws. They impose prohibitions, commands, or obligations for the purpose of maintaining social control, public safety, and civil administration.

Legal history, however, confirms that *customary ethics*, rather than positive laws, have been the prime source of social conformity. For instance, there is ample evidence to indicate that the Code of Hammurabi (1726–1686 B.C.) introduced, in essence, no new laws but reaffirmed prevailing customs (Ferm, 1956:195). In *The Republic*, Plato put little emphasis on laws per se and more on the development of a *polis*—the perfect city—where laws eventually would be unnecessary. Leaders of the *polis* were expected to be "men of gold," endowed with collective rationality and wisdom. The same can be said of common law that emerged during the Norman rule in England essentially to control the "ruffians." The practice of chivalry, common among English noblemen at the time, needed no legal support—it was "law unto itself." The same could be said about social order in traditional Islamic societies, in which relatively few positive laws exist.

The Edwin Meese Syndrome

Given the complexity of the law and the imperative that fairness and equity be adequately served, adherence to the letters of the law can create loopholes that undermine its efficacy. Therefore, to allow for reason and justice in the interpretation of laws, the *spirit* of laws must also be brought into play. The term *spirit of the law* refers to its "original purpose, direction of goodness, and social utility." Failing to consider these elements when the verbiage of the law is unclear or redundant can make the law inflexible or inapplicable. Take, for instance, the case of Edwin Meese, U.S. Attorney General in the Reagan administration. Serious allegations were raised about his involvement in the Wedtech scandal, which were construed as acts of corruption on his part. Speaking in his own defense, Meese allegedly admitted involvement but claimed that his actions, even if substantiated, were not illegal at the time; hence, they were undeserving of any punitive sanctions.

If Meese's "not illegal" doctrine were applied universally, society's ability to protect the interests of victims might be impaired, if not practically demolished. Improper actions by government officials may cease to be culpable as long as they can be massaged to coincide with the literal wording of the law. Unfortunately, the "not illegal" doctrine has often been used to exonerate corrupt politicians, businesspeople, and criminal justice practitioners. While this discussion is obviously not a plea for making more laws, it is a plea for ethical discretion, without which many laws can be too inflexible to apply ethically.

The Imperative of Ethical Discretion

The need for discretion in the conduct of criminal justice has been well documented and its justification well detailed in legal literature, agency rules, and professional journals. The need for discretion in criminal justice grew out of several practical reasons:

- The virtual inability of criminal justice practitioners to give equal attention to enforcement of all the laws and rules on the books. Many minor violations either go unenforced or are handled in an informal manner.

- The ambiguity of the law and its questionable capacity to produce equitable justice as prescribed in legal statutes.

- The substantial variations that exist between seemingly similar criminal situations that may render equal enforcement either unfair or unpopular.

- The demographic and social differences among communities, affluent or underprivileged as the case may be, require different approaches to the administration of justice.

- The intellectual, emotional, and moral differences among criminal justice practitioners compel them to treat even similar situations differently.

Given these considerations, lawmakers are compelled to authorize practitioners to make allowances in their enforcement of laws within recognized parameters (authorized discretion). In other cases the practitioners may find it necessary to exercise their own judgment rather than comply with trivial procedures. In this sense, the practitioners assume an *effective power* to make choices that they are not statutorily empowered to make. Yet the concept of discretion in itself may not be an appropriate remedy, because practitioners still can abuse it in the same way they abuse the law. What is at issue, then, is not discretion per se but *ethical discretion*.

Ethical Discretion

The concept of ethical discretion depends to a large extent on one's *moral commitment* to both the society and the agency served. The concept requires a highly sensitive capacity for moral judgment, because the practitioner must, in essence, determine whether the law or rule is worth complying with—in full, in part, or not at all. The practitioner must decide whether the "glory" of the state (or the agency served) would be substantially affected if the rule was slightly bent or ignored altogether. The soundness of such a decision is the crux of ethical discretion. Decisions of that nature can be difficult to make, because they must be weighed against other occupational and economic values that may be deemed equally important.

A clear example of ethical discretion is the traffic officer who, upon stopping a speeding vehicle and discovering that the driver is his mother, issues a verbal or a written warning instead of a citation. The violation in this case is minor, and the "glory" of the state would not be significantly upset. The traffic officer would essentially be reassigning the hierarchy of virtues in favor of family cohesiveness—by avoiding dishonoring his mother. Such a decision would be more consistent with social reality, and at the same time could hardly violate one's sense of professionalism. Obviously, the officer's discretion should not be the same if the mother were involved in an involuntary manslaughter case. In such a case, the loss of human life outweighs the value of family cohesiveness, and the fact that the driver is related to the officer would be immaterial. As mentioned earlier in the rules of ethical choice in Chapter 1, any moral value—except perhaps denying God and country—can be violated in favor of a higher value. Ethical judgment ultimately will depend on one's level of knowledge, rationality, and devotion to moral excellence, as well as one's ability to distinguish among the finer shades of moral obligations.

Let us consider another example that may better articulate the finer shades of moral analysis—this time from our world of academe. Imagine a professor who discovers a graduating senior cheating on the final exam. University policy in this case requires that the dean of students be notified, the case be investigated, and the student's graduation be suspended pending the outcome of the investigation. Assume that the professor chooses to ignore formal policy and attempts to resolve the matter in her own way. Obviously, the decision must take into consideration individual factors, such as the seriousness of the violation (looking at another student's paper versus stealing the exam from the secretary's office); the student's age and educational level; the student's response (admitting guilt versus accusing the instructor of making difficult tests); the student's cheating record (habitual cheater versus first-time offender); and the injustice that will be inflicted on fellow students if the student is allowed to complete the course. Institutional factors must also be considered: What is "just and reasonable" to the student, to the student body, and to the academic institution as a whole? What is "consistent and universal" in terms of the professor's readiness to offer the same "break" to other students who might be discovered cheating in the future? Furthermore, the professor must take into consideration the consequences of her decision: Would this decision make the students more or less honest in the future, and more importantly, would they benefit personally and professionally from the experience?

Incorruptibility

Discretion has been criticized for its propensity to open the floodgates of corruption. In *Character and Cops* (1989), Delattre points out that nothing is further from the truth—if the decision maker possesses good moral character. Indeed, the only thing incorruptible, Delattre stresses, is a "personal character that refuses to be corrupted." An incorruptible person "is truthful in word and deed just because truthfulness has become second nature with him." If a person is truthful even in matters in which nothing depends on his or her veracity, he or she will be even more truthful when something does depend on it (Delattre, 1989:65).

Incorruptibility is a form of discretion that directs one's life in accordance with standards of excellence and self-respect. According to Delattre, "These traits are more important than anything else, including life itself. No other disposition makes our lives our own, and no other disposition can make anyone trustworthy to the very end." Although few of us may be able to reach full incorruptibility, the principle is undying and should be kept before us (Delattre, 1989:65).

On the other hand, saying that no one is incorruptible and that everyone has a price is a timeworn excuse. If such cynicism is true, then our experiment in ordered liberty simply can no longer endure. Furthermore, it would be impossible to identify any trustworthy public official except by assuming that his or her price had never been offered. Delattre indicates that history is replete with persons who have had the character to resist all sorts of powerful temptations. The story of Socrates is one. The story of Saint Thomas More, the famous English philosopher, is another. He was beheaded by Henry VIII on the strength of perjured testimony. To save himself, More had only to put his hand on a Bible and tell a simple lie, but he remained silent. In the 1970s, hundreds of American prisoners of war in Hanoi were offered return to America if they would provide information and false "confessions" of war crimes. They refused except after torture and then said only as much as they had to. Many preferred to suffer in solitary confinement for years rather than betray themselves, each other, and their country (Delattre, 1989:66).

By the same token, there are thousands of criminal justice practitioners, including police officers, judges, and correctional officers, who cannot be tempted into forsaking their sacred duties to nation, community, or profession. By contrast, many corrupt criminal justice officials may seek consolation by blaming "the system" for their misconduct. Some might say that planting evidence, falsifying pre-sentence reports, and wrongfully writing up inmates are necessary to keep criminals off the streets. But even if such practices were necessary, such behaviors are nevertheless unjustifiable. Respected leaders in the criminal justice system flatly deny that such immoral means are necessary. Like all experienced practitioners of the system, they know that criminals would continue to commit crime, and when they were released from prison, they would be apprehended again—legally—if they were to commit another crime.

Conclusions

To conclude this section on the ethics of law, it is necessary to clarify the relationship between the areas of ethics and law:

1. The purpose of ethics is not to undermine the law or to replace it, but to complement it by deferring to the spirit of the law and to rules of equity.

2. Laws can apply only to behaviors that lawmakers choose to regulate; ethics, on the other hand, addresses all human activities.

3. Laws attempt to change people from the outside inward, while ethics seeks to change them from the inside outward.

4. Laws change frequently, but ethical principles are constant, universal, and everlasting.

5. Laws are "logical instruments" of social control that, for the most part, are not necessarily products of wisdom. Ethics, by contrast, is solidly based on the reasoning process essential to appropriate discretion.

6. Laws are basically reactive instruments, while ethics, for the most part, is prescriptive in nature.

7. Laws depend for their effectiveness upon legal procedures and complex rules of evidence, and ethics is dependent upon knowledge, rationality, and goodwill.

Professional Codes of Ethics

Codes of ethics are *institutional guidelines* used to reinforce ethical conduct by practitioners. They are not constructed as detailed means for resolving ethical problems, but as general principles that can stimulate moral choice. They are basically designed to motivate workers, bolster their ethical stamina, and assist in their occupational development.

Every component of the criminal justice system has some type of a code of ethics. The law enforcement code is perhaps the most widely adopted code of conduct among criminal justice agencies. Originally, the code was developed by the California Peace Officers' Association and then later adopted by the International Association of Chiefs of Police. The current code was adopted by the same institution in 1989. It is generic in the sense that it can be used by any law enforcement agency and fits well within official policy or procedure manuals. Some of the more significant values reiterated in the code are as follows:

- A police officer acts as an official representative of government who is required and trusted to work within the law. The officer's powers and duties are conferred by statute. The fundamental duties of a police officer include serving the community; safeguarding lives and property; protecting the innocent; keeping the peace; and ensuring the rights of all to liberty, equality, and justice.

- A police officer shall perform all duties impartially, without favor or affection or ill will and without regard to status, sex, race, religion, political belief, or aspiration. All citizens will be treated equally with courtesy, consideration, and dignity.

- Officers will never allow personal feelings, animosities, or friendships to influence official conduct. Laws will be enforced appropriately and courteously and, in carrying out their responsibilities, officers will strive to obtain maximum cooperation from the public. They will conduct themselves in appearance and deportment in such a manner as to inspire confidence and respect for the position of public trust they hold.

- A police officer will use responsibly the discretion vested in the position and exercise it within the law. The principle of reasonableness will guide the officer's determination and the officer will consider all surrounding circumstances in determining whether any legal action shall be taken.

- Consistent and wise discretion, based on professional policing competence, will do much to preserve good relations and retain the confidence of the public. There can be difficulty in choosing between conflicting courses of action. It is important to remember that a timely word of advice rather than arrest—which may be correct in appropriate circumstances—can be a more effective means of achieving a desired end.

- A police officer will not engage in acts of corruption or bribery, nor will an officer condone such acts by other police officers.

- The public demands that the integrity of police officers be above reproach. Police officers must, therefore, avoid any conduct that might compromise integrity and thus undercut the public confidence in a law enforcement agency. Officers will refuse to accept any gifts, presents, subscriptions, favors, gratuities or promises that would be interpreted as seeking to cause the officer to refrain from performing official responsibilities honestly and within the law. Police officers must not receive private or special advantage from their official status. Respect from the public cannot be bought; it can only be earned and cultivated.

As in the law enforcement profession, attorneys and bar associations also have formulated various codes of ethics. They are constructed in such a fashion as to define the parameters of ethical conduct within which attorneys should strive to conduct their professional lives. Most legal rules of professional conduct emphasize the following canons of ethics:

- A lawyer should assist in maintaining the integrity and competence of the legal profession.

- A lawyer should assist the legal profession in fulfilling its duty to make legal counsel available.

- A lawyer should assist in preventing the unauthorized practice of law.

- A lawyer should preserve the confidences and secrets of a client.

- A lawyer should exercise independent professional judgment on behalf of a client.

- A lawyer should represent a client competently.

- A lawyer should represent a client zealously within the bounds of the law.

- A lawyer should assist in improving the legal system.

- A lawyer should avoid even the appearance of professional impropriety.

Also, because judges serve an especially sensitive role in the administration of justice, codes of judicial conduct have been developed to guide them in fulfilling their professional responsibilities. Like other professional codes, those for judges are stated in broad terms and place a significant responsibility on members of the judiciary in meeting their public duties. Most judicial codes of conduct include the following canons:

- A judge should uphold the integrity and independence of the judiciary.

- A judge should avoid impropriety and the appearance of impropriety in all his activities.

- A judge should perform the duties of his office impartially and diligently.

- A judge should engage in activities to improve the law, the legal system, and the administration of justice.

- A judge should regulate his extrajudicial activities to minimize the risk of conflict with his judicial duties.

- A judge should regularly file reports of compensation received for quasi-judicial and extrajudicial activities.

- A judge should refrain from political activity inappropriate to his judicial office.

Codes of ethics have also been developed for correctional officers. Perhaps the most widely adopted and well known of these is promulgated by the American Correctional Association. That code consists of two parts. The first prescribes standards of conduct with respect to relationships with clients, colleagues, other professionals, and the public. Some of these standards include the following:

- Members will respect and protect the civil and legal rights of all clients.

- Statements critical of colleagues or their agencies will be made only as these are verifiable and constructive in purpose.

- Members will respect the importance of all elements of the criminal justice system and cultivate a professional cooperation with each segment.

- Subject to the client's rights of privacy, members will respect the public's right to know, and will share information with the public with openness and candor (American Correctional Association, 1981:145).

The second part addresses conduct relative to professional practices in the field. Some of the more significant standards in this section are as follows:

- No member [of the American Correctional Association] will use his official position to secure privileges or advantages for himself.

- No member will act in his official capacity in any matter in which he has a personal interest that could in the least degree impair his objectivity.

- No member will use his official position to promote any partisan political purposes.

- No member will accept any gift or favor of a nature to imply an obligation that is inconsistent with the free and objective exercise of his professional responsibilities.

- Each member will report without reservation any corrupt or unethical behavior which could affect either a client or the integrity of the organization.

- Members will not discriminate against any client, employee, or prospective employee on the basis of race, sex, creed, or national origin.

- Each member will maintain the integrity of private information; he will neither seek personal data beyond that needed to perform his responsibilities, nor reveal case information to anyone not having proper professional use for such.

- Any member who is responsible for agency personnel actions will make all appointments, promotions, or dismissals only on the basis of merit and not in furtherance of partisan political interests (American Correctional Association, 1981:145).

The Function of Codes

Codes of ethics serve two major purposes. First, they provide *moral guidelines* for practitioners of criminal justice. They establish moral obligations that should be met and moral qualities that should be emulated. Furthermore, codes of ethics prescribe *professional standards of conduct* necessary to the agency's well-being. The objective of these standards is to hold the practitioners accountable to the highest level of performance and keep them faithful to the obligations of honesty, fidelity, and duty.

Second, codes of ethics *define professional behavior* in the workplace. When practitioners adhere to a code of ethics, the result is an environment conducive to excellence. Workers know what their responsibilities require them to do without undue supervision. They develop a sense of pride in their jobs. They act with tolerance toward each other and in relationship to their clients. They are able to transcend "petty behaviors" such as jealousy, backbiting, and backstabbing and learn to abhor uncivilized behaviors such as discrimination, favoritism, and egoism. If the code is well adhered to, practitioners can, in essence, become highly civilized individuals.

All codes of ethics seek to cultivate two main virtues: *ethics of public service* and *ethics of professionalism*. These are intrinsic goods, fundamental and nonnegotiable. Without them, a public agency loses its moral entity; it becomes neither "public" nor an "agency."

Ethics of Public Service

In his farewell address in September of 1796, George Washington stressed the virtue of public service, equating it with the sacredness of a public trust. As a profound realist, Washington recognized the fallibility of government employees. He suggested that to suppose that anyone can be infallible in the conduct of public service is arrogant and dangerous. Public trust, he stressed, is based on "good intentions" and the "very best exertions of men" (Delattre, 1989:34).

Dedication to public service is the sine qua non of professional ethics—without the former, the latter cannot exist. The concept establishes the unquestionable primacy of public interest above the interests of practitioners. Dedicated public servants must *intend and resolve* to put the public good above the private gain of everyone—self, family, friends, political allies, or interested groups. They are obliged to identify with the public good and serve it. John Adams also advanced the concept of public service by stating that devotion to public service must be superior to all private passions. Men, he wrote, must be happy to sacrifice their private friendships and dearest connections when they stand in competition with the rights of society (Delattre, 1989:34).

The term *public* relates to an organization or forum bound to serve society. It transcends any identification with a given group or individual. In that sense, public servants are not at liberty to choose whom they serve and from whom they may withhold service. Like doctors and nurses in public hospitals, they must treat all people regardless of whether they are rich or poor, black or white, citizens or foreigners, victims or criminals.

In Western philosophy, obligation to public service traditionally has been analogous to that of a minister or teacher. Whereas the obligation of ministers is to the spiritual welfare of parishioners and the obligation of teachers is to the intellectual advancement of students, the obligation of public servants is to the interests of society as a whole. Indeed, Socrates equated the role of public servants to that of "educators"—they serve society by teaching its youth and sitting in judgment of their performance. This view should not be considered too alien to us; judges routinely appoint public servants as *parens patriae* to oversee the interests of minors and disabled individuals. The virtue of public service can be appreciated even more when public services are rendered at a hardship, such as in the case of soldiers, firefighters, police officers, and correctional officers, who at times may have to sacrifice their lives.

Given these assumptions, the expectation that public servants reflect a higher moral character than average persons should not be a pretentious claim. This is especially true because public servants are usually selected from a large pool of qualified applicants, are rigorously trained in the conduct of their duties, are experts in the arts of their business, and are constantly supervised by responsible superintendents. Furthermore, such an expectation should not be seen as a privilege that civilized governments may or may not extend. It is an obligation that all governments *must* meet by virtue of being the overseers of moral order.

But, "Wait a minute, Professor. Isn't this view a little too idealistic? How can we justify holding public officials to a higher moral standard, especially in a democratic society in which public servants come from the ranks of ordinary people? Isn't it possible that a worker may not be so highly motivated, may not appreciate her job, or may be a victim of occupational stress?" These objections certainly are understandable, yet unjustifiable. An anecdotal illustration may be necessary to make this point. Consider, for example, teachers in public schools. They are expected to be knowledgeable, conscientious, compassionate, and wise. Now imagine a scenario in which a student insults his teacher in the classroom, and the teacher responds by returning the exact insult, *word for word*. Who should be more to blame?

From an ethical viewpoint, both individuals are wrong, of course. But given the ethics of public service, the teacher is more to blame and perhaps deserving of more severe punishment. The justification for this judgment is based on three factors: (1) the doctrine of public officials as the "parents and teachers" of society obligates teachers to be positive role models acting from a higher moral plane; (2) the obligation that teachers, by virtue of their superior knowledge, are wiser than students requires they be better able to control their emotions (losing one's temper in the conduct of public service is an expression of immaturity and weakness); and (3) the principles of learning require that teachers keep a calm and stimulating atmosphere in the classroom. Creating an unsettling environment by trading insults with students can cause tension and disturb the learning process.

Let us take this scenario one step further. Professional persons should not be seen as too helpless, after all. In the example of teachers and students, there are other means by which teachers can effectively handle rude students. Some of these are certainly more effective than trading insults. The ethical teacher can talk to the student in private, call the student's parents, or send him or her to the principal's office, depending on the situation. But what about the defense that the student started the abuse and therefore "got what he deserved"? Ethical reasoning dismisses this defense, because mature persons should be able to control their emotions and be calm. Wise teachers are expected to be able to avoid, or gracefully deflect, minor provocations. Finally, professional teachers should realize that their behavior reflects on the morality of the institution they serve and the dignity of the teaching profession itself. The fact that many teachers fail to demonstrate moral restraint, however, does not relieve them of the moral responsibility to demonstrate higher moral virtue.

Ethics of Professionalism

Associated with the obligation to public service is the obligation to professionalism. The latter is the manifestation of the former. Professionalism has been defined as "striving toward excellence in whatever the practitioner does; a quest for perfection; and a highly civilized state of performance" (Souryal, 1977:396). As such, professional behavior is characterized by self-discipline rather than amateurism, reasoning rather than erraticism, maturity rather than egoism, and principled behavior rather than unbridled passion. In essence, professionalism should be seen as the climax of all work-related values.

Maslow's profile of the ethical person (to which we were introduced at the end of the tour of the Ethics Hall of Fame) elaborates on the attributes of the professional person. It emphasizes one's obligation to shun private gain at public expense; to focus on the service ideal; to transcend hatred, hostility, and prejudice; to respond to the challenge of the job; and to pursue the principles of honor, justice, fairness, and compassion, among other ethical attributes.

John Kleinig (1996:45) explains the significant, yet often unrecognized, difference between membership in a profession and professionalism. He points out that most professions establish a *noble rhetoric* by which they can impress society—the "looking-good syndrome," if you will. As such, professions operate by posturing themselves as the primary providers of the service. They establish a legitimate title by means of certification, or the promulgation of a code of ethics. Yet the ideal of professionalism—as excellence—may be lost in the trappings as long as the essence of professionalism is believed to belong exclusively to the profession rather than to the quality of its members (Kleinig, 1996:45).

True professionalism, on the other hand, is the art of "being good." There is more to it than conformity with institutional rules and disciplinary mechanisms. It embodies a fundamental measure of goodness, a commitment to the service one is providing or the activity in which one is engaging. In no uncertain terms, warns Kleinig, should institutional rhetoric substitute for the ideal of professionalism. Under this rubric, "a janitor or cleaning lady, without associational affiliation, may view and accomplish his or her work with the same professionalism as a skilled surgeon" (Kleinig, 1996:45). As a result, achieving true professionalism should be the goal of criminal justice agencies that aspire to professional status.

But how can true professionalism be achieved? There are two general approaches: *administrative* and *moral*. While these approaches may at times overlap, they are based on two different sets of assumptions. Assumptions of the administrative approach include the following:

- Institutional (agency) ethics are first and foremost derived from the job description stated in the hiring contract.

- The ultimate goal of professionalism is to build effective and efficient performers who always obey agency rules.

- Agency rules are value-free statements that have no bearing on the moral character of workers.

- Workers maintain absolute loyalty to their supervisors regardless of any moral reservations they may have.

- When the agency succeeds, it is because of good management, but when it fails, it is because of bad workers.

The administrative approach underscores the values of discipline, obedience, and organizational loyalty. It operates on the assumption that if the workers are so indoctrinated, they will unquestionably behave professionally when performing their duties.

Assumptions of the moral approach include the following:

- There are fair as well as unfair departmental rules. Fair rules are more likely to be honored and unfair rules to be practically ignored.

- There are "good" and "bad" organizational subcultures. Both can influence the quality of performance beyond the formal rules of the agency.

- Negative subcultures, unless intercepted, can rapidly and widely spread the disease of corruption within the agency.

The moral approach focuses before anything else on building the moral character of employees. In other words, agencies can be only as good as the character of their workers.

Yet for the moral approach to professionalism to succeed, it must focus on a variety of managerial activities. These include an open work environment, motivational techniques, job enrichment, removing the hygiene factors that exist (those conducive to cynicism, resentment, disharmony, and conflict), and the reinforcement of institutional integrity. Such activities, however, can hardly work without ethical leaders and supervisors endowed with reasoning and good faith, an ongoing concern for institutional fairness, and an unwavering courage to see these activities through with the moral zeal of a reformer.

While both the administrative and the moral approach have their own merits, only knowledgeable managers can integrate the two approaches in such a way that maximizes agency professionalism without undermining workers' integrity.

Moral Implications

One question that should be raised at this point is, "How successful are codes of ethics in maintaining ethical conduct among employees?" While there is no conclusive answer, three observations may shed some light on the direction of the question.

First, for codes of ethics to be *meaningful*, they must first be taken seriously. When employees "believe" in certain canons of conduct, ethical behavior is likely to be the result. Conversely, inappropriate or questionable conduct is likely to result when codes of ethics are viewed as inconsequential or meaningless.

Second, for codes of ethics to be *successful*, both administrators and supervisors must acknowledge their importance and follow their canons. Codes of ethics have little chance of success if supervisory personnel are indifferent to them or fail to adhere to their principles. Furthermore, codes are seriously undermined when supervisors insist on employee compliance yet engage in behaviors that are clearly unethical. Supervisory behavior that contradicts ethical conduct has the same effect as parents who tell their children, "Do as I say, not as I do."

Finally, for codes of ethics to be *effective*, the organizational environment must be healthy. Organizations riddled by "hygiene problems" such as inadequate salaries, poor supervision, unrealistic policies, strained interpersonal relations, and poor job security are likely to be beset with ethical problems. In contrast, organizations that attend to these factors are more likely to be able to promote ethical conduct and pride in their members.

Philosophical Theories of Ethics

This source of ethics is so central to understanding the philosophy of ethics that it warrants an independent chapter. In Chapter 4 we will be exposed to the marketplace of ethical ideas. We will learn the literature of a variety of ethical schools of thought. Each will be presented in a consistent manner—introduction, basic theory, and major issues. We also will read about the lives of some of the most influential ethical philosophers in history. This in itself can enrich your knowledge of the heritage of ethical theory and gratify your searching soul.

Chapter 4 will present the "meat" of ethical theory, without which everything we have studied would be incomplete. So far, we have learned only "about ethics," not ethics itself.

Remember that by building on the strong foundation already acquired in the previous chapters, the new materials should not present any real difficulty. I am certain that as you read the new material, you will appreciate your newly acquired knowledge. When you finish reading the Chapter 4, you most likely will agree with Schopenhauer's famous statement: "I can conquer the world because I understand it."

The theories presented in the next chapter include the following:

- The Stoicism school
- The hedonistic school
- The virtue school
- The religious school
- The naturalistic school
- The utilitarian school
- The duty school
- The existential school
- The social justice school

Review Questions

1. Define natural law and discuss four of its implications. How can these implications influence the behavior of correctional officers at a maximum-security prison?

2. Explain the hierarchical rule of identities. How could such a hierarchy influence the decisions of a CIA agent stationed in a foreign country?

3. Explain the Edwin Meese syndrome, giving examples from the fields of probation and parole.

4. Given the fact that there is no national religion in the United States, what application do the ethics of religious testaments have on the average American criminal justice practitioner?

5. Explain the ethics of public service. Why must all criminal justice professionals adhere to such a set of ethics?

6. Explain the ethics of professionalism. Why should public servants be held to a higher standard than private citizens?

7. Why are constitutional ethics held in such high esteem? Explain three such ethics that are most relevant to police officers.

8. What is the highest ethic mentioned in the preamble to the U.S. Constitution? Why is it ranked so high?

9. Explain why discretion is so necessary in policing.

References

American Correctional Association (1981). *Standards for Adult Correctional Institutions* (2nd ed). College Park, MD: American Correctional Association.

Barker, T. (1986). An Empirical Study of Police Deviance Other than Corruption. In T. Barker & D. L. Carter (Eds.), *Police Deviance* (pp. 67–82). Cincinnati, OH: Anderson Publishing Co..

Board of Directors of the State Bar of Texas (1982). *Code of Professional Responsibility.* Austin, TX: Government Printing Office.

Chalfant, H. P., Beckley, R. E., & Palmer, C. E. (1987). *Religion in Contemporary Society* (2nd ed). Palo Alto, CA: Mayfield Publishing.

Chesen, E. (1972). *Religion May Be Hazardous to Your Health.* New York: Peter Wyden.

Delattre, J. E. (1989). *Character and Cops.* Washington, DC: American Enterprise Institute of Public Policy Research.

Durkheim, E. (1933). *The Division of Labor in Society.* Glencoe, IL: The Free Press.

Ferm, V. (Ed.) (1956). *Encyclopedia of Morals.* New York: Philosophical Library.

Gerard, N. L. (1968). The Serpent-Handlers of West Virginia. *Transaction, 5,* 22–28.

Havard, W. C. (1965). *Government and Politics of the United States.* New York: Harper & Row.

International Association of Chiefs of Police (1989). *Code of Police Ethics.* Alexandria, VA: IACP.

Kleinig, J. (1996). *The Ethics of Policing.* New York: Cambridge University Press.

National Opinion Research Center (1985). Chicago: University of Chicago Press.

O'Dea, T., & Aviada, J. O. (1983). *Sociology of Religion.* Englewood Cliffs, NJ: Prentice-Hall.

Porter, B. F. (1980). *The Good Life: Alternatives in Ethics.* New York: Macmillan Publishing.

Richardsen, M. (1975). Anthropologist—The Myth Teller. *American Ethnologist, 2,* 517–533.

Smith, M. L., & Kleinig, J. (1996). *Survey of Criminal Justice Ethics Education.* New York: The Institute of Criminal Justice Ethics, John Jay College of Criminal Justice.

Souryal, S. S. (1977). *Police Administration and Management.* St. Paul, MN: West Publishing.

United Nations (1948). *Declaration of Human Rights.* New York: United Nations.

4

Meeting the Masters
Ethical Theories, Concepts, and Issues

All sects differ because they come from men; morality is everywhere the same because it comes from God.

Voltaire

One part of what is politically just is natural, and the other part legal.
Aristotle, *Nicomachean Ethics*

The urge to punish is, at least in part, the expression of resentment, but this is very different from justice.
Friedrich Nietzsche, *On the Genealogy of Morals*

The first person who, having enclosed a plot of land, took it into his head to say "this is mine" and found people simple enough to believe him, was the true founder of civil society.
Jean-Jacques Rousseau, *The Discourse on the Origins of Inequality*

What You Will Learn from This Chapter

You will learn the major concepts of the Stoicism school, the hedonistic school, the virtue school, the religious school, the naturalistic school, the utilitarian school, the duty school, the existential school, and the social justice school.

You will become acquainted with the works of the following: Epictetus (Stoicism); Aristippus and Epicurus (hedonism); Plato and Aristotle (virtue); Saint Augustine and Saint Thomas Aquinas (religion); Hobbes and Nietzsche (naturalism); Bentham (utilitarian); Kant (duty); Sartre and de Beauvoir (existentialism); and Rawls (social justice).

Key Terms and Definitions

Internal Goodness is the kind of goodness that stems from an active soul and consists of the virtues of justice, courage, temperance, and knowledge.

External Goodness is the kind of goodness that is motivated by culture, geography, laws, or social norms. This type of goodness excludes actions committed out of passion, impulse, or caused by genetic characteristics.

Eudaemonia is Aristotle's concept of well-being. It is an elevated state of mind that can be attained only through a life of reason, moderation, and self-realization.

Golden Mean is Aristotle's concept of balance. It requires people to choose between the two extremes of inadequacy and excessiveness.

Psychological Hedonism is the theory that assumes that all individuals are motivated only by pleasure and pain.

Utility is the concept of usefulness. It assumes that people choose objects or ideas that can produce more good than evil.

Physical Sanctions are punishments that inflict physical pain for unacceptable acts.

Political Sanctions are legal forces that can be mobilized by the state to control criminal acts.

Moral Sanctions are popular sentiments of approval or disapproval expressed by family members, neighbors, and society at large.

Religious Sanctions are blessings or condemnations by one's religion or faith.

Legality is the legal approval or disapproval of an action.

Duties are Kant's definition of ethical obligations. They are either *officia virtutis*, acts performed from reverence to duty, or *officia juris*, acts performed as a matter of duty.

Existential Ethics are moral principles that emphasize individualism, human consciousness, and freedom of choice.

Justice is Rawls's idea of the equal distribution of goods and services among individuals and groups in society.

Overview

We are now ready to meet the masters of moral philosophy and to learn ethical theory. We have become acquainted with the nature, sources, and categories of ethical theory and are familiar with the works of many famous philosophers. Yet some readers may still be apprehensive and wonder why we need to learn more about "ancient people with Greek names!" These are valid concerns that are understandable, yet unwarranted.

There are many reasons for reading the original works by the masters: First, these are pioneers who introduced the truth—or its "closest interpretation" to the literature of ethics. Second, we have been grappling with the question of "What is ethics?" It is now time to address the question of "How does ethical theory work?" Answers to this question can be discerned only from learning the intimate thoughts of those who developed the theory in the first place. If one wants to learn musical composition, one should ask a composer, not a player. Players can describe only what the notes sound like, but composers can explain why the notes are arranged the way they are. Third, by learning the cultural and social heritage of these great minds, we can capture the essence of ethical thought and appreciate its chronological evolution. A brief exposure to the lives of these philosophers can significantly enrich our understanding of ethical theory as a human response to changing environments. Fourth, your aptitude to explore ethical topics must have grown considerably since our tour of the Ethics Hall of Fame. By now you must be eager to investigate deeper into ethical knowledge. Fifth, consider the rule I proposed earlier to my students: *You cannot learn ethics without studying ethics.* Without examining the primary sources of ethics, our command of the subject will continue to be rather soft—heavily based on hearsay, opinions, or emotional arguments. In a nutshell, without studying the works of the masters, our knowledge of ethics will be incomplete at best.

In this chapter, each ethical school will consist of the work of one or more representative philosophers. At times you may encounter philosophers of the same school who disagree or offer different interpretations of the same concept. This is consistent with the fecundity of philosophical inquiry. As a group, however, philosophers from a particular school will more likely advocate the same perspective of reality that characterizes that school and sets it apart from all others.

Finally, as our knowledge of ethical principles continues to increase, we should continue to compare and contrast these principles to the practices of criminal justice agencies. We should note the variation between theory and practice and intelligently discern the reasoning behind these inconsistencies.

Figure 4.1 illustrates the ethical schools that will be discussed in this chapter and the main philosophers of each school.

The Stoicism School: Ethics of Freedom from Passion, Moral Fortitude, and Tranquility (Epictetus)

Introduction

Stoicism is a philosophical and social movement that took ancient Greece by storm around 300 B.C. The Stoic philosophy lasted more than 500 years during the Hellenistic, Roman, and Christian periods. It was described as the "religion" of the upper class prior to Christianity, despite the absence in its tenets of any religious belief in a divine God. Stoicism found expression in the thoughts and practices of a large number of Greek and Roman philosophers, orators, writers, statesmen, and public servants. It was especially dominant among the ranks of the Roman soldiery, who adopted it as a philosophy of indifference to hardship.

The philosophy of Stoicism was founded on the teachings of Zeno of Citium (335–263 B.C.). He lectured to Athenians from the *Stoa Poikile*, or the painted porch, located on the north side of Athens; hence, the name Stoic. His teachings continued through the writings of Cicero, Epictetus, and the Roman Emperor Marcus Aurelius (A.D. 121–180), who has traditionally been recognized as the last great Stoic. With the rise of Christianity, Stoicism declined from its position as the dominant philosophy.

Named the *citadel of the soul*, Stoicism was presented as the philosophy of "tranquility and indifference to pain." In articulating the spirit of Stoicism, Cicero described it by saying, "Once you pronounce anything to be desirable, once reckon anything as good, other than moral

Figure 4.1
Schools of Ethics

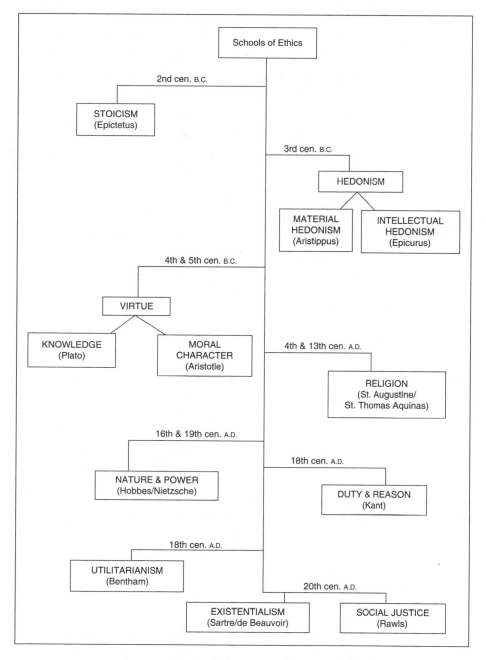

worth, and you have extinguished the very light of virtue, moral worth itself, and overthrown virtue entirely" (Ferm, 1956:589).

Stoical thought is characterized by living in accordance with the universal laws of nature and piety to the gods. Some of its leading beliefs are as follows:

- The universe is a natural whole that is rational, precise, unchanging, and eternal; understanding how it functions can enhance our knowledge of how we ought to function and behave.

- Man, of all things, is most like the gods; he can recognize the harmony of nature, have a feeling for the truth, and be moved by reason.

- Human beings must follow the "rational will" of the universe and live in conformity with the laws of nature.

- Everyone must accept with equanimity his rightful place in the scheme of things and fulfill the necessary purposes of that place.

- Rational choices are to be made in accordance with the dictates of the soul, which is the offspring of the gods.

- Virtues are forms of knowledge, and studying philosophy leads to a virtuous life.

- Reason, courage, justice, and self-discipline are end values that must be internalized without any qualifications.

- Virtuous persons possess *apatheia*: a psychological state of calmness with respect to pleasures and pains, passions and anxieties, or mental elation.

- Morality and moral behavior are the epitome of human existence and must transcend barriers of nationality, race, or class differences.

As such, the theory of Stoicism must be considered *teleological* in nature, because it emphasizes pursuit of the good life.

In Stoic philosophy, goodness is of two kinds: *internal* and *external*. *Internal goodness* stems from an active soul and consists of the virtues of justice, courage, temperance, and knowledge—which are considered equal. Inasmuch as health and wealth are not intrinsic values (beneficial or injurious in themselves), they are not regarded as goods. Even pleasure is not considered good, because there can be many disgraceful pleasures. *External goodness*, on the other hand, is typified by friendship and loyalty. A Stoic's sense of loyalty comprises fondness of one's parents, brothers, countrymen, and friends. Such fondness, however, neither includes nor condones actions committed out of passion, impulse, or inclination (Sahakian, 1974:16).

To the Stoic, the *summum bonum* of all values is moral worth, the chief elements of which are *freedom from passion* and *disinterest in joy or grief*. The Stoic sees the universe as an organic unity in which the form and purpose of each part is determined by *pantheism*, or godliness. The term *pantheism* signifies the Greek doctrine that identifies the universe with God. The Stoic perceives God to be both a vital force that can create things and a cosmic intelligence that can govern the destiny of creatures. Virtue consists of self-sufficiency and living in harmony with nature. Emotional turmoil and depression stem from the element of surprise, which is caused either by ignorance or by one's lack of adjustment to nature. The Stoic believes that only by possessing a passion-free mentality can man live above the conditions of pain and misery. Vices are regarded as diseases that must be expunged from the personality of the "truly healthy" individual.

On a practical level, the Stoic faces and accepts the vicissitudes of life as spiritual tasks ordained by the gods. His sense of security is grounded in self-respect. He harbors no anger, wrath, envy, or pity, nor is he desirous of a fine reputation, a beautiful woman, or a sumptuous meal. The Stoic's conduct exemplifies living in its purest form. By surrendering his life to the gods, the Stoic is ever prepared to accept whatever fate is in store, including death—which he accepts without flinching (Sahakian, 1974:18).

Epictetus is the philosopher who will be studied, because he was most prominent among the Stoics and is considered the authority on Stoic morals.

Epictetus: Inner Peace and Contentment through Self-Discipline

Epictetus was born in about A.D. 50 to a woman slave at Hieropolis in Phrygia. It is believed that as a child he was sold into slavery to a soldier of Emperor Nero's army, who took him to Rome. An apt characterization of young Epictetus is given in an anecdote by Origen: Upon one occasion in which his angry master was twisting his leg, Epictetus commented, "You will break my leg," whereupon his master twisted harder and broke the leg. To this, Epictetus rejoined with utter calm, "Did I not tell you so?" (Albert et al., 1988:67). While a slave, Epictetus studied philosophy under Musonius Rufus, a great Stoic of the period who was impressed by Epictetus's advanced intellectual ability. But Epictetus gained considerable fame as a philosopher in his own right while still a slave. Upon the death of his master, Epictetus became a free man and began to teach philosophy at the street-corner marketplaces of Rome. In A.D. 89, during the rule of the despotic emperor Domitian, all philosophers were banished from Rome and Epictetus was forced to move to Nicopolis, where he started his own school and established himself as a highly regarded teacher. He continued to teach until his death in A.D. 130 (Albert et al., 1988:67).

Epictetus was better known as a lecturer than as a writer. This is probably why none of his original writings survived. It was left to his students to preserve what they considered to be the lasting message of their teacher. One student, Flavius Arrian, succeeded in preserving some of Epictetus's most noted lectures on ethics. These included the *Golden Sayings of Epictetus* and the *Discourses of Epictetus*.

The teachings of Epictetus directly influenced Christian thought through the works of Saint Augustine and Saint Gregory of the

Nazarene, whose writings showed a strong affinity with the ethical philosophy of Epictetus.

Epictetus's Ethical Theory

Epictetus drew heavily upon the Socratic tradition, which advocated that virtue and happiness depend upon the development of character rather than upon material success. To Epictetus, the ultimate virtue for man is maintaining inner peace despite the hardships of life and unsavory events in the world.

According to Epictetus, a person who values virtue for its own sake is a happy person. Happiness is a condition of the will wherein it is governed by reason. Consequently, man should not seek to change what he cannot control. Epictetus proposed that attitudes, rather than events, are the elements that are within one's control. He proclaimed that "externals are not in my power; choice is." Hence, it is one's attitude about events—and not the events themselves—that one can control and modify. Epictetus attributed man's power over attitudes to the force of courage, which he equated with the invincible will. Virtuous individuals must possess an unconquerable will to protect themselves against the events of life and sustain their inner peace.

With the advent of Christianity, much of Epictetus's philosophy was incorporated in Christian doctrine. His views were seen as more pious than probing and more religious than philosophical. His teachings seemed to affirm the existence of an omnipotent and omniscient God who is responsible for the universe and all things within it. His philosophy also appeared to validate the Christian belief that the universe functions in accordance with laws and principles established by God, rejecting the notion that events are mere occurrences attributable to chance.

Major Issues in Epictetus's Ethical Philosophy

Virtue as the Summum Bonum of Value

Epictetus believed that virtue (moral worth) is the ultimate goal of man. It is to be valued for its own sake, because it alone is sufficient for happiness. Consequently, he identified three principal virtues that constitute one's soul: practical wisdom through meditation; self-control through a stubborn will; and justice. Epictetus suggested that when these virtues are properly integrated within the soul, one can be truly virtuous.

The Road to Virtue

Epictetus suggested two means for pursuing virtue: the discovery and acceptance of the nature of the gods, and the acceptance of all events that are beyond one's control. He argued that because man is but a "fragment of God," man embodies God's essence and is intimately connected to Him. Consequently, inner peace and contentment can be attained only when one is prepared to accept one's fate without question, surrendering his or her life to the will of God.

The Virtue of Courage: The Invincible Will

Epictetus was labeled the "apostle of courage." He taught that the only gift the gods have given man that cannot be taken away is the "faculty of will." He insisted that as long as man exercises courage, his control over moral actions will be secure. In illustrating this concept, Epictetus reportedly taught the following: "But the tyrant will chain— what? A leg? He will take away—what? A head? What is there that he can neither chain nor take away? The free will . . . Who, then, is unconquerable? You have power to put me to death, but *hurt me you cannot*" (Sahakian, 1974:16). Epictetus noted that the human will can allow man to remain free even though he may be physically imprisoned. Man's invincible will cannot be broken without his consent; "one may be master over one's carcass, but never over you unless you allow him to break your will" (Sahakian, 1974:17).

Epictetus considered man to be ultimately responsible for his conduct, because the will controls all other faculties. Perceptions, beliefs, and actions are all influenced by the will, which may function as a positive or a negative force. Subsequently, human behavior can be either constructive or destructive, depending on one's firmness of will or simply moral courage. Epictetus proclaimed, *"Only consider at what price you sell your own free will, O man! . . . in the will alone is vice; in the will alone is virtue"* (Albert et al., 1988:78).

Man's Control over Events and Indifference to Events

Epictetus distinguished between events that are within one's control and those that are not. He stressed that man has the power to control his opinions, attitudes, reactions, and desires, because these are "affairs of one's own." But there is also much that is beyond one's control. These include reputation, wealth, longevity, and destiny. Epictetus considered these as matters that are "not properly our own affairs."

Epictetus suggested that while man experiences frustration when attempting to control the "uncontrollable matters," man possesses the capacity to control his reactions to these matters. In order to avoid frustration and disappointment in life, one should be *indifferent* to these matters. For example, death should not be feared, because it is a natural phenomenon that is inevitable and unavoidable. Through man's control over his reactions, death should be taken in stride and certainly should not be feared.

Ethics of the Good Life and Overcoming Sexual Impulses

Epictetus described the "good life" as devoid of emotions and impulses, but not without feelings. Peace of mind, he argued, is not contingent upon external circumstances, but upon the "inner spirit." When one is able to exercise self-control, one can avoid mental anguish and frustration. He noted, for example, that it is not poverty that causes distress, but "covetous desires." Accordingly, man should shun sexual cravings, because "sex is enslaving." In the tradition of the Stoics, who practiced abstinence, Epictetus believed that sexual obsessions interfered with man's ability to maintain inner peace. A "fool," he recriminated, permits himself to be overcome by passion and pleasure. The wise man, on the other hand, is an emancipated individual. Serenity and tranquility will accompany those who harness their desires. Epictetus commented, "To-day, when I see a handsome woman, I do not say to myself, Oh, that I could possess her! and how happy is her husband, nor do I go to fancy her in my arms. On this I stroke my face and say, 'Well done, Epictetus'" (Sahakian, 1974:17).

The Value of Education in Achieving the Good Life

Epictetus proposed that all men are born with an innate sense of moral principles. From birth, man develops an understanding of good and evil, fairness and unfairness, happiness and misery, and what is proper or improper. But education is also essential to teach man the art of good reasoning and its value for self-guidance. Toward that end, one must study logic and science. Nevertheless, Epictetus warned that ethical behavior will not result from one's ability to use reason, because tranquility and happiness are not products of such a mental process. What is essential is one's willingness to apply reason in making decisions pertaining to daily conduct. Epictetus was indeed attempting to present a theory of applied ethics, one that can be practiced successfully in everyday life.

The Hedonistic School: Ethics of the Pursuit of Pleasure (Aristippus and Epicurus)

Introduction

Hedonism is a philosophy that views pleasure as the ultimate virtue. According to this school of thought, pleasure is central to human motivation and the achievement of the good life. The term *hedonism* is derived from the Greek word *hedone*, signifying pleasure, or *he'dys*, which means "sweet." The term refers to a pleasure-producing quality, such as good food or soothing music, or to a human state in which pain is absent (or minimized) and pleasure is present (or maximized). According to hedonistic theory, the only "thing" that is desirable in itself is pleasure. Therefore, pleasure is the *summum bonum* of all values, and happiness is the sum of all pleasures, regardless of how they are obtained or to what they might lead. As such, hedonism must be considered a deontological theory, because it focuses on the value of actions rather than on their consequences. The hedonistic view of ethics was held by a number of distinguished philosophers, including Aristippus and Epicurus in Ancient Greece, and Locke, Hobbes, Hume, and Bentham in later history.

As an ethical principle, the idea of hedonism certainly can be confusing, if not outright contradictory. But in philosophical literature, the concept has been treated in a much broader sense. For instance, while the term *hedonism* strongly suggests sensual enjoyment, as depicted in the philosophy and life of Aristippus, it was used by Epicurus to characterize intellectual and social enjoyment. In the teachings of Epicurus, the term referred specifically to the pleasures of nobility, tranquility, and philosophical reflection. Other hedonist writers agreed that many values besides pleasure can be desirable. These include knowledge and reasoning, because they can influence one's choice among available pleasures. Furthermore, while the theory of hedonism has long been associated with the idea of egoism (one's interest in his or her own private pleasures), many hedonists spurn this implication, arguing that hedonism does not necessarily mean being oblivious to social responsibilities to others. One can be a true hedonist, yet an ardent supporter of social causes. According to these hedonists, the ideas of hedonism and egoism should be considered independent, because one can be interested in pleasures that are desirable in themselves but not harmful to others.

Criticism of the concept of pleasure as a moral value has been due primarily to the difficulty of identifying the term. This difficulty grew out of several realizations:

1. There is little evidence that pleasure is good in itself; the fact that something is desirable does not mean it is "worthy of being desired." For instance, craving rich foods and exotic drinks can be detrimental to health.

2. Many activities can hardly be classified as pleasures in spite of the obvious happiness they can produce; for example, playing sports and exercising strenuously every day.

3. Some pains are, in essence, also pleasurable; for example, giving birth or conducting arduous work in pursuit of a successful career.

4. It is logically erroneous to divorce the idea of pleasure from the concept of social value; otherwise, the pleasures of a madman like Adolf Hitler or Charles Manson would be considered equal to those of Albert Schweitzer or Mother Teresa.

5. Some pleasures may not necessarily be satisfying, as is often the case in sexual pleasures. Schopenhauer noted that sexual pleasures are not fulfilling, but only alleviating. Erich Fromm also pointed out that many persons who seek the satisfaction of love confuse it with sex, believing that a sexual experience can fulfill their need for love.

In the following discussion, we will examine the works of two hedonist philosophers: Aristippus and Epicurus. Aristippus represents the *Cyrenaic* school of hedonism—it is based on material and sensual pleasures. Epicurus represents the *Epicurean* school—it is based on mental and intellectual pleasures.

Aristippus: The Cyrenaic (Egotistic) School of Hedonism

Aristippus was born about 435 B.C. in the affluent city of Cyrene. He traveled to the city of Syracuse, where he taught rhetoric and became an attendant at the court of Dionysius, the elder tyrant of the state. Later in life, Aristippus journeyed to Athens to attend the Olympic games, where he was attracted by the fame of Socrates. He stayed in Athens and joined Socrates's circle of students until Socrates's death in 399 B.C. Aristippus's behavior was reportedly displeasing to Socrates and to his group of serious students, because it sharply contrasted with Socrates's teachings. Aristippus apparently had brought with him from his hometown a lifestyle of luxury and self-indulgence. He further antagonized the Athenians by endorsing many of the Sophists' views, living an extravagant life, and feuding frequently with Plato.

Aristippus eventually settled in his native city and established the Cyrenaic school of philosophy. He died in 366 B.C. without writing anything of significance. Even though Aristippus was an ardent student of Socrates, he disagreed with his mentor's views on the reality of virtue.

Aristippus's Philosophical Theory

Aristippus represented the views of the Cyrenaic school, which also was known as *egotistic hedonism*. His theory was based on the assumption that pleasure can be only physical and is reducible, exclusively, to the immediate gratification of the senses. Aristippus considered happiness as a continued state of pleasure, consisting of separate—but preferably intense—momentary sensations. He believed in a life of sensual enjoyment regardless of any consequential pains. He boasted of worldly luxuries, eating sumptuous food, drinking the best wines, wearing the richest clothing, and an indiscriminate sexual lifestyle.

Aristippus's hedonistic theory stressed the idea that immediate pleasures are good for their own sake—and the more frequent and intense the pleasures, the better. The essence of the theory was, "What is pleasurable is moral, and what is not is immoral." Accordingly, Cyrenaic theorists considered physical pleasure to be the *summum bonum* of all values and the sole embodiment of morality. In the pursuit of pleasure, the Cyrenaics justified all manipulative behaviors by the pleasure seeker, including the use of shrewdness, intelligence, deception, and other dishonorable means. In this sense, Cyrenaic ethics must be characterized as a *deontological* theory, because moral judgment is based on the actions rather than their consequences. Although the Cyrenaics did not consider the values of wealth, fame, or power as good in themselves, they nevertheless were "acceptable" because they can serve as means for achieving physical pleasures. Modern images of Cyrenaic hedonism have long been depicted in Hollywood films that pictured prominent Romans lounging on velvet-covered couches, gobbling grapes, and drinking wine from golden decanters while being entertained by a group of exotic dancers.

Epicurus: The Epicurean School of Prudence, Tranquility, and Intellectual Hedonism

Epicurus was born in 341 B.C. to Athenian parents on the island of Samos. In 323 B.C. Alexander the Great died. This caused great turmoil, because the Greek Empire was being carved into pieces by opposing commanders. As a result, all Athenians, including Epicurus's parents, were forcibly evicted from Samos. After two years of military service, Epicurus rejoined his family in Asia Minor, and the ensuing 10 years were perhaps the most industrious in his life. He spent most of his time studying and teaching in Colophon, where he had the opportunity to reexamine the major principles of his philosophy. At age 30 Epicurus taught philosophy at Mytilene on the island of Lesbos. But like Socrates and Plato before him, Epicurus was driven from the city by local authorities because of his unconventional teachings. He moved to Athens, where he established the Garden of Epicurus and taught philosophy until his death in 270 B.C. The environment in the Garden provided him and his students with secluded comfort and a sense of protection from the turmoils of the outside world. Epicurus's Garden School ranked as one of the great schools of philosophy, along with Plato's Academy, Aristotle's Lyceum, and Zeno's Stoa (Albert et al., 1988:48).

Epicurus's Ethical Theory

Epicurean theory emerged as a dominant philosophy during the decline of ancient Greece. It flourished rapidly as a form of relief from the increasing social turmoil of the time, and in direct response to the mounting criticism of Cyrenaic hedonism. The teachings of Epicurus were a welcome refinement upon Aristippan hedonism, because they advocated spiritual pleasure instead of physical indulgence. His teachings were particularly distinguished because of their constancy of doctrine and simplicity of practice. Epicurus identified pleasure with *ataraxia*—the state of peace of mind and the absence of disturbance. In Epicurean philosophy, the virtues of serenity and prudence were the *summum bonum* of all values. These qualities could be achieved by avoiding the pleasures that cause agony and discomfort. In contrast to the Cyrenaic school, which emphasized momentary sensual pleasures, the Epicurean school stressed mental gratification, contentment, friendship, peace, and aesthetic pursuits. In this sense, Epicurean theory should be considered *teleological*, because it is concerned with the achievement of goodness as a "consequence" of noble human behavior.

Epicurus maintained that people seek what they believe will bring them pleasure and avoid what they believe will bring them pain. An ethical person, therefore, is one who can choose the right pleasures—serenity, peace of mind, and intellectual enjoyment. He also stressed that the duration of pleasure is more important than its intensity. For that reason, mental pleasures are far more valuable than physical pleasures, and passive pleasures are more gratifying than active pleasures. The latter can only trouble the mind and harm the body. Epicurus concluded that enjoying the good life is within the reach of anyone who possesses the prudence of moral choice.

Major Issues in Epicurus's Ethical Philosophy

Nature of the Universe

While Epicurus certainly was not oblivious to Platonian thought, he did not seem enthusiastic about Plato's concern with matters of the "metaphysical world." He rejected Plato's separation between objects of perception (things) and objects of intellect (abstracts), endorsing instead an older Greek view of universal atomism. That view had proposed a mechanistic theory to account for the existence of the universe and all the objects within it. Accordingly, Epicurus advocated that the universe (which is stable and permanent) constitutes a mass of atoms in motion and that all objects came about when these atoms collided and formed matter. All objects therefore are physical entities that can be experienced only by the human senses.

The Composition of the Soul

Epicurus believed that because all objects are products of atoms in motion, the soul also must be made of like atoms distributed throughout the body. Through these fine particles one can experience sensation. At death, the soul dies and sensation no longer is experienced.

Epicurus used the atomistic argument to dispel man's fear of death, which he thought was the primary reason for human weakness and mental anxiety. He taught that while people are alive, they need not fear death. When it comes, either of two alternatives will be possible: an afterlife, or nonexistence. In the first case, fear of death is needless, because man would continue living in a different form. In the second, one obviously would be incapable of worrying. Consequently, fear of death is simply vain, foolish, and unnecessary.

Nature of the Gods and Their Influence on the Good Life

At the time of Epicurus, the idea of the gods and man's obligation to comply with their wishes was of great importance. Epicurus disagreed, suggesting that the idea is too disturbing to the human mind and is a major cause of social anxiety. While he believed in the existence of divine "beings," he rejected the view that man can constantly be held hostage by the idea of gods. Instead, he proposed that man should live a serene and nonthreatened life, free from undue concerns and unrealistic guilt. Epicurus supported his proposition by presenting a two-pronged argument: First, because the gods are truly blessed entities, they would not debase themselves by punishing man; second, because the soul ceases to exist at the time of death, no confrontation with the gods will occur. Consequently, man should concentrate on living a "pleasant" life during his days on earth. Fear of the gods is an unwarranted paranoia.

The Pleasant Life; the Epicurean Way

Epicurus proposed that the logical purpose of all human action is to attain physical and mental happiness. This can be accomplished by maximizing pleasure and minimizing pain. In order to achieve true happiness, Epicurus offered three principles:

1. *Mental pleasures are superior to those derived from sensual experiences or material objects.* Man, therefore, should control his unbridled desires to accumulate great wealth, because this will lead not to riches, but to poverty. Likewise, sensual enjoyment leads not to happiness, but to unhappiness.

2. *The way to happiness is by leading a simple and frugal life.* A luxurious lifestyle will not necessarily lead to happiness. Epicurus

proposed, for example, that a simple diet consisting of bread and water would result in perfectly good health. Conversely, gluttony, lust, and excessive drinking would lead to physical and mental disequilibrium and, ultimately, to misery.

3. *Philosophical contemplation will promote tranquility and cheerfulness.* A prudent person understands that he, not destiny, is responsible for his happiness. Thus, the road to happiness is located within oneself and not the result of external forces. If man makes prudent choices, the outcome will be a pleasant life (Sahakian, 1974:26).

The Epicurean View of Social Justice

Epicurus believed that individuals forge social compacts to ensure protection from harm by others. The chief principle that governs these compacts is justice. Epicurus taught that while injustice is not evil in itself, unjust actions can create fear for those who live in the social compact. Consequently, all laws that create injustice within the community should be abolished. Like Epictetus before him, Epicurus discouraged marriage as a social norm and argued that happiness and tranquility would be greatly enhanced if men sought emotional comfort within a small, select group of friends. He concluded that the pleasant life was possible when people lived within the morals of an ideal community similar to the one he created at his Garden in Athens.

The Virtue School: Ethics of Knowledge and Moral Character (Plato and Aristotle)

Introduction

This school is perhaps the most prominent among all schools of ethics. Its prominence is due, beyond a doubt, to its founder, Socrates, and perhaps more so because of his death than his life. In eulogizing Socrates, Plato wrote in *Phaedo,* "And that was the end of our friend—who was, we may say, of all those of his time whom we have known—the best and wisest, and the most righteous man" (Lavine, 1984:17).

There are many who have come to think of the martyrdom of Socrates as analogous to the martyrdom of Christ. The analogy is based on the idea that the best among us—the wisest, noblest, purest, and most righteous—are unjustly put to death. By contrast, there are others who see his trial and death as an expression of hostility toward philosophy and philosophers in general. Still others may see it as indicative of the unbridled power of the state over the individual and his or her freedom of speech (Lavine, 1984:17). Whichever way one looks at it, the life and death of Socrates were powerful events in the history of civilization. They shocked the world into a new intellectual awakening. Perhaps because of these events alone, Western societies today are much more keen to apply rationality, rely on reasoning, and search for moral truths.

Yet the analogy of Socrates and Christ may not be totally accurate. It would be more fitting if the life and death of Socrates were compared to the life and death of John the Baptist, who prepared the way for Christ and the apostles who followed him. The true messiah of the virtue school of ethics was Plato, who allegorically was "baptized" by Socrates.

Plato, who reportedly possessed more intellectual prowess than his mentor, expanded on Socrates's thoughts. In his famous dialogues, Plato recreated Socrates's philosophy in a more organized fashion, spreading the word among the civilized community of the world. By the same token, Plato was fortunate to have Aristotle as his student for 20 years. Many philosophers contend that Aristotle presented a wealth of knowledge that surpassed the works of Socrates and Plato combined. Thus, the virtue school of philosophy stands uniquely eminent among all others. It included three of the greatest philosophers of all time.

In this discussion, we will focus only on the contributions of Plato and Aristotle.

Plato: The Virtues of Perfection through Knowledge and Justice

Plato (428–348 B.C.) was born in Athens to a distinguished aristocratic family. As a young man, his initial inclinations were toward a career in politics. He believed that the duty of a philosopher was to make the supreme sacrifice of devoting the best of his manhood to the service of his fellow men as a statesman and a legislator. At the age of 20, Plato became a disciple and friend of Socrates. But perhaps due to the influence of Socrates, Plato became disillusioned with the corruption he saw within the Athenian democracy and was further disturbed after his mentor was put to death in 399 B.C. Consequently, he gave up his political ambitions and left Athens. For the next 12 years he traveled in Egypt, Sicily, and elsewhere in search of knowledge.

Upon his return to Athens in 387 B.C., Plato founded the Academy, where he taught and wrote on a wide variety of philosophical issues. The Academy was to become his true calling for the next 40 years. There he formulated his philosophy concerning politics, the ideal community, and justice.

Little is known of Plato's accomplishments during the last 20 years of his life, although it is believed that he continued to write until his death at the age of 80. Plato's teachings had a far-reaching influence on the development of Christian ethics during the Middle Ages and on European social thought during the Renaissance.

Plato's Philosophical Theory

Of the 30 works attributed to Plato, the *Apology*, the *Crito*, and the *Phaedo* describe the trial and death of his beloved mentor, Socrates. Other works that made important contributions to the study of ethics include the *Charmides*, the *Gorgias*, the *Meno*, the *Philibos*, the *Phaedrus*, the *Symposium*, and the *Protagoras*.

Plato's most significant work, however, is the *Republic*, which provides some of his most important contributions to ethics. In the *Republic*, Plato offers his conception of Utopia, the perfect city, the ideal city, or the just city. Utopia is a conceptual model characterized by social harmony, few or no laws, and the stewardship of "philosopher-kings." Plato was certain that social justice depended on the judgment of these "men of gold," who intuitively applied justice, rendering the need for laws unnecessary.

Plato proposed that philosopher-kings could become the political rulers of the *polis* (city-state) in one of two ways: when true and genuine philosophers found their way to political authority, or when powerful politicians, by the favor of Providence, took to the study of philosophy. Plato supported the doctrine of the philosopher-king on the basis of what he called "conviction in absolute truth." He thought that because "absolute truths" can be ascertained only by such intellectual aristocrats, they alone should be rulers.

There is no question that if Plato's premise about absolute truths is correct, then all the features of Utopia would logically follow. However, critics note one difficulty after another in Plato's premise. These include the following:

1. There is no convincing evidence that absolute truths exist at all.

2. Even if these truths exist, there is no demonstrable way by which they could be learned and applied in a uniform manner.

3. There is no guarantee that philosopher-kings would not be corrupted at a later date, given the absolute power they would be able to wield.

Based on this criticism, Plato's views on politics were considered too absolutist, and for a long time doubt lingered over the validity of philosophy. In democratic societies, for example, there is a strong inclination to believe that politics and justice are neither absolute nor certain. Support for the philosopher-king theory therefore defeats the basic principles of representative government in which rulers are to be held accountable to the governed. To this criticism, Plato—who lived the life of an intellectual aristocrat—would reply by discrediting the fundamental idea of democracy. Like his mentor Socrates, Plato thought that democracy was a bad idea because it is founded on government by an "uninformed populace." For Plato, however, government was to be the ultimate instrument of goodness.

The second important doctrine in the *Republic* is Plato's *principle of justice*. He used this principle to convey several meanings:

1. The proper, the correct, or the most rational response to a given situation. In this sense, justice is one's capacity to think rationally and be able to follow proper reasoning based on superior knowledge.

2. A state of human equilibrium wherein the faculties of reason, emotion, and desire are integrated in a well-rounded personality. Plato concluded that unjust individuals were beset by an inner "rebellion."

3. A harmonious state, city, or community functioning within proper social roles whereby each and every part of the community contributes equitably toward the common good.

As such, Plato's philosophy of justice could be viewed in terms of three interdependent elements: knowledge and reasoning at the intellectual level, a well-developed soul at the psychological level, and a functional community at the social level.

Major Issues in Plato's Ethical Philosophy

Morality and Justice

A central question debated by ancient philosophers for centuries was, "Why should men be morally virtuous?" Plato attempted to answer this question by equating the need for morality with the need for justice: "If you want justice, you must be moral." Plato argued the issue of justice with his opponents, the Sophists. They advocated that only the weak would value justice, because it restrains the power of the strong. The Sophists preferred "injustice" to justice, because it would be more rewarding to the powerful, particularly when it is conducted on a large scale. For example, injustice could substantially enrich soldiers who would loot enemy treasures, or slave owners who would exploit the free labor of their slaves. Plato refuted this argument by disassociating the question of justice and injustice from that of pleasure and pain. He argued that while justice and injustice are mutually exclusive (one cannot be both just and unjust at the same time), pleasure and pain are not. It is possible, therefore, for a person to experience pleasure and pain simultaneously, as for instance, in the case of a mother giving birth to a child. While giving birth is often a painful experience, it is considered a pleasurable event that can be most rewarding for the mother. By using this logic, Plato essentially forced his opponents to admit that unjust behavior, while seemingly pleasurable, is in fact immoral, and enduring injustice, while seemingly painful, can indeed be moral.

The Supremacy of Knowledge

Plato believed that knowledge and reason are essential attributes in guiding a person's behavior. He equated knowledge with a "noble" and "commanding" state that cannot be overcome by anger, pleasure, pain, love, or even fear. Like his mentor Socrates, Plato insisted that no knowledgeable person would pursue evil voluntarily. He advocated that when people act wrongly, they do so out of ignorance of the good. Furthermore, he suggested that a person's behavior can be changed by upgrading that person's level of education. In other words, if a person could be shown the outcomes of different behaviors, he would choose the one that would result in the most good. Hence, there is the continuous need to educate people in the use of reason.

But the Sophists continued to argue that in determining proper behavior, pleasure is more important than knowledge. They insisted that regardless of the amount of knowledge one may possess, one's behavior will ultimately be directed by the pleasure that follows from one's actions. Plato, in turn, continued to argue in favor of knowledge, noting that even hedonists must rely on knowledge in order to choose the kind of pleasure they want to pursue. Only by using this logic was Plato able to establish the supremacy of knowledge over pleasure.

The Tripartite Soul and Achievement of Justice

Plato formulated what essentially amounted to a psychological theory of human behavior. He identified justice as the product of a properly functioning soul. The soul, he thought, had three distinct elements, and the influence of each corresponded to a particular virtue. These are *reason* (intellect), *spirit* (passion), and *appetite* (desire). Plato argued that human character depends on the relative development and proper functioning of each of these elements. Therefore, when reason is developed and functions properly, the outcome is the virtue of *wisdom*. People endowed with the gift of wisdom make the best rulers. When passion is developed and functions properly, the outcome is *courage*. Courageous people make the best soldiers. When desire is regulated in a rational manner and functions properly, the outcome is *temperance*.

Temperate people are best suited to join the working class. Plato argued that each of these elements is essential to the development of the soul, or the moral personality. When all three elements are integrated and functioning harmoniously, the result is justice, the all-encompassing virtue. On the other hand, unjust (or immoral) people suffer from a psychological disequilibrium, or imbalance, that is contrary to the natural functioning of the soul.

Plato's Summum Bonum of Values: The Idea of Goodness

Plato proposed that there is a virtue that is even higher than justice—the idea of "goodness." All things become relevant and useful when considered in light of "goodness." Like Socrates before him, Plato argued that the idea of goodness is too exalted to be grasped by the human mind and therefore can be presented only by way of analogy. Plato offered the analogy of human sight, which requires not only the eye and the object of sight, but also the sun, which is the source of light. One cannot see (clearly) in the dark, not because the eye is deficient or because the object is invisible, but because of the absence of light. By the same token, human understanding (wisdom) requires not only an active mind and objects of thought, but also the "light of goodness." When Plato was asked where such light comes from, he suggested the metaphysical world of "ideals, forms, and essences."

Plato's Theory of Ideals, Forms, and Essences

Plato argued that the "world" that appears to our senses is *not* the real world, because there are two world realities—the metaphysical and the sensible. The metaphysical reality exists in the universe (out there in the heavens). It is perfect, unchanging, and eternal. Moral truths emanate from this reality in terms of ideals, forms, and essences (they have approximately the same meaning). These are *absolute moral truths* that can be known only by the intellect. To demonstrate his view of absolute moral truths, Plato compared justice to a "perfect circle"—while no one can draw it to perfection, everyone knows exactly how it looks. Plato considered the metaphysical world much more important than the sensible world in which we live, because the metaphysical world was the first to exist and will forever continue unchanged. Goodness, justice, and beauty are a few forms of that world.

On the other hand, Plato described the sensible world as illusory, consisting of concrete and changing objects that are "imperfect copies" of the metaphysical forms. Plato demonstrated the superiority of the metaphysical forms by using the same analogy of sight: As the eye's vision becomes clearer when objects are exposed to sunlight, so is the understanding of morality when one is exposed to the ideal of "goodness." Without the virtue of goodness, one's soul remains forever in the darkness of immorality.

To summarize, Plato argued that only through the knowledge of ideals, forms, and essences can the ultimate good be grasped. Such good is universal, unchanging, and just in every respect. It is the source of all things and the light that illuminates every human action. Only through this kind of knowledge can man achieve the ideal of perfection.

Aristotle: The Virtues of Moral Character and Self-Realization

Aristotle (384–322 B.C.) was born in the Greek colony of Stagira in Macedonia. His father was physician to the king of Macedonia, who was the father of Philip the Great. At the age of 17, Aristotle was sent to Athens to further his education in philosophy and science. He enrolled in Plato's Academy, where he developed a close relationship with his mentor that lasted until Plato's death in 348 B.C. Soon after, Aristotle was asked by King Philip of Macedonia to return and tutor his son Alexander. In the 3 years of association with Alexander, a strong friendship was formed, and much of Aristotle's subsequent studies were funded by either Philip or Alexander.

When Alexander succeeded to his father's throne in 336 B.C., Aristotle returned to Athens and founded the *Lyceum*, the second greatest school of philosophy (the first being Plato's Academy). For the next 12 years, Aristotle taught, lectured, and produced more than 400 works on various subjects, including theoretical sciences such as physics, biology, astronomy, practical sciences, ethics and politics, poetic sciences, rhetoric and poetics, and logic. According to Aristotle's own classification, his greatest works included *Metaphysics*, *Physics*, *De Anima* (biology), *Del Caelo* (astronomy), *Nicomachean Ethics*, *Eudaemonian Ethics*, *Rhetoric*, *Poetic*, and *Organon* (logic). With such a productive mind, it is not surprising that Aristotle was described at the time as being "knowledgeable of all that was to be known" (Albert et al., 1988:30).

In 322 B.C. Alexander died and his empire disintegrated. As a friend of the fallen regime, Aristotle was accused by the citizens of Athens of seditious teachings. But unlike Socrates, Aristotle was not brought to trial. He fearfully fled Athens, proclaiming "lest the Athenians should sin twice against philosophy" (Lavine, 1984:69). The reference was obviously to Socrates before him. One year later he died at Chalcis on the island of Euboea.

Aristotle's work strongly influenced the evolution of philosophical thought. His rules of syllogism in the field of logic are still in use, and his methods of inquiry continue to enrich the acquisition of knowledge in an all-encompassing manner.

Aristotle's Philosophical Theory

Aristotle's theory of ethics represents a more realistic approach to the study of human nature. In *Nicomachean Ethics* he offered the first systematic treatment of ethics in the Western world. It follows in the tradition of Socrates and Plato, who stressed both the supremacy of a purposeful universe and the rational nature of man. Nevertheless, within this broad framework Aristotle's ethical theory stands in sharp contrast to the views of his teacher and mentor, Plato. Their differences stemmed from conflicting conceptions of the nature of reality and the extent of metaphysical positions.

Aristotle's views differed from Plato's on three subjects: (1) While Plato advocated two independent realms of reality—"the metaphysical and the sensible"—Aristotle believed that both realms are united and neither can have any rational meaning without the other. He emphatically declared that "there is no form without matter or matter without form." (2) While Plato saw metaphysical ideals, forms, and essences as absolutely necessary to assist man in perceiving objects of the sensible world, Aristotle found them unnecessary and argued that moral reality can indeed be grasped by the human intellect alone. (3) While Plato identified the duties of man within the framework of an ideal city or state, Aristotle identified these duties in the context of a common society with all its imperfections. Consequently, Aristotle took a much more commonsensical approach to the moral evaluation of human conduct—one based on practical experience, real personalities, and concrete circumstances (Porter, 1980:30).

Aristotle's ethical theory also tends to take a longitudinal approach to the development of virtue. He argued that because no one is born ethical (or unethical), people must spend their entire lives actualizing their potential in pursuit of happiness. The attainment of happiness is thus a lifelong endeavor that should be regarded not only as a means, but also as an end, desirable in itself.

Aristotle agreed with Plato on the characterization of ultimate happiness as the attainment of intellectual virtue. Yet he was more willing to recognize the forces of culture, socialization, and habit. He identified moral behavior as a soul that is well-habituated to all these forces. Nevertheless, to achieve "moral character," the virtue of reason must be the dominant force. It is essential, therefore, to integrate intellectual virtue and moral virtue. Intellectual virtues pertain to understanding abstract truths such as those derived from the study of science, art, or philosophy. They are superior to moral virtues because they are not subject to opinion and cannot be overcome by sensual enjoyment. In Aristotle's view, ordinary persons are concerned only with mundane moral virtues, while a few gifted individuals possess intellectual virtues as well. Like his mentor Plato, Aristotle believed that only those gifted individuals endowed with intellectual virtue are destined to rule. In a sense, he also condoned the concept of the philosopher-king.

Major Issues in Aristotle's Ethical Philosophy

Nature of Philosophical and Political Inquiry

Aristotle proposed that all philosophical inquiry, whether intellectual or practical, has a teleological basis: the discovery of ultimate good. One of the best methods of investigating the ultimate good is through the study of politics, because it can contribute directly to the betterment of society. But because politics is an inexact science that depends on the establishment of certain truths, it is imperative to first establish "general truth." For instance, no society could establish a procedure for due process without first establishing the doctrine of liberty. Furthermore, because people are not equally capable of discussing political issues, it is the obligation of intellectuals to educate the populace and create a well-informed society. Unlike Plato, however, Aristotle favored a well-informed middle class that can hold the balance of power between the rich, who "can only rule despotically," and the poor, who "are too degraded to rule" (Lavine, 1984:76).

Happiness and the Concept of Eudaemonia

Aristotle noted that most people would agree that the ultimate good in society is "happiness," which he identified with the concept of *eudaemonia*, or well-being. Eudaemonia is not merely a pleasurable experience, but a happy spirit accompanied by an elevated state of mind that can be attained only through a life of reason, moderation, and self-realization.

Aristotle expounded on the concept of eudaemonia by explaining its two major elements. First, an "activity of the soul," which is the moral equivalent of reasoning; this kind of activity can be enhanced by further knowledge and education. Second, "acting in accordance with virtue," which is equivalent to developing good moral habits. Aristotle's notion of happiness is characterized by a high level of knowledge and an environment conducive to moral practices.

Moral Character as the Temple of Virtue

Aristotle proceeded to discover the location of moral virtue. He proposed that what is termed "human personality" consists of three parts: passions, faculties, and a state of character. But because passion (like anger and fear) and faculties (like abilities and skills) are not in themselves praiseworthy or blameworthy, the only part that can influence moral virtue is the state of character. Aristotle considered the state the "temple of virtue" where moral choices are made. A state of character is what distinguishes moral individuals from immoral individuals and motivates people to do good and achieve happiness.

Moral Character as the Activity of the Soul

Aristotle moved his investigation of moral character one step further. He raised the question, "If moral character is a product of the soul, then why are not all men who are endowed with the same soul capable of producing the same moral character?"

Aristotle answered his question by explaining that the soul itself is divided into three parts that control one's perception of moral truths. These include sensation, desire, and reason. Of these, sensation has no part in determining moral choice, because it can be said that even animals of a lower order share that capability. Only desire and reason, then, can play a part in determining moral character.

Desire refers to one's willingness to choose a course of action perceived to be in one's best interest, despite one's knowledge to the contrary. *Reason*, on the other hand, refers to one's ability to make rational decisions on the basis of knowledge, despite one's desire to do otherwise. Reason and desire are considered opposite forces that operate in the mind and the soul, respectively, determining moral judgment. When reason dominates desire, the result is a rational decision, but when desire dominates reason, irrational decisions are made. In other words, knowledge alone cannot make moral choices. In addition to possessing knowledge of what is moral or immoral, one must have the desire to behave in a morally correct manner.

This view sharply contradicts Socrates's view that knowledge—and knowledge alone—is sufficient for moral behavior, and that all other behaviors are the products of ignorance. Aristotle, the more realistic thinker, envisioned that "knowledgeable people" may act immorally out of moral weakness.

Moral Virtues and the Golden Mean

Aristotle proposed the idea of the "golden mean" as a fundamental moral guide that can best direct man's choices. He noted that in nearly every situation human actions fall within two "end choices." On one end there is the choice of under-quality (or insufficiency); on the other there is the choice of over-quality (or extreme). In other words, all moral evaluations range between the extremes of *inadequacy* and *excessiveness*.

Aristotle designed the "golden mean" as a moral index that identifies "end choices" and designates the proper quality that falls equidistant between the two extremes. For instance, he proposed that the "mean" virtue of temperance is the middle ground between the qualities of pleasure and pain; the "mean" virtue of truthfulness is the middle ground between the qualities of irony and pretentiousness; the "mean" virtue of modesty is the middle ground between the qualities of shamelessness and bashfulness; and the "mean" virtue of pride is the middle ground between the qualities of humility and vanity. Regarding the virtue of justice, Aristotle noted that the "mean" virtue is the middle ground between two extremes of "injustice": the "injustice" of insufficiency and the "injustice" of excessiveness. He advised that in making moral judgments, one should choose the middle ground value.

Moral Development as the Actualization of Potential

Aristotle discussed the principle of moral development, which he viewed as a progression from "potential" to "actualized" conduct. This principle enabled him to account for developmental changes in moral behavior and explain the stages of moral growth. He argued that as an acorn grows to become an oak tree, so moral character grows from a modest potentiality to a full-grown actuality. Moral potentiality represents the seeds of one's moral character as formed by a universe of bodies, objects, and experiences around him. One's character is then gradually actualized as one increases in knowledge, better understands the moral ideals, and improves in attributes. Another way of grasping this process of actualization is Aristotle's analogy of a stone with a rough surface that can be polished and made smooth. Furthermore, Aristotle asserted that as one grows in knowledge and better understands moral ideals, one's actualization process would be accelerated accordingly. Aristotle envisioned that the ultimate product of the actualization process is the realization of eudaemonia, or perfect happiness.

Man's Three Dimensions, a Profile of Moral Character

Aristotle offered a profile of the ideal moral character: one that is fully actualized on the road to perfection. According to Aristotle, man at this level would have developed three distinct dimensions: man as *knower of the truth, doer of goodness*, and *maker of beauty*. As knower of the truth, man would be a learned person who has acquired knowledge of all sorts—not only of nature, society, and humanity, but also of knowledge itself. As doer of goodness, man would be an activist individual who can make a difference not only in his own life, but also in the lives of others—one who can see wrong and correct it, see injustice and rectify it, and influence others in order to improve the quality of life for all concerned. As maker of beauty, man would be a polished artisan, a producer, and a creator of things—not only in terms of natural things but also in terms of efficient things, beautiful things, and things that can be used for the making of other things.

Aristotle's Rules of Syllogism

One of Aristotle's unparalleled contributions to inquiry was his contribution to logic. Logic is essential to the understanding of ethical philosophy, because it serves as a method for testing the validity of propositions forwarded in a philosophical argument. An *argument* is a demonstration of proper evidence in support of a thesis or premise, or a refutation of a thesis by introducing evidence that detracts from its validity. Because much of ethical philosophy is based upon argumentation, logic is considered the master skill in proving the validity of one's position.

Aristotle's contribution was confined to the area of *deductive logic*: reasoning from the general to the particular. His "rules of syllogism" constitute an advanced method of deductive logic. One of his classic rules, the "categorical syllogism," is a simple one. It consists of a major premise, a minor premise, and a conclusion. For example:

Major premise:	All humans are mortal.
Minor premise:	Socrates is a human.
Conclusion:	Socrates is mortal.

In logical analysis, the categorical syllogism is considered a solid and irrefutable proof.

Aristotle has also been credited with more complicated and complex syllogisms. Many involved the use of declarative propositions in testing contradictions and inferences. His "square of opposition" is often used to illustrate this principle.

Aristotle devised the "square of opposition" syllogism to illustrate all possible logical relationships among the A, E, I, and O propositions (see Figure 4.2). He assumed that A and E represent statements of

Figure 4.2
Square of Opposition

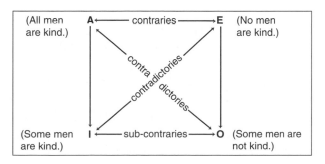

universal quantity, while I and O are statements of particular quantity. Furthermore, A and I are affirmative statements, while E and O are negative statements. Therefore, certain logical relations can exist among the four statements on the square. Statements that are diagonally opposite are contradictories (either of the pair is true and the other must be false). On the other hand, a statement at the top of the square implies the one below it. For example, A implies I, and E implies O. While the nature of logic is certainly much more complex, this discussion does not intend to offer an in-depth examination of all the uses of syllogism. It should be noted, however, that Aristotle's syllogisms continue to be considered the primary tools for testing the validity of any dialectic proposition.

The Religious (Scholastic) School: Ethics of the Love of God (Augustine and Aquinas)

Introduction

The religious school of ethics (also known as the scholastic school) emerged in medieval Europe. Its main writers were students and professors who served in universities under the dominion of the church. This school was characterized by (1) an immense interest in logical and linguistic analyses, because the writers were essentially concerned with producing profound essays in defense of church beliefs; (2) an unequivocal belief in the Bible as the revealed word of God; (3) the use of reason and deductive logic in order to explain and justify the controversial tenets of Christian creed; and (4) an attempt to reconstruct Greek thought so as to make it appear consistent with the pretexts of Christian faith.

The scholastic school must be considered a deontological theory, because a Christian life consists of a set of obligations that are considered right in the eyes of God. Therefore, actions are justified not by their consequences, but by the fact that they are willed by God. The biblical story of Abraham best illustrates this deontological view, because the consequences of slaying one's own son could not be considered "good" by any ethical standard. The fact that the slaying was commanded by God made all the difference. The fact that God commands an act makes it intrinsically good (therefore moral) and establishes an unequivocal obligation on the believer's part to complete it. The ethical worth of an act must therefore be accepted or rejected on the basis of faith in the word of God and belief in the existence of miracles. As such, Christian ethics cannot be explained or proved in terms of human reason; the basis for its acceptance is foregone conclusions dictated by church dogma and preserved as unquestionable eternal truths.

Christian ethics constitutes a set of moral standards that a Christian (precisely because he or she is a Christian) must apply in determining what is moral and what is immoral. Christian ethics begins with the assumption that all answers to human and social problems are to be found in the sacred revelations made available to man through God's messengers and apostles. The Old Testament consists of a set of sacred books produced by Hebrew apostles and presents a strict deontological ethic based on obedience to God's will. This ethic requires certain duties to be performed in accordance with precise rules and rituals. Wrongdoing in the Old Testament is not considered the result of ignorance, as Socrates or Plato would say, but of disobedience to God's laws. Beginning with the Book of Genesis, and throughout the Old Testament, the *summum bonum* of Hebrew ethics has been obedience to God and the obligation on the part of man not to question his commandments (Porter, 1980:195).

In contrast to Hebrew ethics, the New Testament provides a reconstructed philosophy of ethics based on God's eternal love for man and man's redemption through the blood of Jesus Christ. The ethical obligations of a Christian thus revolve around two significant doctrines attached to the person of Jesus Christ: (1) belief in his ministry, crucifixion, resurrection, and ascension to heaven; and (2) belief in the redemption of sins if one accepts Christ as one's Savior and lives a sanctified life as recommended by the ministry of Jesus and his apostles.

In this section, the philosophies of Saint Augustine and Saint Thomas Aquinas will be presented. Saint Augustine was so influenced by the ideas of Plato that he was called the "Platonizer of Christianity." Saint Thomas Aquinas, on the other hand, was chiefly influenced by Aristotelian thought and was known as the "Christianizer of Aristotelianism." Thomistic ethics was declared the official philosophy of the Roman Catholic Church by Pope Leo XIII in 1879. There are nevertheless certain Catholic orders that do not adhere to Neo-Thomistic ethics. The Franciscan order, for example, continues to embrace the Stoical philosophy of ethics, while members of the Augustinian order obviously follow the tradition of Saint Augustine.

Saint Augustine: Spiritual Safety and the Happiness of Salvation

Saint Augustine (A.D. 345–430) was born Aurelius Augustine in the Roman town of Thagaste in what is now Algeria, North Africa. He grew up in a period of history that saw the decline of the Roman Empire and the rise of Christianity both as a political force and as the central theme of intellectual activities. He was born to a Roman family, and although his mother was a Christian, Augustine did not convert to Christianity until he was 32. Prior to his conversion, Augustine was a teacher of Latin literature and rhetoric. During that phase of his life, he spent much of his time introspectively searching for philosophical answers to questions that troubled him (Albert et al., 1988:84).

Augustine studied the teachings of the Manichaeans, which explained the universe as a struggle between God and Satan. He aligned himself with the philosophy of Neo-Platonism and used it in his claim that ultimate knowledge is a mystical intuition of the supreme reality that can be experienced by only a few (Albert et al., 1988:85). It was not until he came under the influence of Saint Ambrose, Bishop of Milan, that Augustine turned to Christianity.

In A.D. 391 Augustine entered the priesthood and eventually became the Bishop of Hippo. It was here that he was able to apply his knowledge of philosophy and his talent as a thinker to the study of the Holy Scriptures. He produced many works on Christian doctrine, including *Confessions*, in which he chronicled many autobiographical details; *The City of God*, an extensive philosophy of history within the structure of Christianity; the *Enchiridion*, in which he set forth his understanding of the virtues of faith, hope, and love; and *De Musica*, the clearest expression of his theory of knowledge (Albert et al., 1988:85).

Saint Augustine died in A.D. 430 during the siege of Hippo by the Vandals. His death marked the beginning of the medieval era and the end of the Roman Empire. The teachings of Saint Augustine continued to dominate Christian belief for more than nine centuries and had far-reaching influence on the contemporary doctrines of the church.

Saint Augustine's Ethical Theory

Saint Augustine's philosophy had a profound effect on the development of Christian ethics primarily because he was the first philosopher to analytically address Christian doctrines. He assigned himself two basic but sacred tasks: to clarify the route that Christians must take to achieve spiritual safety and salvation; and to expose heretical beliefs that he felt were responsible for misleading too many people in their search for true union with God (Albert et al., 1988:85).

Although many passages in Saint Augustine's work suggest an outstanding technical ability, such as his famous analysis of time in *Confessions*, his overall philosophy was almost ancillary to a religious preoccupation. He saw philosophy and religion as essentially two quests for wisdom through which one can ultimately achieve *beatitude*, or eternal bliss. The main difference he saw between them was that Christian faith eventually succeeded in its quest, while philosophy (unaided human reason) failed.

Saint Augustine began reconstructing the Christian creed by reemphasizing the assumption that God is perfectly good and all things come from Him. Because God in His goodness cannot create anything evil, it then follows that evil cannot be a characteristic in itself. Evil is only "evil" insofar as it lacks the goodness of God. And because man was born to sin (Adam's sin), then all human behavior must be sinful. But because God is not only the omnipotent Creator, but also the benevolent Forgiver of mankind, He would not want the human race to be destroyed by sin. He therefore sent His redeeming grace through His son Jesus Christ. Consequently, whoever believes in Christ and seeks salvation will be saved—and those who choose not to are doomed to eternal death.

Throughout his ethical theory, Saint Augustine insisted that man needed God's grace in order to effect his reconciliation with Him, because "fallen men" are powerless in their endeavor to achieve that goal by themselves. This particular thought raised some serious questions about Saint Augustine's view of free will. Although he attempted to address these questions and agreed that man has a measure of freedom to receive or reject God's offer of grace, his arguments did not seem conclusive to many critics.

Saint Augustine portrayed the entire history of humanity from the fall of Adam to the Day of Judgment as a struggle between the "City of God" and the "City of Man." Those who live in the earthly city pursue material interests and carnal pleasures. They suffer not only from the frustrations brought about by their false beliefs while on earth, but also endure everlasting alienation from God. The Last Judgment will be a day of reckoning, where virtuous deeds and evil deeds will be examined and just rewards and punishments administered. The City of Man eventually will be dissolved and its citizens condemned to eternal death. The reward of those who hold fast to their faith is the eternal blessedness of reigning with God in heaven (Albert et al., 1988:86).

According to Saint Augustine, the ethical foci of Christian belief were as follows:

1. God is the omnipresent, the omniscient, and the benevolent Creator of the entire universe.

2. Human beings were created a "little below angels" and are endowed with free will, but unless they are aided by faith, they are unable to choose between good and evil.

3. Adam's evil choice caused him to fall from God's grace, and his original sin was inherited by all humans.

4. God in His mercy provided redemption through His son Jesus to those who have faith in Him.

5. People who seek redemption must follow the example of Jesus and live a sacred life of humility, love, compassion, and obedience to God's commandments.

Saint Augustine's theory of ethics bears no earth-shattering revelations to the Western world, because it is founded upon basic Christian assumptions. When considered from a reasoning point of view, however, these assumptions may be hard to accept, especially by someone who does not subscribe to the Christian faith.

Major Issues in Saint Augustine's Ethical Philosophy

The Paradox of Good and Evil

One of the most problematic issues in Christian ethics is the existence of evil: If God is so benevolent, why, then, should there be evil in the world? Saint Augustine responded to this question by first explaining that although God is perfectly good and incapable of creating anything evil, He nevertheless allows the existence of evil. Saint Augustine tried to explain evil by arguing that it is not an independent characteristic but only the absence or the mutilation of goodness. As such, it is caused by the defilement of the sinful man. What God originally created was goodness. But in the hands of sinful persons, goodness can be diminished or derailed. Consequently, evil is a product of the human corruption of the perfect nature of God—it is "nature disordered." By the same token, evil can be eradicated when man admits his sins and accepts God's offer of redemption through the blood of Jesus Christ.

The Will of God and the Will of Man

The second major issue that Saint Augustine had to face in constructing his ethical theory was the question of human will. Based on the thesis that evil is "nature disordered," one might ask, "Why, then, does God permit or tolerate man's disruption of nature?" Augustine replies by stating that while God has the power to put a stop to evil by divine decree (thus abolishing the will of man), He chooses not to, knowing that a great number of men eventually will choose to disrupt the orderly nature of goodness. It is preferable for God to grant man the freedom to do good rather than to create human puppets incapable of sinning because of their lack of freedom.

Saint Augustine explained that morality cannot exist without free will, because only by virtue of possessing a free will can the soul (and its activities) be designated good. Furthermore, the will itself is neither good nor bad. It becomes evil only when man abuses it by turning from the "superior to the inferior." For example, when a man appreciates a beautiful woman, he does not commit sin until his mind turns to lust—the will assenting to evil desire. On the other hand, to assert that something can automatically vitiate the will of man is to affirm that God created evil (Sahakian, 1974:79).

Predestination and Foreknowledge

Saint Augustine proceeded to reconcile the concept of freedom of will with the concept of *predestination* (God's determination of who eventually will be saved and who will not). Augustine made the reconciliation by introducing the concept of "foreknowledge." Accordingly, God knows in advance who eventually will follow His commandments and who will not. But God's foreknowledge lacks the causal power to control, or change, the will of people, because He operates in a timeless state of eternity, while man's will functions in the present world of time. In later writings Saint Augustine seemed to concede more toward predestination by assuming that only the first man, Adam, had a truly free will. But because he abused it by choosing to disobey God, he became the first sinner. His sin subsequently corrupted the nature of all mankind. Man's redemption, therefore, can no longer be achieved by choice, but only by God's grace, which elects those who will be saved.

The City of God and the City of Man

The controversy between good and evil continued throughout the teachings of Saint Augustine. To illustrate this controversy, Augustine described the existence of two cities. First is the *City of Man*, which is inhabited by those who choose evil (living after the flesh), pursue physical pleasures, or harbor heretical beliefs. Second is the *City of God*, the heavenly abode of those who are saved by the grace of God. To live in the heavenly city, one must follow the spirit as well as the teachings of Jesus. The City of God is the ideal state, where man lives in accordance with the grace of God.

Saint Augustine's depiction of these two cities distinguishes the differences between life as it is and the Christian life that man should strive to achieve. The City of Man represents a world of imperfection and defiled existence, but the City of God is a blissful state of beatitude in which man is rewarded for his faith and devotion by reunion with God in a perpetual "Sabbath." Saint Augustine believed that those who live in the City of Man will be condemned to eternal death, which is the wage of sin.

Man's Search for Virtuosity and Morality

Saint Augustine believed that Greek ethical philosophy is flawed in several ways. First, it concerns itself with only the "earthly nature" of life and is limited to man's brief existence on earth—as signified by the teachings of Socrates, Aristippus, Epicurus, and others. Christian ethics, on the other hand, must be seen as a segment of eternity, because man (as an extension of God) will continue his relationship with God in perpetuity. Second, Greek philosophy is based primarily on human intellect and the faculty of reason as a method of understanding and resolving the evils of the world. Saint Augustine stressed that reason *alone* is incapable of solving human problems. Only when reason is guided by divine revelation can it truly be possible for man to deal with the evils of life. Third, the virtues of prudence, temperance, justice, and fortitude, as identified by the Greek philosophers, are simply prideful vices unless applied in accordance with religious doctrine. In Saint Augustine's view, without true religion there is no true virtue.

Summum Bonum *of Ethical Values, the Love of God*

Saint Augustine pointed out that ultimate virtue is the love of God. All other virtues are only mirrorings of that relationship. For example, temperance is loving God by surrendering one's pleasures entirely to Him; fortitude is loving God by bearing all hardships for His sake; prudence is loving God by finding the correct avenues for reaching His grace; and justice is loving God by distributing His virtues equally within one's community.

Based on these principles, Saint Augustine exhorted Christians to manifest love in three hierarchical levels: love of God; love of neighbor; and love of self. It is the responsibility of the true Christian not only to love God before all things, but also to love one's neighbor as oneself and to love oneself by keeping in constant union with God.

Saint Thomas Aquinas: Morality as the Vision of God

Thomas Aquinas (1224–1274) was born near Naples, Italy. He was the seventh son of the Count of Aquinas, the head of a noble and powerful family in Southern Italy. Thomas received his early education from the Benedictines of Monte Cassino and pursued his studies at the University of Naples. While at Naples, Aquinas came to admire the religious order of the Dominicans. He was so impressed by their ideals of chastity and poverty that he joined the order at the age of 20. His family was so distressed over the event that his brothers forcibly returned him to the Castle of Rocca Secca, where they kept him prisoner for 1 year. He was released only after they were unable to force him to abandon his convictions.

As a Dominican monk, Aquinas was sent to Paris to study philosophy under Saint Albertus Magnus (Albert the Great), who recognized the genius of young Thomas and openly shared his vision with him. In 1252 Aquinas completed his study of theology, and his reputation as a theological philosopher grew steadily thereafter (Albert et al., 1988:107).

In 1259 Aquinas began serving in the Papal Courts at Anagni and other locations. In 1268 he was dispatched to Paris to resolve a theological controversy that was brewing between the Franciscans, who followed the teachings of Saint Augustine, and the Dominicans, who held an Aristotelian view of theology. It fell upon Aquinas to reconcile these conflicting views and reconstruct an official stand for the church, which he did with unparalleled knowledge and skill. Aquinas returned to Italy in 1272 as director of the Dominican Stadium in Naples. He died in 1274 at the age of 49, and in 1323 he was canonized.

Saint Thomas Aquinas wrote prodigiously. His best-known treatises are *Summa Contra Gentiles* (A Summary against the Gentiles), composed to provide missionaries with a means to convert pagans, and *Summa Theologica*, a textbook designed to give novices a systematic understanding of Christian theology. His writings show a profound ability to discuss formidable subjects such as the existence of God and the supreme good for humanity. More importantly, Saint Thomas's work proved that philosophy and theology are not only compatible, but indeed complement one another.

Aquinas's Ethical Theory

Saint Thomas Aquinas was perhaps the greatest philosopher of the scholasticism school. Throughout history he has been distinguished as a realist. In fact, one of the titles he earned was "Angelic Doctor" of the Catholic Church. In his realist approach he advocated that there are no innate ideas; all knowledge originates from sensory experience. When the mind acts upon such experiences, the result will be the formation of abstract and universal ideas.

Aquinas was both a theologian and a philosopher. He kept a clear distinction between the two disciplines, even in their closest alliance. He pointed out that philosophy works to its conclusions by the unaided use of human reason, while theology depends on divine revelation and authority from the church. The two disciplines also differ as to their subject matter. Some truths can be known only from revelation. These belong to the realm of theology; for example, the mysteries of the Trinity and the Immaculate Conception. Other truths belong to the realm of philosophy; for example, the constitution of the universe and other related bodies. Still other truths belong to both disciplines, such as the existence of God, which can be ascertained by revelation as well as by reasoning.

While Aquinas followed the Aristotelian tradition, he tried to Christianize Aristotelian thought. In his ethical theory, he reformulated Aristotle's views and applied them to the Christianity of his time. Much of his work attempted to show that Christian beliefs and Aristotelian philosophy were in general agreement. At the same time, he suggested that while Aristotle's formulations were correct for the most part, they were incomplete without the incorporation of Christian beliefs. For example, he endorsed Aristotle's metaphysical position but highlighted the role of God as the epitome of the metaphysical phenomenon. He accepted Aristotle's distinction between the actual and the potential but added that in finite beings there is always a mixture of both. An infant, he pointed out, is complete and perfect as a child, although his potential is yet unfulfilled. The only being that is devoid of all potential and completely actualized (perfect) is God. Thus, man's ultimate goal must be the "beatific vision of God," the direct knowledge of Him or seeing Him as He is (Albert et al., 1988:109).

In *Summa Theologica* Aquinas developed a rather comprehensive moral system. He analyzed the nature of human action and discussed the subjects of virtue and vice. He elaborated on the theological virtues of faith, hope, and charity, and on their achievement through the practices of prudence, justice, and fortitude. Aquinas also offered concrete solutions to common problems such as homicide, theft, and dishonesty.

The influence of Saint Thomas was overwhelming. During his time, and until the sixteenth century, he was considered the official interpreter of the Roman Catholic Church. Nevertheless, his influence waned between the sixteenth and nineteenth centuries due to the rise of Protestant doctrines championed by Martin Luther and others. Since the middle of the nineteenth century, however, there seems to be considerable revival of Thomistic theological views.

Major Issues in Aquinas's Ethical Philosophy

The Moral Problem: Freedom and Finality

In discussing the moral problem, Saint Thomas Aquinas held beliefs similar to those of Saint Augustine. Both agreed that God is absolutely perfect, that all things were created in his image, and that the goal of human activity is the achievement of happiness. Aquinas, however, defined happiness in an Aristotelian manner: the sum of goods that brings appetite to rest because there is nothing else to desire. In Aristotelian terms, that probably equals the full actualization of one's potential.

According to Aquinas, the moral problem is a human problem. Unlike nonintelligent beings (for example, animals and birds), who are driven toward the end of their nature by extrinsic causes, man can direct himself toward happiness and away from destruction. God gave man both intelligence and free will in order to enable him to determine moral action. Man has the freedom to choose and adapt by varied means. In this sense, man is truly judge and master of his own acts and ultimately responsible for his own actions.

Like Aristotle, Aquinas believed that all human actions are designed to achieve some end and that the highest end is capturing the truth. This, he argued, cannot be achieved without first contemplating the divine. Man's ultimate happiness is indeed the contemplation of God.

The Significance of Laws: Eternal, Natural, Human, and Divine

Aquinas emphasized the role of laws in making human choices. He defined *law* as a dictate of practical reason that emanates from a ruler who governs a perfect community. But the origin of all laws, he declared, is God, because He ordains them directly or indirectly to guide man in his search for the common good.

Aquinas identified four types of laws that are essential to ethical judgment:

1. *Eternal laws:* These are God's laws that are not revealed to humankind. They constitute the source of all other laws. They are non-temporal (not subject to time) and everlasting. Aquinas believed that eternal laws are absolute dictates of divine wisdom. They include laws that govern the cosmos, gravity, motion, and the revolution of planets.

2. *Divine laws:* These are God's laws that are revealed to humankind through divine revelation. They include biblical commandments, church doctrine, articles of faith, and rituals of worship.

3. *Natural laws:* These are laws that are discernible to people by virtue of their rational nature and their ability to distinguish between good and evil. While they may be culturally based, they are difficult to change, because they are tied to human nature. They include such laws as self-preservation, justice, equality, and the rearing of offspring.

4. *Human laws:* These are laws that are made by people to govern the actions of others and to represent the collective reason of the community. They include such laws as criminal laws, civil laws, tax laws, and labor laws.

Man's Moral Responsibility

One prevailing view prior to the time of Aquinas was that man cannot be morally responsible for his actions if he is overcome by fear or overwhelmed by desire—"the spirit is strong, but the flesh is weak." Aquinas rejected that view, observing that while fear can be inhibiting, man is indeed morally responsible because of his failure to avoid the evil that brought about the fear in the first place. Based on the same theory, he rejected the idea that man cannot be held responsible when he is overcome by desire. Man, he insisted, is responsible, irrespective of the introduction of fear or desire.

Aquinas noted, however, that in some cases man may not be held morally responsible for his actions, on the grounds of ignorance. For example, a man should not be held responsible when, after taking proper caution, he shoots an arrow that kills a passerby of whom he was unaware. In this example, the archer neither intended to kill, nor was he bound to know that his act would result in harm. Alternatively, Aquinas noted that ignorance provides no excuse for moral irresponsibility when one voluntarily elects not to learn about things that he has a responsibility to know. In this sense, "ignorance of the law" was as unacceptable a defense for Aquinas as it now is in modern legal systems.

Human Reason and Human Will

Aquinas distinguished between two kinds of sin: the sin of *reason* and the sin of *will*. He considered reason to be a function of the conscience and will to be a function of choice. Immoral acts based on following a "mistaken" conscience are less sinful than those motivated by ignoring conscience. Therefore, while some find it plausible to deny all moral responsibility to those who willfully follow their conscience, such judgment should be inaccurate. Aquinas explained that if the conscience is in fundamental error—basically wrong about a moral principle—one's act would be labeled an *accidental evil*. But if one's conscience is correct about the morality of what ought to be done, and the actor chooses to override the dictates of that conscience, that person would be guilty of committing an *absolute evil*. For example, if an Amish person refuses to take her sick child to the hospital for religious reasons, and the child dies as a result, the woman would be guilty of committing an accidental evil. But if someone's conscience dictates that fornication is morally wrong, yet he fails to refrain from such conduct, then his will is *unresponsive*—not strong enough to check the wrong choice. In this case, he would be guilty of committing an "absolute evil" (Albert et al., 1988:121).

Intentions and Consequences

Saint Thomas Aquinas taught that in judging morality it is the *intention* behind the act that makes it good or evil, rather than its *consequences*. An example of this is when an ordinary person observes a homeless person and out of the goodness of her heart gives him money for food. Instead of buying food, the homeless person buys heroin, injects himself with it, and dies. In this case, Aquinas would not hold the person morally responsible for the street person's death, because her intentions were good and she had no opportunity to foresee the consequences that followed. On the other hand, if the donor is a veteran police officer, then most likely Aquinas would find her morally accountable, because by virtue of her experience, she would be expected to know that some homeless people use the donations they receive to satisfy their drug habits.

The Naturalistic School: Ethics of Egoism and Power (Hobbes and Nietzsche)

Introduction

Most of the schools of ethics discussed so far (with the exception of the Aristippan school of egotistical hedonism) identified ethics with normally acceptable virtues. The Stoic school emphasized the morals of "tranquility," the Epicurean school emphasized the morals of the "contemplative mind," the Platonian and Aristotelian schools emphasized the morals of the "elevated soul," and of course the Christian school emphasized the morals of the "love of God." All these schools seem to follow a similar, if not fairly predictable, script of morality that we can all claim to have learned in childhood.

There is more to the study of ethics, however, than what we have covered to this point. The school of ethical naturalism is radically different; it presents a scientific explanation of ethics and prescribes a controversial set of morals. Ironically, the morals of scientific naturalism might be easier to identify and relate to if you closely observe the behavior of classmates, roommates, or coworkers whom you do not particularly like. This school of ethics examines the nature of man from a different perspective—the "naked reality" of the human race, with all its imperfections, weaknesses, and inclinations toward power, egoism, selfishness, and brutality.

The classical school of ethical naturalism denies the "romantic" view of man and holds that what is observed by the natural sciences is all that there is to observe and study. Champions of this school reject any explanation that goes beyond the practical universe in which we live. Furthermore, they do not consider man to be the son of God; they do not even consider him a particularly noble creature. Human behavior, they argue, is closer to that of animal behavior than we are willing to admit. As a general rule, these philosophers subscribe (with some variations, of course) to Darwin's theory of evolution, which asserts that human beings evolved from lower forms of life, which in turn may have evolved from nonliving matter. They endorse the premise that the most vital moral among men is competition for survival.

Champions of the classical school of naturalism view human morality as a purely empirical topic; a branch of natural sciences akin to those of geometry, physics, or biology. Rather than evaluating moral values, they consider such values to be neutral statements of fact—including statements of a theological nature. They point out that when the "romantic" ethicists discuss moral issues, they indeed describe a natural phenomenon, but instead of focusing on "what is" and "what is not," they simply emphasize "what ought" and "what ought not."

To ameliorate the harshness of the classical school of naturalism, John Dewey (1859–1952) presented an ethical theory based on what he termed the *scientific method*. He argued that the leaders of the classical school have been following an absolutist view supported by outmoded methods of observation. He contended that there are new behavioral and reflective techniques of inquiry that the classical school philosophers were reluctant to apply in their treatment of ethics. Consequently, truths must be seen as relative rather than absolute and changing rather than dogmatic. Dewey attributed this lag in knowledge to the rigid view of the classical philosophers, who perceived human beings as passive spectators living in a fixed universe, and to the misguided belief in the truth as static and unchanging. To bridge that gap, Dewey proposed a theory of pragmatic naturalism that is based on the scientific method but also takes into account the view of mankind as socially adaptable and psychologically adjustable.

In this section we will study the works of two classical ethical naturalists, Thomas Hobbes and Friedrich Nietzsche. This should not detract from the great value of Dewey's work or the works by modern naturalists such as Ralph Barton Perry or Moritz Schlick. Hobbes and Nietzsche are classical theorists whose works have dramatically opposed the conventional view of ethics. Their contributions have been especially significant because they represented the first departure from traditional ethical thought at a time when expressing such views was not merely unfashionable but taboo.

Thomas Hobbes: Ethics of "Might Makes Right"

Thomas Hobbes (1588–1679) was born in Malmesbury, England. The son of poor and uneducated parents, his father deserted the family early in Hobbes's life. But fortunately for Thomas, his education was taken over by a wealthy uncle who sent him to Oxford, where most professors at the time were great devotees of Aristotle and his metaphysical thought. These views were neither amusing nor convincing to young Thomas.

Upon graduating from Oxford, Hobbes became a tutor to Lord Cavendish, son of the Earl of Devonshire. His relationship with the Cavendish family was to last his entire lifetime, affording him the opportunity to meet many distinguished people, including Francis Bacon, Ben Jonson, and Galileo Galilei.

During that period, English politics were in turmoil. In 1640, when tension between King Charles I and Parliament was at its peak, Hobbes defended the rights of the king as an absolute sovereign. Consequently, he was threatened by Parliament. To avoid reprisal, he chose a self-imposed exile in France, which was at that time an enemy of England. While in France, he further studied physics and physiology. Upon returning to England, he continued to write political critiques, even when civil disturbances in England indicated that civil war was imminent. It was within that period of political upheaval that Hobbes formulated his views in favor of the king as an absolute sovereign and the need to force a social compact among subjects of the realm. His first political essay, *The Elements of Law*, was published in 1642 and followed by his celebrated masterpiece, *Leviathan*, in 1651. It is alleged that Hobbes wrote *Leviathan* while in France to flatter Lord Cromwell, whom Hobbes hoped would expedite his return. The *Leviathan* indeed impressed Cromwell, who allowed him to return to England soon after (Albert et al., 1988).

Parliament continued to harass Hobbes, however. Because of his continuing unpopular political and religious views, an act of Parliament was passed in 1666 forbidding him from publishing any works in England. But being a vigorous man, both mentally and physically, Hobbes continued to publish in Holland. The last of his works appeared when he was 87. He died in 1679 at the age of 91.

Hobbes' Ethical Theory

Hobbes was indeed the philosopher of power. As a pragmatic thinker, he was suspicious of all metaphysical configurations, eternal truths, and unrealistic exhortations concerning the "shoulds and oughts" of human behavior. He had little respect for reason, the great mother of philosophy since the time of Socrates. For Hobbes, reason was no more than mere reckoning that is detached from physical reality. Instead, he was so impressed with Galileo's work in the area of science that he developed a systematic "science of politics" on a par with the mathematical formulations of Galileo.

Hobbes's ethical theory presented a remarkable attempt to examine the observable nature of man and, more particularly, what man would be like "if all restraints of law and society were removed." From Galileo's work, Hobbes borrowed the idea of a "universe in motion," which he applied to the social universe. He argued that just as atoms travel restlessly in the astronomical universe, so do human beings in the social universe. Subsequently, he advocated the concept of "mechanistic materialism," by which every body, object, or idea is ultimately reducible to material elements in motion, not excluding (indeed, including) the structures of man, government, or state.

Hobbes noted that every ethical philosopher among his contemporaries was careful to identify an "incorporeal spiritual substance" such as God, soul, or conscience by which human behavior could be explained. He despised the use of such metaphysical fabrications, exclaiming: "What if all of these incorporeal spiritual substances are not really there!" He added, "It is no better than absurd—when a man is dead and buried—for anyone to say that his soul can walk separated from his body and he is seen by night amongst the graves." Infuriated by that kind of "silliness," Hobbes offered instead a naturalist theory of psychological egoism based on what he termed "the wolf desire" that lies inside all natural men (Flew, 1979:141).

In his ethical theory, Hobbes offered the following propositions:

1. The free *will* of people (liberty) and the *necessity* of state (control) are indeed compatible. In making that point, Hobbes used the analogy of water flowing downward: Not only does it have the liberty, but also the necessity of descending down the channel.

2. The natural life of man is completely and exclusively egotistical, because it is solitary, poor, nasty, brutish, and short. Subsequently, people must be controlled by a binding "social contract" under the authority of a strong-willed ruler who must maintain absolute authority. Otherwise, Hobbes believed, the entire social structure of the commonwealth will collapse.

3. Religion, in particular the Catholic faith, is not only unscriptural but also incoherent and unreal. Any use of religious principles, therefore, should be excluded from the exercise of moral valuation.

Major Issues in Hobbes's Ethical Philosophy

Human Motions: Endeavors and Aversions

In accordance with the scientific method, Hobbes's first task was to isolate the intimate components of human behavior. He argued that human beings possess two types of motions: a vital motion, such as the functions of blood circulation, breathing, digestion, and so forth, and a *voluntary* motion that requires prior thought, such as the functions of walking, moving, or speaking. Before a voluntary motion can occur, the mind must initiate a thinking process, which Hobbes called *endeavor*.

Endeavors are of two kinds: *appetite*, or desire, and *aversion*, or avoidance. These represent the motions of approaching and of retreating, respectively. When individuals seek items that motivate a desire, they call them "good," because they further their vital motion. On the other hand, when they avoid items that induce retreat, they call them "bad," because they frustrate the vital motion. Therefore, people love items that cause an appetite and hate those that cause an aversion. But when people neither desire nor hate an item, they hold it in *contempt* and harbor a feeling more of indifference. On the basis of this analysis, Hobbes concluded that all statements made about moral conduct are descriptive rather than evaluative, because they do not have a scientific base—what one man may call good, another may call evil.

Happiness as Self-Preservation

Hobbes held a fairly dismal view of man in his natural state. He argued that in presocial existence (prior to the establishment of civil authority), self-preservation was the primary objective of all human beings. He termed any object or means that is used to achieve self-preservation *power*. While he noted that self-preservation is neither a pleasurable nor painful feeling, he pointed out that man associates happiness and unhappiness (mere subjective sentiments) with success or failure of his endeavor to achieve self-preservation. When one succeeds, one feels happy, and when one fails, one feels unhappy.

Nature and the Origin of War

Hobbes stressed that in the absence of a civil authority, the natural condition of man is a state of war. Because self-preservation is the ultimate goal, every man would be against all others. Hobbes's concept of war is based on the assumption that human beings are naturally inclined to secure power in order to achieve self-preservation—a state that will make them happy. But in the struggle to secure power, conflicts are bound to occur. This is due in part to the natural equality of men: All people have approximately the same mental and physical capacity to attain power, and all have the capacity to hurt one another. Hobbes concluded that an external power is essential. Furthermore, such a power must be stronger than the powers of any individual or group of individuals. Moreover, such a power must be absolute; it cannot be restricted to any law, even its own. If it does, Hobbes argues, it would appear weak in the eyes of the conflicting groups, who may find it advantageous to band together and defeat it.

Self-Interest and the Need for Authority

Hobbes believed that the chief motivation of man is fear of unexpected violent death—both in the present and in the future. He proclaimed that "the origin of all great and lasting societies consisted not in the mutual goodwill men had toward each other but in the mutual fear they had of each other" (Albert et al., 1988:135). He explained mutual fear in terms of the ability of men to inflict a relatively equal amount of pain on each other—causing fear to become a real passion.

Hobbes argued that in the natural state of man, "everyone has a right to all—what one man calls his own could be claimed by any other." Furthermore, the dominating passion is simply self-interest without regard to considerations of rightness and wrongness, justice and injustice. Anyone has the right to invade the property of another, thereby claiming his right, just as any other man has the right to resist that claim. Hobbes emphasized that without civil authority, there is no law; and where there is no law, there is no peace. Only through the establishment of a strong civil authority can order be maintained in the "commonwealth" (Albert et al., 1988:137).

The Golden Rule

In order to maintain peace in the "commonwealth," Hobbes presented a negative Golden Rule, which he thought would sum up all natural laws and be acceptable to everyone. His rule states: "Do not do unto others what you do not want them to do unto you."

Hobbes's rationale was based on his absolutist view of social contract theory. In order to achieve peace and self-defense, people, he advocated, should be willing to lay down their natural rights to all things and be content with as much freedom to act against others as they will allow others to act against them. As long as people believe they can do anything they like, they will remain in a state of war. On the other hand, if a person unilaterally gives up his rights, he will be preyed upon. Hobbes believed that the Golden Rule should be the primary ethic in a civilized society, especially because many members of the commonwealth might be unable to understand the complicated lexicon of the laws or uninterested in learning them.

Friedrich Nietzsche: Ethics of the Superman

Friedrich Nietzsche (1844–1900) was born to a Lutheran minister in Rocken, in the Prussian province of Saxony. When he was four, his father suffered a serious accident and died, leaving Friedrich the only male child in an all-female household. His home life and early education were in keeping with the family tradition of piety. In 1850 the family moved to Nuremburg, where he began his education. He later attended the University of Bonn, where he studied divinity and philology. However, he was much more impressed with other subjects: Greco-Roman civilization and Darwin's theory of "survival of the fittest."

In 1867 Nietzsche began a year of military service with the Prussian army, but an accident put an end to his military career. He next attended the University of Leipzig, where he was exposed to the "pessimistic and anti-rationalistic" writings of Arthur Schopenhauer. Schopenhauer's *The World as Will and Idea* (1909) had a profound influence on Nietzsche. It drastically changed his outlook on life and led to his renunciation of Christianity. At the age of 24, Nietzsche was appointed

Professor of Classical Philology at the University of Bale in Switzerland. There he met Wagner, the great German composer, as well as Schopenhauer himself.

Despite protracted sickness and loneliness, Nietzsche produced a succession of brilliant works. He published *The Birth of Tragedy* in 1871 as a homage to Wagner; *Thoughts Out of Season* in 1876; *Beyond Good and Evil* in 1886; and *The Antichrist* and *The Will to Power* in 1889. His works were considered radical, and hostility to his views grew among the educated Germans of his time.

During the latter part of his life, Nietzsche's health gradually declined, making it impossible for him to write on a regular basis. Yet he continued to write aphorisms in which he further developed his own radical philosophy. In 1879, when his health completely deteriorated, he resigned his professorship and resided at Saint Moritz. For the remainder of his life he traveled from place to place in search of health, friends, solitude, and truth. In 1889 he became mentally ill and was placed in a mental institution. His madness is thought to have been caused by the stress of constant writing, worry, loneliness, illness, and the effect of drugs he was taking. In 1900 Nietzsche died of pneumonia.

Nietzsche's Ethical Theory

Friedrich Nietzsche was a revolutionary thinker who challenged traditional ethics by raising unconventional questions. He accused his predecessors of taking for granted what was good and what was evil without adequately investigating the nature of man. He believed that traditional philosophers made it their business to simply rationalize the moral idiosyncrasies of their environments.

In Nietzsche's ethical theory, he raised two main questions: "How does morality in one society compare with morality in another?" and "What does that say about the theory of morality in general?" In response to these questions, he voiced his utmost disfavor with Western morality, because it was characterized as divine or supremely venerable. He had no wish, any more than did Freud 25 years later, to accept any claim to surpassing wisdom.

Nietzsche questioned the value of both the Judeo-Christian religion and Greek rationalism. He accused Christian morality of being antagonistic to excellence, with a predisposition for mediocrity—if not downright baseness. He rejected the Christian belief that sex was sinful and resented the devaluation of both the body and intellect in favor of the soul.

Nietzsche opposed Greek rationalism on at least two counts: its "baroque and unreasonable nature" of generalizing when generalizations were impermissible; and its overrated sense of reason, which was unnatural to ordinary people. While he credited the Stoics and the hedonists with a great deal of wisdom, he believed that their work "should be taken with a grain of salt," because no moral code can be unconditionally derived from their thoughts (Ferm, 1956:396).

Nietzsche also saw hypocrisy in traditional European morality, which led him to believe that radical changes in moral thinking were necessary. Indeed, his reputation as a philosopher was based on his "campaign against morality." He was particularly distressed by the moral indiscretion of the ruling classes, who treated their populations as slaves. Subsequently, he called for a "moral revolution" through the doctrine of *transvaluation of values*, in which he advocated a set of radical values based on his innate obsession with power. In his new inventory of virtues, he replaced humility with *pride*, sympathy and pity with *contempt* and *aloofness*, and instead of love of one's neighbor, mere *tolerance* (Albert et al., 1988:240–241).

To justify his radical view, Nietzsche set out to redefine human nature. He identified man's natural state with an aggressive "will to power" that seeks to dominate the environment. He believed that power is a universal drive found in all men, both masters and slaves (Ferm, 1956:398). He further stressed that the strongest and highest "will to live" does not express itself in a miserable struggle for existence. It only manifests itself in the will of the "superman," a person with a free spirit who towers high above the "common herd." He consequently advocated that abidance with reason is inadequate—man must not hesitate to exercise power, the true agent of human nature.

Criticism of Nietzsche's ethics has been prevalent because his influence has been generally perceived as harmful. Bertrand Russell, a philosopher who was neither favorable nor negative to Nietzsche, thought that his values were driven by universal hatred and an exaggerated inventory of twisted facts. He accused Nietzsche of embracing some of the egotistical aspects of human instincts while rejecting some of the most benevolent ones, such as the needs for love, peace, and justice. Russell concluded that Nietzsche's reductionist view of humanity portrayed men as beasts who simply destroy each other for the ostentatious display of power. Other critics thought that Nietzsche's philosophy projected his own sense of fear and inadequacy and that his "noble" man was merely a creation of his daydreams. Still others thought that Nietzsche's dangerous influence led to the popularity of the Nazi party in Germany and to the eventual devastation of the Second World War at the hands of Germany's "superman," Adolf Hitler.

Major Issues in Nietzsche's Ethical Philosophy

View of Christian Ethics

Nietzsche criticized Judeo-Christian ethics, accusing it of being in direct conflict with what he called "true" or natural values. These, he asserted, were founded in individualistic values that expressed themselves in the quest for power, aggressiveness, and domination. Christian ethics, by contrast, promoted weakness, submission, exhaustion, and fatalism. He explained that at the heart of Christianity was resentment of everything "strong and healthy" (for example, body, sex, and intellect). These, he thought, were the very ideals of individualistic ethics.

Nietzsche accused Christianity of being the most seductive lie that ever existed. He charged Christian morality with allowing men to "emasculate" themselves when it teaches "Love ye your enemies," because nature's injunction is to love one's friends and hate one's enemies. He considered Christian morality suited only for paltry and mediocre people who are duped into believing that power, aggressiveness, and sex are immoral. In *The Antichrist* he urged people to declare open war against Christianity, the degenerate doctrine.

Master Morality and Slave Morality

Nietzsche identified two distinct sets of moral values within society: a *master morality*, which reflects moral values of the ruling class, and a *slave morality*, which is held by the ruled class. Members of the ruling class are the "creators of all values"—they need no approval from others. They believe in the ethics of power, which is based upon the dictum "What is harmful to me is harmful in itself." Slave morality, on the other hand, originates among the oppressed classes. Members of these classes are skeptical of everything their masters call "good." In persuading themselves that the morals of the ruling classes are not genuine, they choose an opposite set of values. They endorse submissive values such as sympathy, patience, humility, pity, and endurance. These values are especially honored in the lexicon of slave morality, because they furnish the only means by which the oppressed can endure the hardships of their existence. Slave morality, Nietzsche emphasized, is essentially a morality of cheap utility (Sahakian, 1974:151).

The Origin of Slave Morality

Nietzsche believed that the morals expressed by the ruled class (slaves) are merely an attempt on their part to justify their weaknesses. He pointed out that the slave understands "I am not worth much" and translates this feeling into a religious principle that justifies lack of self-worth (Albert et al., 1988:246). By adopting such a principle, slaves interpret their unfortunate condition as a result of being sinners or as the fault of society, and not as the result of lack of self-worth, ambition, or aggressiveness. In order to reverse slave morality, Nietzsche urged members of the ruled classes to ignore religion, to overcome the illusion of life after death, and—instead of worshipping gods in an alleged "beyond"— to aggressively improve their lives on earth.

The Concept of Repressed Resentment (Ressentiment)

Nietzsche believed that the idea of "good" evolved out of an aristocratic idea of "nobility," or the state of being of a "high calibre." Conversely, the idea of "bad" was associated with members of the ruled class, who did not fit the description of "noble." In order to prove this point, Nietzsche introduced the concept of *ressentiment* (a repressed resentment toward the ruling class) in order to explain why slaves choose opposite ethics from those adopted by the ruling class. Thus, healthy values held as moral by members of the ruling class become immoral when defined by slave ethics; power is replaced by obedience; aggressiveness by humility; and sex by chastity (Sahakian, 1974:152). As a result, the natural will to power is vanquished among the poor, furthering their state of servitude.

The Superman Doctrine

Nietzsche pointed out that men should not hide their instinctive desires for power in order to appear culturally acceptable. Accordingly, he exalted the individual who would express his independence, act as a law unto himself, and reach above the standards of master morality to become a *superman*. Nietzsche believed that supermen are great individuals, capable of creating everlasting civilizations without having to cater to slave morality or submit to Christian values.

Nietzsche associated his concept of superman with the theory of evolution. But unlike Darwin, who identified evolution as a passive adaptation to the environment, Nietzsche saw evolution as an active and endless drive to achieve the "will to dominate the environment" and eventually gain superiority over nature.

Nietzsche identified Jesus, Caesar, and Goethe as men who embodied the superman doctrine. He recognized that unique circumstances allowed these men to break from the grasp of the common herd. The ideal superman, in Nietzsche's view, however, was "a Roman Caesar with Christ's soul" (Sahakian, 1974:152).

Ethics of Utilitarianism (Bentham)

Introduction

Utilitarianism was a leading moral and political theory that dominated England for approximately 100 years beginning in the middle of the nineteenth century. It represented the most prominent normative ethics doctrine in the English-speaking tradition. Although it also was championed by several continental theorists, such as Helvetius in France and Beccaria (the father of classical criminology) in Italy, the theory was essentially

English. Its most noted proponents were Englishmen and Scotsmen, including John Gray, Henry Sidgwick, Jeremy Bentham, James Mill, John Stuart Mill, and, to a limited extent, David Hume (Ferm, 1956:620).

From a political perspective, utilitarian theory was a movement aimed at extending social reform, expanding political privileges, realizing a higher standard of living for the less fortunate, and correcting the injustices caused by harsh and corrupt penal codes. It sought to provide the masses with a greater amount of material comfort combined with a wide range of opportunities to achieve human dignity. Utilitarian philosophers were interested not only in theoretical speculation, but also in direct action and participation in political activities. Indeed, their pursuits brought about sweeping political and social reforms in nineteenth-century Britain.

From an ethical perspective, utilitarianism was the first modern movement toward recognizing Greek hedonism as an ethic capable of social application. The theory attempted to unite individualistic hedonism with social hedonism. Although it rejected unbridled egoism as advocated by Aristippus in the distant past and Hobbes in the recent past, it recognized the force of selfishness as natural to mankind. In a sense, the theory endeavored to reconcile two opposing views: the hedonistic nature of man (as an individual) and the altruistic obligation of society (as a collectivity of individuals). The result was to create a civilized community that takes into account both concern for self and concern for the common good (Ferm, 1956:620).

In its original form, utilitarian theory is a rather simple principle, perhaps deceptively so. Its central theme is based neither on a religious command nor on a metaphysical principle. It is derived inductively from understanding the role of man in society. According to this theory, utility is the only intrinsic good and, as such, the only criterion for moral judgment. Actions are considered right only in proportion to their propensity to promote happiness (pleasure), and wrong insofar as they are capable of producing unhappiness. A moral act, therefore, is one that can bring about more pleasure than displeasure—under the circumstances. All actions are judged by their consequential pleasure or denial of pleasure: The greater the happiness, the greater the moral merit of the act; and the more persons made happy by the act, the more praiseworthy it is. Utilitarianism is therefore a teleological theory whose *summum bonum* is clearly the greatest happiness for the greatest number.

Utilitarian philosophers differed widely as to how pleasure can be measured. The classical philosopher Jeremy Bentham, for instance, believed that happiness and pain can be measured quantitatively only in accordance with a specific matrix he called a "hedonistic calculus." On the other hand, John Stuart Mill, in rejecting this view, thought that pleasures can hardly be subjected to any mathematical or scientific rule. In addition, he advocated a qualitative approach based on the judgment of "expert jurors" who are familiar with the particular kind of pleasure or pain. Other utilitarian philosophers suggested alternate methods of measurements such as Rashdall's "axiom of equity" and Sidgwick's "intuitional utilitarianism."

Like all other ethical theories, utilitarianism suffers from several theoretical weaknesses. First, the central principle—the greatest happiness for the greatest number—is ambiguous. Based on the language of the statement, it is impossible to determine whether the emphasis is placed upon the *nature of good* (the quality of happiness) or the *number of recipients*. The difference is critical because if the emphasis is weighed in favor of the quality of pleasure, then a small number of people at the top could claim their right to indulge themselves in pleasures of the first order, while the rest would receive low-quality pleasures. Conversely, if emphasis is weighed in favor of the numbers involved, the good of the minority would have to be sacrificed in favor of the good of the majority, regardless of how superficially the majority will benefit or how severely the minority will be required to sacrifice.

Second, the theory fails to take into account personal rights as seen from an individualistic point of view. The principle of utility seems to ignore certain pleasures that are favored by specific individuals, such as the sports of bird watching, mountain climbing, or skydiving. How could these pleasures be subjected to a general rule, let alone adequately measured? Furthermore, even if two individuals were exposed to the same event (pleasurable or painful), how can we accurately assess the amount of happiness likely to be felt by each? Should such a judgment be based on personal appreciation or upon the tyranny of a general rule?

In the next section, the works of Jeremy Bentham will be discussed. Bentham has been acclaimed as the most typical and influential among the classical utilitarianists, and his works represent the quantitative approach to utilitarianism.

Jeremy Bentham: Ethical Hedonism and Social Happiness

Jeremy Bentham (1748–1832) was born in London, England. His father enrolled him at Oxford at the age of 12 to study law. He graduated at the age of 16 and was admitted to the bar at the age of 19. But Bentham was not interested in merely practicing law—he had an overwhelming desire to reform society's penal laws and institutions.

Bentham was independently wealthy. That enabled him to spend his entire life writing about ethical and social issues. Included in his writings were critiques of the economic, moral, religious, educational, political, and legal institutions of England. The guiding thought behind these critiques was his fierce conviction of the principle of utility, which he had introduced in 1780 in his essay *An Introduction to the Principles of Morals and Legislation.*

Soon after his first publication, Bentham became involved in reviewing the English penal system. He found punishment at the time to be unduly severe and the condition of prisons inhumane. Bentham felt that the penal system was failing to serve the common good, and in 1791 he publicized a plan for building more humane prisons. He proposed a new model of prisons, the *Panopticon*, which was shaped like a wheel, with the central management of the prison located at its hub. Bentham believed this design would lend itself to more humane prison conditions. Although he had signed a contract with the British government to build such prisons, none were built, due to the ongoing French Revolution. The British Parliament, however, later paid Bentham a handsome amount of money in compensation for expenditures he incurred in association with the prison project. Interestingly, the Illinois state prison system adopted the panopticon model in the early 1890s, and the first and only such prison opened in Stateville in 1925.

In 1823 Bentham helped found the first utilitarian journal, *Westminster Review*, which at the time was considered a radical publication. He also was instrumental in founding the University College in London as an alternative to the two main British universities, Oxford and Cambridge.

Bentham died in 1832, leaving his body to science. But rather than being dissected for the benefit of medical research, as he had instructed, his body was embalmed, dressed in his accustomed attire, and preserved in the college he helped to found (Borchert & Stewart, 1986:182).

Bentham's Ethical Theory

The idea of utility was not created by Bentham. Earlier formulations are found in the writings of Joseph Priestly, Cesare Beccaria, and David Hume. Bentham's fame, however, was essentially due to his adaptation of the idea to ethical theory and issues of social reform. Nevertheless, Bentham has generally been regarded as one of the founding fathers of utilitarianism.

Fundamental to Bentham's ethical theory was the old notion of *psychological hedonism*, by which all individuals are assumed to be motivated by pleasure and pain. They naturally seek to maximize pleasure and minimize pain. Accordingly, pleasure alone is the goal of all people and the measure of all actions. Bentham recycled that notion and called it the *principle of self-preference*.

Bentham defined *utility* as "the principle which approves or disapproves of every action, whatsoever, according to its tendency to augment or diminish the happiness of the party whose interest is in question." He also characterized happiness as one kind, differing only in quantity. It is enjoyable regardless of whether it proceeds from listening to

Beethoven's music or from "sticking pins in baby's bottom." Each person is his own judge as to what constitutes pleasure (Sahakian, 1974:29).

In a later edition Bentham labeled the principle of utility as *the greatest happiness or greatest felicity principle*. The new principle expanded his original notion by identifying the morality of an act with the amount of happiness that act can yield to those whose interests are concerned. Through this expanded version, Bentham was able to adapt the principle to the broader needs of a given community, thus justifying his involvement in issues of political and social reform. Bentham also defined *community* as the body of individuals who constitute its membership. The interests of a community are thus the sum interests of its members. Through the notion of community, Bentham was also able to establish the moral responsibility of government to provide maximum happiness to the largest number of citizens.

Bentham realized that for a person to choose the "right" action (one that can bring the most pleasure or the least pain) there must be a system of measures to determine the value of diverse pleasures and pains. Believing that he was indeed rescuing ethics from the fickle sentiments and intuitions of uninformed people, he presented the hedonistic calculus as a measurement system based solely on quantifiable portions of happiness.

Major Issues in Bentham's Ethical Philosophy

Psychological Hedonism

Bentham's theory of utilitarianism stemmed directly from his belief in psychological hedonism. He argued that nature has placed mankind under the governance of two sovereign masters: pain and pleasure. Only these two sensations govern what we do, what we say, and what we think. More importantly, they determine what ought to be done and what we eventually do. While most individuals in day-to-day activities deny or pretend to ignore their subjugation to these forces, in reality they always exist.

Nature of Utility

Based on his belief in psychological hedonism, Bentham explained the principle of utility in terms of five succinct premises:

1. Utility is the foundation of determining morality.

2. Utility is the property of an object whereby it tends to produce benefit, advantage, pleasure, good, or happiness. By the same token, an object that prevents the occurrence of pain, evil, or unhappiness also constitutes utility.

3. The greatest and sole good in the principle of utility is pleasure.

4. All pleasures are of one quality, and one quality only, regardless of their nature or sources.

5. All pleasures are calculable in accordance with a quantitative formula.

Utility as a Tool of Social Reform

Bentham moved from the concept of utility to its applicability to individuals and communities. He stressed that community interests have been neglected in the vocabulary of morals to the extent that their meaning has practically been lost. He reiterated that because government is the custodian of the collective interests of communities, the rules that regulate such interests must also be subjected to the law of utility. Therefore, social policies should be characterized as moral or immoral on the basis of whether they provide or fail to provide maximum harmony, comfort, and happiness. Bentham declared that any governmental law, rule, or policy that violates the essence of utility "must necessarily be a wrong one" (Borchert & Stewart, 1986:186).

The Hedonistic Calculus

To measure happiness, Bentham proposed a hedonistic calculus that was both profoundly simple and bewilderingly complex. Pleasure-producing actions and pain-producing actions must first be identified according to their specific characteristics; for instance, educational, recreational, or entertaining (or by the absence of such characteristics). Each action is then evaluated in terms of the degree of pleasure or pain of its characteristics. These are computed in terms of stated variables, or "differences." Each difference is assigned a number of points that adds to, or takes away from, the sum value of the characteristic in question. The overall value of the action is thus determined by the sum total of points assigned to each difference. Actions that produce the most points of pleasure (or the fewest points of misery) would be the most utilitarian, thus the most moral.

The hedonistic calculus furnished seven "differences," by which the characteristics of happiness can be measured. These are as follows:

1. *Intensity*—the force of pleasure as felt by the individual experiencing it (for example, watching a good movie versus a mediocre movie)

2. *Duration*—the length of time a person experiences the pleasure or pain (for example, punishing a mischievous child by three swift strokes of a paddle versus grounding him or her for a week)

3. *Certainty*—the chance the action will in fact lead to pleasure or pain (for example, choosing to stay at a quality hotel versus staying at a second-rate hotel)

4. *Propinquity*—the delay time, or distance, between the action and its anticipated pleasure or pain (for example, accepting a manual labor job that pays minimum wage or attending college, whereby upon graduation one can have a better-paying job)

5. *Fecundity or fruitfulness*—the chance that the pleasure will be followed by continued pleasure or the pain leading to further pain (for example, completing a college education, which can improve one's career, versus pursuing a private business, which may not improve one's future)

6. *Purity*—the chance that the pleasure will not be followed by pain, guilt, or remorse (for example, choosing to attend church versus frequenting a drug-infested bar)

7. *Extent*—the number of people to be affected by the pleasure or pain (for example, practicing a narrow medical speciality versus offering general medical care to a multitude of people in a refugee camp)

Critics of the hedonistic calculus, however, were quick to point out one logical error after another. These included Bentham's neglect of qualitative distinctions among varying pleasures; the teleological significance of the consequences of certain actions; the impracticality of adequate quantification within such a narrow framework; and the overlapping of some of the differences designated in the calculus. Criticism led Bentham to later admit that his calculations might not be precise, although "able moralists" should still be able to apply these calculations successfully.

Bentham's Four Sanctions

One of Bentham's main objectives was to integrate the philosophy of individual egoism with society's broader concern for human benevolence. He argued that the motivations of hope and fear can unite one's concerns for self and one's social concerns for others, thus making selfishness and benevolence concurrently possible. Bentham called these motivations *sanctions*, which he defined as "forces governing human conduct." Through these sanctions, the individual and the society can be drawn together, because one would be compelled to recognize the coincidence of his or her own happiness and that of his or her fellow citizens.

Bentham identified four specific sanctions:

1. *Physical sanctions*—the natural sensations of happiness or pain as they affect an individual's welfare

2. *Political sanctions*—the legal forces that can be mobilized by the state to curtail immoral acts by citizens

3. *Moral sanctions*—the popular sentiments of approval or disapproval expressed by family members, neighbors, and society at large

4. *Religious sanctions*—the blessings or condemnations by "the supreme invisible being" in accordance with one's faith, which may be experienced in the present life or in the afterlife

Ethics of Duty and Reason (Kant)

Introduction

Immanuel Kant (1724–1804) was born in Konigsberg, Germany, to a middle-class family. His father was a saddler, and both his parents were simple but sincere Pietists. At an early age, Immanuel displayed superior intellectual ability and was sent to the local Pietistic college to study theology. Soon after, however, he became disinterested in the subject and developed a greater interest in natural sciences and philosophy. While at the University of Konigsberg, Kant supported himself as a private teacher for various families in the area. He was later appointed instructor at the University of Konigsberg, where he eventually became a full professor of logic and metaphysics. Kant spent the rest of his life lecturing at the university until his retirement in 1796 at the age of 72.

Kant lived a life of routine, never marrying and never traveling more than 40 miles from Konigsberg. Heine, the famous German writer, labeled Kant an "automaton," describing his daily routine as "rising, coffee drinking, writing, lecturing, dining, walking, each had its own time" (Sahakian, 1974:107). Though Kant's personal life appeared uneventful, one of his biographers remarked that like the "most regular of regular verbs," Kant's philosophical theory was a radical innovation. His scholarly abilities have been linked to the great philosophers of history. He probably came as near as anyone ever has to combining the speculative originality of Plato with the encyclopedic thoroughness of Aristotle. As Albert comments, Kant's inner strength was apparently as dramatic as his outer life was drab (Albert et al., 1988:178). Two major factors in Kant's background were particularly important: first, the Pietistic form of Protestantism in which Kant was reared; and second, the ideas of enlightenment that characterized philosophical thought in Germany at the time.

Kant wrote extensively on science and philosophy. In *Fundamental Principles of Metaphysics of Morals* (1785), he examined the foundations of genuine morality; in *Critique of Practical Reason* (1788), he investigated the implications of morality for religion; and in *General Natural History and Theory of the Heavens* (1755), he hypothesized on the origin of the solar system. Kant's technique of writing was unique. It consisted of formal symmetry that he called "architectonic." Although his writing was rather formidable to read, the depth of his insight and his profound knowledge of history made him a central figure among ethical theorists. His writings were cited as a prerequisite for all who desired to understand nineteenth- and twentieth-century thought.

Kant's Ethical Theory

The starting point in Kant's ethical theory is his concern for the moral experience of the "ordinary man." He noted that philosophers and statesmen may agree or disagree on what constitutes morality, but ordinary men tend to be unanimous. At the core of that agreement is the natural distinction between inclination and duty—what is "expedient" and what is "morally required." He argued that only actions performed in accordance with duty have moral worth. Duty is the master principle and the *summum bonum* of all virtues.

Kant's ethical theory is intuitionist in nature and deontological in form. Its fundamental premise is the immediate apprehension and reverence to duty. His philosophy broke away from contemporary ethics on two fundamental points. First, he rejected the claim that people possess a "special" faculty for making ethical judgments—a conscience. He argued instead that people apply the same faculty of *reasoning* in making ethical decisions as they do in making other judgments. Second, Kant rejected the idea of *consequences* as a measure of rightness or wrongness. He advocated that morality is unequivocally predicated on duty; an act is *always* right if performed in accordance with duty, and always wrong if it is not. To Kant, virtue is doing one's duty regardless of the consequences—one ought to do his or her duty even if "the Heavens fall" (Borchert & Stewart, 1986:197). This orientation in Kant's ethical philosophy can be traced to his famous reflection: "two things fill the mind with ever new and increasing admiration and awe . . . the starry heavens above and the moral law within" (Albert et al., 1988:179).

Kant was the first modern philosopher to propose an absolute deontological theory of ethics. His position obviously contradicts the teleological or *consequential* views advocated by Hobbes and Bentham. As a result, Kantian thought has long been debated by philosophers who accused him of inflexibility and ignorance of the dynamics of human choice. His supporters contended that Kant did not intend to refer to all consequences across the board—only to the immediate consequences. They agree that Kant's views are justifiable given his intense interest in the nature of the universe and the morality of duty as culturally practiced in his Prussian homeland.

Major Issues in Kant's Ethical Philosophy

The Principle of Duty

Kant defined *duty* as the expression of free and autonomous will, self-legislating and commanding. For instance, to tell the truth when one is forced to do so does not constitute a moral action, but to tell the truth when prompted by reverence to duty does. In Kant's view, if an act is performed as a *matter of duty*, it is one of mere rote or what Kant termed *officia juris*, or *legality*. He defined legality as "the mere agreement or disagreement of an action without regard to the motive from which the action springs" (Sahakian, 1974:108). Ethical duties, on the other hand, are *officia virtutis*, or performed *from reverence to duty*. They are not promulgated by law, but are motivated by intent and prudence. Consequently, performing an act simply because it is legal must be considered devoid of moral content. But performing an act from reverence to duty is virtuous. Furthermore, the more one acts from ethical principle rather than from legality, the more virtuous the person is.

The Concept of Universality

Kant's theory of ethics was characterized by an intense pursuit of "certainty." All moral obligations must be judged in the same manner and regarded as scientific facts. Based on this assumption, Kant argued that for a moral principle to be genuine and acceptable, it must be capable of universal application. Therefore, if a person would say to another "do this or don't do that," she must be willing to say the same to every other person in the same situation. Moral principles must be applied equally to all members of the human race. That rule may sound difficult to accept, but from a Kantian perspective, because morality is founded on "the rule of reason," all moral principles must be reasonable—thus universally accepted.

Definition of Happiness

In a radical departure from Greek ethical theory, Kant rejected the idea that happiness is the reward of virtuous behavior. He insisted that happiness is an "ideal" that cannot be realized, at least in one's lifetime, because its fundamental aspects cannot fully be realized in practice. Supporters of Kant's view concur, suggesting that if the Greek philosophers were correct in their view (living a good life is the realization of virtue), then one should conclude that a drug dealer living a luxurious life is a virtuous person. There is definitely a moral contradiction in viewing an evil individual enjoying unbounded happiness, because reason dictates that it should not be so. In a perfectly rational world, evil persons are supposed to be miserable and virtuous persons are supposed to be happy. But because the world is not an entirely rational model, Kant's view should be considered accurate.

Kant's view of happiness was not based on asking, "Will my action make me happy?" but rather, "Will my action make me *worthy* of happiness?" Kant compared one's appreciation of happiness to one's appreciation of fortitude; a resolute force to resist injustice and other immoral influences. In Kant's analysis, the ideal of happiness is a state that must include (1) self-sufficiency, (2) harmony with self, and (3) self-determination (freedom of will). Nevertheless, he emphasized that all of these are not practically attainable attributes.

The Virtue of Goodwill

Kant emphasized that no value can be considered intrinsically good or bad. "Things" are good only when they are accompanied by *goodwill*—the "only good without qualification." Goodwill is virtuous, not only in terms of what it can accomplish, but also because of its pure intention. To illustrate his point, Kant used the examples of intelligence and power. They cannot be considered good or bad without qualification, because they could be used constructively (thus contributing to public good), or otherwise destructively. The goodness of any action must depend on the goodwill of the person doing it. When intelligence or power is handled by an evil person, it most likely would be conducive to great evil (Borchert & Stewart, 1986:200). In Kantian thought, goodwill is man's only relief from this dilemma, because it can determine one's true obligation toward the pursuit of goodness or badness.

Duty as the Manifestation of Goodwill

Kant proceeded to explain how goodwill can resolve the ethical dilemma of right and wrong. He argued that the only manifestation of goodwill is acting out of duty. And because all actions that are motivated by duty are morally worthy, goodwill constitutes moral worth. All actions that are not motivated by duty must be motivated by *inclination*, *self-interest*, or *impulse*. In evaluating moral duties, Kant considered it totally irrelevant whether the action does (or is designed to) make anyone happy or is even conducive to human pleasure. People must always be motivated by duty, because it is the supreme manifestation of goodwill.

The Concept of Maxims

Kant argued that because moral actions are to be guided solely by duty, they must be based upon a "dutiful principle," or law. Kant called such principles *maxims*, or rules of conduct. Examples of such maxims are "honesty is the best policy" or "an eye for an eye, and a tooth for a tooth." But because anyone can claim any rule that suits his desire or whim as a dutiful principle, moral maxims must be of such a nature as to be *accepted universally by all people.* One "should never act in such a way that he could not will that such a way (maxim) should become a universal law" (Ferm, 1956:270). In other words, everyone must be able to act in the same manner without contradiction or exception. As an illustration, the duty to pay one's taxes is a valid maxim, because one should pay his taxes and, at the same time, *will* that everyone else does so. On the other hand, the maxim that "killing is wrong" is invalid, because one cannot will that "all" killings be prohibited, including killing in war or in self-defense.

Maxims as Imperatives: Hypothetical and Categorical

Kant further explained moral maxims in terms of directives or commands that are expressed by the words *ought* or *shall*. He divided moral maxims into two kinds: *hypothetical* and *categorical*.

Hypothetical imperatives are "conditional commands." They direct behavior regarding what ought to be done if a desired goal is to be achieved. They qualify an action as good or bad only in terms of its capacity to achieve such a desired goal, regardless of whether it is actual or potential. Examples of the hypothetical imperative include "If I want people to like me, then I ought to be friendly," or "If I want to get good grades, then I ought to study hard." Kant did not favor these kinds of imperatives, because they fail to establish criteria for morality or lend themselves to universal performance or certainty. Worse still, they fail to prescribe what duties constitute "friendliness" or "studying hard."

Categorical imperatives, on the other hand, are "unconditional directives." They prescribe actions that must be done, regardless of purpose or consequence. A categorical imperative is a command that does not seek a particular goal to be achieved, but only a "principle" to be followed. For example, the maxim "one ought to tell the truth" is a perfect categorical imperative, whereas "If you want to avoid punishment, you ought to tell the truth" is a hypothetical imperative (Albert et al., 1988:189). Kant steadfastly supported the categorical imperative maxims, because they place the essence of morality on an impersonal basis and are universally applicable. What is valid for one person is valid for everyone, including oneself. Categorical imperatives imply that what is right for one person is right for all, and what is wrong for one is wrong for all. They are morally binding on all rational beings, and no exceptions can be made.

The Categorical Imperative

Although Kant proposed one categorical imperative, he formulated it in several versions to encompass the fundamental aspects of basic morality. The original imperative states, "Act only on that maxim whereby thou cans't at the same time will that it should become a universal law." This signifies the virtue of duty as the *summum bonum* of all values. Duties are obligations that are morally binding and universally applicable. If a duty cannot be right for one person to do (regardless of one's particular situation), then it is wrong for all.

Another version of Kant's categorical imperative pertained to the treatment of people. In that version he stated, "Act so as to treat humanity, whether in thine person or in that of any other, in every case, as an end and never as a means." This formulation calls attention to the moral imperative of treating all human beings with dignity and impartiality, regardless of what we may gain or lose from the relationship. The maxim has traditionally been cited as a moral condemnation of exploiting fellow men. According to this version, respect for man's dignity is the basis of all morality, and all persons are duty-bound to preserve and regard human dignity as holy.

Yet another version of Kant's categorical imperative emphasized freedom and autonomy in taking a moral action. Kant's formulation reads, "Act as if the maxim of thy action were to become, by thy will, a universal law of nature." By this formulation, Kant reasserts that no praiseworthiness or blameworthiness can be attributed to an action unless it is taken freely. This maxim sets the Kantian theory of ethics apart from divine or authoritative doctrines that are forced upon people. In Kantian thought, the principle of freedom is central: "Without freedom, there is no morality" (Borchert & Stewart, 1986:210).

The Existential School: Ethics of Moral Individualism and Freedom of Choice (Sartre and de Beauvoir)

Introduction

Existentialism is an ethical school that focuses on individuals and their almost unrestricted freedom to make choices. Existentialists suggest that people are ultimately alone—subjective beings in an objective world; consequently, they have absolute freedom over their nature. The first philosopher labeled as an existentialist was Soren Kierkegaard (1813–1855). Although the roots of existentialism were planted much before him in the schools of romanticism and antirationalism, Kierkegaard was the first to emphasize human existence (Oliver, 1999). Among the most famous philosophers of existentialism, however, were Jean-Paul Sartre and Simone de Beauvoir. These French philoso-phers met while they were classmates at the *Ecole Normale Superieure.* While Sartre focused mainly on the ideas of individualism and free will, de Beauvoir became one of the first feminist philosophers in European history. Also, while there was rivalry between them, Sartre and de Beau-voir would spend the rest of their careers developing the theory of existentialism.

The existential school proposes to answer three questions: (1) What is human freedom, and what limitations restrict its exercise? (2) What is human happiness, and how can it be achieved? and (3) What ethic or way of life can emerge from a position that emphasizes individuality? In response to these questions, existentialists argue that because individ-uals are alone in the world, they should decide for themselves how to live their sorrows, pains, fears, and joys. People can judge each other's emotions based only on their objective view of each other's action. How-ever, such judgment should be considered subjective because some peo-ple may react to their fears with timid behavior, while others may interpret that as being defensive and become angry. Existentialists argue, therefore, that the truth about a person's emotional state is known only to that person. In fact, the only sentiments people can experience directly (and therefore know to be true) are their own. When people feel, taste, or smell something, they are aware only of the signals it sends to their brain and their brain's interpretation of it—not the thing itself. A good illustration of this is optical illusion (Banach, 1991).

Arguably, the most popular concept of existentialism is that of free will. Existentialists explain that what makes human beings different from animals is their freedom to choose. As such, they are not slaves of fate or nature, as animals and plants are. However, human beings vary in their levels of self-control. Each person is a unique creation, con-stantly making choices that create new options and opportunities. The key to making full use of free will, therefore, is appreciating one's exis-tence. Jean-Paul Sartre (who will be discussed later) defined existence as one's ability to make choices, including the decision not to choose. Existentialists further argue that because people are free to choose, they must then accept the responsibility of the consequences that follow. Existentialist ideas have permeated criminal justice literature. Criminological theory has been, to a large measure, based on the classical the-ories of Cesare Beccaria and Jeremy Bentham, who argue that "man is rational and can freely choose to become deviant." From an ethical per-spective, therefore, if people are free to choose and take responsibility for their choices (as the existentialists argue), then society is justified in punishing them when they violate social norms (Banach, 1991)

Existentialist philosophy can be pessimistic at times, because it often reminds people of the "worthlessness of their lives" and the "trap of individual will." However, this is not always true, because many existential philosophers also discuss human happiness. For instance, Albert Camus states that life is not quite so dismal. He illustrates this view in his essay *The Myth of Sisyphus*. The gods had condemned Sisyphus to ceaselessly rolling a rock to the top of a mountain. Upon reaching the top, the rock would fall back because of its own weight. The gods then noted that there is no harsher punishment than inflicting helplessness on human beings. Camus argues that although people may find their life distasteful and meaningless, they still should find happiness in what they do, because sadness would be "the rock's victory." Furthermore, no matter the external pressure, there can always be the "freedom to rebel" (Camus, 1955). Existentialists emphasize that the despair people encounter is the necessary cost of obtaining greater happiness, one that comes from within. Again, the existentialists place the emphasis on the individuals and their experiences (Banach, 1991). If only people can find value within themselves, that value will be all that they need to experience happiness (Oliver, 1999).

Sartre and de Beauvoir

Jean-Paul Sartre was born in Paris on June 21, 1905. Son of a naval officer, Sartre had a childhood wrought with rejection. In his autobiography, *The Words*, he wrote, "I hated my childhood and everything that remains from it." Sartre's father died when Sartre was only 15 months old, from an intestinal disease caught while on duty in French Indochina. Sartre's mother, having no money or vocation, had to take her infant son and live in her parents' house. While there, Sartre's mother was mistreated and exploited, a situation that Sartre recognized and deeply resented. As a small child, he vowed to one day marry his mother and free her from her life of bondage (Lavine, 1984). When his mother remarried in 1917, Sartre and his new family moved to La Rochelle. He attended school at the *Lycee Louis-le-Grande*, the *Ecole Normale Superieure*, the University of Fribourg, and the French Institute in Berlin (Banach, 1991). While at the *Ecole Normale Superieure*, he met Simone de Beauvoir, an inspiring writer. Though they never married, Sartre and de Beauvoir would spend the rest of their lives as companions and intellectual associates. In 1929 Sartre began teaching at various *lycees* (high schools). He developed his existentialist philosophy by combining the phenomenology of Edmund Husserl, the metaphysics of Hegel and Heidegger, and the social theory of Karl Marx. Sartre began writing in the Left Bank cafes of Paris because they were warm, giving him the nickname the "café philosopher." Some of Sartre's most influential works include *Nausea*, *No Exit*, *Being and Nothingness*, and *Truth and Existence*.

Simone de Beauvoir was born in 1908 in Paris to a bourgeois family, the very social class she would later despise. Her father was a lawyer, and her mother was a devout Roman Catholic who raised her daughters in the fashion the church dictated. At an early age de Beauvoir studied philosophy at the Sorbonne. Many historians believe that her academic career was inevitable due to the strain between her father's pagan morals and her mother's strict Catholic teachings. As de Beauvoir matured, her religious beliefs began to dwindle as she became more and more interested in human nature. She learned to appreciate earthly joys and believed they should be embraced, not abandoned, as her religion suggested. She began to live for the moment and embrace every natural joy available. At that time, de Beauvoir seemed to have abandoned her religion and all beliefs about eternity. She joined a group of philosophy students that included Jean-Paul Sartre. De Beauvoir taught philosophy at several schools until becoming a professor at the Sorbonne in 1941. In 1945 she wrote *Le Sang Des Autre*, a novel that dealt with the politics of the French Resistance, and in 1954, *Les Mandarins*, a call to liberal intellectuals to discard their "elitist" status (Albert et al., 1988).

De Beauvoir's most influential work was *The Second Sex* (1949). In this book she condemns male-dominated societies that treat women as less than human. De Beauvoir went on to be a champion of the feminist movement in the late 1960s by speaking out on issues of abortion and sexual violence. One of her last publications, *Adieux: A Farewell to Sartre*, chronicled her life with Sartre, his death, and their eternal separation.

Although Sartre considered himself a philosopher and de Beauvoir a writer, their influence on each other was clearly evident. Sartre's influence on de Beauvoir characterized most of her ethical theory. In return, Sartre borrowed many of his ideas about feminism from de Beauvoir's writings. Because of this intimate relationship, it would be difficult to separate their work. Therefore, in this chapter they will be treated collectively.

Major Issues in Existential Theory

Evolution of Human Consciousness

Sartre argued that the only way to explain "being" is through human consciousness. He pointed out that human "thinking" cannot prove existence, because it is our nature to think. Consciousness, on the other hand, is the beginning of philosophy; it is focused, profound, and intentional. Sartre identified two regions of being. The first is "being-in-itself," as with existing things such as a tree or a rock. These objects have no consciousness and are unaware of themselves. The second is "being-for-itself." In this case, consciousness is based on possessing seven properties: (1) being conscious of objects and of one's consciousness of them; (2) being able to think of what one *lacks*, what one's *possibilities* are, and what one is *dissatisfied* with; (3) being free from other objects, free to doubt and to say no; (4) being totally free and spontaneous, because the past does not determine what people are at present; (5) being responsible for one's own situation; (6) being totally alone and independent—"condemned to be free"; and (7) being able to escape self-deception, a condition that presumes that fate exists (Lavine, 1984).

Moral Individualism

Since its beginning, existentialism has echoed Kierkegaard's claim, "I must find a truth that is true for me." An existentialist, therefore, must be able to choose his or her own path without the influence of others. The social and criminological ideas of the time aligned themselves with this view of rational choice—people choose their behaviors on the basis of their objective notions of right and wrong. Furthermore, existentialists deny that any characteristics of right and wrong can be found for all individuals—what is right for one person may not be right for another. Even before the existentialists, Friedrich Nietzsche taught that individuals must decide for themselves which situations are morally applicable (Banach, 1991).

Human Nature—Existence or Essence?

Existentialists argue that while each person can shape his or her nature, a pattern evolves only when people follow, and herein lies the idea of human nature. Sartre emphasized that what all existentialists have in common is that "existence precedes essence," or if you prefer, subjectivity is the starting point of life (Sartre, 1957). This focus on human nature underscores that (1) people have no predetermined essence that controls what they are, what they do, or what their values should be; (2) people are radically free to act independently of outside influences; and (3) people create their human natures and values through free choice. As such, the existentialists view human nature as diametrically opposed to the old belief that people were first given an essence that determines what their purposes in life are to be. This "cookie-cutter" theory of human nature assumes that an artisan (possibly God) created people with a determined plan for their happiness as long as they submitted to that plan. In contrast, the existentialists believe that people are first thrown into existence without a predetermined essence, and only later do they create their own natures through choices they make through their free will (Banach, 1991).

Sartre's Existentialist Ethics

Using the philosophy of consciousness and being, Sartre developed what later would be referred to as "existentialist ethics." While Sartre doubted whether there can be existentialist ethics, he raised three ethical issues: (1) *What choices should I make?* Sartre once told a story about a student whose brother had been killed during the French Army's effort to stop the German invasion in 1940. The student wanted to avenge his brother's death, but in so doing, he would abandon his mother, who was living alone and only for him. Sartre told his audience that the young man was torn between the morality of personal devotion and the morality of defending society as a whole. His reply to the young man's question was simply, "You're free, choose." (2) *What is the spirit of seriousness?* Sartre claimed that one of the worst violations of oneself is living in "bad faith." Bad faith (sometimes referred to as *inauthenticity*) is the lie people tell themselves when they feel they are not really free and conscious, that some things are unavoidable, and that they are not responsible for their occurrence. Sartre warned that living in bad faith leads to alienation from oneself, a sentiment that causes a void to occur. As a result, one fills that void by adopting the moral rules of the dominant social class—the bourgeoisie. (3) *Why should one have moral laws?* Sartre argued that they are necessary to exercise choice and to be independently responsible for these choices. Beyond these situations, Sartre added, no moral code can, or should, guide how people live (Lavine, 1984).

De Beauvoir's Influence on Feminism

De Beauvoir has been regarded as the champion of the feminist movement. Her book *The Second Sex* remains one of the best literary works on modern feminism. Although her interest in feminism was largely intellectual, she emerged in the late 1960s as a champion of women's rights. De Beauvoir's emphasis was mainly in the areas of abortion and sexual violence. She lived her life by the ideals of feminism as she articulated them in *The Second Sex*. She never married, although Sartre once proposed to her. She remained totally independent, exemplifying the main stances of feminism. She stood up in protest against those who discriminated against her or against the poor and the impoverished. While contemporary feminists attempt to develop new ideas, most such ideas are indeed extensions of de Beauvoir's views (Kopaczynski, 1994).

De Beauvoir on Motherhood

Though de Beauvoir devoted a large portion of *The Second Sex* to the topic of motherhood, she spent her whole life avoiding it. She felt that motherhood was a restriction that could limit her talent as a writer. As a feminist, she urged women to either avoid motherhood completely or choose it carefully. De Beauvoir stressed the importance of timing for motherhood, even going as far as repeatedly suggesting that to better one's plan in life, motherhood should be carried out by means of artificial insemination (Kopaczynski, 1996).

De Beauvoir's Trap of Human Knowledge

De Beauvoir argued that human nature and animal nature are fundamentally the same. Both must eat, drink, and die. She pointed out, however, that while these necessities do not separate human beings from animals, knowledge of them does. While human beings know that their death is imminent, their awareness of mortality is often difficult to acknowledge, and attempting to escape it is often self-deceptive. De Beauvoir calls this the "trap of human knowledge." This trap provides conditions that force people to be pessimistic. By the same token, rationality can also be a "trap," one that condemns the human mind to bleakness. The freedom to make choices is all that mankind desires. However, upon achieving this freedom, mankind must be committed to acting responsibly (Albert et al., 1988).

De Beauvoir's Moral Responsibility

While the existentialists argue that human choice makes people more responsible for their actions, critics argue that it can promote moral irresponsibility. They explain that if people are left alone and independent (as the existentialists argue), they can make awful mistakes simply by acting in whatever manner they choose. De Beauvoir argued against this view, stating that free people are more responsible people. She further explained that in God's absence the earth is their creation; therefore, they can appreciate the outcomes of their actions and take pride in their successes. People, de Beauvoir insisted, are solely responsible for their destiny, and if such destiny is pleasing, they should unapologetically take the credit (Albert et al., 1988).

Ethics of Social Justice (Rawls)

Introduction

Justice is a paramount moral doctrine second only to goodness. It is fundamental to the morality of individuals and public agencies, as well as to states. It was reported that the Greek term *dikaiosyne* (roughly translated as "justice") was the term most frequently used by Plato throughout his philosophy. The term implied a generic idea that could mean rightness, lawfulness, judiciousness, and at times, penalty (Angeles, 1981:63). Aristotle also viewed justice as the supreme virtue, but he proceeded to explain it in more definitive terms. He is well known for his three-pronged model: *distributive justice, rectificatory justice,* and *commutative justice.* In this sense, Aristotle saw justice as an exchange commodity: a system of social agreements that relate to each other according to a "going rate of exchange." This obviously left open the problem of how the rates are to be established and whether they conform to a fundamentally fair exchange rate between commodities.

In contemporary literature, justice has been defined in numerous ways: "fairness," "due process," "equal protection," "impartial treatment," and "assignment of merited rewards or punishments," among others. All these definitions share a particular emphasis on the morals of *fairness, equality,* and *impartiality* (Pollock-Byrne, 1989:38).

But justice can also be defined in terms of what it is not. It certainly differs from benevolence, generosity, gratitude, friendship, and compassion. It is not a virtue for which we should feel grateful, but rather *a virtue to which we have a right.* In that sense it should not be confused with the concept of "goodness," because some actions may be considered good but cannot, for that reason alone, be considered "just." For instance, giving to charity is considered good, but it is not necessarily just. A person not inclined to contribute cannot be accused of injustice. Furthermore, if one contributes $100 to the American Heart Association and $1 to the National Rifle Association, one could not be considered as acting unjustly, even though unequal contributions were made. (Pollock-Byrne, 1989:39).

Controversies about the meaning of justice have caused great social strife. Nevertheless, they have been historically related to the shifting tides of consensus and conflict that characterize social life. The interpretation of justice and injustice often shape and reshape the nature of society, at times peacefully, but often violently. Examples include the issues of slavery and prohibition in the past, and abortion and euthanasia at present. Such controversies keep resurfacing because theories of justice have both "cutting" and "dulling" edges. Based on assumptions society makes concerning the distribution of goods and services, justice theories establish a number of limitations on individual or group freedoms. But in enforcing these limitations, societies discover new areas of social inequality that must be rectified if those limitations are to work. Invariably, when a theory of justice suggests new changes, it exposes unraveled inequalities that have their own disruptive effects. These in turn require a new formulation of justice, and so on. Distributive justice and criminal justice are two of the best illustrations of the changing nature of justice; for instance, what rights should criminals have as opposed to victims? How much freedom should inmates enjoy while they are incarcerated versus how many services the state is morally committed to offer them? Concerns in these areas are primarily with what minimal standards of freedom or living conditions should be allowed even to the poorest and most deviant person, and how the state should react to criminal behavior in a civilized society.

Although there are numerous widely recognized theories of social justice, the scholarly attention given John Rawls's recent work, *A Theory of Justice* (1971), and the critical literature it has since stimulated are formidable, to say the least. His theory is considered one of the most prominent contributions to social justice in the twentieth century. It specifically addresses the way modern society distributes its goods and services. In the tradition of Hobbes, Locke, and Rousseau, Rawls is considered a modern social-contract theorist, and that alone requires examination of his theory in greater detail.

John Rawls: Ethics of Social Justice

Rawls (1921–2002) received his Ph.D. in philosophy from Princeton University in 1950. He continued his studies as a Fulbright scholar at Oxford and from 1962 held appointments as Professor of Philosophy at Cornell University, the Massachusetts Institute of Technology, and Harvard University, respectively. While at Cornell, he was coeditor of *Philosophical Review*. Prior to his death, Rawls was James Bryant Conant University Professor Emeritus at Harvard University.

Rawls' Ethical Theory

Rawls sets out to offer a theory of justice that is more refined than the theory of utilitarianism. He asserts that the primary subjects for studying justice are the basic structure of society, because they exert a profound influence on the life prospects of individuals. By basic structure, Rawls refers to an entire set of political, legal, economic, and social institutions (Cohen, 1986:27). When society is fortunate enough to have a fair and impartial social structure, justice will be done and citizens will receive their fair share of *primary goods and benefits*.

Primary goods and benefits are one's basic entitlement to rights and liberties, to powers and opportunities, as well as to incomes and wealth. The fair distribution of these primary goods and benefits is a legitimate concern for each and every rational person in society. Rawls terms these goods *primary* because they are preeminently desirable. The proper and smooth distribution of these goods and benefits makes a society moral, and their absence makes it immoral (Borchert & Stewart, 1986:302).

As an interactionist, Rawls is concerned with justice as it applies to situations of "social agreement." To understand the idea of social agreement, one must first understand how the concepts of society and justice are defined. Rawls defined *society* as "the participation of both individuals and government institutions (whether they are educational, medical, criminal justice, etc.) in social agreements." He defined *justice* as "the equal distribution of society's goods and services" among the individuals and groups that constitute society.

In a free society, social agreements are necessary to determine the criteria and procedures that should govern the distribution of goods and benefits. In a democratic society it is even more incumbent upon social agreements to be conducive to justice. But for that to occur the state must first establish a *condition of equality* without which individuals and groups would be unable to enter into legitimate and meaningful agreement.

Building upon the "presumption of equality," Rawls presents three requisite principles of justice that are essential for the smooth distribution of goods and benefits:

1. *The principle of the greatest equal liberty.* Each person is to have an equal right to the most extensive array of liberties available to anyone else. This principle is fairly simple for most Americans to understand, because it is directly based on the constitutional dicta stated in the Bill of Rights.

2. *The principle of the greatest equal opportunity.* Offices and positions are to be open to all, and all persons with similar abilities and skills are to have equal access to such offices and positions.

3. *The difference principle.* Social and economic institutions are to be arranged so as to offer maximum benefit to those who are worst off (Cohen, 1986;27). This principle, admittedly, constitutes one of the more controversial aspects of the theory. Rawls seems to suggest (and aptly so) that a just society is a civilized society; one that can, and should, tolerate differences in wealth, privileges, and other goods without acting unfairly to those concerned. If a society cannot bring itself to that level of justice, it must be lacking in civility.

Rawls's idea of social justice can be perceived as being closely related to the concept of social tolerance. It specifically points out two social obligations:

1. If inequalities should occur, they must be a product of individual inabilities rather than systemic discrimination; hence, all opportunities in society must be available to all.

2. If inequalities must occur, society should favor the least advantaged. Civilized societies are expected to exercise *noblesse oblige*: the capacity to be tolerant, compassionate, merciful, and even magnanimous in the treatment of their underprivileged populations (remember Maslow's profile of the ethical person).

Major Issues in Rawls's Ethical Philosophy

Justice and Fairness

Rawls considers justice to be the primary virtue of government institutions. Public agencies must therefore eliminate all "arbitrary distinctions" that may upset a balanced and impartial treatment of competing claims. Each claim to a "primary good or benefit" should be judged on its own merits.

Rawls emphasizes that for institutions to meet their obligation to justice, they must operate from the perspective of an ideal observer—one who would systematically ignore the personality of participants, their talents and inclinations, their social status, their political ideology, and all the incidental features of their lives. Rawls calls this perspective "acting under the veil of ignorance"; that is, operating as a free and rational person with all factors of inequality eliminated from one's thinking.

In distinguishing between the concepts of justice and fairness, Rawls points out that while they are two different concepts, they share a fundamental element—*reciprocity*. Justice represents reciprocity as applied to situations in which one has no option whether to engage in them or not—everyone must play; for example, the freedoms of expression, of religion, of assembly, or of travel. Fairness, on the other hand, represents reciprocity as applied to situations in which individuals have an option and may choose to decline the invitation; for example, the opportunity to work in a government agency, to attend a university, or to engage in a commercial enterprise.

Some theorists, however, contend that Rawls's principle of the "veil of ignorance" coincides with the utilitarian viewpoint expressed by Mill. The object of morality in both theories is promoting the greatest happiness for the greatest number of people. But Rawls refutes that view, offering slavery as an example. He asserts that a typical utilitarian would argue that the sacrifice of a few slaves for the benefit of the majority would be moral because it would contribute to the happiness of the greatest number. Under the "veil of ignorance," Rawls adds, no one would know who was to be a slave. Thus, with the possibility that "any one person" could be a slave, slavery should be considered unacceptable and immoral (Borchert & Stewart, 1986:311).

Society as a Network of Social Agreements

Rawls defines *society* as a network of social agreements or "practices" that are conducted among individuals or institutions (businesses, churches, government, and so on). This implies that participants must be allowed to enter into agreements as free and rational persons. This, of course, is a departure from Hobbes's view, which suggests that a social contract is not a matter of rational choice, but a condition imposed by a sovereign ruler, simply because it is society's only way out of the "unpleasant nature of life." In contrast, Rawls suggests that in order to rid society of its unpleasant conditions, fair agreements must be put in place as original positions. For that to be possible, two conditions must be met:

1. First, agreements should be reached by participants despite their relative class or place in society. Everyone must have the opportunity to enter into an agreement as a free and rational person. Only when free and equal persons recognize that the conditions of agreement have been met can social agreements be considered fair.

2. Second, everyone's commitment to the social agreement must increase as one's understanding of these commitments grows. For example, parties in a trial are expected to follow the rules of criminal procedure (an agreement), but as new evidence is revealed, the parties should continue to participate in an orderly manner despite the fact that the outcome of the case might be dramatically different from the original position.

The Concept of Social Justice

Having developed the concept of social agreement, Rawls defines *social justice* as the kind of justice that governs the ways and means in which society distributes goods and services. Central to this definition are such issues as (1) What minimum standards of living should even the poorest person in society be allowed? and (2) What right of access to society's institutions (educational, medical, governmental, and so on) should be guaranteed to everyone? (Borchert & Stewart, 1986:301).

Rawls responds by identifying two principles associated with social justice that if followed would allow for the equal distribution of society's goods and services:

1. Each person participating in a social agreement or affected by it has an equal right to the most extensive liberty compatible with a like liberty for all.

2. Inequality is permissible to the extent that it serves everyone's advantage. This can be justified only under conditions of equal opportunity (Albert et al., 1988:368).

The First Principle of Justice: The Greatest Equal Liberty

Rawls's first principle of justice states that "each and every person should have the right to liberties equal to those of everyone else having that same right." This principle simply affirms the need for equal liberty, which includes (1) freedom to participate in the political process;

(2) freedom of speech; (3) freedom of conscience (religion, privacy, and the like); (4) freedom of the person; (5) freedom from arbitrary arrest and seizure; and (6) freedom to hold personal property (Borchert & Stewart, 1986:303).

The Second Principle of Justice: The Equal Opportunity Principle

Rawls's second principle of justice states that all participants who interact with public institutions must be offered an equal opportunity to compete. Without an unobstructed opportunity to compete on equal footing, social justice cannot be administered. Therefore, for agencies to fail or refuse to hire an individual, to withhold information or privileges, to deprive or discriminate against a participant, would be acts of social injustice. As Rawls emphasizes, the rights of citizens for an equal opportunity are not subject to political bargaining or to the calculus of social interest.

The Third Principle of Justice: The Difference Principle

This is probably the most controversial aspect of Rawls's theory. While he stresses the extreme importance of equality in the practice of social justice, he also recognizes that social and economic inequalities (for example, wealth, income, power, and authority) can promote injustice.

Rawls accepts inequalities under one condition: if they are arranged in such a manner as to offer the greatest benefit to the least advantaged (Borchert & Stewart, 1986:303). In other words, inequality can be justified if it benefits the underprivileged. Suppose, for example, that a firm is required to raise its capital investment and produce more goods. By doing so, the firm would be able to employ a larger number of disadvantaged members of society. Furthermore, it would be able to pay higher wages to those who are already employed. So far, no inequality occurs. But suppose the firm's board of directors decides against taking the risk of expansion and committing more capital investment unless the owners of the firm have an opportunity to reap larger profits. In this case Rawls's difference principle would justify allowing special tax advantages on the capital investment and lowering the taxes on the profits of the expanding firm. Even though the owners of the firm would end up enjoying a larger share of profit, the inequality would be justified because it will improve the prospects of a much larger group of disadvantaged persons (Borchert & Stewart, 1986:304).

Rawls extends the difference principle to include competition for positions (offices) in society. He proposes that society must do more than just ensure the equality of opportunity for individuals with equal skills and abilities. He suggests that society must provide for the education of the unskilled, who otherwise would be deprived of the opportunity to compete with the skilled. For example, he advocates that a person should not be denied the opportunity to become a lawyer only because he or she cannot afford to attend law school. The just government must be obliged to assist. Rawls thus reiterates his central position: "Positions to which inequality is attached should be open to all" (Borchert & Stewart, 1986:305).

The Lexical Priority of Justice

Rawls completes his theory by introducing an inborn system of priorities reminiscent of Maslow's hierarchy of needs. He calls it the *lexical priority*. The system dictates that societies (and for that matter, governments and public agencies) cannot move from one level of justice to the next until demand for the previous level has been met. Accordingly, Rawls's first principle of justice must always have priority over his second, and his second principle must always have priority over the third. In adherence to the lexical priority, the "greatest equal liberty principle" must be considered Rawls's *summum bonum* of social justice; it cannot be subjected to any subsequent principle. It would be unjustifiable to restrict anyone's freedom of speech or of assembly as a trade-off for offering him or her greater access to education or health care. By the same token, it would be unjustifiable to undermine the "equal opportunity principle" even if it violates the "difference principle," which benefits the least well off in society. In order to achieve social justice, Rawls exhorts civilized societies to abide with the lexical priority and to adjust their laws and rules to conform accordingly.

Review Questions

1. Suppose a fellow class member asks you, "Why do we study these dead people with Greek names?" Based on your understanding of ethical theory, what is your response?

2. List five central elements of Stoicism. Who is its leading philosopher? What are some implications of this philosophy on the performance of police officers in a high-crime area?

3. Define *hedonism*. Who are its primary spokespersons? What are the implications of this principle on the subculture of male correctional officers who serve in a women's prison?

4. Plato theorized that the *summum bonum* of all values is the realization of justice. How can this theory influence the decision of a detective who is required by her supervisor to clear a number of burglaries based on an admission by a suspect whom the detective knows did not commit all of them?

5. List the characteristic ethics of the religious school. How can a "born again" Christian criminal justice practitioner maintain his values when working with a group of partners who commit corrupt acts? Should he report his observations to a supervisor or keep quiet? Why?

6. Explain the Hobbesian principle of "might makes right." Discuss some of the unethical implications of this principle in the worlds of police and corrections.

7. Define *utilitarianism* and name its two leading spokespersons. If all criminal justice practitioners in the country allowed utilitarianism to guide their thinking, what would the implications be for the administration of criminal justice?

8. Explain Kant's principle of the categorical imperative. How can a criminal justice professional reconcile conflicting duties; for example, the duty of an African American correctional officer to treat everyone equally and the specific needs of an African American inmate in the cell block to which she is assigned?

9. Rawls theorized that the difference principle should be applied to those who are the least advantaged. How does the ethics of affirmative action fit into this theory? How can a criminal justice professional justify being passed over for promotion in favor of a less qualified minority person in the name of social justice?

10. The term *summum bonum* has been used frequently in this chapter. Define the term. List the *summum bonum* of each of the schools of thought discussed in this chapter.

References

Albert, E. M., Denise, T. C., & Peterfreund, S. P. (1988). *Great Traditions in Ethics* (6th ed.). Belmont, CA: Wadsworth Publishing.

Angeles, P. A. (1981). *Dictionary of Philosophy.* New York: Barnes and Noble Books.

Banach, D. (1991). *Ethics of Absolute Freedom*. Saint Anselm College. *www.anselm. edu/homepage/dbanach/sartrelecture.htm*.

Borchert, D. M., & Stewart, D. (1986). *Exploring Ethics*. New York: Macmillan Publishing.

Camus, A. (1955). *The Myth of Sisyphus and Other Essays*. New York: Vintage Publishing.

Cohen, R.L (Ed.) (1986). *Justice: Views from the Social Sciences*. New York: Plenum Press.

Ferm, V. (Ed.) (1956). *Encyclopedia of Morals*. New York: Philosophical Library.

Flew, A. (1979). *A Dictionary of Philosophy*. New York: St. Martin's Press.

Fromm, F. (1941). *Escape from Freedom*. New York: Farrar & Rinehart.

Kopaczynski, G. (1994). Abortion's Mother: Early Works of Simone de Beauvoir. *Faith & Reason*, (Winter). www.ewtn.com/library/PROLIFE/FR94401.TXT.

Lavine, T. Z. (1984). *From Socrates to Sartre: The Philosophic Quest*. Toronto: Bantam Books.

Oliver, M. (1999). *History of Philosophy*. New York: Barnes and Noble Books.

Pollock-Byrne, J. M. (1989). *Ethics in Crime and Justice: Dilemmas and Decisions*. Pacific Grove, CA: Brooks/Cole Publishing.

Porter, B. F. (1980). *The Good Life: Alternatives in Ethics*. New York: Macmillan Publishing.

Rawls, J. (1971). *A Theory of Justice*. Cambridge, MA: Harvard University Press.

Sahakian, W. S. (1974). *Ethics: An Introduction to Theories and Problems*. New York: Barnes and Noble Books.

Sartre, J. P. (1957). *Existentialism and Human Emotions*. New York: Philosophical Library.

Schopenhauer, A. (1909). *The World as Will and Idea*. London: Kegan Paul, Trench, and Trubner.

5
The Ambivalent Reality
Major Unethical Themes in Criminal Justice Management

To turn a young man into a piece of clockwork should not surely be seen as a triumph for any government save one proud of its oppressiveness.
Anthony Burgess

The so-called new morality is too often the old immorality condoned.
Hartley Shawcross

Very great bravery was required to say no in the midst of that roaring chorus of approval.

Aleksandr Solzhenitsyn

Since we cannot move Leningrad, we must move the frontier.
Josef Stalin

What You Will Learn from This Chapter

To understand the role of ethics in criminal justice, you will learn the characteristics of unethical management in terms of how it can negatively affect the practices of criminal justice, causing the harvest of shame.

You will learn the truth about professionalism, integrated thinking, and moral agility. You will also learn the extent of corruption in criminal justice agencies and its "root sins."

Key Terms and Definitions

Principle-Based Management is a philosophy of management that is characterized by ethical principles, enlightened reasoning, moral responsibility, and good faith.

Integrated Thinking is a broader talent for wisdom. It is based on the use of reasoning and deductive logic independent of any bias or interest.

Moral Agility is the ability to distinguish between the fine shades of moral choice.

Overview

There is no field in which ethical dilemmas are more prominently noted, perhaps, than criminal justice. Despite the multitude of departmental rules, training manuals, management seminars, and disciplinary actions, making moral choices continues to bewilder practitioners at all levels. It is perplexing, nevertheless, that when ethical education is proposed as a possible remedy, it is usually shunned with condescendence. While most criminal justice practitioners applaud maturity, morality, and decency as worthy human values, when ethical principles are proposed as work strategies, they are usually disregarded as naive and unworkable. Despite the fact that we formulate codes of ethics for police and correctional officers, lawyers, and judges, expecting workers to behave ethically at the workplace and holding them accountable to ethical standards somehow seems alien to workplace dynamics.

Nowhere has this ambivalence been so manifest as at an in-service training course I recently taught at a leading police academy. The hallways of the academy had high cathedral ceilings and were magnificently decorated. On the walls were exotic plaques donated by graduating classes. The majority of these plaques had biblical inscriptions with verses such as "Let Not Mercy and Truth Forsake You," "Wisdom Is Better than Weapons of War," "Beareth Not the Sword in Vain," and "Let Integrity Preserve Me."

In discussing the subject of ethics in the classroom, however, most of the officers were "unmoved," to say the least. In a Nietzschean manner, they seemed infatuated with power and the will to overpower. They described policing as a field of action that must be matched with a mind and heart of steel. They exclaimed, "We've got a war going on out there, Professor ... and you want us to think ethics!" In justifying their exclamation, vitriolic references were made to the "scum of the earth out there" who are victimizing society, and to the number of police officers killed in the line of duty. Most gratifying, however, was watching the demeanor of the veteran officers who slouched on the back benches. They had a faint smile on their faces and acted stoically, even "Epictetusly." By way of symbolic interaction, they made it clear that they disagreed with those "pugnacious neophytes up front" who "knew not what they were saying!"

As an "ethical reasoner," what is your response to the neophytes' claims? First, one should sincerely empathize with the officers' plight, because death and danger in any occupation are serious concerns that people, *ethical or not*, cannot ignore. Second, one should examine the truth of such claims to danger, because studies show that policing may not be the most dangerous occupation, as many officers want to believe. French (1975), Hageman (1978), and Terry (1985) confirm that it is more dangerous to work in construction, agriculture, or mining than in policing. As to the issue of officers who are killed in the line of duty, their number has been steadily decreasing (U.S. Department of Justice, 1987). Third, one should question the utility of the so-called steel mentality theory: "What has this mentality accomplished so far, and what good has it produced?" While crime rates have been declining recently for reasons *unrelated* to police preparedness, data show that between 1982 and 1987 the rate of violent crime per 100,000 population increased by approximately 2.8 percent, while the number of police officers killed in the line of duty decreased by 29.8 percent (U.S. Department of Justice, 1987). The logical conclusion must be that "The steel mentality did not work." Furthermore, the steel mentality may be especially inconsistent with community-oriented policing, the philosophy based on forging partnership with the community at every level.

The following line of questioning, though fictitious, portrays a typical case of prejudging the role of ethics in criminal justice, whereby it is unfairly equated with naiveté, weakness, powerlessness, and defeatism.

Q. Have you exhausted all methods of dealing with criminal behavior?
A. *No, how could we have?*

Q. Have you tried the ethical approach, community-oriented policing, community supervision of inmates, perhaps?

A. *No, we didn't.*

Q. On what grounds can you reject these if you haven't tried them?

A. *Because they don't work; they are "old wine in new bottles."*

Q. How do you know they won't work if you put your minds to it?

A. *There you go again, Professor!*

The truth nevertheless remains: When ethical principles are faithfully applied, they can yield an awesome power. Ethical practitioners can be firm, practical, and realistic. Ethical theory, it should be emphasized, does not object to the use of force, *including deadly force*, as long as it is morally justifiable "to bring about justice, stop cruelty and exploitation, and punish evil" (remember Maslow's profile of the Ethical Person). In the conduct of criminal justice, professional workers must realize that it is not the "principle of power" that matters, but the "power of principle."

The Imperative of Ethics in Criminal Justice

To speak of criminal justice while ignoring "justice" is a contradiction. The analogies of heaven and hell, life and death, light and darkness—in which one cannot exist without the other—highlight this contradiction. The tendency of any society to commit crime cannot be separated from its concern to establish justice, because in the broader sense all crimes are violations of an "assumed order of justice." Criminal acts are distinguishable from noncriminal acts only when they are seen "under the light of justice." Murder, rape, robbery, and theft are considered criminal because they are "unjustifiable acts," whereas saving lives and assisting the needy are "justifiable acts." Hypothetically, therefore, if it can be shown that everyone is acting "justly," it should be true that no one is acting "criminally."

In support of this logic, criminological literature indicates a positive relationship between the propensity to commit crime and social perceptions of justice and injustice. Indeed, a substantial amount of crime is directly or indirectly related to the presence (or the perception) of social, political, or economic injustices (Quinney, 1977; Turk, 1982; Vold & Bernard, 1986; Williams & McShane, 1988). Conflict and radical theories of criminology are cases in point. They identify strain in society as a legitimate cause of crime. When poor and disenfranchised people seek the goals of society but cannot meet them by legitimate means, they turn to illegitimate means (Felson, 1994:15). By the same token, nations throughout history revolted against unjust governments and the imposition of unjust laws. The history of the United States presents perhaps the best proof.

Furthermore, because justice is so integral to ethical theory (indeed, justice is more closely aligned with ethics than with law), the primary concern of criminal justice practitioners must be a de facto concern for ethics. Lawmakers should comply with ethical standards in the making of laws, and judges, prosecutors, and peace officers should comply with ethical principles in their enforcement procedures. In carrying out their responsibilities, criminal justice practitioners should always keep the "moral brakes" on their personal beliefs, sentiments, and biases. Their mental and emotional state should be directed to preserving the public good and attending to the well-being of citizens. To ensure responsible behavior, ethical practitioners must operate within the ethical parameters previously discussed in Chapters 1 and 2: (1) distinguishing between intrinsic and non-intrinsic values; (2) following the fundamental hierarchy of professionalism, Americanism, and humanism; and (3) striving for the *summum bonum*, the highest good.

In urging the ethical imperative, Lozoff and Braswell (1989) captured the attention of the criminal justice community by exposing one of its most misguided beliefs—violence. In *Inner Corrections* the authors stated,

> The criminal justice system in our country is founded on violence. It is a system which assumes that violence can be overcome by violence, evil by evil. Criminal justice at home and warfare abroad are of the same principle of violence. The principle sadly dominates much of our criminology. Fortunately, more and more criminologists and practitioners in criminal justice are realizing that this principle is fundamentally incompatible with a faith that seeks to express itself in compassion, forgiveness, and love.

In emphasizing the ethical imperative in policing, A.C. Germann (1976) stated,

> We seem to be prisoners of our clichés and the thinking of 25 and 50 years ago. Our police and their predecessors seem wholly unable to emancipate themselves from thinking about weaponry and repression as the key social control solution and often act as "gunmen" bearing a "social worker" designation ... we have been, are, and will be, almost totally ineffective in controlling anti-social behavior by our current police interventions, no matter how many times we double our forces, no matter how many computers we purchase, no matter how contrived our public relations. Yet, we go on, replicating the useless efforts of the past ... it is no wonder that sensitive, intelligent, motivated, liberated, and humanistic people are discouraged from affiliating with police.

But not having adequately learned our lessons during the 1980s, Goldstein echoed Germann's theme with his focus on problem-oriented policing in the 1990s. In *Problem-Oriented Policing* (1990) he writes,

The dominant perspective of policing is heavily influenced by the primary method of control associated with the work—the authority to enforce the criminal law ... that police officers are commonly referred to as law enforcement officers [is] a misnomer that uses only one of the methods they employ in their work ... efforts to improve policing should extend to and focus on the end product of policing—on the effectiveness and fairness of the police ... much more is required than simply law enforcement.

In underscoring the ethical imperative in probation and parole, John Whitehead (1989) states,

It is assumed that there are certain values to guide the ethical choices, such as truth, honesty, fairness, hard work, and consideration for others ... it does not matter whether these values are absolutes or simply mutually agreed upon conventions ... the effectiveness of probation or parole can be considered an ethical question.

To put it succinctly, criminal justice practitioners must be intellectually alert and morally judicious so as to be able to distinguish between the *ends of justice* and the *means of justice*. The former pertain to one's moral responsibility to preserving civic righteousness, and the latter to one's concern for shunning the seduction of pragmatism and popular justice. Given the cultural, social, and constitutional values we cherish in the United States, sustaining the ends of justice is a "categorical imperative." It cannot be sacrificed for the "hypothetical imperative" of efficiency.

A House on the Sand: The Spoils of Management

Unenlightened management philosophies continue to stifle criminal justice agencies. Symptomatic of these philosophies is how dispassionately criminal justice managers view their role as "peace officers" and "renderers of justice." Field observations indicate feelings of cynicism, indifference, and a tendency to pursue their own agendas (Crank et al., 1986). Such feelings are usually rationalized by the following precepts: (1) justice is in the eye of the beholder; (2) the ethical doctrines embodied in natural law, constitutional law, and religious testaments are of little importance—power and control of workers come first; (3) codes of ethics have no value beyond being instruments of social and political propaganda; (4) the oath of office—presumably sacred, because it solicits God's help—is an insignificant formality; (5) practitioners are rewarded primarily for their loyalty to superiors. Such observations, if true, are troubling. They are inconsistent (if not outright contradictory) with the basic tenets of truth, professionalism, and moral responsibility.

Consistent with these philosophies, unenlightened managers view their task as simply one of controlling employees and keeping them on "a tight leash." Implicit in this task are several managerial fallacies:

1. The view of "management is management is management." Management, therefore, is not in the business of searching for truths or pursuing ethical outcomes.

2. The belief that power is the "super ethic"—workers are to do or die, and management is to reason why.

3. The perception of management as simply pigeonholing workers in little "boxes" and subjecting them to strict supervisory measures.

4. The view that allowing workers to make ethical choices is an indication of management "wimpiness," and perhaps foolishness.

While most criminal justice practitioners understand and comply with ethical principles (with varying degrees of conviction, of course), many do not. Protected by a bureaucratic environment that often promotes the "equality of ignorance," uninformed practitioners often end up being unable to see, or are disinterested in discovering, the truths of good management.

While the relationship between unethical management at the workplace and workers' performance in the field has not been adequately researched, studies indicate that those who are treated "shabbily" at the workplace tend to treat their clients in a shabby manner. For instance, Shernock (1990) suggests that police officers who are frustrated and resentful about the lack of respect shown to them by supervisors compensate by acting overly authoritarian on the street, where it is safer to express themselves without the fear of being accused of insubordination. Carter (1986) points out that as job satisfaction among police officers decreases, their tendency to discriminate on the basis of race or ethnicity increases. Price (1983) reports that when correctional officers are dissatisfied with their work environment, they develop serious conflicts in moral judgment. And Whitehead (1989) reveals that when the organizational structure of probation departments is inadequate, probation officers suffer from accelerated burnout.

The Cunning of Unethical Management

Although this book is not intended to be a management book, the dangers of unethical management cannot be overstated. Although students are taught to think that management can "fix" all problems, they are usually unaware that uncivilized management can also create enormous problems.

While the fundamental purpose of management is to stimulate *workers' productivity*, this objective seems to be perverted in many criminal justice agencies by the managers' ignorance, arrogance, or both. Authoritarian managers, especially by the absolutist followers of the Weberian and Taylorist schools, rule by fear and intimidation rather than reasoning and consensus. As a result, productivity is perceived as a "flurry of activities" to be performed by an army of operatives in an organizational trance; pseudo-efficiency is pursued by displaying showy progress charts and neat statistical forms; discipline is maintained by a *tyranny of proceduralism* that ensures unquestionable loyalty to the agency's elite; and regulations, for all practical purposes, are used to silence the nonconformists who are unscrupulous enough to publicly deviate from the agency line.

More importantly, uncivilized managers come to view authority as an opportunity to reward their friends and punish their enemies, leadership as giving orders rather than guiding and coaching workers, and loyalty to themselves as more important than loyalty to the agency mission. Such managers tend to treat supervision as a method of catching subordinates doing something "wrong" instead of catching them doing something "right," and view communication as a method of exchanging favors within a small circle of "good old boys." Such practices, which usually benefit a small number of "cronies," have been detrimental to agency performance—they blunt productivity by demoralizing the larger group of unsuspecting professionals.

The Harvest of Shame

The product of uncivilized management is a *harvest of shame*—a disjointed organization that stifles creativity, destroys morale, penalizes initiative, encourages waste, and rewards snitching. The inevitable consequence of such a harvest is a dynasty of immature, inward-bent, morally disenfranchised, and corruption-prone workers. The chief loser in this case is, of course, the unsuspecting society that ends up holding a "bag of chaff" instead of the "bag of wheat" on which it counted and for which it paid dearly.

This harvest of shame has been detrimental to national productivity. The integrity of government has recently been brought into question over a number of serious affairs (for example, rape and sexual harassment at the U.S. Air Force Academy, the army's Aberdeen Proving Ground, the navy's Tailhook case, the FBI's Ruby Ridge case, and the Atlanta Centennial Olympic Park bombing case). As a result, the increasing number of whistle-blowers (employees who publicly disclose unethical or illegal practices) has given impetus to the silent practice of "ethical resistance." Since the 1960s, there has been a continuous stream of whistle-blowers who, not acting out of self-interest, aggressively expose policies that endanger or defraud the public. Not surprisingly, the most crucial factor behind that movement has been widespread disillusionment with the dishonesty of government that occurred during the Vietnam War and continues to increase today (Glazer & Glazer, 1989:6). This evidentially confirms the truth of the statement that "governments self-destruct when they violate their own laws."

On the other hand, while it is true that unethical management practices have been challenged in recent years by innovative theories such as "Total Quality Management," "Quality Circles," "Theory Z Management," and "Problem-Oriented Policing," the old practices ostensibly refuse to be dislodged, primarily because of unprincipled managers. Like those described in Plato's allegory of the cave, they seem to operate in a closed habitat rather than in the sunshine of principle-based management. This tendency seems to provide them with a warm (albeit foul) atmosphere of security and a false sense of invincibility. In this management style they clandestinely push "hidden agendas," use favoritism to divide workers, and manipulate the rules to perpetuate their domination. To give the appearance of "professionalism," however, they—like the Sophists of Greece—speak of leadership, duty, and courage either as a matter of lip service or administrative gimmickry.

Principle-Based Management

Ironically, the most notable weakness in criminal justice management today is its most rudimentary: failure to understand the true role of management. It is an unsettling yet common commentary on the state of criminal justice today that "when institutions succeed, it is attributed to good management, but when they fail, it is attributed to bad workers." This commentary underscores incoherent thinking, to say the least. Not only is it illogical, it also perpetuates egoism, elitism, and scapegoating in the workplace. Managers who subscribe to this view must be oblivious to the contradictory nature of such a statement. Consider the following reasoning:

1. Workers are the creation of management, not the other way around. Therefore, talk of "bad workers" may reveal a management system that is uncaring, insensitive, or unethical.

2. Institutional policies are only as good as the ethics and integrity of the managers who make them. It would be contradictory to demand ethics and integrity from workers without offering them honesty and fairness in return.

3. Workers' performance is a function of the institutional culture tolerated by management. Workers act professionally in support of fair management and unprofessionally when the institutional culture is deficient or when managers themselves violate it.

4. Institutional culture can be changed by management. However, doing so takes a caring, sensitive, and ethical management that is committed to changing the prevailing culture.

5. A caring, sensitive, and ethical management can "move mountains," so to speak. It can increase productivity, improve workers' performance, prevent workplace misbehavior, and rehabilitate/ terminate aberrant employees.

6. Without adopting a principle-based management system to be conducted in good faith, institutions will continue to act the way they always have.

7. The first step toward incorporating a principle-based management system is to publicly commit the agency to the practices of ethics and integrity and always act in accordance with "moral principles." Nothing else has worked before or can work in the future.

The Challenge of Principle-Based Management

At this point one may ponder what specifically ethics-based management is and how it is different from other management styles. *Principle-based management* is a "philosophy of management that is characterized by vision, enlightened reasoning, moral responsibility, and good faith." Principle-based managers are agents of reason who are driven by principle rather than whim, by democratic principles rather than egoism, by substance rather than appearance, and by collaboration rather than hostility.

The objective of principle-based management is to bring the workers together in dynamic organizations to make things happen—all consistent with ethical principles and good faith. In their pursuit of solutions, principle-based managers harness their workers' energy, mix values with technology, encourage multilateral relationships, negotiate with colleagues, and adjust their strategies to vaguely defined environments. Principle-based management operates like a chemical reaction in a fluid solution: cheerful, collegial, consensual, and consultative. Reminiscent of the old Stoics, principle-driven managers are motivated by a sense of welfare, a sense of equity, a concern for achievement, and a strong commitment to virtue. As such, principle-based managers are diametrically opposed to practices of dishonesty, deception, manipulation, secrecy, or bad faith.

The basic tools of principle-based management are knowledge, reasoning, decency, and good faith. When these tools are used properly, any need for exploitation or manipulation becomes unnatural. At its core, principle-based management promotes the capacity for goodness among workers and reduces the need for trickery, secrecy, double-talk, or hidden agendas. If these basic assumptions are invalid, then either our fundamental doctrines of civility are flawed or our claim to professionalism is misleading.

In civilized societies, principle-based management is essential (Cleveland, 1985:xvi; Herzberg, 1976:9–11; Williams, 1980:xi) and principle-based managers are called "Rushmoreans" (after Mount Rushmore) (O'Toole, 1995). Rushmorean managers are *transcendent* individuals who (1) respect all people, (2) do not inflict unjustified pain, and (3) are faithful servants of the public interest (O'Toole, 1995:44).

Yet exercising principle-based management is by no means easy. It requires keen understanding, moral stamina, and a considerable amount of hard work. It is no surprise that many managers are intimidated by its practice. There are several reasons principle-based management can be intimidating:

1. Its appeal to the principles of honesty, fairness, and obligation gives it the impression of being a tool of the weak. Managers naturally want to appear all-powerful, a state more easily sustained by imposing penalties rather than by worrying about ethical principles.

2. Its reliance on workers' performance, rather than on managers' crude prowess, gives it an image inconsistent with the "can-do" posture that most managers would like to project.

3. Its inability to cure bureaucratic ills within a short period gives it the appearance of being ineffectual. This inability is clearly not a function of principle-based management, but of change in general.

4. The overriding fear of legal liability that constantly threatens public employees deters managers from making choices unless they are legally based and politically correct.

While these reasons are not entirely without foundation, when considered under the "canopy of wisdom," they reflect more dismally on the moral fortitude of managers than on the merits of principle-based management. The fact remains, however, that principle-based management is ineffectual mainly in third-world societies where concern for liberty, equality, and human dignity is lacking, and that the term "traditional management" has been associated with abusive bureaucracies in which ethical principles have no significance. On the other hand, it does not seem coincidental that only until the United States demanded that the world community honor human rights has the whipping of blacks in South Africa, the detainment of "refusnicks" in the former communist countries, and the mysterious disappearance of undesirable persons in Latin American countries, all but ceased.

Rethinking Professionalism

Professionalism is hardly a new concept. Perhaps because of the exalted image of the Praetorian Guards of Rome, it has been traditionally characterized by unquestionable devotion to duty regardless of the hardships one may confront. Throughout history, professional groups have been exalted in one form or another. Socrates described them as "men of wisdom"; Plato, as "philosopher kings"; John Mill, as "hedonistic experts"; Thomas Carlyle, as "great men"; and Friedrich Hegel, as "leaders of Zeitgeist." Regardless of label, however, these groups have had one feature in common: They were faithful custodians of the public trust—the unsleeping sentinels who guard the outposts of society.

Given today's political expectations, however, this exalted view of professionalism may be more nostalgic than realistic, and the achievement of true professionalism may be far too elusive. There are several reasons for this contention:

> First, *the difficulty of distinguishing a profession from an occupation or a guild on the basis of their declared goals*. For example, the medical profession has been hailed as the epitome of professionalism, yet many doctors continue to overcharge patients, operate on patients unnecessarily, and commit other professional infractions. By the same token, the legal profession, despite its most worthy goals, represented the largest group of defendants indicted in the Watergate scandal, and many lawyers are routinely disbarred every year for unethical practices. On the other hand, while soldiers and athletes often are referred to as professionals, police and correctional officers are not. Even in the world of crime, serial murderers and rapists who elude apprehension are considered professional, and a crime executed meticulously is labeled a "professional" hit.

> Second, *the negative influence of traditional management that ignores the ethical dimension of work*. In this management style, professionalism has been associated with the qualities of unquestionable obedience and catering to the whims of superiors. Therefore, a "company man" who knowingly pushes the sale of a defective item is considered a business professional. By the same token, leaders of organizations such as the SS troops of Hitler, the KGB, and crime syndicates are considered professional. Obviously, this characterization is clearly illogical, because the infamous truths of these organizations are overlooked. No mention is made of their true purpose (moral or immoral), their real direction (conducive to life or to death), or their real motives (serving humanity or serving an oppressive regime).

> Third, *the inaccurate perception of professionalism as a characteristic of organizations, not of individuals*. According to this view, all those who work for the FBI, the Marine Corps, the Army Corps of

Engineers, and for that matter, anyone who is associated with Harvard, IBM, or American Airlines must, by virtue of such association, be a professional. This reasoning is obviously flawed for three reasons:

1. Professionalism is not a characterization of things (for example, large offices, advanced technology, impressive uniforms, or elegantly produced manuals); it is a quality of human beings—their enlightenment, reasoning, and ethical principles.
2. Professional agencies cannot exist, let alone function, without professionals. Only through the devotion of ethical personnel can the integrity of the agency be achieved.
3. Professionalism is not a constant state; it can flourish or suffer depending on the leaders' commitment to ethical performance. An act of misfeasance, for instance, by a police chief or a chief probation officer can undermine the professional integrity of an agency for years to come (remember the impact of Richard Nixon on the White House in 1973 and Edwin Meese on the Justice Department in 1987).

The Truth of Professionalism: Looking Good versus Being Good

James Madison stated in the 51st *Federalist Paper* that "if men were angels no government would be necessary, [and] if angels were to govern men neither external nor internal controls on government would be necessary" (Hamilton et al., 1961:322). But because man is neither an angel nor an ape, civility must be nurtured through an effort of moral building. Short of divine intervention, the responsibility for such an effort must fall upon a group of *professionals* who, on behalf of society, are committed to protecting social order, justice, and the "good life."

But what is the truth of professionalism, and what does it entail? One way to answer these questions is by examining how the term is defined by criminal justice practitioners, in particular, police officers, who seem to set the tone for all others. When police officers define professionalism, they invariably use such terms as *demeanor, authority, maintaining the edge*, and *loyalty to partners*. While these terms are admirable, they define only the appearance of professionalism—the "looking good" version. They fail to define the essence of professionalism. In a Platonic sense they describe only the shadow of what ought to be, but may not be there.

True professionalism, on the other hand, is "being good"—having a passion for humanity, legality, and compassion; telling the truth (unless there is a compelling reason for concealment); fulfilling the promises that one makes; and taking every obligation seriously. It is one's devotion to reasoning, service, duty, and goodwill—in short, to ethical principles. In the objective reality of public service, the difference between the "looking good" version and the "being good" version of professionalism can be enormous.

In the practice of criminal justice, the "looking good" version of professionalism is dangerous and can lead to widespread corruption. To better appreciate this indictment, one should ask, what good is criminal justice if the practitioners can pretend to be what they are not? ... if they can claim to "serve humanity," yet lie, cheat, and steal? ... if they can appear to "act legally," yet arrest suspects without probable cause, search homes without warrants, and falsify evidence?

In ethical management the answer to these questions should be an unequivocal *none*. "Looking good" professionalism is cosmetic and cannot replace "being good" professionalism. If mere appearance can substitute for the truth, then one must conclude that the most professional police in the twentieth century must have been the SS troops of Nazi Germany; they were all Aryans, tall, good-looking, well-disciplined, and well-educated, yet they were merchants of death. They most likely knew what they were doing, yet they acted differently as a matter of loyalty to "bosses" rather than to principles. As a result, they failed to distinguish between truth and untruth, innocence and guilt, life and death. While they certainly were very efficient in whatever they did, they clearly dishonored themselves for generations to come.

The Lungs of Professionalism: Integrated Thinking and Moral Agility

To achieve "being good" professionalism, one must be endowed with two moral virtues: *integrated thinking* and *moral agility*. Like the human lungs, they must work in unison, if at all. Without synchrony, each component will undermine the other.

Integrated thinking is a talent for wisdom. It is based on the use of reasoning and deductive logic, independently from any particular bias or interest. It is a higher-level thinking that transcends the immediate question at hand. Its purpose is to enhance the quality of life, explore all possible solutions, and adhere to the commonwealth of ethical principles (Rush, 1991:252). Cleveland describes integrated thinkers as persons who—in the middle of anarchy—have the wisdom to point out directions, negotiate priorities, allocate scarcities, settle arguments, and calm tempers (Cleveland, 1985:xv). As such, they have the capacity to think globally yet act locally.

Moral agility, on the other hand, is a talent for distinguishing between the fine shades of moral choice. It is based on intelligently capturing the principle (or principles) that bears on the matter and figuring out its justification under the circumstances. In a sense, moral agility is the art of *mastering the formula* $E = PJ^2$ introduced in Chapter 1.

Persons who are endowed with moral agility are identified with the qualities of intelligence, maturity, flexibility, and the ability to make analytical distinctions when distinctions are hardly visible. Such people possess moral agility and are able to free themselves from the sentiments of emotionalism, amateurism, authoritarianism, egoism, self-interest, or whim (Souryal, 1977:397). To them, the qualities of arrogance, selfishness, unfairness, or hypocrisy are simply unacceptable.

Given the concepts of integrated thinking and moral agility, criminal justice professionals are expected to always act wisely. They naturally recognize the virtues of liberty and justice; honesty and fidelity; decency and social righteousness. Furthermore, because ethics in public service cannot be forced upon workers, criminal justice professionals are internally driven. They are able to distinguish between the "legal and the right," the "is and the ought," the "convenient and the obligatory," and have the courage to stand their ground when they are required to make difficult decisions.

Finally, in the management of criminal justice, one fact is undeniable: Without "being good" professionals who can master the arts of integrated thinking and moral agility, the goals of liberty and justice will not be achieved, nor will the purpose of criminal justice institutions make any sense.

Institutional Integrity

As alluded to earlier, institutions can violate professional conduct in the same way individual practitioners can. Institutions have a tendency to act unprofessionally when they are threatened, need to appease their political overseers, or are forced to release information that can tarnish their reputation. In these cases, the institution's decision invariably reflects its prevailing culture. If the prevailing culture is cynical about morality and about the moral seriousness of its leaders, the agency would be more willing to act unprofessionally, violating its own rules.

Unprofessional conduct by a criminal justice agency occurs when an orchestrated scheme is made to alter the truth concerning an event or situation that would otherwise find the agency culpable or tarnish its image. Such conduct occurs, for example, when the leadership of a prison unit, a probation agency, or a sheriff's department publicly denies that an act of brutality or financial mismanagement has taken place (when in reality it has) and, toward reinforcing this denial, uses false evidence, propaganda, or disingenuous explanations. Examples of such conduct, in recent history, include the cases of My Lai, Watergate, the Iran-Contra affair, Ruby Ridge, the Rodney King incident, and the Centennial Olympic Park bombing in Atlanta. In each of these cases, legal and ethical principles were trampled upon and a "looking good" facade was presented to cover up the truth.

To be able to gauge the institutional integrity of public agencies, the following matrix may be useful. While it cannot explain all institutional misconduct, it provides an exposition of the propensity of public agencies to engage in such behaviors. Figure 5.1 explains the matrix of institutional integrity.

As Figure 5.1 shows, the institutional integrity of public agencies

Figure 5.1
Professionalism of Agencies

	Knowledge of Principles	Ignorance of Principles
Acting in Good Faith	Professional	Naive
Acting in Bad Faith	Corrupt	Unprofessional

may be a function of two factors: (1) the agency's cultural knowledge (or ignorance) of ethical principles, and (2) the agency's propensity to act in good faith (or in bad faith).

The agency's *knowledge of ethical principles* is the cumulative talent the workers gain from their official experience. This knowledge is also known as "cultural literacy" (Siegel & Zalman, 1991; Souryal, 1993; Thornberry, 1990). It is usually developed through four formal means:

1. The level of education initially required for appointment. For instance, federal police agencies and probation agencies require a college degree, while local police agencies may require 60 college credit hours or less.

2. The amount of in-service training the agency requires. Most criminal justice practitioners (including judges and prosecutors) are now required to attend between 20 and 40 hours of professional training every year.

3. Agency policies regarding ethical behavior and the disciplining of workers who act unethically.

4. The presence of a union or a professional association that can monitor agency matters and keep the workers abreast of how the agency handles its own affairs.

The agency's *propensity to act in good faith*, on the other hand, depends on informal and rather intangible factors. These include (1) the agency's tradition of ethical performance—its history of honest behavior rather than reliance on "egoism," "looking good," or "institutional deception"; (2) the agency's managerial experience in terms of team working, credit sharing, and dedication to the public interest; (3) the ethical stamina of agency leaders; their willingness to make hard decisions, clean up messy situations, bring about good workmanship, and help the self-actualization of workers.

Given these factors, four categories of public agencies emerge: (1) agencies that know the ethical principles and, at the same time, act in good faith are *professional*; they fulfill the demands for both knowledge and good faith; (2) agencies that do not know the ethical principles yet act in good faith are *naive*; despite their ignorance of what they ought to do, they still offer good faith service; (3) agencies that know the ethical principles yet act in bad faith are *corrupt*; while they know what they ought to do, they override their goodness obligation by betraying their trusting constituents (the case of the religious groups that allow priests to sexually violate children is a good example); and (4) agencies that neither know the ethical principles nor act in good faith are *unprofessional*; they basically exist in Plato's cave of ignorance.

Rushmorean Criminal Justice Agencies

In *Leading Change* (1995) James O'Toole coined the term *Rushmorean* to describe distinguished corporate leaders in the United States, those who are endowed with courage, authenticity, integrity, vision, passion, conviction, and persistence. The adjective O'Toole used was fashioned after the Mount Rushmore monument and the faces of the four presidents carved on it—Washington, Jefferson, Lincoln, and Roosevelt. O'Toole used the adjective Rushmorean specifically to characterize leaders who had the moral courage and professional resolve to change the world around them and succeed. The analogy here is that Washington succeeded in founding a nation, Jefferson in creating a democracy, Lincoln in preserving the Union, and Roosevelt in expanding the country. O'Toole described the four presidents as "the best representatives of the school of principle-based leadership dedicated to democratic change." He suggested they all shared four moral principles: integrity, trust, listening to people, and respect for followers.

Without getting into a detailed evaluation of the characteristics of each of these great presidents, it is hardly debatable that they all were leaders of remarkable knowledge and an intense determination to do the moral obligation. O'Toole adds that the most significant manifestation of their courage "did not occur in battle, their real courage was moral. Their courage surfaced after they refused to become discouraged when their ideas, principles, visions—even their very selves—were publicly rejected, attacked and vilified" (p. 22).

Following up on O'Toole's concept of Rushmorean leadership, it may be appropriate to use the label "Rushmorean" to describe successful criminal justice agencies. By that I mean robust agencies that can succeed in combating crime, establishing justice, and serving the public, all without sacrificing goodness or depriving citizens of their constitutional rights. The following four characteristics distinguish an ethically daring culture conducive to "Rushmoreanism" in criminal justice agencies:

1. *Duty*—the imperative that agency leaders, managers, supervisors, and operatives honor their obligations toward agency goals even when there is no hope for reward or fear of punishment. As such, the practices of "covering up to obstruct criticism," "masking the truth for looking good," "snatching credit from subordinates," or "favoring the good old boys" should be individually and institutionally avoided.

2. *Integrity*—the imperative that agency leaders, managers, supervisors, and operatives understand the obligation of integrity (which is here defined as doing the right thing when no one is watching) and faithfully comply with moral principles even at a personal hardship. As such, the use of "hidden agendas," "cooked-up books," and "personal interests" should be avoided.

3. *Self-control*—the imperative that agency leaders, managers, supervisors, and operatives realize that self-control is the highest level of agency control and the most effective means to guard against corruption. When self-control is routine, the practices of "economic opportunism," "social exploitation," "sexual harassment," and "egoism" can be avoided.

4. *Democracy*—the imperative that agency leaders, managers, supervisors, and operatives understand the advantages of democratic administration and pleasantly treat everyone within the agency, and without, democratically. As such, "management by intimidation," "violating the constitutional rights of citizens," "refusal to listen to subordinates," or "unfairness" must be avoided.

A Profile of Rushmorean Courage: Coleen Rowley, the FBI Agent Who Directed Her Boss

On May 21, 2002, Coleen Rowley, an FBI special agent and the Minneapolis Chief Division Counsel sent a 13-page memo to FBI Director Robert Mueller. Ms. Rowley questioned what she considered flawed responses to a previous memo she had written related to the terrorist attacks on the World Trade Center Towers on September 11, 2001. In her memo, Rowley pointed out failures in the FBI's organizational decision making and its management procedures. Until then the fact that a middle-management-level employee could send a memo directly to the director was unprecedented. What made Special Agent Rowley's memo especially controversial was that it was explicitly critical of both the workings of the FBI and the management skills of its director. The memo amounted to an indictment of the director's neglect in the face of the biggest terrorist operation ever mounted on U.S. soil. As a result, the memo sent shudders through Congress, the federal bureaucracy, and the nation (Rowley, 2002).

Rowley, a graduate of the University of Iowa Law School, joined the FBI in 1980. She was a mother of four, the breadwinner in her family, a competitive long-distance runner, and an ardent admirer of the FBI. Over the years, she won a reputation as a highly disciplined agent, principled and supremely devoted to her job. A colleague of Rowley described her as "the kind of person who always does what is right when nobody is watching ... that is why she came out." She was also described as "a loyal public servant who clings to her belief in the system until a betrayal of that faith makes it impossible to stay silent" (Rowley, 2002). Unable to sleep at 3:00 A.M. one night in early May, Rowley drove to the office and wrote the first draft of her famous memo. She spent a week fine-tuning it, setting it aside for days, anguishing and at times doubting whether she could go through with it. Summoning her courage on May 21, she fired off the 13-page letter to her ultimate boss.

Rowley began her memo as follows:

> I feel at this point that I have to put my concerns in writing concerning the important topic of the FBI's responses to evidence of terrorist activity in the United States prior to September 11th. The issues are fundamentally ones of integrity and go to the heart of the FBI's law enforcement mission and mandate.

Rowley continued,

> To get to the point, I have deep concerns that the delicate and subtle shading/skewing of facts by you and others at the highest levels of FBI management has occurred and is occurring. The term "cover up" would be too strong a characterization which is why I am attempting to carefully (and perhaps over laboriously) choose my words here. I base my concerns on my relatively small, peripheral but unique role in the Moussaoui investigation in the Minneapolis Division prior to, and during and after, September 11th.
>
> I feel that certain facts have, up to now, been omitted, downplayed, glossed over and/or mischaracterized in an effort to avoid or minimize personal/or institutional embarrassment on the part of the FBI and/or perhaps even for improper political reasons.
>
> In a day or two following September 11th you, Director Muller, made a statement to the effect that if the FBI had only any advance warning of the attacks, we (meaning the FBI), may have been able to take some action to prevent the tragedy ... finally when similar comments were

made weeks later, in Assistant Director Carouso's congressional testimony in response to the first public leaks about Moussaoui, we faced the sad realization that the remarks indicated someone, possibly with your approval, had decided to circle the wagons at FBIHQ in an apparent effort to protect the FBI from embarrassment and the relevant FBI officials from scrutiny. After the details began to emerge concerning the pre-September 11th investigation of Moussaoui, your statement has changed.

With all due respect, this (new) statement is as bad as the first! It is also quite at odds with the earlier statement (which I'm surprised has not already been pointed out by those in the media!). I don't know how you or anyone at FBI headquarters, no matter how much genius or prescience you may possess, could so blithely make this affirmation without anything to back the opinion up other than your stature as FBI Director.

Rowley concluded,

Mr. Director, I hope my observations can be taken in a constructive vein. They are from the heart and intended to be completely apolitical. Hopefully, with our nation's security on the line, you and our nation's other elected and appointed officials can rise above the petty politics that often plague other discussions and do the right thing.

Like no other document to emerge from the firestorm over the mistakes and missed signals that may have led to the September 11th attacks, the Rowley memo highlighted the depth of government's need for Rushmorean officials to bolster bureaucratic inability to serve perfectly when national interests are so seriously imperiled.

The attitude and performance of Special Agent Rowley is highly consistent with the Rushmorean model. She exhibited enormous leadership talent, one that excited the nation and shook it out of its apathy. She stood alone against a mighty organization. She grasped the truth and did not let it go, but instead courageously acted upon it. She exhibited moral character by choosing not to be silent, but to be radically vocal as long as that was necessary to save the country (remember Aristotle). She took a professional risk, one that almost all other professionals would have dreaded taking (remember Epictetus). She clearly violated the FBI rules of hierarchical communication, a matter that could have resulted in her being summarily terminated. But given the degree of danger to the country, she turned the risk into a mission that brought immediate attention to that danger. She confidently addressed her ultimate boss without fear or frailty. She saw wrong in the way the FBI functioned and tried to correct it. She addressed issues of trust in government, particularly in the way the FBI should respond to changing conditions. She demanded public integrity, and her message was heard loudly and clearly, not only by the FBI community, but also by the nation and the world. She cared for responsible action by the FBI to the extent of publicly criticizing her "beloved agency." She presented her views in a logical, businesslike manner. She exhibited a higher level of loyalty, one that transcended the traditional ones—to the organization, the coworkers, the supervisors, or the agency's leadership. Indeed, her loyalty was to a much higher entity—the wounded nation itself. She fulfilled her professional calling not only by acting out of duty, but acting in "reverence to duty"(remember Kant). In her approach to calling attention to the possible damage to the country, she was constructive. She systematically stated her case, demanded itemized reform, proposed rational solutions, and wished her leaders all success. In summary, her attitude and performance reflected some of the most difficult moral challenges addressed in this book: the truth, moral courage, integrity, indifference to hardship, reverence to duty, self-control, and principle-based leadership. As a result, Ms. Rowley was selected by *Time* magazine as one of three women of the year for 2002.

The Extent of Corruption in Criminal Justice Agencies

But how much corruption is there in criminal justice today? And how much can be tolerated? In response to the first question, each of us may have a different perspective. If you are a veteran practitioner, you will probably have a more dismal view, based on your years of experience. If you are a student, you will most likely maintain a more idealistic perspective. The proper response, however, should be "no one really knows for sure." Much of what we know about widespread corruption in criminal justice occurs in large cities such as New York, Philadelphia, Chicago, Houston, or Detroit. In these cities a cyclical pattern of corruption seems to exist—"when it surfaces, some officials are then fired, and the situation quiets down for a few years until another scandal breaks" (Bartollas et al., 1983). Also, given the lack of comparative data among criminal justice institutions and the inherent difficulty of identifying and measuring uniform units of corruption, it would be invalid, if not wrong, to speculate on the scope of the problem in any particular agency without improved research methods.

In response to the second question (how much corruption can be tolerated), the ethical reasoner should answer, "None." The administration of justice in a democratic society must be one of *the highest quality attainable to man*. This view can be supported by both a theoretical and a practical argument:

- The theoretical argument is founded on two basic premises: (1) democracy is based on the ideal of liberty—without liberty there cannot be democracy; and (2) liberty emanates from the ideal of justice—without justice there cannot be liberty. The Founding Fathers regarded the impartial administration of justice as the foundation of liberty. Given these two premises, it must be concluded that any denial of justice is a betrayal of liberty, and any denial of liberty is a betrayal of democracy. Consequently, any attempt to ration justice is tantamount to courting tyranny. Tolerating corruption, therefore, not only diminishes justice, but also threatens the survival of a democratic society.

- The practical argument is based on the premise that laws are imperfect instruments of justice. They present an *assumed state of legal rightness* that may or may not be consistent with the expectation of justice. Civilized societies, on the other hand, demand equitable justice that cannot be attained without ethical principles. It would be contradictory, therefore, for agencies to demand ethical discretion on the one hand while they tolerate corruption on the other.

The Root Sins in Criminal Justice Management

While unethical behaviors may vary substantially from one criminal justice situation to another (for example, from a contemptuous look by a police officer to a complex cover-up scam by a prison warden), this section will focus only on four "root sins" that I consider most detrimental to the practice of criminal justice. These are not subjects that practitioners would wish to discuss publicly, nor are they usually included in regular training programs. Bringing such issues to the fore may cause a sense of uneasiness, embarrassment, and at times, shame. Nevertheless, under the sunshine of ethics, these subjects must be confronted and their moral implications exposed. The darkness of concealment can only perpetuate their sinfulness and further diminish social goodness.

The behaviors to be discussed represent the most common, infamous, and critical. These behaviors, it should be emphasized, are seldom committed independently of one another. They often feed on one another; the commission of one leads to the commission of the other, often making the next one easier. Obviously, this is not an empirical view that can be conclusively proved or disproved; rather, it is an ethical observation based on many years of field and teaching experience in criminal justice agencies. Furthermore, the observation seems to perfectly fit the "rules of reasonableness" discussed earlier in ethical theory (see Chapter 2).

These root sins are as follows:

Lying and deception (the most common)

Prejudice and racial discrimination (the most infamous)

Egoism and the abuse of authority (the most critical)

Misguided loyalties (the most troublesome)

These root behaviors will be addressed in a thematic approach in the following chapters. They will cover the areas of police, corrections, and probation and parole. Examples from each area will be used to highlight basic theories, applications, justifications, and excuses. But more importantly, ethical guidelines will be proposed whenever possible to guide our understanding of the "ambivalent world" of criminal justice. These guidelines may be helpful to assist both the "neophyte" professionals in learning the intricacies of moral judgment and the "veteran" professionals in addressing the problems that may trouble them. Through a fresh look at criminal justice based on *integrated thinking* and *moral agility*, it is hoped that the moral bleeding in criminal justice will be minimized, the recalcitrants may be able to extricate themselves from their past, and the idealists may double their efforts to make a difference.

References

Bartollas, C., Miller, S. J., & Wice, P. B. (1983). *Participants in American Criminal Justice: The Promise and the Performance.* Englewood Cliffs, NJ: Prentice-Hall.

Carter, D. L. (1986). Theoretical Dimensions in the Abuse of Authority by Police Officers. In T. Barker & D. L. Carter (Eds.), *Police Deviance* (pp. 147–170). Cincinnati, OH: Anderson Publishing Co.

Cleveland, H. (1985). *The Knowledge Executive: Leadership in an Information Society.* New York: Dutton.

Crank, J. P., Regoli, R. M., Poole, E. D., & Culbertson, R. G. (1986). Cynicism among Police Chiefs. *Justice Quarterly, 3*(3).

Felson, M. (1994). *Crime and Everyday.* Thousand Oaks, CA: Pine Forge Press.

French, J. R. P., Jr. (1975). A Comparative Look at Stress and Strain in Policemen. In W. H. Kroes & J. J. Hurrell (Eds.), *Job Stress and the Police Officer: Identifying Stress Reduction Techniques.* Washington, DC: U.S. Department of Health, Education, and Welfare.

Germann, A. C. (1976). Law Enforcement: A Look into the Future. In A. S. Blumberg & E. Niederhofer (Eds.), *The Ambivalent Force: Perspectives on the Police* (pp. 401–405). New York: Holt, Rinehart, and Winston.

Glazer, M. P., & Glazer, P. M. (1989). *The Whistle Blowers: Exposing Corruption in Government and Industry.* New York: Basic Books.

Goldstein, H. (1990). *Problem-Oriented Policing.* New York: McGraw-Hill.

Hageman, M. J. C. (1978). Occupational Stress of Law Enforcement Officers and Marital and Familial Relationships. *Journal of Police Science and Administration, 6,* 402–412.

Hamilton, A., Madison, J., & Jay, J. (1787, 1788/Repr. 1961). *The Federalist Papers.* New York: Mentor Books.

Herzberg, F. (1976). *The Managerial Choice: How to Be Efficient and Be Human.* Homewood, IL: Dow-Jones-Irwin.

Lozoff, B., & Braswell, M. (1989). *Inner Corrections.* Cincinnati, OH: Anderson Publishing Co.

O'Toole, J. (1995). *Leading Change: Overcoming the Ideology of Comfort and the Tyranny of Custom.* San Francisco: Jossey-Bass, Inc.

Price, K. (1983). *Job Satisfaction as a Means of Increasing Productivity among Correctional Officers in Texas.* Unpublished doctoral dissertation. Huntsville, TX: Sam Houston State University.

Quinney, R. (1977). *Class, State and Crime: On the Theory and Practice of Criminal Justice.* New York: McKay.

Rowley, C. (2002, June 20). Memo to FBI Director Robert Mueller. Minneapolis, MN: Time.

Rush, G. E. (1991). *The Dictionary of Criminal Justice* (3rd ed). Guilford, CT: Dushkin Publishing.

Shernock, S. K. (1990). The Effects of Patrol Officers' Defensiveness Toward the Outside World on Their Ethical Orientations. *Criminal Justice Ethics*, 9(2), 24–42.

Siegel, L., & Zalman, M. (1991). Cultural Literacy in Criminal Justice: A Preliminary Assessment. *Journal of Criminal Justice Education*, 2(1), 15–44.

Souryal, S. S. (1977). *Police Administration and Management.* St. Paul, MN: West Publishing.

Souryal, S. S. (1993). What Am I Supposed to Fall Back On? Cultural Literacy in Criminal Justice Ethics. *Journal of Criminal Justice Education*, 4(1).

Terry, W. C., III. (1985). Police Stress: The Empirical Evidence. In A. S. Blumberg & E. Niederhofer (Eds.), *The Ambivalent Force: Perspectives on the Police* (3rd ed., pp. 357–370). New York: Holt, Rinehart, and Winston.

Thornberry, T. (1990). Cultural Literacy in Criminology. *Journal of Criminal Justice Education*, 1(1), 33–49.

Turk, A. (1982). *Political Criminality: The Defiance and Defense of Authority.* Beverly Hills, CA: Sage Publications.

U.S. Department of Justice, (1987). *"Uniform Crime Reports." Crime in the United States.* Washington, DC: U.S. Government Printing Office.

Vold, G. B., & Bernard, T. J. (1986). *Theoretical Criminology* (3rd ed.). New York: Oxford University Press.

Whitehead, J. T. (1989). *Burnout in Probation and Corrections.* New York: Praeger.

Williams, F. P., III. & McShane, M. D. (1988). *Criminological Theory.* Englewood Cliffs, NJ: Prentice-Hall.

Williams, J. D. (1980). *Public Administration: The People's Business.* Boston: Little, Brown and Company.

6
Lying and Deception in Criminal Justice

The trouble with our society consists in the phenomenon of "lie," which modern man has invented and "introduced into nature" as synonymous to truth.

Kahlil Gibran

False words are not only evil in themselves, but they infect the soul with evil.

Socrates

There are truths which are not for all men, nor for all times.

Voltaire

Let me have no lying; it becomes none but tradesmen.

Shakespeare

What You Will Learn from this Chapter

You will learn the general theory of lying, the origins of lying, the doctrine of veracity, the rules of moral justification, and the idea of institutional lying in criminal justice.

You will also learn the conservative and liberal views that justify lying, and the characteristics of lying in policing, corrections, and probation/parole.

Key Terms and Definitions

The Religionist View of Lying is the view that prohibits all lies on the basis of the *fall from grace* theory that equates lies with sin.

The Sociological View of Lying is the view that considers lying a learned behavior and requires that individuals transcend the need to lie as they increase in socialization.

Pseudologia Phantastica is an extreme condition of compulsive lying. It is commonly known as *pathological lying*.

The Ultraconservative View of Lying is the view that assigns extreme negative weight to lying and considers all lying moral sins.

The Liberal View of Lying is the view that considers lying a choice between competing opportunities and interests. It justifies lying in certain conditions.

Institutional Lying is a term that explains lying as an unspoken agreement between agency members to make their agency look good and to hide its organizational weaknesses.

Introduction and Confession

Before I am to be accused of plagiarism, I must admit that most of the thoughts, principles, and ideas in this section have been gleaned from a relatively small number of sources. Foremost among these is Sissela Bok's *Lying: Moral Choice in Public and Private Life* (1978). Bok's work presents the most comprehensive analysis of lying as a moral choice. Her views remain basically unquestioned for several reasons: (1) not many people are willing to grapple with the issue of lying, let alone write about it, because the subject can evidently arouse strong feelings of self-guilt; (2) not many scholars have devoted as much of their lives researching the topic of truth and falsity as Bok; and (3) most philosophers tend to agree with the truism of her analysis. Although Bok's analysis does not lend itself to empirical scrutiny, it has been widely recognized as rational and accurate. It certainly meets the criteria for reasonableness—it is consistent, takes available scientific facts into consideration, and fits the human experience.

General Theory of Lying

Bok distinguishes between two conceptual domains: the abstract question of *truth and falsity*, and the moral question of *intended truthfulness or deception*. She states that veracity, in most cases, cannot be settled by establishing the truth or falsity of what one says, but on the basis of whether one *intends* to mislead. For instance, if one states that God resides on planet Zook, the statement can be either truthful or deceptive depending on the level of proof—which is virtually impossible. But regardless of whether the statement is true or false, the person making it can be accused of lying if he or she made the statement with the intent to deceive.

Obviously, the two domains of lying often overlap and, up to a point, are inextricable from each other, as in the case of scientific statements. For our purposes, however, we will leave the domain of the "abstract truth" alone and proceed with Bok's investigation of lying as an "intention to deceive."

According to Bok, a deceptive person is not one who is merely wrong or mistaken; he is *one who is intentionally deceitful or treacherous*. A liar is one who intentionally undertakes to deceive others by communicating messages meant to mislead them. A lie must therefore include any intentionally deceptive message that is stated. Such a statement may be verbal, written, or conveyed via smoke signals, Morse code, sign language, and the like (Bok, 1978:14). The statement of a message can also be implied by way of a gesture (as by nodding one's head for "Yes" and shaking it for "No"), through disguise, by means of action or inaction, or even through silence.

Bok's definition of lying is similar to those given by other philosophers, but not all. The definition of lying has presented a moral dilemma all its own, because "never telling a lie" can be inconsistent with human nature and therefore unreasonable. According to Bok, people lie to be sociable, to be humorous, to cheer each other up, or to avoid being the bearers of bad news. People are also justified in lying when faced with imminent danger to their lives or safety, because killing and maiming are intrinsic evils, whereas lying is an instrumental one. Consequently, while certain moralists were rigorously opposed to lying, others tended to recognize at least a few circumstances in which misleading statements can be allowed. For instance, Grotius, as well as a long line of Protestant thinkers, argued that speaking falsely to liars—like thieves, to whom truthfulness is not owed—should not be considered lying. Other moral thinkers developed a variety of "mental reservations," which in some extreme formulations can justify a completely misleading statement as long as one can add a silent qualification in his or her mind to make it true. Thus, if you were asked whether you broke somebody's vase, you could answer "No," adding in your mind the mental reservation of "not last week" to make the statement technically true (Bok, 1978:15).

Bok further explains that all deceptive messages can be affected, more or less, by the factors of self-deception, error, or variations in one's intent to deceive. She calls these factors "filters" that alter the way in which a message can be experienced by both the deceived and the deceiver. Bok adds that when people intend to deceive, they usually work with such filters in order to manipulate their victims; they can play on the biases of certain persons (for example, affirmative action can destroy one's chances for promotion), on the imagination of others (for example, strategic defense initiative is a panacea against all attacks by foreign powers), or on the confusion throughout the system (for example, the national debt could be wiped out in 23.8 months if federal income taxes were increased by 3.497 percent, compounded daily).

The Origins of Lying

The origin of lying has been perceived from two viewpoints: the *religionist view* and the *sociological view*. The religionist view is based on the "fall from grace" theory that equates all human behavior with sin. According to Christian belief, all human beings are products of Adam's sin, and everyone is born with the propensity to commit evil. Lying is therefore a manifestation of evil. Based on this view, as one grows into adulthood, the propensity to lie is actualized due to increasing unsavory social demands and the inevitable need to compete with other "sinners." Consequently, all adults will eventually lie whenever deception is deemed serviceable either for gaining an advantage or avoiding pain. This tendency will cease, the religionists submit, only when the human character is sanctified and cleansed from sin. This transformation can occur only when one is touched by God's grace, repents of one's sins, and devotes one's life to worshipping God.

The sociological view of lying has been championed by physical and behavioral scientists who disagreed with the religionist view. They contend that lying is a learned behavior that thrives more or less in proportion to one's level of socialization. The sociological view has been supported by two main arguments: (1) Scientific findings have not (as yet) shown that lying is genetically based. These scientists argue that all human beings start out as innocent infants who have no particular inclination either to lie or to tell the truth. (2) Learning theory indicates that moral character is an acquired trait and lying is a product of deficient learning (learning the wrong things). Psychiatrists assert that the initial process of moral development starts at age 2, when children begin to understand reality. For instance, a child accepts food from a parent's hand because his parent tells him it is good, and abstains from touching a hot stove because he is told it is bad. Truth-telling at that level is considered a matter of life and death.

Sociologists advocate that children begin telling lies because of their inability to distinguish right from wrong. Their lies are mostly attributed to messages they receive in associating with their parents; for instance, those who lie to a police officer when stopped for a traffic violation, or accept too much change from a cashier without calling the error to his or her attention. Such messages seem to continue ingraining themselves in the child's moral character. Tarnow, a well-recognized psychiatrist, states that "overall, the determinant of whether children will cheat or lie [as adults] is whether their parents cheat or lie—their moral standards" (*Houston Post*, May 12, 1990). By the age of 6, a child would have developed the cognitive ability to understand right from wrong and realize when he or she is trying to deceive. From that point on, Tarnow stresses, the pattern of moral character continues through adulthood.

According to the sociological view, while parents and family members play a major role in the moral development of children, society as a whole also contributes to their developmental process. Ideas of honesty and dishonesty come from playmates and schoolmates, but more significantly from those who play the role of societal parents. Adult children begin noting television commercials that portray political candidates as liars, television evangelists who are disgraced for lying to their congregations, or businesspeople indicted for cheating and embezzling. They may also learn the advantages of lying as acts done in self-interest, or as tools for getting ahead in competitive situations. At school they may realize the benefit of lying to a teacher (for example, "I forgot my homework"), to the athletic coach (for example, "I was sick"), and to other students. In time, especially if lies continue to go unchecked and internal controls fail to develop, the choice to lie becomes seductive and compulsive, if not addictive. Under extreme conditions, compulsive liars develop *pseudologia phantastica*, a combination of a disease and a habit, commonly known as "pathological lying." Its exact condition depends largely on the extent to which the individual confuses falsehood with reality. In acute cases, pathological lying is known to cause false recollection or fabrication of memory (Swanson et al., 1988:131).

The Doctrine of Veracity

Veracity is a fundamental doctrine in the social sciences because it is central to the stability of society. Without it there can be no continuity in human conduct across situations or through time. In a sense, there would be no "human personality," because people would cease to be persons, acting more like mechanical units reacting to changing situations (Nettler, 1982:13).

Consistent with the doctrine of veracity, lying is immoral because it can destroy confidence among people. When society ceases to presume "mutual truthfulness," social order is eroded and substantial harm can follow. People would be continuously fearful of being tricked, and those who share a lie would fear the effects of their undiscovered lies on others and might resort to violence. Moreover, healthy societies must consider the long-term results of lying if everyone resorted to denying the truth. As Samuel Johnson stated, even "the devils themselves do not lie to one another, since the society of Hell could not subsist without truth any more than others" (Bok, 1978:20). Imagine, for instance, how miserable life would be in a neighborhood where one could not trust one's neighbor, the police officer, the postal worker, or the utility meter reader; or working in an agency where one cannot trust his bosses, colleagues, or subordinates. It would be a miserable life indeed.

The presumption of veracity is necessary to stress the positive worth of truthfulness. A high degree of veracity is essential for proper social relations. People who do not trust other people may not treat them fairly, may not have their interests at heart, and may be encouraged to do them harm. Furthermore, if there is no confidence in the truthfulness of others, there is no way of assessing one's intentions to help or harm. Trust, therefore, is the atmosphere in which veracity thrives. When trust is shattered or wears away, human institutions of all kinds collapse.

From a moral viewpoint, the doctrine of veracity assigns an *initial negative weight to lying*. As such, lies are not considered neutral statements; they require explanation, whereas truth ordinarily does not. The doctrine places the burden of proof on those who assume the liar's perspective (Bok, 1978:32). It is necessary, therefore, that we accept the initial premises that (1) lying is a mean and culpable choice, and (2) truthful statements are preferable to lies, in the absence of extenuating considerations (Bok, 1978:33).

Can Lying Be Morally Justifiable?

Building on the doctrine of veracity, Bok proceeds to analyze when, if at all, lies can be justified. Her analysis covers a continuum between two extreme views: the *ultraconservative view*, which categorically prohibits all lies, and the *liberal sociological view*, which considers lying as a choice between competing opportunities and interests. Bok neverthe-less recommends an ethical view somewhere on the continuum, one based on rationality and consistency with the human experience.

Proponents of the ultraconservative view not only assign a negative weight to lies, they also see that weight as so overwhelming that no cir-cumstances can outweigh it for any reason. This view has been voiced by orthodox religionists on the basis of biblical verses such as "You shall not bear false witness against your neighbor" (Exod. 20:16) and "Let what you say be simply 'Yes' or 'No,' anything more than this comes from evil" (Matt. 5:37) But if one accepts this view, there is obviously no room left for consideration, even in the most extreme cases, such as lying in self-defense. It would be illogical, if not contradictory, to justify killing in self-defense, but not lying—an evil of much lesser harm.

Foremost among those who prohibited all lies was Saint Augustine. He initially defined lying as having one thing in one's heart and uttering another, with the intention to deceive. He claimed that God forbids all lies and that liars endanger their immortal souls. His definition left no room for justifiable lies. But Saint Augustine later confessed that this troubled him. He worried about lies to ailing persons, for instance, and lies to protect those threatened by assault or defilement. He conse-quently reconstructed his view, admitting that there are differences among lies, and that some are much more abhorrent than others. Saint Augustine ended up organizing an *eightfold distinction scale*, beginning with lies uttered in the teaching of religion, which he thought were the worst of all, and ending with lies that harm no one, such as white lies of little moral import. While Augustine still considered white lies to be sins, he thought they could be much more easily pardoned.

Saint Thomas Aquinas followed upon Augustine's eightfold hierar-chy by setting a pattern still followed by the Catholic Church. He distin-guished three categories of lies: (1) the *officious*, or helpful lies (for example, a physician giving a placebo to a patient); (2) the *jocose* lies, or those told in jest (for example, calling an athletically built friend a gorilla); and (3) the *mischievous* or malicious lies that are told to harm someone. Aquinas considered the last category to be a serious moral sin. Although he agreed with Augustine that all lies are sins, he regarded the officious and jocose lies as far less serious than the mischievous lies.

Another view of justifiable lies found powerful expression in Gro-tius's *On the Law of War and Peace*, in which the author argued that a falsehood can be a lie only if it conflicts with the right of the person to whom it is addressed. Blackmailers, Grotius argued, have no right to information they try to exhort; therefore, lying to them is perfectly justi-fiable. People, Grotius added, are expected to use proper judgment when they communicate with others. Consistent with such judgment is one's right to withhold the truth if the listener has evil intentions; has no judg-ment, as in the case of children or the mentally ill; or freely gives it up, as when two persons agree to deceive one another in a poker game. Grotius's views (he was a lawyer, by the way) led many to believe that lies may not be unlawful or even morally unacceptable (Bok, 1978:39).

Bok proceeds by stating that only two beliefs support the rigid rejection of all lies: (1) that God forbids all lies; and (2) that he will punish those who lie. These beliefs, however, cannot be proven or disproven by reason, because religious doctrines are based on faith. Bok further asserts that many theologians indeed refuse to accept either belief or both. Judaism, Christianity, and Buddhism, for example, all allow exceptions to lying. Therefore, Bok asserts that there are circumstances that justify telling a lie. While she acknowledges that deceptive practices are certainly harmful and that white lies (which harm no one) should be treated with extreme care, she accepts justifiable lies, but limits them to (1) when innocent lives are at stake, provided that only a lie could deflect imminent danger; and (2) when a lie can help achieve a "higher moral value," such as keeping national secrets, helping a patient recover, or sustaining vital family relations.

Basic Rules on Lying

Based on the doctrine of veracity, lying is intrinsically "immoral and culpable." But given the window of justifiable exceptions previously discussed, the following guidelines should be instrumental when one is confronted with a moral choice of whether to lie:

1. In any situation in which a lie is a possible choice, one must first seek truthful alternatives.

2. If lies and truthful statements can achieve the same result, lying should always be ruled out.

3. Only where a lie is considered "a matter of last resort" should one begin considering whether a lie can be morally justified.

4. A morally justifiable lie must be conducive to a "higher moral good." Higher moral goods include acting in self-defense or the defense of others; maintaining the security of classified information; acting undercover; and, arguably, defending the honor of God and country.

5. The justification of a higher moral good must be publicly recognized in advance of the lie—*the test of publicity*. The alternative would obviously allow liars to keep inventing bogus reasons for justifying their lies, thus defeating veracity by acting in bad faith.

As simple as these guidelines may sound, if taken seriously, they would eliminate a great number of lies told out of hatred, prejudice, selfishness, carelessness, bad taste, or unexamined intentions.

The Extent of Lying

Lying is perhaps the most common vice in any society. People lie at home, on the street, and in the workplace. Liars include all kinds of people: apostles and bishops, kings and presidents, generals and privates, professors and students, business executives, salespeople, and laypeople. People lie for many reasons: to protect their own interests, to defend peers and clients, to support common beliefs, or for fun. People who are lied to are too pervasive to enumerate; they include family members, friends and enemies, and coworkers, as well as an entire population of strangers. The methods of lying also vary; they may be verbal, in writing, by gesture, or even by silence. The seriousness of lies can also differ considerably; some lies are of little issue, others can be much more troublesome. Nevertheless, all liars invariably believe that their lies are either justified or excused.

The *Washington Post Magazine* (December 27, 1988) devoted a 19-page section to the topic of lying. The section highlighted what modern societies have sadly concluded: "Greed is the universal motive, sincerity is a pose, honesty is for chumps, altruism is selfishness with a neurotic twist, and morality is for kids, saints, and fools." Articles in this section were editorialized, "Revenge of the Dupes," "According to Our Poll, You're Lying," and "The Academy Awards of Untruth." The *Post* stated that 1987 was the "Year of the Big Lie," typifying the age of disbelief—when people stopped believing politicians, journalists, employers, Madison Avenue, TV, clergy, doctors, police officers, lawyers, insurance agents, bankers, stockbrokers, undertakers, labor leaders, and business executives. Consequently, the *Post* states, 70% of Americans are dissatisfied with the current standards of honesty.

Bok points out that the loss of confidence reaches far beyond government agencies. She states, for instance, that from 1966 to 1976, the proportion of the public who had a great deal of confidence in major medical institutions dropped from 73% to 42%; in major business companies from 55% to 16%; in major law firms from 24% to 12%; and in advertising agencies from 21% to 7% (Bok, 1978:xviii). Bok further acknowledges that government officials and candidates running for office often deceive when they assume that the state of affairs is beyond the comprehension of citizens, or when they can get away with it. In the legal profession, deception is considered routine when it is felt to be excusable by those who tell the lies or by those who make the rules. In the medical profession, doctors have become accustomed to lying to seriously ill patients in order to avoid disturbing them. They also prescribe placebos, such as sugar pills or salt-water injections, that have no physiological effect on the patient's condition but may a have powerful psychological effect leading to relief from pain or depression. It is also not unusual for psychiatrists to distort information to protect client confidentiality. In the academic profession, educators often write "inflated" letters of recommendation for graduating students in order to give them a competitive edge in the job market. In the fields of sales, advertising, and promotion, it is generally considered permissible to mislead the public and one's competitors in order to increase profits.

Turning to the field of academe, it is not uncommon (as I am sure you well know) for instructors and students to lie. Instructors may justify cancelling their classes because of illness when, in reality, that was not necessary; showing videotapes in class because they were unprepared to lecture; requiring students to read certain materials only because their names are mentioned in them; or giving the class a "walk" (or adjourning night classes early) because they have a social engagement.

Students, too, may not always act saintly. A study of University of Virginia students found that the chance that students lied to their parents or strangers is 50%. For instance, when college students talked to their parents, they lied about once in every two conversations. When they talked with strangers, they lied even more. According to the study, student participants recorded every conversation they had and what lies they told for a week. The student group reportedly lied a total of 1,000 lies throughout that period, an average of about two a day for each student. The diaries kept by students showed that they lied in 28% of their conversations with a best friend or a regular friend; in 48% with an acquaintance; and in 77% with a stranger. Lying to Mom came in at 46%, and to lovers, 34%. Among the more common lies told to parents were inflating the cost of books they buy for classes, and claiming they were staying in to study for a test. Among the more common lies told to others were "getting out of baby-sitting some 'brats' by claiming a prior commitment," and "telling an interesting man she's not dating someone else regularly so he'll ask her out" (*Detroit News*, August 16, 1995).

The ethical dilemma associated with lying, however, is much more complex, because most liars do not find themselves in situations that justify telling a lie. Consider, for example, the case of the apostle Peter, who reportedly lied three times when asked whether he knew "Jesus the Galilean." Do you consider him justified? The answer can be "Yes," but only if Peter was genuinely afraid for his life. On the other hand, the answer can be "No," because as a disciple, his spiritual commitment to Christ should have been a much higher obligation, one that outweighed any concern for earthly living. Also consider the case of President Nixon and his White House zealots who, in 1973, lied to the nation about involvement in the Watergate affair. On second thought, maybe we need not look for reasons in this case. A quick trip to the library can easily produce the main reason—absence of ethical restraint.

Institutional Lying in Criminal Justice

Institutional lying is a term that characterizes deceptive actions or statements that are unjustifiably made in violation of the institution's laws or procedures. Institutional lying is usually consistent with the agency's organizational subculture or the product of customary practices over a period of time. Such actions or statements seek either to project the image of effectiveness most preferred by the agency or to dispel a negative image that is unacceptable to society.

From the practitioner's point of view, institutional lies are invariably taken for granted and would cause the practitioner little or no anguish. In some agencies, institutional lies are accepted simply as functional means of doing business, as occupational patterns of behavior, or as legitimate "tricks of the trade." Not infrequently, institutional lies are rationalized as the "rite of passage" essential to continued employment or as conditions for acceptance by peers. As such, institutional lies are seldom subjected to reasoning or ethical scrutiny.

In the field of criminal justice, institutional lying permeates the ranks of prosecutors, police officers, probation and parole officials, and correctional officers, casting a "cloud of duplicity" over the legitimacy of the system. For instance, Skolnick states that "deception by police—and courts as well—is as normal as pouncing is to a cat" (Skolnick, 1982:40). In corrections, McCarthy states that deceptive practices range from simple acts of theft and pilferage to large-scale criminal conspiracies (for example, drug trafficking, counterfeiting rings, sale of paroles, and so on) (McCarthy, 1998:252). In probation, Rosecrance reports that deception in preparing presentence reports is routinely used to take judges "off the hook" for unpopular sentences. In such instances, judges can easily deny responsibility for harsher sentences by implying that their "hands are tied" (Rosecrance, 1988:254).

Institutional lying in criminal justice agencies begins at the point of entry into the organization. During preservice training, instructors tacitly encourage the trainees to lie in certain situations, while strongly discouraging them to do so in others. For instance, new practitioners are invariably taught that the use of deception in court is risky, socially unacceptable, and would subject the practitioner to legal and departmental sanctions. At the same time, they are taught that it is "routine performance" to lie to substitute guile for force in situations of crisis intervention, investigation, and interrogation, especially when dealing with the downtrodden or the mentally ill.

Job experience seems to broaden the practitioners' view of institutional deception and the circumstances under which it is justified. For instance, police officers learn on the job that officers routinely participate in a variety of illicit activities that reduce the discomfort of the job, such as drinking, sleeping on duty, or staying inside during bad weather. Correctional officers learn that to keep the cell block quiet, it may be necessary to spread a false story among inmates that would inspire an inmate to silence a troublemaker on the cell block floor. Probation and parole officers learn that using illegal threats can help subdue a defiant client.

Because patterns of institutional lying may result in discovery, practitioners also quickly learn the need to manufacture explanatory stories or misrepresentations of the truth. Such stories are used to rationalize the utility of illegitimate behaviors either by making them appear consistent with agency policy, or as harmlessly motivated by the need to support a colleague or supervisor. Common stories usually either invoke claims to propriety, such as "acting within the letter of the law," or refute an allegation on the basis of "malicious information," "misunderstanding the situation," or even on the basis of a "bad telephone connection."

In the following sections, institutional deception in criminal justice will be discussed briefly.

Lying in Policing

In "Deception by Police," Skolnick aptly describes police work as a "morally dangerous" endeavor, whereas the temptations faced by the average patrol officer are much greater than those confronted in other occupations. Police officers perform within a severe and often agonizing moral order. The police environment, Skolnick adds, can be contradictory, almost to the point of being schizophrenic. Such an environment may demand certain fidelities and repudiate certain betrayals. Hard and fast rules limiting police conduct may challenge common sense, while the absence of such rules may invite arbitrary and abusive conduct. As a result, police officers may be confused as to the propriety of employing trickery and deceit as part of their practices (Skolnick, 1982:41).

Consider, for example, the extent of lying involved in the "Collars for Dollars," allegedly practiced by police officers from the Miami, Florida, Police Department and the surrounding departments. Officers allegedly turn arrests on the streets into profits by listing each other as witnesses in drunk-driving and misdemeanor cases—even if they did little or no police work. As a result, more officers get to go to court, where they make overtime pay they do not deserve (*Herald Link*, July 29, 1997). The practice allegedly involves hundreds of officers and costs millions of dollars. It burdens the courts with thousands of unnecessary witnesses, leads to lost cases, and traps innocent people. In the end, a simple DUI costs taxpayers as much as $5,400 in overtime, and a night of prostitution arrests can cost as much as $7,500 (*Herald Link*, July 29,

1997). Dade County Judge Wendell Graham described the lying associated with this practice as "some form of racketeering." The Miami
Beach Police Chief described the practice as a kind of "train: if they
[the officers] can get on it, they will do so" (*Herald Link,* July 29, 1997).

Police officers normally learn the situational utility of lying when
they need to overstep their authority, largely under the pretext of the
"ends justify the means" doctrine. They may have to use certain ruses
to gain entry without a search warrant or to obtain a search warrant
with a false affidavit. Patrol officers, in particular, may have to "rough
up" a defiant subject, to extend the parameters of "probable cause" so
as to make their arrest appear legal, or to justify the use of excessive
force. The "usual" stories may involve claiming self-defense or accusing
the subject of resisting arrest, acting disorderly, hitting his or her head
against the wall, or attempting to commit suicide. Officers also learn
to lie from observing supervisors changing official reports to avoid
unnecessary paperwork or to enhance their clearance rate.

Detectives may be more prone to lying than others. Cases initially
defined as robberies, assaults, and burglaries may be reduced to lesser
offenses (Hunt & Manning, 1989). They may also operate on the
assumption that institutional lying is necessary to reduce the time and
effort spent on "bullshit jobs" that are unlikely to be cleared. Patrol officers who may oppose this practice and insist on filing cases as legally
required are ridiculed or labeled naive, uncooperative, or "troublemakers." As a result, most detectives give them minimal cooperation.

Some police tasks, especially those in specialized units such as vice,
narcotics, and internal affairs, may reward lying. The unfulfilled and
perhaps impossible expectations in drug enforcement may be seen as justifying lies in the "war on drugs," further reducing public trust when
officers' lies are exposed. According to Manning, most detectives, at
one time or another, participate in some form of illicit or illegal activity
that varies from violating the police code of ethics to the use of excessive
force. In this regard, there is always the blanket justification that it is
impossible to police by the book (Hunt & Manning, 1989).

Lying in Probation

Probation officers use deception in their court reports as well as in
their relations with clients and supervisors. Like the police, they learn
that lying in court is most unacceptable because it is extremely dangerous and unnecessary. Only "stupid" officers would attempt that. But
lying in an oral or written report to be presented to a judge is common,
especially if done in a subtle, defensible manner. If the lie is discovered,
there are usually the common excuses that put the blame on the heavy
workload, the irrelevance of certain information, the difficulty of

including all minor details, or simple forgetfulness. Consequently, while probation officers invariably state the basic facts of the case in their presentence reports, they frequently use deceptive means to influence the judicial decision. In a report narrative, they can paint the suspect as a hard-core criminal, a dangerous person, or a threat to society. Especially in revocation cases, probation officers can insert certain unfavorable comments that are not significant or deemphasize information that is significant. Specifically, in cases in which a probationer is charged with a new offense, probation officers can impede the probationer's chances of receiving a favorable judicial outcome by presenting an unduly negative background report.

In their relationship with clients, probation officers can be deceptive by offering probationers promises, or breaks, knowing that they are illegal or futile (for example, "I will speak to the judge"). They can deceive a probationer by threatening harm or harassment in order to enforce a probation condition. They can enter false information in the "contact log" of an unsuspecting probationer, creating contrived probable cause to justify revocation of probationary status. They may insert notations indicating a probationer's failure to respond to a telephone call that was never made, or absence from home when a reported home visit never took place. Based on such methods of deception, probation officers could obtain an arrest warrant and place the seemingly uncooperative probationer in jail.

In their relations with supervisors, probation officers can lie about their attempts to find jobs for probationers or to collect court-ordered fines on time as expected. They can also lie about their whereabouts when they are supposed to be making home visits to supervise probationers. Due to the unstructured nature of this practice, many probation officers waste valuable agency time and transportation costs spending an entire morning or afternoon running personal errands. Furthermore, when they are authorized to travel on agency business, it is not uncommon that they "fudge" on their travel expenses, indicating higher expenditures for food and lodging than were actually incurred. While this behavior is obviously not limited to probation officers (just about all unethical practitioners choose to do so), due to the untraditional nature of probation agencies it seems easier to engage in such behaviors with a decreased risk of being detected.

Lying in Parole

Parole duties are not categorically different from probation duties, especially at the federal level, as well as in the 35 states where probation and parole are combined. Like probation, parole duties serve investigatory and regulatory functions. Parole officers investigate candidates for parole and present preparole (or postsentence) reports to the parole board, recommending granting or denial of parole. As in presentence reports, parole panels can influence the outcome by incorporating misleading statements or basing their recommendation on a twisted portrayal of the truth. If parole is granted, parole officers must supervise their parolees by regulating their behavior and enforcing the conditions of their "release plan." As a method of coping with an excessive workload, many parole officers may use deception in constructing (or reconstructing) the Risk Needs Assessment Report to be authorized by the parole board, thus reducing the frequency of home visits, work visits, and other contacts with the parolee. Other means of deception include playing one parolee against another, coercing parolees into offering personal favors to officers, and in extreme cases, carrying on an intimate relationship with a parolee.

Lying in Corrections

Correctional officers normally serve in prisons and jails. Their role has developed an unsavory stigma over the years because of their relatively low status, inadequate salaries, and involvement in the "dirty work" of guarding society's malefactors (Bartollas et al., 1983:244). While there are obviously ethical and unethical correctional officers, deception is ordinarily used as an institutional defense to keep inmates in line. Officers learn early in their careers that order can be maintained through a series of unethical trade-offs, and using "con-wise" tactics can make them less vulnerable to manipulation by inmates. They can "run some slack" to certain inmates, for example, by shaking them down and claiming they were unarmed (but when another officer then shakes down the same inmates, weapons are found), or by lying to certain inmates in order to entice or settle a racial conflict. Correctional officers may also lie in their incident reports in order to manufacture disciplinary actions against defiant inmates. Corrupt officers obviously lie outright when they bring contraband into the prison unit and further lie about the price of drugs they bring, in order to pocket even larger profits (Bartollas et al., 1983:254).

Unethical correctional officers also lie to their supervisors in order to avoid disciplinary actions (for example, letting an inmate in or out when they are not supposed to). They also lie to cover their tracks when an inmate files a complaint citing brutality or discrimination. When ordered to investigate a situation concerning, for instance, the behavior of a subordinate, they also often lie by presenting either a "half-truth" to vindicate a supportive subordinate, or by offering an exaggerated account of the truth to "nail" an unfriendly one. In informal "raps," they may also lie, denigrating the integrity and reputation of colleagues and supervisors to block their chances for promotion or transfer to an authority-wielding assignment.

Conclusions

The relationship between criminal justice practitioners and the public is one essentially characterized by trust. This is based on the centrality of their functions as representatives of the moral and political orders (Manning, 1978:241). In matters of crime and punishment, it certainly is more harmful when one is lied to by a police officer, a prosecutor, or a judge, than by a neighbor, a colleague, or a stranger. It is important for society that disputes be resolved in a fair, honest, and dignified manner. Criminal justice practitioners must realize, and always be reminded, that lying and deception are fundamentally mean and culpable choices that cannot, and should not, be tolerated in any ethical agency. Deception, however, can only be justified—as a matter of last resort—in accordance with the moral rules previously cited; namely, when a serious threat to life is imminent, when it is necessary to conduct covert operations, to keep classified information, or when it is directly conducive to a higher good. Aside from these moral justifications, criminal justice practitioners—who are bound "to protect society against deception"—cannot be justified in using "deception against society." Any argument to the contrary must be a product of ignorance, an unjustified rationalization, or outright hypocrisy.

Review Questions

1. How does the "ethical reasoner" respond to claims of neophytes within the police force? What is the logical conclusion concerning the response to social disorder?

2. What must be the primary concern of criminal justice practitioners? Distinguish between the "ends" and "means" of justice.

3. What is the most notable weakness of criminal justice management? What fallacies are found in this weakness?

4. Describe the "harvest of shame" in the management of your agency. What are some of its causes?

5. Why is the idea of professionalism often confusing by today's standards? Explain the concept of the new professionalism. What are the characteristics of the new professional?

6. Define *professionalism*. Why is it a deceptive term? What are the characteristics of the professional criminal justice practitioner?

7. What are the domains of lying defined by Sissela Bok? How are they related? In what ways can an intentionally deceptive message be stated?

8. Discuss two viewpoints in the origin of lying. What is *pseudologia phantastica*?

9. Discuss the views of Saint Augustine and Saint Thomas Aquinas regarding lies. What was Grotius's view of justifiable lies?

10. Using Bok's discussion of lying, determine how many of her views apply to your agency. What kinds of lies are considered justifiable in your agency?

References

Bartollas, C., Miller, S. J., & Wice, P. B. (1983). *Participants in American Criminal Justice: The Promise and the Performance*. Englewood Cliffs, NJ: Prentice-Hall.

Bok, S. (1978). *Lying: Moral Choice in Public and Private Life*. New York: Vintage Books.

Braswell, M., McCarthy, B. R., & McCarthy, B. J. (1998). *Justice, Crime and Ethics* (3rd ed.). Cincinnati, OH: Anderson Publishing Co.

Collars for Dollars (1997, July 29). *Herald Link*.

Commentary (1990, May 12). *Houston Post*.

Hunt, J., & Manning, P. K. (1989). *The Social Context of Police Lying*. Unpublished paper.

Manning, P. K. (1978). Lying, Secrecy and Social Control. In P. K. Manning & J. Van Maanen (Eds.), *Policing: A View from the Street*. Santa Monica, CA: Goodyear Publishing.

McCarthy, B. J. (1998). Keeping an Eye on the Keeper: Prison Corruption and Its Control. In M. Braswell, B. J. McCarthy & B. R. McCarthy (Eds.), *Justice, Crime and Ethics* (3rd ed.). Cincinnati, OH: Anderson Publishing Co.

Nettler, G. (1982). *Explaining Criminals*. Cincinnati, OH: Anderson Publishing Co.

Revenge of the Dupes (1988, December 27). *Washington Post Magazine*.

Rosecrance, J. (1988). Maintaining the Myth of Individualized Justice: Probation Presentence Reports. *Justice Quarterly, 5*, 235–256.

Skolnick, J. (1982). Deception by Police. *Criminal Justice Ethics, 1*(2).

Study Tells Truth about Students' Lies to Mom (1995, August 16). *Detroit News*.

Swanson, C. R., Jr., Chamelin, N. C., & Territo, L. (1988). *Criminal Investigation* (4th ed.). New York: Random House.

7
Racial Prejudice and Racial Discrimination

If A. can prove, however conclusively, that he may, of right, enslave B., why may not B. snatch the same argument, and prove equally, that he may enslave A.?—You say A. is white and B. is black. It is color, then; the lighter, having the right to enslave the darker? Take care. By this rule, you are to be slave to the first man you meet with a fairer skin than your own. You do not mean color exactly?—You mean the whites are intellectually the superiors of the blacks, and, therefore have the right to enslave them? Take care again. By this rule, you are to be slave to the first man you meet with an intellect superior to your own. But, you say, it is a question of interest; and, if you can make it your interest, you have the right to enslave another. Very well. And if he can make it his interest, he has the right to enslave you.

Abraham Lincoln

I never knew a man who wished to be himself a slave. Consider if you know any good thing that no man desires for himself.

Abraham Lincoln

What You Will Learn from This Chapter

You will learn the nature of racial injustice, the basic theory of prejudice and discrimination, the roots of racism, and the moral guidelines that condemn racism. You will also learn the current state of racism in policing, corrections, and probation/parole.

Furthermore, you will learn the origins of racial injustice, the relationship between prejudice and knowledge, the targets of prejudice, institutional racism, and reverse discrimination.

Key Terms and Definitions

Justifiable Inequality is unequal treatment that is considered socially necessary to serve the interests of the population as a whole (for example, restrictions on children, military personnel, and prison inmates).

Unjustifiable Inequality is unequal treatment that is knowingly practiced by institutions or individuals. It can harm innocent victims (for example, the violation of civil rights of workers).

Prejudice is an adverse judgment or an opinion formed before examining the facts or having sufficient knowledge.

Prejudgment is a generic term that means making certain decisions in advance when the facts are not available.

Stereotyping is the practice of automatically treating a person as an exact duplicate of a group to which he or she belongs.

Discrimination is the injurious treatment of people on grounds rationally irrelevant to the situation.

Mystical Conception of Racism is the view that explains racism in terms of some people being born inferior.

Biological Conception of Racism is an anthropological approach to understanding racial and ethnic discrimination in terms of physical features and proportions.

Social and Legal Conceptions of Racism are views that explain racism in social and legal terms. They include laws and Supreme Court cases that support racial views.

Institutional Racism is the practice by public or private organizations to discriminate against workers or customers on the basis of race.

Overview

The U.S. Constitution was created essentially as an instrument for advancing human civilization among a population with more or less uncommon values. The Constitution's primary means was through "establishing justice" between the governors and the governed. Since 1789, however, thousands of laws have been passed to accomplish just that: the equal treatment of everyone. Nevertheless, inequalities in society continue to exist at all levels—social, economic, and political.

There are two basic categories of inequality: *justifiable* and *unjustifiable*. The first category refers to unequal treatment that is socially necessary, such as the treatment of underage persons, prison inmates, or the mentally ill. Inequality in this case is intentionally designed to serve the interests of society as a whole. The other category refers to unequal treatment that is inflicted by institutions or individuals against other individuals or groups. These inequalities are unjustifiable because they can cause harm to innocent victims. As such, these inequalities must be products of malice, prejudice, oppression, or misappropriation of justice. Most infamous among these are discriminatory acts committed on the basis of race, sex, religion, natural origin, age, or disability, among other emerging differences. The infamy of these inequalities stems from the fact that they victimize innocent individuals who, given the nature of their difference, are unable to protect themselves or seek relief from their oppressors.

Among all government institutions, criminal justice agencies are perhaps the most active in combating prejudice and discrimination. Yet the practitioners' experience in this endeavor may be paradoxical. On the one hand, they are expected to be experts in the constitutional doctrines of due process and equal protection (as well as criminal and civil liability) when they make arrests, prosecute suspects, or supervise probationers or parolees. On the other hand, it is not unusual to find those who are assigned to combat discrimination in the field having to protect themselves from discrimination in the workplace.

Obviously, while all aspects of discrimination should be examined, this book will address only racial discrimination, because it is arguably the most infamous in a civilized society. Furthermore, the discussion will be limited to white–black relations. The moral lessons to be learned from this discussion should be equally applicable to all other types of racial discrimination.

Glimpses of Racism in Criminal Justice

Racial injustice by the criminal justice system represents an even more dismal commentary on race relations in the United States— the full dimensions of which may be just beginning to unfold.

Two commission reports seem to verify a significant level of racism in criminal justice.

The first report comes from the State of California: the 1991 report by the Independent Commission on the Los Angeles Police Department (also known as the Christopher Commission report) that was formed in the wake of the Rodney King incident. The commission stated, "Bias within the LAPD is not confined to officers' treatment of the public, but is also reflected in conduct directed to fellow officers who are members of racial or ethnic minority groups ... minority officers are still too frequently subjected to racist slurs and comments and to discriminatory treatment within the Department" (Independent Commission on the Los Angeles Police Department, 1991:xii).

The second report came from the State of New York. A 3-year study by a special commission concluded that New York State courts are "infested with racism." The New York State Judicial Commission on Minorities (a 17-member panel consisting of judges, attorneys, law professors, and others) released its report in June 1991, stating that "there are two justice systems at work in the courts of New York State; one for whites, and a very different one for minorities and the poor" (New York State Judicial Commission on Minorities, 1991). The commission based its findings on public hearings, meetings with judges and court administrators, and surveys of judges and attorneys, as well as a thorough review of literature research and other data.

Some of the more deplorable findings released by the commission are as follows:

1. Inequality, disparate treatment, and injustice remain the hallmarks of the justice system.

2. Many minorities in our courts receive "basement justice" in every sense of the phrase—from where courts are located, to the "assembly line" manner in which their cases are decided.

3. The process by which minorities are "stripped of their dignity" often begins when they must enter court facilities that are "unfit for visitation"—they are infested with rats and cockroaches.

4. Minority defendants and their family members are often treated with disrespect and lack of courtesy by court officials, especially court officers; white court officers "revel in exercising their power over an individual who is basically helpless and at their mercy."

5. Racist graffiti is scrawled on the walls of court facilities and is "left untouched by court personnel." The locker rooms for the Supreme Court of Bronx County were "segregated until the commission brought that fact to the attention of the administrative judge."

6. New York State has a "court system, 81 percent white, that holds the keys to a prison population that is 82 percent minority."

7. Minority cases take "only four or five minutes of the court's time." This assembly-line justice undermines the confidence of minority defendants, family members, and witnesses in the justice system.

8. Black defendants outside New York City often have their cases heard by all-white juries. Even though the U.S. Supreme Court has barred use of peremptory challenges to remove minority group members from juries, some New York judges still uphold the practice.

The information released in this report is self-evident; no amplification can make it more graphic. The commission's five-volume report, which totaled 2,000 pages, also found problems with legal representation of minority group members, bias in pretrial processing and criminal penalties, inadequate language interpretation in courts, barriers to minority careers in the law, and other issues. Chief Judge Wachtler, who appointed the commission, praised the report and accepted its recommendations for reform. He promised to appoint a panel to implement and monitor such reforms in the near future. Although similar panels have been appointed in a dozen other states, it must be emphasized that few have criticized the state of racism in American justice in terms as scathing as the New York State Judicial Commission's.

Nature of Racial Injustice

At no time in recent history has the problem of racism been so ubiquitous—involving so many and lasting for so long—as in the United States. Racial prejudice and racial discrimination stand out as the most conscience-shocking types of social injustice. They are rooted in *irrational convictions* that are very difficult to reason away or legally suppress. Racial injustice continues to embarrass the moral conscience of the American nation—one that prides itself on the principles of liberty, justice, and equality. Moreover, the "color line," as W.E.B. DuBois puts it, does not seem likely to go away, and unless the "leprosy of racism" is totally cured, the "crack in the melting pot" may have to be permanent (Zinn, 1980:23).

While recent civil rights acts must be credited with reducing the cruelty of racial discrimination (we no longer lynch or brand people), the same cannot be said about the frequency of its occurrence or the reasons for its continued existence. As Allan Bloom (1987:30) states in *The Closing of the American Mind*, "The equal protection of the laws did not protect a man from contempt and hatred as a Jew, an Italian, or a black." Bloom adds, "There is obviously more to resolving racial prejudice than invoking the mechanical forces of the law." History shows that legal forces can be rendered ineffective by man's ingenious ability to circumvent their sanctions. Succinctly, it must take a "reasoning mind" and a "civilized heart," if we are to succeed in making equality work. As if, in a clinical sense, ridding ourselves of racial discrimination requires *forces of reason* that can block away the forces of prejudice and free our minds of its seductive grip.

Forces of reason can be divided into two groups: forces of knowledge and forces of democracy. While both of these forces will be explained later in greater detail, it suffices to mention that true openness is a prerequisite of true knowledge—without it, ignorance will be rampant. Based on this principle, when natural laws, religious laws, and constitutional laws all reason that racial discrimination is inconsistent with human civility, knowledgeable people should not act out of transience. Failure to be open-minded betrays knowledge and perpetuates ignorance. *Forces of democracy*, on the other hand, take hold where the forces of knowledge end; when knowledgeable people understand, they should commit their support. To understand the primacy of human equality yet withhold one's support of it is tantamount to denial of democracy. The continuing reluctance of the German people to denounce Hitler's views on race is a case in point. Only when knowledge and courage are combined can irrational behavior be overcome.

One of the best examples of this combination of knowledge and courage was William Wilberforce, a young Christian member of the British Parliament. He almost single-handedly succeeded in abolishing the slave trade in nineteenth-century England. Due to the significant—and rather romantic—contributions to human civilization by Wilberforce, his story warrants a special exposition.

The Wilberforce Story

William Wilberforce (1759–1833) was the only son of prosperous English merchant parents. At 21 he ran as a conservative for a seat in Parliament from his home county of Hull. Soon after, he began the abolition movement with a small number of social reformers and a china maker named Josiah Wedgwood. The latter designed a cameo that became the equivalent of a modern-day campaign button. The cameo depicted a slave kneeling in bondage whispering the plea that was to become the movement's battle cry: "Am I not a man and a brother?" After several years of moral struggles and defeats, the Parliament, in 1807, passed the motion to abolish the most prosperous slave trade, 283 to 16. And as the votes were being counted in the House of Commons, Wilberforce sat bent in his chair with his head on his hands and tears streaming down his face. Wilberforce's conviction triumphed over a two-centuries-long "practice of bondage" that "employed upwards of 5500 sailors, upwards of 160 ships, and whose exports amounted to 800,000 pounds sterling every year" (Colson, 1987: 102–108).

The Ethical View of Racial Injustice

Racial injustice in the United States is no longer overt. It is subtle, making it much more difficult to document or measure. Even in the literature of criminal justice—which is obligated by virtue of its nature to expose racial injustice—few reports are made of racial misconduct by practitioners. But whether it is explicit or implicit, racial injustice must be considered an intrinsic act of social oppression. And the only effective way to defang oppression, Bloom asserts, is by persuading those who practice it that they are "ignorant of the good," while at the same time resisting their prejudice.

In the philosophy of ethics, equality is an integral quality of humanity; without it, the fundamental essence of humanity is diminished. Subsequently, racial inequalities must be equivalent to human degradation, because the dignity of one reflects the dignity of all. In ethical theory, only nature and rationality can be considered the standard virtues by which people can judge their lives and the lives of others, and philosophy, not history or anthropology, is the most important human science. Furthermore, only through reasoning and social enlightenment can prejudice be shamed (as Socrates shamed his detractors). This can best be accomplished by exposing racial prejudice to the light of rational thinking. On the other hand, in a civilized society, the dogmatic belief that racial prejudice is cultural must be discredited, because it can only reinforce discrimination. As will be shown, when examined from an ethical standpoint, racial prejudice is irreconcilably a problem of ignorance and a weak conscience.

Basic Theory of Prejudice

Generally stated, *prejudice* is "an adverse judgment or opinion formed without examining the facts or before having sufficient knowledge." It is an irrational belief regarding reality or what it ought to be. A prejudicial view reflects an absolutist thinking that systematically misinterprets the facts or seriously distorts judgment. Prejudice causes people to select the facts that can reinforce their position, while blinding their view of other facts (Wilbanks, 1987:13).

At this point, it is necessary to distinguish between prejudice and nonprejudicial attitudes that are heavily laden with emotion. For instance, if one is asked whether he or she can have a strong belief in capitalism without being prejudiced in its favor, the answer could be "Yes," but only if such a belief takes into consideration facts concerning other economic systems. Sociologists, however, tend to limit the term *prejudice* to the area of human interaction. This limitation has an etymological justification because the Latin term *judicum* (a preceding judgment) was used specifically to examine litigants in the courts of Rome. The status-defining connotation associated with the term, however, has not been lost and continues to mean "putting an individual in his place or class."

In a sociological sense, *prejudice* can be defined as "thinking ill of a person or a group without sufficient justification, or a disposition to respond to a certain stimulus in a certain way regarding a group of people." A more analytical definition was developed by Wilbanks, who studied prejudice as a feature of attribution theory. He defined *prejudice* as the assignment of positive traits and motives to one's self or group while assigning negative traits and motives to other groups (Wilbanks, 1987:24).

The relationship between prejudice and the concepts of *prejudgment* and *stereotyping* may need further clarification, because they have been mistakenly used to mean the same. *Prejudgment* is a generic term that means making certain decisions in advance where the facts are not available. The term is used to describe both good and bad situations (for example, we prejudge the motives of a suspect prior to conducting an investigation or the performance of students prior to taking an exam). In this sense, prejudice is a subcategory of prejudgment, one directed at irrational differences (for example, whites cannot jump, fundamentalists are terrorists, and foreign students cannot handle multiple-choice tests).

Stereotyping can be distinguished from prejudice by its greater degree of rigidity. When we stereotype someone, the person is automatically treated as an exact duplicate of the group to which he or she belongs. Furthermore, whereas prejudice usually occurs when the facts are unavailable or inadequate, stereotyping is characterized by lack of concern for difference—actually, when the facts attesting to such differences are indeed available. Moreover, while stereotyping does not necessarily constitute prejudice (for example, all students experience anxiety prior to exams), only when used to justify an irrational intent is it considered to constitute prejudice. A good example from our world of academe is the practice of grade "curving" by professors. The practice is not prejudicial if it is carried out in good faith. It can more realistically measure student performance in difficult courses. Only when the instructor chooses to curve with the intent of hurting certain students whom he or she "does not necessarily care for" does prejudice occur.

Prejudice and Knowledge

The relationship between prejudice and knowledge is of great significance, because regardless of how prejudice is rationalized, it is indisputably a type of ignorance. Prejudice is a state of mind based on belief, a level of knowledge lower than reasoning (remember Plato's divided line in Chapter 1). As such, it is not inherent to the human brain (no one is born with prejudice); rather it is acquired over extended periods because of the messages the brain receives. In a sense, all human beings are prejudiced one way or another (for example, one dislikes chocolate ice cream, while another dislikes vanilla ice cream). To overcome prejudice, however, individual persons must develop enough reasoning to block its negative effect. A mind bereft of reasoning is an ignorant mind.

Prejudicial beliefs evolve early in childhood and progressively solidify as a result of being subjected to continuing "irrational" messages—prescriptions, meanings, gestures, or symbols. Such messages originate from several sources, principally (1) the influence of role models (for example, attitudes of parents, teachers, clergy, friends, and significant others); (2) indoctrination (for example, ideological views published in books, journals, or magazines or shown on TV); (3) propaganda (for example, misleading statements usually made by political officials or marketing enterprises); and (4) socialization (for example, experiences learned from associating with others, discriminatory practices, unequal treatment, or unsuccessful relationships). Yet, like IQ or stature, prejudice is not an absolute character trait that one either has or does not have—it is usually a point on a continuum or signified by degree.

As human understanding increases through formal education, socialization, and personal experience, beliefs are modified, intensified, or reduced in proportion to the amount and quality of knowledge acquired. For instance, knowledge of social and behavioral sciences, moral principles, and logic tends to reduce prejudice by reinforcing human tolerance. On the other hand, knowledge of ethnocentrism, egoism, and authoritarianism reinforces detachment and hatred. Ideally, reaching the level of nonprejudice is achieving *civic consciousness*—the *summum bonum* of self-actualization. Individuals at that level are considered truly exceptional; they view all people as equals and treat them with equal dignity and fairness. The ratio of such persons to the general population, however, is disappointingly small. A Harvard study estimated that "four-fifths of the American population lead mental lives in which feelings of group hostility play an appreciable role" (Allport & Kramer, 1946:9).

The degree of one's prejudice can be measured by one's station on the ethical continuum. Individuals who are closest to the point of reasoning are considered *civic transcendents*. They are rational, logical, and moderate. They refuse to believe that they are more worthy than others, that their race is superior to that of others, or that their gender is higher than that of others. Critics of this view disagree, however, suggesting that regardless of one's station on the ethical continuum, one may never be able to eliminate prejudice. While this may be theoretically true, Socrates would have explained the matter in terms of residual ignorance—"they are not knowledgeable enough."

Nontranscendents, on the other hand, are individuals who are typically mindless of the wider aspects of humanity and indiscriminately rely on stereotyping all others. When faced with another individual, nontranscendents tend to hastily apply a label—for example, African American, Hispanic, foreigner, liberal, conservative, or crazy. In the objective reality of ethics, however, most theorists would agree that nontranscendents are simply acting out of ignorance and that the essential purpose of social institutions is to assist them in their transcendence to the level of civic consciousness.

Targets of Prejudice

Historically, the targets of prejudice have been determined by conflicting values that dominated the socioeconomic scene at the time. The most evident targets have been groups whose relationships with the prejudiced are marked by competition or opposition. Often one group has been singled out as a target for a period and then replaced by another group. For instance, at the outset of American history, the chief target of prejudice was the Loyalists, who opposed the movement toward independence. After the Civil War, blacks and immigrant groups were handy targets of prejudice. Economic competition was a crucial factor in the earlier outbreaks of prejudice; immigrants willing to work for lower wages often eased American workers out of jobs in an era of rapid industrialization and explosive capitalism. Another factor of hostility pertained to an ideological conflict between the Protestantism of most of the Americans and the Catholic faith of the immigrants. This was especially true after 1890, when southern Europeans began to outnumber immigrants from Germany, Great Britain, and Scandinavia. The Protestant–Catholic friction erupted in the growth of "Native American" and other nativist movements. Foremost among these movements was the Ku Klux Klan, which flourished in 1919 (Coffey et al., 1982:9).

Types of Prejudice: Cultural and Psychological

Theories of prejudice distinguish between two types: *culture-conditioned prejudice* and *character-conditioned prejudice*. Culture-conditioned prejudice is the most typical. Persons who are victims of culture-conditioned prejudice are referred to as *sociologically prejudiced*. This type of prejudice is quickly learned through the normal socialization process (family, church, school, place of employment). Thus, white persons who are raised in an environment that verbalizes antipathy toward African American culture soon assume a prejudicial belief that treats African Americans as different and inferior. By the same token, and perhaps in response to a long history of discrimination, African American persons may develop a negative view of whites that attributes evil motives to them. They tend to see whites as an insensitive group intent on denying them equal rights and opportunities. This cultural bias has led to a growing tendency to look for "facts" that can confirm this negative view of whites (Wilbanks, 1987:32).

There are differences, of course, in one's susceptibility to culture-conditioned prejudice even among those reared in the same general culture. These differences are invariably related to the extent and quality of knowledge one possesses. It has been found, for instance, that the more prejudiced persons, in contrast to the less prejudiced, are more likely to (1) have had less formal education; (2) be either a farmer or an unskilled laborer; (3) live on a farm or in a very small town; (4) take less interest in civic affairs; or (5) receive a smaller income (Coffey et al., 1982:10).

Character-conditioned prejudice, on the other hand, is rigidly embedded in one's personality. Persons afflicted with this kind of prejudice are often referred to as *psychologically prejudiced*. They harbor early-absorbed sentiments of hate, deeply embedded frustrations, and insecurities as distinct as personality deficiencies. They are more likely to be "sick," and their sickness is not of their doing, but is the outcome of a deficient upbringing. These persons can be particularly dangerous because they are (1) found in all segments of the population—among the educated, the wealthy, and the influential, as well as the poor and the uneducated; (2) more likely to be in high positions that can channel their prejudice into political or social action; and (3) far more difficult to cure. Postwar studies of the more avid Nazis and members of the American Fascist movement have uncovered all the earmarks of character-conditioned prejudice (Coffey et al., 1982:12).

Having explored these two types of prejudice, it must be emphasized that they reflect only the more traditional view of understanding race relations. They leave three other concerns that continue to cloud our understanding of prejudice: First, the view of prejudice as a product of a deep feeling of inferiority and threat. According to this theory, people who feel inferior tend to direct their bias at those whom they perceive to be even more inferior yet threatening. A good example of this is the irrational view of the Japanese by American autoworkers during the 1970s and 1980s when Japanese cars outsold most Detroit products that lacked in value or workmanship. Second, the view of prejudice as a distinct and separate type of behavior that should be studied independently of all other types of irrational behaviors. A good example of this is the irrational view of Jews by many, especially by Arabs, who share the same Semitic race with their Jewish neighbors. Third, the tendency to explain prejudice as a product of frustration, authoritarianism, displacement, or even an unidentifiable personality disorder.

Given the advancements we have made in behavioral sciences today, understanding the truth of prejudice should be sought in the broader body of sociological and psychological literature. One cannot be a "wise" student of race relations without being a student of human behavior, cultural anthropology, and the whole range of human dynamics. To simply claim that prejudice is a human "instinct," an inevitable urge to "dislike the unlike," or a natural reaction to inferiority is to fail to examine prejudice in the light of analytical thinking.

Basic Theory of Discrimination

The term *discrimination* literally means "drawing a distinction." This meaning can be expressed either positively or negatively. It is positive when one shows a "faculty for nicely distinguishing according to generally accepted standards" (for example, telling a woman that she is pretty). It is negative when one draws an "unfair or injurious distinction" (for example, questioning a person's ability because she is a member of a minority group that one disfavors). It is this latter expression that constitutes discrimination—the making of distinctions in a way that violates widely accepted social values.

Based on this definition, *discrimination* is "the injurious treatment of persons on grounds rationally irrelevant to the situation"; in other words, the "differential treatment" of individuals based on their social group or class. As social distinction, however, discrimination cannot be based on one or a few isolated acts. It must be based on a behavior pattern that identifies continual practices consistent with an ongoing tradition, social sanction, or ideology (Antonovsky, 1960:81).

Distinguishing between discrimination and prejudice is significant to understanding both concepts. It must be emphasized that discrimination is an act based on prejudice or a system of applied prejudice. Prejudice, by contrast, is *an attitude*—albeit hostile—that may or may not materialize in action. Many prejudiced individuals and groups never involve themselves in discriminatory acts, either because no situation arises, or because other considerations inhibit the open expression of discrimination. For example, although I may have an unforgiving attitude toward the former system of *apartheid* in South Africa, my attitude may remain unchanged because I did not have an opportunity to meet a member of the South African ruling party, or because I may have met with one during a Christmas party where protocol forbids discussing such political matters.

But saying that prejudice and discrimination are two distinct phenomena does not mean they are mutually exclusive. One may indeed discriminate against a minority group member—without harboring a personal prejudice—simply because members of his or her group hold a prejudice against such a minority group. A correctional officer, for instance, may treat a minority inmate more harshly than others because he or she thinks that not doing so would undermine the officer's relationship with his or her supervisor or with a wider circle of colleagues who expect such treatment to take place. By the same token, identification of certain practices as discriminatory (such as in the widely publicized cases of reverse discrimination) could lead an unprejudiced person to become prejudiced. Consequently, discrimination can exist without prejudice inasmuch as prejudice can exist without discrimination.

From a moral viewpoint, however, it is imperative that criminal justice practitioners scrutinize each prejudicial relationship they are confronted with in terms of the facts and values involved—regardless of the social or psychological pressures that bear on such a relationship. While this is obviously easier said than done, moral courage (remember Epictetus and the Stoics) should be considered the overriding value in one's judgment.

Roots of Racism

Justifying racism on the basis of economic, social, political, or psychological factors (or even on the basis of free choice) is neither logically misleading nor theoretically disturbing. Numerous philosophers, including Plato and Aristotle, have done just that with varying degrees of persuasion. In that sense, you, I, or anyone else, can present a defensible theory in support of a racist practice. But justifying racism on the basis of a moral principle is a different matter. Moral judgment, lest we forget, must be based on principles derived from reason, advanced knowledge, universal values, religious testaments, and matters of the conscience.

Before we examine the moral issues of racism, however, it is appropriate to first examine the basic conceptions, or theories, that explain racism. Some of these are of a universal nature, such as the *mystical conception* and the *biological conception*. Others are more closely associated with contemporary experiences, including the *social and legal conception* and the *institutional conception*.

The Mystical Conception of Racism

This is a view that attempted to explain racism in a rather unintelligent way. Although it dates back to ancient times, it may have indeed influenced the American experience of slavery. According to this conception, racism and slavery emanated from a common origin, one that was amoral regarding the possession of "inferior" human beings. It was based on the premise that some human beings are born inferior to others, or are so made when captured as spoils of war. As such, these individuals were to be enslaved. This view, of course, did not attempt to raise—let alone attempt to answer—such critical questions as what characterizes inferiority and what the owner–slave relationship entailed.

From a purely practical perspective, slavery was considered a legitimate endeavor in the pursuit of the "good life," and racist behavior was as natural as any other "romantic" or "literary" behavior. Slavery was inherent in most societies and practiced, in one form or another, in almost every nation. Indeed, it was old when the Pharaohs of Egypt were young and continued in Plato's Athens, Cicero's Rome, Confucius's China, Charlemagne's Europe, as well as in Jefferson's Virginia. It was practiced in Africa and the Moslem world, and it thrived in Christian Europe. Given the level of knowledge at the time, owning slaves was by no means a badge of shame. It is interesting to note, however, that slavery was not a culturally bound practice, and contrary to common belief, the white man was not the only immoral actor in the unfortunate drama. The slave trade involved African kings and chieftains who raided their own villages to capture slaves and trade them for brandy, beads, weapons, or anything else the white man had to trade (Jackson, 1990:7–12).

It is surprising that many enlightened thinkers at the time succumbed to the mystical conception. One of those was Aristotle, the master logician. In *Politics* he justified the practice of slavery on the basis that "slaves may perceive reason, but are incapable of using reason." As such, they are "by nature fitted to become the chattel of another man, and that makes it so" (Jackson, 1990:8–13). Nevertheless, being the kind and civilized gentleman he was, Aristotle urged Athenians to be fair to their slaves. Despite his undeniable genius, Aristotle was morally wrong in his treatment of the subject. The only justification for his error can be attributed to the narrow realities of the world at the time and perhaps his falling victim to the naturalistic fallacy—"what is must be what it ought to be." Bentham, the eighteenth-century utilitarian, called out Aristotle's error, cautioning that such "mistaken beliefs concerning human nature can become entirely tyrannical when they lapse in dogmatic statements" (Jackson, 1990:14).

The mystical conception of racism was used as a convenient rationalization by those who opposed social change. Subsequently, the nobility of Europe considered themselves of better ancestry than the common people. In France, the Count of Boulainvillers declared that there were two races: the nobles, who were descended from the Germanic conquerors, and the masses, who were the descendants of the Celts and Romans. After the French Revolution, the Count de Gobineau continued to applaud the mystical approach in *Essay on the Inequality of the Human Races*. He argued that "everything great, noble, and fruitful in the works of man on this earth, in science, art, and civilization, derives from a single starting point, to one family alone—the Aryans" (Martindale, 1981). Gobineau, who was opposed to democracy, admitted that his purpose was to strike at liberal ideas. His racial theory, which reiterated the old defense of feudalism, became popular among the slave owners of the Old South in the years preceding the Civil War (Simpson & Yinger, 1972:34).

In an attempt to liberalize the mystical conception, Velben and Gumplowicz (1989) identified slavery with the spoils of conquest. Velben noted that the earliest form of slavery was the seizure of female captives in warfare. As such, it became an objective of acquisition. Ownership of slaves became an institution unrelated to subsistence, and the acquisition of wealth as a means of distinction was the new incentive. Gumplowicz added a "moral reservation" to Velben's view by separating the moral question from the controversy of racism. He asserted that individual conscience and morality had nothing to do with racism, because "individuals have a conscience; but societies don't" (Jackson, 1990:7).

Nevertheless, the mystical conception continued in the works of numerous writers, including Lothrop Stoddard, Adolf Hitler, Carleton Putnam, Madison Grant, Henry Garret, Wesley George, and Robert Gayre. They all attempted to rationalize racism by using different excuses. The views of the first three writers are of specific significance. Stoddard's *Rising Tide of Color* included the thesis that the intermixture between higher and lower races can only produce a race that reverts to the lower type, and that the downfall of civilizations has been due to the crossing of racial lines. Hitler's *Mein Kampf* presented perhaps the most repercussive racial dogma. He declared that "If we divide the human race into three categories—founders, maintainers, and destroyers of culture—the Aryan stock can be considered as representing the first category." Carleton Putnam focused on the doctrine of the innate inferiority of the American Negro.

The Biological Conception of Racism

The biological conception represents an anthropological approach to racial and ethnic discrimination. According to this conception, racism was an intense concern for the purity of a given race by avoiding admixture with any another race. People are assumed to carry certain traits that if mixed with the traits of other races will produce an inferior race. This view has been used as the sorting criteria for denigrating members of the black race, first in Europe and subsequently in the United States, and of the Jewish race, especially in Nazi Germany.

To a great measure, the biological conception was reinforced by the reading (and certainly the misreading) of Darwinist thought as presented in *On the Origin of Species by Means of Natural Selection*, or *The Preservation of Favored Races in the Struggle for Life* in 1859, and in *The Descent of Man* in 1871. Darwinist theory emphasized, in particular, the part played by the survival of the fittest in the process of natural selection. While Darwin's views were supported by great enthusiasts at the time, including Galton, Prichard, and Weismann, it was seriously criticized by equally eminent scholars such as Bagehot, Gumplowicz, and Kidd (Banton, 1967:37–42). Darwin, who made no attempt to classify races, observed considerable differences that had been "nearly constant for a very long time" and therefore concluded they could not be the product of environmental factors. Based on these observations, he concluded that human differentiation was due to sexual selection; "the choice by men and women of partners whom they found most to their taste" (Banton, 1967:36). Indeed, the biological theory relied heavily on Darwin's idea that attempted to ensure the continuance of the best-adapted types.

Early biological theories identified three basic races—*Negroid, Mongoloid,* and *Caucasoid*—on the basis of a variety of feature classifications. These included shape of body, head, and nose; color of skin, hair, and eyes; and texture of hair, among others. Each classification had several subcategories. For instance, the Caucasoid classification included the Mediterranean, the Nordic, and the Lapps; the Negroid classification included African Negroid, Oceanic Negroid, Asian Negroites, and others. Groups that did not fit any of those classifications were either ignored or squeezed into one of the three racial pigeonholes regardless of their lack of conformity (Coffey et al., 1982:5). For example, Arabs and Jews, who are both Semitic, are considered Caucasoids despite noticeable differences. By the same token, Sudanese and Nubians are considered Negroids despite the fact that they are descendants of Arab Hamite (Caucasoid) stock.

More recent biological theorists used a numerical method to formulate other classifications that focused on combinations of three or more characteristics such as skin, hair, and eye color; facial counters; nasal indexes; and stature or height. Some of these classifications are as complex—and perhaps as silly—as they are limited in utility. Take, for instance, Broca's measurement known as the "cephalic index." According to the model, to distinguish dilicho-cephalic (long-headed) populations from brachycephalic (broad-headed) ones, the lengthwise diameter of the skull is to be divided into the crosswise diameter and the result multiplied by 100 (Banton, 1967:38). By the same token, the nasal index examines the relationship between the width of the nose measured between the wings and the length of the nose from the juncture of the septum to the upper lip. If the percentage of the width relative to the length is less than 70, the index is called *leptorrhine* (narrow-nosed); if it is 84 or over, the indexes are known as *platyrrhine* (broad-nosed). Intermediate indexes are *mesorrhine* (medium-nosed). Hair color and eye color are exceedingly complex, and technical subjects and details concerning them cannot be presented here.

The biological theory became even more complex when new factors related to genetics, blood groups, and diseases were added. Nevertheless, it became increasingly apparent that the theory overlooked several critical elements that could radically alter the understanding of race theory. Consider, for instance, the following reservations that focus on the ethical factor among races:

1. *The myth of racial cultures*: Studies of race show no correlation between race and culture. Indeed, one looks in vain for a "Negroid culture," a "Mongoloid culture," or a "Caucasoid culture." There are, of course, variations in family roles, religious beliefs, government systems, artistic traditions, and other aspects of culture from one section of Africa to another. The same is true for Latin America, Europe, and the United States. But since the development of rapid means of communication and transportation, the inventions and systems of diverse peoples have been transplanted to all habitable regions of the earth. The young children of any race today seem to have no difficulty absorbing any set of cultural norms, provided they are constantly exposed to it. Indeed, in spite of all preoccupations about racial differences, where white and black slaves in seventeenth-century America found themselves with common problems, common work, and common enemies, they behaved toward one another as equals (Zinn, 1980:31). Perhaps one of the best examples of the absence of a relationship between race and culture is seen in the African American population, in which relatively few still retain African culture traits. Current differences in behavior between white Americans and African Americans are mainly attributable to class, education, occupation, and other nonracial factors (Simpson & Yinger 1972:58).

2. *The doctrine of mentally superior races*: The belief that some groups have greater intellectual capacity than others goes back at least to the time of Aristotle. Mythical dogmas have reinforced that belief. Nevertheless, numerous studies indicate the invalidity of this belief. For instance, C.S. Myers, professor of experimental psychology at Oxford, concluded after many years of study of local populations in Australia and Africa that "the mental features of the rural populations in Europe correspond essentially to those observed in primitive peoples and that differences where they occur must be ascribed to environmental influences" (Simpson & Yinger 1972:50). Another significant study was conducted by the Department of the Army during World War I. In the study, 15,000 southern blacks and 8,000 northern blacks were tested

for differences in IQ. Northern blacks were clearly superior to the southern blacks. The study also revealed that although northern blacks ranked below northern whites, the median IQs for blacks from Ohio, Illinois, New York, and Pennsylvania were higher than the median IQs for whites from Mississippi, Arkansas, and Georgia (Simpson & Yinger 1972:51).

3. *The fallacy of racial morality*: A widespread belief suggests a strong connection between racial traits and ethical standards. Deviation from genteel middle- or upper-class norms on the part of members of racial minorities are often credited to the "wild blood" of the recently domesticated savages, or the "low-grade blood" of peasant hordes. Such explanations seem to indicate that untamed people are controlled by whim and passion rather than by reason and self-restraint. The practices traditionally cited to show the brutality and undeveloped moral sense of nonwhite groups include infanticide, incest, and premarital sexual intercourse, which also occur in other cultural contexts. By the same token, mention is rarely made of the immoral practices prevalent among white societies. Such practices include the bloodbath atrocities committed by the Crusaders in the eleventh century, by the Catholic Inquisitors in the eighteenth century, by the colonialists in the nineteenth century, by the Aryans under Hitler, by the Bolsheviks under Stalin, or by the Bosnians against the Moslems in the twentieth century. In the United States one can cite only the high violence rate; the high delinquency rate; the high divorce rate; the increasing rate of homelessness, child abuse, drug-addicted babies, gangsterism; and, of course, racism.

Given these reservations, a "reasoning person" would be at a loss trying to answer the questions "What is a moral race?" and "Which ones, if any, are and which ones are not?" Franz Boas, in *The Mind of the Primitive Man* (1938), states that we unwittingly pursue a false reasoning by believing that "since the aptitude of the European is the highest, then every deviation from the white type necessarily represents a lower feature" (Boas, 1938:3–10). While Western civilization is especially notable for technological and economic development, these do not necessarily imply greater advancement or a keener sense of justice. In some ways they may even be adverse to the "good life." Consider, for example, the damage to the global environment due to acid rain, or the threat to the health and well-being of individuals due to radioactive waste and carcinogenic materials produced by large-scale, self-serving industries. Given these observations, I always tell my students that "civilization was never meant to be summed up in skyscrapers and industrial leviathans, but rather in the *eudaemonia* of citizens. Unless intellect is brought to life as widely as possible, and with the unmistakable purpose of enriching civilization, it is valueless."

Reasoning, as well as history, may attest to the fact that none of the world's civilizations was the product of the genius of a single people. Lowie asserts that ideas and inventions were carried from one culture to another and disseminated by people that came into contact with one another. Neither race nor language limited their diffusion. And because many races worked together in the development of the ancient civilizations, it is only logical to bow to the genius of all. Lowie further explains that, notwithstanding undeniable differences in outward manifestations, all cultures display the same sentiments toward basic human relations. Savage and civilized cultures alike seek not unbridled self-indulgence, but restraint; not brutality, but kindness; not neglect of one's neighbors, but regard for them. What differs is essentially the extent to which these sentiments are applied in the group (Lowie, 1941:33).

Social and Legal Conceptions of Racism

These conceptions focus on the social settings that breed racism and give them impetus. Racist attitudes can develop because of social interaction with others even without actually seeing them. All human beings are considered "perceivers," because their beliefs are influenced by the meanings, symbols, and values of society. But because of one's ignorance of other factors that may bear on the issue, or because of the applicability of the same factors to other groups, perceivers selectively recognize certain factors as their "total world." Over time, these factors become socialized in their perception of others, and judgment becomes "unavoidably" colored by a social filter.

Social stigma (more than physical features or facial expressions) is what truly determines how one is perceived and therefore treated. The more a target group is described in derogatory terms, the more its members are subjected to racist treatment. The conception is essentially consistent with Sutherland's theory of differential association that you may have already encountered in criminology courses. Examples of stigmatized populations include the Jewish race in Nazi Germany, the Japanese during World War II, the Iraqis during the Gulf War, and, of course, African Americans in America.

Because race relations are so critical to the conduct of criminal justice, the following sections will focus on the social and legal conceptions of racism and point out ethical dilemmas and ethical remedies.

The Social View

Perhaps the best way to illustrate the social view of racism in the United States is through the anecdotal method. The title of our story will be "The Social Drawing of the Color Line," a title taken from Zinn's work, *A People's History of the United States* (1980). The story begins like this:

Once upon a time there was a Negro race. Unlike the white or the Indian races, it was the easiest to enslave. Within 40 years after the first Negroes landed in Jamestown in 1619, they became a group apart, separated from the rest of society by custom and law. Treated as servants for life, forbidden even to wed whom they chose among their own group, deprived of their African traditions, and dispersed among Southern plantations, they became an outcast class. They were stigmatized as "dirty, soiled, foul, sinister, iniquitous, and horribly wicked" (Zinn, 1980:31). Because most Americans at the time were in favor of slavery, they harassed those who sought to educate Negro children and attacked those involved in reforming their living conditions. A pervasive body of literature was also already in circulation that the mystical approach showed that the Negro was imperfectly developed in mind and body, that he belonged to a lower order of man, and that slavery was right not only on economic grounds, but also on social grounds.

The conditions in which Negroes lived were despicable and slave protest was unavoidable. The despair of the Negroes was evident and malingering, and sabotage tormented every slaveholder. The problem of runaway slaves became endemic. Some slaves—Gabriel Prosser in 1800, Denmark Vesey in 1822, Nat Turner in 1831, and others—turned to violence, and the sporadic uprisings that flared demonstrated a deep protest against a demeaning way of life. Subsequently, the laws of bondage became even more institutionalized. Masters retained absolute authority over their slaves, who were unable to leave their masters' properties without written permission. Even if they wanted to run away, unlike the Indian slaves, they had "no countrymen a hill or a forest away" to help. They could own no property, could enter into no contract, and had no right to assemble in public places unless a white person was present. Above all, they had no standing in the courts. In both North and South they were regularly victims of mobs. In 1829, for instance, white residents invaded Cincinnati's "Little Africa," killed the Negroes, burned their belongings, and ultimately drove their entire population from the city (Report of the National Advisory Commission on Civil Disorders, 1968:209).

In the nineteenth century, Negroes' despair increased, but so did the moral anguish among the whites who sought to "uplift the whole human race" by abolishing slavery. In 1834 the American Moral Reform Society was founded, and in 1852 *Uncle Tom's Cabin* appeared and sold more than 300,000 copies the first year. The book dramatized the cruelty of slave masters and overseers and condemned a society based on human degradation and exploitation. When Frederick Douglass, the distinguished Negro abolitionist, addressed the citizens of Rochester, New York, on Independence Day, 1852, he told them,

The Fourth of July is yours, not mine. You may rejoice, I must mourn.
To drag a man into the grand illuminated temple of liberty, and call
upon him to join you in joyous anthems, were inhuman mockery and
sacrilegious irony ... Fellow citizens, above your national tumultuous
joy, I hear the mournful wail of millions, whose chains, heavy and
grievous yesterday, are today rendered more intolerable by the jubilant
shouts that reach them (Report, 1968: 211).

The Civil War did not offer much relief to the enslaved race. The
Union victory promised freedom, but not equality or immunity from
white domination. More violence and deaths occurred as a result of
further racial confrontations. During World War I, Negro combat units
had to fight under French commanders (because their own white
officers refused to command them) and performed exceptionally well,
vindicating the French commanders' belief that Negro soldiers were
not inferior people. As a result, perhaps, when the war was won, the
returning Negro soldiers expected to be treated equally to white soldiers.
However, they were mobbed for attempting to use facilities open only to
white soldiers, and of the 70 Negroes lynched during the first year after
the war, a substantial number were soldiers. Some were even lynched
while in uniform (Report, 1968:219). By 1919 the Ku Klux Klan flourished, basically in response to the popular movement for equality by the
victorious Negro soldiers. The Ku Klux Klan program that emphasized
"uniting native-born white Christians for concerted action in the preservation of American institutions and the supremacy of the white race"
was implemented by flogging, branding with acid, tarring and
feathering, hanging, and burning. The program contributed to the
destruction of the elemental rights of many Negroes and of some whites
(Report, 1968:219).

While violence and death continued on both sides of the color line,
and despite the establishment of the federal Civil Rights Commission
(1957) and the ensuing generations of civil rights laws, rules, and regulations, racism in America left deep imprints on the American perception
as an unmistakable social, but irrational, doctrine.

The Legal View

This view holds that in addition to socialization, laws (including
Supreme Court and federal court decisions) are particularly powerful
instruments of racism. They reinforce social order by compelling people
to alter their behaviors, attitudes, and beliefs. Legalism establishes an
obligation to adhere to social rules. Failure to comply with these rules
can demonstrate absence of civic duty or an indication of social delinquency, or can constitute a crime. Consequently, constitutional and legal

traditions, which were discussed in Chapter 2, have for centuries been considered primary sources of moral reasoning.

In a previous draft of the Declaration of Independence, Americans indicted the king of England only for waging "cruel war against human nature itself." The king was accused of "violating the most sacred rights of life and liberty in the persons of a distant people who never offended him, and carrying them into slavery in another hemisphere" (Report, 1968:208). In the final version of the Declaration, however, Americans proclaimed that "all men are created equal," presenting a radical change in the social contract. The document nevertheless ignored the blacks who were held in bondage and the few who were set free.

The first test of the Declaration came when blacks were barred from serving in the Revolutionary Army. Recruiting officers were instructed in 1775 to enlist no "stroller, vagabond, or Negro" (Report, 1968:208). The *Dred Scott v. Sanford* case in 1857 not only legalized discrimination, but also abolished the humanity of the Negro altogether. The decision involved a Negro slave who had lived with his master for 5 years in the Illinois and Wisconsin Territories, which were free at the time. The Court decided that because Mr. Scott was a slave, he was not a citizen and not entitled to the constitutional safeguards enjoyed by other Americans. The decision was upheld as law of the land until 1868, when it was over-ruled by the Fourteenth Amendment. The amendment applied to "All persons born or naturalized in the United States, and subject to the juris-diction thereof." It declared that "No state shall make or enforce any law which shall abridge the privileges or immunities of citizens . . . without the due process of law; nor deny to any person within its jurisdiction the equal protection of the laws." The amendment extended the principle of equality under the law to all human beings.

For many years, however, the courts interpreted the law in accor-dance with socially held doctrines of equality. In *Plessy v. Ferguson* (1896) the Supreme Court upheld the doctrine of "separate but equal" as the criteria of equality for American blacks. Government-endorsed segregation thus became the established moral doctrine. Blacks and whites were separated on public carriers and in all places of public accommodation, including hospitals and churches. In courthouses, whites and blacks took oaths on separate Bibles, and in most commu-nities whites were separated from blacks in cemeteries. Justice Harlan, expressing a minority opinion in *Plessy v. Ferguson*, wrote,

> In view of the Constitution, in the eye of the law there is in this country no superior, dominant ruling class of citizens. There is no caste here. Our Constitution is color blind, and neither knows nor tolerates classes among citizens. In respect of civil rights, all citizens are equal before the law. The humblest is the peer of the most powerful. The law regards man as man, and takes no account of his surroundings or of

his color when his civil rights as guaranteed by the supreme law of the land are involved (163 U.S. 537, 559, 1896)

As we learned earlier, legal segregation has led to legal discrimination. On trains, blacks—including those holding first-class tickets—were allotted seats in the baggage car. Blacks in public buildings had to use freight elevators and toilet facilities reserved for janitors. Schools for black children were, at best, a weak imitation of those for whites, as states spent 10 times more to educate white youngsters than blacks. Racial discrimination virtually became the moral of the land until 1954, when *Brown v. Board of Education* declared the practice unconstitutional. In the 1960s the civil rights movement began to erase the moral stigma, but the social conception of racism refused to die, giving rise to a new conception of racism—institutional racism.

Institutional Racism

Institutional racism involves discriminatory practices that are inflicted by institutions (public or private) rather than by individuals. In other words, no identifiable person or group can be held directly accountable. The concept defines "situations in which there is disparity in outcome by race, though there may be no evidence of an intent to cause such an effect." Racial disparity appears commonly in matters of housing, education, hiring, and promotion but, more alarmingly, in practices of criminal justice as well.

The concept of institutional racism is undoubtedly controversial and can raise a great deal of ethical concern. More African Americans today seem to invoke this argument, indicating that regardless of intent by any given individual, "racism is racism is racism," and the fact that the culprit is the system offers no acceptable justification. People can be equally hurt by systems as by individuals.

To alleviate institutional racism, a gamut of laws have been passed by federal and state governments since the 1960s pertaining to affirmative action programs, the assignment of quotas associated with minority hiring, and the promotion of minority groups ahead of their peers, as methods of ensuring fair and equal treatment. As amended by the Equal Employment Opportunity Act of 1972, the Civil Rights Act of 1964 requires that government and businesses undertake affirmative action programs. These programs are designed "to correct imbalances in employment that exist directly as a result of institutional discrimination" (Barry, 1982:311). But while these measures were designed to overcome legal racism against blacks and minorities, they also raised serious reservations concerning justice and unfairness to "disenfranchised" white Americans. Such reservations are commonly known as "reverse discrimination."

Reverse Discrimination

Without sounding too legalistic, affirmative action refers to positive measures legislated beyond normal nondiscriminatory and merit-hiring practices. It is an aggressive program designed to identify and remedy discrimination against people who are qualified for jobs. *Preferential hiring* is an employment practice that gives special consideration to persons victimized by racism, sexism, or other forms of discrimination. *Quota hiring* is a practice of hiring and employing people in direct proportion to their numbers in the community. According to affirmative action guidelines, preferential and quota hiring go hand in hand. Courts today increasingly require government and private institutions to provide apprentice and re-apprentice training to hire, promote, and train minorities and women in specified ratios, in specified job categories, *until* remedial goals are reached.

Critics, on the other hand, charge that at least in some instances, implementing affirmative action guidelines has led to *reverse discrimination*— the unfair treatment of majority members—usually white males (Barry, 1982:306). For example, in 1996 the State of California passed Resolution 209, which dismantled many of the affirmative action programs designed to admit women and minorities to state colleges and universities, in the hiring of faculty members, and in state contracts. By the same token, the City of Houston recently defeated a similar proposition designed to end racial preference in the receipt of city contracts. While the California position does not seem to have extended much beyond the state of California, ethical arguments for and against reverse discrimination continue. For the purpose of this discussion, only the main points will be presented. They have been gleaned rather liberally from Barry's thesis.

Arguments for reverse discrimination include the following:

1. *Compensatory justice demands reverse discrimination.* This point is based on the assumption that black minorities and women traditionally have been discriminated against, often viciously. As individuals and as a nation, we cannot ignore the sins of our fathers and mothers—indeed, we are obligated to repair their wrongs. This point is also consistent with both Bentham's "most good for most people" utilitarian theory, and Rawls's doctrine of the difference principle: "Social and economic institutions are to be arranged so as to offer maximum benefits to those who are worst off—regardless of who they are." And because minority members and women happen to be the worst off (among the most people) at

this point in history, preferential treatment is justified and reverse discrimination is a "sound method" of compensatory justice.

2. *Reverse discrimination defuses social unrest.* This point is based on the fact that the social conditions in our society are volatile. Blacks are pitched against whites, and females against males. At the core of this tension is the fact that minority members and women do not share in the economic bounty of this land. Furthermore, minority members perceive white males and the establishments they "man" as bent on preserving the white males' preferred social and economic position. Whether or not this perception is accurate is irrelevant, but a potential "class war" must be avoided. Hence the need to renegotiate the social contract to accommodate this eminent danger; otherwise, Hobbes's fears may materialize and citizens may revert to their "natural state" of violence. Thus, preferential treatment is justified as a method of unnecessarily avoiding "social turmoil."

3. *Reverse discrimination is a last-ditch attempt to curb existing discrimination.* The salience of this point is that it is analogous to that of the *Miranda* rule, which was required by the Supreme Court to clean up illegitimate police acts. The argument goes as follows: "If there is any other way to root out racism and sexism in society, we would favor it over reverse discrimination, but since there is not, we have no choice but to support it." Proponents of this argument assert that it would be "nice" if we could count on the good graces of the population to rid society of inequalities, but because there is nothing to suggest that it will, a last-ditch effort must be attempted. This argument supports the historical view that "Until people are forced to change, they will not, and unless they are forced to play fair, they will not relinquish their preferred positions."

Arguments against reverse discrimination include the following:

1. *Reverse discrimination is unequal treatment.* This point is based on the fact that in the final analysis, reverse discrimination boils down to recompensing one race or sex over others, solely for biological reasons. Equality can exist only where all individuals are treated the same, where they are rewarded or punished to the same degree for the same behavior, regardless of race or sex. Reverse discrimination precludes this—and, as such, violates natural and constitutional law.

2. *Reverse discrimination victimizes white males.* This point is based on the psychological concept of "self-identity," a concept that must be preserved; otherwise, people would experience unhealthy feelings of anxiety, frustration, and hostility. When people have poor self-concepts, they are unhappy—and indeed can hardly

pursue happiness. Therefore, because reverse discrimination makes white males feel unequal, inadequate, or incomplete—due to no fault of their own—we are doing them far greater harm. Admittedly, this is one of the most potent arguments against reverse discrimination. But the argument also can be reversed and applied to the initial discrimination against women and minorities: Do they not also have equal rights to self-identity and self-concept? And was violating these rights not what created the need for preferential treatment in the first place?

Is the Criminal Justice System Racist?

There is considerable debate about whether the criminal justice system—in particular, the application of capital punishment—is racist. An increasing number of notable researchers have been involved, including Wilbanks, Wilson, Hagan, Blumstein, Hindelang, Kleck, Petersilia, and others.

Not surprisingly, this is a ubiquitous question, answers to which warrant an entire volume if it is ever possible to conclusively ascertain. At the time of this research there are allegations and counter-allegations. Each allegation is based on one or more studies—the findings of which may be indicative yet, if taken separately, are inconclusive. But given the significant ethical issues involved in this debate, a brief and a rather uncomplicated attempt will be made to explain the main arguments. Discussions will be based to a large measure on Wilbanks's work, *The Myth of a Racist Criminal Justice System* (1987), but also to a lesser measure on Pepinsky and Jesilow's *Myths That Cause Crime* (1984) and Petersilia's *Racial Disparities in the Criminal Justice System* (1983).

The Debate

White and black Americans differ sharply about whether the criminal justice system is racist. The vast majority of blacks argue that the police and courts discriminate against blacks, whereas a majority of whites reject the charge. In Dade County, Florida (Miami), for example, a poll by a television station found that 97% of blacks believed the justice system to be racist and 58% of whites disagreed (Wilbanks, 1987:1). This disparity in views between blacks and whites also appears to exist among those who work in the criminal justice system. In a supplemental study for the National Advisory Commission on Civil Disorders in 1968, it was found that 57% of black police officers but only 5% of white officers believed that the system discriminated against blacks. Some black critics conclude that the criminal justice system is so characterized by racism that blacks are no longer within the protection of the law. Others charge that when whites speak of justice, they really mean "just us." Another black critic indicted the criminal justice system as "more criminal than just" (Wilbanks, 1987:1).

A sizeable minority of whites, on the other hand, charge that the criminal justice system actually discriminates for blacks in bending over backward for them in reactions to charges of racism from the black community, liberal white politicians, and elements of the news media. White police officers have reported that they often ignore criminal activity by blacks out of fear of criticism from the department, the black community, or the media. Because officers are seldom criticized for inaction, "they find themselves tempted to overlook a situation that might lead to physical conflict and subsequent criticism" (Wilbanks 1987:1).

Although numerous charges of racism have been levied against the criminal justice system (mostly by black communities and liberal white critics), encompassing the entire gamut of police, prosecution, conviction, sentencing, and prisons, reference will be made only to the areas of police, corrections, and parole. Doubts in the area of courts (conviction and sentencing) have probably been cleared (at least to some measure) by the publication of the report by the New York State Judicial Commission on Minorities (1991), presented at the outset of the discussion on racism. By the end of this segment, Wilbanks's thesis refuting the allegations of racism in the criminal justice system will be examined.

Accusations against Police

Pepinsky and Jesilow (1984) accuse police departments of racial discrimination by deploying officers in such a fashion that crimes disproportionately committed by blacks are the focus of patrol and detection efforts. If the police were so concerned with "crime in the suites" as they were with "crimes in the street," the authors charge, blacks and whites would be arrested in proportionate numbers. Current police deployment strategies give the false impression that most criminals are black. Another charge accuses the police of racial discrimination on the grounds that officers are more likely to arrest blacks than whites. One study often cited in support of this charge examined the impact of race on 5,688 police/citizen encounters in 24 police departments in the metropolitan areas of St. Louis, Rochester, and Tampa/St. Petersburg. The study, which was controlled for race, sex, age, and demeanor of offender, among other variables, showed that blacks were arrested in 21.4% of their encounters with police, as opposed to 13.1% for whites (Smith & Visher, 1981).

Accusations against the Correctional System

Critics accuse the prison system of chronic and pervasive discrimination, especially because segregation was the rule in northern as well as southern prisons until the late 1960s. Perhaps the most blatant form of racial discrimination by American prison systems was the post–Civil War practice in the South of leasing black adult male felons to private parties. This practice not only helped to achieve the racial subordination of blacks, but also was highly profitable to southern states at a time when they were hard-pressed for revenue (Wilbanks, 1987:126). Among the more serious charges of racial discrimination is the fact that blacks are incarcerated at a rate 8 times that of whites. This alone, in the minds of critics, is evidence of discrimination.

Accusations against Parole

Critics suggest that black inmates are discriminated against by white parole boards so that blacks serve longer terms in prison than whites with comparable sentences. In a study of racial differences at various points in the criminal justice systems of California, Texas, and Michigan, Petersilia has shown racial discrimination in time served in prison and on parole. She states, "It was evident that although minorities received equal treatment in prison, they did not when it came time for release. Controlling for factors that could affect the release decision (including participation in prison programs and prison violence) we found consistent evidence that race made a difference" (Petersilia, 1983:49).

The Wilbanks Rebuttal

In *The Myth of a Racist Criminal Justice System* (1987), Wilbanks, who makes no claims to resolving all the issues involved, attempts to articulate the major areas of dissonance. Although his thesis is beyond a doubt "the system is not racist," his explanation hinges on many qualifications that cannot be resolved in the absence of another set of research techniques—those that could measure human endeavors and aversions, reasons for action, and sensitivities toward fellow human beings. As to when such techniques might be available for use, no one can speculate.

Taking Wilbanks's defense at face value, however, the author makes some penetrating and rather convincing defenses of his thesis. Some of the more significant arguments Wilbanks makes are as follows:

1. There is no doubt that there is racial prejudice in the criminal justice system, in that there are individuals, both white and black, who make decisions partly on the basis of race. Nevertheless, the system is not characterized by racial discrimination against blacks.

2. The denial of a racist justice system at present does not deny the existence in the past of systematic racial prejudice and discrimination in designing and operating the system.

3. The view that the criminal justice system is racist is problematic in view of the myriad definitions of the term *racist* and is valid only if one accepts the view that racism is proven simply by blacks being disproportionately represented at arrest through incarceration.

4. The assertion that the criminal justice system is not racist should not be confused with the issue of whether blacks commit more crimes at a greater rate than whites because of discrimination by the sociopolitical system.

5. The arguments that the system is racist imply that the system in itself (from the point of arrest to the point of incarceration) tends to accentuate the oppression of black offenders. This is inaccurate, because the black–white ratio of 8:1 at incarceration is not a product of the system. The racial gap remains relatively stable from arrest to sentencing and does not cumulatively increase from point to point across the system.

6. The racial gap at arrest is a product of a gap in offending rather than of racial discrimination by the police.

7. The assertion that racism in the criminal justice system is a myth does not suggest that the opposite thesis has been proven. Neither thesis has been proven.

Exploratory Issues in Racism

From the previous discussions, it becomes clear that racial discrimination is a complicated social problem. Yet it is essentially an "ethical problem" that cannot be fully rectified by constitutional or legal sanctions. While laws, rules, and regulations are certainly of a corrective nature, they alone cannot alleviate the implications of racial discrimination, improve social justice, or cleanse a conscience that is loaded with ignorance and hatred. As shown from the Wilbanks thesis, discrimination is a product of ignorance of facts, incorrect reasoning, or the absence of an active conscience.

To further articulate the moral issues in racism, two sets of exploratory questions will be raised. An intellectual examination of these questions can promote an insightful appraisal of the thorny issues of racism and put it to rest, once and for all.

1. Is race a matter of free choice? In other words, do human beings
    choose their race? Could it not be that individuals are created (or
    evolved) into a race not of their choosing? The answer to the first
    two questions must be an unequivocal "No," because a choice of
    race is impossible to the unborn, and no spiritual or metaphysical
    evidence to the contrary has been discovered. Although some
    could argue that given today's genetic engineering technology,
    scientists can manipulate the characteristics of infants, the embryos
    in question are neither consulted nor capable of making a choice.
    And because the answer to the first two questions is "No," the
    answer to the third question must logically be "Yes," for the same
    reason.

2. Given the determinacy of race, on what grounds can one then
    claim racial superiority over another? Can existence based on
    "random birth" justify claiming superiority over someone who
    was "randomly born" to another race? From a reasoning perspec-
    tive, the answer to the first question must be "None," because, in a
    democracy, offering privileged treatment, especially on the basis of
    birth, is unjustifiable (see Rawls, for instance). By the same token,
    the answer to the second question must be "No," for the same rea-
    son. Consequently, whereas no one could claim credit for the way
    he or she "came to being," no superior or inferior status can be
    assigned on the basis of race, and no apology should be necessary
    for being a member of another race. The chances of one being born
    white, black, Hispanic, or otherwise depends unequivocally on the
    genetic combination of the parents. Claims to superiority, there-
    fore, must be considered fallacious.

The issue of racial superiority, as you may have gathered, is as complex as it is fallacious. Let us examine, for intellectual stimulation only, a
quandary I often share with my students: the race of Jesus Christ. "Was
he of a superior or an inferior race?" If he was in fact the son of God, it
should be safe to assume that he must have been able to choose his
race—for instance, Aryan or Roman. Yet he was born a Semitic Jew,
supposedly an inferior race at the time. Based on that choice, then,
should the Semitic race not be the master race? Yet it is not. On the
other hand, if he chose to be born to a modest race to demonstrate his
humble origins, how did Semitic Jews end up being God's chosen
people? Where would that leave the legacy of racial superiority?

Moral Guidelines in Understanding Racism

Based on the previous discussions and explorations, criminal justice
students and practitioners should intellectually consider the following
conclusions as moral guidelines:

1. *Racism is a mindless belief*, because it violates the basic truths of nature and reasoning. In the universal reality of humankind, one cannot be rewarded or victimized on the basis of race. Furthermore, if this logic is erroneous, then racial discrimination against white people in African or Asian cultures should be legitimately acceptable. A black or Hispanic person has as much right to liberty, equality, and dignity as a white person—simply by virtue of membership in humankind.

2. *Racism is an artificial social label* manufactured by "uncivilized" social groups to manipulate the articles of the "social contract." As such, the label can be attached to any group, at any time, for any reason, given favorable sociopolitical conditions. In this sense, racism is egotistically immoral, potentially dangerous, and not conducive to social goodness.

3. *Racism violates religious doctrine.* Pope John Paul II declared that "Harboring racist thoughts and entertaining racist attitudes is a sin." In an 800-word document published by the Pontifical Commission for Peace and Justice, the Vatican denounced apartheid in South Africa, tribal conflicts in Africa, the violation of the rights of aboriginal peoples in Australia, and the discrimination encountered by migrants in European and Asian countries. The document added that in the United States, "Much still remains to be done to eliminate racial behavior in what can be considered one of the most interracial nations in the world" (*New York Times*, May 15, 1990).

4. *Racism is constitutionally and legally wrong.* The Thirteenth Amendment (1865) and the Fourteenth Amendment (1868) began a long list of prohibitions against racist behaviors, and federal and state civil rights laws continue to ban such behaviors.

5. *Racism may reflect a character deficiency*, one that signifies a lack of integrity, because it violates the agencies' code of ethics as well as obligations to "liberty and justice for all." It furthermore renders the practitioner's oath of office in affirmation of this pledge a morally indictable lie.

6. *All participants in the criminal justice system, including suspects and inmates, should be treated equally despite their racial differences.* They are entitled to the same immunities and privileges accorded by natural law, religious testaments, constitutional and legal provisions, and ethical codes of civilized behavior.

7. *All practitioners in the criminal justice system, including managers and subordinates, should be treated as ends rather than means.* They should receive fair and equal treatment for what they are. Racial differences do not translate to racial status, and racial discrimination in the workplace only adds to deterioration of productivity.

8. *At all times, practitioners should exercise noblesse oblige in the treatment of members of other races.* Such treatment must

manifest respect, honor, and goodwill, rather than suspicion, egoism, self-interest, or intimidation. When in doubt, the reasoning practitioner should consider Kant's test of universalization: "What if everybody were subjected to this kind of treatment ... Would that bring about more or less civic righteousness?"

Conclusions

Racial discrimination is an intrinsic social evil. It has led to increased injustice, oppression, and hatred in a society bent on justice, tolerance, and morality. The potency of racial discrimination stems from collective ignorance, rigid belief, and indifference to the dictates of conscience. Ironically, however, racism in America may have served, in part, as a moral antidote against tyranny and ethnocentrism. Racial struggles have kept the nation humble and forced Americans to search for a renewed faith in virtue. While vitriolic strides have been made toward racial harmony and nowhere are minority groups as protected as in the United States, "subliminal" discrimination continues, contaminating the mental and emotional state of the unenlightened and the morally feeble.

Criminal justice professionals are, by definition, moral agents and shapers of values. As such, they must form the front line of defense against racial discrimination and, individually, should be on their guard as to its potential destructiveness. While antidiscrimination laws are essential to preserving social justice, without a persistent concern for racial tolerance the situation can hardly improve. In the final analysis, the practitioner's resolve to reduce racial prejudice may be the only "difference" that can truly "make a difference."

Review Questions

1. Discuss the two basic categories of inequality. How are criminal justice agencies directly involved with issues of prejudice and discrimination?

2. Define *prejudice* in a sociological sense. What is the relationship between prejudice and the concepts of "prejudgment" and "stereotypy"?

3. Distinguish between "culture-conditioned prejudice" and "character-conditioned prejudice." Define *discrimination*.

4. Explain the mystical conception of racism and compare it to the biological conception of racism.

5. What is the "social and legal conception of racism"? Discuss the presence of "institutional racism" in your agency.

6. What are the arguments for reverse discrimination? What are the counterarguments? Where do you stand, and why?

7. Provide examples of charges of racism levied against the criminal justice system. Explain Wilbanks's rebuttal.

8. Why is racial discrimination an ethical problem? Discuss two sets of exploratory questions that emphasize the moral issues of racism.

9. Outline intellectually the moral guidelines of racism. What are the chances of their success in your agency?

References

Allport, G. W., & Kramer, B. M. (1946). Some Roots of Prejudice. *J Psychol, 22,* 9–39.

Antonovsky, A. (1960). The Social Meaning of Discrimination. *Phylon* (Spring), 81–95.

Banton, M. (1967). *Race Relations.* London: Social Science Paperbacks.

Barry, V. (1982). *Applying Ethics: A Text with Readings.* Belmont, CA: Wadsworth Publishing.

Bloom, A. (1987). *The Closing of the American Mind.* New York: Touchstone.

Boas, F. (1938). *The Mind of the Primitive Man.* New York: Macmillan Publishing.

Brown v. Board of Education (1954). 347 U.S. 483.

Coffey, A., Eldefonso, E., & Hartinger, W. (1982). *Human Relations: Law Enforcement in a Changing Community* (3rd ed.). Englewood Cliffs, NJ: Prentice-Hall.

Colson, C. (1987). *Kingdoms in Conflict: An Insider's Challenging View of Politics, Power, and the Pulpit.* New York: Morrow.

Dred Scott v. Sanford (1857). 60 U.S. (19 How.) 393.

Independent Commission on the Los Angeles Police Department (1991). Los Angeles: City of Los Angles.

Jackson, J. E. (1990). *Ethics and Racial Discrimination.* Unpublished paper.

Lowie, R. H. (1941). Intellectual and Cultural Achievements of Human Races. In H. S. Jennings (Ed.), *Scientific Aspects of the Race Problem.* New York: Longman.

Martindale, D. (1981). *The Nature and Types of Sociological Theory.* Boston: Houghton Mifflin Company.

New York State Judicial Commission on Minorities (1991). *Criminal Justice Newsletter, 22*(12), 1–2.

New York Times (1990, May 15).

Pepinsky, H., & Jesilow, P. (1984). *Myths That Cause Crime*. Cabin John, MD: Seven Locks Press.

Petersilia, J. (1983). *Racial Disparities in the Criminal Justice System*. Santa Monica, CA: RAND Corporation.

Plessy v. Ferguson (1896). 163 U.S. 537.

Report of the National Advisory Commission on Civil Disorders (1968). New York: The New York Times Company.

Simpson, G. E., & Yinger, J. M. (1972). *Racial and Cultural Minorities: An Analysis of Prejudice and Discrimination* (4th ed.). New York: Harper & Row.

Smith, D. A., & Visher, C. A. (1981). Street-Level Justice: Situational Determinants of Police Decisions. *Social Problems*, 29(2), 167–177.

Velben, T. B., & Gumplowicz, H. (1989). In J. E. Jackson (Ed.), (1990), *Ethics and Racial Discrimination*. Unpublished paper.

Wilbanks, W. (1987). *The Myth of a Racist Criminal Justice System*. Monterey, CA: Brooks/Cole Publishing.

Zinn, H. (1980). *A People's History of the United States*. New York: Harper Perennial.

8

Egoism and the Abuse of Authority

Right and wrong is originally a concept connected with power and having to do with the motivation of those who are not bound to obedience.

Bertrand Russell

Once nature was half-tamed and game-hunting no longer crucial to survival, the skills of the hunt were transferred to human prey. The invention of metallurgy provided the means, the acquisition of settled wealth the provocation.

Oliver Thomson

Man was born free and everywhere he is in chains.

Jean-Jacques Rousseau

The Cheka was the only prosecuting organisation in history that combined investigation, arrest, interrogation, prosecution, trial, and execution.

Aleksandr Solzhenitsyn

What You Will Learn from This Chapter

You will learn the blindness of egoism, the types of egoism, and the role of official responsibility as an antidote for egoism. You will also learn that unjustified corporal punishment and acts of brutality are inconsistent with criminal justice principles; that the ethics of means and ends may be harmful; and that ethical guidelines prohibit all acts of natural egoism.

You will learn the current practices and perceptions of egoism in criminal justice, the limits of authority and power, and the view of egoism as deadly force. You also will become acquainted with the arguments for and against capital punishment.

Key Terms and Definitions

Egoism is an exaggerated concern for self-love or one's administrative position.

The Natural View of Egoism is the theory that human beings will naturally act only in fulfillment of their self-interest.

The Altruistic View of Egoism is the view that considers human nature a harmonious combination of both self-interest and common good.

Authority is the right to control the behavior of others within legally determined parameters.

Power is the means for controlling the behavior of others beyond the standards of authority.

Overview

Egoism and the abuse of authority are formidable viruses that permeate the administration of criminal justice. Like flu viruses, they infect criminal justice practitioners at all levels. Egoism debilitates the psychological defenses of practitioners, making them indifferent to unfair practices, and abuse of authority reinforces the administrator's sense of egoism. Together they form a toxic character deficiency that makes practitioners giddy, proud, and vain. The fumes of this deficiency invade the unsuspecting organization, short-circuiting its ethical circuits and disabling the moral reasoning of its members.

While all public officials can be accused of egoism, by virtue of their authority, egoism by criminal justice practitioners may appear more sinful. There is no other government system, perhaps, in which so much power is held by so few who are so vulnerable to so much temptation. Consider, for instance, the damaging influence of an unethical judge presiding over a criminal proceeding in which the outcome could mean life or death; an unethical jailer in charge of a cell block (especially on a slow graveyard shift) whose judgment can preserve or violate the civil rights of a prisoner; or an unethical probation officer whose decision can primarily determine the freedom or imprisonment of a probationer.

Abuse of authority is a perennial characteristic of irresponsible government. In the eighteenth century B.C., Hammurabi tried to prohibit such abuse by passing sweeping accountability standards; Christ condemned it by issuing the commandment "Give to Caesar what is Caesar's and to God what is God's"; and the noblemen of England sought to terminate it in 1215 by creating the Magna Carta. In recent history most governments have passed laws against abuse of authority. Specific federal and state laws have criminalized a variety of such abuses, including oppression by public servants, misconduct by government officials, misuse of official information, sexual harassment, record tampering, obstruction of justice, and, of course, violating the civil rights of citizens. Nevertheless, abuse of authority continues, perhaps for no other reason than the *seduction of egoism*. Failure to remedy this character deficiency renders the central concept of authority ineffectual and its abuse ever more enticing.

Glimpses of Egoism in Criminal Justice

Although it would be foolish to single out members of any criminal justice component with egoism and overstepping authority, the most visible manifestation of such behavior is likely to be the police. Allegations of police misconduct, including the unjustified use of deadly force and the excessive use of force, have been known for decades. The Wickersham Commission (1931) drew attention to them, the National Advisory Commission on Civil Disorders (1968) investigated them, the President's Commission on Law Enforcement and the Administration of Justice (1967) cautioned against them, the Knapp Commission (1972) and the Mollen Commission (1993) verified them, and the Independent Commission on the Los Angeles Police Department (1991) condemned them.

It must be stressed, however, that while police agencies operate at the edge of society's ills and their tasks can typically be extraordinarily stressful, thousands of decent police officers carry out their duties with great attention to ethical principles. Yet when egoism and overstepping authority are tolerated, if not implicitly encouraged, by unethical supervisors, the "reasoning observer" must set personal affiliation aside and focus on loyalty to the truths of reasoning and good faith.

As an example of egotistical behaviors in criminal justice, the report by the Independent Commission on the Los Angeles Police Department (the Christopher Commission Report, 1991), focusing on the aggressive culture of the department, stated,

1. There are a significant number of LAPD officers who repeatedly misuse and ignore the written policies and guidelines of the Department regarding force (ix).

2. Of approximately 1,800 officers against whom an allegation of excessive force for improper tactics was made from 1986 to 1990, more than 1,400 had only one or two allegations. But 183 officers had four or more allegations, 44 had six or more, 16 had eight or more, and one had 16 such allegations (ix).

3. Of nearly 6,000 officers identified as involved in use-of-force reports from January 1987 to March 1991, more than 4,000 had fewer than five reports each. But 63 officers had 20 or more reports each. The top five percent of the officers (ranked by number of reports) accounted for more than 20 percent of all reports (x).

4. In the years covered, one officer had 13 allegations of excessive force reports, five other complaint allegations, 28 use-of-force reports, and one shooting. Another had six excessive force/ improper tactics allegations, 19 other complaint allegations, 10 use-of-force reports, and three shootings. A third officer had seven excessive force/improper tactics allegations, seven other complaint allegations, 27 use-of-force reports, and one shooting.

5. On the Mobile Digital Terminals (computer messages sent to and from patrol cars throughout the city), the Commission's staff examined 182 days of transmissions from November 1989 to March 1991 and discovered hundreds of improper messages including scores in which officers talked about beating suspects. Such messages included: "Capture him, beat him, and treat him like dirt," "I would love to drive down Slauson with a flame thrower ... we could have a barbecue," "I almost got me a Mexican last night but he dropped the damn gun to[o] quick." Officers expressed eagerness to be involved in shooting incidents. The transmissions further indicated that some officers enjoyed the excitement of a pursuit and viewed it as an opportunity for violence (x).

6. Former Assistant Chief Jesse Brewer testified that the lack of management attention [to such behaviors] is the "essence of the excessive force problem ... We know who the bad guys are. Reputations become well known, especially to the sergeants and then to

lieutenants and captains.... But I don't see anyone bring these people up." Assistant Chief David Dotson also testified that "we have failed miserably" to hold supervisors accountable for excessive force by officers under their command (ix).

7. Too many LAPD patrol officers view citizens with resentment and hostility; too many treat the public with rudeness and disrespect. While the relative number of officers who openly make racially derogatory comments or treat minority officers in a demeaning manner is small, their attitudes and behavior have a large impact because of the failure of supervisors to enforce rigorously and consistently the department's policies against racism (xiii).

8. FTOs (Field Training Officers) in four representative divisions revealed that many FTOs openly perpetuate the "siege mentality" that alienates patrol officers from the community and pass on to their trainees confrontational attitudes of hostility and disrespect for the public.

At this point, delving any further into the report's findings may not be necessary. The chief purpose of citing the report in this discussion is to give a tangible example of the concept of egoism and abuse of authority.

Perceptions of Egoism in Criminal Justice

Given the extent of harm that unethical criminal justice practitioners can inflict on society (as well as on their own agencies), the popular perception of criminal justice institutions as brutal, unfair, and unreasonable may not be entirely without foundation. The following are among the more significant reasons for such a view:

First, *the ideal of justice inherent in criminal justice institutions makes them radically different from other government agencies.* More than any other institution, criminal justice agencies are society's enterprise in charge of justice and therefore are supposed to act fairly. The "business" of criminal justice is safeguarding freedom, equality, and fairness. This business has been especially signified in the Preamble to the Constitution as second only to "forming a more perfect union." Furthermore, with the Bill of Rights almost entirely devoted to curbing government abuses, it is only logical to view criminal justice abuses as unconscionable. Imagine, for example, the frustration one would feel if jailed for a crime one did not commit and the court administrator refused to entertain a writ of habeas corpus.

Second, *the mechanics of criminal justice are particularly conducive to the amplification of wrong.* A great deal of social harm can occur as a result of a single act of abuse of authority. A simple act of malfeasance could lead to an inexplicable episode of human misery. Consider, for instance, the social and occupational embarrassment of being wrongly arrested for rape, child molesting, or embezzlement. Such a wrong would be further aggravated by a seemingly unstoppable conveyor belt from one component of the system to the next. The output of a police decision to "pick up a suspect" becomes the input for prosecution. Likewise, the courts, grand jury, bondsman, and defense counsel would have a continuing impact on the allocation of justice. By the same token, decisions by correctional officers can be influenced by the sentencing modes of judges and the revocation decisions of parole officers.

Third, *the excessive range of discretionary powers available to criminal justice practitioners can seduce unethical agents into making irresponsible decisions.* This can be especially damaging when proper checks and balances are ineffective. When discretion is unchecked, it is naturally difficult, if not impossible, to hold agents firmly accountable. Consider, for example, the wide range of behaviors listed under the charge of disorderly conduct in the Texas Penal Code. They include 11 possible categories (each with several subcategories), ranging from discharging a firearm in public, to using abusive language, to making an offensive gesture, to creating an unreasonable odor (Texas Penal Code, 42.01). Without proper role-model supervisors it would be extremely difficult for the young practitioner to make a sound moral choice.

Criminal justice agencies, however, are neither hapless nor beyond reform. Indeed, many police, corrections, and probation and parole agencies are making admirable progress. Interestingly, progress cannot be brought about only by immense budgets, new technology, or modern facilities, but also by thoughtful and responsible managers as well (DiIulio, 1987; McCarthy, 1998; Skolnick & Bayley, 1986). Skolnick and Bayley (1986:11), for instance, state that "success seemed to rise out of the capacity of police leaders to imbue a sense of responsibility and accountability to the citizenry into the police enterprise." DiIulio, in *Governing Prisons*, states that "the quality of prison life depends far more on management practices than on any other single variable ... prison officials can form a government that produces safe, civilized conditions" (DiIulio, 1987:6). By the same token, McCarthy, in "Keeping an Eye on the Keeper," indicates that the best security that society can have in keeping corruption out of prisons is "the character of the men [and women] to whom the government of the prison is entrusted ... The character and mentality of the keepers may be of more importance than the character and mentality of the kept" (McCarthy, 1998:252).

At this point, we should be reminded that the purpose of this discussion is not to expose corruption by criminal justice practitioners (for example, accepting bribes, free meals, and favors) but to focus on the tendency of many practitioners to abuse their authority under the intoxicating seduction of egoism.

The Blindness of Egoism

On several occasions I have been invited to speak on management at criminal justice meetings. I usually begin by asking the attendees (who usually are high-ranking officials) to define *management* and explain what public managers are supposed to do. Almost every time, I receive one or more of these answers: "to run the agency my way," "to tell my deputies what I want," or "to take care of my friends and to punish my enemies." To these answers I usually respond by asking for a clarification: "But whose agency is it, after all?" Invariably, a long moment of silence follows as the audience appears baffled. The intended clarification is to call attention to three critical facts that are often overlooked: (1) practitioners do not "own" the agency; (2) practitioners serve the public interest, not their own; and (3) practitioners are the servants of the public, not the other way around.

Egoism, in uncomplicated terms, is "an exaggerated concern for self-love or an infatuation with one's official position." *Ego* in Greek is a pronoun used for the first person, "I," and *egoism* came to mean "for my part," or "for myself." Other meanings of *egoism* include (1) preoccupation with oneself; (2) exorbitant pride in one's own power, knowledge, experiences, abilities, or beliefs; (3) gratification in teaching others a harsh lesson by showing them "who is boss"; and (4) a firm belief that "might makes right" and "the ends justify the means" (Angeles, 1981:70).

Egoistical behaviors in criminal justice are manifest both in the *field* and in the *workplace*. In the field, such behaviors include brutality, reneging on professional obligations, denigrating nonconforming members of society, violating the civil rights of suspects, and similar demonstrations of power. All such behaviors are consistent with arrogance, irrationality, disregard for duty, and the absence of ethical restraints. The qualities opposite egoism are altruism, self-restraint, compassion, humility, and self-sacrifice.

Minor abuses of authority can at times be justified, as, for example, when a supervisor uses excessive measures to deter employees' carelessness or scolds them for a good cause. Examples of unjustifiable use of authority, on the other hand, are too numerous to mention. They may range from expressing an air of superiority—the "don't you know who I am?" syndrome—to the all-out persecution of employees. These include harassing employees; making inequitable assignments; favoring the "good old boys"; unfair performance evaluations in retaliation against defiant workers; claiming personal credit for accomplishments made by subordinates; or coercing employees into compliance with unreasonable rules, among others. The underlying motivation in all such behaviors is arguably feeding one's ego.

The blindness of egoism is critical to criminal justice, because it can destroy the doctrine of responsibility. Public officials, as mentioned earlier, do not "own" the agencies they serve—they are temporary custodians of the public trust, and as such, their primary obligation is to carry out the agency's goals. While public officials obviously should not be precluded from enjoying the benefits of their positions, such benefits, when legitimate, are only ancillary to performing the job.

Types of Egoism

Public officials may act egotistically in two settings: when they are *obsessed with self-love*—the blind pursuit of personal power, and when *excessively enamored with position power*—the "ends justify the means" mentality. In the first setting, they are overly concerned with self-image, and in the second, with their ability to control workers.

To better understand the nature of egoism and its negative influence on the administration of criminal justice, it is necessary to first understand (1) the theoretical views of egoism—the *natural view* and the *altruistic view*; and (2) official responsibility—the antidote for natural egoism.

Egoism—The Natural View Theory

The natural view theory of egoism is as old as the story of creation. Adam and Eve reportedly violated God's law to gain knowledge so as to glorify themselves and perpetuate their blissful existence. In their natural state, they apparently believed that they were doing the "right thing" and were justified in their endeavor. According to biblical sources, the consequences of their egoism were catastrophic not only to themselves, but also to the entire human race. The natural view of egoism may be even better appreciated by recounting the story of Cain. In his preoccupation with self, he went one step further. He reportedly destroyed his only competition on the planet—his brother Abel, a man described as being kind, gentle, and of a caring nature.

According to the natural theory of egoism, human beings are constituted to act only in their self-interest. It is the "nature of the beast" that compels people to seek satisfaction even at the cost of destroying others. Furthermore, the theory affirms that because people always act in their own interest, selfishness must be "good" and therefore ought to guide moral behavior (an evident naturalistic fallacy). This view seems to have been reinforced by the misreading of Darwin's evolutionary thought that led to the idea of the survival of the fittest. In Darwinian thought, man is ostensibly self-serving, therefore, a cause for society to be consistently in a state of war, wherein only the fittest can win. The winners are those characterized by power, manipulation, or deception. The losers are the feeble, powerless, and naive.

This view of egoism came to signify a belief that despite great strides made toward the socialization of man, human nature has not substantially changed since the time of Cain. Socialization continues to be considered "second nature," which is merely as useful to humans as domestication is to wild animals—regardless of how tame and well-trained, they are still beasts and may bite. Natural egoists argue that in the reality of human development, civility is transient and, to a great measure, superficial. Even Aristotle's principle of self-realization (an acorn grows to be an oak tree) was interpreted to support that view: Because the "first nature" of the acorn does not become an olive tree or an apple tree, so too man's "first nature" never changes. Socialization cannot change the unchangeable. Selfishness is therefore natural, and what is natural is "good."

Hobbes' Theory of Natural Egoism

As discussed in Chapter 4, Hobbes argued that the mind and the body are not different substances—they work together to produce voluntary *psychological motions*. Such motions represent undying animal instincts that are impossible to change or suppress completely. Accordingly, no objects or actions are intrinsically good by their very nature. Rather, people call "good" the objects of their desire and call "bad" the objects of their aversions. Consequently, *all individuals are justified in seeking their own interests at all times*. Furthermore, acting in one's best interest should not be considered selfishness, because it is only consistent with human nature. Moreover, there are no unselfish acts. All endeavors are consciously or unconsciously motivated by a desire on the part of the actor to serve his own interest—to show power, instill fear, rally support, please God, appear charitable, or just feel good.

In the final analysis, natural egoists argue that when man feels so strongly that his survival is at stake or that his essential interests are endangered, he is justified in reverting to naked power. They assert that knowledge, rationality, and moral teachings (in sum, civilization) are fragile social mechanisms designed to inhibit—but not replace—man's natural instincts. The role of ethics must therefore be limited and ineffectual.

Egoism—The Altruistic View Theory

Altruistic egoism presents a radically different view of human nature. It was most popular among the Stoics of Greece and Rome and continues to be cherished by humanist writers. According to these,

Hobbes and his supporters overlooked the "goodness attribute" of nature. If by *nature* it is meant acting the "way one pleases," it would indeed be ridiculous to use nature as a moral guide, because deviating from the "way we please" doctrine would be meaningless. According to the altruistic view, "human nature" is not a free-for-all property, but one that is harmoniously ordered around a purpose, a direction, and a capacity for goodness.

Altruistic philosophers further argue that the view of human beings as "glorified beasts" is absurd. Man is shaped in "God's image" and characterized by ethical intuition—a capacity for the *immediate apprehension of right and wrong*. As such, man has a unique moral faculty comparable to other sensory faculties. Therefore, decisions concerning what is right, good, just, or duty-bound should be pursued independently of any endeavor to please oneself or harm others. Furthermore, although actions can be made better or worse depending on motive (Hobbes's desires and aversions theory), human judgment is strictly related to one's *intention* to do the right thing. The fundamental human issue, as Aristotle advocated, revolves around the purpose of man. As the constitution of the watch is adapted to "measuring time," so man's constitution is adapted to "doing goodness." Subsequently, the strongest drive to please oneself is not necessarily the best, nor does it possess the greatest moral worth (Sahakian, 1974:95).

In critique of natural egoism, altruistic thinkers agree that although self-love is important, it is not always incompatible with the interests of others. Indeed, many people donate money and services anonymously, and thousands of soldiers die for their country without the expectation of compensation or glory. Such behaviors cannot be properly regarded as aimed at self-love without doing a disservice to the English language. The ethic of altruism promotes the good of others; it embodies selfless love for humankind and dedication to the well-being of fellow human beings. Butler's theory of altruistic egoism exemplifies this highly refined ethic.

Butler's Theory of Altruistic Egoism

Joseph Butler (1692–1752) was a famous English priest and philosopher who disagreed with Hobbes's psychological egoism. In "Fifteen Sermons Preached at the Rolls Chapel" (1726) he presented a critique of Hobbes's natural theory, advocating as an alternative the practice of altruistic egoism. Butler accused the Hobbesian view of being discordant with human nature, and as such, unnatural and evil. Butler rejected psychological egoism, attacking its two main claims: (1) that people are exclusively egoistic—that is, they are committed solely to promoting their own good; and (2) that no moral obligation is valid if it runs counter to the way people are, by nature, capable of acting.

Butler dismissed the first claim as "bad psychology," accusing Hobbes of failing to distinguish between the *immediate gratification of desire and the basic goal of achieving self-preservation*—the heart of Hobbes's natural theory. The former, being merely a momentary satisfaction of a given drive, may not serve a person's self-preservation. Consider for instance, the case of a correctional officer who uses unnecessary cruelty against an inmate. She may indeed be gratifying a Nietzschean desire to "overpower," but is she acting in her self-interest or in a manner conducive to her self-preservation? In all likelihood, the act might trigger aggression on the part of the inmate that might threaten the safety of the officer. Furthermore, if the act is properly reported and investigated, the officer may stand a good chance of being fired.

As to the second claim, Butler accepted—with reservations—the idea that people can act only within their natural impulses. He hastened to add that "introspection" reveals that people also possess the means to regulate these impulses. These means include *benevolence* and the *power of conscience* (Butler, 1726:147). Butler identified benevolence as social love and caring for others. It is a disposition of compassion toward parents and siblings, friends and neighbors, coworkers and subordinates, and all members of society. The end of benevolence, he insisted, is collective and social happiness. As such, benevolence to society becomes what self-love is to the individual. And given that parallel, both are perfectly coincidental. The greatest satisfaction to oneself is the greatest benevolence one offers to others—one cannot be promoted without the other, because human nature is made of both (Butler, 1726:150).

The second means Butler suggested for regulating egoistic impulses is the *power of conscience*. He considered it the criterion of morality that is equally natural to all men, thus making them the moral agents they are. He identified conscience in several ways, including (1) the moral arbitrator that sets all priorities, controls, and judgments; (2) the source of understanding that approves or disapproves actions; and (3) the guiding power that distinguishes between right and wrong. Butler further asserted that conscience is more than just a feeling. It is an *introspection* whereby a person intuitively discerns moral and immoral behavior even prior to its actual occurrence. It is by this faculty (conscience) that man becomes a "law unto himself." For behavior to be designated moral, it must come under the scrutiny of the conscience. Natural impulses can be prohibited by conscience, and moral life can be perfected by living in accordance with conscience. The essence of conscience, Butler insisted, is the achievement of perfect harmony and its rule is final (Sahakian, 1974:97). In the final analysis, Butler implores people to renounce Hobbesian egoism and adopt a life of benevolence and altruism.

Official Responsibility: The Antidote for Natural Egoism

Egoism in public service is acting *irresponsibly* to feed one's best interests. While there are, of course, individual reasons for egotistical behavior at the workplace, such as ignorance, jealousy, or greed, a typical pattern of egoism emerges when practitioners lose sight of the demarcation between what constitutes authority and what constitutes power.

Supervisors, in particular, can be seen as egotistical when, *without valid justification*, they (1) overstep their authority by persistently meddling, opposing, or criticizing workers' performance; or (2) abuse their power by dominating workers (or members of the public) or treating them arbitrarily. The only way, however, to minimize egotistical behavior is by asserting the concept of official responsibility. And the first step toward this assertion is to understand the differences between authority and power.

Generally stated, authority is the practitioner's *right* to control the behavior of others. Power is the *force* a practitioner can use in controlling the behavior of others. In almost all situations, both of these elements are necessary, because to act without a right to intervene is *tyranny*, and to intervene without effectiveness is *meaningless*. The role of responsibility, therefore, is to provide the proper balance between authority and power.

In a bureaucratic sense, the concepts of authority and power have also developed a dubious application. Because intervention by practitioners can vary from one situation to another, *authority* has come to mean "the right to apply a standard response," whereas *power* has come to mean "the application of additional force." The concept of *official responsibility* remains the critical arbitrator.

To further articulate the differences between authority and power, an important distinction must be pointed out. Authority is usually well defined in the laws society applies; therefore, it need not be justified. Power, on the other hand, is unclear and therefore always must be justified. For example, when police officers make routine arrests (without the need for using extra force), they are considered "responsible." Yet if they choose to exercise extra force, their decision must be justified. Examples of using power (extra force) include situations such as having to hog-tie a destructive jail inmate, putting handcuffs on a 12-year-old, or pepper-spraying civic protesters. In such cases, the practitioners must explain why it was necessary to take more severe measures. If their explanation is found to be unjustified, they are assumed to have acted irresponsibly. In criminal justice, practitioners must always show that their use of power is necessary and reasonable and that their decisions are not motivated by prejudice, personal gain, or an intention to deprive citizens of their civil rights.

Official Responsibility

Like other misused concepts, the term *responsibility* can mean different things to different people. Indeed, it is easier to talk about responsibility than to define it. One way to clarify this confusion is by examining some distinctions derived from the general usage by scholars: responsibility as *accountability*, responsibility as *cause*, and responsibility as *obligation* (Spiro, 1969:15). The first two of these are of lesser significance to the study of ethics; the last is particularly significant.

1. *Responsibility as accountability.* According to this view, practitioners are to be held accountable for the manner in which they conduct their duties. For example, a county attorney or a prison warden is duty-bound to render an account of the way the official tasks are carried out to the county commissioners' court or to the board of corrections. These, in turn, are held accountable to the governor and to the electorate, respectively.

2. *Responsibility as cause.* According to this view, individual practitioners cause the actions anticipated by the agency. Popular parlance illustrates this meaning as "If it is said that the police are responsible for law and order, it does not mean that police officers are held accountable to a designated board; rather it simply means that the police (as individuals or a group) cause law and order to prevail."

3. *Responsibility as obligation.* According to this view, practitioners are committed to seeing their assignments through in accordance with the laws of the land, the agency's rules and regulations, and their own discretionary reasoning. As such, officials are obliged to (a) remain within their limits of authority; and (b) avoid using additional force unless it is reasonable and necessary. Overstepping these limits, as in the case of using excessive force, discrimination, intimidation, sexual harassment, or improper behavior, constitutes irresponsibility. As an obligation, criminal justice practitioners should not only respond effectively to criminal situations, but they also should do so without violating the principles of justice, fairness, or equality or institutional procedures.

Authority Defined

Authority is the *right* to control the behavior of others within legally determined parameters. These include constitutional and professional limitations, which are designed to resolve conflicts in an orderly fashion. Authority stems from the practitioner's official position and applies only to the territory or jurisdiction to which he or she is assigned. The limits of authority are usually stated in penal codes, the codes of criminal procedure, agency rules and regulations, training manuals, and often in codes of ethics. In brief, authority is compliance with the legal and professional rules of operation.

Authority applies to the handling of standard cases because, contrary to popular belief, criminal justice practitioners encounter more similar situations than dissimilar situations. Examples include suspects who resist arrest, probationers who violate conditions of probation, and inmates who hide contraband in their cells. Agency rules specify when practitioners can intervene, how to deal with the situation, and what they should guard against during the intervention process. If the case turns out to be different or if the practitioners are faced with unexpected complications, they must then resort to the use of power—a deliberate decision that they must explain.

Power Defined

Power is the *means* for controlling the behavior of others beyond the standards of authority. Its purpose is not to punish or discriminate, but to protect one's safety (or the safety of others) when necessary or to reinforce authority in unconventional cases. Power is a legitimate means of exercising responsibility when it is justified. When it is not, the practitioner can be accused of a variety of acts ranging from first-degree murder to minor ethical violations.

Acts of power range from the physical, such as assaulting an inmate in prison, to the symbolic, such as ignoring an inmate's request for medical assistance. Because of this wide variance, judging power abuse—especially when committed within confined facilities—can be frustrating and difficult. The situation becomes more difficult when the practitioners feel threatened and "stonewall" the truth. They may perjure themselves, destroy evidence, or cover up significant facts. The situation is further compounded when high-ranking officials are implicated in the matter. In such a case, the practitioners usually end up being torn between loyalty to superiors and loyalty to professional principles. This brings us back full circle to the concept of official responsibility and the need to minimize egoism in public service.

Egoism as Deadly Force

As mentioned earlier, the use of power must be justifiable. For an act to be justified, it usually must be exercised in self-defense (or the defense of others), in support of authority, and only to the extent of being reasonable and necessary. Conversely, an act is unjustified if it is exercised in lieu of authority, as a means of retribution, or to gratify an egotistical desire to overpower.

In the case of fleeing felons, for instance, the constitutional standard set in *Tennessee v. Garner* (1985) has practically outlawed killing unless circumstances reasonably suggest that the suspect is dangerous to the officers or to others. Furthermore, the use of deadly force must be necessary and "where feasible, some warning has been given" (More, 1998:100). Consequently, in most jurisdictions today, the use of deadly force against fleeing felons is seldom justifiable otherwise.

The use of deadly force by police nevertheless continues to be a national tragedy (Roberg & Kuykendall, 1990:355). Since 1949, when data first began to be collected by the National Center for Health Statistics, 15,000 citizens, and possibly more, have been killed by police. About one-half of those killed were minority citizens, with the majority of them African Americans. Furthermore, research by Sherman and Langworthy (1979) suggests that the center's statistics are approximately 25% to 50% lower than reality. Roberg and Kuykendall (1990:355) estimate that since modern police departments were first established, it is not unreasonable to assume that 30,000 to 40,000 citizens have been killed by police.

The following observations gleaned from Roberg and Kuykendall's research of shootings by police are of particular significance, because they bear directly on the issue of official responsibility:

1. Although the frequency of shootings varies among cities and neighborhoods on the basis of crime rate, in general, the frequency of police killing citizens tends to vary on the basis of the restrictiveness of shooting policies, the quality of police training, and departmental subculture.

2. Minorities are shot disproportionately to whites when compared with their numbers in the population, but not when compared with the minority arrest rate or frequency of police contacts. Nevertheless, in some cities, minorities are shot at in situations in which whites are not.

3. A substantial number of citizens have been shot at who posed no threat to police officers. This, however, has been changing, as more police departments adopt restrictive "defense of life" policies.

4. The decision to shoot or not to shoot, especially in spontaneous situations, appears to be largely the result of the officer's instinctive perceptions of the situation—the perception of danger to oneself or others, as well as the requisites of justice perceived by one's inner emotions.

5. Female officers utilize deadly force less frequently than male officers, because they have no ego involvement with suspects. Male officers tend to personalize violent encounters to such a degree that the encounter becomes a survival competition governed more by "macho rules" than by organizational training and policy.

From an ethical standpoint, it should be safe to conclude that (1) killing police or correctional officers (or for that matter, any innocent person) is a serious crime that should be avoided by all means possible; (2) police or correctional officers are justified in shooting suspects who present a serious danger to the officers' safety or the safety of others; (3) initiating an unjustifiable shooting by police or correctional officers is a regrettable crime intolerable in a free society; (4) police or correctional officers should avoid, whenever possible, the use of deadly force unless justifiable; (5) under no circumstances should the decision to use deadly force by police or correctional officers be based on considerations of race, color, or any other personal bias; and (6) if a decision to shoot by police or correctional officers is to be made, it should be made as a matter of last resort and only to avoid more serious harm.

Capital Punishment as State Egoism

This section addresses the controversy over capital punishment as state egoism—how far can the state go toward punishing its criminals? The term *egoism* here is being used to characterize positions that are unreasonable, inhumane, too punitive, or simply uncivilized. The main questions to be raised are whether punishment is a morally acceptable concept, and if so, is capital punishment justified?

The answer to the first question is fairly simple, because it is difficult to imagine any society functioning without a system of punishment. Most ethical philosophers agree that punishment is morally justified because it is essential to achieving a higher good—*the effective support of the rule of law.* For laws to be effective, individuals must be warned that in the interests of society, certain acts are forbidden and if they (the individuals) commit such acts, they will be punished. In essence, without effective punishment of law violators, society cannot continue to exist (Barry, 1982:260).

The answer to the second question is much more complex, if it can be answered from an ethical perspective. This perspective forces reasoning—arguing the point and the counterpoint. On one side there is the realization that capital crimes are heinous crimes; that victims die or suffer irrevocable harm; that would-be criminals must be effectively deterred; and that the scales of justice must be balanced. On the other side there is another set of dictates: the issues of reasoning over emotion; civility over vengeance; life over death; and social utility over individual vengeance, among other moral principles. Two overriding factors, however, impose themselves on the argument: (1) the view of the death penalty as barbaric and (2) the fact that capital punishment has been abolished in all civilized countries and 12 of the United States. One abolitionist state that particularly stands out is Israel, which continues to resist its application despite the exorbitant price in death and injuries inflicted upon its citizens by unrelenting terrorist attacks.

The debate about capital punishment continues between the *abolitionist view* and the *retentionist view*. Each side is trying to reinforce its logic (see, for instance, Ehrlich, 1975; Greenfield & Hinners, 1985; Marquart & Sorensen, 1988; Van den Haag, 1969). It should also be noted that while advocates of each side may not agree among themselves on the conditions under which capital punishment may be retained or abolished, the abolitionists as a group agree that the practice is immoral, while the retentionists disagree. To articulate this debate, a brief analysis of the issues raised by each side will follow, with substantial reliance on Barry's thesis on the morality of capital punishment.

The Abolitionist View

Proponents of this view argue that

1. *Life is sacred.* This is a natural law principle that religious and moral institutions have traditionally upheld. The sanctity of life precludes any person or state from taking what God has created in "his own image," whatever the circumstances or provocations.

2. *Capital punishment does not deter crime.* There is sufficient evidence that the threat of capital punishment does not convince potential murderers to forgo criminal activity. Comparisons between states with the death penalty and those without it show that states without the death penalty generally have far lower murder rates. Of the 12 states without a death penalty, 8 are in the bottom 15 of murder rates. In 13 of the instances in which borders of non-death penalty states and death penalty states meet, the murder rate is higher in the death penalty states (*Boston Globe*, October 31, 1997). Because most murders involve people who know each other (very often friends and family members), and because murderers are often under the influence of drugs or alcohol or are suffering psychological turmoil, it is unlikely that the threat of capital punishment can have a deterrent impact (Senna & Siegel, 1987:474).

3. *Capital punishment is implemented with a class bias.* About 41% of the inmates on death row are black, and this number is disproportionate to their representation in society. While there is conflicting research on this issue, acknowledged by both sides, the abolitionists argue that doubt should be disposed in favor of their view, because the punishment is clearly final and any possible error is too great a burden to bear.

4. *The innocent may die.* About 350 wrongful convictions of crime that carry the death penalty have occurred in the last century, of

which 23 led to executions. In addition to the 23 innocent persons who were executed, 128 of the falsely convicted served more than 6 years on death row (Radelet & Bedeau, 1987:21). According to the *Boston Globe* (October 28, 1997), included among those who were wrongly executed were Nicola Sacco and Bartolomeo Vanzetti, in 1927. Half a century later, the State of Massachusetts publicly acknowledged in a proclamation that their trial was unfair and directed that their names be cleared. Furthermore, in the last 24 years, 73 persons were released from death row (including 21 since 1993) across the nation after evidence of innocence was found. Of greater alarm is the situation in New Jersey, where 30 of the 46 persons sentenced to death since 1976 (until 1997) have had their sentences overturned because of legal defects (*Boston Globe*, October, 28, 1997). Obviously, while society cannot bring back the innocent from the grave, the very existence of capital punishment can allow for such barbaric errors to occur.

5. *Retribution is uncivilized.* Because putting someone to death cannot bring back the victim or in any meaningful way repay the victim's loved ones, the purpose of capital punishment must be to satisfy the primitive urge for revenge. While the question of revenge is almost always justified by the religious belief in "an eye for an eye and a tooth for a tooth," this belief may be gravely misunderstood. The Hebraic reference, in its original intent, was not meant as a license to kill, but as a plea for restraint if the victim, or his family, were unable to forgive the wrongdoer. In this case, the victim or his family were prohibited from inflicting more than equal harm.

6. *Capital punishment precludes rehabilitation.* By putting individuals to death, the chance that they can ever be rehabilitated and restored to a useful place in society dies with them.

7. *Capital punishment injures the criminal justice system.* Capital punishment can make judges and juries soft on crime. Where capital punishment has been a mandatory sentence, juries have been known to strain the evidence to acquit rather than sentence to death. And to make matters worse, cases of capital punishment inevitably involve years of costly appeals. This may not only delay justice, but also subject the people involved to cruel and inhuman punishment.

The Retentionist View

Supporters of this view argue that

1. *Capital punishment is the only prevention against certain crimes.* Certain heinous crimes cannot be deterred in any way other than by capital punishment. Take, for example, child rapists and

traitors. These will not be deterred from crime by threats of life imprisonment, because in their view they will eventually gain freedom. Then there are those who are prone to violence, unreformable individuals whose very existence constitutes a potential danger to society. The only way society can possibly protect itself from that danger is to carry out capital punishment.

2. *Capital punishment balances the scales of justice.* When someone wantonly takes another's life, that person upsets the balance of equal limitations under which everyone in society ought to live. The disruption must be balanced, and the only way to do this is to impose a punishment equal to the offense. Those who murder forfeit their own claim to life—so to speak.

3. *Capital punishment deters crime.* When potential murderers realize that they may have to pay for crime with their lives, they will think twice before killing. Isaac Ehrlich, using a highly advanced statistical technique, found evidence that in the United States each additional execution per year would save seven or eight people from being victims of murder (Ehrlich, 1975:397).

4. *Capital punishment is an economical way to manage offenders.* Because there is no conclusive evidence that violent criminals can be rehabilitated, society is faced with having to pay for their incarceration. It is unfair for innocent people to be made to pay for the care of those who wantonly violated society's conventions when there is no evidence that such care will rehabilitate them.

Comments and Questions to Ponder

The following discussion is not meant to shake your beliefs regarding the rightness or wrongness of capital punishment. It seeks to make you recognize the wider range of issues involved. There are obviously many reasons other than one's beliefs that influence one's mind. These include religion, tradition, social status, and political ideology. While these are significant factors to reckon with from an ethical perspective they are not necessarily based on reason, the *inner sanctuary of ethics*. The following are statistical comments to ponder regarding the use of capital punishment:

1. **Twelve States and the District of Columbia Do Not Have It:** While the death penalty continues to appeal to many states in the United States, 12 states (more than 20% of the states) disallow it. Massachusetts recently voted not to restore capital punishment despite ferocious politicking by legislators who were swayed by the increasing rate of murders and rape. The vote of 81–79 in favor of restoration was later changed to 80–80 when House member John Slattery changed his vote, creating a tie, thus killing the

bill. In defense of his position, Slattery stated that the bill "under-scored the absence of guarantees that innocent people would not be executed ... and could open the door to the execution of juve-niles as young as 14" (*Boston Globe*, November 7, 1997).

2. **We Are Alone in the Civilized World:** Most countries of the civilized world have concluded that other punishment is better, even for the most outrageous crimes. Since South Africa outlawed capital punishment on June 5, 1995, the United States now stands alone among the Western and civilized countries that allow it (*Boston Globe*, October 28, 1997). The only other countries in the world that continue to practice the death penalty are basically the fundamentalist states (for example, Iran, Iraq, Pakistan, Syria, Libya, and Bangladesh), the totalitarian states (for example, the now-defunct Soviet Union countries and Chile), and a long line of African states.

3. **To Deter or Not to Deter:** One of the most legitimate arguments about the death penalty is whether it deters capital crime. The issue then must be, "If it can be shown that capital punishment is not a deterrent to capital crime, there should be no real reason for supporting it." The following statistical observations are ger-mane to this issue and may shed more light on what we as ethical reasoners should accept as truth. They have been gleaned from the *Boston Globe* (October 28, 1997):

a. Since the Supreme Court restored the death penalty in 1976, the *annual* number of executions around the country has gone from 0 to 60, while the national murder rate has remained the same. It was 10.8 per 100,000 in 1980 and 10.7 per 100,000 in 1993.

b. The distribution of murder rates by state neither supports the premise that capital punishment deters capital crime in the states that apply it, nor increases capital crime in the states that prohibit it. For instance, in Illinois, a death penalty state, the murder rate is nearly triple that of Wisconsin, a non-death penalty state. The murder rate in Missouri, a death penalty state, is 5 times that of non-death penalty Iowa. Massachusetts's 1993 murder rate of 4.1 per 100,000 was higher than the 2.3 rate of New Hampshire, which has the death penalty. Massachusetts's murder rate was nev-ertheless less than Connecticut's rate of 6.4, a state that has the death penalty. Although it too has the death penalty, New York's murder rate of 13.5 per 100,000 was more than triple that of Massachusetts.

c. States that have executed the *most* people since 1976 have the *highest* murder rates. Texas is by far the nation's leader, with 138 executions, including 31 in 1997 alone. For all that, Texas's mur-der rate is still the seventh highest in the nation.

d. The average murder rate in the eight states with the highest num-ber of executions—Texas, Virginia, Florida, Missouri, Louisiana, Georgia, Alabama, and Arkansas—is 12.8 per 100,000. The highest murder rate in a non-death penalty state is 11 per 100,000 in Michigan. Eight of the 12 non-death penalty states have murder rates under 5 per 100,000.

  e. The idea that the death penalty is a deterrent has been so discredited that 386 police chiefs ranked it last in a 1995 poll among ways to reduce crime. The chiefs were far more interested in substance abuse, improving the economy, family values, community policing, and longer prison sentences. In their explanations, four of five chiefs indicated that they do not believe that murderers think about punishment while doing the act.

  f. While the cost of executions should not be a factor in this discussion because the sanctity of life cannot be measured in dollars and cents, evidence shows that the death penalty is a drain on state coffers rather than a saving. For instance, the average cost of a death penalty case in Texas is $2.3 million, 3 times the cost of locking up a murderer in maximum security for 40 years. In Florida the cost per execution is $3.2 million, 6 times the cost of life in prison, and the cost in North Carolina is $2.16 million per person (*Boston Globe*, October 31, 1997).

  4. **The Obsession with Spilling Blood:** Aside from the questionable morality of fundamentalist and totalitarian ideologies, capital punishment societies seem obsessed with spilling blood as the ultimate punishment. The act in itself seems to provide a fetish not too different from those that characterized Hobbes's "primitive man." Strikingly opposed to this view is the Israeli position that (except in the case of the Nazi war criminal Adolph Eichmann in 1962, for which a special law was passed) rejects the death penalty *precisely* because of its repulsion to the notion of "spilling blood." The Jewish people realize that throughout history, Jewish blood was so easily sacrificed that they no longer can stand the memory or want to be reminded of it. On the other hand, jurists in capital punishment societies (for example, China, Saudi Arabia, Libya, Iraq, and Pakistan) argue that if carrying out executions can produce more long-term benefits than capital punishment's abolition, they would support it regardless of reason or justification.

To conclude this discussion, it should be added that the U.S. Supreme Court in two recent capital punishment decisions (June 2002) seemed to push back the death penalty in America, at least a couple of steps. By making these rulings the Court may have spared the life of up to a quarter of the country's death row inmates. The Court has indeed reconsidered its own views on the ethical application of the death penalty. In the first case the Court ruled six to three that executing the mentally retarded violates the Eighth Amendment's ban on "cruel and unusual punishment." The Court has long held that the judgment of what is cruel and unusual must reflect "an evolving standard of decency," and cited a trend among 18 states that banned executions of the retarded. The ruling stopped the execution in Virginia of Daryl Atkins, who is said to have an IQ of 59, and stayed those of approximately 160 people whose IQs were less than 70, the generally accepted definition or retardation (*Economist*, June 2002).

In the second decision, the Court ruled that only juries can impose the death penalty, overturning an Arizona law it upheld 12 years ago in another case. With the two justices from Arizona, Chief Justice William Rehnquist and Justice Sandra Day O'Connor dissenting, the majority ruled that under the Sixth Amendment's guarantee of a jury trial, a judge cannot displace a jury in imposing a death sentence or, for that matter, any harsher penalty.

The next likely concern for opponents of the death penalty is the execution of offenders who committed murders while minors, a practice that—as mentioned earlier in the previous debate—puts America in the company of Iran, Saudi Arabia, Pakistan, and other totalitarian countries. Although several states have banned the execution of criminals for crimes committed before they were 18, other states set the age limit at 16, and 83 juvenile offenders are currently on death row. Yet in the retardation case the Court said that there is not yet a comparable consensus on juveniles, so this issue will have to wait a few more years (*Economist*, June 2002).

Other questions may arise over the defenses available to inmates. The court has recently agreed to hear the appeal of a Tennessee death row inmate on the issue of introducing new evidence in capital appeals, which could reopen many other cases. On the other hand, the Court refused to hear, and therefore let stand, a lower court's decision that a Texas man's death sentence was invalid because his lawyer was asleep for large chunks of his trial (*Economist*, June 2002).

Egoism—Ethics of Means and Ends

In 1513 Niccolo Machiavelli held up a mirror in the city-state of Florence to enable Giulano de Medici to see what he would have to do to rule successfully. Machiavelli suggested that the prince should be part fox and part lion; part trickery and part strength:

> Men, in general, judge by their eyes rather than by their hands. Everyone sees what you appear to be, few experience what you really are, and those few dare not gainsay the many who are backed by the majesty of the state. In the actions of all men, and specially of princes where there is no court of appeal, one judges by the result.
>
> (Machiavelli, 1911 translation:101)

Machiavelli, incidentally, never wrote the phrase "end justifies the means" in his original text. References to that phrase appear in inaccurate translations in which translators were certain that this was what Machiavelli "must have meant." When translated accurately from Italian, Machiavelli simply stated that "every action is designed in terms of the end which it seeks to achieve" (Friedrich, 1967:139).

Machiavelli's concern was basically with the notion of state expediency, a purely pragmatic rationality in the conduct of politics. It is this pragmatic rationality that the term *reason of state* is meant to designate (Friedrich, 1967:139). Machiavelli advocated that the state—for that matter, the organization, the department, or the agency—is the highest value in society, beyond which there is no other. The logic here is clear: "Whatever strengthens or protects the state's interest is *justified* by the ends it is pursuing" (Williams, 1980). In democratic societies, however, this logic is unacceptable on the basis of two arguments: (1) the state—being the embodiment of its citizens—is as fallible as its citizens; and (2) it is society that creates the state, not the other way around. By the same token, the organization, the department, or the agency can also be fallible and should therefore be governed by rational rules rather than by decrees by "unnamed officials." A modern Machiavelli, therefore, should realize that in a democratic state, "the ends can justify the means only if the ends are noble and the means are legitimate." Anything else can be tyranny.

The ethical dilemma raised by Machiavelli trickled down through the centuries into contemporary government basically because most politicians believed that it works. Whether that belief is justified or not has been a secondary concern as long as the "reason of state" was fully served. In accordance with this logic, President Lincoln during the Civil War years suspended habeas corpus in support of the war effort; President Roosevelt in 1942 concluded that national security considerations justified incarcerating Japanese Americans without trial; President Nixon claimed executive privilege to cover up his involvement in the Watergate scandal; and President Reagan denied any knowledge of the Iran-Contra affair, which involved the trading of weapons to Iran for the release of American hostages.

In criminal justice the FBI reportedly has conducted surreptitious entries and illegal burglaries as investigative techniques; initiated counterintelligence programs aimed at domestic political groups to "disrupt and neutralize" targeted groups; and used informants as agents' provocateurs to initiate violence or illegal activity, among other activities (Poveda, 1990:65). At state and local levels, there is ample evidence to suggest that criminal justice agencies are no less inhibited than federal agencies, except perhaps in terms of the relative triviality of what they attempt to accomplish.

Some of the better known and more dramatic literature in the ethics of means and ends is in policing, especially Klockars's "The Dirty Harry Problem" (1980) and Cohen's "D'Angelo's Behavior versus Kirkham"

(1987). Both are popular topics in police courses. A brief summary of these two cases will follow for the purpose of emphasis.

The Dirty Harry Scenario

The problem draws its name from the 1971 film *Dirty Harry* and its chief protagonist, Inspector Harry Callahan. The film features a number of events that dramatize the need for the ends to override the means. But the one that does so most explicitly places Harry in this situation: A 14-year-old girl has been kidnapped and is being held captive by a psychopathic killer. The killer, "Scorpio," who has already struck twice, demands $200,000 ransom to release the girl, who is buried with just enough oxygen to keep her alive for a few hours. Harry gets the job of delivering the ransom, and after enormous exertion, he finally meets Scorpio. During the meeting, Scorpio decides to renege on the bargain, let the girl die, and kill Harry. Harry, however, manages to stab Scorpio in the leg before the latter carries out his decision, but not before Scorpio seriously wounds Harry's partner. Scorpio escapes and Harry tracks him down and breaks into his apartment, finding guns and other evidence of his guilt. He finally confronts Scorpio and shoots him in the leg as he tries to escape. Standing over him, Harry demands to know where the girl is buried, but Scorpio refuses to disclose her location, demanding his rights to a lawyer. As the camera draws back from the scene, Harry stands on Scorpio's bullet-mangled leg to torture him into a confession of the girl's location (Klockars, 1980:34).

As it turns out, the girl is already dead. Neither the gun that was found in the illegal search nor the confession Harry extorted, nor their fruits—including the girl's body—would be admissible in court. Legally, Harry overstepped his authority; he acted egotistically because no case could legally be made against Scorpio. Nevertheless, Harry thought that the ends in this case justified the means—what he did was therefore right. He was meting out justice "for the glory of the state."

The D'Angelo versus Kirkham Scenario

These were police officers patrolling a ghetto area one night. D'Angelo, a much more experienced officer than the rookie Kirkham, notices two black subjects in their late teens in an alley, slowly stepping from behind a pile of wooden crates. The officers stop them and D'Angelo frisks the first while Kirkham begins frisking the other. D'Angelo finds a nickel-plated revolver on the first subject. This constitutes a legal search, because he first felt an object that any police officer would have good reason to believe might be a weapon. Frisking the other suspect, Kirkham feels something soft and spongy in the man's left sock. Under the Supreme Court's decision in *Terry v. Ohio*, it is illegal, Kirkham murmurs, to go beyond the extremely limited "search" and examine the man's sock without first having actual grounds to make an arrest. D'Angelo growls and commands Kirkham to continue the search, whereupon Kirkham finds a plastic bag of heroin. Both suspects are consequently transported to the city jail and booked (Cohen, 1987).

According to Cohen, D'Angelo was not acting from ignorance of the law; rather, he treated the encounter as a matter of public safety. He realized the suspects were drug users or dealers, and he did not want to give them the message that they were safe from him. His concerns were less with law enforcement than they were with public safety. He intimidated, threatened, searched one of them illegally, and arrested them. Nevertheless, D'Angelo felt he was justified in removing a gun and a bag of heroin from the street—it was the right thing to do.

Discussion

These scenarios accentuate the ethics of means and ends: To what extent does a morally good end justify an illegal or unethical means to its achievement? Is overstepping authority in order to achieve what one perceives to be a higher good justified? If it is, would that still make the practitioner an egoist, or an ethical person deserving of praise? Similar examples are, of course, plentiful in the fields of prosecution, corrections, or probation and parole. Most, however, are not as graphic as those just described. For instance, is a probation officer justified in violating office rules prohibiting the release of personal information related to probationers if she knows that the probationer has AIDS and is carrying on a relationship with a person the officer knows? Is a correctional officer justified if he uses a fictitious reason to lock up an inmate for an extended period if he thinks that will protect the inmate from the drug dealers who are exploiting him?

Answers to these questions are complex because they presuppose that the decision maker is (1) aware of all the facts, (2) able to predict the ends before the means are used, (3) cognizant of the wide range of "higher goods," and (4) acting in good faith. Scenarios of that kind fall within the nebulous area of "situational ethics," which I have continually discouraged throughout this book. Nevertheless, assuming that the decision maker can answer the previous presuppositions in the affirmative, and given the gravity and immediacy of the situations, the actor can be justified under five stringent conditions. These conditions have been suggested by Cohen (1987):

1. *The end must be good in itself.* For an end to justify the means, the end's own goodness must not be open to question. For instance, if the end is evil (for example, personal gain, deprivation of liberty, or increasing the misery of the poor and needy), then the means to achieve such an end are unjustifiable. In both of the previous scenarios, the ends were good in themselves: saving a life and removing drugs from the street, respectively.

2. *The means must be directly conducive to achieving the end.* Given the value of the end, the selected means must be necessary to achieving it, rather than being a remote or delayed response. In the previous scenarios, the means were directly and immediately related to rescuing the buried girl and removing the drugs from the street, respectively. The effective application of these means would directly achieve the desired ends.

3. *The means must be the best alternative to achieving the end.* This condition requires that the decision maker examine all possible alternatives that could achieve the end. In the first scenario, the inspector wisely chose a restrained means by shooting Scorpio in the leg rather than "blowing his head off," when he indeed would have been justified in acting in self-defense. In the second scenario, the officers honestly reported what they found on the suspects without using excessive force or "padding" the charges against the suspects.

4. *The means must be applied in good faith.* This requires that the means are not selected on the basis of a bias or prejudice against the person or persons involved. In other words, the decision must be made under Rawls's "veil of ignorance," regardless of whom the suspect is. In both scenarios it appears that this condition had been met. In the first case the inspector would have used the same means to rescue the imperiled girl regardless of who the kidnapper was. In the second case the officers were justified in frisking the suspects, because they would have done the same had they observed anyone creeping out of a pile of crates in a dark alley about midnight.

5. *The means cannot undermine an equal or greater end.* This is probably the most critical condition, because it relates directly to the "hierarchy of goodness" and the formula of $E = PJ^2$ discussed in Chapter 1. It is obvious that torturing Scorpio for a confession in the first scenario and conducting an illegal search (of the second suspect) in the second scenario both involved violating the rights of suspects and promoting disrespect for the law. As such, it should be safe to assume that Inspector Callahan and Officers D'Angelo and Kirkham were at least aware of the negative consequences of their actions. Yet they also may have believed that their actions were justified on the basis of a higher good—the presence of extenuating circumstances. In the case of Callahan, this may have been

true. Extenuating circumstances existed—saving the life of a human being buried alive certainly "outweighs" any negative perception of illegality in the police profession. In the case of D'Angelo and Kirkham, no such circumstances could be shown. In light of these conditions, it would be more reasonable to justify Callahan's behavior under the circumstances that existed and to condemn D'Angelo's and Kirkham's behavior. The inspector seems to have acted illegally but ethically. The other officers seem to have acted illegally and egotistically.

Ethical Guidelines

To conclude this discussion of egoism and the abuse of authority, the following are moral guidelines that can help all criminal justice practitioners regardless of whether they serve in policing, prosecution, courts, probation and parole, or related functions. They should also be considered applicable both in the field and in the workplace:

1. Egoism as a concern for self-love is a natural human quality. It is neither condoned nor condemned. Excessive egoism, however, is inconsistent with proper moral judgment, because it violates the principle of equality by placing one's concern for self at a higher plane than one's concern for others. Excessive egoism leads to irresponsibility, which in turn allows for abuses of authority. Excessive egoism can induce such abuses in proportion to the level of excess.

2. Egoism that is pursued solely for the sake of self-aggrandizement and personal supremacy is a character deficiency. It is tantamount to moral tyranny. It can potentially create an environment in which abusing authority becomes more frequent and its toleration easier. If untempered, this could lead to corruption.

3. Egoism in public service can be justified only when it is altruistic—motivated by benevolence and regulated by conscience.

As such, altruism can be an admirable ethic that can help achieve the noble ends of government without violating the means of justice. When it is practiced in criminal justice agencies, it can reinforce justice and create an environment of civic righteousness.

Conclusions

Egoism stimulates the urge for unjustified power. It weakens responsibility and diminishes respect for authority. Natural (Hobbesian) egoism should be considered morally wrong, because it violates natural law ethics (equality among all mankind), constitutional law ethics (the dictates of liberty, rule of law, due process, and equal protection), religious ethics (humility and the love of others), professional duty (rules of operation), and the obligations of codes of ethical conduct.

The appropriate use of power, on the other hand, can reinforce authority and bolster responsibility. Its use is praiseworthy, especially when applied in moderation and accompanied by goodwill. Wilson describes ethical practitioners as *altruistic* individuals: They are able to "take into account the feelings of others and sympathize with the joys and sorrows of those with whom they deal to the extent that those joys and sorrows are justifiable and proportional to the circumstances" (Wilson, 1993:241). They do not inflict unjustified harm on innocent parties. They possess "prudent self-control" and do not act while in the grip of extravagant passions (Wilson, 1993:241). Nevertheless, altruistic practitioners are not deterred from taking strong actions or expressing justified anger when important matters are at stake (Wilson, 1993:241). In a sense, they somehow manage to love the world as it is and try to improve it. As Maslow stated in the "Profile of the Ethical Person" (Chapter 1), they enjoy taking on responsibilities and bringing about law and order in a situation that is chaotic, messy or confused, or dirty and unclean.

Review Questions

1. Where can egoism be found in the criminal justice system? What is the essence of the excessive force problem described by former Los Angeles Assistant Chief Brewer?

2. On what grounds is the criminal justice system accused of egoism? Are the reasons well founded? Why or why not?

3. Define *egoism*. Where are egotistical behaviors found in the field? Where are they found in the workplace?

4. What is the "natural view" theory of egoism? Give examples of "misunderstandings" that support this view.

5. What is the "altruistic view" theory of egoism? What arguments reinforce this theory?

6. Explain three popular meanings of the term *responsibility*. How does ethical choice affect responsibility?

7. Define *authority* and *power*. How are these concepts used in your agency?

8. Is capital punishment morally justified? Why is this question so complex from an ethical viewpoint?

> 9. What are the arguments in favor of capital punishment? What are the arguments against capital punishment? Where do you stand on this issue, and why?
>
> 10. On what basis is the criminal justice system considered racist? What is your experience at your agency? Do you agree or disagree, and why?

References

Albert, E. M., Denise, T. C., & Peterfreund, S. P. (1988). *Great Traditions in Ethics* (6th ed.). Belmont, CA: Wadsworth Publishing.

Angeles, P. A. (1981). *Dictionary of Philosophy.* New York: Barnes and Noble Books.

Barry, V. (1982). *Applying Ethics: A Text with Readings.* Belmont, CA: Wadsworth Publishing.

Braswell, M., McCarthy, B. R., & McCarthy, B. J. (1991). *Justice, Crime and Ethics.* Cincinnati, OH: Anderson Publishing Co.

Butler, J. (1726). Fifteen Sermons Preached at the Rolls Chapel. In E. M. Albert, T. C. Denise & S. P. Peterfreund (Eds.) (1988), *Great Traditions in Ethics.* (6th ed.) Belmont, CA: Wadsworth Publishing.

Cohen, H. (1987). Overstepping Police Authority. *Criminal Justice Ethics, 52,* Fall.

Commentary (1990, May 12). *Houston Post.*

DiIulio, J. (1987). *Governing Prisons.* New York: The Free Press.

The Economist (2002, June).

Ehrlich, I. (1975). The Deterrent Effect of Capital Punishment: A Question of Life or Death. *The American Economic Review, 65.*

Friedrich, C. J. (1967). *An Introduction to Political Theory.* New York: Harper & Row.

Greenfield, L. A., & Hinners, D. (1985). *Capital Punishment.* Washington, DC: Bureau of Justice Statistics.

Independent Commission on the Los Angeles Police Department, (1991). Los Angeles: City of Los Angeles.

Kleinig, J. (1993). Symposium: Editor's Introduction. *Criminal Justice Ethics* (Winter/Spring), 12–34.

Klockars, C. B. (1980). The Dirty Harry Problem. *The Annals, 452.*

Knapp Commission Report on Police Corruption (1972). New York: George Braziller.

Kroes, W. H., Margolis, B., & Hurrell, J. J., Jr. (1974). Job Stress in Policemen. *Journal of Police Science and Administration, 2,* 145–155.

Machiavelli, N. (1911). *The Prince* (G. Bull, Trans.). New York: Penguin Books.

Marquart, J., & Sorensen, J. (1988). Institutional and Post-release Behavior of Furman-Commuted Inmates in Texas. *Criminology*, 26.

McCarthy, B. J. (1998). Keeping an Eye on the Keeper: Prison Corruption and Its Control. In M. Braswell, B. R. McCarthy, & B. J. McCarthy (Eds.), *Justice, Crime and Ethics* (3rd ed.). Cincinnati, OH: Anderson Publishing Co.

More, H. W. (1998). *Special Topics in Policing* (2nd ed.). Cincinnati, OH: Anderson Publishing Co.

Morris, N., & Hawkins, G. (1977). *Letters to the President*. Chicago: University of Chicago Press.

Morris, N., & Tonry, M. (1990). *Between Prison and Probation*. New York: Oxford University Press.

National Commission on Law Observance and Enforcement. (1931). *Wickersham Commission*. Washington, DC: U.S. Government Printing Office.

No Death Penalty, By One Vote/Momentum for a State Law Is Halted as House Member Changes His Mind (1997, November 7). *Boston Globe*, A1.

Paying for the Death Penalty (1997, October 31). *Boston Globe*, A23.

Poveda, T. (1990). *Lawlessness and Reform: The FBI in Transition*. New York: Brooks/Cole.

President's Commission on Law Enforcement and the Administration of Justice. (1967). *Task Force Report: The Police*. Washington, DC: U.S. Government Printing Office.

Price, K. (1983). *Job Satisfaction as a Means of Increasing Productivity among Correctional Officers in Texas*. Unpublished doctoral dissertation. Huntsville, TX: Sam Houston State University.

Radelet, M., & Bedeau, H. (1987). Miscarriages of Justice in Potentially Capital Cases. *Stanford Law Review*, 40.

Roberg, R. R., & Kuykendall, J. (1990). *Police Organization and Management: Behavior, Theory and Processes*. Pacific Grove, CA: Brooks/Cole Publishing.

Sahakian, W. S. (1974). *Ethics: An Introduction to Theories and Problems*. New York: Barnes and Noble Books.

Senna, J., & Siegel, L. (1987). *Criminal Justice* (5th ed.). St. Paul, MN: West Publishing.

Sherman, L. W., & Langworthy, R. H. (1979). Measuring Homicide by Police Officers. *Journal of Criminal Law and Criminology*, 70, 4.

Skolnick, J., & Bayley, D. (1986). *The New Blue Line*. New York: The Free Press.

Spiro, H. J. (1969). *Responsibility in Government: Theory and Practice*. New York: Van Nostrand Reinhold Company.

Tennessee v. Garner. (1985). 105 S. Ct. 1694.

Van den Haag, E. (1969). On Deterrence and the Death Penalty. *Journal of Criminal Law, Criminology and Police Science*, 26, 2.

Van Raalte, R. (1986). *Law Enforcement News*, March 24.

Vito, G., & Keil, T. (1988). Capital Sentencing in Kentucky: An Analysis of the Factors Influencing Decision Making in the Post-Gregg Period. *The Journal of Criminal Law and Criminology, 79*(2).

Williams, J. D. (1980). *Public Administration: The People's Business*. Boston: Little, Brown and Company.

Wilson, J. Q. (1993). *The Moral Sense*. New York: The Free Press.

Wrongful Death, (1997, October 28). *Boston Globe*, A14.

9

Misguided Loyalties
To Whom, to What, at What Price?

Loyalty means nothing unless it has at its heart the absolute principle of self-sacrifice.

Woodrow Wilson (28th President of the United States)

Our loyalties must transcend our race, our tribe, our class and our nations, and this means we must develop a world perspective.

Martin Luther King Jr.

Masters who sacrifice for their servants will receive the gift of loyalty.

Ancient proverb

Loyalty to the country always. Loyalty to the government when it deserves it.

Mark Twain

The best way to keep loyalty in a man's heart is to keep money in his purse.

Irish proverb

What You Will Learn from this Chapter

In this chapter you will explore the major concepts of loyalty and loyalties in the field of criminal justice. You will learn why criminal justice practitioners must be able to distinguish between personal loyalty, institutional loyalty, and integrated loyalty. You will be able to understand the hidden dangers of being personally loyal (that is, dependent) to a specific superior, especially when such loyalty is inconsistent with the agency's mission or its professional values. You will also learn that organizational subcultures that emphasize personal loyalty to superiors (for example, loyalty to the person of the boss rather than to the agency and its shared values) are questionable, troubling, and at times dangerous. Instead, the primary loyalty of criminal justice practitioners should always be to constitutional, legal, and moral principles, as well as to the ideals of public service, rationality, and common decency.

Key Terms and Definitions

Professional Accountability is the agency's obligation to comply with its rules and regulations, be faithful to its mission and procedures, and enforce its policies fairly, without favoritism or discrimination. Toward this objective, public service practitioners must be true to the values of professional accountability and organizational identification. Only then can the agency maximize its productivity while acting constitutionally, legally, and ethically.

Personal Loyalty is the lowest level of workplace loyalty. It is seductive in nature and constitutes the subordinate's unexamined obligation to obey, accept, and support all of the superior's directions and wishes, often when such directions and wishes are illegal or morally questionable. Such a level of loyalty is normally associated with the absence of enlightenment and the failure of moral courage.

Institutional Loyalty is the next level on the ladder of workplace loyalties. It is organizational in nature and constitutes the practitioner's obligation to support the agency's mission and honor its ends–means strategy. It is based on intelligently supporting the institution by being faithful to its purpose and mission. This level of loyalty should not be confused with, nor replaced by, the practice of personal loyalty to superiors.

Integrated Loyalty is the highest and most virtuous level of workplace loyalties. It is idealistic in nature and constitutes the practitioners' obligation to uphold, above any other value, constitutional and legal principles, the ideals of public service, and the interest of any third party that might be involved either locally or globally. This level of loyalty transcends all others by honoring reason, justice, goodness, duty, and goodwill. It represents the workers' commitment to mankind, public service, impartiality, and transcendence.

Overview

One of the most perplexing issues in public service in general, and in criminal justice institutions in particular, is that of misguided loyalties. On the one hand, the practitioners are required to be loyal to the U.S. Constitution, state laws, and professional values, yet they are also culturally required to be *personally* loyal to their supervisors and superiors, as well as to one another. While resolving this conflict may seem common-sensical, in reality, it may be one of the most challenging issues in public service. It can lead to illegal, unethical, or unprofessional behaviors that are detrimental to one's job performance as well as to one's career.

Students with prior service in criminal justice agencies may recognize that when issues of workplace loyalties are raised, three global assumptions are usually made: First, personal loyalty to superiors is essential and must be demonstrated without any reservation on the practitioner's part. Second, loyalty to the United States Constitution, to the laws of the land, and to organizational rules and regulations is formalistic; it can be manipulated (for example, the "looking good" posture) to fit the agency's needs when necessary. Third, if a clash arises between the previous two assumptions, the practitioners are left to fend for themselves; they must intuitively figure out where their primary loyalty lies, and if they err, they may have to face the consequence of being labeled "disloyal."

These are hard options, especially for inexperienced workers. They are options that can make criminal justice practitioners nervous, especially because the mere accusation of disloyalty can undermine one's employment and, eventually, one's career. This situation is exacerbated by the fact that there is no preservice training that can prepare the practitioners to handle such issues, nor is there in-service training that can help them resolve the ensuing conflicts. As a result, a great number of criminal justice practitioners may silently agonize over the matter, much more perhaps than over any other workplace issue. Ironically, and rather axiomatically, the answer may be easier than generally thought: If the practitioners and the superiors were to be loyal to the agency's legal, organizational, and moral principles, they would be, by natural association, loyal to each other, making the issue of personal loyalty to superiors irrelevant.

The Continuing Controversy

This chapter is certainly *not* intended to apply a wrecking ball to the ideal of loyalty to God, country, family, or friends. Nor is it intended to discredit loyalty to one's organization, profession, colleagues, or even superiors under more enlightened conditions. This chapter only examines the unreasonable and (as you may soon learn) unnecessary practice of *subservience* to superiors, especially when such practice undermines the worker's loyalty to the public interest or to higher professional concerns. Subsequently, criminal justice practitioners should consider developing and supporting an integrated loyalty perspective throughout the organization if they are keen to promote a civil and productive institution. Endorsing such a perspective can make the workers more confident, the public more satisfied, and society more appreciative.

Understanding where one's primary workplace loyalty lies is a matter of enlightenment and freedom. In criminal justice agencies, this might be especially difficult because of the organizational culture that pervades some ultraconservative agencies where first-line supervisors *traditionally* demand absolute personal loyalty from their subordinates. And given the amount of power that criminal justice superiors possess, or are perceived to possess, especially in paramilitary criminal justice organizations, the unexamined practice of personal loyalty to superiors may hinder progressiveness and enlightenment within criminal justice agencies. As "protectors of the faith," unenlightened superiors may mistakenly believe that the practice is essential to guide the practitioners' choices as to what is important, acceptable, or tolerable, while in reality, it may repress individuality, encourage isolationism, and prohibit the circulation of fresh and useful ideas. Given this kind of thinking, it is not surprising that new criminal justice practitioners (for example, police, courts, prisons, and probation and parole) learn very early in their careers that personal loyalty to superiors is paramount and absolute, and that if unheeded, it can ruin one's career (Kleinig, 1996).

Supporters of the personal loyalty tradition have been numerous. They include kings, popes, governors, and generals, as well as public and private bureaucrats (Wiener, 1973:108–16). They justify the practice on a variety of reasons, including obeying God, deterring defection, reinforcing discipline, bolstering responsibility, increasing productivity, and ensuring institutional integrity. Yet, although many of these reasons may sound plausible, their validity has not been intellectually and ethically debated.

Critics of the misguided practice of personal loyalty to superiors view it as an artificial excuse by superiors to further control the practitioners as a class, reduce their freedom to think and act, make them more dependent on their superiors, and instill fear in the hearts of those who disagree with them. More critical observers argue that the practice is a contrived scheme devised—over generations of bureaucracy—to legitimize the right of superiors to retaliate against recalcitrant practitioners. The practice makes it easier for the superiors to get rid of free-minded practitioners simply by accusing them of disloyalty, a charge so bureaucratically serious it required the United States Congress to pass whistle-blowing legislation in 1999 to protect practitioners from its arbitrariness (Blamires, 1963; Denhardt, 1987; Souryal, 1998).

The Ideal of Loyalty

Loyalty has been defined as "a virtue, a state, or a quality of being faithful to one's commitments, duties, relations, associations, or values ... it is fidelity to a principle, a cause, an idea, a religion, a nation, or a government" (Konvitz, 1973:108). Other definitions include "a life in which interaction with others becomes the primary means for solving problems" (Fletcher, 1991:171); "an emotional tie that can lead people to be unreasonable and to overlook or override proper claims on them" (Ewin, 1993:36); and "the thoroughgoing devotion of a person to a cause" (Royce, 1908:155). David Hume described loyalty as a virtue that holds "less of reason than of bigotry and superstition" (Kleinig, 1996:70). In criminal justice management, loyalty has been identified as the "workers' obligation to do *what it takes* to protect their organization without exposing themselves to criticism" (Souryal & McKay, 1996:57).

The ideal of loyalty has its roots in the virtue of sympathy, which is at the foundation of all human experience. It continues to be held at the heart of commonsense morality because of its importance to communal and social life. Evidence of its importance can be shown by its adaptive value; were it not so, the process of natural selection would have worked against loyal people and in favor of disloyal ones (Wilson, 1993). But loyalty cannot be mere sympathy; otherwise, it would be reducible to mere feelings. For instance, we may sympathize with the people of Darfur but that does not mean that we are loyal to them. If there is any loyalty involved, it is indirectly through the *principle of humanity*, the obligation to assist "our kind" by aiding those who are in a crisis. The sentiment underlying this obligation is the recognition that humankind is our kind and, therefore, the demise of any person diminishes us all.

Yet unexamined loyalty can be dangerous and often has threatened world peace. The cases of personal loyalty to Hitler or Stalin may be extreme examples of *bad* loyalties, the kind that produce disastrous consequences. Blamires likened that kind of loyalty to an intoxicant. He noted that "we breathe the word loyalty and immediately a sentimental warmth floods our minds" (Souryal & McKay, 1996:46). Fletcher also stressed loyalty's natural bias when he commented, "by definition, [loyalty] generates interest, partiality, an identification with the object of one's loyalty rather than with the cause it serves" (Souryal & McKay, 1996:46).

Issues of loyalty cannot be divorced from issues of disloyalty, a sentiment viewed as "the forsaking of an object of loyalty for self-serving and individualistic or self-assertive reasons" (Kleinig, 1996:74). Criminal justice practitioners who are accused of disloyalty (perhaps because of their agencies' paramilitary nature) are considered pariahs, and their chances for survival as practitioners may be demonstrably blunted. In ultraconservative agencies—the kind where the practitioners are called upon to circle the wagons and take no prisoners—disloyal workers are routinely targeted for elimination as the Jacobeans were during the French Revolution. During Watergate, for example, not much reflection was needed to realize that the "loyalty of a G. Gordon Liddy or John Mitchell generated about as much admiration as the honor amongst thieves, and that for all their soul-stirring qualities, [they] were frequently jingoistic and exclusionary" (Souryal & McKay, 1996:53). Because of its notorious ambiguity, perhaps, loyalty has also been labeled an "uneasy virtue" and the "last refuge of scoundrels" (Kleinig, 1996:71). Blamires was much more suspicious, pointing out that "[O]ne can say fairly that whenever loyalty is quoted as a prime motive or basis for action, one has the strongest reasons for suspecting that support is being sought for a bad cause" (Blamires, 1963:24).

The Grammar of Workplace Loyalties

Maintaining loyalty relationships in criminal justice agencies can be particularly stressful because, although the work itself is exhilarating, the work environment may be disappointing. A gratifying loyalty relationship, therefore, may not be "a fair-weather commitment"; it often has a "self-sacrificial dimension" (Kleinig, 1997:71). For that reason alone, perhaps, it is important that criminal justice practitioners fully understand the grammar of their workplace loyalties. The term *grammar of loyalties* is here used to mean "the skillful conjugation of three levels of loyalty, which, while not interchangeable, may overlap with varying degrees of intensity" (Souryal & McKay, 1996:48). Moreover, because the ethical weight of these levels is critical, they will here be rank-ordered from the least valuable to the most valuable.

Personal loyalty is the lowest rung on the ladder of workplace loyalties. It is mechanical in nature and constitutes the subordinate's unexamined obligation to accept, comply with, and support a superior's directions and wishes. Examples include the obligation of police officers or correctional officers to be personally subservient to their sergeants and lieutenants. As a result, they may agree to make an illegal arrest, give an inmate a break, or recommend the revocation of a probationer in violation of the rules. The guiding statement at this level is "from each practitioner based on his or her performance."

Institutional loyalty is the next rung on the ladder of workplace loyalties. It is organizational in nature and constitutes the practitioners' obligation to accept, comply with, and support the agency's mission and to honor its ends–means strategy. Examples include the obligation of probation officers to revoke a person's probation solely on the basis of agency rules and regulations, professional standards, and ethically accepted practices. The officers involved should objectively examine the circumstances of the case, solicit legal advice, and use justified judgment. The guiding statement at this level is "from each practitioner based on his or her devotion to honor the agency."

Integrated loyalty is the highest and most virtuous level of workplace loyalties. It is idealistic in nature and constitutes the practitioners' obligation to observe, above all else, the constitutional principles of the land and the ideals of public service. Examples include the practitioners' obligation to honor freedom, privacy, honesty, rationality, and goodwill. It represents the unadulterated commitment to the doctrines of equality, impartiality, decency, and compassion—indeed, to the pursuit of civility. The guiding statement at this level is "from each practitioner to the highest constitutional, professional, and moral ideals."

This grammar of loyalties can also be identified by its durability. Personal loyalty to superiors is short lived and transient; it seldom outlives the subordinate–superior relationship. Institutional loyalty is more profound; it lasts as long as the practitioner is currently employed by the agency. Integrated loyalty is lifelong and transcendent; it continues throughout the practitioners' life, regardless of which agency they serve. Compliance with this grammar of loyalties requires a great deal of caution and good faith. It is, therefore, important that criminal justice practitioners consider the following triadic criteria:

1. Personal loyalty to superiors, being the most temporary and volatile, should be the least necessary workplace loyalty.

2. Institutional loyalty, being the more comprehensive and durable, should be the normal workplace loyalty, and cannot be replaced by personal loyalty.

3. Integrated loyalty, being the cornerstone of all professional and
    moral loyalties, should be the highest level of all workplace loyal-
    ties. It should always be aspired to in the *supreme* name of crimi-
    nal justice. As such, Royce may have said it best when he referred
    to integrated loyalty as *loyalty to loyalty* (Royce, 1908).

The Physiology of Personal Loyalty to Superiors

In the objective reality of public agencies in general, and criminal
justice agencies in particular, concern for personal loyalty to superiors
enters into *every* decision the practitioners make. Subconsciously, yet
unceasingly, the practitioners ask themselves, if they do this or that,
whom will they please or offend; who will support or ostracize them;
and, inescapably, will their careers prosper or suffer as a result. To articulate this point, I ask you to consider, for example, the symbolic, yet not
uncommon, case of a police officer who pulls over a young female driver
suspected of speeding who, after questioning, turns out not only to have
a violated traffic law but *also* to be the police chief's daughter. What is
the first thought that will overcome the majority of officers in such a
situation? No one knows for sure, because police officers usually don't
talk about such incidents (basically out of personal loyalty to their
superiors) and no pertinent research exists.

What seems typical, however, is that the officer agonizes over the
high probability of a negative reaction from the police chief (even
though the issued ticket was perfectly legitimate), whereas if the driver
had been another person, the officer would not worry. What makes this
situation particularly stressful is the unspoken, yet questionable, tradition of personal loyalty to superiors. From an ethical perspective, the
officer's decision to issue a ticket should depend on the gravity of the
offense, observance of departmental rules, enlightened sense of discretion, and trust in the department's sense of fairness. The issue of personal loyalty to superiors should not be a factor, because if it is,
the officer is logically justified in over-ticketing or under-ticketing the
daughter of any superior (or for that matter, citizen) to whom they
owe no personal loyalty at the time.

While this scenario can be casually dismissed as insignificant or
benign, it exemplifies, at least in principle, the dangers of unexamined
personal loyalty to superiors. Such danger signifies the misguided belief
that, by virtue of one's personal loyalty, one is expected to act more
favorably toward one's superiors, including in situations that might violate the concepts of the rule of law and equal protection. From an ethical
perspective, the issue is not only legal but also strongly moral: practitioners' reluctance to freely and honorably perform their constitutional
duties for fear of retaliation by a slighted superior. Allowing for such
a mental reservation can lead to more serious consequences if, for

instance, the chief's daughter is underage, driving under the influence of alcohol, or fleeing the scene of an accident. Furthermore, criminal justice practitioners face much more serious situations than issuing traffic tickets. In police and correctional settings, it is not unusual for probationers to be accused of abusing authority, falsifying evidence, lying on the witness stand, or covering up for corrupt acts. Historically, such acts marred numerous national cases, including Watergate, Iran-Contra, My Lai, and Abu Ghraib. Furthermore, because criminal justice practitioners take an oath to faithfully execute all laws, and because the basic integrity of justice is at stake, it is all the more crucial that issues of workplace loyalty be carefully examined and morally discussed.

The Peculiar Nature of Personal Loyalty to Superiors

Personal loyalty to superiors can be defined as an act of "intentionally upholding higher commitments to specific superiors for periods of time at the risk of undermining personal commitments to the truth." As such, the practitioners (unless justified, as in the case of an emergency) invariably suspend their judgment about what is right or wrong and act on the basis of unsubstantiated sentiments. Examples include one's loyalty to clan members, classmates, and friends. But personal loyalty also must be seen as having a self-sacrificial dimension. For the sake of the object of loyalty, the practitioners set aside significant personal and public interests. Gordon Liddy epitomized this sentiment in 1973 when he accepted a prison sentence rather than tell the truth about President Nixon's illegal activities during Watergate.

The peculiarity of personal loyalty to superiors stems from the concept's moral fragility. Consider, for instance, the following scenarios:

- Personal loyalty to superiors can be offered to a worthy object but for an unworthy reason (for example, power, egoism, personal gain, or corruption). Kleinig points out that personal loyalty can create conditions that make it vulnerable to exaggeration and distortion.

- Loyal people may not always be loyal; their ambitions change, and with them, their loyalties. The betrayal of George Washington by Benedict Arnold (one of Washington's most loyal generals) is a case in point (Bayh, 1972).

- The superiors themselves may not value the submissive practice of personal loyalty; many may even loathe it. It is not surprising that, as a result, middle managers may not hesitate to file grievances against their managers, and chief deputies may not hesitate to run for office against their sheriffs.

- For personal loyalty to be genuine, it should be a two-way-street relationship. Yet while subordinates are silently required to demonstrate loyalty to their superiors, the latter do not consider themselves obligated to reciprocate. Consequently, being aware of such contradictions is essential to truly understanding the dangers of personal loyalty to superiors.

On the basis of this discussion, it should be safe to suggest that if public service is to be based on rationality, due process, and equal protection, then reliance on personal loyalty to superiors demonstrates incoherence. This can be explained by the *primary–secondary obligation* paradigm. By virtue of organizational citizenship, the practitioners' primary loyalty must be to serving the public, and, if so, every other loyalty must be considered secondary. Subsequently, if criminal justice practitioners are expected (or, worse still, compelled) to exercise personal loyalty to superiors as the primary obligation, they will be acting either illogically or disingenuously. Such acts are illogical if made on the basis of ignorance, and disingenuous if made on the basis of prior knowledge; in either case, the agency's integrity is impugned and its reputation tarnished.

The Paradoxical Nature of Personal Loyalty to Superiors

The obligation of personal loyalty to superiors, especially in criminal justice agencies, is paradoxical. Although it is hardly mentioned at the workplace, it is considered essential to workers' survival—they must adhere to it, or at least pretend to do so. While the superiors emphasize the significance of such loyalty, it can more frequently cause administrative embarrassment (remember the letter FBI agent Colleen Rowley wrote to the FBI director in 2002 in Chapter 5). Consequently, unless it can be shown that personal loyalty to superiors is legally or morally justified, the practice must be deemed unnecessary and possibly dangerous.

Consider, for instance, the troubling statements by two high-ranking criminal justice officials cited by Kleinig (1994) during a meeting he had with them. The first statement was, "when an organization wants you to do right, it asks for your integrity; when it wants you to do wrong, it demands your loyalty." The second was, "when I make an appointment, I look for two things: loyalty and competence, in this order" (Kleinig, 1994:10). Unless one is a neophyte, the former statement should be dismissed as hyperbole, and unless one is a cynic, the latter should be considered a naturalistic fallacy: If it is true that the value of competence is lower than the value of personal loyalty, how then can society be assured that its practitioners are competent enough to make intelligent decisions for the good of all concerned? Kleinig further added an even more repugnant note by stating, "the more ethically troubling implication of this citation was not what the official stated, but the fact that it was *not* too troubling to those who were present" (Kleinig, 1994:10–11).

To further articulate the paradox of misguided personal loyalty to superiors in criminal justice agencies, practitioners and students should be familiar with the following facts:

1. Despite the cultural support for the practice of personal loyalty to superiors, there is no mention of it in agency rules and regulations. This may compel one to ask, if personal loyalty to superiors is such a great virtue, why are agency rules and regulations so reticent about it? On the other hand, if personal loyalty to superiors is optional, why are the practitioners who offer it rewarded so handsomely? Wouldn't that raise suspicion concerning the integrity of the organization and the good-faith efforts of its leaders?

2. The more it is that agency leaders are subjected to external scrutiny (for example, a state audit, criminal investigation, or charge of misappropriation of funds), the more they demand personal loyalty from their subordinates. By contrast, no loyalty demands are usually made when the agency is stable and safe. The more likely reason for this behavior is to deter the practitioners from leaking adversarial information that could embarrass the superiors.

   As an illustration, consider the undocumented story of a state governor who had just lost a favorite legislative bill by a single vote and who, upon discovering who the responsible legislator was, accused him of disloyalty. According to the story, the legislator responded apologetically, "but Governor, I have always been loyal to you when you are right." At that moment, the governor rudely interrupted, "but ... I do not need you when I am right!" Even if this story is fictitious, it demonstrates how disingenuous the practice of personal loyalty to superiors can be.

3. The practice of personal loyalty to superiors ignores the fact that some superiors are not worthy of loyalty. This can be shown by the fairly large numbers of supervisors and administrators who are fired or disciplined at all levels of government each year. And if that is the case, it is inappropriate to expect criminal justice practitioners to be loyal to unworthy superiors, and hypocritical if they are compelled to do so.

4. The excuse that personal loyalty to superiors is simply a *knee-jerk reaction*, one akin to saluting commanders on military bases, is misleading. While saluting military commanders is required by military rules, personal loyalty to superiors is not. Furthermore, while no harm to third parties occurs when military commanders are saluted, serious harm can occur when criminal justice practitioners comply thoughtlessly with their superiors' unrestrained desires. Moreover, if personal loyalty to superiors were

truly intended as a reflex action, the entire argument in favor of loyalty would be pointless.

5. The common tendency of superiors to treat personal loyalty as a one-way-street relationship (that is, the superiors need not return the loyalty) destroys the essence of loyalty. Any one-sided relationship in a free society should be considered suspect and potentially abusive. Furthermore, because institutional effectiveness requires that superiors and subordinates trust one another, then practicing one-way-street loyalty can destroy this trust.

Cases in Point

The following cases illustrate the dangers of personal loyalty to superiors in real criminal justice conditions: the first, in a police department; the second, in a correctional institution.

Case No. 1: A Police Situation

On April 27, 2000, Miami Mayor Joe Carollo fired City Manager Donald Warshaw over a disagreement pertaining to Police Chief William O'Brien. Following the raid on the home of Elian Gonzalez's Miami relatives, Carollo demanded that Warshaw fire O'Brien for failing to inform the mayor's office of the raid and for allowing a Miami police officer to participate in the action after the mayor had announced that the police department would not assist federal agents if such a raid occurred. When Warshaw refused to fire Chief O'Brien (his successor at the department), Mayor Carollo dismissed Warshaw, although the city charter did not grant the mayor the authority to do so. Sixteen hours later, O'Brien announced his resignation, stating, "I refuse to be chief of police when someone as divisive and destructive as Joe Carollo is mayor" (Bridges, 2000:IA).

Carollo defended his decision to dismiss O'Brien by claiming that he had "lost all confidence" in the chief because he had refused to warn Carollo of the raid by the federal authorities (LaCorte, 2000:5A). O'Brien, in turn, defended his decision not to inform the mayor of the raid, calling it "a police issue and not a political issue" (LaCorte, 2000:5A). The Immigration and Naturalization Service, which eventually led the raid, requested that the police department keep the plans for the action confidential and not disclose the purpose of the federal search warrant. An INS agent later called O'Brien "a hero" (Bridges, 2000:18A).

Case No. 2: A Corrections Situation

In 1997, Wayne Garner, the commissioner of corrections in Georgia, allegedly authorized a mass beating of inmates at Hays State Prison in northwestern Georgia. He reportedly watched while the inmates—some already handcuffed and lying on the floor—were punched, kicked, and stomped until blood streaked the walls. When the officers who participated in this beating were later interrogated, they stated, "we were all under the impression that it was OK to do it." Furthermore, Ray McWhorter, the highest-ranking prison official participating in the assault, allegedly covered up the entire affair. He publicly denied that any abuse had occurred (*Houston Chronicle,* July 1, 1997).

Discussion

These two cases clearly demonstrate the dangers of unrestrained personal loyalty in the workplace, the first at the executive level and the second at the operational level. They demonstrate the need for *moral fortitude* in the proper conduct of criminal justice activities. In the first case, the police chief proudly resigned in protest and, in the second, the correctional officers failed to protect the inmates from acts of unjustifiable abuse by higher officials. Both cases show the vulnerability of public good when unprotected by watchful ethical subordinates. On the one hand, it was the seemingly disloyal act of Chief O'Brien that carried the day by making the INS raid successful. On the other, it was the abdication of professional judgment by the correctional officers that allowed illegal and unjustified physical assault to be so brutally inflicted on the inmates.

The moral of these two cases can be troubling and calls attention to the hierarchical nature of loyalties in criminal justice agencies. To Mayor Carollo, Chief O'Brien's cooperation with INS agents constituted an act of disloyalty of the most egregious kind. To Chief O'Brien, keeping the INS raid confidential and allowing his second in command to participate was by far a higher good. As a result, the raid's objectives were accomplished, America's honor was preserved, and no one was hurt in the process. By so doing, O'Brien remained loyal to the constitutional provisions of the land and his obligation to protect the lives of fellow officers on duty. By the same token, in failing to fire O'Brien, Warshaw demonstrated loyalty to higher administrative values by halting further disruption in city government rather than obeying the mayor's agenda.

In the second case, another pattern is clear: the dangerous nature of an occupational culture gone afoul. It seems far less plausible to believe that the participating correctional officers were naturally evil or suddenly confronted with a situation they had never been trained to face. On the other hand, it is much more plausible to believe that they willingly submitted to the commissioner's desire because "it was the way it was always done" at the unit. Organizational culture seems to have prevented the officers from thinking independently, intelligently, or consistently with the universal ACA (American Correctional Association) Code of Ethics.

Evidence of such a sullied organizational culture was more evident when McWhorter (the highest-ranking prison official participating in the assault) tried to cover up the entire affair, denying that any abuse occurred. It seems clear that personal loyalty to the commissioner and his men was the overriding reason for the brutal assault. If that was not the case, one would think that at least a few officers would have questioned the extent of force applied or have reported the episode later. Because that did not occur, the belief may be reinforced that the participating officers elected to "suspend their own judgment about right and wrong and act on the basis of unsubstantiated sentiments" (Fletcher, 1991:61). Furthermore, the fact that the commissioner himself led the assault must have triggered the officers' "personal loyalty effect," prompting them to act without much concern for legality or propriety.

There are three ethical lessons to be learned from these cases. First, criminal justice practitioners, superiors as well as subordinates, should be held accountable for accomplishing their official duties legally and ethically, each at his or her own level. Second, while subordinates are obviously inferior in rank, they cannot be written off as inferior in professional judgment. Third, superiors cannot act on the prescription that "the ends justify the means" unless the means themselves are legitimate.

Two Controlling Realities

In an ideal organizational setting, two controlling realities must be recognized: first, the *primary* obligation of workers is to the ideals of public service; second, the values of public interest and those of private interest are basically incompatible.

If these two realities are accepted, it should logically follow that the conduct of government would be fundamentally flawed if the practitioners were to be loyal to a specific "person," or a group of persons, rather than to the organization itself. Though critics may trivialize the distinction between *loyalty to the ideal* and *loyalty to the instrument*, one should consider, for example, the dire consequences of being loyal to the person of the doctor rather than to medical science, or to the person of the judge rather than to the law. If these distinctions are noted, then the primary loyalty of criminal justice practitioners cannot be identified with specific superiors. If they are so identified, then the entire discipline of public service will lose a whole dimension of what is necessary to make it legitimate.

To emphasize this point, consider, for instance, the public service consequences that can ensue if correctional officers or police officers are primarily loyal to a sergeant who is egotistical, racist, corrupt, or advocates harassing minorities or immigrants. A careful consideration of such consequences may not only reveal that personal loyalty to superiors *can* lead to evil, but that evil activities may be the organizing principle behind the practice of personal loyalty to superiors (Ewin, 1993). If Ewin is to be believed, then the practice can hardly be considered a moral principle or a basis for moral theory.

Unlike the *intrinsic virtues* of honesty, fidelity, or courage, personal loyalty to superiors should be seen as a negative relationship, one that can encourage collective evil and discourage collective good. Furthermore, it may well create a "master–slave" relationship that makes the practitioners either unable or unwilling to serve the public good as they are trained to do. Subsequently, yet sadly, many criminal justice practitioners who practice this relationship may eventually find themselves involved in justifying untruth, impeding justice, supporting cover-ups, or falsifying evidence, all under the incoherent tradition of personal loyalty to superiors.

Five Investigatory Questions

To accentuate the debate about unexamined personal loyalty in public agencies, the journal of *Criminal Justice Ethics* (Winter/Spring 1993) devoted an entire issue to examining the hermeneutics of loyalty and loyalties. While this issue renewed interest in the subject, it also challenged some of the most rudimentary assumptions of workplace loyalty.

Some of the more significant questions the journal raised were (1) Why—in the conduct of public service—should personal loyalty be an issue at all? (2) If personal loyalty to superiors is such a great virtue, why is it not stated in agency rules and regulations? (3) Is it safe to assume that all superiors, as a class, are worthy of loyalty? (4) Is the absence of loyalty to superiors the moral equivalent of organizational disloyalty? Is it not possible that the practitioners may not like their superiors *without* being disloyal to their agency? (5) What, specifically, are loyal workers (commonly referred to as the "good old boys") supposed to do beyond fulfilling their official duties to the best of their abilities? If there is anything more that they should do, then what is it? If there is nothing, then why are they treated affectionately and offered special privileges? (Souryal & McKay, 1996).

With these questions in mind, enlightened criminal justice agents should "reason" whether personal loyalty to superiors (unless otherwise justified, as in the case of an emergency or matters of a classified nature) is a true moral principle or, as the critics argue, another "organizational drama" designed to intimidate the subordinates into submission to the unreasonable demands of a "ruling class" that is motivated more by personal power than by promoting the agency's mission (Manning, 1985).

Three Self-Evident Truths

Before presenting the arguments for and against personal loyalty to superiors, three self-evident truths should be made clear. They are essential to understanding the theoretical construct of personal loyalty to superiors in the organizational setting.

First: Contractible and Noncontractible Obligations

The practice of personal loyalty to superiors is diametrically different from those related to organizational control, discipline, or even effectiveness. The latter are *contractible obligations,* while the former is a *noncontractible* one. The difference between these two categories is as clear as expecting schoolchildren to bring the teacher an apple, under the tacit risk of being treated differently, and requiring them to take exams to graduate. It would be rather naive, for instance, to expect that when police or correctional officers put their lives in danger, they do so because they cherish their personal loyalty to any particular superior. It is much more plausible to believe that when they do so, they are motivated by a professional sense of devotion that calls upon their inner strength to overcome "impossible" odds.

Concerns for organizational control, discipline, or effectiveness, on the other hand, are *contractual obligations.* They are embedded in the organizational structure and enforced through the agency's rules and regulations. Contractual obligations are *primary relationships* that are complete in themselves; they alone constitute the agency's authority to achieve its stated goals. Subsequently, while all criminal justice practitioners are required to comply with agency rules and regulations, no one should be required to enter into personal loyalty pacts with the superiors.

Second: The Primacy of Justice in the Equation of Criminal Justice

Criminal justice is not just another field of public service. It is critical to establishing justice, a concept without which the idea of crime cannot exist. The field of criminal justice embodies the ideals of liberty, democracy, and freedom, values inextricably associated with the primacy of justice (criminal justice without justice is a farce, as discussed in Chapter 13). Accordingly, if the value of personal loyalty to superiors is considered higher than the value of justice, the equation of criminal justice will be seriously skewed. The entire field of criminal justice will be endangered and the democratic system of government will limp.

Third: Institutional Integrity

In a free society, any system of government that condones unrestricted submission to an individual or to a small group of individuals—whether they are governors, mayors, or chief administrators—undermines society's institutional integrity. While totalitarian and fascist governments are extreme cases, the principle is, nevertheless, the same. Consider, for example, the public embarrassment the United States government had to endure because of the Watergate scandal, the Los Angeles Police Department because of the Rodney King case, or the New York City Police Department because of the Abner Louima case. In each of these cases, it seems safe to assume that justice would have been better served had the practitioners been more loyal to the constitutional obligations enshrined in the Bill of Rights than to the dictates of their organizational culture.

Logical Findings

Based on what has been said, personal loyalty to superiors must be seen as a *nonintrinsic* virtue, one that is "good" not in itself, but only for achieving certain desired ends at the time and place. While personal loyalty to superiors seems to expect that those superiors be helpful and wise, it cannot override or replace public service obligations or subvert the employees' *intrinsic* loyalty to the Constitution or to their organizational rules and regulations. For this reason alone, personal loyalty to superiors should be seen as a means to an end, *not* the end itself. Subsequently, it should be exercised extremely carefully and weighed most intelligently. If not done so, it can then *freeze* the workers' own intellect and discretion, creating conditions reminiscent of fascism and communism, where loyalty to superiors was considered sacred and workers trapped by artificial realities. The dangers of unexamined personal loyalty to superiors stem from its *counter-reasoning*, whereas the superiors' desires—at that time and place—can be unsavory, foolish, self-serving, contradictory, and subsequently dangerous (for example, they can support or reject war, affirmative action, or the human rights of all people). Subsequently, submitting to such illegal or inhumane desires can be justified by claiming that the employee's behavior was consistent with the principle of personal loyalty to superiors—therefore, no one is to blame (the Watergate scandal during the seventies is a perfect example!).

The claim of personal loyalty to superiors can also undercut the essential value of *good-faith* decision making by making it attractive to employees to justify their wrong behaviors or decisions at will. They can always claim loyalty to the community, the group, the partners, or self on the basis of what they perceive can enhance their standing in the organization. As a result, public accountability may be diminished (or even lost) when the employees switch their claim to loyalty in order to survive when they perceive "work conditions are too inconvenient, too costly, or too contrary to their expectation of how things should be" (Kleinig, 1994:10). In this context, consider, for instance, the case of the apostle Peter, who found it convenient to switch his personal loyalty to Jesus Christ after the Christ had been arrested. Although Peter had been a loyal disciple of Jesus, when danger was imminent, Peter quickly and repeatedly switched loyalties for personal safety.

Consequently, personal loyalty to superiors should be neither assumed nor expected, and the practitioners' primary loyalty should be *only* to the dictates of law and conscience. Failure to support this view may reveal a management system that favors power over reasoning, status over obligation, and coercion over freedom. In criminal justice agencies, such a system can be especially troubling, because the discipline's *original condition* is anchored in the principles of justice, due process, equal protection, and democracy.

It should also be emphasized that the routine practice of misguided personal loyalty to superiors in criminal justice agencies may substantially alter the "original position" of what makes the criminal justice system legitimate. Throughout organizational theory, especially in the works of Max Weber, Herbert Simon, and Frederick Taylor, "impartiality" has been a prerequisite for professional public service. This requirement was incorporated to dissipate the feudal and misguided loyalties that existed between the owners of industry and the workers. What these theorists envisioned was establishing a higher kind of loyalty, one that—while legitimate, rational, and durable—did not impede the workers' freedom to serve the public good, speak the truth, and uphold the moral precepts of honesty, fidelity, and obligation (Denhart, 1993; Kleinig, 1996; Simon, 1997; Souryal & McKay, 1996).

While the revisionist view expressed here is not meant as a blanket indictment of all criminal justice agencies, it should be emphasized that the civility of each agency will be measured by the *moral agility* of its members and the *moral courage* of its leaders.

Cultural and Ethical Concerns

Criminal justice practitioners seem more squeamish about issues of loyalty and loyalties than their counterparts in other public agencies. Each time they make an arrest, lock up an inmate, or revoke a probationer, they ponder where their primary loyalty lies: the Constitution, the community, the public good, agency rules, the boss, their partner, or themselves? While several of these loyalties compete, the practitioner's primary loyalty should remain first and foremost. Also, while politics at the workplace can blur the practitioners' ability to figure out where their loyalties lie, most criminal justice practitioners seem unconcerned. This may be due to the fact that most of them serve at the pleasure of their superiors, are organized along paramilitary lines, perform under extraordinary conditions (for example, police and correctional officers), or operate under ultraconservative cultures. Subsequently, many practitioners seem *ideologically* comfortable with the belief that personal loyalty to superiors is a moral obligation and that deference to the superiors' wishes is a proper and fitting duty. Without much circumspection, many criminal justice practitioners may conclude that upholding personal allegiance to a specific superior is more beneficial and assuring than having to comply with a litany of agency rules and regulations, mission statements, and codes of ethics. What seems to reinforce this belief is the fact that matters of workplace loyalties in criminal justice agencies are almost never mentioned in the rules and regulations of any known agency.

Having said that, I must add that it may be safe to assume that criminal justice employees learn the practice of personal loyalty to superiors from experiencing their agencies' organizational culture. Through real or fictitious experiences, they are made to believe that the primacy of personal loyalty to superiors is *intrinsically good* and that any deviation from it would automatically constitute disloyalty. So ingrained is this belief in the psyche of some criminal justice practitioners, it appears, that many have exploited the practice by using it as a crutch to success. Due to such a warped logic, perhaps, it is not accidental that many police, corrections, and community supervision practitioners are attracted to "brownnosing" (some may call it "sucking up") and overtly flattering their superiors (Klockars, 1999:23). Yet, unknown to most of them, the more they do so, the more competitive practitioners become and the more vulnerable their careers can be.

What seems to further complicate this matter is the ghastly silence that surrounds the practice, chiefly out of fear. Even as criminal justice practitioners attend management seminars at academic institutions, many are uncomfortable commenting on loyalty issues. Bringing up the subject, especially by police and correctional practitioners, even with the best of academic intentions, seems to make the attendees nervous. Not unlike joking about bombs or explosives when walking through airport metal detectors, many such practitioners believe that discussing issues of workplace loyalties can get them into trouble for "suspicion of disloyalty."

Unionized versus Nonunionized Agencies

At this juncture, it might be necessary to explain that while personal loyalty to superiors in unionized criminal justice organizations may be different from nonunionized organizations, the principle is basically the same. This is due to the fact that the purposes and objects of loyalty are the same. The practitioners' willingness to comply with the personal wishes of superiors in unionized organizations is no less attractive than in nonunionized organizations. Also, because of the wide variety of unionization models (for example, hard trade unions, professional associations, fraternity unions, and so on), criminal justice practitioners may believe that they owe more or less loyalty to their unions.

In general terms, however, criminal justice practitioners are not nearly as intimidated by their unions as they are by their superiors. There are two reasons for this assertion: (1) as unionists, the practitioners stand to benefit or suffer collectively rather than individually; and (2) loyalty to unions is normally seen in *hypothetical* terms, while loyalty to superiors is always seen in *realistic* terms—they are right here and now. In some cases, however, the rewards for personal loyalty to superiors in unionized organizations may be more gratuitous and durable than in nonunionized organizations. For example, a promotion to a managerial position in a nonunionized organization is more likely to be rescinded once the agency's CEO leaves office, while in unionized organizations, such a promotion is more likely to be permanent. A critical difference, however, exists between unionized and nonunionized criminal justice organizations: In the unionized ones, practitioners invariably have legal protection provided by the "due and fair representation" clause when they are threatened by dismissal or made to pay monetary fines. In the nonunionized ones, by contrast, the practitioners may have to obtain legal protection and pay for it themselves. Ironically, this difference may have been the strongest motivation for practitioners to seek protection by espousing personal loyalty to superiors in the first place.

The Goliath of Disloyalty

Throughout history, disloyalty has been recorded as the most shameful of defections. Kleinig (1995:122) describes disloyalty as "the forsaking of an object of loyalty for self serving and individualistic or self-assertive reasons." In this context, it should be clear that *disloyalty* is an ethical rather than a legal term. It can be defined as "an act of social or occupational betrayal." Subsequently, disloyal practitioners are considered pariahs whose chances for survival on the job are demonstratively low.

In management literature, being accused of disloyalty is one of the most serious and frightening events, if for no other reason than the general nebulousness of the accusation. This is due, in part, to the common misuse of the dichotomous rule. As in love, patriotism, or religiosity, the opposite of loyalty is *not* disloyalty, but the absence of loyalty, and the opposite of disloyalty is *not* loyalty, but the absence of disloyalty. This clarification can be better understood by remembering Aristotle's rule (as it is here adapted): There is a fundamental difference between not supporting organized religion or classical music and wanting such religion or music to be defeated or destroyed. Accordingly, an accusation of disloyalty to a superior may have little or nothing to do with disloyalty to the department. Indeed, such an accusation may reveal a higher level of departmental loyalty, one that signifies "safeguarding lives and property, protecting the innocent against deception, and the weak against oppression or intimidation," to quote the Law Enforcement Code of Ethics (2000).

To better understand issues of loyalty and disloyalty at the workplace, the dichotomous rule of loyal–disloyal should be replaced by an *operational continuum.* Such a continuum naturally has two extreme positions—loyalty and disloyalty—and a huge "bubble" in the middle, one consisting of those practitioners who are *neither loyal nor disloyal,* depending on the issue being addressed at the time. Criminal justice practitioners inside this bubble are naturally expected to faithfully and peacefully carry out their official duties without becoming entangled in the agency's political allegiances (that is, to be left alone). These bubble practitioners—who here will be labeled *a-loyal*—can be considered neither disloyal to their superiors, since they faithfully fulfill their legal and/or moral obligations (that is, duty, professionalism, justice, and compassion or humanity), nor blameworthy for distancing themselves from superiors they fear are unwise, prejudiced, or corrupt. As a case in point, the number of a-loyal public officials has been increasing lately. This can be shown by the huge recent increase in the number of employees who report agency violations committed by their own superiors. That number almost quadrupled between 2003 and 2005 (see Sarbanes-Oxley complaints/Department of Justice/www.usatoday.com: 4-11-2006). In the absence of more plausible arguments, it should be safe to believe that a-loyal criminal justice practitioners are motivated by a different set of loyalties, and that they differ from other employees only in how they identify their primary objects of loyalty.

To avoid the accusation of disloyalty to superiors, many criminal justice practitioners are made to play the personal loyalty card when they feel bullied, threatened, or discriminated against. They find it safer to adopt a self-protective mode. Like turtles, they "crawl into their shells and hide" (Morris, 1997:123). To survive, they tend to act even more subserviently toward their bosses (or so they pretend), not infrequently allowing their allegiance to devolve into a master and slave relationship (remember Nietzsche in Chapter 4), bringing humiliation to themselves and embarrassment to their profession (Denhardt, 1987).

The Strain of Personal Loyalty to Superiors

Among the most anxiety-causing areas in criminal justice organizations, perhaps, are those related to workers' loyalty or disloyalty, to whom and at what price. No other value or concern carries a heavier emotional strain because loyalty-based issues can, by themselves, create a clash between two principle moral senses: *commitment to the sanctity of public service* and *loyalty to the immediate supervisor*, the one who controls the worker's destiny at the time. Resolving this clash is critical to the construction of social reality in the workplace. Kleinig describes such a clash as a form of "psychological dismemberment," one that can cause delusions and undermine the worker's self-esteem. If such a conflict is not resolved, *moral schizophrenia* may set in, turning hard-working practitioners into confused and disoriented mercenaries.

The strain of moral schizophrenia can be enormous. If untreated, it can diminish productivity, increase cynicism, and encourage corruption. Because of the slow-radiation type of moral schizophrenia in the workplace, few employees may realize (or admit) to its debilitating effect. It is not atypical that after a major scandal erupts, the workers find it necessary to communicate their fears surreptitiously during lunch or coffee breaks in the same manner in which teenagers of the past found it necessary to smoke in school bathrooms. The resulting condition is usually a lingering "internal bleeding" that reduces institutional integrity and diminishes the moral stamina of workers. Historically, perhaps, it was moral schizophrenia that led to the killing of 34 postal supervisors and coworkers between 1983 and 1993 by disgruntled postal employees who, for one reason or another, were unable to collect on their personal loyalty stocks.

Arguments in Support of Personal Loyalty to Superiors

Proponents of traditional personal loyalty to superiors in criminal justice agencies argue that this practice is essential for four reasons: (1) it motivates the practitioners into fostering supererogation; (2) it bolsters institutional responsibility; (3) it inhibits organizational disloyalty; and (4) it ensures institutional integrity. Each of these reasons will be discussed in detail.

Personal Loyalty to Superiors Fosters Supererogation

According to this view, personal loyalty obligates workers to perform *above and beyond the call of duty*. The idea of supererogation lies in Christian theology, particularly the story of the Good Samaritan, who paid the innkeeper "over and above for taking care of the robbed and wounded man" (Heyd, 1982:18). Typically, supererogatory acts are seen as "saintly and heroic, those in which people make sacrifices to achieve a morally good end" (Heyd, 1982:118). Perhaps with the exception of police and prisons, most supererogatory deeds in criminal justice are relatively low-level acts, such as staying after hours to finish paperwork or perform extra tasks that are not specified in the work contract (Souryal & McKay, 1996).

Although supererogation is an admirable virtue, there is no evidence that supports the view that supererogatory acts by criminal justice practitioners are products of personal loyalty to superiors. It is implausible to suggest, for instance, that when correctional officers risk facing armed rioting inmates, they do so because of personal loyalty to any specific supervisor. It would be much more logical to argue that when they so act, they do so because they are faced with a professional situation that calls for a response of extraordinary courage. Furthermore, one should realize that not all supererogatory acts are good; some may be arbitrary, and even foolhardy (Souryal & McKay, 1996). Consider, for example, the controversy about General Custer's last stand. Was his decision to fight until death an act of supererogation, or was it a military duty? Was it more consistent with proper military strategy or with personal egoism? Finally, was it really worth doing? With these questions in mind, one may legitimately conclude that supererogatory acts in criminal justice may have nothing to do with personal loyalty to superiors, and everything to do with embracing a professional commitment.

Personal Loyalty to Superiors Bolsters Institutional Responsibility

This view suggests that personal loyalty to superiors enhances discipline by maximizing compliance with agency rules and minimizing dissention. This practice, so the argument goes, can reduce rule violations and acts of misfeasance. Although this assumption sounds reasonable, compliance with agency rules and regulations hinges essentially on an effective system of quality supervision. If this is the case, then failure to comply with agency rules and regulations may be entirely unrelated to matters of personal loyalty to superiors. It would be more plausible to argue that failure to comply with rules and regulations can be minimized if the supervisors dutifully watch for errors, set quality controls, and enforce disciplinary actions impartially.

Yet these supervisory activities are antithetical to criminal justice agencies that endorse and protect the practice of personal loyalty to superiors. When superiors and workers enter into loyalty pacts, they naturally believe that by virtue of such pacts, they are committed to "taking care of each other." This implication suggests that errors can be overlooked, support offered, and misbehaviors systemically forgiven. This can obviously undermine the effectiveness of discipline in such criminal justice agencies, whereas, in the name of personal loyalty, the practitioners can underreport the "seriousness" of their violations, and the supervisors—interested in keeping these loyalty pacts active— disingenuously oblige.

Personal Loyalty to Superiors Inhibits Organizational Disloyalty

This view assumes that if the workers had no loyalty to their super- iors, they would, by implication, have no loyalty to their organization. This logic is incorrect for two reasons. First, superiors are only tools for achieving organizational ends; withholding loyalty from the former is not the moral equivalent of denying loyalty to the latter. Second, sen- timents of loyalty and disloyalty are not mutually exclusive. The essence of personal loyalty is offering unwavering support while the essence of disloyalty is committing professional betrayal. As mentioned earlier, a-loyal criminal justice workers may be equally loyal, albeit to higher institutional or professional loyalties.

This assertion may explain the "whistle-blowing" phenomenon whereby a-loyal workers can publicly denounce lower loyalties in favor of higher ones. As a case in point, in 1955, Frederic Whitehurst, an FBI forensic scientist, blew the whistle to call attention to the problems prev- alent in the FBI crime lab. When he was accused of disloyalty, he defended himself by invoking loyalty to higher professional values, ones he accused his superiors of ignoring. In the final analysis, however, Whitehurst's act of a-loyalty may have been a supererogatory act—the crime lab underwent monumental reforms.

Personal Loyalty to Superiors Enhances Institutional Integrity

This view suggests that building a chain of personal loyalty to super- iors can enhance institutional integrity. While this argument sounds plausible, it may also be flawed for two reasons. First, it is doubtful that any chain of loyalty can exist in any but the smallest of criminal justice agencies. Even if this is possible, loyalty chains invariably break when power arrangements change from within or without the agency. For example, when a correctional lieutenant is promoted to the rank of assistant warden, creating a situation in which her former captain now serves under her new command, the existing chain of loyalty changes. Loyalty chains can also break when supervisors are hired laterally or when professional jealousy and conflict permeate the ranks.

Second, even if a perfect chain of loyalty existed, the agency's institutional integrity would be only as strong as the integrity of its weakest link. Furthermore, if the chain argument is pushed to its extreme, there logically cannot be any acts of disloyalty committed by middle managers, deputy directors, or assistant bureau heads, yet such acts continue to occur without any noticeable loss of agency efficiency (Souryal & McKay, 1996).

Arguments against Personal Loyalty to Superiors

When personal loyalty to superiors eclipses the obligation of *institutional loyalty* (that is, professionalism, fairness, duty, and the truth), the agency loses its legal equilibrium, and when it eclipses the obligations of *integrated loyalty* (that is, reason, justice, decency, and civility), it loses its moral equilibrium. In the latter case, the agency may act irresponsibly, producing as many illegal or immoral behaviors as laudable ones. Just as courage and religiosity can lead to injury and fanaticism, respectively, so can personal loyalty to superiors lead to extremism and managerial misconduct. Evidence of this can be seen in the occasional failure of criminal justice agencies to prevent constitutional violations, cover-ups, and acts of cronyism and racism, as well as abuse of authority (Ewin, 1993:36).

It is also noteworthy to mention that most of the governmental crises that our nation has endured in the latter part of the last century (for example, Watergate, the Iran-Contra affair, Whitewater, Travelgate, Waco, and Ruby Ridge) have virtually been products of misguided personal loyalty to superiors. The practitioners indicted in these scandals chose personal loyalty to superiors over concerns for constitutional principles, public duty, and institutional integrity. Although critics may blame this on the continuous political pressure at the workplace, the fact remains that such pressure could be more effectively ameliorated if the practitioners observed the proper grammar of workplace loyalty. Consider, for example, Nixon's demand to dismiss Archibald Cox, the special prosecutor in the Watergate Affair in 1972. Nixon's demand was rejected by both Attorney General Elliot Richardson and Assistant Attorney General William Ruckelshaus. They both chose to resign in protest, alerting the Congress and the nation to the dangerous constitutional standoff. Like many others, perhaps, they could have granted the president his wish without risk to their careers; indeed, they might have been rewarded for so doing. They, nevertheless, chose to invoke *integrated loyalty.* As a result, what was politically labeled America's Saturday Night Massacre turned out to be its defining moment.

The Ethical Imperative: The Duty-Based Thesis

To replace the controversial tradition of personal loyalty to superiors in criminal justice agencies, it seems logical to rely on the ideals of duty and public service (remember Immanuel Kant in Chapter 4). *Dutifulness* is the "workers' obligation to do the best they possibly can in the service of their publics, rather than themselves or each other" (Souryal & McKay, 1996). In Kantian terms, dutifulness is a *categorical imperative,* because it is consistent with ideals that are fairly abstract, objective, and universal. Because dutifulness commits practitioners to carrying out their assignments as legal and moral contracts, they would by virtue of such contracts be uninterested in compromising themselves by seeking personal gain.

The duty-based thesis consists of two metaphorical "lungs": commitment to *professional accountability,* and commitment to *organizational identification.* The former reinforces compliance with agency rules and regulations, the latter with individual responsibility. The former focuses on *procedural* matters, the latter on *substantive* matters. The former signifies *policy* decisions, the latter *discretionary* decisions. The use of the word *lungs* here is significant because it emphasizes unison of action—no lung can function independently from the other. Yet, together, they can maximize productivity without being subjected to the risk of personal loyalty to superiors. To incorporate this duty-based module, the following three cultural changes should be considered.

First: The Use of the Word *Loyalty* Should Be Avoided in the Context of Relationships between Superiors and Subordinates

Loyalty in the workplace is an emotionally charged word. It implies "taking sides," "offering one's all," "supporting one's camp at any price," and, in extreme cases, engaging in a *jihad.* Although the perceptions associated with these terms can enable the practitioners to separate acceptable behaviors from unacceptable behaviors, they also can lead to irrational conclusions (Zerubavel, 1991). The workers may be persuaded to see the workplace as consisting of two warring camps: those in the social cluster and those outside its confines; those favored regardless of what they do and those disfavored despite what they do; and possibly those who deserve justice and those who do not.

By contrast, the environment of criminal justice agencies should be dignifiedly serene. Although stressful at times, it should be fundamentally embedded in the principles of veracity, impartiality, tolerance, and good faith. Subsequently, in lieu of using the loyalty paradigm, criminal justice agencies should use concepts such as *collaboration, cooperation,* and *support.* Such concepts have a calming sociological effect that can bind workers and superiors together in a social reality that transcends obsessions with ranks, boundaries, antipathies, salutations, and betrayal.

Second: Dutiful Supervision Should Be Strengthened

When criminal justice practitioners make procedural decisions, they should be firmly held accountable to agency rules and regulations. Yet for this to occur, a system of "dutiful supervision" must be set in place. Supervisors should devise reasonable standards, apply fair sanctions, and, when necessary, terminate "uncooperative" workers. Dutiful supervision, however, cannot be performed in a strictly Kantian context; it requires a human essence, one that can stimulate the sentiments of self-control, responsibility, accountability, and good faith (Wilson, 1993). Yet any such system cannot succeed without the ideal of fairness, the absence of which can be calamitous to any criminal justice agency regardless of which loyalty level it embraces.

Third: Professional Accountability Should Be Maximized

When criminal justice practitioners make discretionary decisions, they should always be cognizant of their obligation to professional accountability. Their determination of what is reasonable, legal, or moral must reflect both institutional and integrated loyalties. Although the practitioners can, and always should, seek guidance from their superiors, their acquiescence must be based on reason and logical justification (remember $E = PJ^2$ in Chapter 1). The relationship between the practitioners and the superiors should be civil; characterized by maturity, not subservience; respect, not fear; strength, not feebleness; and optimism, not dejection. If these traits are patiently cultivated within the agency culture, both the workers and the superiors will be able to defer to organizational identification, the institutional imperative of serving the public interest, before any other.

When professional accountability and organizational identification are nourished within a criminal justice agency, it would be only natural that the practitioners develop a philosophical conviction of justice and a dignified understanding of themselves. The more they learn, the more they can wish to serve the public good. As a result, the practitioners should eventually be able to *support their superiors when they are right and correct them when they are wrong.* The superiors, in turn, should be able to transcend the need for personal loyalty and respond to their workers with *noblesse oblige,* a fundamental sentiment that emphasizes understanding, appreciation, and patience. Finally, with the growth of mutual trust between the practitioners and the superiors, the practitioners may finally be able to see their superiors as philosopher-kings, role models, serious mentors, and (when mutually agreeable) friends.

In the News: An Example That Says It All

GI Chose Morality Instead of Loyalty/Abu Ghraib Whistle-Blower Has No Regrets

By RICHARD PYLE
Associated Press, August 11, 2006

NEW YORK—The soldier who triggered the Abu Ghraib prisoner-abuse scandal by sending incriminating photos to military investigators says he feared deadly retaliation by other GIs and was shocked when Defense Secretary Donald Rumsfeld mentioned his name at a Senate hearing.

Within days, Joe Darby was spirited out of Iraq at his own request. But his family was besieged by news media, and close relatives called him a traitor. Ultimately he was forced to move from his hometown in western Maryland.

"I had the choice between what I knew was morally right and my loyalty to other soldiers. I couldn't have it both ways," the 27-year-old military policeman said in the just-released September issue of *Gentleman's Quarterly.*

In an interview with the Associated Press on Wednesday, Darby said that if presented with the same circumstances at Abu Ghraib today, he would do the same thing. "It was a hard decision to make when I made it, but it had to be done," he said.

Darby also said he later learned that Rumsfeld was not the first to identify him, and he did not see "anything intentional or malicious" on the Pentagon chief's part.

Iraqi detainees at Abu Ghraib were brutalized and sexually humiliated by military police and intelligence agents in the fall of 2003. Photos of the abuse—the same ones that Darby provided to investigators—stirred global condemnation of U.S. military practices in Iraq. At least 11 U.S. soldiers have been convicted in the scandal.

Darby has not previously detailed his role at Abu Ghraib to the media, according to Dan Scheffey, a spokesman for GQ. In the as-told-to article, he said he never expected the Abu Ghraib story to "explode the way it did."

Darby is scheduled to leave the Army and the Reserves on Aug. 31, after eight years of duty. He said he has returned to his hometown, Cumberland, Md., only twice, for a wedding and his mother's funeral.

"I'm not welcome there. People there don't look at the fact that I knew right from wrong," he said.

"They look at the fact that I put an Iraqi before an American."

Reprinted with the permission of the Associated Press.

Review Questions

1. Suppose a cynical colleague asked you, "What is loyalty; is it not all about feelings?" How can you intelligently answer this question?

2. Do you agree that there is "good" loyalty and "bad" loyalty? On what basis you can distinguish these two categories?

3. Do you think criminal justice practitioners should be more loyal to each other than to their obligation to constitutionalism and legality? If you disagree, explain how some of them justify giving "special breaks" to one another in violation of the laws.

4. Define the concept of "a-loyalty." Do you agree with the concept? Should criminal justice practitioners act "a-loyally" at times in order to be fair and just?

5. Define and distinguish among the three levels of loyalty: personal loyalty, organizational loyalty, and integrated loyalty. What should an honest practitioner do if two levels are in conflict?

6. Define *disloyalty* and explain whether it is truly the opposite of loyalty. Give examples.

7. Discuss the statement "All superiors are worthy of loyalty by virtue of their rank." Give examples of unworthy leaders.

References

Barker, T. & Carter, D. L. (Eds.) (1994). *Police Deviance*. Cincinnati, OH: Anderson Publishing Co.

Bayh, B. (1972). *Great Court-Martial Cases*. New York: Grosset and Dunlap.

Blamires, H. (1963). *The Christian Mind*. London: Society for Promoting Christian Knowledge.

Bridges, T. (2000, April 29). Elian Fallout Topples Second Miami Official. *The Houston Chronicle*, IA, 18A.

Clarendon, R. J. (1908). *The Philosophy of Loyalty*. New York: Macmillan.

Delattre, E. (1996). *Character and Cops: Ethics in Policing*. Washington, DC: American Enterprise Institute.

Denhardt, R. B. (1987). Images of Death and Slavery in Organizational Life. *Journal of Management*, *13*, 529–541.

Denhart, R. B. (1993). *Theories of Public Organization*. Wadsworth: Belmont, CA.

Drucker, R. E. (1974). *Management: Tasks, Responsibilities, and Practices.* New York: Harper & Row.

Ewin, R. E. (1993). Loyalties, and Why Loyalty Should Be Ignored. *Criminal Justice Ethics*, 12(34), 36–42.

Fletcher, G. P. (1991). *Loyalty: An Essay on the Morality of Relationships.* New York: Oxford University Press.

Haughey, J. C. (1993). Does Loyalty in the Workplace Have a Future? *Business Ethics Quarterly*, 3(l), 1–16.

Herzberg, F. (1976). *The Managerial Choice: To Be Efficient and to Be Human.* Homewood, IL: Dow Jones-Irwin.

Heyd, D. (1982). *Supererogation.* New York: Cambridge University Press.

Hummel, R. P. (1994). *The Bureaucratic Experience.* New York: St. Martin's Press.

Kleinig, J. (1994). Loyalty and Public Service. *The Public Interest (RIPA)*, Queens Land, 1(3), 10–11.

Kleinig, J. (1995). Loyalty. *Criminal Justice Ethics*, 13(1), 34–36.

Kleinig, J. (1996). *The Ethics of Policing.* New York: Cambridge University Press.

Klockars, C. B. (1999). The Rhetoric of Community Policing. In S. Stojkovic, J. Klofas & D. Kalinich (Eds.), *The Administration and Management of Criminal Justice Organizations* (pp. 19–36). Prospect Heights, IL: Waveland Press.

Konvitz, M. R. (1973). Loyalty. In P. Wiener (Ed.), *Dictionary of the History of Ideas-* Vol. 3. New York: Charles Scribner Sons.

LaCorte, R. (2000, April 28). Miami Mayor Dismisses Official Who Refused to Fire Police Chief. *The Houston Chronicle*, 5A.

Law Enforcement Code of Ethics (2000). Accessed at http://www.co.riverside.ca.us/sheriff/general/law-code.htm.

Manning, P. K. (1985). The Police: Mandate, Strategies, and Appearances. In W. C. Terry III (Ed.), *Policing Society: An Occupational View* (pp. 133–154). Newark, NJ: Wiley.

McGregor, D. M. (1960). *The Human Side of Enterprise.* New York: McGraw-Hill.

Merton, R. (1938). Social Structure and Anomie. *The American Sociol Review*, 3, 672–682.

Morris, T. (1997). *If Aristotle Ran General Motors.* New York: First Owl Books.

Prison Commissioner Is Implicated in Abuse, (1997, July 1). *The Houston Chronicle.* 5A.

Richards, D. (1971). *A Theory of Reasons for Action.* Oxford: Oxford University Press.

Schaar, I. (1957). *Loyalty in America.* Berkley, CA: University of California Press.

Simon, H. A. (1997). *Administrative Behavior.* New York: The Free Press.

Souryal, S. (1998). *Ethics in. Criminal Justice: In Search of the Truth* (2nd ed.). Cincinnati, OH: Anderson Publishing Co.

Souryal, S. (1999). Personal Loyalty to Superiors in Criminal Justice Agencies. *Justice Quarterly*, 4(16), 871–895, with permission.

Souryal, S., & Diamond, D. (2001). The Rhetoric of Personal Loyalty to Superiors in Criminal Justice Agencies. *Journal of Criminal Justice* 543–554, with permission.

Souryal, S., & McKay, B. W. (1996). Personal Loyalty to Superiors in Public Service. *Criminal Justice Ethics*, 15(2), 41–45, with permission.

Wiener, P. (Ed.) (1973). In: *Dictionary of the History of Ideas* (Vol. 3). New York: Scribner.

Wilson, J. Q. (1993). *The Moral Sense*. New York: The Free Press.

Zerubavel, E. (1991). *The Fine Line: Making Distinctions in Everyday Life*. New York: The Free Press.

10
Ethics of Criminal Justice Today
What Is Being Done and What Can Be Done?

The meaning of life is the most urgent of questions.

Albert Camus

The greater the power, the more dangerous the abuse.

Edmund Burke

If you have some respect for people as they are, you can be more effective in helping them to become better than they are.

John Gardner

Men must have corrupted nature a little, for they were not born wolves, and they have become wolves.

Voltaire

What You Will Learn from This Chapter

To better understand the ethics of criminal justice, you will learn the dual essence of criminal justice—the social order and the moral order. You also will learn another duality that exists in criminal justice—the ideal model and the serviceable model.

Key Terms and Definitions

Social Order is a cohesive structure designed to produce a secure and stable life within an orderly community.

Moral Order is a moral structure that can preserve the principles of humanity, fairness, righteousness, and civility.

Overview

The human species is struggling to end its extended infancy. In a recent essay on ethics, Carolynne Stevens, peering into what she calls "Glimpses on the Horizon," envisioned the human race as being galaxy-beckoned into a new celestial environment where it will establish itself amid new challenges. Stevens wondered what the human race will have learned in its earthly cradle that is worthy to spread among the stars (Schmalleger & Gustafson, 1981:211). Expanding on Stevens's "glimpses," let us imagine that each earthly profession will first have to dispatch a delegation of experts to meet with board members of the Celestial Life Forms (CLF) to account for the professional achievements of which they are most proud. What will the delegation from the American Criminal Justice Association (ACJA) be able to say? What great knowledge has the profession accumulated?

It is doubtful that the delegates will be able to speak about issues such as high crime statistics, intolerable prison conditions, nationwide drug abuse, homeless people sleeping under bridges, gang warfare, and organized crime killings. If asked about the values of criminal justice in America, the delegates will certainly be reluctant to bring up such romantic slogans as "presumption of innocence," "justice for all," "due process," and "equal protection." In sheepish embarrassment, they most likely will vaunt the material accomplishments of the last 30 years or so. Like children boasting of their precious marbles, they may recount the near-explosive increases in the size of law enforcement agencies that are armed with state-of-the-art weaponry, the proliferation of prisons that are equipped with Plexiglas walls and sophisticated security systems, the ingenious electronic monitoring devices that can keep thousands of probationers and parolees under house arrest, and the burgeoning intelligence technology that can record the movement of each and every citizen at any time. One achievement the delegates will not be able to mention is advances in human wisdom, rationality, and goodness—without which all material accomplishments are meaningless, if not indeed dysfunctional.

During the interview phase, the ACJA delegates will continue to argue incoherently. To force their theses, they will use elaborate official statistics, flowcharts, and research graphics in an attempt to "romance the stones" of earthly justice. But the CLF members will remain grim—having not seen that before among earthly creatures—they are unimpressed.

In the judgment phase, a disappointed CLF board chairperson will most likely admonish the ACJA experts by stating,

> Go to the ant, thou slugger; consider her ways, and be wise (Proverbs 6:60).

> The memory of the just is blessed: but the name of the wicked shall rot (Proverbs 10:6–7).

> Keep thy heart with all diligence; for out of it are the issues of life (Proverbs 4:23).

Before concluding the celestial visit, the delegates will, of course, be taken on a tour of the celestial tabernacles of justice. They will be shown tabernacles of Plato's "Perfect Circle," Aristotle's "Tripartite Soul," Aquinas's "Natural Law," Butler's "Benevolence," Kant's "Categorical Imperative," and Rawls's "Social Justice," among other ideas and forms they never thought existed. Before the delegates head home, they will be handed a sealed envelope with a message to the ACJA national meeting. The message reads,

> The fool hath said in his heart, There is no God.
>
> Psalms 14:1

Although the message should not be interpreted in a strictly biblical sense, its meaning to criminal justice practitioners is poignant: *The fools are us, ethics is the civic religion of criminal justice, and wisdom, rationality, and righteousness are the forgotten gods.*

The Dual Essence of Criminal Justice: The Social Order and the Moral Order

The dream of quality criminal justice is as ancient as it is universal. It emanated from the natural law of humanity and flourished in Europe since the Enlightenment. The truism of criminal justice, however, continues to elude human understanding because of its dual, often contradictory, nature. For the dream to come true, however, attention must be given to the dictates of two autonomous but commingled entities—*social order* and *moral order.*

Social order pertains to man's concern as an individual for a secure and stable life within an orderly community. As such, attention is focused on the social norms and legal sanctions that ensure public safety, economic well-being, and the freedom to pursue happiness, among other contractual relations.

Moral order, on the other hand, relates to man's collective concern for superior values within the realm of the spiritual. As such, attention is focused on the principles of humanity, fairness, and righteousness, among other standards of civility. Focus on one order *to the exclusion of the other* fails to fulfill all the needs of a civilized community. For instance, while it is considered antisocial for adults to raise havoc with their neighbors, a policy that involves locking up all unfriendly neighbors is frowned upon.

Understanding the dual nature of criminal justice requires a vision that rises above daily existence and congruously combines man's need for "social control" with the need for "spiritual transcendence." In a philosophical sense, the essence of criminal justice is achieving the *proper balance between matters of the world and matters of the soul.* If the balance is tilted toward the former, concern for humanity suffers, and if it is tilted toward the latter, concern for individuality is diminished. Precisely, the moral of criminal justice should be "How much social control is necessary before a community of citizens is turned into a community of barbarians?" or "How much humanity should accompany punishment in the equation of justice?"

In years past, Plato, Aristotle, Jesus, Bentham, Kant, Beccaria, and Durkheim all agonized over the duality of that relationship. In modern literature, Quinney, Douglas, Blumberg, Schmalleger, Braswell, and numerous others continue to grapple with the same dilemma. For instance, Quinney, writing in *Providence*, asserts that the task of criminal justice is to adjoin both the existential form and the spiritual form into a workable concordance conducive to man's individual and collective well-being (Quinney, 1980:x).

Within the constructs of this duality (the social and the moral), three philosophical issues dominate the body of criminal justice knowledge:

(1) the social reality of crime in terms of its relationship to power, law, politics, economics, class, and racial configurations, among others; (2) the nature of justice in terms of its retributive aspects (for example, proportionality of punishment and consistency of sentences) and its distributive aspects (for example, right to possess goods and entitlement to equal benefits); and (3) the role of social control agencies that are entrusted with balancing the criminal issues and the justice issues in a fair and rational manner (for example, the impartiality of police, fairness of grand juries, and effectiveness of corrections). The first two issues are more germane to the study of criminology and law, respectively. The third is central to the study of ethics, because it addresses the fundamental probity in the conduct of criminal justice.

The Dual Practice of Criminal Justice: The Ideal Model and the Serviceable Model

Once more, credit must be given to Samuel Walker for his persistent effort to sort out the truths and fallacies of criminal justice in America. In *Sense and Nonsense about Crime* (1989), he examines many of the myths that dominate the discipline. In his Socratic endeavor, he identifies another duality of a much greater significance to the study of criminal justice ethics: *the ideal (moral) model* and *the serviceable (morally questionable) model*.

The ideal model represents a civics book image of the administration of justice. It is the vision of law and justice by which hard-working practitioners diligently handle each case on its merits. Any person who commits a crime is arrested and prosecuted. If convicted, the offender receives a punishment commensurate with the crime. Fair trials are conducted in an adversarial system of justice in which questions of guilt and innocence are determined through a public contest between prosecution and defense under the impartial eye of the judge. As Walker points out, this version of the criminal justice process expresses an ideal, "but [let] no one mistake it for a description of reality" (Walker, 1989:20). "Things" may not be what they appear, and the ethical reasoner should not be fooled into believing they are.

The serviceable model ("the cynical view," as Walker calls it, or the "bureaucratic garage sale model" [Braiden, 1991]), permeates all aspects of the administration of justice. The model portrays a criminal justice system awash in arbitrary and irrational decision making. Critics of this model cite one deception after another: the questionable motive for arrest, deviance by police, railroading of suspects by prosecutors, the revolving door practice of courts, and the failure of corrections, among other deficiencies that victimize the poor and weak of society.

Consider, for instance, this observation by Skolnick (1996): In an instance in which an individual burglar was caught red-handed during the commission of a burglary, the police suggested that he should confess to many unsolved burglaries that they knew he had not committed. In effect, they said, "Help us out, and we will help you out." The burglar confessed to 400 burglaries. Following the confession, the police were satisfied because they could say they had "solved" many burglaries, and the suspect was pleased because the police had agreed to speak to the judge on his behalf (Skolnick, 1996:179).

In particular, critics of the serviceable model accuse the police of serving a political culture that favors selective law enforcement (Manning & Van Maanen, 1978; Wilson, 1968). Consequently, police officers are often unable to arrest the guilty—even when they have probable cause—while they often arrest others without legal justification. Prosecutors are accused of widely abusing the practice of plea bargaining for political purposes. They drop charges or recommend lenient sentences in return for guilty pleas, while poor and minority defendants are railroaded through overcharging and harsh sentences. By the same token, judges are accused of fashioning standard sentences on the assumption that up to 90% of the defendants plead guilty. Moreover, court congestion seriously impedes the due process rights of the underclass and the less fortunate.

Critics of the serviceable model accuse corrections of flagrant and consistent abuses of justice. Prisons, they argue, have become inhumane places for warehousing inmates (Fleisher, 1989). Prisoners are treated as the "dust and ashes" of the criminal justice system, to be heard from only when they attempt to riot or escape. Concern for the treatment and rehabilitation of inmates, critics argue, has become inconsequential to the administration of justice. Parole boards have been the "passive politicians" of the system, granting release of inmates with little rationale beyond making room for newcomers to move in.

Walker notes that much criminal justice decision making remains irrational and arbitrary. Vast numbers of criminals (especially among the rich and the influential) escape punishment even when they have been caught. That discrimination continues to pervade the system, and gross disparities exist in the outcomes of similar cases. To underscore his argument, Walker reports that convicted murderers in Philadelphia get either 2 or 20 years in prison, and rape defendants in New York City can expect either dismissal of their cases or 20 years in prison. In this chaotic model, Walker asserts, "there is neither law, order, nor justice" (Walker, 1989:20).

The implications of Walker's powerful indictments cannot be overlooked by the ethical reasoner. Not only do they violate the dictates of the social and moral orders, but they also render any attempts toward reform "nonsense," because they attack the wrong problems. Walker submits that all too often reform is based on irrational grounds that have little relevance to the requirements of fairness, equity, or moral principles (Walker, 1989:20).

The Serviceable Model: Moral Double Bookkeeping

Given the reluctance on the part of many criminal justice practitioners to comply with professional standards and their unfamiliarity with ethical principles, many find it beneficial to support the serviceable model. For all practical purposes, the model allows them the freedom to practice *moral double bookkeeping*, whereby the quality of services delivered is substantially inferior, yet the "salesperson" can hardly be held accountable. Not only does the double bookkeeping method appeal to the bureaucratic nature of practitioners, but it also is perhaps the safest method of survival in the *bureaucratic bazaar* of criminal justice.

Packaged in the guise of efficiency, moral double bookkeeping is maintaining at least two sets of operational ledgers: one for public use and the other for internal use. The public ledger contains what ambitious politicians and an uninformed public want to hear—a glowing chronicle of achievements and accomplishments that "look" impressive. By contrast, the internal ledger includes a sad inventory of illegal and unethical practices routinely performed by officials in what amounts to an institutional conspiracy of silence. Such practices are often contrived to circumvent legal or professional restrictions, on one hand, and allow the practitioners the opportunity to administer justice their way, on the other. The sad inventory may include well-thought-out strategies, both offensive and defensive, that seek to accomplish four primary aims: (1) keeping the good image of the agency; (2) serving the ends of justice as *interpreted* by the practitioners themselves; (3) allowing the agency the flexibility to handle difficult or undesirable clients; and (4) forestalling potential criticism by civil authorities, mass media, or society at large (Manning & Van Maanen, 1978:227).

Foremost among these strategies is ensuring that the practitioners are not caught, and that if they are, they have a plausible denial story. Examples of this strategy include how to "effectively" deal with a police informant who no longer wants to snitch, how to "throw the book" at a prison inmate who threatens to blow the whistle on a corrupt guard, or how to manipulate the testimony of witnesses who refuse to perjure themselves despite pressures by the prosecutor to coerce a particular testimony.

Compounded by organizational subculture and impeded by political meddling, many criminal justice agencies improvise on their double bookkeeping strategies—at times, beyond imagination. As a result, the ideals of responsibility and accountability give way to mutual accommodation, obligation gives way to convenience, and devotion to duty gives way to bureaucratization. To lend legitimacy to such strategies, many criminal justice agencies turn to the "old faithful" ploy of number crunching. Unsubstantiated numbers are presented as certain figures, and "micro-dots on flowcharts" are forwarded as unimpeachable proof. Consequently, any view of justice that goes beyond the mere processing of "sorry lost souls" is thought of by practitioners (especially in corrupt agencies) as having little place in the "real world." The idealistic view of criminal justice, unprofessional practitioners believe, survives only in the heads of academicians who need not face life "on the streets" (Schmalleger & Gustafson, 1981:2).

Physiology of the Serviceable Model

In denouncing the serviceable model, Douglas explains in *Crime and Justice in American Society* (1971) that police, prosecution, courts, and other agencies have ceased to be truth-seeking agencies. They operate in synthetic environments that are considered both comfortable for practitioners and responsive to their egotistical need to appear omniscient and omnipotent. Such environments, Douglas submits, fit no universal standard of justice beyond the shell of legalism that protects practitioners from legal and administrative liability. Within this shell, Douglas adds, proceduralism lends itself to favoritism, venality, arbitrariness, and disregard for the rights of individuals. As a result, Douglas adds, the principle of adversarial adjudication ceases to be real, and the fundamental presumption of innocence is reduced to a casual slogan. Even the expectation that the accused will ultimately have "his day in court" may be treated as a farce (Douglas, 1971:54).

Dershowitz (1982) asserts that in the objective reality of criminal justice, the accused rarely goes to court. In most communities, he submits, only about 6% of criminal cases at the felony level ever go to trial. What customarily passes for full, fair, and open hearings are reduced to superficial and hasty negotiation sessions conducted in secret by the defense counsel and the prosecutor. In such sessions, the reasons for the final guilty plea are usually shrouded in mystery and rarely subject to review.

In underscoring the danger of the serviceable model, Chief Justice Warren Burger remarked on the state of court proceedings by stating, "The entire profession, lawyers, judges, law teachers, have become so mesmerized with the court-room contest, we have forgotten our fundamental mandate—healers of conflict" (Houston Police Academy, 1991:19). By the same token, Braiden (1991) made the same point with regard to police by stating,

> Today most organizations have twice as many boxes on the organization chart compared to twenty years ago. But what improvement in product quality has resulted? None that I can discern. On the contrary, I believe this preoccupation with specialization has done more harm

than good. It has reduced peacekeeping in law enforcement tradecraft. What has come to be known as the professional police model is, in reality, a corruption of the original mandate of the police, which according to the Oxford dictionary is "A better state of society." With the passage of time, dedication to the function becomes counter-productive to the original idea. Bertrand Russell had this on the subject: "Organizations have a life of their own independent of their founder. The most striking of these is the Catholic Church, of which Christ would be astonished."

Braiden, 1991:24

As mentioned earlier, the occupational subculture of criminal justice agencies can further exacerbate the dangers of the serviceable model. Under the myth of solidarity, unethical practitioners, like the Sophists of Greece, find it more plausible to continue to ignore the truths of criminal justice, conveniently shrouding them in propaganda, lip-service claims, and administrative gimmickry. To ensure their occupational survival, many such practitioners continue to resist efforts to operate in the sunshine that they may have never before seen.

Critique of the Serviceable Model

From an ethical standpoint, the failures of the serviceable model warrant no further condemnation. While many practitioners mistakenly accept it as "business as usual," or regard it as "critical to their survival," the model must be considered utterly immoral. This judgment is based on the realization that the model (1) destroys the soul of justice, the central virtue and the *summum bonum* of all criminal justice principles; (2) denudes the agencies of their reason for being by exposing their lack of commitment to the public interest; (3) betrays constitutional ethics by denying citizens their rights to due process and equal protection; (4) violates the social contract that binds communities together and sustains social order in a civilized society; (5) discredits the practitioners' sacred oath to be faithful to the office they serve; and (6) encourages corruption among new employees who join the agency with sincere intentions to serve their country faithfully.

Given this analysis, it should be safe to suggest that unless the entire class of behaviors associated with the serviceable model mentality is exposed and repudiated, it is almost certain that the essence of criminal justice will further deteriorate.

Where Do We Go from Here?

In the following chapters a discussion of ethics in the institutions of police, corrections, and probation and parole will be presented. The reader should be mindful, however, of the following two important caveats.

First, based on the relatively long history of the police, more research has been produced in the area of police ethics than perhaps all other criminal justice components combined. As a result, most of the studies in the ethics of corrections, probation, and parole have followed the same methodologies first introduced in police studies (Crouch & Marquart, 1980; Hepburn, 1985; Price, 1983; Rosecrance, 1968; Toch, 1978). Therefore, the disproportionate discussion of police ethics that follows should not reflect a bias for or against the other components. Indeed, if it indicates anything at all, it confirms that either the other components are more ethical, or simply that we know less of their transgressions. Also, it should be safe to add that there are no "substantive differences" between abuses committed by police officers and those committed by correctional or probation officers except, perhaps, that the former abuses are usually witnessed by more people.

Second, while the generic term *corrections* does include the functions of probation and parole, the systematic examination of ethics in corrections will be limited only to institutional corrections—prisons. Probation and parole agencies will be discussed separately.

References

Braiden, C. (1991). Ownership: Who Paints a Rented House? *Leadership Journal*, Houston Police Department in-house publication.

Cole, G. F. (1976). *Criminal Justice: Law and Politics* (2nd ed.). North Scituate, MA: Duxbury.

Crouch, B. M., & Marquart, J. W. (1980). *The Keepers*. Springfield, IL: Charles C Thomas.

Dershowitz, A. M. (1982). *The Best Defense*. New York: Random House.

Douglas, J. D. (Ed.) (1971). *Crime and Justice in American Society*. Indianapolis, IN: Bobbs-Merrill.

Fleisher, M. S. (1989). *Warehousing Violence*. Newbury Park, CA: Sage Publications.

Hepburn, J. R. (1985). The Exercise of Power in Coercive Organizations: A Study of Prison Guards. *Criminology, 23*(1), 145–164.

Houston Police Academy (1991). Striving for Excellence. *Leadership Journal*, Houston Police Department in-house publication.

Manning, P. K., & Van Maanen, J. (Eds.) (1978). *Policing: A View from the Street*. Santa Monica, CA: Goodyear.

Price, K. (1983). *Job Satisfaction as a Means of Increasing Productivity among Correctional Officers in Texas*. Unpublished doctoral dissertation. Huntsville, TX: Sam Houston State University.

Quinney, R. (1980). *Providence: The Reconstruction of Social and Moral Order*. Cincinnati, OH: Anderson Publishing Co.

Rosecrance, J. (1968). Maintaining the Myth of Individualized Justice: Probation Pre-sentence Reports. *Justice Quarterly, 5*(2), 235–256.

Schmalleger, F., & Gustafson, R. (1981). *The Social Basis of Criminal Justice: Ethical Issues for the 80s.* Washington, DC: University Press of America.

Toch, H. (1978). Is a 'Correctional Officer,' by Any Other Name, a 'Screw'? *Criminal Justice Review, 3*(2), 19–35.

Walker, S. (1989). *Sense and Nonsense about Crime: A Policy Guide* (2nd ed.). Pacific Grove, CA: Brooks/Cole Publishing.

Wilson, J. Q. (1968). *Varieties of Police Behavior.* Cambridge, MA: Harvard University Press.

11
Ethics and Police

Either justice is always and in all circumstances sacred, or intrinsically of no account; it is inconceivable that it should be in some cases the one, and in some the other.

Malcolm Muggeridge

Pride grows in the human heart like lard on a pig.

Aleksandr Solzhenitsyn

As a law enforcement officer ... I will keep my private life unsullied as an example to all.

Law Enforcement Code of Ethics

Purely structural arrangements for achieving accountability do not, on their own, reach the problems citizens most want to reach.

Herman Goldstein

What You Will Learn from This Chapter

You will learn the problematic nature of policing, the peculiar environment of the police, the ethics of democracy, and the ethics of shunning corruption. You will also learn the semiprofessional characteristics of police, the reasons why police sometimes abuse their powers, and the obligation of police to shun corruption.

You will learn the nature of police power, the imperative of trust in the police, the basic principles of democracy, the extent of police corruption, and the hedonistic and obligatory types of police corruption.

Key Terms and Definitions

Hedonistic Corruption is the type of corruption that is practiced for personal gain or comfort. It is generally related to economic matters including gratuities, bribery, thefts, and similar dishonest behaviors.

Obligatory Corruption is the type of corruption that knowingly violates agency rules and regulations for egotistical purposes. It entails abusing authority in the performance of one's duties and the demonstration of crude power, egoism, or self-aggrandizement.

Overview

Contrary to misguided belief, policing is one of the noblest functions in society. In biblical times it was entrusted almost entirely to the clergy and the wise men of society. With the emergence of European cities, police became an extension of the polis, or city, signifying its emphasis on serving society. In addition to crime-related functions, the police were expected to aid those who were sick, injured, lost, abused, disturbed, or abandoned. While in earlier periods police developed a degenerate image by associating themselves with oppressive government, the police today are generally regarded as a semiautonomous institution of social order.

In the United States, the role of the police signifies a variety of complex functions that are so interwoven that clinical separation of these functions appears impossible. Such functions include crime fighting, peacekeeping, community service, problem solving, and more importantly, order maintenance. In this myriad of functions, good police work seems to have been identified with problem-solving policing—the practice of ultimately finding the truth of things. This is clearly a capacity that depends more on knowledge, understanding, judgment, initiative, and restraint than on physical or technological prowess (Goldstein, 1990). It is no surprise that a vitriolic scramble is under way among police agencies today to recruit officers of good character and keen mind—individuals who can responsibly and tactfully accomplish such complex tasks without undermining public demands for ordered liberty and professional decency.

But policing a free society is by no means an easy task. This is in part because liberty is a fairly recent human experience and the moral contract between the governed and the governors is still in its infancy. Despite numerous theories, no one knows for certain what policing a free society entails, if it is at all possible. The controversy between freedom and privacy on one hand, and social control on the other, is probably one of the most problematic tasks that faces a civilized society. The controversy has been the center of debate during the past three decades and, regardless of merit, has resulted in the primacy of law and order above all other goals. But the heart of the debate was not really about goals; rather, it was about the means by which society can operate an *effective and humane system of control.*

Given the popular "conflict view" of society as a heterogeneous dynamic, and essentially in competition within itself, there is no question that the need for an *effective but fair* police system is critical. Absent that role, society may not survive and free societies may cease to be free. People will prey on one another, personal safety will be endangered, conflicts will remain unresolved, and social justice will be undermined. More predictably, the very freedoms that make up the institution of democracy will be denied to those who need them most. As mentioned earlier, the rich and the powerful do not need the protection of police, because they can protect themselves. It is the poor, the weak, and the minorities who most need police protection, because the alternative would be either their demise or their uprising in civil disobedience.

The Problematic Nature of Policing

While the vast majority of police officers are professional and dedicated practitioners, it should be noted that among the most pressing concerns in policing today are issues of fairness, rationality, and dedication to public service. Central to these concerns, of course, is the question of discretion: "How can the police make professional decisions in difficult situations that, at times, must render their judgment questionable?" In answering this question, Manning (1978) contends that no rational reply can be found, because policing is an "impossible mandate" and the practice of policing is inherently fraught with contradictions.

Others, including Goldstein, Bittner, Niederhoffer, Wilson, and Skolnick, each reflecting his own philosophical view, recommend changes that range from restructuring discretion to radically revamping the entire criminal justice system—indeed, the entire social system.

In discussing the inherent contradictions in policing, Manning explains that police are victims of an irrational society. Officers must fight crime to keep the peace; act publicly to control private events; prevent new forms of crime for which they have no knowledge, training, or tools to combat them (for example, computer fraud, political corruption); and appear to serve the community while selectively applying force to whomever they choose. Manning further adds that these contradictions have compelled the police to forge "legal dramas" to conceal them, and "ideologies" to cloak them, thus forcing themselves into lying to mislead the public (Manning & Van Maanen, 1978). In sum, he seems to indicate that there is virtually nothing that the police can do, because they are helplessly part of a misguided society.

While Manning's explanation, to a large extent, is realistic, even logical, it falls short of offering a plausible moral argument. The implication that the police have no choice but to continue acting unethically because their occupation is fraught with contradiction neither makes their acts less unfair nor justifies the continuance of contradiction. It is a *naturalistic fallacy* to argue that because contradictions exist they ought to continue. Throughout history there have been contradictions in the governance of societies, and a great many of these contradictions were resolved by rational means. Indeed, democracy is designed to reason away social and economic contradiction in a peaceful manner. And because policing in a free society is an integral part of the democratic process, it is incumbent upon the police to rationally square away inconsistencies without undermining the moral values of honesty, fidelity, and obligation. Displacing the moral responsibility of police by blaming it on a misguided society may be a forced argument, because, at least in part, "the system is us" and begging one's responsibility, problematic as it may be, is ethically unjustifiable.

Literature of comparative policing indicates that the quality of life in industrialized societies like the United Kingdom, Scandinavia, and Japan depends in large measure on the ethics and vision of police leaders in bringing about wisdom in chaotic situations and proper judgment to questions of right and wrong (Bayley & Mendelsohn, 1969; Skolnick & Bayley, 1986). In explaining the "family doctor" approach to policing in Edmonton, Canada, Inspector Braiden remarks, "As police administrators, we cannot always deliver on a promise to reduce crime, no matter how hard we try. We can, however, deliver on a promise to care, and to try harder about people's problems." It is against these "moments of truth" that the ultimate success of the organization is measured (Braiden, 1991).

But while the Canadian approach to policing may not be very different, especially in metropolitan areas, many police agencies in the United States have begun to resolve these contradictions. Many such agencies have been hailed as models of courage, innovation, and vision (Skolnick & Bayley, 1986:226). After all, in a free society, people do not accept police "legal dramas" because they are legal or dramatic; rather, they demand "moral dramas" because they accomplish social good.

The Peculiar Environment of the Police

Police functions were traditionally defined in terms of criminal and regulatory matters. But given the complexity of deviance in today's society (for example, drugs, gangs, and terrorism), a politically convenient—albeit irrational—view emerged, redefining the role of the police as the "fixers of all wrongs." The police were assigned to what amounts to eradicating the ills of a failing social system, a mandate for which they are neither mentally prepared nor adequately trained. For such a monumental task to succeed, coordinated efforts by the social, political, economic, and legal institutions at all levels must be mobilized and faithfully deployed.

Toward accomplishing this extraordinary task, the police were given an impressive array of power, weaponry, and technological gadgets with which they became personally and institutionally infatuated. Furthermore, as the spoils of crime and violence became more politically intolerable, new legal and administrative demands were made on the unsuspecting police. In many departments, politically savvy chiefs were hired to implement politically motivated programs in order to score politically desirable successes. To demonstrate effectiveness, superfluous restrictions and work quotas were imposed on the practitioners, stringent performance standards were implemented, lengthy paper trails were required, and legal and administrative liabilities emerged as the order of the day. As a result, occupational stress and managerial pressures continued to mount, creating an obtrusive fog of confusion, paranoia, and despair.

Police practitioners, particularly in the 1960s and 1970s, reacted imprudently. They responded with hostility toward those who supported them and "those who did not." Many officers became disillusioned with the ambivalence of their profession and the hypocrisy of a society they depended upon to support them. Many realized that while they were required to enforce all current statutes, the public did not tolerate full enforcement of all laws; while they were held responsible for eradicating drugs and apprehending drug dealers, their ability to cope with the drug problem was substantially limited; while they were expected to act in an impartial and apolitical manner, the infiltration of politics into policing compelled them to use compromising deals, deceptive means, and collusion with criminals (Manning & Van Maanen, 1978). Frustrated with unfair department rules and regulations, many police officers found solace in corruption as a way of getting even (Souryal, 1977:424).

These disheartening conditions must have further eroded police ethics. Many officers found justification in having to ignore their oath of office; to overlook much of the professional principles they were taught in the academy; to bluff and lie—not necessarily out of malevolence—but out of a desperate attempt to reconcile unfair and contradictory demands. As Goldstein aptly describes, the police became a "super-structure without an adequate foundation" (Goldstein, 1977:9–11). Not surprisingly, most of the recommendations made in the latter half of the last century for improving the quality of police officers have focused on their state of knowledge, rationality, and professional training. Examples include the President's Commission on Law Enforcement and Administration of Justice in the 1960s; the Knapp Commission Report and the National Advisory Commission on Higher Education for Police Officers in the 1970s; the Report on the State of Police Education in the 1980s; and the Independent Commission on the Los Angeles Police Department in 1991. The last report, in particular, was critical of the aggressive mentality, brutality, racism, and improper preparation of officers.

The Semiprofessional Professionals

Delattre (1989), Blumberg and Niederhoffer (1970), Manning and Van Maanen (1978), Goldstein (1977), and others characterize the police in a free society as an anomaly. Delattre calls them the "unprofessional professionals," Niederhoffer used the term "ambivalent force," while Manning, as mentioned earlier, refers to their mandate as "impossible." These are disappointing characterizations that can be understood only in the broader context of American government. Unlike in European systems, the police in America are vested with powers under a unique form of government in which authority is reluctantly granted, and when granted it is sharply curtailed (Goldstein, 1977:1). This unique form of government may have been a dominant factor behind the politicization of police and the failure of federal and state governments to fully support law enforcement at the local level.

In criticizing the political environment of police, Patrick Murphy suggested that much of what is wrong is the result of the "absurd, fragmented, unworkable, non-system of more than 17,000 local departments" (Murphy, in Delattre, 1989:xv). Consequently, he adds, individual officers, chiefs, and entire departments have been inhibited from taking actions that would better serve the true goals of law enforcement. Political meddling in police matters by elected officials, party leaders, and campaign contributors is a common handicap. Mismanagement and discrimination against qualified persons in hiring, assigning, promoting, and disciplinary matters are far from rare. Moreover, professional standards that could be used to correct such abuses or to support principled practitioners have not been generally accepted. Consequently, many police departments are stymied in their efforts to provide better police services (Delattre, 1989:xv).

While democracy has many desirable traits, it is an ideal that is difficult to live by. While, on one hand, the police are responsible for social control, the public, on the other hand, cannot be expected to submit to oppression. Untempered abuses by police (for example, unjustified excessive force, discrimination against the poor, racism, and brutality) should legitimately worry a democratic society. The perception of police as semiprofessionals may have been further tarnished because abuses that are ordinarily committed by ill-prepared officers at the lowest level are tolerated, in most instances, without adequate scrutiny by supervisors (Goldstein, 1977:1). Subsequently, given the lofty values of democracy, it would be illogical, if not irrational, to expect society to endure police abuses rather than demand that the police act responsibly. If government is to be truly representative of the people, its first obligation must be to the people, rather than to the agencies it creates. Intensifying efforts to improve the moral quality of the police, therefore, must be a categorical imperative, not only because it is good in itself, but also because it must be the only way to govern a democratic society.

When compared to other components of criminal justice, the public perception of police seems to range from "unsettling" at one end of the continuum, to "out of control" at the other. There are three reasons for this perception: First, in the vast majority of cases, the police are the initiators of the criminal justice process that, regardless of the outcome, can cause immense social harm to the implicated party. Second, as custodians of social order, the police are entrusted with hard-to-standardize powers. They can stop and frisk people when they see fit, detain suspects for "unspecified" periods, and settle disputes between individuals who seem equally guilty. Unlike judges, prosecutors, and grand jurors, the police have what appears to be a license to manipulate, to chase people in the streets, to embarrass them in public places, and to invade the inner privacy of their homes. Third, the police have the distinct discretion not to initiate the criminal justice process. By so choosing, they can effectively reinterpret the law and redefine social morality (for example, not issuing speeding tickets until the motorist is at least 10 miles per hour in excess of the speed limit, or not enforcing minor drug laws in certain areas of town). Unlike police decisions to invoke the law, such choices are of extremely low visibility and seldom the subject of review (Goldstein, 1977). In extreme cases, a corrupt officer could technically let an individual "get away with murder" with insignificant risk to his or her career. In such cases, a corrupt officer can avoid responsibility by invoking the "never saw" or "never heard of it" defense (Souryal, 1977:48). Based on these reasons, it should be safe to suggest that the image of the police suffers, not because of their statutory authority, but because of their likelihood to abuse their professional duties.

The Police Prerogative to Abuse Power

Once again, while the majority of police officers are professional and dedicated practitioners, it is the small minority among them that drive their dedication. Given the problematic nature of policing and its peculiar environment, the police—who also happen to have a monopoly on the use of force in the community—are perceived as possessing "something extra" that can intimidate, if not frighten, most citizens. While this "something" is hard to identify, it is manifest in sentiments of suspicion, skepticism, and fear. Such sentiments could be better sensed when the characteristics of the police are compared to those of other public officials, such as the military, schoolteachers, mail carriers, or engineers. Upon closer analysis, the causes of this "something" may reveal two sets of concerns: concerns related to *the nature of police power*, and concerns related to *the lack of trust in police personnel*. In the following segments, both sets of concerns will be explained.

Concerns Pertinent to the Nature of Police Power

These concerns include (1) *Casualty:* Any arrest decision, even in a simple situation involving a defendant who may ultimately be exonerated, can cause serious punitive consequences. These include the loss of a job, a period of jail detention, or the indignity of being fingerprinted and photographed. (2) *Permanence:* Once a police decision has been made to arrest or charge, the decision invariably remains for the duration of one's life. Furthermore, the procedure necessary to undo such a decision is usually lengthy, complicated, frustrating, and costly. (3) *Secrecy:* The "real" criteria employed by the police in determining which persons are candidates for arrest are usually "known only to the police." Manning stresses that rookies learn how to be police officers by watching "what other police officers do, say, feel, and otherwise act in routine situations—they do not learn it in books" (Manning & Van Maanen, 1978). The secret criterion to arrest, Manning adds, is more distinctively shaped by the subculture of the department and by the moral qualities of the supervisors at the time than by legal or administrative rules. (4) *Inadequacy:* Given the relatively modest educational background of police officers and their limited preservice training, the police have not been particularly noted for making visionary or nonconformist judgments. Most often their judgments reflect the conservative middle class to which they normally belong. Such biases include, especially in the past, aggressive behavior toward nonconforming persons, minority members, and lower-class males—both white and black. Subsequently, the police continue to be seen as "petty tyrants" by many groups—especially the poor and the underprivileged (Bittner, 1967; Goldstein, 1963; Westley, 1953).

Concerns Pertinent to Lack of Trust

These concerns include several fears on the part of the unsuspecting public, such as the following four examples. (1) *Physical fear:* What if the police used undue force? What would I do if they overreacted? (2) *Anticipatory fear:* What are the police really "up to"? How do I know they are not attempting to frame me? (3) *Ghost fear:* How can I forget what the police did to poor Johnny the other day? (4) *Escape fear:* Why should I get involved or cooperate with the police? To whom can I complain if they get me in trouble?

The police prerogative to abuse power may also be a product of their ubiquitous stature within the criminal justice system. Police agencies are most likely to be the (1) largest, (2) most visible, (3) most armed, (4) most specialized, (5) most costly, and (6) most discretionary. With the exception of the last assumption, all others are inconsequential to police ethics, because they are structural in nature and can be restructured only by political and administrative policy. The last assumption, however, is both the easiest and the most important, because it is behavioral in nature and can be corrected by the individual officers themselves. Based on this premise, it should be safe to argue that despite the good intentions of many police organizations, there is little that departmental rules can do to improve the conduct of officers who knowingly operate unethically. The integrity of any police department is the sum total of the integrity of its members; collectively, they can create it, preserve it, or lose it.

The Police in Search of a Soul

Given the voluminous literature on police corruption, the perennial question continues to go unanswered: "How can the police prerogative to abuse power be minimized, and honesty, decency, and civility be maximized?" In response to this question, it may be safe to suggest that, short of endangering democracy or radically impairing police effectiveness, the only rational alternative is actualizing the soul of police by promoting "street-corner morality." On one hand, the street is where the propensity for abuse is highest and the potential for social harm greatest. On the other hand, the individual officer is perhaps the only person who can effectively suppress evil and promote righteousness. Hence, the plea to focus on the moral character of officers—the soul of police—by transforming street-corner cops into *street-corner moralists*.

In 1969 the foundation of the Hastings Center in Hastings-on-Hudson, New York, began a movement toward strengthening ethics in public service. Rapidly proliferating moral problems in the fields of medicine and biology were the initial impetus behind the center. Soon afterward, the center expanded to include similar concerns in other fields. In 1982 the Institute for Criminal Justice Ethics at John Jay College of Criminal Justice was founded as the spiritual offspring of the Hastings Center. Its objectives were to upgrade ethical standards in criminal justice, stimulate research in the field, and ensure ethical performance in policing. At present, the institute produces ethical training programs for police academies throughout the country. While the institute is gradually growing, it is hoped that its influence will outgrow concern with mundane police corruption and address moral issues in policing, rethinking the police mentality, reversing police myths, and stimulating institutional repugnance to lawlessness.

Yet how in the objective reality of police culture can the soul of police be actualized? While the answers to this question are complex, the challenge, as we will later learn, is not insurmountable. Recalling Aristotle, two virtues are necessary to actualize the soul of any public organization: an *intellectual virtue* and a *moral virtue*. Each virtue complements the other, forming a wholesome moral character. For Aristotle, nothing else is necessary.

In the following segments, both virtues will be discussed in the context of policing; the intellectual virtue will be presented as "Ethics of Democracy," and the moral virtue as "Ethics of Shunning Corruption."

The Intellectual Virtue: Ethics of Democracy

In *Policing a Free Society*, Goldstein (1977) points out that the police model that has emerged in this country has been a neutral one. It represents a sterile kind of organization, devoid of a clear commitment to any values other than operating efficiency. Absent an effort to build a set of values into policing, those that prevail are the values of the subculture. In large measure, this accounts for the radically different assessments made of the quality of police service by police personnel when compared with those made by critics on the outside (Goldstein, 1977:12).

Goldstein underscores that failure to build a set of democratic values into policing is "all the more disturbing" because of the peculiar nature of policing a free society. Under a system of government in which so high a value is placed on democratic virtues, an extraordinarily heavy responsibility must fall upon those who are assigned to defend these virtues. The police mission, after all, is not only limited to exercising authority in accordance with constitutional and legal limitations; it also extends to the protection of the constitutional rights of citizens from infringement by others.

The absence of intellectual virtue can be detrimental to the quality of policing. Particularly in large cities, the police continue to place a higher priority on order maintenance than on operating in a democratic manner. Constitutional and statutory requirements—such as those that limit the police right to arrest, search, or interrogate—continue to be viewed by many police officers as technicalities that interfere with "effective law enforcement." Consequently, many police officers may fail to appreciate their obligation to provide equal law enforcement to seemingly undeserving individuals, provide due process when it is too ambivalent to ascertain, protect the rights of minorities who may be unaware of their rights, and ensure the dignity of someone who may have no dignity. As Goldstein remarks, most bothersome is the fact that talk about supporting democratic virtues in the context of police operations has come to be equated, by many police officers, with a soft and permissive attitude toward criminals and toward unruly elements in society (Goldstein, 1977:14).

Why Not Democracy?

From a philosophical point of view, it would be contradictory to argue that in a democratic society effective policing cannot be administered democratically. It is equally contradictory to contend that democratic principles may be essential at the trial level but not at the street level, where the facts of the trial are mostly found. Goldstein challenges this twisted rationale, questioning why "democratic policing" should be such a tall order to fill. Democratic values, he asserts, *cannot* logically be ignored if police legitimacy is to be real and the public recognizes it as such. In a Kantian sense, perhaps, Goldstein asserts that government should be unequivocally committed, "aggressively, overtly, and unashamedly," to creating a system of policing in which democratic ethics is a standard practice.

There are three reasons for Goldstein's powerful exhortation: (1) recognition that the police function is governed by a complicated set of rules and that a high social value attached to conforming to those rules would make policing much more challenging and rewarding;

(2) compliance with democratic ethos, especially in "critical incidents," such as protecting the right of an unpopular speaker to speak, or sheltering from attack a person accused of a heinous crime, would most spectacularly demonstrate professionalism; and (3) the example set by police in conforming to the law and in acting even-handedly to protect the constitutional rights of citizens would, in the long run, win greater respect and cooperation from the community (Goldstein, 1977:13).

As to reasons many police officers appear uncommitted to democratic principles, one can only speculate. Two sets of factors, however, may shed light on this question: the first is *sociologically oriented*, and the second is *work oriented*.

Sociologically oriented factors include the following. (1) Police officers are mostly employed at a young age (between the ages of 18 and 22), before they would have had any real experience with democracy. Few would have had significant jobs or been exposed to the trauma of being subjected to unfair treatment. (2) Most police officers belong to lower-middle-class households that are not noted for being cradles of democracy nor for offering an exemplary democratic environment. (3) Most of the educational institutions that police officers attend prior to employment pay lip service to democracy. They neither emphasize democratic principles nor provide an environment that is conducive to independent critical thinking. Indeed, when the U.S. Constitution is taught in many high schools, it is often presented in a dry, abstract, and rather sterile fashion, as if it has little relevance to career life. (4) Many rookies are hired soon after they complete military service, bringing along with them a rigid style of thinking. If they are not retrained away from that style, they may tend to pursue an autocratic model of treating people—the only model they know.

Work-oriented factors exacerbate the previous conditions in significant ways:

- *Police academies may be lagging behind the professional movement.* Traditionally, police academies follow a quasimilitary model, and when democratic principles are presented, they usually are neither explained intelligently nor endorsed sincerely. Aside from legal and technical studies, police academies tend to focus more on superficial criteria, such as demeanor and physical appearance, rather than on democratic and ethical behavior. Consequently, most rookies are trained to apply "rule by law" rather than "rule of law," a subject that requires advanced reasoning and understanding. As Harris observes, "One of the main purposes of the police academy seemed to be to develop uniform behavior in order to lessen the member's need to depend on his own judgment. . . . ethos of police professionalism assumes that the impersonal rules of law enforcement are correct and appropriate regardless of what the citizenry may think" (Harris, 1973).

- *Police subculture, as mentioned earlier, reinforces the image of police work as a bureaucratic activity that has little in common with democratic principles.* As such, it is to be pursued, first and foremost, to ensure efficiency and control. The values of honesty, fidelity, obligation, and compassion, if raised at all, are usually considered irrelevant to the practice of law enforcement.

- *Police departments, which are traditionally organized and managed along the military model, neither recognize democratic accomplishments nor reward those who pursue them.*

- *Popular television programs seldom exhibit episodes of democratic policing and instead glorify officers who demonstrate the so-called John Wayne and Dirty Harry syndromes.* By implication, the message is clear to all those who are eager to hear.

Toward instilling democratic virtues in the police, Goldstein proposes a two-pronged approach: (1) education and training should be intensified in order to provide officers with a better understanding of the principles of democracy and the ways in which they could be exercised; and (2) the day-to-day operation of police agencies and the manner in which individual performance is rewarded should be revised to elicit greater support for democratic conduct by frontline enforcers (Goldstein, 1977:15).

Democratic Ethics

True democracy is an advanced state of mind that can be achieved only through learning, experience, and soul-searching. Democratic ethics should be seen, therefore, as a set of principles that characterizes the working of a democratic society—how people can live freely despite their diversity, frailties, and follies.

In accordance with the dictum of "anything that can be learned can be taught," there is no reason to believe that democratic ethics cannot be taught in a classroom setting in the same way other subjects can. Obviously, completing a course in democratic ethics can hardly make a person any more "democratic" than a course in religion can make a person any more "saintly." Nevertheless, by emphasizing democratic ethics at all levels of police development (for example, preservice training, in-service training, and executive training), it should be possible—at least in incremental portions—to improve the officers' democratic character in the same way that teaching investigative techniques can improve their technical skills. Furthermore, the more that police officers experience democratic treatment at the workplace, the greater their devotion to democracy, and the more they are likely to apply it on the street when dealing with others.

Basic Democratic Principles

Without repeating an introductory political science course, I can say that democracy is neither the easiest nor the most efficient form of government. The original philosophers of democracy never meant it to be either. Nevertheless, democracy is the most cherished form of government as far as the reasoning mind can determine. It is based on rational assumptions that are closest to, and complementary of, the true purposes of man. The basic tenets of democratic theory assume that people are self-motivated, know their own interests, and have enough sense to give way when another person's interests are more reasonable.

Democratic principles include the following:

1. Individualism is the essence of human existence; citizens want to be, and can be, different.

2. Liberty is the foundation of justice; *oppression* and *justice* are contradictory terms.

3. Equality is a human property—never to be traded or taken away.

4. Sovereignty is by popular choice; an imposed government is not only illegitimate, but it also causes social misery.

5. Government is the creation of society, rather than the other way around.

6. Checking the behavior of government is the responsibility of each citizen; all officials are hired hands who must be held accountable to elected officials.

7. Rule of law is the only equitable means for judging free and equal people; everyone is under the law and no one is above the law.

8. Workable laws are the product of majority rule; anything else is tyranny.

9. The dignity of man is the *summum bonum* of civilized society, more so than economic or social power.

10. Civil liberties are immunities from governmental oppression—they are not options to be offered or withheld upon personal whim or animosity.

In confirming Goldstein's prescription for instilling democratic values through knowledge, Carter, Sapp, and Stephens in *The State of Police Education* (1989:134) recount the case of an ethical officer:

> One college-educated officer (a white male) with whom we rode on patrol in a high-crime, low-income, predominantly black area said: "You know, I feel myself becoming more prejudiced. I try not to let it affect the way I treat people, but I still can't help the way I feel." ...

The value of education for this officer was that "he recognized the prejudice, understood its potential effects, and consciously attempted to control it." In observing this officer on patrol, dealing with people and his responsibilities, we felt that we saw the best application of liberal arts education in a trying environment. After patrolling down the dark, litter-covered streets with this officer ... [he] abruptly stated: "Let us go somewhere else." He drove a short distance outside his patrol area to a street brightly lighted with signs from businesses, frequent street lights, attractive homes, and the trappings of a middle-class neighborhood. As he drove down the street, the officer visibly seemed to relax and simply said: "Sometimes I need to see the light."

The inference from this encounter is powerful. The officer's environment was depressing and stressful—it was affecting his judgment with citizens. He needed a source of relief to help him regain perspective. His knowledge of democratic ethics was the ballast. It gave him not only clarity of direction, but also the introspective ability to determine when the judgmental equilibrium was beginning to shift. The officer's thought clearly reflects the philosophy of wisdom in action, and perhaps this alone is a sufficient benefit of learning democratic ethics (Carter et al., 1989:134). In contrast to this encounter, consider the events of the Rodney King incident referred to in Chapter 4.

The Rodney King Case

Rodney King was severely beaten by officers of the Los Angeles Police Department. While beating a suspect is a rare event in many communities, what gave this event critical significance was the fact that the beating was captured by an amateur videographer and broadcast nationally for several days. The film showed 11 or more white officers, 3 of whom ferociously beat and kicked a handcuffed African American man for nearly 2 minutes. The suspect, who had been arrested for a speeding violation, was also shocked more than once by a Taser. As a result of this incident, he suffered nine skull fractures, a shattered eye socket and cheekbone, a broken leg, a concussion, injuries to both knees, and nerve damage that left his face partially paralyzed. The event resulted in embarrassment to the police department and the city of Los Angeles, stunned the nation, rocked the law enforcement community, and further outraged minority groups that have contended for years that they are targets of an abusive police force (*Dallas Morning News*, March 18, 1991).

Several observations heightened the gravity of the King incident. First, at least 11 officers, including a sergeant, stood by while 3 others administered the beating, and no one made a serious effort to stop it. Also, no one reportedly attended to King after he was hog-tied, dragged to the side of the road, and left bleeding. Second, the beating was carried out with impunity, with no apparent concern for the fact that barely 60 feet away as many as 20 local residents were watching, or that the officers were acting in full view of motorists who slowed down to look as they drove by. Third, subsequent information confirmed by the investigative commission revealed that some of the officers who accompanied King to the hospital flippantly remarked that "we played a good game of hardball" and "we hit quite a few home runs" while smashing their batons against King's body (*Los Angeles Times*, March 21, 1991). Fourth, court records depicted a history of similar cases, some of which seem to differ from King's only in not being recorded on camera.

While the King case may reveal evidence of police lying, practicing racial discrimination and official oppression, and conspiring to commit a felony, in a broader sense it represents a textbook case of the breakdown of democratic ethics. Regardless of how heinous King's crimes allegedly were, the officers appear to have violated a number of basic democratic principles; namely: (1) the presumption of innocence—by meting out punishment before the suspect was taken before a magistrate; (2) the principle of rule of law—by setting themselves above the authority delegated to them as peace officers; (3) preserving the civil rights of a prisoner—by assaulting and humiliating him; (4) equal protection under the law—by failing to protect a suspect from unnecessary harm; and (5) public accountability—by giving conflicting accounts about the facts of the case.

As a result of the King case, three patrol officers and a sergeant were indicted. On April 29, 1992, a 12-person jury in Ventura County, California, acquitted the four officers. The jury was unable to reach a decision on one assault count against one of the officers. A retrial of the charge was ordered. Upon word of the verdict, African Americans in south central Los Angeles rioted, attacking citizens and looting and burning businesses across the city to show their outrage at what they considered further injustice toward not only Rodney King, but also all African Americans. Consequently, damage to the "moral consciousness" of the Los Angeles Police Department appeared to be complete and perhaps irreversible for many years to come.

Haven't We Learned Anything Yet?

As mentioned earlier, in 1991 the Rodney King case helped provoke one of the worst riots in American history, leaving 54 people dead and 2,000 injured, and causing more than $1 billion in damage (*Economist*, July 13, 2002). Yet, on July 6, 2002, another amateur video taken by a tourist, Mitchell Cooks, again showing the arrest of an African American motorist, raised similar doubts about the capacity of the police in California (this time in Inglewood) to restrain themselves from the seduction of using unjustifiable force.

The video showed a white officer, Jeremy Morse, hoisting a hand-cuffed black teenager to his feet and smashing his head on a car trunk. Morse then punched the teen in the face, while several other officers, some black and some white, stood behind him. Eventually one of the officers intervened.

Although the encounter was not as prolonged or ugly as the King beating, the incident, which brought unhappy memories to TV watchers across the country, involved considerably less provocation. While Mr. King was reportedly a strong man, allegedly high on drugs, who tried to flee from the police in a high-speed car chase and attacked them when they tried to arrest him, the victim in the Inglewood case was a slender 16-year-old, a special education student with no arrest record. The problem that provoked the clash was a routine traffic stop (the license plate on the victim's family car had expired). When Mr. Cooks, the tourist who filmed the video, was asked how he felt while recording the event, he stated that he was not shocked: "I just thought it was standard procedure; I thought it was normal in Los Angeles" (*Economist*, July 13, 2002). Officer Morse's case was not helped by the fact that another victim has since come forward claiming to have been handcuffed and beaten by Morse.

As a result of this altercation, hundreds of angry protestors marched on Inglewood City Hall calling for Officer Morse to be dismissed from the force and prosecuted to the full measure of the law. Congresswoman Maxine Waters also sent a letter to the attorney general's office demanding an investigation into the incident—all that while Mr. Jackson's lawyers went to the federal courthouse in Los Angeles to file a lawsuit.

With this scenario in mind, one should legitimately ask whether the lessons learned from the Rodney King case had any meaning or were sufficiently learned, and whether the impact of police subculture is indeed more potent than the impact of police training in the state of California during the last 11 years. One should also ask whether the local political establishment in Inglewood will be able to put an end to such notorious cases before social anger again turns to social alienation and outright violence. One should also inquire into the effectiveness of police supervision, especially when the videotape allegedly showed a police corporal assisting officer Morse in the beating. Finally, one should ask what good is police leadership if it cannot effectively turn the bureaucratic culture of police departments into an enlightened environment, one based on reason, duty, self-control, and "serving mankind" (to quote the police code of ethics).

The Farther Reaches of Democratic Ethics

In addition to the conventional principles of democracy mentioned earlier, specific values are associated with the American democratic experience. Westermann and Burfeind, in *Crime and Justice in Two*

Societies (1991), identified two important value clusters that are of great significance to American policing and that should be emphasized in any police training course. These are *freedom, individualism, equality*, and *diversity* (Westermann & Burfeind, 1991:19). A fair amount of the following discussion will be based on Westermann and Burfeind's views.

First, if there is one primary value in American society—perhaps other than the value of success—it must be the value of *freedom*. The United States boasts that it is the "land of the free," and though it is in no way perfect, no other society in the world has accomplished so much to protect individual freedom and liberty. Whether they are peacekeepers or peace breakers, citizens must be conscious and protective of their civil rights as well as the civil rights of others. The notion of *rights* means being endowed with innate entitlements that cannot, under the law, be abridged. The concept of civil rights, by definition, establishes a set of claims that the citizen possesses and an unquestionable legal obligation by government to protect these claims. Any infringement thereof, without due process, is a serious violation of democratic ethics—regardless of excuse or justification. Such violations would be considered even more sinful when committed by the police—the stewards of civil rights.

Second, the concept of freedom is organically related to the doctrine of *individualism*. Rights are endowed to individuals by virtue of being citizens and apart from any relationship to race, color, or social status. Individuals in America are free to travel where they wish, speak as they please, and criticize the government within the boundaries of the law. Infringements on these rights, without due process, constitute betrayal of democratic ethics.

Third, closely intertwined with the doctrines of freedom and individualism is the ethic of *equality*. These three values form an equilateral triangle. For freedom and individuality to be able to stand, equality must be the supportive ethic. The presumption of equality extends to the realization that any person has as many rights and responsibilities as everyone else, regardless of individual or class differences, because, philosophically, no one can be equal unless all are equal. Consequently, police subculture that classifies people into *desirables* and *undesirables* (among other categories with less complimentary labels)—ironically, for operational direction—ends up destroying the very soul of democratic direction.

Fourth, the next most important value in American democracy is *diversity* and the values that cluster around it. One historical fact that cannot be overlooked is that the United States was framed from a polyglot of immigrants that continues to bring a mixture of peoples and cultures from virtually all lands. The United States is a quilt of diversity, patched together out of a multitude of racial and ethnic groups. Compounding this quilt is the diversity of lifestyles brought about by the socioeconomic distinction this division brings. At one time, people in the United States believed in a melting pot theory of cultural assimilation, predicting that the sharp differences in ethos and culture would ultimately be blended into a new synthesis. Today, people are more likely to speak in terms of cultural pluralism and to value the diversity it brings. Police personnel must realize that valuing diversity not only strengthens the American yearning for democracy, but also brings about human virtue in its most salient essence.

The Moral Virtue: Ethics of Shunning Corruption

Out of life comes death, and out of light comes shadow. This has been the controversy between good and evil that for centuries has mystified moral philosophers. In applying the same principle to police ethics, one should be able to say, "out of nobility comes greed" and "out of professionalism comes the dust and ashes of corruption."

Until recently, it was almost impossible to generate an open discussion of corruption by the police. That was perhaps rationalized on the basis that (1) the police are being made scapegoats for the corruption of society; (2) by painting the police as corrupt, certain segments of society hoped to convince themselves that their corruption was less serious; and (3) because police are responsible for controlling the conduct of others, certain elements of society delight in alleging police corruption. The subject of corruption was subsequently seldom referred to in law enforcement texts and rarely covered in police training programs. Most strikingly, the leaders of some of the most corrupt police departments publicly denied the existence of corruption (Goldstein, 1977:188).

There is a greater willingness today to discuss the problem of police corruption. Three books, titled *Police Deviance* (Barker & Carter, 1994), *Character and Cops* (Delattre, 1989), and *Ethics of Policing* (Kleinig, 1996), deal exclusively with the problem of corruption. While the titles may sound surprising to an ordinary citizen or to a student of law enforcement, when perceived from the vantage point of a young African American person, a long-haul truck driver, or even a veteran patrol officer, the titles may sound most appropriate.

Corruption Defined

There is considerable disagreement about what constitutes police corruption. Sometimes it is defined so broadly as to include all forms of police wrongdoing, including questionable behavior off the job. At other times it can be defined so narrowly that serious unethical behavior is excluded (Goldstein, 1977:188).

Consistent with the narrower perspective is the legal definition of *corruption* that can be found in federal or state penal codes. These include acts such as theft, bribery, perjury, falsification of evidence, record tampering, and official oppression. While such behaviors are clearly unethical, they are also illegal and their practice by police makes perhaps the worst kind of corruption in the minds of citizens (Souryal, 1977:418).

Consistent with the broader perspective is the sociological view of corruption. It focuses on the issue of arbitrary *power*, because arbitrariness presupposes an intent to achieve an end other than that for which the power was granted. Accordingly, all acts of arbitrariness, including abuse of authority, brutality, and violation of civil rights, are considered corrupt. While in police subculture many acts of arbitrariness may appear justifiable (for example, surreptitious entries by FBI agents for intelligence purposes, provocative law enforcement in combating gang crimes, or physical overreaction in protecting one's partner), none, perhaps, can withstand the categorical tests of duty, honesty, or obligation. From an ethical point of view, corruption is prima facie culpable behavior. It is generally characterized by malice, greed, or an intention to exploit. While corrupt acts may also be products of ignorance (remember Socrates's view of wrongdoing), ethicists tend to be more stringent when immoral acts involve betrayal of public office. As such, Goldstein defines *police corruption* as "acts involving the misuse of authority by a police officer in a manner designed to produce personal gain for the officer or for others" (Goldstein, 1977:189). Given the noble cause of police, corruption by police should be viewed as a particularly sinister form of public misconduct.

Scope of Police Corruption

Subjective evidence indicates that police corruption has been with us for a long time, perhaps since the inception of organized policing. Walker calls it a problem of enormous magnitude, and Sherman observes that "for as long as there have been police, there has been police corruption" (Walker, 1983:174). In a study of crime in colonial New York, Walker reported that numerous complaints about misconduct by law enforcement officials were noted. He also reported that the office of sheriff was often auctioned off to the highest bidder in pre–Civil War Kentucky, and in both New York and Chicago scandals involving the police have been regular occurrences.

In New York City, scandals seemed to erupt once every 20 years with almost perfect regularity (Walker, 1983:174). The *Knapp Commission Report on Police Corruption* (1972) revealed that corruption in the city was "widespread and took various forms depending upon the activity involved, appearing at its most sophisticated among plain-clothesmen." Corrupt acts, the report indicated, involved gambling, narcotics, prostitution, construction, bars, parking and traffic, and tow trucks, to mention just a few (*Report*, 1972:1). The Pennsylvania Crime Commission (1974) also reported that police corruption in Philadelphia is "ongoing, widespread, systematic, and occurring at all levels of the police department" (Walker, 1983:174). Studies by Barker and Carter (1994) pointed out sustained patterns of occupational deviance including perjury, brutality, sex on duty, drinking on duty, and sleeping on duty. In an empirical study, the authors found that the perceived extent of corruption as reported by officers represented (in a multicategory-reporting fashion) approximately 39% brutality, 22% perjury, 31 % sex on duty, 8% drinking on duty, and 39% sleeping on duty (Barker & Carter, 1994:132).

The Dust and Ashes of Corruption

Institutional corruption is especially immoral because of its fallout of dust and ashes. By *dust* I mean the moral degradation of the profession in general and the agency one serves in particular. By *ashes* I mean the social tax that society must pay—either directly, as payoffs to police, or indirectly, in terms of social embarrassment.

The cost of police corruption is significantly high. According to Walker, four "hidden social costs" exist. First, the hedonistic nature of corruption represents a "secret tax" on businesses that must pay off the police in order to avoid harassment. Second, disregarding the law, especially by those who are paid to uphold it, strikes deep into the Kantian theory of duty. Police officials who disregard the law violate the very "categorical imperative" of institutional and personal integrity. They also undermine the principle of rule of law by allowing illegal activity to flourish. Third, betraying the professional values of policing destroys the essence of policing by robbing the officer of self-respect and the potential for self-realization. Effective discipline, including self-discipline, becomes nearly impossible when corruption is systematic. Fourth, the existence of corruption undermines the public faith in the police and their commitment to serve society. These costs can further impede police professionalism by undermining public trust and confidence (Walker, 1983:174).

To reduce the fallout of dust and ashes, serious thought must be given to police corruption. Reasoning, rather than old myths; sagacity, rather than rationalization; and ethical reasoning, rather than organizational subculture, should be used to examine its nature and causes. One reason, perhaps, police corruption has persisted for so long is because police practitioners have been wrapped in its fog, unable to see the light overhead or the hills of dust and ashes under their feet.

Hedonistic and Obligatory Corruption

As Delattre remarks in *Character and Cops*, "If greed is simple, the variety of temptations to which police officials succumb is not." While temptations of this sort are too numerous to count and may vary in volume and intensity from one agency to another, two broad categories of police corruption can be identified: *hedonistic corruption* for personal gain or comfort, and *obligatory corruption*, or ignoring the rules for egotistical reasons.

Hedonistic corruption relates to low-visibility economic temptations that include gratuities, bribery, thefts, and similar behaviors. They are described in great detail in most police textbooks that discuss the subject. They will therefore be only briefly mentioned here.

Gratuities, Bribes, and Payoffs

These are perhaps the most extensive forms of hedonistic corruption. For example, officers may receive free meals at a restaurant, a free haircut at a barber shop, or discounts on merchandise they purchase at a store. While gratuities are generally viewed by police as a minor form of corruption, Delattre considers them the beginning of more sinful deviance, namely, bribes. Truck drivers may clip money to their drivers' licenses to avoid traffic citations, contractors may pay the police to ignore city ordinances, and bar owners may pay to allow double-parked cars or violations of Sunday-closing laws. As petty bribery becomes commonplace, police may even make frivolous inquiries to collect bribe money.

Bribes may in turn escalate into payoffs. These are usually mutually arranged and strictly honored. When payoffs are routinely paid to the police, especially to those at the top of the organization, the formal control structure of the agency becomes increasingly ineffective. Rules and operating procedures promulgated by the agency are held in contempt because, as Goldstein asserts, "You can't expect those on the take to take orders" (Goldstein, 1977:190). Subsequently, as the *Knapp Commission Report on Police Corruption* (1972) reveals, a number of officers (characterized as "meat eaters") spend a good deal of their working hours aggressively seeking out situations they can exploit for financial gain. What Delattre, Goldstein, and others are warning of is the notion of "slippery slope of moral career"—the deeper one is involved, the more difficult dissociation becomes. From an ethical point of view, this notion is hardly new. Aristotle, Saint Augustine, Kant, and Butler all warned of its dangers when they advocated moral character as the anchor that can prevent the "temple of virtue" from slipping into apostasy.

Theft and Burglary

These types of corruption are usually committed when, during the course of their work, police appropriate goods or money that do not belong to them. Examples would include an officer who picks up a drunk on the street, finds $100 in the person's wallet, and keeps half of it. The individual was unconscious at the time, and when he wakes up, he has a difficult time persuading anyone that he actually had $100 in his wallet when he was arrested. Another often-cited example is the "disappearance" of weapons and valuable goods from the police property room, where they are held for safekeeping. Officers may appropriate weapons for their personal use or for sale (Walker, 1983:177).

Organized burglary rings by the police are not uncommon. Examples include the 1958–1960 scandals that erupted in Chicago, Denver, and Omaha, when it was revealed that groups of officers were actively engaged in burglary. In some instances, the officers committed the burglaries themselves. In others, they provided protection while a professional burglar committed the act (Walker, 1983:177).

Sexual Misconduct

In Barker and Carter's *Police Deviance* (1994), Sapp reports that demanding sexual favors from prostitutes, homosexuals, or citizens involved in illegal activities is perhaps the most serious of all forms of sexual misconduct by police. Sapp points out that sexually motivated misconduct by police includes contacts with crime victims, offenders, and young females; sexual shakedowns; and voyeuristic contacts. The author further states that perhaps no other occupation presents the opportunities for sexual misconduct that policing does. This he bases on both the extent of police authority and the constant contact police officers have with members of society in relative isolation. As a prescription for controlling sexual misconduct, Sapp suggests that police departments take an aggressive ethical view of sexual misconduct and that the attitude that "boys will be boys" should not be allowed to prevail. Only when administrators and supervisors educate their subordinates that sexual misconduct is intrinsically wrong and will not be tolerated is the behavior likely to decrease (Barker & Carter, 1994:198).

When Police Are Out of Control

Wallkill is an Orange County town of 25,000 in New York State, and for the past few years its residents have had to put up with a variety of torments from the 25-member police force. Problems with the police department first came to light in 1998 when officer Ari Moscowitz went to superiors with allegations of officers working side jobs while in uniform and taking cash under the table. In January 2001 the town had enough clues that its police department was out of control. One of the widely reported discoveries was that the police chief was seen having sex with a woman in the backseat of a police vehicle (*New York Times*, January 25, 2001). That was deftly characterized in an official report as "the chief's dalliance." Then there was the harassment, intimidation, and outright coercion of women by Wallkill cops, both on and off duty. Teenage girls employed at a local store took to hiding in a back room because of the repeated pawing and suggestive comments of an on-duty, uniformed police officer.

When the voluntary civilian police commission conducted an investigation of the department (prompted by complaints about its crime-fighting ineptitude), members of the commission found themselves and their families being harassed by the police. Predatory behavior seemed to be the rule (*New York Times*, January 25, 2001). As a result, New York State Attorney General Eliot Spitzer, responding to the insanity, filed a federal lawsuit against the town of Wallkill charging that it had failed to reign in its lawless police department. He also demanded that the Wallkill police department be placed under a federal monitor. To that the town board grudgingly agreed 3 weeks after the attorney general filed the lawsuit, calling the police department a "rogue" police force. The monitor would serve for 3 years. Details of the lawsuit included the following information.

In the spring of 2001 a 23-year-old woman driving alone was stopped and arrested for drunken driving. "In fact," according to court papers filed by the state attorney general, "she was not intoxicated." A videotape of the stop showed that the woman had the field sobriety test." Nevertheless, the woman was taken into custody. The following week the arresting officer approached the woman and suggested he could get the charges dropped if she would go out with him. The woman declined and the judge later dismissed the charges.

In another case, a cop who had arrested a woman on a petty larceny charge ordered her into a holding cell and told her to take her pants down so he could search for contraband. The woman, frightened, complied. Later the officer told the woman that he would try to have the charges reduced if she would meet with him privately.

The Wallkill cops even had a special vehicle, known as the "stealth car," that was used for following women drivers. The front of the car had no markings to indicate that it was a police vehicle. Late one night, a cop in the stealth car followed an 18-year-old woman as she was driving home from her job at a movie theater. On a particularly dark, almost deserted road, the officer began flashing his headlights. "Not seeing any police marks on the car, she became afraid for her safety and continued driving." The woman pulled in the driveway of her parent's home and began blowing the horn. By the time her mother came out of the house, the driver was crying. When the mother attempted to comfort her daughter, the cop pulled his gun, cursed, and told her to stay back. The teenage driver was arrested and taken to jail, where she was held for a couple of hours and then released on $500 bail.

In addition, the attorney general's report said police harassed citizens who spoke of their conduct by following them and repeatedly driving by their houses. The town's police also ticketed eight newspaper delivery trucks in one day to retaliate against articles about how officers were working simultaneously at one police department while also "punched in" at another. "It's certainly a good ol' boy slapping group who likes to run around and play cowboys and Indians. All of a sudden, their party's interrupted, and they're angry about it," said John Lovett, the lawyer for Officer Moscowitz (*Houston Chronicle*, January 26, 2001). Furthermore, the agreement between the town and the attorney general required the town to equip each police car with a video camera to document each traffic stop as well as requiring the town to develop a civilian-complaint procedure and annually evaluate each officer's performance.

If the allegations made in the attorney general's report are true, the behavior of the Wallkill police force should be condemned by both the police and the citizens. Not only did the officers in question bluntly violate articles of the penal code, they also betrayed their professional contract with the citizens of Wallkill and made a mockery of the police code of ethics, which they had taken an oath to preserve.

Obligatory Corruption

Obligatory corruption, on the other hand, entails abusing the rules of office in performing one's duties. Such abuses are usually committed for no gain other than power, egoism, or self-aggrandizement. While this category may be closely related to the ethics of democracy, the fact that it entails abrogating one's oath of office warrants special attention.

According to Heffernan and Stroup (1985), obligatory corruption in policing can take one of the following forms:

1. *Meting out justice via violations of the Constitution*. This includes illegal searches or arrests, which are frequently undertaken to punish persons whom officers believe to be systematically engaged in crime but who are relatively immune from the formal processes of the courts. Such violations amount to illegal punishment, although they may be motivated by the officer's desire to "clean up the beat," or his belief that "known criminals" should receive their due punishment.

2. *Meting out justice via selective enforcement of the law.* This is usually undertaken by a deliberate decision not to enforce the law and amounts to offering illegal clemency. A good example is not issuing tickets to fellow police officers when they are stopped for traffic violations. The officer in these cases may see herself as a merciful administrator of justice and her act as conducive to enhancing police solidarity and professional status.

3. *Promoting social order via violations of the Constitution.* This includes making illegal stop-and-frisk detainments or questioning suspects believing that the courts do not understand the critical benefits of such actions to the maintenance of public order. Furthermore, the officers may believe that criminal activity can be more efficiently detected when such violations are undertaken than when they are not.

4. *Promoting social order via selective enforcement of the law.* This includes declining to enforce the law without thinking of the harmful implications of not taking all laws seriously. Activities of this type include whether an arrest is necessary to promote public order when some college students are having a party rather late at night. In such a case, the decision by the officer would be limited only by one's interpretation of what a party entails and one's fidelity to the rules of office. The decision to ignore the rules of office may also be influenced by the officer's perception of whether enforcing the law is worth one's energy that late at night (Heffernan & Stroup, 1985:9-10).

The Obligatory Ethic Not to Deceive

Police work has been called a "morally dangerous" endeavor—with good reason. Not only are the temptations faced by average police officers much greater than those encountered in other occupations, but the nature of the work requires activities that can easily cross the line from acceptable to unethical conduct (Braswell et al., 1998:47). Let us examine, for instance, the police obligatory ethic not to lie.

The ideal of legality implies that those convicted of crimes will be not only factually guilty, but legally guilty as well. A commitment to legality, after all, is what distinguishes democratic governments from totalitarian ones. As alluded to in Chapter 4, this establishes the police obligatory ethic to tell the truth at all times, unless certain conditions justify sequestering the truth—working undercover, dealing with secret information, and the like. Nevertheless, as Skolnick indicates, for every ideal there seems to be a practical challenge. In the reality of policing, deception is considered "as natural as pouncing is to a cat" (Skolnick, 1982:41). Take, for instance, the function of detection, without which the criminal justice process is not initiated. This function occurs in the context of fluid moral constraints that are circumscribed by an indistinct tradition of due process of law, unclear interpretations of what constitutes individual rights, and a police subculture that imposes its own moral norms. The detective may therefore find it justifiable to lie in order to ensure conviction. The law even permits the detective to pose as a consumer or purveyor of vice, but does not allow the patrol officer to employ certain ruses to gain entry without a search warrant (*United States v. Ressler*, 530 F.2d 208, 1976).

In explaining deception in the detection process, Skolnick suggests that it occurs at three stages: *investigation*, *interrogation*, and *testimony*. When placed within the framework of the moral cognition of the police, the acceptability of deception varies inversely with the level of the criminal process: Deception is most acceptable at the investigation stage, is less acceptable during the interrogation stage, and is least acceptable in the courtroom (Skolnick, 1982:41). It appears that the police are offered more latitude to deceive by the courts during the investigation stage. The ethical justification is the assumption that when detectives deceive suspects in the course of criminal investigations, they typically are not seeking to promote their own self-interest (as a detective would if he had lied about accepting a bribe). On the contrary, the sort of deception employed to trap a narcotics dealer or a fence is used in support of the public interest.

The paradox that Skolnick raises is interesting because even the most professional detective may accept employing psychological intimidation (another word for lying and deceiving) in order to elicit the truth, as he or she sees it. Thus, in this framework, the end of the truth justifies the means of denying the truth. Skolnick further explains that in rationalizing such a logic, the detective indeed applies a utilitarian calculus for ascertaining the truth. The detective measures the costs of lying against the benefits that can accrue to the victim and the general public. However, unlike the civil libertarian, who measures public good in terms of protecting the long-range interests of all citizens, the deceptive investigator narrowly focuses on the conviction of suspects.

At the interrogation stage, Skolnick states that the courts make deception much more difficult, because at that level it is more definite that society would not permit police authorities to employ tactics that are regarded as intrinsically immoral against those who are accused of crime. At the testimonial level, the moral standard is even higher, because the proceeding is public, the detective's testimony is given under oath, and the quality of evidence is sustained through examination and cross-examination by the prosecution and the defense.

Skolnick concludes by stating that in light of the different perceptions of police deception at these three stages, "it is hard to make consistent common sense out of it." Such inconsistency, he adds, "makes law look more like a game than a rational system for enforcing justice."

Consequently, "police are not likely to take the stated rules of the game seriously and are encouraged to operate by their own codes, including those which affirm the need for lying whenever the means justify the ends" (1982:53).

The moral in Skolnick's investigation is the need to reaffirm the obligatory ethic of telling the truth at all stages of investigation—indeed, in all police functions. The moral is a plea, once again, especially to those officers who tend to take the principle of veracity lightly, to forgo subcultural ethics and consistently tell the truth unless otherwise justified under the specific conditions discussed in Chapter 4.

Can Corruption Be Administratively Stopped?

Despite the numerous manuals, policies, and measures designed to deter police corruption, they may all amount to an effort that has little chance for success. This is precisely because all such efforts focus solely on administrative techniques: designing indicators to detect corruption, determining levels of corruption, developing an anticorruption policy, strengthening internal affairs divisions, and intensifying disciplinary actions. Despite these well-intended measures, in the mind of the officer they may represent another "flurry of activities" reminiscent of the previous others.

Because no one is born corrupt, and because police officers undergo such a rigorous background investigation when they are hired, police corruption is a behavior learned on, or in association with, the job. Also, assuming that corrupt officers are rational, they should have no reason to believe that the restrictions that failed to deter them from "being corrupt" can deter them from "staying corrupt," especially after many years of hedonistic experiences with corruption.

A major weakness persists in the administrative approach to combating corruption: the perception of corruption as an occupational hazard rather than an occupationally induced problem. As such, the administrative approach attempts to pierce its way from the outside in, relying solely on the power of discipline to instill fear in the hearts of officers. Clearly, corrupt officers cannot be so easily deterred and may not change until they have more "occupational reason" to do so. A realistic effort would require more than just intensifying investigations and disciplinary actions. If corruption is to be shunned, a conscious choice must be made by the individual officer originating from an "occupational concern." Such a choice requires a "mental revolution" on the part of all, from top to bottom, one that can enhance ethical awareness, promote pride in the agency, propel moral fortitude, and establish a work environment conducive to self-realization—in sum, restoring the occupational soul of policing. No other way has worked in the past, and from an ethics standpoint, no other way is likely to work in the future.

Toward achieving this end, police leaders should be as creative as their enlightened minds can be. Methods to be considered may include (1) creating an environment that is conducive to dignified treatment on the job; (2) increasing ethical awareness among the ranks through formal and informal socialization; (3) avoiding deception and manipulation in the way officers are assigned, rewarded, or promoted; (4) allowing for openness and the free flow of unclassified information; (5) fostering a sense of shared values and incorporating such values into the subculture of the agency; (6) demonstrating an obligation to honesty, fairness, and decency by example; and (7) publicly discussing the issue of corruption, exposing corrupt behavior, and rewarding ethical behavior. While these methods may not work in the short run, they can most likely succeed when combined with goodwill and a sense of moral obligation. The first step, however, must be taken by police leaders who have the moral reasoning and fortitude to incorporate ethics as a standard mode of operation.

Review Questions

1. Discuss the concerns of citizens regarding the power of police. To what extent are these concerns valid?

2. What fears expressed by the public demonstrate a lack of trust in police officers? Why is it often assumed that police have the prerogative to abuse their power?

3. Describe "intellectual virtue." What reasons does Goldstein provide for aggressively dealing with a system of policing in which democratic ethics is standard practice?

4. Explain the sociologically oriented factors that explain why many police officers appear uncommitted to democratic principles. What work-oriented factors contribute to these conditions?

5. Discuss the author's 10 democratic principles. Explain how they can be applied to current situations.

6. Who is Rodney King? What violations of basic principles were present in his encounter with the police?

7. Explain the significance of freedom, individualism, and equality as presented in police training courses. Explain the "patchwork quilt" of diversity in the United States.

8. Why does considerable disagreement exist about what constitutes police corruption? How does the police subculture sometimes justify corruption?

9. Explain the phrase "dust and ashes of corruption."

10. Define the primary function of police. What stages of detection occur in this process?

References

Barker, T., & Carter, D. L. (1994). *Police Deviance* (3rd ed.). Cincinnati, OH: Anderson Publishing Co.

Bayley, D. H., & Mendelsohn, H. (1969). *Minorities and the Police*. New York: The Free Press.

Bittner, E. (1967). "The Police on Skid Row: A Study of Peace Keeping." *American Sociological Review*, 32(5), 699–715.

Blumberg, A. S., & Niederhoffer, E. (1970). *The Ambivalent Force: Perspectives on the Police*. New York: Holt, Rinehart and Winston.

Braiden, C. (1991). "Ownership: Who Paints a Rented House?" *Leadership Journal*, Houston Police Department in-house publication.

Braswell, M., McCarthy, B. R., & McCarthy, B. J. (1998). *Justice, Crime and Ethics* (3rd ed.). Cincinnati, OH: Anderson Publishing Co.

Carter, D. L., Sapp, A. D., & Stephens, D. W. (1989). *The State of Police Education: Policy Direction for the 21st Century*. Washington, DC: Police Executive Research Forum.

Cole, G. F. (1976). *Criminal Justice: Law and Politics* (2nd ed.). North Scituate, MA: Duxbury.

Delattre, E. J. (1989). *Character and Cops: Ethics in Policing*. Lanham, MD: University Press of America.

Douglas, J. D. (Ed.) (1971). *Crime and Justice in American Society*. Indianapolis, IN: Bobbs-Merrill.

Goldstein, H. (1963). "Police Discretion: The Ideal versus the Real." *Public Administration Review*, 23, 140–148.

Goldstein, H. (1977). *Policing a Free Society*. Cambridge, MA: Ballinger.

Goldstein, H. (1990). *Problem-Oriented Policing*. New York: McGraw-Hill.

Harris, R. N. (1973). *From the Police Academy: An Inside View*. New York: John Wiley and Sons.

Heffernan, W. C., & Stroup, T. (1985). *Police Ethics: Hard Choices in Law Enforcement*. New York: John Jay College of Criminal Justice.

Kleinig, J. (1996). *Ethics of Policing*. New York: Cambridge University Press.

Knapp Commission Report on Police Corruption (1972). New York: George Braziller.

LA Beating Case Points to Pattern, Police Critics Say Abuse Now an Issue Nationwide (1991, March 18). *Dallas Morning News.*

Los Angeles Times (1991, March 21). Los Angeles.

Manning, P. K., & Van Maanen, J. (Eds.) (1978). *Policing: A View from the Street.* Santa Monica, CA: Goodyear Publishing.

Opinion (2001, January 25). *New York Times.*

Skolnick, J. H. (1982). Deception by Police. *Criminal Justice Ethics*, 1(2).

Skolnick, J. H., & Bayley, D. H. (1986). *The New Blue Line: Police Innovation in Six American Cities.* New York: The Free Press.

Souryal, S. S. (1977). *Police Administration and Management.* St. Paul, MN: West Publishing.

Terry, W. C., III. (1985). *Policing Society: An Occupational View.* New York: John Wiley & Sons.

Town Deals with Troubled Police Force (2001, January 26). *The Houston Chronicle.*

United States v. Ressler. (1976). 530 F.2d 208.

Walker, S. (1983). *The Police in America: An Introduction.* New York: McGraw-Hill.

Westermann, T. D., & Burfeind, J. W. (1991). *Crime and Justice in Two Societies: Japan and the United States.* Pacific Grove, CA: Brooks/Cole Publishing.

Westley, W. A. (1953). Violence and the Police. *American Journal of Sociology, 59,* 34–41.

12
Ethics and Corrections (Prisons)

How many of our citizens do we want to turn into criminals before we yell "enough"?

Milton Friedman,
American Nobel Prize Winner

The worst sin toward our fellow creatures is not to hate them but to be indifferent to them.

George Bernard Shaw

To put people behind walls and bars and do little or nothing to change them is to win the battle and to lose the war—it is expensive, and it is stupid.

Chief Justice Warren Burger

While society in the United States is the example of the most extended liberty, the prisons of the same country offer the spectacle of the most complete despotism.

Alexis de Tocqueville

What You Will Learn from This Chapter

You will learn the arguments for the conventional and unconventional perspectives of correction. These are described as *life for life* and *man and corrections*, respectively. You will also learn aspects of corruption by prison personnel.

In addition, you will learn the principles of moral punishment, the moral justifications for prisons, the ethics of contemporary corrections, the scapegoating theory, the holier-than-thou syndrome, and the idea of rehabilitation through inner corrections.

Key Terms and Definitions

Retribution is a concept that justifies punishment as a legitimate form of revenge. It seeks to inflict pain on the offenders equal to that which they inflicted on their victims. The purpose of retribution is to restore social balance.

Deterrence is a concept that confronts criminals with risks they cannot take. It justifies punishment as a method to scare would-be criminals from committing crime.

Rehabilitation is a concept that seeks to restore wholesomeness to convicted criminals. It advocates the use of treatment as long as it can change the behavior of criminals, making them law-abiding citizens.

Lex Talionis is an ancient law that requires punishment to be equal to the amount of harm caused by the offender.

Brutality is the intentional use of force against anyone when the use of such force is illegal or unwarranted.

Scapegoating Theory is a theory that explains imprisonment in terms of a social need to exclude those believed to be undesirable. These include criminals, the mentally ill, and the physically deformed.

Inner Corrections is the practice of rehabilitating criminals through the use of humane treatment. It includes religious training, meditation, proper diet, and spirituality.

Overview

Prisons are a major stock in the moral order of society. They symbolize the ultimate instrument of punishment the state can wage against those who renege on the social contract. Besides death, imprisonment remains society's most ominous response to social disorder. Included among the purposes of a civilized society are maintenance of law and order and control of violence. To accomplish this purpose, it is imperative that deviant persons be, at some point and for some time, incarcerated.

Yet the moral utility of prisons depends on how they are used, because prisonization, as a social experience, may have a more damaging impact upon individuals than any other social sanction. Not only does it restrict the body and space of those incarcerated, but it also expiates their soul, will, and thought. Therefore, determining who is sent to prison, the deprivations imposed upon inmates, and the authority vested in the custodians of prisons can reveal much about society's values. This insight has been captured in the common rubric that the civilization of any society is judged by the state of its prisons (Jacobs, 1983:17; Lozoff & Braswell, 1989:5; Travis et al., 1983:50).

But sociopolitical and humanitarian changes occur in all dynamic societies, especially among those inspired by democratic values. Researchers have documented major changes occurring within prisons throughout the United States (Carroll, 1974; Crouch & Marquart, 1989; Irwin, 1980; Jacobs, 1977; Jacobs & Kraft, 1983; Poole & Regoli, 1980). Of critical concern has been the shifting philosophies that address the social and moral issues of imprisonment. To a large measure, a serious debate about the morality of corrections has begun, and the final destination is not yet in sight. Toward exploring where the destination should be, the "reasoning person" should be attentive, open-minded, and motivated only by principle.

If police are to be viewed as the most visible component of criminal justice, institutional corrections (prisons) are its least visible. Until recently—when building prisons became a fashionable and increasingly profitable enterprise—prisons were the "forgotten component" of the criminal justice system. Relatively few citizens knew where they were or why they were there. Even fewer people cared to know. Discussing the state of prisons made for a relatively distasteful topic, and visiting a maximum-security prison invoked a depressing reminder of human debasement with its trappings of viciousness and worthlessness. What happens to criminals after they receive a prison sentence has not been a humanitarian, social, or moral concern of society. Aside from the broad requirement to refrain from "cruel and unusual punishment," no other concerns are deemed necessary.

From an ethical standpoint, this observation may be particularly true, because neither natural law nor religious testaments particularly stressed better treatment for offenders. Indeed, most religions, including the Judeo-Christian faith, emphasized the "rightness" of punishment, including capital and corporal punishment. Not surprisingly, the torture and crucifixion of Christ has been treated as a messianic experience rather than a question of social injustice.

The Corrections Debate

With the renaissance of criminal justice in the mid-1960s, debate about the role of corrections in society erupted. Current concerns are rightfully based on the fear of crime and what to do with criminals. Changing sentiments regarding these concerns have been reflected in responses by the criminal justice system. Notably, the death penalty has been resurrected, more retributive community-based programs have been implemented, and long prison sentences continue to be imposed (Weisheit & Alexander, 1988:57).

On the other hand, the idea of imprisonment cannot be separated from the societies it serves; advanced societies maintain civilized prisons, while undeveloped societies are not offended by uncivilized prisons. Associated with this idea is the criterion of utility; the recognition that traditional prisons may neither deter nor rehabilitate offenders, and that the cost of operating professionally managed prisons that provide humane conditions is more economically advantageous, presents the impetus of the ongoing debate (Fleischer, 1989:236).

But unlike the debate about police that produced a fairly distinct set of priority functions, at no time did one key function of corrections predominate. Pollock points out in *Ethics in Crime and Justice* (1989) that corrections has become "a schizophrenic system paying homage to several masters including the principles of retribution, incapacitation, deterrence, and rehabilitation" (Pollock, 1989:128).

Yet the essence of the corrections debate continues. It focuses essentially on two perspectives—the conventional and the unconventional. The conventional perspective, with which you are probably familiar, is based on the theories of *social defense* and *retribution*. Social defense is a process by which society protects itself from crime, and retribution is punishing those who commit crime against society. When these two theories are viewed from an ideology of pragmatism and conservative economics, the conventional perspective appears rational because it seems to effectively serve as a center of punishment.

The unconventional perspective, on the other hand, may be rather alien to you and may cause some surprise, if not bewilderment, at times. This perspective ranges from denying the social legitimacy of prisons altogether, to accepting certain types as social purgatories—as long as they are humanitarian and perhaps spiritual in nature. As such, the unconventional perspective associates prisons with the "repairing" of misguided citizens and distinguishes prisons as centers for treatment and rehabilitation.

Of great significance, however, is the danger of equating the conventional–unconventional perspectives with the politically popular "liberal–conservative" label. Applying such a label—especially when inappropriate—serves no rational purpose and may constitute an error of reasoning. Labeling perspectives of corrections in such a manner was a common ploy by the Sophists when reason was counterproductive to the beliefs they advocated. If any labeling is necessary, the conventional–unconventional perspectives should be labeled the ethical–unethical views.

For the purposes of this chapter, the conventional perspective will be presented under the rubric of "Ethics of Life for Life." The unconventional perspective will be introduced under the rubric of "Ethics of Man and Corrections." Both perspectives are important. Regardless of where one stands on these issues, understanding both of these perspectives is of particular significance: (1) any new knowledge is useful knowledge, regardless of its nature or aim and (2) this knowledge can stimulate new insights into the chronic problem of prisons, especially by exploring the wider implications of reason and civility. We will begin with the conventional perspective—the "Ethics of Life for Life."

Ethics of Life for Life: The Influence of Beccaria

Although Cesare Beccaria (1735–1794) may be best known to those in criminology, it was he who inspired our basic debate about the role of prisons. Born in Milan to aristocratic parents, he received his schooling at the Jesuit College in Parma and graduated with a degree in law from the University of Pavia in 1758. Within 6 years he would be famous. His *Dei dilitti e elle pene*, later published under the title *An Essay on Crimes and Punishment* (1767), was enthusiastically received and widely acclaimed. As a result, the Italian government offered Beccaria a professional chair in law at the Palatine College in Milan (Massaro, 1991–1992).

Beccaria's work, although not lengthy, provided a great deal of root thought during an era characterized by intellectual confusion, emotionalism, and social cruelty. Beccaria conceptualized the rational relationship between crime, punishment, and law, advocating that there can be no crime without punishment and no punishment without law. He warned, however, that in a civilized society any punishment that is not founded upon the *absolute necessity* to defend the rights of all the people is tyrannical. By the same token, he advocated that laws should apply equally to all, regardless of station. In subsequent chapters, Beccaria examined various types of crimes and penalties along with their classification.

In his theory of punishment, he stressed that for punishment to attain its ends, the evil that it inflicts has to exceed the advantage derivable from the crime; society should consider the certainty of punishment and the loss of the good that the crime might have produced. Nevertheless, Beccaria cautioned against cruel punishment, because "if torments become more cruel, the spirits of men, which are like fluids that always rise to the level of surrounding objects, become callous and the ever lively force of the passions brings it to pass that after a hundred years of cruel punishment, the wheel inspires no greater fear than imprisonment once did." Nevertheless, Beccaria did not waver on the need for strict punishments—including corporal punishment—as a method of deterring serious crime. Such deterrents, he held, should be "stronger when the crimes are more harmful to the public good" (Massaro, 1991–1992:211).

In stressing the importance of swiftness in the conviction of criminals, Beccaria stated, "The more promptly and more closely punishment follows upon the commission of a crime, the more just and useful ... so much stronger and more lasting in the human mind is the association of these two ideas, crime and punishment; they then become inseparable, one to be considered as the cause, the other as the necessary inevitable effect" (Massaro, 1991–1992:211).

It is interesting to mention that while it is conventionally thought that Beccaria was against the death penalty, this may be an inaccurate assumption. Although he never showed infatuation with a penalty that he considered a "useless prodigality of torments," he nevertheless thought that at least two crimes justify the imposition of capital punishment. First, when it is evident that even if deprived of liberty, the offender still has the connections and power such as "to endanger the security of the nation" (for example, crimes of treason, terrorism, and gangsterism by today's terminology). The death of a citizen, he wrote, was necessary when the nation is recovering or losing its liberty, or during times of anarchy. Second, Beccaria saw a need for the death penalty when executing the offender is the "only true way" to restrain others from committing crimes (that is, the case for deterrence theory in today's terminology). In this case, Beccaria believed that the death penalty was just and necessary (Massaro, 1991–1992:213).

Beccaria's influence on the morality of punishment in the United States has been both spectacular and enduring. His views were quoted by John Adams when he took up the defense of the British soldiers implicated in the Boston Massacre in 1770, endorsed by Benjamin Franklin while he served as American minister to France, and quoted by Thomas Jefferson in *Commonplace Book* (written between 1774 and 1776) no less than 26 times. Jefferson's writings heavily influenced Virginia law at the time, resulting in the adoption of strict punishments for violent crimes, but limiting capital punishment, to no one's surprise, to crimes of treason and murder (Massaro, 1991–1992:213). By the same token, Beccaria's views on crime and punishment continue to constitute the backbone of our penal philosophy today.

Ethics of Life for Life: The Morality of Punishment

Mainstream philosophers agree that punishment is a morally acceptable social defense mechanism. As such, it is an essential component of the social contract, which announces to individuals that certain acts are forbidden and that an adverse response is necessary to minimize their occurrence. Having laws without punishment denudes them of utility and renders them ineffectual. Of course, there are others who disagree with this view of punishment, suggesting that society should be restructured in such a way that punishment is unnecessary. But just how this can be accomplished is problematic. The methods most often proposed involve some kind of therapeutic treatment, behavior modification, or a startling advance in biomedicine (Barry, 1982:260). While in an abstract sense such views may be of value, society as a collectivity of human beings has not yet discovered how such treatments could be administered, especially when offenders object to their use or react violently to their application.

But for punishment to be morally acceptable, five principles are essential. Punishment must (1) involve an amount of suffering, (2) be administered for a violation of a law or rule, (3) be administered only to those judged guilty of an offense, (4) be imposed by someone other than the offender, and (5) be imposed by a rightful authority (Barry, 1982:259). These principles will be briefly clarified as follows:

1. *Suffering.* Given that the essence of nature is equilibrium, punishment is a natural instrument for restoring a disrupted equilibrium. As such, it must involve an amount of pain, harm, or some other consequences that are considered unpleasant. Humankind has not yet been able to devise another method that can be equally certain and effective. Because crime disrupts the social balance of communities, the only rational response to this imbalance is to cause suffering to the transgressor. Inflicting pain as an instrument of exacting justice has long existed in human communities and is explicitly supported in religious testaments. The critical question at this juncture is not whether to punish, but how to punish: "How much suffering is necessary to constitute morally acceptable punishment?"

2. *Violation of the law.* While punishment involves suffering, not every instance of suffering involves punishment. Many people may feel (and at times enjoy) pain after a stressful endeavor such as work or an athletic competition without intending to punish themselves. As a method of punishment, however, suffering must be in response to a transgression of a rule prescribed by society. In such a case, it is not limited to corporal punishment, but may include spiritual pain (imprisonment) or economic pain (payment of fines). Imprisonment, especially for long periods under harsh

conditions, may be considered cruel and unusual punishment. As Rotman (Smarto, 1989:81) states, "Offenders are sent to prison as punishment, not *for* punishment."

3. *Punishment only of the guilty.* As a refrain from old methods of punishment that often allowed for the imprisonment of innocent individuals along with their family members, friends, and acquaintances, for punishment to be moral it must be limited to those who have been found guilty of violating a law or rule. Any violation of this principle constitutes blatant injustice, a legitimate reason for nullifying the system of justice that imposed the punishment.

4. *Punishment by someone other than the offender.* It is true that some people sometimes speak of "punishing themselves," such as a spiritual person who might flagellate himself as an atonement for sin. While self-punishment is not amoral, it is morally unacceptable in lieu of social punishment, because it fails to provide equality of punishment for those who commit the same crime. For punishment to be morally acceptable, it should be consistent, with fairness to all those who may be in the same situation.

5. *Punishment by rightful authority.* For punishment to be morally acceptable, it must be administered by a rightful authority—one that is legally constituted to maintain social and moral order. While rightful authorities may, for instance, include parents or teachers, in today's society it must be judicially condoned and administered within prescribed boundaries. Therefore, even in the harshest prisons there are rules that specify the duration of solitary confinement and the privileges inmates can receive during periods of confinement. Any attempt to prolong punishment or to augment its severity constitutes tyranny (Barry, 1982:259).

Ethics of Life for Life: The Moral Justifications for Prisons

In the years between 1820 and 1840, when prisons were first built in the United States, imprisonment was justified on philosophical and moral grounds. Indeed, early prisons were designed as utopian societies, not only as models for control, but also as the reincarnation of a social order lost in the free world. Regardless of the type of prison (for example, penal colony, penitentiary, reformatory, correctional facility, and so on), justifications for imprisonment continue to underlie today's penal philosophies.

The moral justifications for imprisonment can be seen from two viewpoints: (1) consistent with the kind of punishment transgressors are considered to deserve or (2) consistent with its utilitarian consequences. The first viewpoint supports the retributive theory of imprisonment; the second, the rehabilitative theories of imprisonment.

Retribution

This justification explains imprisonment in terms of just deserts for a wrong that has been done. This philosophy reflects a Kantian view that holds that offenders must be punished because they deserve it. Traditionally, retribution was considered a form of revenge, whereby offenders were made to suffer in kind for the amount of harm they caused others. In support of this view, retributionists cite natural law sanctions, *lex talionis* (equal retaliation) sanctions, and religious sanctions that condoned the morality of an "eye for an eye and a tooth for a tooth." Arguments for capital punishment clearly accentuate this view.

Another version of retributive theory distinguishes punishment from revenge by associating it instead with the doctrine of social balance. This argument is based on a two-pronged philosophy: First, punishment is an attempt to restore the disrupted balance between the offender and the victim. Therefore, when the state imprisons an offender for stealing someone's car, punishment restores the balance. By restoring the balance, respect for the parties involved is also restored. This view obviously focuses on the rights of the victim. Second, failure to punish the transgressor is tantamount to treating offenders with disrespect, because it denies them autonomy and responsibility for their actions. Showing respect entails giving people what they deserve, whether that be reward or punishment. By the same token, denying punishment to a deserving person is an act of disrespect (Barry, 1982:261).

Opponents of the retributive theory obviously disagree with this philosophy, claiming that to punish a person because he or she deserves it is merely revenge wrapped in sophisticated terms (the word *sophisticated* originated from the Greek Sophists, remember) and therefore is immoral. The only legitimate motives for imprisonment, these opponents argue, is either to deter others or to mend the offender—inflicting pain has no value in and of itself. What these opponents aim for is removing the concept of "desert" from imprisonment. While this endeavor, as mentioned earlier, seems ethically plausible, its propagation can be harmful to society as a whole, because desert is the only connecting link between punishment and justice. It is only as deserved or undeserved that punishment can be just or unjust.

Prevention/Incapacitation

This justification is far less problematic. By using imprisonment, society ensures that the incapacitated offender is no longer able to injure society during the period of imprisonment. No ethical argument can refute this assumption except perhaps under one condition: if imprisonment —as a pathological experience—would cause intensive damage to the incarcerated individual and subsequently to society as a whole, as in the adage "prisons are schools for crime." Under this condition, society may cause more social harm by creating a more hardened offender than by absorbing the harm caused if he or she was placed under an alternative mode of punishment, such as probation. In this context, an insightful comment was made by Senator Mark Hatfield (Smarto, 1989:28): "If one accepts that a prisoner deserves whatever he or she gets in prison, one must also be prepared to accept that society deserves whatever it gets when the prisoner is eventually released!"

Deterrence

This view suggests that people contemplating crime will be deterred from committing the crime because of the harsh conditions of prisons. In theory the concept assumes that potential law violators are rational, thoughtful, and possess a free will. Perhaps because most law-abiding people are like this, deterrence seems to make good sense (Newman & Anderson, 1989:493). As such, deterrence should be a worthy utilitarian principle because it can benefit a large number of people despite the side effect of having to imprison a few. Based on this theory, prisons are built and utilized, at least in part, to bolster the deterrent effect, both specifically and generally. Specifically, offenders are assumed to be deterred from committing further crime by the fact that prison conditions are harsh. Generally, potential criminals are supposed to be deterred by the prison experience of those before them.

Critics of the deterrence philosophy argue that the deterrent effect of imprisonment is, to a large extent, taken for granted and is so deeply ingrained in the "commonsense thinking" of society that questions about its occurrence frequently are not raised (Mathiesen, 1990:48). While critics do not dispute the concept in principle, they discredit its utility from a practical point of view. They deny the basic assumption that would-be criminals could be deterred by sentences given to others. They further assert that most violent criminals, about whom society should be primarily concerned, may indeed be irrational. Many suffer from impaired choice, given the proliferation of drugs and alcohol in society. They may pursue a criminal career because it pays, given the ineffective nature of the criminal justice system. We cannot discuss this controversy in greater detail here, especially because evidence presented by each side of the argument remains inconclusive.

Rehabilitation

This view holds that society is justified in imprisoning offenders to avail them of the opportunity to reform and to return to society in good standing. The rehabilitation ideology, like that of punishment, seems to have been given expression in connection with the treatment of the youth. In the *Hopital General* in Paris, a youth section was established by a decree in 1684 for boys and girls younger than the age of 25. The decree emphasized that work was to occupy the greater part of the day, accompanied by "the reading of pious books" (Mathiesen, 1990:23). Based on this tradition, imprisonment has been justified in terms of moral reform. This theory will be explained in greater detail as we move on with the discussion.

Ethics of Life for Life: A Society That Loves Walls

Corrections today has rapidly become a gigantic business. In the United States it costs somewhere in the neighborhood of $28 billion a year for operating expenses. The average cost of maintaining a maximum-security cell is estimated at $20,000 per year. Correctional agencies employ more than 500,000 employees who incarcerate about 1.14 million people in addition to another 3 million who are under correctional supervision. As 1995 figures show, the incarceration rate varied between 636 per 100,000 in Texas to 78 per 100,000 in North Dakota, which translates to a national average of 387 per 100,000 population (Maguire & Pastore, 1995). In the state of Texas alone, 11 prison facilities have been built and 14 more are in the planning stages.

Robert Frost once wrote, "Before I build a wall, I would want to know what I was walling in or walling out." American society today has come to love walls; it does not want them down, but it does not want to pay for them. It has not yet realized the phenomenal price it must pay to house, feed, clothe, supervise, and manage the people behind the walls. The cost of those walls has been high and is increasing with each passing year (American Correctional Association, 1990:11).

More astounding is the fact that correctional facilities in America have turned into shelters for a substantial number of African Americans and, to a lesser degree, Hispanics. One of every four African American males is currently under some form of correctional supervision (American Correctional Association, 1990:123). As Samuel Sublett Jr., President of the American Correctional Association pointed out, "We have practically lost a generation of young black males to the correctional experience; it is not unusual for many jurisdictions to have 40, 50, 60 percent black population in corrections" (American Correctional Association, 1990:112).

For those who equate volume and size with goodness, the correctional scene is viewed as positive. Perhaps in a twisted logic it is even utilitarian—if it offers more services to more people. But for those who can understand what the growth of corrections means to the well-being and values of society, the current scene must be deplorable.

Regardless of one's view, however, the mentality of a "society that loves walls" continues, and correctional agencies seem to be warehousing more citizens and doing it at an increased rate.

The state of corrections today, however, is in many respects much like it was a decade ago (some might say even worse). Despite new programs of unproven validity such as shock incarceration and boot camps, crime continues to run rampant, recidivism has not abated, professionalism of correctional officers is still some distance away, and the system's effectiveness remains in doubt. Society nevertheless cannot turn its mind away from these problems in the way prison officials turn on electronic cell block doors each night. While the number of people committed to prison every year is not directly related to the kind of treatment they receive, the rate of recidivism may be. Furthermore, the presence of overcrowded prisons tends to develop a quality of its own, causing a serious challenge to the integrity of corrections as a social institution. The politically popular practice of building new prisons at a rate that exceeds the increasing rate of crime may in the long range prove shortsighted, if not unwise. This judgment is not based on economic factors alone, but on the moral assumption that solving the crime problem by warehousing larger segments of the population every year cannot, under any rationale, be conducive to the overall welfare of a civilized society. *Radical*—but knowledgeable—responses must therefore be found before the jagged image of prisons in America becomes an even greater national disgrace.

Ethics of Life for Life: Putting Pain Back into Prisons

In an editorial on the future of prisons in the state of Texas, Professor Raymond Teske, a well-known criminologist, reaffirms the perspective of life for life by stressing the need for "putting pain back" into prisons. In his thesis Teske asserts that being sentenced to prison should be made painful, "a statement that one's deeds, as well as the individual himself, were so repulsive to society that one had to be officially separated for a period of time" (Teske, 1987).

Teske contends that the purpose of imprisonment is to inflict pain, primarily psychological pain, but also the physical pain that accompanies legitimate punishment. During the past several years, Teske adds, "step by step, each of the elements of pain previously imposed by the Texas prison system has been neutralized to the point that imprisonment has become essentially a painless process, only an interlude, perhaps even a positive interlude, in the life of the convicted." In questioning the trend by the Texas Board of Corrections to build new prison units in locations where prisoners from these locations might be closer to their families, Teske points out that such a trend "undermines the foundations of the prison system and nullifies the fundamental effectiveness of the criminal justice system." The deterrence of criminal acts, Teske argues, "is dependent on the threat of, and infliction of pain" (Teske, 1987).

In supporting his view, Teske regrets the disappearing pains that have been traditionally associated with each step of the criminal justice process. Teske identifies three such steps: (1) the humiliation associated with arrest, the sudden loss of liberty, the pain associated with being jailed—even temporarily in an environment of strangers being helplessly under the control of strangers, and the fear of condemnation; (2) the pain of formal accusation by society before a public forum representing society; and (3) the pain of public condemnation, which, according to Teske, has in most cases been eliminated. To be publicly chastised for having offended society, and to be made to feel the burden of public condemnation, Teske points out, can be the most painful experience of all.

Focusing his attention on the pain of imprisonment, Teske suggests that true deprivation of liberty should be a source for the infliction of pain. As such, deprivation of liberty should be accompanied by several serious "pain-inducing circumstances." Among these, Teske emphasizes the following: (1) the pain of physical separation from family and friends by restricting the number of visitors and limiting visitation to short periods of time every 2 weeks—taking place through wire screens without physical contact. The modern practices of picnic-type areas with tables on the prison grounds reduce the true pain of physical separation. (2) The pain of harsh accommodations, including bare cells, the absence of radios and televisions, and lack of decorations on the walls. Furthermore, Teske adds, pain could be further augmented by frequently moving the inmate from cell to cell and from unit to unit as deemed fit without undue concern. The modern layout of cells that Teske describes as "homes, cozy, comfortable, and entertaining" are not effective means of pain-inducing circumstances. (3) The pain of restricting the movement of inmates—to be told when to turn out the lights, when to rise, when to come and when to go, what and when to eat, and when to go to the toilet. According to Teske, current policies that allow inmates specific periods to have access to recreation, to remain and relax in their cells, and not to be physically restrained as to where to go or what to do severely erodes the impact of pain. (4) The pain of humiliation—and not being treated as a social equal. While Teske disagrees with the overhumiliation of inmates, including, for instance, the use of the term *boy* when referring to an inmate, or expecting inmates to "step aside when a prison employee walks by," he does not seem to mind the humiliation of being shouted at, berated, or disgraced in front of one's peers. The point, Teske stresses, is that the impact of humiliation is real, but to a large measure has been diminished (Teske, 1987).

How would you view Teske's thesis on prisons? It certainly heightens the "life for life" perspective by requiring not only strict discipline, deprivation of liberty, and harsh treatment, but by emphasizing the need for pain, humiliation, and suffering. As could be expected, Teske's thesis received mixed responses in the corrections community in Texas and elsewhere. Many in the prison community praised it for being poignant, truthful, bold, and consistent with the purposes of corrections. Others were skeptical and considered it a serious setback to the aspirations of a society liberated from medieval thought, oppression, and misguided ethics. Most of the latter, however, associate themselves to some degree or another with the nonconventional view of prisons—the "Man and Corrections" view.

From the Ethics of Life for Life to the Ethics of Man and Corrections: Changing Attitudes about Prisons

Originally, the term *correction* (as the word has come to be known) did not exist in any society. In early communities those who violated the laws, mores, or taboos of society were either banished or executed. There was no attempt to salvage the individual or to return him to a constructive lifestyle. Perhaps the earliest recorded penalty of banishment was the case of Adam and Eve (Travis et al., 1983:15). Banishment was an extreme penalty in earlier societies, because removal from one's clan or village often meant death. Nonetheless, banishment became particularly popular in some societies because, while the result was identical to capital punishment, the sentencers were not held directly responsible for the demise of the offender.

The penalty of death was also imposed with regularity, primarily because it provided a certain solution to the problem of crime. It also seemed consistent with the practice of *lex talionis* (the rule of "an eye for an eye and a tooth for a tooth"), which was institutionalized in religious doctrine. Less serious penalties included flogging, mutilation, branding, and public humiliation. Although history is replete with cases of prisoners who were incarcerated for political reasons (for example, Joseph, Socrates, Machiavelli, and Thomas More), the practice of holding large numbers of wrongdoers prisoner was alien to early societies. This can be explained in two ways: (1) society's inability to provide the logistical means for keeping people under guard for long periods and (2) the social assumption that "once a criminal, always a criminal" negated the reasoning for imprisonment, and death was clearly a more sensible option.

As societies advanced, however, the ability to hold and manage large bodies of prisoners became possible. More importantly, by the sixteenth and seventeenth centuries there was a dire need for slave labor. Warships were driven by oars, requiring many men to work for the navies of the newly emerging world powers. Prisoners were also needed to work in the expanding mining industry, in which wretched and hazardous working conditions inhibited the growth of a volunteer workforce. When new technology later decreased the need for slave labor, the policy of transporting offenders to remote locations became popular. The British sent convicts to the American colonies, the French shipped them to Devil's Island, and the Russians, to Siberia. By this time, the concept of incarceration as a source of labor as well as punishment for crime had become established (Travis et al., 1983:17).

Punishment in early America most often took the form of "blood punishment," including death, maiming, and branding. But the rationale for such cruel penalties soon came to be questioned, particularly by the Quakers and other humanitarian groups. Such groups demanded reforms in criminal penalties that would eliminate the "retributive factor" of society. The idea of punishment was equated with exacting revenge that was reserved to God alone, or with official violence. The Quakers, in particular, were pacifists by conviction and resented both the harsh treatment of prisoners, which went against the "deep respect for every person's dignity," and a system of punishments administered by "a government which was much more criminal than the prisoner" (American Friends Service Committee, 1971:17-22).

The Quakers continue to resent the harshness of American prisons and base their objections on three broad moral values:

1. *The fallacy of the paternalistic notion in A's assumption that he knows better than B what is in B's best interest.* The Quakers consider this notion treacherous and reflective of colonialism, especially when invoked by middle class whites to run the lives of blacks, Hispanics, Native Americans, and the poor.

2. *The natural tendency of any coercive program to escalate*—the more coercion is exercised, the greater the violence that will have to be applied.

3. *The likelihood of coercive measures to reduce efforts toward discovering and experimenting with more humanitarian alternatives.* Such coercive measures, the Quakers argue, would inhibit the development of voluntary programs and impede solving the problem of crime by peaceful means.

In addition to the reform movement spearheaded by the Quakers in the United States, similar movements in Europe (for example, the John Howard Society) contributed to developing better conditions for prisoners. The idea of the social contract, so basic to the American Revolution, was aligned with arguments against the imposition of harsh penalties. Quetelet and Guerry, among other reformists, recognized that some groups of people could not be held entirely responsible for their actions and therefore should not be punished. The insane and the young, for instance, were among such groups and considered moral infants—not possessing enough sense to refrain from wrongdoing. Furthermore, the "treatment ethic," which was developed by the positivist philosophers, influenced penal philosophies to the extent that imprisonment was viewed as mentally unhealthy and its continuance reflective of the broader unhealthiness of society (Pollock, 1989:128).

Ethics of Contemporary Corrections

As a result of changing attitudes, it is not surprising that when correctional leaders of today attempt to explain the purposes of corrections, they frequently offer a contradictory rationale (American Correctional Association, 1990). While it should be assumed that all correctional leaders in America have good intentions, their judgment naturally reflects their perceptions of what is just and what is effective. Nonetheless, the following discussion will highlight the contemporary views of corrections in the two dominant areas of *retribution* and *treatment*.

Ethics of Retribution

As mentioned earlier, the oldest rationale for corrections was *retribution*, a modern term for what used to be revenge and the infliction of suffering because offenders deserve it. From a humanist standpoint there is nothing inherently wrong with the idea of retribution, because it is logical, coherent, and conveniently simple. But for this rationale to be morally justifiable, one must first accept a Hobbesian view of society (man is by nature selfish); a dogmatic view of religion (people are either sinners or nonsinners); and a narrow view of the law as *the* predominant instrument of social order.

Regardless of where one stands, however, the traditional rationale for retribution has been supported by two powerful principles: (1) *lex talionis*, which was incorporated in religious testaments under the tutelage of "an eye for an eye and a tooth for a tooth"; and (2) the utilitarian concept of "punishment works."

Lex Talionis

While most writers refer to *lex talionis* as an obligatory ethic—"If you take my eye, I must take yours"—the law in Hebrew jurisprudence has a different thrust. It is not viewed as a license to kill or maim, but rather as an instrument of restraint. What the Hebrew scholars originally meant was, "If I take your eye, you cannot *take any more than one* of mine, and only if you must." Instead of allowing people to return harm in equal portions, the law was an exhortation for restraint; only if the injured party was unable to settle the dispute peacefully or to control his emotions was he justified in exercising reciprocity. In the Christian era the traditional belief continued, mostly by secular rulers who were more concerned for political stability than for Christian doctrine. This indifference is especially noteworthy, because in Christian teaching the same God who allowed retaliation also commanded forgiveness and loving one's enemy. It would be illogical to claim that both commandments were equally moral. Indeed, if retribution (as traditionally believed) had been applied against Cain for murdering Abel, the entire human race would not have existed, because according to biblical sources, Cain was the only male left to father mankind.

Punishment Works

This view of punishment was originally transferred from the punishment of children to the punishment of adults; if punishment works for deviant children, it must also be a valid method for disciplining deviant adults. There is a naturalistic fallacy involved in this reasoning: First, no evidence shows that all children are, or can be, deterred by paternal disciplining. At a certain age, children resent punishment by parents and may even fight back. Second, children may accept parental punishment because they depend upon their parents and have no alternative but to accept this way of life. Third, when children accept parental discipline, they usually take it in the specific context of a love relationship they share with the parents. Most children resent discipline if imposed by a relative or a stranger. Furthermore, children who harbor little or no love for their parents are not usually afraid to challenge the parent's right to punish them. Fourth, the premise that disciplining children works may be based on insufficient knowledge, because in many cases punishing a child could cause considerable rage, humiliation, and feelings of inadequacy that may cause neurotic reactions or contribute to deviance at a later age.

Based on the previous observations, the validity of retribution has been questioned as a socially acceptable practice. Furthermore, from a geometric point of view, retribution seems to have a *multiplying negative quotient:* If I harm you and you harm me, then two persons will end up being harmed instead of one—regardless of who the attacker is or who the victim is. To understand the seriousness of this quotient, we need to universalize the issue. Imagine, for instance, a community of 100 individuals living on an island. Also imagine that the community is divided into two equal groups, A and B. Because of disagreement about who hunts on Saturday and who enjoys the beach on Sunday, members of Group A become irate and each of them attacks and seriously injures a member of Group B. But before members of group B are down, each of them is able to hurl a big rock and inflict equal harm on the attacker. What will the outcome be? Obviously, a community of individuals, all of whom are injured, would have little hope of survival. However, if retribution is avoided, the community will survive with only 50 wounded individuals. Members of Group A who undoubtedly need the services of Group B to survive will most likely regret their offensive deed and nurse members of Group B back to health. The entire community will eventually recover and perhaps learn to design a fair method of alternating Saturday and Sunday duties and resolving their conflicts peacefully.

Retributive thought has also been criticized for being too deontological; it fails to consider the consequences of its application. If the principle of "an eye for an eye and a tooth for a tooth" is to be the rule, it is highly probable that society will end up with a substantial population of "blind and toothless," especially in a society in which violence is rampant. Furthermore, retribution theory fails to take into consideration pertinent scientific data on recidivism. Can retaliation truly put an end to criminal behavior? If so, why do so many offenders continue to commit crime even after losing an "eye or a tooth," so to speak? Retributive thought, moreover, tends to debase the collective soul of society, because "if one person is diminished, the entire society is diminished as well."

The product of retributive thought in American prisons, especially in the past, has been a policy intent on the harsh treatment of offenders—one characterized by hard labor, shackling, poor diet, poor medical care, and solitary confinement, to mention just a few. Schmalleger comments in *Criminal Justice Today* (1991) that the punitive era was lackluster in American corrections. An "out-of-sight, out-of-mind" philosophy characterized American attitudes toward inmates. Popular accounts of the time portrayed convicts as "mad dogs" and rehabilitation-oriented officials as "sob sisters" and "cream puffers" (Schmalleger, 1991:420). Writing in the midst of the punitive era, Barnes and Teeters observed in *New Horizons in Criminology* (1959) that

> Even earnest administrators who sincerely believe in rehabilitation are afraid to introduce a whole-hearted program that might improve treatment of offenders. Such rehabilitative treatment requires flexibility and experimentation, but these increase escape risks and even the most enlightened warden realizes that his work will be judged by newspapers, politicians, and the public on the basis of how successful he is in preventing escapes.
>
> Barnes & Teeters, 1959:357

As another product of retributive policy, correctional officers developed a subculture bent on a single-minded view of their duties; namely, an obsession with security measures. Their mental habits revolved around the mania of keeping the prisoners locked up or scrupulously accounted for. Consequently, considerations for humanity, compassion, and rehabilitation evaporated in the face of this inexorable and all-encompassing anxiety (Schmalleger, 1991:420). In further confirming this occupational subculture, Jacobs observes, "Not merely prison practices but the prison itself has been declared violative of standards of decency which were the mark of a civilized society" (Jacobs, 1983:31).

Ethics of Treatment

Chief Justice Warren Burger has been quoted as saying, "To put people behind walls and bars and do little or nothing to change them is to win the battle and lose the war. It is expensive, and it is stupid" (Schmalleger, 1991:405). The era of treatment that had begun in America soon after World War II illustrates the concerns raised by the chief justice. Amid the bounty of the postwar boom economy, politicians and public officials pressed the humanitarian view of punishment, ushering the movement toward rehabilitation in prisons. As if to echo the chief justice's observation, Sol Wachtler, the former chief justice of New York's court of appeals, described the harsh treatment of drug offenders in prison, saying, "after 10 to 20 years of humiliation and loss of self-esteem, those non-violent offenders—almost all of whom have lost their families—come home to a hostile community with no jobs, no skills, and a prison mentality ... And then we wonder why we have repeat offenders" (Wachtler, 1997).

Rehabilitation is a term that has been often used and abused. The term derives from the French and Latin word *rehabilitare* (*re* + *habilitare*, meaning "ability"). The term thus denotes "returning to a former capacity," or bringing something back to functioning order. In corrections, the term came to mean a variety of activities: work programs, educational programs, therapeutic programs, and, essentially, a treatment associated with decency (Mathiesen, 1990:28–31). Most rehabilitative programs today are somehow directed toward changing the behavior of offenders one way or another. Some programs, such as deferred adjudication and probation, intervene early in the criminal justice process, and others, such as parole, at the end of the process. Despite a considerable number of impressive programs, however, the view of rehabilitation today suffers from a mistaken attitude created by the controversial Martinson Report, which is purported to have found that rehabilitation "does not work" (Walker, 1989:202).

Does Rehabilitation Work?

The Martinson Report was a bombshell dropped on the criminal justice community. It analyzed all evaluations of correctional programs in the country between 1945 and 1967. The report, which first appeared as an article, concluded that "with few and isolated exceptions, the rehabilitative efforts that have been reported so far have had no appreciable effect on rehabilitation" (Martinson, 1974). The article was originally titled "What Works?" but because of its findings, it came to be known as "nothing works." As Walker explains, the phrase became an instant cliché and exerted an enormous influence on both popular and professional thinking.

Martinson, a well-known criminologist, did not actually state that "nothing works." As several critics have pointed out, he found positive outcomes from a large number of correctional rehabilitation programs. Indeed, 48% of the programs he examined had at least some success. Nevertheless, the popular and professional audiences that were motivated more by *belief* than by *reasoning* heard the message as "nothing works," because it was an idea whose time had come (Walker, 1989:202).

By the mid-1970s, disillusionment with the emerging rehabilitation programs in prison was widespread. Politicians and the public were fed up with a decade of soaring crime that was attributed to the failure of rehabilitative programs conducted in prisons. Conservative groups led a revival of the concepts of retribution, deterrence, and incapacitation. Liberals, on the other hand, attacked established rehabilitation programs because of the due process problems associated with their implementation. For example, because there was no scientific way to measure a prisoner's rehabilitation, parole decisions were invariably considered arbitrary. The Martinson Report nevertheless continued to cast a cloud of doubt on the value of rehabilitation in correctional establishments.

Martinson's singular accomplishment, however, was his thrust to change the direction of the rehabilitation debate. He in effect threw down the gauntlet to the correctional establishment, demanding that it prove, in a scientific, verifiable way, the effectiveness of its programs (Walker, 1989:203). Martinson's findings were indeed embarrassing for a correctional community that had claimed a wide array of successes. According to the report, the correctional community failed to (1) develop a systematic process of evaluation, (2) use reliable measures in its evaluations, (3) prescribe proper treatment for the diverse groups of inmates, and (4) draw accurate conclusions from available data. The report, which was correct in some aspects and incorrect in others, exposed considerable professional irresponsibility. The truth of the matter still remains, however: The principle of rehabilitation is rational, but its implementation by politically oriented, ideologically driven, and emotionally disinterested managers creates a serious ethical dilemma.

Supporters of the rehabilitation theory argue that it is beneficial to both the inmate and society because (1) It maximizes goodness by extending it to all those concerned (for example, the inmate, his family, his neighborhood, society at large, and the national economy). (2) It provides a fundamentally different approach from the "moral rejection" implicit in retributive theory. It demonstrates acceptance rather than rejection, support rather than hatred, tolerance rather than revenge, and decency rather than brutality (Pollock, 1989:129). (3) It is more consistent with the "New Testament ethic" of loving and caring rather than the "Old Testament ethic" of reciprocal harm. (4) It is Epicurean in nature, because it is based on the principle of "Any man's debasement diminishes Me, because I am involved in Mankind!" (5) It is goal oriented, because it seeks to prevent crime by changing the nature of the offender.

Methods of Rehabilitation

The traditional methods of rehabilitation have basically been either individual treatment or group therapy. Both methods operate on the psychological principle of encouraging the inmate to accept responsibility for his or her own life. Treatment programs include education, self-discipline, and religious conviction. Individual treatment requires a face-to-face relationship between the offender and the therapist. Most individual approaches depict the offender as someone who has failed to realize his human potential (an Aristotelian theme). Personal development may have been thwarted into a detour of criminality by experiences in early life that the therapist will try to uncover.

Group therapy, on the other hand, relies upon the members of the therapeutic group themselves to facilitate treatment, often by first revealing to the client the emotional basis of criminal behavior. What the inmate regards as personal strength may be shown to be nothing more than ignorance or an excuse for his or her inability to "own up" to responsibility. Some group strategies are known as attack therapies, in which group members are verbally pummeled by other members in order to rid themselves of old self-concepts and criminal values. While these therapies may uncover past personal traumas, they cause more trauma in their relentless destruction of all personal armor (Schmalleger, 1991:421).

The State of Rehabilitation Today

Rehabilitation is in a state of limbo today, not because the principle is unsound, but because of the inability of correctional institutions to serve as instruments of change. "Uninformed" correctional practitioners reject its appeal, misjudge its moral worth, and seem unwilling to give it a chance to succeed. Wardens are told that they "will never lose their jobs, because recidivism rates rise"; however, they may very well lose them if inmates escape or riot. In the objective reality of correctional administration, however, all but today's most hardened wardens acknowledge (perhaps more privately than publicly) that correctional facilities can indeed do a lot of good for prisoners. But correctional officers, who control the cell block, rarely share this view. Perhaps because of their insecurity on the job, the prison subculture they cannot escape, or their relative unfamiliarity with the philosophy of corrections, most correctional officers remain oblivious. If officer and inmate slang is an accurate guide to the reality of prison management, a correctional officer is still considered a "hack" or a "screw" by the inmates, and solitary confinement is still a "hole," not an "adjustment center" (Crouch & Marquart, 1980; Toch, 1978a; Walker, 1989).

But even well-informed correctional leaders today are pressured into disavowing rehabilitation. The subject has become politically unfashionable, expensive, and to a large measure, socially unpopular. Legislators who can also exert strong influence on the business of corrections continue to demand political solutions to humanitarian problems. But political solutions are seldom ethical solutions. Correctional leaders are expected to appear tough, accomplish quick results, and enhance the legislator's chances of getting reelected (Williamson, 1990:33). This brings us back to the ethics of public servants, those who know the virtue of rehabilitation but choose to remain silent.

Given this predicament, it appears necessary that prison institutions reexamine what Toch calls the "correctional lag," by thinking less "custodial" and more "correctional." Prison officials who "talk corrections and act custodially" should seriously reconsider their moral orientation toward corrections in general and rehabilitation in particular. They should perhaps recognize that the ethics of corrections is inherently an "ethic of support," wherein they function more as "brother's keeper—caring, relating, and helping" (Toch, 1978a). But to successfully develop such a character, prison officials must be familiar with the philosophies of Socrates (knowledge as virtue), Epictetus (courage and tenacity), Saint Augustine (doing goodness as serving God), Kant (reverence of duty even if the heavens fall), and Rawls (social justice as social goodness). Given the comedy of errors that envelops prisons today, the state of rehabilitation may perhaps be best described as a "battle of ethics" between legislators who care not to dare, and correctional officials who dare not to care.

Ethics of Man and Corrections: What Good Is Brutality?

In *A Critique of Prison Building*, Newman describes prisons as the cruelest institutions that society has devised. In his view, everything from the basic architecture of walled, turreted, maximum-security facilities to rules and regulations creates an environment that is degrading, repressive, and punitive. Prisons are more than simply a collection of the worst among us; they are the symbolic embodiment of the awesome power of society to compel conformity. Newman further argues that "everyone familiar with American prisons—whether inmates or not—agrees that correctional facilities, particularly maximum security prisons, are brutal by their nature" (Newman, as cited in Travis et al., 1983:93). The major effects of imprisonment on those serving time, Newman concludes, are shattered self-esteem and acceptance of unjustified oppression as a way of life.

Newman's description of prisons is certainly a depressing commentary on the state of prisons in any society. What makes it especially depressing is that he is describing American prisons, and that he is not alone in his conclusions. Similar assessments have been made by Jacobs, Irwin, Carroll, Conrad, DiIulio, Fleischer, Hawkins, and Lombardo, among others, whose works will be cited throughout this chapter. If Newman's assessment is accurate or even broadly resembles reality, no rationale can be accepted for such treatment without causing great damage to the English language. Conrad comments that "granted that society, or at least judges and legislators, will demand high levels of incarceration, there is no reason we have to maintain dehumanizing brutal holding tanks for inmates" (Travis et al., 1983:60). Conrad emphasizes that the continued use of brutal prisons not only affects the inmates, but also degrades society. In *Warehousing Violence* (1989), Fleischer points out that "Americans don't know what happens inside maximum-security prisons; they don't understand the serious, even fatal consequences of failed correctional management, particularly among violent criminals" (Fleischer, 1989:237).

On the other hand, the view of American prisons as centers for inhumane treatment has not been a mystery—to a large measure, society has simply chosen to ignore it. There is certainly no shortage of information confirming the presence of physical and spiritual violence in American prisons. Studies have been made of the role of age in prison violence (Mabli et al., 1979; MacKenzie, 1987); overcrowded conditions as causes of violence (Ekland-Olson, 1986; Ellis, 1984; Farrington & Nutall, 1980; Gaes & McGuire, 1985; Nacci et al., 1977a, 1977b); alienation, boredom, and idleness as interludes to violence (Sykes, 1958; Sykes & Messinger, 1960); ethnic and racial rivalries (Carroll, 1974; Davidson, 1974; Jacobs, 1977, Jacobs & Kraft, 1983); and sociopsychological causes of inmates' violent behavior (Toch, 1969; Toch & Adams, 1986).

The conclusions of these studies can be summed up in three general realizations: (1) when convicts are powerless, mistreated, bored, sexually frustrated, and cramped, they cannot be prevented from committing violent acts; (2) prison violence will continue as a normal product of

prison life; and (3) punitive correctional policies neither deter nor rehabilitate America's miscreants. Surprisingly, these realizations are rarely
contested by traditional prison administrators who employ hardheaded
custodial officers and rely on harsh shakedown squads, routine unoffi-
cial force, and harsh retaliatory actions against nonconforming inmates
(Fleischer, 1989:197; Jacobs, 1976:80; Toch, 1978b:21).

The Brutality Issue

In light of the previous discussion, a critical question must be raised
and confronted: Can brutality be justified in responding to inmates
when self-defense, the defense of others, or preserving order is not at
stake?

In response to this question, it is necessary to first define brutality
and establish its intrinsic culpability. *Brutality* is a generic term that
means "the intentional use of—or the threat of using—unauthorized
acts of force against an inmate, or indicating by statement or attitude
a readiness to cause bodily harm when harm is unwarranted." The
intrinsic culpability of brutality stems from its immoral sanctions. Three
of these sanctions are particularly significant: (1) using violence for its
own sake is an act of egoism—it serves no legitimate purpose and can
cause substantial social harm to all concerned; (2) prison conditions
are, in themselves, conducive to restlessness and frustration—the use
of brutality can exacerbate unnecessary violence; and (3) prisons are,
by definition, *correctional institutions*—the use of brutality by prison
officials defeats the stated mission of prisons and embarrasses state officials. Based on these sanctions, the practice of brutality in any of its
forms must be considered prima facie unethical.

The most common justification for prison brutality, on the other
hand, is the "dangerous nature of inmates." This justification tends to
support a seemingly irresistible tendency to treat all prisoners as despicable individuals. Nonetheless, this justification is ethically flawed on two
counts.

First, this justification implies that brutality is necessary, if not
indeed essential, to control murderers, rapists, and habitual robbers—
where the potential for unrest is the highest and the likelihood of harm-
ing fellow inmates is considerable. Yet when this justification is carefully
examined, it does not stand the test of factuality, because the vast majority of inmates do not belong to any of these categories. Figures indicate
that the percentage of inmates convicted in state courts in 1992 was 1.0
for murder, 2.4 for rape, and 5.8 for robbery (Flanagan & Maguire,
1994:485). The remainder of prison inmates, which amounts to
90.8% (based on previous figures) of the general population, are sentenced for burglary, larceny, drug trafficking, and lesser felonies. Yet

the fallacy of labeling all inmates as despicable and dangerous continues unexamined. Even if the fallacy is correct and all prisoners are indeed hard-core criminals, reasoning dictates that the state (the parent and teacher of society) is still obliged to react to violence *only* in the most rational and restrained manner.

Second, the justification cannot stand the test of reasonableness, because, if valid, doctors and nurses should be justified in treating patients in a "sickly" manner, and teachers should be justified in treating students in an "immature" fashion. We know that even in the conduct of warfare, enemy prisoners are universally protected from acts of brutality, including humiliation, parading in public, or being forced to do undignified work. Similar arguments have, of course, been made by animal lovers and environmentalists advocating better treatment for animals, birds, trees, and the earth itself. Somehow the justification becomes so intellectually disparaging when prison officials insist that brutality and harsh treatment are the only language inmates understand and therefore must be "good" for their self-concept. Such an argument is not only unintelligent, it is also inconsistent with behavioral science theories, the assumptions of natural law, religious testaments, and, of course, the principles of conduct in a civilized society. Any argument in support of brutality, it must be concluded, places the administrators' morality, and perhaps their knowledge, in question, rendering their claims to professionalism indistinguishable from vileness.

Ethics of Man and Corrections: The Scapegoating Theory

Since the beginning of time, questions of citizenship have ubiquitously polarized the human mind. Like the natural contradictions of life and death, good and bad, light and darkness, the contradiction of criminal and noncriminal may have been taken for granted as a social phenomenon giving rise to the *scapegoating theory*.

The concept of scapegoating is not altogether new; it was known to primitive tribes as sacrificial rituals. When societies were confronted with catastrophes, real or imaginary, that were beyond their comprehension, they were interpreted as wrathful acts of the gods, caused by the sinful or the unclean. To end the suffering, chiefs isolated those members and made sacrifices (physical or symbolic) to appease the gods. Consequently, sacrificing a person, an animal, or an object became a cultural ritual, institutionalizing the practice of social scapegoating. To prevent future catastrophes, isolation of the sinners and the unclean had to continue and sacrifices had to be offered on a routine basis. If that practice discontinued, it was believed that a catastrophe would occur. In early Hebrew societies, the lepers, the defiled, and menstruating women were likewise isolated, because they were considered unclean. Sacrifices were also made as atonements for sin. In Christian doctrine, the practice became even more common, because Jesus Christ spilled his blood to cleanse all sin-stained souls.

The Influence of Foucault

Foucault, a noted French psychologist and journalist, pointed out that there may be an unspoken relationship between the scapegoating theory and the purpose of corrections. In *Madness and Civilization* (1973) he wrote that the current warehousing of criminals may indeed be an exercise in social scapegoating. He explained that there appears to be a cultural need to exclude from society those believed to be sinners or unclean. By today's definition, these are the murderers, rapists, robbers, and thieves, as well as anyone who is socially embarrassing, such as the mentally ill or the physically deformed.

Foucault reported that since the Middle Ages there were literally thousands of leprosariums in Europe where lepers were incarcerated. While their isolation was in fact the proper "cure" and the disease almost completely disappeared, this left Western society with a moral void. To fill these leprosariums that were left empty for years, Western societies looked for scapegoats who fit the images and values of the leper, as well as the reasoning for their exclusion. The significance of isolating society's members and physically penning them up in a "circled pit" served two purposes: atonement from sin on the part of society, and giving the offenders an opportunity to achieve a state of grace (Pollock, 1989:130). Foucault's perspective is certainly interesting and should not be dismissed as farfetched. In his discussion of police subculture, Skolnick identified the police officer's view of the world with the concept of the "symbolic assailant," an anonymous source of fear that presents danger to the community of policemen. Skolnick explained that "the underlying moral sentiment among cops was to round up and isolate persons who represent a prelude to violence by fitting the symbolic assailant profile" (Skolnick, as cited in Blumberg & Niederhoffer, 1970:82).

Foucault later turned his attention to the problem of corrections and the role of prisons. In *Discipline and Punish* (1977) he suggested that another reason for the development of prisons was the disappearance of torture as a public spectacle. Foucault wrote that a few decades saw the "disappearance of the tortured, dismembered, amputated body, and those exposed alive or dead to public view ... the body as the major target of penal repression disappeared" (Foucault, 1977:7–8). Foucault then asks, "If the penalty in its most severe forms no longer addresses itself to the body, on what does it lay hold?" His answer was simple, almost obvious—it must be the soul. The public spectacle of punishment was banished into the unconscious of society—the prison fortress. The expiation that once rained down upon the body of the prisoner has been replaced by a punishment that acts in-depth on his heart, his thoughts, his will, and his inclinations (Travis et al., 1997:67).

Foucault, of course, is not the only observer to see modern prisons as tools to break the human spirit rather than skin and bones. Horkheimer and Adorno—who wrote during World War II about Nazi Germany—argued that since the mid-nineteenth century, "bourgeois" governments have attacked man's soul, whereas the monarchies attacked his body. According to the authors, prisoners no longer die a slow death in the torture chamber; they simply waste away spiritually in the great prison building that differs in little but name from madhouses (Horkheimer & Adorno, 1972:228). It is little wonder that Germann, in his classic *Introduction to Law Enforcement and Criminal Justice*, refers to imprisonment as "spiritual punishment" (Germann et al., 1988:39).

In describing today's prison, Smarto (1989), in *Justice and Mercy*, presents a horrific view of the prison environment. While his description can be very depressing at times, his analysis emphasizes four basic features: (1) the total loss of choice that turns inmates into infantile creatures; (2) the continuous threat of violence that can be neither ignored nor overcome; (3) the terrifying fear of sadism and rape—more than half of the inmates are raped within the first 30 days of their incarceration; and (4) the continuous abuse by correctional officers. Smarto, a former assistant superintendent of a maximum security facility, asserts that the prison environment makes inmates "sicker" and wonders how any rational policy can seek to "make sick people well by making them sicker."

Ethics of Man and Corrections: The Holier-than-Thou Syndrome

Americans show greater righteous indignation when it comes to criminals than to the abstract issue of crime, and to prisoners than the abstract issue of imprisonment. While each of these sets is naturally inseparable (there cannot be criminals without crime or prisoners without imprisonment), personalizing sin somehow seems to make it more sinful. By the same token, while praying for forgiveness is one of the most common prayers universally offered, when the issue of prisoners is mentioned, the most frequent refrain echoed is, "Lock them up ... and throw away the key. Let them suffer. Who cares if they are in inhumane, overcrowded, and filthy prisons?" (Fleischer, 1989:235).

While the tendency to separate causes from effects in some cultures can be understood, in a civilized society it is irrational. It is hardly logical that because one has not encountered a prison sentence, one should be considered a social saint and is justified in denigrating all those in the *camp of outcasts.*

Crime as Virus

Unconventional theorists argue that the holier-than-thou syndrome accentuates moral stratification (for example, he is a criminal, I am not) giving rise to a false perception of social problems. However, the ethical reasoner should ask, "Who are these prisoners, and why are they there?" While the purpose of this discussion is certainly not to "coddle" criminals or to "overlook" their antisocial behavior, it is to put the problem of prisonization in perspective and to treat it maturely and objectively. As mentioned earlier, issues of crime and punishment cannot be separated from issues of justice. And because justice is the hallmark of civility, the way prisoners are treated—despite their shameless transgression—reflects on our sense of civility. As citizens of a civilized society, we must realize that "while all societies have crime, only civilized societies can offer justice."

For the most part, inmates begin their lives as American children, raised on an American diet and taught American values (or whatever they were able to receive and internalize). They will eventually be released from prison and, in time, die as American citizens. Yet under certain conditions that are too complex to understand or predict, what appears to be a "criminal virus" becomes active—impairing their choices about right and wrong. As a result, they begin to commit crime as failure of their socialization process occurs.

The virus analogy is of special significance to the criminological researcher, because viruses are known to (1) be ubiquitous—throughout the environment; (2) adapt to changing cultures—whenever a cure is found, the virus changes; (3) spread rapidly among unexposed populations; and (4) remain dormant *only* when confronted by persons with stronger immune defenses. Still, cognizant of the theory of choice, the virus view may confirm the perspective that "character is made for us rather than by us."

Criminological theorists have exhausted themselves discovering what causes this criminogenic virus. In an assortment of sociological, psychological, economic, political, and biological theories, three questions remain unanswered: (1) How much crime do we know is caused by weaker immune defenses to crime (loosely translated, the free choice theory)? (2) How much crime do we know is determined by environmental temptations (the determinant theory)? (3) How much crime is a product of both? No theory, as of yet, has provided any satisfactory answers to these questions. This is more likely because of our inability to measure in advance the strength of an individual's *immune defenses* and the *amount of temptation one can withstand* before turning to crime. Unless "crime viruses" are identified and measured, and unless people at risk are "vaccinated," so to speak, all human beings, by virtue of their existence, may be considered "crime carriers" (Marcus, 1996). Gordon Hawkins observes that "in all the impediments to human development and social change, none is more fundamentally disabling than our lack of knowledge, both the blamed and the blamers are uninformed" (Travis et al., 1983:57). Given this knowledge shortage, individuals cannot be justified in their righteous indignation of inmates, nor can societies be justified in denying them humane treatment.

A more sobering observation, perhaps, is the probability that the mysterious "virus" may have already infected millions and that it may well infect millions of unborn children (that is, as with children born with AIDS or an addiction to alcohol or cocaine). Furthermore, it is generally assumed that prison inmates account for approximately 1% of all lawbreakers who could have been brought to the prison gate but were not. This technically allows for 99% of all wrongdoers to live as "honorable" citizens, were it not for flaws in the criminal justice system. This may also confirm, at least in part, that an unidentified number of prisoners may indeed be victims of ignorance, stupidity, or bad luck.

By the same token, it should be equally safe to assume that an unidentified number of "honorable persons" in society today may in fact have no moral grounds for not being in prison.

A Camp of Outcasts

Now let us now examine the other side of the coin. It is equally contradictory to argue that because one has been imprisoned (perhaps for a minor offense), one is forever relegated to the *camp of outcasts*. Theories of recidivism indicate that while "we think we know" why some prisoners recidivate, we are in no position to know why others do not. Indeed, a study shows that 80% of all death row convicts who were saved by the *Furman* decision (the Supreme Court's ruling in 1972 that temporarily stopped capital punishment) did not recidivate (*Newsweek*, May 7, 1991:57). Moreover, many spiritual and world leaders in history have served prison terms (either as regular criminals or as political activists). These include Jeremiah, Joseph, Peter, Paul, Andrew Jackson, Gandhi, Martin Luther King Jr., and Nelson Mandela, to name just a few. Paul, who as Saul should have been condemned as a mass murderer, perhaps because of his unique prison experience, exhorted Christians to "Remember the sufferings of those in prison as though you are suffering with them" (Hebrews 13:3). The assumptions, therefore, that "once criminal, always criminal" and that prisoners *cannot* be salvaged through some means of rehabilitation must be inaccurate. Although it is true that a large number of prisoners do recidivate under the present methods of treatment, it cannot, by the same token, be assumed that under more developed methods their behavior cannot be changed.

Ethics of Man and Corrections: We're All Doing Time

There is general agreement that the distribution of crime in society is normal. This creates at least two categories of criminals: *convicted criminals*, whom we know have a criminal record, and *shadow criminals*, who violate the law without ever being charged with a crime. Shadow criminals are found among all races, social categories, and economic classes. They are male and female, old and young, rich and poor, educated and uneducated. While this category is technically not considered criminal, its members may be actively engaged in serious crimes, such as treason, organized crime, corporate crime, environmental crime, or in domestic crimes such as incest and spouse battering.

Even in the area of minor crimes, shadow criminals include high- and low-level government officials who falsify travel vouchers, violate the civil rights of subordinates, or simply take pencils and erasers from the office. To bring it closer to home, shadow criminals may include those involved in student crimes; for example, those who commit date rape, steal exams, plagiarize term papers, drive under the influence of intoxicants, or use illicit drugs. All of these are culpable individuals who technically qualify as criminals and should be punished, perhaps by a prison term.

The notion of "we're all doing time" has been emphasized in criminological literature; criminality is a "normal" factor, not a pathological one, because the criminogenic virus permeates all social climates. The neo-positivist school of criminology, in particular, views crime as determined by social or environmental factors (internal or external) that influence personal behavior. Thus, individuals *will* commit crime if their immune defenses are weaker than the criminal temptation with which they are faced. By the same token, crime *will not* occur if one's immune defenses are greater than the criminal temptation one faces.

In support of this view, Durkheim points out that "a society exempt from it [crime] is utterly impossible and the fundamental conditions of social organization logically imply it." He further stresses that "crime is not due to any imperfection of human nature or society any more than birth and death may be considered abnormal or pathological," and "a society without crime would necessitate a standardization of the moral concepts of all individuals which is neither possible nor desirable" (Mannheim, 1970:390). By the same token, Sutherland's explanation of white-collar crime makes reference to shadow criminals even more clear. He points out that the financial cost of organized crime in the United States is "probably several times as great as the financial cost of all crimes customarily included in the crime problem." Nonetheless, most white-collar criminals neither end up in prison, nor are they usually denigrated as social deviants (Sutherland, 1949:51).

Ethics of Man and Corrections: Postcards from Prison

Our next episode is even more controversial. It certainly is not a plea to favor criminals or to strike some "terms of endearment" with prison inmates. It is simply an exposé of the truth as presented by well-meaning theorists. In Lombardo's study of correctional officers (1989), he presents a view that prisoners are not, in effect, very different from people outside prison. Lombardo surveyed hundreds of correctional officers in Auburn prison, asking them how they felt toward inmates. While many correctional officers across the country may disagree, especially because prison populations can vary dramatically from one prison to another, the responses in Lombardo's study were enlightening. In response to questions related to "Contact with Reality," the officers in the sample population offered the following responses:

> I was amazed. I found out there that they were normal people, not two heads, eight feet tall and grotesque.

> One day I asked a guy what he was doing. I thought it was a Morse Code. He was making something in braille. Just doing their time, occupying themselves. Probably no different from the rest of us.

> I always expected they'd have a different look. Like a murderer would be a mean and tough guy. A lot of them have baby faces and you look at their records and see murder. What you expect doesn't always go with the person you see. You expect lifers to escape, but they get in and they're the opposite. The big timer is the best inmate. They do their time the best they can and the easiest way.

> When I first went to Sing Sing, I thought they were all killers and tough and difficult to talk to, but I don't think that way now. The majority you can talk to and get to know. He'll come to you with problems, and sometimes he can help you out.

Lombardo concluded in his study that the general perception of what prisoners are like is "deceptive." While correctional officers may have had a stereotypical image of the convict, the stereotype breaks down in the diversity of human character. Furthermore, the study showed that convicts, rather than "being aloof, were viewed as people with whom one can communicate" (Lombardo, 1989:35).

More revealing perhaps is Jacobs's study of "What Prison Guards Think" (1978). In this study, 75% of Illinois prison guards surveyed agreed with the statement that "only a few inmates are troublemakers; most of them are decent people." Furthermore, in response to the question, "In your opinion, when considered as people, how similar are correctional officers and inmates?" a majority of the officers answered "very similar" (Jacobs, 1978:193).

In addition, in a study of Texas prisons that indirectly affirms this view, Crouch and Marquart indicated that a specific objective of the guards' subculture was to teach new recruits to perceive inmates as "fundamentally different and inferior" (Crouch & Marquart, 1989). The authors reported that veteran officers had to make a special effort to convey to recruits that inmates are abnormal persons by telling them fictitious atrocity stories. Telling lies was evidently necessary to socialize the rookie guards into a discriminatory prison subculture.

Additional support for this view was offered by a former warden of three prisons, including Auburn and Sing Sing, cited in *Corrections: An Issues Approach* (Schwartz & Travis, 1997:65). The warden was reported as saying,

1. Prisoners are human beings; for the most part remarkably like the rest of us.

2. Prisoners can be clubbed into submission, but cannot be reformed by that process.

3. Prisoners cannot be reformed by bribery in the shape of privileges, special favors, or tolerant behavior.

4. Prisoners will not respond to sentimentality; they do not like gush.

5. Prisoners appreciate a "square deal" when they get one.

6. Prisoners are not "mentally defective"; on the contrary, the majority are embarrassingly clever.

Based on the previous discussions, it should be safe to conclude that (1) *most* prisoners are not "dangerous and despicable characters"; (2) "we're all doing time," because it is certainly difficult to think of a healthy adult who has not at least once violated a law, the consequence of which—if caught and properly prosecuted—would have possibly been a prison sentence; and (3) while shadow criminals remain hidden from public scrutiny, their *potential* for crime could become active again when unstable social, economic, or political factors (external to them) are aligned. This explains, at least in part, the increased crime rates during economic hard times, periods of social unrest, and wartime (Thomson, 1993:6–11).

Ethics of Man and Corrections: Rehabilitation through Inner Corrections

The strongest advocates of the rehabilitation theory of corrections today are not chaplains, as might be expected, but a group of professors reminiscent of the students who championed the scholastic movement in medieval times. That group, which includes Quinney (1988), Pepinsky (1989), Fleischer (1989), and others, has been calling attention to the immorality of a prison system that treats people inhumanely. They argue that no "goodness" could come out of an environment that offers neither hope nor kindness. Hope, they assert, is about all that inmates have to hold on to, and peacemaking is the only vehicle for kindness. For corrections to be effective, these scholastic moralists argue, the prison must be lawful, safe, industrious, and hopeful.

The concept of *Inner Corrections* has been particularly popularized by Bo Lozoff and Michael Braswell. The concept is specifically based on the notion of "we're all doing time" and the imperative of peacemaking in correctional thought. The concept, which is holistic in nature and metaphysical in tone, reflects a close similarity to the Epicurean philosophy of tranquility, prudence, and peace. It is directed at everyone in the field of corrections—the keepers and the kept, the offender and the victim, the parent and the child, the teacher and the student, and the incarcerator and the liberator (Lozoff & Braswell, 1989:iii).

Inner Corrections

Inner corrections is a relatively uncomplicated concept that is identified as a human experience rather than a correctional agenda. The cornerstone virtues of the concept represent universal virtues that are not only independent of race, creed, or culture, but also of time and place, "whether one is talking about ancient Mesopotamia or modern Manhattan." These virtues are self-honesty (remember Aristotle's moral character), courage (remember Epictetus's invincible will), kindness (remember Saint Augustine's love of God), and a sense of humor. But putting inner corrections into practice, the authors admit, requires a great deal of motivation, spirituality, and hard work.

The philosophy of inner corrections presents an alternative to the conventional theory of retribution. It is based on the assumption that people, including prisoners, are not necessarily bad or wicked—they are only *spiritually clumsy*. They are out of balance because they see life from the view of the "mouse"; worrying endlessly about the terrible world at the tips of its whiskers. Wisdom, peace, and even joy can come only from learning to appreciate a wider and more interesting world, and the only power that inner corrections can offer comes from the spirit within (Lozoff & Braswell, 1989:1). The primary goal of inner corrections has been stated as follows:

> to help build a happier, peaceful person right here in the prison, a person whose newfound self-honesty and courage can steer him or her to the most appropriate programs and training, a person whose kindness and sense of humor will help him or her to adjust to the biases and shortcomings of a society which does not feel comfortable with ex-offenders.

Lozoff & Braswell, 1989:2

Component programs of inner corrections, especially in the category of spiritual development, include kindness, peace, proper diet, and prayer. Through these means, inner corrections addresses the soul of the inmate and attempts change from the inside out rather than the other way around. Needless to say, it frowns on traditional treatment programs that come in steps, phases, and formulas. Instead, it promotes a nearly limitless variety of practices that revolve around empowering the prisoner to gain more self-control as a means of personal liberation.

The Future of Inner Corrections

While some programs in the inner corrections package seem so morally meritorious as to represent perhaps the *summum bonum* of any correctional theory, their chances for recognition, given the current "get tough on crime" attitude, appear limited. There are at least three reasons for this judgment: (1) The effectiveness of such programs, like the effectiveness of medical and educational programs before them, hinges absolutely on the vision, rationality, tenacity, and inner peace of those who apply them. Furthermore, the shortage of well-paid professional personnel trained in spiritual counseling may well be a case in point. (2) The bureaucratic nightmare of administering individualized programs on such a wide scale may render their implementation prohibitively costly, if at all manageable. Given the large numbers of inmates in prison today, obsession with security and custodial needs runs so high as to obliterate all other "frivolous" needs. This sets inner corrections at the bottom of all needs, with the distorted image of "coddling the inmates"—an image that policy makers find detrimental to political survival. (3) The concept of inner corrections is not suited to all prisoners—only a small minority may qualify at any time. There obviously may be too many prisoners whose severe orientation toward crime and violence (or because of their mental or emotional state) may make them not only nonresponsive to such therapies, but may even make them resent those who attempt them.

The irony of inner corrections, nonetheless, is a trademark of the dual reality of choice; as an ideal, it encompasses some of the most admirable virtues ever known to man, but as a social policy it may indeed be a victim of its own virtuousness. Given the social politics of the times, it seems less likely that correctional leaders will be persuaded to accept a policy of inner corrections than it was 2000 years ago to persuade Plato to accept democracy.

Corruption of Prison Personnel

Prisons are complex bureaucratic institutions that have a rather depressing environment, and correctional officers invariably suffer from stress, low morale, and lack of job satisfaction (Crouch & Alpert, 1982; Fleischer, 1989; Jacobs, 1977; Lasky et al., 1986). As a result, the popular thesis is that corruption in prisons is normatively higher than in other institutions. The validity of this thesis is hard to prove or disprove, given the closed nature of correctional institutions and the inadequacy of available research techniques. As in all bureaucratic agencies, there are more ethical and less ethical prison units, depending on the ethics of the workers who staff them.

While patterns of corruption in prisons should not be seen as different from those of police or, for that matter, of any other criminal justice agency, certain characteristics exist. Given the seclusion of the prison environment and the jealous protection by prison officials to keep them from public view, information about prison corruption is scarce, and whatever is known is mostly anecdotal or based on hearsay. In order for corruption to be substantiated, there must be a corrupter and a victim, but more importantly, a defender who cares for the interests of the victim. In a sociological sense, however, inmates are members of an "orphan group"; they are not significant enough to be able to act on their own as a pressure group, and influential pressure groups do not associate themselves with the inmates' seemingly small causes. As a result, most people would likely be more agitated if a suspect were mistreated by police than if an inmate were physically assaulted by a prison guard. This leaves inmates, in most cases, prey to exploitation and may lend credence to the widely publicized image of corruption in correctional institutions.

Moreover, given the highly political nature of correctional institutions, small corruption in prisons, such as theft of products, trafficking in contraband, and sexual favors by correctional employees, frequently goes unreported or unpublicized. Incidents of this nature are usually resolved administratively by firing the party involved. The publication of such information can be politically damaging to prison officials who seek to appease the politicians who fund their agencies. On the other hand, the majority of publicized prison corruption is usually related to abuse of authority by correctional officers. These are considered transient workers whose "questionable" behavior could be used by prison officials as leverage to receiving more funding (for example, for improving selection processes, upgrading training, or increasing salaries). Publicizing such cases does not usually create serious collateral damage to the image of the institution, because it could conveniently be blamed on the modest background of prison guards, bad work conditions, or burnout caused by dealing with inmates for prolonged periods.

Patterns of Prison Corruption

Mundane Corruption: The most common category of prison corruption is usually committed by low-ranking correctional officials and involves manipulating inmates and abusing prison rules. These activities seem to go hand in hand. Most correctional officers do not seem bothered by the end–means dilemma when they find it necessary to make a particularly annoying inmate pay for his or her defiant behavior. This seems to be especially true when correctional officers believe that established procedures are ineffective in preventing inmate violations or in providing "just" punishment for habitual offenses (Lombardo, 1989:101). For instance, to make an inmate pay, and knowing that no action will be taken during the weekend, an unethical officer may submit a violation report on Friday afternoon—thus effectively placing the inmate in "keep lock" for 2 days—while the actual penalty for the violation would be of lesser gravity.

Most correctional officers work in a precarious environment, having to physically deal with inmates. Consequently, in order to avert such contingencies, the first rule of thumb is to establish dominance over inmates by word and behavior. The classical strategy for establishing dominance is the use of profanity and "bluster." The assumption here is obvious: In order to make inmates accept their inferior status, directives must be delivered loudly and profanely (Crouch & Marquart, 1980).

Other, more humiliating tactics to establish dominance include strip searching in view of other inmates when such a search is clearly not called for; locking an inmate out of his or her cell for a period of time while others are locked in, thus making the inmate fear that he may be targeted for harm; turning off the inmate's water supply or electricity; or keeping a "keep lock" tag on a cell door lever so as to keep the inmate locked up until someone discovers that the tag was in error. Not notifying inmates when they have a scheduled appointment is another way of "getting back" at persistent rule violators. An ingenious example of similar acts of oppression cited by Lombardo involved making an inmate wait for a sergeant while he held three pints of ice cream from the commissary. The salient point in all such cases is to make certain the inmates understand that the correctional officers can and will find ways to make the inmates' lives miserable whenever they want to. In all such cases, the officers also make it almost impossible for inmates to prove a case of harassment (Lombardo, 1989:101).

Another means of inmate oppression is to keep them *off balance*—to manipulate their daily needs so as to remind them of their subordinate position. One of the more serious instances of keeping inmates off balance was reported by Crouch and Marquart (1980) and was labeled as "messin' with their minds." According to the authors, correctional officers deliberately "act crazy" in order to confuse inmates. Acting crazy means that the officer may respond to the inmate in ways quite unrelated to the inmate's question or problem; in this way, the inmate is put on the defensive or made to feel uncertain of what is happening. Examples of such behavior include structuring situations so as to place inmates at a disadvantage, or confronting them with feigned seriousness while questioning them about things that would not make sense to them (Crouch & Marquart, 1980:84).

Crouch and Marquart (1980) point out other means by which correctional officers' authority is corrupted: trade-offs with inmates. In exchange for willingness on the part of select inmates to keep the cell block quiet, officers may tacitly agree to overlook minor transgressions committed by those prisoners. Illustrations of trade-offs include offering special privileges to inmates who aid the guards. Examples include allowing them freedom to choose cell partners, keep prohibited commodities in the cell, smoke where prohibited, dress out of uniform, allow for sexual favors, all the way to providing alcohol, drugs, and, in extreme cases, weapons (Allen & Bosta, 1981).

Bringing contraband into the institution for profit can be lucrative for corrupt correctional officers. Narcotics have been among the most marketable contraband in prison institutions. Inmates seem to have a greater drug appetite than ever before, because so many of them were drug users when they entered prison. Furthermore, these prisoners have drug contacts and can obtain money to pay anyone who can bring in the drugs to them; all they need is someone to make the pickups and bring the drugs into the prison (Bartollas et al., 1983:255). Yet, given the recent no-smoking policy adopted by most states, tobacco may well be the most marketable contraband. The unethical, low-paid correctional officer may thus have a far better chance of becoming a well-paid middleman who provides this highly valued service.

Corruption by Higher-Ups: Prison corruption is not limited to mundane corruption by low-level correctional officers; higher-up officials can also be involved. There are basically two types of corruption at this level: (1) using brutality to appear in control and (2) accepting kickbacks. While such cases are not very common, one example of each type will be presented.

The Use of Brutality to Appear in Control: Inmates in the Georgia prison system have long complained of officers' brutality, yet no attempt was seriously made to resolve their complaints. This prompted a number of prison officials, including officers, counselors, and prison employees, to support inmate claims, implicating, at least on one occasion, the state corrections commissioner himself. They testified that the commissioner had condoned, watched, and celebrated a mass beating of inmates (*Houston Chronicle*, July 1, 1997).

A sworn statement by Ray McWhorter, a lieutenant in charge of a riot squad at Hays State Prison in Georgia, alleged that the commissioner had touched off a bloody attack on prisoners in July 1996 when he grabbed an unresisting inmate by the hair and dragged him across the floor. On the same day, the lieutenant added, the commissioner watched in another cell block while inmates, some handcuffed and lying on the floor, were punched, kicked, and stomped until blood streaked the walls. Later, the lieutenant added, the commissioner applauded the guards at a celebratory chicken dinner. The celebration was described as "everyone was high-fiving ... shaking hands ... congratulating each other, and patting each other on the back bragging about how much butt was kicked" (*Houston Chronicle*, July 1, 1997).

Lieutenant McWhorter admitted that he himself had taken part in the attack after the commissioner's aide had begun the melee by dragging the prisoner across the floor by the hair. "We were all under the impression that it was OK to do it," the lieutenant added. "If Thomas can slam one, then we can slam one, too ... that is just the dad-gum way it was ... folks were still getting forced to the floor and slammed into the wall and Flexicuffed ... and all that stuff. It was a dad-gum shark frenzy. It was a free-for-all, you know, how sharks do" (*Houston Chronicle*, July 1, 1997).

Accepting Kickbacks by Chief Administrators: A Louisiana sheriff pleaded guilty to taking kickbacks in connection with the lease of a detention center in the county in which he served (*Corrections Journal*, September 22, 1997). According to a statement by the U.S. Attorney for the Western District of Louisiana, the sheriff of East Carrol Parish, Dale Rinicker, pleaded guilty to one count of engaging in monetary transactions in property derived from mail fraud and public bribery. Prosecutors said Rinicker entered into an arrangement in which the sheriff's department leased the detention center from East Carroll Corrections Systems. Rinicker used the detention center to house prisoners for the state, which pays counties a per-prisoner fee as reimbursement. Under the lease arrangement, East Carroll Corrections Systems received 25% of the money that the state paid the sheriff's office to house state prisoners.

Prosecutors said that Rinicker received kickbacks from the portion of the state money that went to East Carroll Corrections Systems. Part of the scheme also entailed receiving a hidden ownership interest in East Carroll Corrections Systems. As a result, from May 1993 through October 1995, Rinicker reportedly received $340,142. Under a plea agreement, Rinicker agreed to vacate his office as sheriff and never be associated with law enforcement in Louisiana. He also faced up to 10 years in prison and a fine of $680,000 (*Corrections Journal*, September 22, 1997).

Assessment of Prison Corruption

How should the ethical reasoner view these corrupt acts by correctional officers and administrators? Can manipulation and theft be justified, especially when committed by veteran officials entrusted with leading thousands of others?

From an ethical standpoint, the answer should be an unqualified "No," because (1) The correctional institution is expected to be the civilized party in these relationships, not the prisoner. The inmate is not presumed—or even supposed—to be ethical, but correctional officers are. They are obligated by the laws of the state and professional codes of ethics to act fairly and decently. (2) The fact that the other party to the relationship is a "nasty, wicked inmate" makes such a party no less deserving of justice. (3) If treatment and rehabilitation are the true purposes of corrections, correctional officers should be obliged to act as role models for inmates to emulate once they are ready to reenter society. Through the acts and words of treatment officers, inmates can be induced to rethink their criminal habits and reshape their behavior. However, if prison life continues to reinforce practices of lying, cheating, and stealing, then the process of corrections is not only mutilated, but utterly wasted. (4) The fact that misconduct by correctional officers may seem minor does not make it any more legitimate—given the diminutive world of prisoners. To inmates, the prison is their entire world, the cell is their home, and each action or reaction is amplified as it echoes off the walls surrounding them. (5) The excuse that correctional officers have little choice but to use unethical conduct to maintain control over inmates, while tactically logical, is as unjustifiable as excusing lying to liars or biting the arm of one's child in return for him or her biting yours. Despite the threatening environment in which correctional officers have to operate, in a free society such manipulative behaviors violate natural law (dignity of man), constitutional law (preserving the rights of others), the American Correctional Association's code of ethics (treating inmates fairly), and the obligation of professional officials to develop self-restraint and "maintain courageous calm in the face of danger, scorn, or ridicule."

At this juncture, a few of my students, especially those who work at nearby prison units, display uneasiness and start grumbling, "It is impractical, Professor; it is just unfair to expect prison guards to be so moralistic." "How could a prison be run like that?" In response, I ask, "Would you want your brother or sister to be treated that way if they were over there?" To this, a *fewer* number of students retort, "But no way will they be there." To that I respond, "How sure can you be?" At this point the grumbling begins to dissipate. Nevertheless, they still question: "Well, you tell us, Professor, how can prisons be administered ethically?" To this I rejoin, "Just because we haven't discovered the solution yet doesn't mean we can't. In the meantime, go back and read Maslow's profile of the ethical person; read Plato's treaties on justice; read Rawl's theory of fairness … and if you are still in doubt, try democracy."

What, then, are the characteristics of a "professional" correctional officer? In general terms, they are the same as those expected from any honorable public agent; one who is deeply concerned for issues of honesty, fidelity, and obligation; for the ethical hierarchy of professionalism, Americanism, and humanitarianism, and above all else, for acting in good faith. In specific terms, Pollock identifies such a person as one who treats all inmates fairly, with no favoritism; who does not "always" follow rules to the letter; who is not quick to use force, but is not afraid of using it if it becomes necessary; and who treats inmates in a kind manner, giving them the respect they deserve as human beings (Pollock, 1989:146). More specifically, however, observing the virtue of social justice and denouncing egoism, vindictiveness, and racial prejudice are critical to the makeup of the professional correctional officer in America.

Review Questions

1. Describe the debate about the role of corrections that erupted in the mid-1960s. Address the issues of social defense and retribution.

2. Explain Beccaria's influence on the role of prisons. Under what circumstances did he believe capital punishment was justified?

3. Define the principles that are essential for punishment to be morally acceptable.

4. Explain the moral justification for "retribution" concerning incarceration. On what grounds do opponents disagree?

5. What are the preventative, deterrent, and rehabilitative roles of imprisonment?

6. Explain why we are a "society that loves walls." How does overcrowding cause a serious challenge to the integrity of corrections?

7. Why do some experts believe that pain should be put back in prisons? How do you respond to their statements?

8. How did the advancement of societies in the sixteenth and seventeenth centuries affect the concept of punishment? Discuss how the moral values of the Quakers influenced the treatment of prisoners.

9. Explain how the term *rehabilitation* has changed over time. Do you agree with critics who state that "nothing works"? Why or why not?

10. Describe the classical methods of rehabilitation. Discuss the state of rehabilitation today.

11. Explain the difference between *convicted criminals* and *shadow criminals*. Do you believe that "we're all doing time"? Why or why not?

References

Allen, B., & Bosta, D. (1981). *Games Criminals Play*. Sacramento, CA: Rae John.

American Correctional Association (1990). *The State of Corrections: Proceedings. ACA Annual Conference*, Laurel, MD: American Correctional Association.

American Friends Service Committee (1971). *Struggle for Justice: A Report on Crime and Punishment in America*. New York: Hill and Wang.

Barnes, H. E., & Teeters, N. K. (1959). *New Horizons in Criminology* (3rd ed.). Englewood Cliffs, NJ: Prentice-Hall.

Barry, V. (1982). *Applying Ethics: A Text with Readings*. Belmont, CA: Wadsworth Publishing.

Bartollas, C., Miller, S. J., & Wice, P. B. (1983). *Participants in American Criminal Justice*. Englewood Cliffs, NJ: Prentice-Hall.

Blumberg, A. S., & Niederhoffer, E. (1970). *The Ambivalent Force: Perspectives on the Police*. New York: Holt, Rinehart and Winston.

Carroll, L. (1974). *Hacks, Blacks, and Cons: Race Relations in a Maximum Security Prison*. Lexington, MA: Lexington Books.

Corrections Journal. (1997, September 22).

Crouch, B. M., & Alpert, G. (1982). "Sex and Occupational Socialization among Prison Guards: A Longitudinal Study." *Criminal Justice and Behavior, 9*(2), 159–176.

Crouch, B. M., & Marquart, J. W. (1980). *The Keepers*. Springfield, IL: Charles C Thomas.

Crouch, B. M., & Marquart, J. W. (1989). *An Appeal to Justice: Litigated Reform for Texas Prisons*. Austin: University of Texas Press.

Davidson, T. (1974). *Chicano Prisoners: The Key to San Quentin*. New York: Holt, Rinehart and Winston.

Ekland-Olson, S. (1986). Crowding, Social Control, and Prison Violence: Evidence from the Post-Ruiz Years in Texas. *Law and Society Review, 20*(3), 289–421.

Ellis, D. (1984). Crowding and Prison Violence. *Criminal Justice and Behavior, 11*(3), 277–307.

Farrington, D. P., & Nutall, C. P. (1980). Prison Size, Overcrowding, Prison Violence and Recidivism. *Journal of Criminal Justice, 8*(4), 221–231.

Flanagan,, T. J., & Maguire, K. (Eds.) (1994). *Source Book of Criminal Justice Statistics—1989*. Albany, NY: Hindelang Criminal Justice Research Center.

Fleischer, M. S. (1989). *Warehousing Violence*. Newbury Park, CA: Sage Publications.

Foucault, M. (1973). *Madness and Civilization: A History of Insanity in the Age of Reason*. New York: Vintage Books.

Foucault, M. (1977). *Discipline and Punish: The Birth of the Prison*. New York: Pantheon.

Gaes, G. G., & McGuire, W. J. (1985). Prison Violence: The Contribution of Crowding versus Other Determinants of Prison Assault Rates. *Journal of Research in Crime and Delinquency, 22*(1), 41–65.

Germann, A. C., Day, F. D., & Gallati, R. R. J. (1988). *Introduction to Law Enforcement and Criminal Justice*. Springfield, IL: Charles C Thomas.

Horkheimer, M., & Adorno, T. (1972). *Dialectic of Enlightenment*. New York: Heider & Heider.

Irwin, J. (1980). *Prisons in Turmoil*. Boston: Little, Brown and Company.

Jacobs, J. B. (1976). Prison Violence and Formal Organization. In A. K. Cohen, G. F. Cole & R. G. Bailey (Eds.), *Prison Violence* (pp. 79–87). Lexington, MA: Lexington Books.

Jacobs, J. B. (1977). *Stateville: A Penitentiary in Mass Society*. Chicago: University of Chicago Press.

Jacobs, J. B. (1978). What Prison Guards Think: A Profile of the Illinois Force. *Crime and Delinquency, 24*, 185–196.

Jacobs, J. B. (1983). *New Perspectives on Prisons and Imprisonment*. Ithaca, NY: Cornell University Press.

Jacobs, J. B., & Kraft, L. J. (1983). Race Relations and Guards' Subculture. In J. B. Jacobs (Ed.), *New Perspectives on Prisons and Imprisonment* (pp. 160–177). Ithaca, NY: Cornell University Press.

Lasky, G. L., Gordon, B. C., & Srebalus, D. J. (1986). Occupational Stressors among Federal Correctional Officers Working in Different Security Levels. *Criminal Justice and Behavior, 13*(3), 317–327.

Lombardo, L. X. (1989). *Guards Imprisoned: Correctional Officers at Work* (2nd ed.). Cincinnati, OH: Anderson Publishing Co.

Lozoff, B., & Braswell, M. (1989). *Inner Corrections: Finding Peace and Peace Making.* Cincinnati, OH: Anderson Publishing Co.

Mabli, J., Holley, C. S., Patrick, J., & Walls, J. (1979). Age and Prison Violence: Increasing Age Heterogeneity as a Violence-Reducing Strategy in Prisons. *Criminal Justice and Behavior, 6*(2), 175–186.

MacKenzie, D. L. (1987). Age and Adjustment to Prison: Interaction with Attitudes and Anxiety. *Criminal Justice and Behavior, 14*(4), 427–447.

Maguire, K., & Pastore, A. (1995). *Source Book of Criminal Justice Statistics.* Albany, NY: Hindelang Criminal Justice Research Center.

Mannheim, H. (Ed.) (1970). *Pioneers in Criminology.* (2nd ed.). Montclair, NJ: Patterson-Smith.

Marcus, J. (1996). *The Crime Vaccine: How to End the Crime Epidemic.* Baton Rouge, LA: Claitor's Publishing.

Martinson, R. (1974). What Works? Questions and Answers about Prison Reform. *Public Interest, 35,* Spring.

Massaro, D. R. (1991–1992). Of Crimes and Punishment. In *Annual Editions, Criminal Justice.* Guilford, CT: Dushkin Publishing Group, Inc.

Mathiesen, T. (1990). *Prisons on Trial.* London: Sage Publications.

Nacci, P. L., Teitelbaum, H. E., & Prather, J. (1977). Population Density and Inmate Misconduct Rates in the Federal Prison System. *Federal Probation,* June, 27–38.

Nacci, P. L., Teitelbaum, H. E., & Prather, J. (1977). *Violence in Federal Prisons: The Effect of Population Density on Misconduct.* National Institute of Justice/National Criminal Justice Reference Service.

Newman, D. J., & Anderson, P. R. (1989). *Introduction to Criminal Justice* (4th ed.). New York: Random House.

Newsweek. (1991, May 7).

Pepinsky, H. E. (1989). Peacemaking in Criminology. *The Critical Criminologist, 1*(3), 6–10.

Poole, E. D., & Regoli, R. M. (1980). Role Stress, Custody Orientation, and Disciplinary Actions: A Study of Prison Guards. *Criminology, 18.*

Pollock, J. M. (1989). *Ethics in Crime and Justice: Dilemmas and Decisions.* Pacific Grove, CA: Brooks/Cole Publishing.

Prison Commissioner Is Implicated in Abuse/Georgia Guard Says He Witnessed Incident (1997, July 1). *The Houston Chronicle.*

Quinney, R. E. (1988). The Political Economy of Crime. In R. A. Farrell & V. L. Swigert (Eds.), *Social Deviance* (3rd ed., pp. 134–148). Belmont, CA: Wadsworth Publishing.

Schmalleger, F. (1991). *Criminal Justice Today.* Englewood Cliffs, NJ: Prentice-Hall.

Schwartz, M. D., & Travis, L. F., II. (1997). *Corrections: an Issues Approach* (4th ed.). Cincinnati, OH: Anderson Publishing Co.

Smarto, D. (1989). *Justice and Mercy.* Wheaton, IL: Tyndale Publishers.

Stojkovic, S., Klofas, J., & Kalinich, D. (Eds.) (1990). *The Administration and Management of Criminal Justice Organizations.* Prospect Heights, IL: Waveland Press, Inc.

Sutherland, E. H. (1949). *White-Collar Crime.* New York: Holt, Rinehart and Winston.

Sykes, G. M. (1958). *The Society of Captives.* Princeton, NJ: Princeton University Press.

Sykes, G., & Messinger, S. L. (1960). The Inmates' Social System. In D. Cressey (Ed.), *Theoretical Studies in Social Organization of the Prison* (pp. 5–19). New York: Social Science Research Council.

Teske, R. H. C. (1987, December 20). Putting the Pain Back into the Prisons. *The Houston Chronicle.*

Thomson, O. (1993). *A History of Sin.* New York: Barnes and Noble Books.

Toch, H. (1969). *Violent Men: An Inquiry into the Psychology of Violence.* Chicago: Aldine.

Toch, H. (1978). Is a 'Correctional Officer,' by Any Other Name, a 'Screw'? *Criminal Justice Review, 3*(2), 19–35.

Toch, H. (1978). Social Climate and Prison Violence. *Federal Probation* (December), 21–25.

Toch, H., & Adams, K. (1986). Pathology and Disruptiveness Among Prison Inmates. *Journal of Research in Crime and Delinquency, 23,* 7–21.

Wachtler, S. (1997). *After the Madness: A Judges' Own Prison Memoir.* New York: Random.

Walker, S. (1989). *Sense and Nonsense about Crime: A Policy Guide* (2nd ed.). Pacific Grove, CA: Brooks/Cole Publishing.

Weisheit, R. A., & Alexander, D. M. (1988). Juvenile Justice Philosophy and the Demise of Parens Patriae. *Federal Probation, 52.*

Williamson, H. E. (1990). *The Corrections Profession.* Newbury Park, CA: Sage Publications.

13

Ethics of Probation and Parole

Healing a limb is inspiring, but isn't the healing and restoration of a shattered life a greater miracle?

Manford Craig

I was in prison and you came to visit me.

Matthew 25:36

Remember those in prison as if you were their fellow prisoners, and those who are mistreated as if you yourselves were suffering.

Hebrews 13:3

Incarceration is a life in an evil and corrupting atmosphere with hope dimmed and common decencies smothered.

Karl A. Menninger

What You Will Learn from This Chapter

You will learn the professional orientation of probation and parole, the dilemma of the borderless community, and the ethics of community-based corrections. You will also learn the work strategies of probation/parole practitioners, the common unethical practices in probation/parole, and the four typologies of probation/parole officers.

You will also learn the historical background of community-based corrections, the arguments for and against these programs, the views of Morris and Tonry, who consider community-based corrections too lenient, and of von Hirsh, who considers them too severe.

Key Terms and Definitions

Ethical Imperative of Probation/Parole is the obligation of probation and parole officers to protect the community and the offenders.

Community-Based Corrections is an alternative to institutional corrections. Instead of relying totally on incarceration, it places more offenders on probation, therefore enhancing their chances for rehabilitation without separating them from their communities or contributing to prison overcrowding.

Intensive Probation is a method of probation that imposes more severe restraints on the probationers than those imposed by normal probation conditions. It involves stricter supervision, closer monitoring, restrictions on one's freedom of movement, and mandatory participation in treatment programs.

Overview

Traditionally, probation and parole were the stepchildren of American corrections. The dominant feature—both politically and financially—has been institutional corrections. Consequently, probation and parole have always been starved for attention. Today, this picture has almost totally vanished. Probation and parole have become the most rapidly increasing forms of corrections, with probation being the most common sentence given to offenders (Walker, 1989:210).

Probation is a sentence meted out by a court in lieu of a prison term, and parole is a form of pardon granted before a prison sentence is completed. From a correctional standpoint, probation and parole represent perhaps the most rational model, because under the rubric of community-based corrections, they seem more humane, cost effective, and successful than prisons. The philosophy of probation and parole is fairly basic: Society is willing to take a chance on the offenders who are willing to help themselves; they are allowed to remain in the community, have a job, raise a family, and earn a living, as long as they abandon crime. Offenders are to be supervised in accordance with a prestructured plan crafted by the court and the probation expert. If the offender reneges or fails to keep his *parole* (simply meaning "promise"), his privileges are revoked and he is returned to prison.

There is not much doubt that the initial purposes of probation and parole were as noble as they were motivated by goodness. Probationers and parolees were far less risky individuals than they are today; indeed, most of them were property offenders. There were not many mentally retarded, psychologically disturbed, or chemically dependent offenders, as is the case today. By the same token, probation and parole officers' jobs were substantively challenging. They were drawn to the field because they were interested in people, took pride in their personal skills, and worked with offenders in both the office and the field (Friel, 1990).

Probation and parole officers came from a background in the social sciences and believed that they had the capacity to substantively change other people. They did not use scientific methods like risk-needs assessment and instruments with complex grids and boxes, and viewed themselves as intuitively competent to perform such tasks. Probation and parole administrators came from the ranks of good probation and parole officers. They were good role models of what probation and parole stood for, and society understood what those institutions were and what the core technology was. These managers were people who rose to the top because they were devoted to the mission, upheld a high work ethic, and were able to effectively supervise the supervisors of probation and parole (Friel, 1990).

The Professional Orientation of Probation and Parole

Compared with police or corrections personnel, probation and parole officers reflect an exceptional knowledge orientation. Probation and parole agencies require a college degree for employment. Unless a department requires additional experience (which is becoming more common today), new practitioners are hired from college or university settings, where they probably have majored in social work, sociology, or criminal justice studies (Bartollas et al., 1983:206). Hired at a relatively mature age (as opposed to many police officers and correctional officers), they bring with them an impressive social service orientation, an informed view of criminal behavior, and in most cases, a professional orientation toward the delivery of social services.

Another reason for the professional orientation of probation and parole officers is the "civilian" nature of their departments. Most agencies are organized along a "corporate" structure in which they serve a professional commission, as in the case of probation, or an executive board, as in the case of parole. Unlike the semi-military structure of police and correctional institutions, in which emphasis is placed on discipline and obedience, the environment of probation and parole departments lends itself to more reasoning and greater reliance on self-control. This professional orientation is further enhanced as new officers learn the information necessary to provide probation and parole services. Focus is usually on learning the general philosophy, the goals and objectives of the profession, and the ways and means of effectively achieving such objectives. Of particular note, moreover, is the fact that most probation and parole officers tend to take professional training much more seriously than police or corrections officials and eagerly absorb the new technologies offered by qualified in-house and outside instructors.

A third reason for the professional orientation of probation and parole officers is their method of operation. In the vast majority of cases, probation and parole officers face no emergencies of the kind faced by police or corrections officers, usually carry no weapons, and are relatively less concerned for their own safety. Officers are assigned a "case-load" of offenders, who become their personal "clients." They meet them on a regular basis, evaluate their family backgrounds, and pursue a treatment plan that can fit their individual needs. Improvement in the offender's behavior produces instant gratification for the handler. Unlike the "herdlike relationship" that exists in police and corrections, this "client relationship" entails a personal investment, allowing the practitioner an opportunity to "see the result" in a more tangible manner.

A fourth reason for the professional orientation of probation and parole officers is the sense of professional worth that they develop by their proximity to the centers of justice allocation—the courts. Especially in probation, in which the officer normally serves under the intimate guidance of a judge, practitioners become more able to appreciate their impact on exacting justice. Involvement in the presentence investigation (PSI) is a perfect example. It can provide a gratifying sense of accomplishment when contrasted with the meaninglessness and powerlessness experienced by other criminal justice practitioners. Unlike issuing traffic tickets or filing mundane criminal charges, as most police officers do, or performing "turnkey" functions, as most correctional officers do, preparing a PSI report can represent involvement in the justice process, because the officers assess the past and the present, as well as the future of an offender on trial. PSI reports can be detrimental to the continued liberty of the offender, because judges consider them integral to the sentencing process, often relying on them as "the best guide to intelligent sentencing" (Murrah, 1963, as cited in Stojkovic et al., 1990:400). Indeed, national studies show that PSI recommendations are adopted by judges between 66% and 95% of the time (Abadinsky, 1991). Moreover, PSI reports have far-reaching implications in devising a plan for probation or parole supervision. While criticism of PSIs is abundant (Dawson, 1969; Gaylin, 1974; Kingsnorth & Rizzo, 1979; Rosecrance, 1968), the power that PSIs offer the probation officer can certainly reinforce his or her professional orientation.

The Probation Mystique

The probation mystique has been altogether different from that of police or institutional corrections. It began as a peaceful movement, devoid of violence, malice, deceit, or even indifference. It was based on the presumption of goodwill and giving offenders a second chance. The probation movement, at its core, glorifies the story of humanness, voluntariness, sympathy, self-denial, and mercy. John Augustus (1784–1859) was recognized as the "apostle" of probation and the hero of the story. He was a man who "voluntarily attended sessions of criminal court in the 1850s, and willingly offered to take selected offenders *into his home* as an alternative to incarceration (Souryal, 1996:6).

The Augustus mystique tells a very "ethical" story that should be internalized in the minds of all criminal justice students and practitioners. He was not famous, rich, or intellectually prominent, nor did he hold a public office (indeed, he was a shoe repairman). Yet Augustus was a rational man who was gifted with moral values and a unique sense of vision. He saw social wrong and tried to correct it, and saw an opportunity to do good and took advantage of it. What he offered was neither socially necessary nor economically attractive, yet he saw it as a moral imperative. "Why," he most likely asked, "should society subject its people to the dangers of imprisonment if it were able to treat them by more ethical means?" The answer to this question constitutes the principle of *social obligation*—the duty of a "good society" to make every effort possible to redeem its delinquents, especially because "we are all fallible, and the demise of anyone diminishes us all." He probably also realized that "the civility of any society can be measured by how few prisoners it keeps" (Souryal, 1996).

For all practical purposes, the Augustus legacy reflects Maslow's image of the transcendent person (the profile we first met in Chapter 1). Augustus must have been one who delights in bringing about justice; tries to set things right; tries to clean messy situations; and sacrifices his time and money to accomplish all that. Had Augustus lived today, he most likely would have disagreed with boot camps, wearing uniforms, and carrying a weapon, and would have approached probationers armed only with *knowledge* and *goodwill*.

Idealistic as Augustus must have been, his legacy produced a viable probation system. By the end of the nineteenth century, probation in America became a widely accepted form of community service. By 1925 all 48 states had adopted probation legislation and the National Probation Act enabled federal district court judges to appoint probation officers and impose probationary terms (Schmalleger, 1995:407). Probation today is not only a well-established social institution, but also a fairly universal phenomenon as well. Its meteoric progress attests to its moral sensibility. The validity of present-day probation, however, cannot be divorced from the moral idealism of Augustus, because without the "ideals" he started, there could not have been the "realities" we now possess (Souryal, 1996).

The Borderless Community

Perhaps the most significant responsibility of probation and parole officers is supervising offenders. Underlying this responsibility is a utilitarian obligation to protect the community, on one hand, and a Rawlsian obligation to protect the interests of the offender, on the other. Balancing these two obligations represents the *ethical imperative* of probation and parole. But in order to better understand the "reality" of this imperative, we should first be familiar with the environment of community-based supervision from the standpoint of both the offender and the probation or parole officer.

Offenders placed on probation or parole today may have committed almost any type of criminal offense and may range from first-time offenders to career criminals. The number of offenders placed on probation or released on parole can also vary considerably, depending on the political and fiscal climate in the jurisdiction, existing laws, levels of prison overcrowding, and the prevailing philosophy toward probation and parole. Naturally, there are bound to be substantial variations with respect to the type and extent of supervision conditions imposed by the court or the parole board. Moreover, the individuals under supervision may vary considerably in terms of the personal problems they face (for example, family difficulties, unemployment, educational needs, or alcohol or drug abuse) (Travis et al., 1983:159).

The officers, on the other hand, are expected to be "all things" to all people. They are expected to perform paradoxical functions: surveillance, much as police do, and treatment, much as correctional officers do. But unlike police or corrections, probation and parole officers are inundated with excessive caseloads, progress reports, and unnecessary paperwork. It is not unusual that community resources are unavailable or disorganized, or that those in charge are unwilling to offer the service (Travis et al., 1983:160). As a result, the professional orientation probation and parole officers bring to their jobs suffers in several aspects. As Friel describes, this ambivalent environment forces devoted officers to "trash out the definition of their profession and get hoodwinked into the shell game" (Friel, 1990:41).

Some of the factors contributing to the borderless community of probation and parole are as follows.

First, probation officers are seen as notoriously underpaid. If they are under county jurisdiction, as are more than two-thirds of juvenile probation officers, their pay is likely to be even less (Bartollas et al., 1983:213). This situation makes it nearly impossible for an officer with a family to survive without a second job or without the spouse working. Low pay also contributes to low self-esteem, which in turn impedes one's sense of self-realization.

Second, the unsettling attitudes of the public and other criminal justice practitioners continue to frustrate the officers' sense of professionalism. Probation and parole officers operate in a system that has been widely criticized for being ineffective (Cullen & Gilbert, 1982; Sechrest et al., 1979). Parole agencies, in particular, have been labeled the "unwanted child" of the criminal justice system, a label that arouses the fury of both conservatives and liberals. Conservatives accuse parole agencies of turning dangerous criminals loose too soon to prey on law-abiding people, while liberals indict parole boards for making arbitrary release decisions that discriminate against or victimize minority group members.

Third, the politicization of probation and parole agencies seems to continue unabated. Managers of parole agencies, in particular, are compelled to accommodate the whims of uninformed policy makers who demand that they carry out illegitimate diversionary measures as political ploys to alleviate prison overcrowding. In this regard, Friel, in "Intergovernmental Relations: Correctional Policy and the Great American Shell Game," writes,

> The policymaker says, "Psst, parole guy, I don't know what you do, but they tell me you watch guys for 50 cents a day. Here is what I want you to do. Every time we need a bed in the prison, you get a guy out. Around midnight, you slip him out and keep him out. You take this huddled mass yearning to breathe free, drug dependent, mentally retarded, illiterate with no work ethic, psychopathetic deviant, and you keep him out, right? We will tell the public we are tough on crime, and no taxes. OK? ... Everybody agree?"
>
> Friel, 1990:41

Given this perplexing environment, it comes as no surprise that probation and parole officers—despite their professional orientation—resent their "borderless community"—one that is ambiguous, contradictory, and politically vulnerable. Consequently, in such an environment, job dissatisfaction, stress, and burnout are considered "very real occupational problems," and disillusionment with the noble cause of community corrections becomes common. In *Burnout in Probation and Corrections,* Whitehead points out that in most organizations, employment is seen as an early-career position that most people eventually leave. Few people, Whitehead adds, "stay in community corrections work for their entire professional careers. Turnover is often high, burnout is epidemic, and work cynicism pervades the office" (Whitehead, 1989:3).

The Yellow Wind

In Israeli mythology a "yellow wind" is a nasty east wind that comes once every few decades. It brings with it high temperatures, deafening noise, and mountains of dust. It aggravates the "shepherds and the sheep, but neither the lizards nor the locust." After a short while, the yellow wind suddenly stops, accomplishing nothing. The wise man sets his back to the yellow wind, and turns not around until it blows over.

By the late 1960s and early 1970s, a yellow wind blasted the institutions of probation and parole. As a product of increased violence, attributable to the baby boom generation hitting puberty, the civil rights movement, and the antiwar movement, people began to see an America that was nasty and violent. Subsequently, as Friel chronicles in "Intergovernmental Relations: Correctional Policy and the Great American Shell Game," "Society declared war on everything—we had a war in Vietnam, a war on illiteracy, and a war on crime." (Friel, 1990:38). The rhetoric of war is particularly pleasing because it galvanizes society. The rhetoric presupposes that there are good guys and bad guys, that there are strategies and tactics, and that there is an ultimate victory—all of which, Friel believes, is a myth when it comes to crime; the unending plague common since Cain. As a result, Friel asserts, society demanded action and government acted with severe countertrends.

Among the first victims of the yellow wind were the legacies of prisons. They were envisioned as a defunct concept: expensive and ineffective. Consequently, a moratorium on prison construction was put into effect, giving rise to a scramble for alternative methods of corrections. Community-based corrections—as a "new and improved" version of traditional probation and parole—emerged, capturing the imagination of a perplexed correctional community. Many states were attracted to the concept because they did not have to spend money on prisons (which do not bring any votes anyway), satisfying society's outcry for "getting tough on crime" and avoiding raising taxes.

In 1996, for instance, the number of adults on probation and parole reached a record high. State and federal agencies reported that 2,343,220 were on probation, 555,183 on parole, and 155,327 under mixed supervision—at an annual budget of $3,166,286,652. In the same year, the male population on probation and parole constituted 83% of the population of all those under correctional supervision and about 2.86% of all adult males (Criminal Justice Institute, 1996).

Probation and parole practitioners felt the brunt of the yellow wind more than anyone else in criminal justice. With large numbers of offenders came the need for modernization, which brought about bureaucratization, which in turn led to occupational stress and premature burnout. Many of the practitioners became disenchanted with their jobs, many succumbed to the *bureaucratic trance*, and many sought employment elsewhere. In order to accommodate the sudden change, scientific methods were introduced, including electronic monitoring and surveillance techniques, in effect destroying the original philosophy of personal attention and compassion. Instead of a benign work environment, an officious environment analogous to a prison environment emerged—one that such agencies were originally designed to replace.

Because probation and parole agencies have so much in common and practitioners of both agencies face similar role conflicts and frustrations, in the following discussion no distinction will be made between them. To avoid undue complexity, both functions will be discussed as one and the same.

Romancing the Stone or Stoning the Romance: Ethics of Community-Based Corrections

In a well-known Hollywood action film, a couple of adventurers went to the Amazon jungle in search of a precious stone, but after dangerous encounters with native tribesmen, professional thieves, and, of course, encounters with exploding trucks and man-eating crocodiles, they almost lost what they had fought for—the stone itself. In a sense, this illustrates how society today handles the jewel we call community-based corrections.

In a less romantic scene, Americans can be seen as experts in building walls when the bricks are straight; if the bricks are not straight and the wall is warped, they pass it off to the next generation to fix. The nation has repeatedly done so with regard to the national debt, national health care, and education, and we may be doing the same today with corrections. While the goals of community-based corrections represent the admirable virtues of human dignity, self-realization, and a utilitarian concern for the welfare of society—all under the canopy of social justice—the means of conducting probation and parole duties indicate a "comedy of errors" similar to that in policing and prisons. Once more, society fails to stand up to the ends–means dilemma: the seduction of accomplishing glorious things the wrong way.

Community-based corrections is, in essence, a value-neutral concept; it is neither inherently good nor does it threaten unexpected harm. As such, the practice produces goodness when it is applied ethically, and produces evil the rest of the time. However, the concept of community-based corrections seems to have degenerated in a miasma of indifference wrapped in political propaganda. What some may view as the most moral reform package ever invented, others may consider a social cop-out—either disproportionate to the gravity of crime, or unduly intrusive on human dignity or the privacy of third parties (von Hirsh, 1990).

Proponents of community-based corrections justify its goodness on the basis of its apparent effectiveness and record of success—the lower rate of return to crime. Critics, on the other hand, argue that the system may only appear successful in a "corporate sense," yet it is qualitatively deficient—it falls short of delivering the benefits it is billed to deliver. It is noteworthy, however, that while supporters of community-based corrections focus invariably on its contribution to humanity (as opposed to harsh treatment in prisons), detractors, while equally critical of prisons, raise a broader, rather contradictory range of ethical issues. These include leniency of punishment, on one hand (the Morris and Tonry thesis), and undue severity (the von Hirsh thesis), on the other.

The Case for Community-Based Corrections

Advocates of community-based corrections argue that the practice is ethically superior to institutional corrections because it offers several distinct benefits: freedom from incarceration at the humanistic level; cost effectiveness at the utilitarian level; and maintaining family relationships at the socio-organic level. Nothing else is considered to be of greater moral significance. In sum, the case for community-based corrections seems to be artificially constructed as a convenient scheme to alleviate the adverse image and high cost of incarceration. A brief summary of the principal benefits of community-based corrections, from the prescriptive of its advocates, follows.

Freedom from incarceration. Even with the considerable advances in penological practices in the twenty-first century, the perception of prisons as doing more harm than good lingers. Community-based corrections, on the other hand, maintains some semblance of the social qualities of free life. Community-based programs are not considered "total institutions," and penalties involved are not perceived as "real punishments." After all, they do not involve high walls, cell blocks, window bars, curfew requirements, and other degrading trappings of imprisonment. Furthermore, community-based programs make every effort to spare offenders the psychological damage of living under a totalitarian community created and administered to reinforce inferiority and debasement. Critics, as we will see, question this benefit, asserting that probation, despite any benevolent label given to it, is still punishment and, at times, can be as cruel as imprisonment.

Cost effectiveness. The cost of incarceration has escalated in recent years. In 2005, the estimated daily cost per bed was $48.23, not including capital investment, costs of operation, food, medical services, and other "invisible" costs (Bureau of Justice Statistics, 2005). Community-based programs, on the other hand, are operated at an estimated annual cost of $3,425 per probationer/parolee (Amnesty International Report, 2004). Moreover, because the offender usually maintains employment while under supervision, the "invisible" costs do not accrue. Instead, the offender usually contributes to his or her upkeep through taxes, social security, family support, and in some cases, restitution to victims. Thus, the general perception is that while prisons are financial liabilities, community-based corrections programs are assets. Critics refute this benefit by suggesting that the idea of immediate savings as a result of substituting a prison sentence by probation is a false assumption. True savings, they assert, cannot accrue unless substantial numbers are taken out of prison so that a prison or a wing of the prison may be closed. That, critics add, does not seem an immediate likelihood in most American jurisdictions (Morris & Tonry, 1990:18).

Family relationships. As Newman and Anderson (1989) state, community-based corrections help avoid "social surgery"; that is, the severing of a person's family and community relationships. In contrast to prison, community-based corrections provide a local base from which the offender continues to receive support from family members, friends, church members, and other sources. Furthermore, depending on the offender's needs, agencies such as Alcoholics Anonymous, drug treatment centers, and marital and vocational counseling, as well as religious organizations can all be utilized toward the person's self-realization. Such services tend to satisfy the offender's psychological needs, reinforce his or her self-esteem, and perhaps help purify his or her sinful soul. Critics, as we will also see, question this benefit, asserting that the punitiveness of probation may very well disturb family relations and further complicate one's self-esteem (von Hirsh, 1990:163).

From an ethical standpoint, the case for community-based corrections must be considered a worthy step on the road toward instilling humanity in the conduct of criminal justice. In contrast to the degradation of prison, this method of corrections signifies a moral concern for

ETHICS IN CRIMINAL JUSTICE: IN SEARCH OF THE TRUTH

the individual, one that is consistent with the natural law ethics of "dignity of man," the constitutional ethics of individualized treatment, and perhaps the religious ethics of redemption. The offender in community-based corrections is treated as a responsible person, capable of upholding moral obligations toward self, family, and community, as well as making restitution for the offense committed. More important, however, is the common perception of community-based programs as a huge economic saving, regardless of whether they advance the objective of rehabilitation—the principal purpose behind its theory.

The Case against Community-Based Corrections

Critics of community-based corrections do not question the movement's tendency to humanize the correctional process. Harsh as imprisonment is, its deprivations are manifest, and so is the need to limit its use. Critics nevertheless argue that this real—or contrived—focus on humanity may obscure more serious moral issues related to justice and equity and the rights of offenders.

Two notable critics have examined the state of community-based corrections in considerable detail and forwarded adequate reasoning for criticism. Morris and Tonry, in *Between Prison and Probation* (1990), argue that the practice of probation is essentially too lenient and should be integrated into a more effective system of intermediate sanctions. In contrast, in "The Ethics of Community-Based Corrections" (1990), von Hirsh argues that community-based corrections may be too severe and may violate significant ethical principles that must be addressed before the practice is considered an appropriate means for noncustodial penalties.

The Leniency View of Morris and Tonry

In their thesis, Morris and Tonry point out that the correctional system in America is, in general, both too lenient and too severe; too lenient, as there are many on probation who should be subject to tighter controls in the community; and too severe, because many of those in prison and jail would present no serious threat to community safety if they were under control in the community (Morris & Tonry, 1990:3).

In reference to the current theory of corrections, the authors state most directly that

> convicted criminals should not be spared punitive responses to their crimes; there is no point in imposing needless suffering, but effective sentencing will normally involve the curtailment of freedom, either behind walls or in the community, large measures of coercion, and enforced diminutions of freedom; this is entirely properly regarded as punishment. The language of treatment, reform, and rehabilitation

has been corrupted by unenforced and uncritically evaluated good intentions. We fool ourselves—or worse, pretend—if we fail to acknowledge that the intrusions into people's lives that result from criminal punishment are unpleasant and painful.

Morris & Tonry, 1990:5

Having explained their view of what punishment ought to be and justifying the need to restore "real punishment" to the correctional process, Morris and Tonry characterize the state of contemporary probation by stating,

> [Probation] in many cities has degenerated into ineffectiveness under the pressure of excessive caseloads and inadequate resources. For certain categories of offenders now on probation, some though not all could be better subjected to more intensive controls than probation now provides.

Morris & Tonry, 1990:6–10

In their quest to propagate a system of *intermediate punishments* as a rational (and, presumably, more just) sentencing system, the authors proposed a hierarchy of sanctions, starting with capital punishment and ending with electronic monitoring. Intermediate levels include prison, fines, house arrest, probation, intermittent imprisonment, forfeiture, and restitution. Details of these punishments will not be discussed, because they are fairly complex and are of lesser relevance to the discussion of ethics of probation. At the probation level, however, the authors particularly noted the propriety of intensive probation. The authors underscore intensive probation as "a mechanism by which reality can be brought to all intermediate punishments" (Morris & Tonry, 1990:11). They further assert that "intensive probation has the specific capacity of both controlling offenders in the community and facilitating their growth to crime-free lives" (Morris & Tonry, 1990:11). In the next segment we will discuss intensive probation because of its significance to effective probation and electronic monitoring, two of the most attractive—yet perhaps ethically questionable—intermediate sentences.

Intensive Probation

Morris and Tonry characterize this method of probation as a more intensive withdrawal of autonomy than ordinary probation. While conditions of intensive probation may vary from state to state, the central feature is that more control is exerted over the offender than with standard conditions of probation. These extra control mechanisms invariably involve restrictions on liberty of movement, coercion into treatment programs, employment obligations, or all three.

The intensive probation program in Georgia has been highly acclaimed as a model for other jurisdictions. The program is a judicially imposed package (as opposed to Massachusetts, where the decision is made administratively by the probation department), the characteristics of which are (1) small caseloads for team supervision, each team consisting of two officers (a probation officer and a surveillance officer); (2) each team supervises about 25 offenders; (3) each team is authorized to enforce a variety of conditions, including curfews, employment, community service, and drug and alcohol monitoring; (4) at least five face-to-face contacts each week; and (5) offenders pay fees for service ranging from $10 to $50 per month, the amount being set by the sentencing judge.

From an ethical perspective, however, Morris and Tonry do not address the moral implications of intensive probation; namely, the *direction of intensification* in terms of any added capacity to promote rehabilitation. Little mention, if any, is made regarding visionary means by which the probationers' behavior can be modified or their relationships with society improved; for example, intensified psychological or spiritual counseling, intensified academic or vocational schooling, or intensified means for locating gainful employment. If these directions are not the impetus for intensification, then what is being described as "intensive" is simply an intensified effort at individual deterrence—not to commit crime during the duration of probation. But in the philosophy of probation, this goal must be considered secondary at best. All offenders would eventually be released from probation, whether intensive or standard, and unless a redeeming change away from crime could be started "within" the person, no real merit can be claimed by intensive programs over standard programs, except perhaps the negative merit of wasted cost. Furthermore, it is rather peculiar reasoning to argue that a probationer who has been compelled to meet with his or her probation officer five times per week (as opposed to once or twice) and was forced to endure greater punitive restrictions would turn out to be a better citizen than someone who was not, for that reason only.

Another ethical consideration can be raised pertaining to the requirement of paying service fees. Although most offenders will probably not object to such a condition because it is their exit tax out of prison, in principle the requirement is ethically questionable on at least four counts: (1) As the sovereign entity, the state has an obligatory interest to reform all of its "delinquent children" as a means of protecting society, and because the state governs the correctional system, it is then obliged by social arrangement (remember Rawls), by legal tradition, or for that matter, by the absence of alternative means, to accommodate its "offenders," free of charge, for as long as it takes. If that is not the case, prison inmates should be required to pay for their cell space, meals, showers, medical services, and custodial costs. And because placing offenders on probation is a "greater interest" to society than keeping them in prison (where they remain idle, cost more, and pay nothing), requiring probation fees must be unreasonable and inequitable. While some may argue that the probationer has an option to accept or refuse probation, given the "boogey man of prison," such an option does not amount to a fair choice. The requirement to pay service fees can, of course, be even more unjust if the individual cannot afford to pay or would be seriously harmed by diverting badly needed earnings to pay for probation purposes. While there are certainly legal safeguards against revoking the probation of indigents, such provisions, in themselves do not make the original issue of paying fees any more ethical. (2) To impose a probation sentence, but make it contingent upon paying service fees can be equally unjust, because it could lead to the imprisonment of low-risk criminals who cannot afford to pay and the release on probation of more dangerous offenders who can. (3) Because one of the prominent claims of probation is to create the opportunity for offenders to be gainfully employed so as to be able to pay their taxes, requiring a service fee—without which one's opportunity to become gainfully employed may be seriously impaired—amounts to the imposition of a poll tax, a policy prohibited in all civilized laws. (4) If, hypothetically, all probationers decided not to pay service fees, the only alternative left for the state is to imprison them at a much greater cost to society than keeping them on probation at no cost. Would that be a rational or desirable choice by the state, especially given the astronomical rise in prison costs today?

Electronic Monitoring

Electronic monitoring in itself is an enforcement mechanism for the practice of house arrest, a form of intermediate punishment. As a result, an industry has developed to market monitoring devices. Obviously, none of the systems in use is foolproof; each has its share of failures, false alarms, and hidden costs. The presumption, however, is that these problems will be solved and the system will become reliable and affordable (Morris & Tonry, 1990:215).

At present, there are three main systems of electronic monitoring: *active, passive,* and *tracking.*

Active telecommunication systems consist of a small transmitter, strapped to the ankle or wrist of the offender, that emits a signal to a receiver-dialer unit connected by the offender's telephone to a centrally located computer. Provided that the offender remains within a 150- to 200-foot radius of the receiver-dialer, no interruption in the signal occurs. If there is an interruption, the receiver-dialer conveys this fact to the central computer. Such a signal is also transmitted if there is interference with the strap that attaches the transmitter to the offender. This system provides constant monitoring.

Passive systems are slightly different, but are still based on the technology of connecting a telephone and a centrally located computer. Tracking systems are considerably different because they are built on radio technology that has been used to track wild and domestic animals. A transmitter worn by the offender emits a constant radio signal to a portable receiver in the monitoring officer's car when he or she is sufficiently close to pick up the signal (at present, about a city block). The probation or parole officer can, at any time, locate the offender (Morris & Tonry, 1990:215).

Several ethical concerns have been raised regarding electronic monitoring. They revolve around the issues of class bias and ability to pay for the service. The latter issue is similar to the requirement to pay probation fees, which has been discussed. The difficulty of paying service fees can of course be more severe in the case of electronic monitoring. Given the higher amortized cost for installing and maintaining such sophisticated equipment, not many offenders are in a position to meet such fees. This leaves us with the other major issue—class bias.

The issue of class bias stems from the fact that for offenders to qualify for electronic monitoring, they must first have a home and a telephone; however, not every offender has both. This requirement unavoidably creates a tendency to apply house arrest and electronic monitoring to the more privileged and to deny it to the indigent. For example, all offenders, regardless of offense, who are homeless or staying at public shelters or cheap motels are prima facie ineligible. This is a striking violation of the basic principle of equality under the premises of social justice theory; "inequalities can only be accepted if in such a manner that offers the greatest benefit to the least advantaged (Borchert & Stewart, 1986:303).

Class bias is particularly worrisome because most electronic monitoring legislations do not define "a home." Without a clear definition, electronic monitoring programs may raise serious constitutional concerns related to the provision of equal protection under the law. The Kentucky house arrest program is one that has defined what a "home" is for the purposes of electronic monitoring. The Kentucky legislation defines a "home" to include hospitals, hospices, nursing centers, halfway houses, group homes, and residential treatment centers. However, the enabling act does not include a single property in which more than one family, other than the offender's, reside (Morris & Tonry, 1990:2). While this omission may not sound alarming, the question, in principle, may lead to a wider variety of inequities that may not be easy to explain or justify.

Evidence of class bias has been apparent in the increased use of electronic monitoring for those convicted of driving under the influence of alcohol, a tendency resented by victim groups, such as Mothers Against Drunk Driving, who see it as both an insufficiently severe sanction and as a class-biased sanction (Morris & Tonry, 1990:218). Consider, for example, the 1988 case of John Zaccaro Jr., the son of former vice presidential candidate Geraldine Ferraro. He was sentenced to 4 months of house arrest for selling cocaine. He spent his sentence in his $1,500-a month luxury apartment in Vermont, with maid service, cable TV, and other expensive amenities. Zaccaro's prosecutor has reportedly observed, "This guy is a drug felon and he's living in conditions that 99.9 percent of the people of Vermont couldn't afford" (Schmalleger, 1995:394).

The Severity View of von Hirsh

This view is based on the assumption that community-based corrections—and probation in particular—may not be a benign, friendly, or ethical intermediate sentence, as is popularly thought. The punitive character of probation and parole is often less visible to those who espouse them. Because these sanctions are often packaged as more humane alternatives to the harsh sanction of imprisonment, the deviations they themselves cause are often overlooked. Von Hirsh comments, "Because the offender no longer has to suffer the pains of confinement, why cavil at the pains the new program makes him or her suffer in the community?" (von Hirsh, 1990:163).

Von Hirsh raises three specific issues pertaining to the severity of community-based sentences: (1) proportionality or desert, (2) restrictions against humiliation and degradation, and (3) concerns for the intrusive nature of punishment upon the privacy of third persons. In the enthusiasm for community-based sanctions, von Hirsh argues that such issues have been easily overlooked. The following is a brief discussion of von Hirsh's views.

Proportionality and Desert

According to von Hirsh, the proportionality of punishment (its level of severity or leniency) has been sacrificed in community-based corrections, because such programs have principally been evaluated in terms of their effectiveness rather than fairness. If a program (for example, an intensive supervision scheme) seems to "work" in the sense that its participants have a low rate of recidivism, then it is said to be a "good" program (von Hirsh, 1990:163). Part of the attraction of these programs has been that their more punitive character gives them greater public credibility.

Yet noncustodial measures, especially those pertaining to intensive supervision, home detention, and day fines, are also punishments that involve substantial deprivations, according to von Hirsh: Intensive supervision and home detention curtail an offender's freedom of movement; a community-service program exacts enforced labor; and a day fine may inflict substantial economic losses. Advocates of community-based corrections seem to overlook the fact that many offenses committed by those under supervision are not serious enough to make the sanctions proportional in response. In a sense, von Hirsh seems to imply a hypocritical streak—if not an outright deception—on the part of community-based enthusiasts. He states, "Intensive supervision programs tend to be applied to offenders convicted of the least serious felonies because program organizers feel that such persons would be more likely to cooperate" (1990:164). Some sanctions, remarks von Hirsh, are nevertheless quite severe, given the low level of seriousness of the crime committed.

Restrictions against Humiliation and Degradation

In his examination of what constitutes "dignified treatment" of offenders, von Hirsh reiterates several of the previously mentioned themes in this chapter: (1) Punishment is unjust if it is of such a nature as to be degrading or dehumanizing in terms of its intrusion on the individual under supervision. (2) Intrusion depends not on technology, but on the extent to which the practice affects the dignity and privacy of those intruded upon. For instance, frequent unannounced home visits may be much more disturbing than an electronic telephone monitor that verifies the offender's presence. (3) Legal intrusion (in accordance with constitutional provisions) may not meet the minimum obligations of community-based personnel to treat offenders with dignity. Convicted felons, adds von Hirsh, are still members of the moral community and should be treated as such. (4) Enforcement sanctions that are grossly humiliating should be ruled out, because justifying indignity on the basis of creating (or reinforcing) a noncustodial sanction with a "punitive bite" is ethically unjustifiable.

Implications Concerning the Privacy of Third Parties

Because community-based corrections places the offender into settings in which others live, the offender's punishment spills over into the lives of others. Von Hirsh suggests that concern for the privacy of others has been grossly overlooked. He points out, for example, that home visits may be potentially shaming to the offender, in part because of the presence of unconvicted third-party witnesses. Such visits could affect those witnesses, diminishing their own sense of privacy. Von Hirsh proposes that community-based corrections personnel should be sensitive to these dangers and earnestly attempt to reduce their adverse impact. Toward that end, he suggests that because the impact on third persons can be so critical, probation officers—in choosing among noncustodial penalties—should be extremely cognizant of the need to ameliorate such embarrassments (1990:171).

The very notions raised by von Hirsh bring us back to the imperative of ethics in the treatment of offenders, whether in prison or in the community. This imperative should be universally accepted because (1) regardless of how we view offenders, human beings should be treated with dignity—it is the law of nature that preceded the human existence; (2) regardless of how we view offenders, inequitable treatment is inconsistent with constitutional law and the spirit of justice; (3) regardless of how we view offenders, it is in the interest of a civilized society to treat people with decency, especially in light of the doctrine of "we are all doing time"; (4) regardless of how we view offenders, carrying out the ethical imperative can purify our souls and realize our yearning for a more peaceful society; and (5) regardless of how we view offenders, extending goodness to others can also bring us more into God's grace.

Work Strategies of Probation and Parole Practitioners

Given their professional orientation, the complexity of their work environment, and their career challenges, probation and parole officers engage in and pursue numerous work strategies. Abadinsky (1991) cites a variety of such strategies. The following are among the more significant strategies:

1. *Detection*. This strategy involves identifying when a client is at risk or when the community is at risk. It serves three basic objectives: (1) identifying the individuals who are experiencing difficulty or who are in danger of becoming a risk to the community; (2) identifying conditions in the community that may contribute to the client's personal problems (for example, lack of jobs, lack of training, availability of drugs); and (3) determining whether the community is at risk from the probationer or parolee and taking steps to protect the community.

2. *Brokering*. This strategy seeks to steer clients to existing services that can be beneficial to them. The essential benefit of this strategy is the physical hookup of the client with the source of help. Examples include locating a job or a training facility where a client can be educated or retrained.

3. *Advocating*. This strategy attempts to fight for the rights and dignity of clients who need help. The key assumption in this strategy is that there will be instances in which practices, regulations, and general conditions prevent clients from receiving services or obtaining assistance. Advocacy aims at removing the obstacles that prevent clients from exercising their rights and receiving available resources. Examples include advocacy on the part of the Parole Officers' Association in New York to change restrictions on parolees who need to operate a motor vehicle in order to pursue legitimate employment needs.

4. *Mediating*. This strategy seeks to mediate between clients and resource systems. The key assumption is that problems exist neither within people nor within resource systems, but rather in the interaction between people and resource systems. As opposed to the advocate role, the mediator's stance is one of neutrality.

5. *Enabling*. This strategy seeks to provide support and facilitate change in the client's behavior patterns, habits, and perceptions. The key assumption is that problems may be alleviated and crises prevented by modifying, adding, or extinguishing discrete bits of behavior by increasing insights or by changing the client's values and attitudes.

6. *Educating*. This strategy involves conveying and imparting information and knowledge as well as developing various skills. A great deal of what has been called "social casework" or "therapy" is simple instruction.

7. *Community Planning*. This strategy entails participating in and assisting neighborhood planning groups, agencies, community agents, or governments in the development of community programs to assure that client needs are represented and met to the greatest extent feasible.

8. *Enforcing*. This strategy requires the officer to use the authority of his or her office to revoke the probationer/parolee's standing due to changes in status quo, which involves heightened community or client risk outside the control of the officer.

Common Unethical Practices in Probation/Parole

The following is a listing of unethical practices common to probation and parole agencies. The term *common* does not mean that the practice happens every day in any given department; it simply means that it is identifiable within probation and parole agencies. Officers may never violate such practices, yet they are familiar with them once they are mentioned.

1. *Adjusting numbers on assessment instruments that would reduce a probation or parole officer's workload.* Officers, especially those who have exceptionally high caseloads, may finagle to reduce the frequency of contacts they have with the probationers or parolees assigned to them. They may justify such reduction by indicating that the supervisee has "cleaned up his/her act," has become "less of a risk to society," or has been "making progress" while indeed he or she has not. If such a recommendation is made on the basis of knowledge and good faith, it would be considered ethical. If, on the other hand, it is made for the selfish purpose of working less, it should be considered unethical.

2. *Not making field visits and claiming that they were made.* This practice is one of the more infamous ones. It institutionalizes the practice of lying and deception; it encourages the supervisee to violate his or her supervision contract; it increases the supervisee's risk to society; and it sets an unethical example to junior officers who may be watching their seniors' "modus operandi."

3. *Claiming mileage on personal vehicles that are not driven for business purposes.* This practice compounds the previous one by adding theft to the other unethical actions.

4. *Taking care of private business during work hours under the pretense of making field contacts with probationers or parolees.* In this case, officers may use agency time for getting a haircut, shopping or returning merchandise, getting their car fixed, or simply playing golf. This practice adds another vice—service betrayal.

5. *Having a relationship with a probationer or a parolee, or with someone related to them.* In this case, the officer may have a sexual relationship with a supervisee or one of his or her relatives or friends, or a business relationship by which the supervisee (or one of his or her relatives) may be asked to paint the officer's house, build furniture, or fix the plumbing. In the first case, the officer could be accused of sexual harassment or sexual assault; in the latter cases, the officer could be accused of theft of services, in addition to violating the principles of the agency's code of ethics.

6. *Discriminating against supervisees on the basis of gender, color, race, or age.* In this case, the officer not only violates the ethical principles of fairness, equality, and decency, but he or she may also violate the Fourteenth Amendment, as well as the civil rights of the supervisee.

7. *Revealing confidential information regarding the history or status of offenders.* This may be one of the more common violations, and is usually caused by egoism and abusing one's authority. Officers violate the rules of confidentiality to appear important, in return for other information, or to intentionally make the supervisee "look bad." Regardless of the reason, this behavior may not only violate the ethical principles of fidelity and obligation, but also the state penal code.

Ethical Choices in Probation/Parole

Based on the work strategies mentioned earlier and the unethical situations mentioned previously, some questions must be raised: "What are *professional* probation and parole officers expected to do? How can they maximize goodness and minimize social harm?" In answering these questions, four typologies of probation and parole officers may be explored, each emphasizing an ethical view or a cluster of views (Abadinsky, 1991:305).

These typologies cannot be taken in an absolute manner. Probation and parole officers may fit one type or another. Furthermore, practitioners within a given type may not always practice uniformly; some of them may be more knowledgeable (Platonian), more compassionate (Epicurean), more duty-bound (Kantian), more religious (Augustinian), more democratic (Jeffersonian), or simply more gentlemanly (Aristotelian). Nevertheless, these typologies have been widely recognized for their consistency.

The Punitive/Law Enforcement Practitioner

Practitioners of this type see the *summum bonum* of community corrections as *serving the interests of the community*. Any other interest can, and must, be sacrificed. This model underscores a dogmatic utilitarian view that seeks to maximize "goodness" through serving the largest number of benefactors—the community. Toward achieving this goal, anything goes, including the welfare of the probationer, her family, her career, and her destiny. In this model, *control* of the supervisee is viewed as the main purpose, and the strategy of *enforcement* is the chief tool. All rules and regulations are enforced to the letter, including surveillance, checks for drug use, intimidation, and a detective-like enforcement style. The practitioner of this type is generally characterized by depersonalization and extreme detachment. Contacts with the individual are frequent, formal, short, and abrupt. Concerns for the family welfare of the supervisee are unimportant, and whether the supervisee "makes it" or returns to prison is irrelevant. A hedonistic streak may also appear in this type—an overemphasis on efficiency as a tool for securing a promotion or career advancement. In this model, recognition of the "true" purpose of supervision, of the obligation to assist a fellow human being in distress, or of fidelity to the ethics of treatment are all but ignored. An excellent example of this type of ethics is the case of Captain Balian, whom we met in Chapter 2.

The Welfare/Therapeutic Practitioner

Practitioners of this type see the *summum bonum* of community corrections as *rehabilitating the individual supervisee*. Of primary concern is the welfare of the individual, even if it violates the conditions of supervision or the popular interests of the community. For this practitioner, emphasis is placed on advocating, brokering, educating, enabling, and mediating. The practitioner recognizes the relationship with the individual as a "clientship," rehabilitation as a therapeutic treatment, and the client's needs as preeminent. Of paramount concern is providing the client with adequate employment, housing, and psychological assistance, among other support services. Clients are treated with dignity, fairness, openness, and personal sympathy. A streak of religiosity may also pervade this type of practitioner, making his or her role rather missionary in nature. They may invite the individual into their homes or volunteer to pay for the cost of schooling his or her children.

While this model may be hailed for its ethical overtones, it can be criticized for its lack of moderation—extreme affection for the client combined with neglect of the broader interests of society. Another criticism of this type may be the practitioner's limited knowledge of behavior modification methods, leading overzealous practitioners to cause more psychological harm to the client than originally intended (Abadinsky, 1991:307). Finally, there is also the danger of becoming too personally involved with the client, a situation that may lead to considerable disappointment on the part of the officer if he or she fails in rehabilitating the supervisee.

The Passive/Time Server Practitioner

Practitioners of this type see the *summum bonum* of community corrections as *inactivity* and *avoidance*. They have minimal concern for either the welfare of the community or that of the client. They adhere to the serviceable model of management and practice double bookkeeping each time it is necessary. They see their work as meaningless and requiring no ethical attention. Many such practitioners are political opportunists who fail to see the truth of the community service ideal, are burned-out employees who await retirement, or are simply amoral creatures.

The Combined Model Practitioner

Practitioners of this type see the *summum bonum* of community corrections as *moderation between the welfare of the supervisee and protection of the community*. Focus in this model is placed on the provision of social and therapeutic services to the client, while attending to the control functions.

The practitioners in this category integrate their community protection role with the enforcement role, while maintaining the flexibility to use one more than the other in an individualized response to each case.

They adapt work strategies that are useful while sacrificing others, sometimes cynically, on the altar of reality (Abadinsky, 1991:306). Practitioners of this type are loyal to the humanitarian model of community corrections. Their decisions are usually based on balancing the interests of "community" and those of "corrections." For that reason, they are considered experts in a vast range of human problems far beyond the possibilities of ordinary competence. Their role is often seen as "Solomonian" (after Solomon, the prophet of the Old Testament who threatened to cut a baby in half to determine who the child's mother was). These practitioners are also "Aristotelian," in terms of being rational and consistent, yet practical. When endowed with goodness and morality, an appreciation for social justice, and inspired by good faith, these practitioners may be the most ethical practitioners (remember Maslow's profile of the ethical person).

Most probation and parole agencies fall somewhere between the combined and therapeutic models, with parole departments leaning more toward the combined model and probation departments leaning more toward the therapeutic model (Abadinsky, 1991:306). Ethical probation and parole managers cannot overlook the damage that unethical practitioners can inflict upon their agency. Intensive yet sincere efforts are therefore essential for reclaiming these practitioners, and motivation and education—or otherwise termination—should be considered viable options. Termination, however, should be a matter of last resort. Cumbersome and undesirable as it may be, it might, in the long range, be the most ethical way to better serve the interests of the community as well as those of the clients.

Review Questions

1. Compare the professional orientation of probation officers to that of police officers. Why are probation officers considered to have a higher level of professionalism?

2. Define the "borderless community" of probation and parole officers. Why is it considered "borderless"?

3. Discuss the politicization of parole agencies as described by Friel. What are the main reasons for that state as opposed to other agencies of criminal justice?

4. What is the "yellow wind?" What was its effect on the state of parole agencies in recent years?

5. Identify and discuss the main benefits of community-based corrections. Do you agree that these are benefits? If not, why?

6. Identify and discuss the basic views that oppose community-based corrections.

7. Explain the theory and practice of intensive probation. In what sense is it different from standard probation?

8. What is electronic monitoring? How many kinds are presently in use, and how do they differ?

9. Explain the argument that electronic monitoring involves an inherent class bias. How could this bias be ameliorated?

10. Identify and explain five of the work strategies common in probation and parole practice.

References

Abadinsky, H. (1991). *Probation and Parole: Theory and Practice* (4th ed.). Englewood Cliffs, NJ: Prentice-Hall.

Bartollas, C., Miller, S. J., & Wice, P. B. (1983). *Participants in American Criminal Justice*. Englewood Cliffs, NJ: Prentice-Hall.

Borchert, D. M., & Stewart, D. (1986). *Exploring Ethics*. New York: Macmillan Publishing.

Bureau of Justice Statistics (2005). *Budget Summary*. Washington, DC: Bureau of Justice Statistics.

Criminal Justice Institute (1996). *The Corrections Yearbook*. South Salem, NY: Criminal Justice Institute.

Cullen, F. T., & Gilbert, K. E. (1982). *Reaffirming Rehabilitation*. Cincinnati, OH: Anderson Publishing Co.

Dawson, R. O. (1969). *Sentencing*. Boston: Little, Brown and Company.

Friel, C. M. (1990). Intergovernmental Relations: Correctional Policy and the Great American Shell Game. In *Proceedings of the Bureau of Justice Statistics Search Conference, Criminal Justice in the 1990s: The Future of Information Management*. Washington, DC: U.S. Department of Justice.

Gaylin, W. (1974). *Partial Justice: A Study of Bias in Sentencing*. New York: Knopf.

Jankowski, L. (1990). *Bureau of Justice Statistics Bulletin*. Washington, DC: U.S. Department of Justice. November.

Kingsnorth, R., & Rizzo, L. (1979). Decision-Making in the Criminal Court: Continuities and Discontinuities. *Criminology, 17*.

Morris, N., & Tonry, M. (1990). *Between Prison and Probation*. New York: Oxford University Press.

Newman, D. J., & Anderson, P. R. (1989). *Introduction to Criminal Justice* (4th ed.). New York: Random House.

Rosecrance, J. (1968). Maintaining the Myth of Individualized Justice: Probation Presentence Reports. *Justice Quarterly*, 5(2), 235–256.

Schmalleger, F. (1995). *Criminal Justice Today*. Englewood Cliffs, NJ: Prentice-Hall.

Sechrest, L., White, S. O., & Brown, E. D. (Eds.), (1979). *The Rehabilitation of Criminal Offenders: Problems and Prospects*. Washington, DC: National Academy of Sciences.

Seiter, R. P. (2002). *Correctional Administration*. Upper Saddle River, NJ: Pearson Education, Inc.

Souryal, S. S. (1996). Probation as Good Faith. *Federal Probation*, 60(4).

Stojkovic, S., Klofas, J., & Kalinich, D. (1990). *The Administration and Management of Criminal Justice Organizations*. Prospect Heights, IL: Waveland Press, Inc.

Travis, L. F., III., Schwartz, M. D., & Clear, T. R. (1983). *Corrections: An Issues Approach* (2nd ed.). Cincinnati, OH: Anderson Publishing Co.

von Hirsh, A. (1990). The Ethics of Community-Based Sanctions. *Crime and Delinquency*, 36(1).

Walker, S. (1989). *Sense and Nonsense about Crime: A Policy Guide* (2nd ed.). Pacific Grove, CA: Brooks/Cole Publishing.

Whitehead, J. T. (1989). *Burnout in Probation and Corrections*. New York: Praeger.

14
The Truth Revealed
Civility—The Mother of All Virtues

It is a mark of an educated mind to be able to entertain a thought without accepting it.

Aristotle

All nations have crime, but only civil countries can offer justice.

Sam Souryal

Civility is a holistic phenomenon that requires societies to rise to a higher level of brotherhood, collaboration, persistence, and a higher brand of imagination.

Sam Souryal

The DNA of civility is the inalienable right of man.

Sam Souryal

The higher the civility, the lower the crime rates.

Sam Souryal

Nations are great because they are civil; they are not civil because they are great.

Sam Souryal

We are what we repeatedly do. Excellence then is not an act, but a habit.

Aristotle

What You Will Learn from This Chapter

You will learn the role of practical ethics. You will learn that ethics is a set of abstract moral theories akin to those of social theory, psychological theory, or economic theory. Thus, ethical theory should be treated as a tool rather than an end. To put ethics to work, however, ethicists identified two subethics, *morality* and *civility*. Morality works when ethical principles are internalized into the mind and heart of *the individual* and used to sustain one's integrity and guard one's personal goodness. This includes, for instance, honesty, fidelity, mercy, and self-control. Civility works when *the individual interacts with other individuals, groups, societies, or nations*. In sum, morality is a set of individually constructed sentiments and civility is a set of interactive sentiments—how to treat others.

Key Terms and Definitions

Morality is the branch of ethics that is concerned with internalizing moral principles within one's self as an ethical regulator on a daily basis.

Civility is the other branch of ethics which deals with how one relates to other people, singularly or collectively, such as offering respect and willingness to serve.

Compassion is the sentiment of caring for others and sacrificing one's time and effort to make them feel happier, such as helping a stranger who was hurt in a car accident.

In Essence

Because people in general, and criminal justice practitioners in particular, cannot be held ethically or legally to a set of standardized moral *beliefs* or denied their freedom to achieve their personal ambitions and preferences (for example, factors that change with maturity, education, religion, or social obligations), this chapter will not discuss the subject of personal morality because it is individually based and no two persons can accept it or interpret it alike. This chapter will focus only on the topic of civility because, as in the cases of professionalism and codes of ethics, it is collectively upheld and universally used to compare the levels of advancement, moral standards, peacefulness, sophistication, wealth, and stability.

Overview

The connection between criminal justice and happiness is not too hard to understand if criminal justice practitioners and institutions would act more honestly, more responsibly, and more humanly. Yet, critics argue, how can reading ethics books change the minds and hearts of practitioners who face the brunt of crime, violence, or even life and death? Another concern they may raise is, why should we read all the ethics masters who might have been devils or divines? They were still fallible human beings limited by the orthodox methods of their time. Specifically, critics continue to doubt whether, at the end of the day, criminal justice institutions can change the behavior of their practitioners and clients and help them transcend their bad habits, let alone their ingrained attitudes. Furthermore, how can studying ethics change the organizational culture of institutions, let alone their leadership? It is certainly difficult to change the old cultures of violence, power, or worse into an exercise of transparency, justice, dignity, and transform the institution into more honest and less corruptible gathering.

To calm doubts, one should first recognize that learning ethics and internalizing its principles requires a long time of schooling and reflection. Thus, it has been recommended that teaching ethics to American students should begin at the junior high school level or the preservice police or correctional academies. Second, realize that ethics is *not a matter one can mold; it is a human sentiment that can last throughout one's entire life*. Moreover, and especially to those who ignore these questions and mistakenly claim they are ethical because their parents raised them well, this reader should think again more logically. Not all parents are capable of, or interested in, raising their children ethically because many parents themselves are ignorant, selfish, greedy, or even criminals. The state of Texas alone incarcerates about 160,000 inmates basically because their parents were "ethical illiterates" (*Crime and Justice in Texas*, 1995: 4). Third, building more dysfunctional prisons cannot effectively rehabilitate inmates. Almost like dervishes, imprisoned inmates gradually become brutish, antisocial, and prone to committing *more* violence. For example, many well-trained priests are known to have fathered illegitimate children, several CIA personnel turned double agents, and more well-behaved girls turned prostitutes. Moreover, being ethical under certain conditions does not make one ethical under all conditions. Conclusively, it is no exaggeration to say that we live at a time when criminal justice as a discipline needs to be reinvented.

It should be understood that learning ethics is only a *tool* that can be used to promote civility wherever and whenever possible. The esoteric reason for that is simple: "no person can live alone," and if we must engage with one another, we must create a climate of laws and moral principles to live a decent life. Higher levels of civility (for example, as in the Scandinavian countries, Switzerland, and New Zealand) do not guarantee a better life, but its likelihood is increased by children socializing with their peers in school or in the neighborhood in a manner that instills ethics as their "second language." With time and the evolution of enlightenment, children internalize ethical principles wherein people are accustomed to treating each other with dignity, nobility, honesty, and duty-bounded courtesy.

The Machination of Ethics: Morality and Civility

Imagine the story of the burning bush as a metaphor of trees that never die. Like these trees, *civility* does not usually die or abandon its DNA. Once the machination of a tree is examined and understood, the tree continues to live and bring forth fresh leaves on the same old branches, perpetuating its growth and collusion with adjacent trees. At the human level, civility, as the burning bush, brings about a template of moral *Rushmoreans* (strongly moral people named after Mount Rushmore; see "Rushmorean Criminal Justice Agencies," Chapter 5). These include Abraham Lincoln, Robert E. Lee, Pope John Paul II, Mother Teresa, and Nelson Mandela. Now imagine ethics again as one of those burning bushes. They consist of roots (usually underground), trunks (above the ground), and a canopy of branches and leaves at the top that keeps the tree cool, healthy, and productive. Given this metaphor, it would be safe to assume that *ethics* is at the roots of every tree, *morality* as its trunk, and *civility* as its canopy of leaves. As a trinity, they are all connected, yet each has a time, place, and task. At this point, it should be understood that ethics is the theory of all goodness and its offshoots are both *morality* and *civility*. They are not identical, but like the wheels of a bicycle, the faster the front wheel goes, the faster the back wheel goes. Based on this image, the machination of ethics works as follows:

1. *Ethics as the mother of all virtues:* It is the blueprint for humanizing mankind. As in Chapter 1, among the ancient hunters and gatherers, there existed a crude scheme of consensus and integrity to minimize violence, share food, and trust each other (for example, I hunt tonight and you hunt tomorrow). Over time, patterns of docility and discipline become routine, and the burning bush keeps producing small branches and little leaves of *moral principles*. Over time, the masters of philosophy (see Chapter 4, Meeting the Masters) continued to refine this intellectual enterprise, perhaps before historians, sociologists, and political scientists. Yet, sadly, in modern times ethicists focused on the heuristics of ethical principles rather than on their application to serve mankind. As a

result, while ethics continues to be normally taught as an old language, when addressing a university commencement, legal defense, or scriptural literature, practical ethicists ponder how to make it serviceable to human development. In a sense, they continue to focus on the roots but ignore how it can be harvested to bring forth their fruits with tangible attributes of "kindness, decency, respect, graciousness, and sacrifice." World religions continue to reinforce this universal movement but, as with the burning bush, they couldn't quite turn it into a workable culture.

In time, while physical technologies blossomed, the roots of ethics remained rather stagnant as a *theory* with its two offshoots of *morality* and *civility* scrabbled together in whichever way philosophers envision. While morality addresses *the effects of ethics on oneself* (for example, I should not lie, cheat, or steal), civility addresses *the effects of ethics in relationship to others* (for example, we don't do that to neighbors, we don't keep people waiting too long, we treat people with dignity, we fight in defense of our country). Finally, because liberal arts education is basically a rehearsal for dealing with differences among knowledge(s), the requisite talents remain as honesty, fidelity, and obligation among other intellectual virtues we are called upon to master (Roune, 2000: 17).

2. *Morality* is a personal commitment to use ethical principles to direct *oneself*. Examples include manifesting self-control, humility, mercy, charity, and kindness (more silently than publicly). Such principles are used to bring about happiness, self-contentment, telling the truth, patience, and respecting the dignity of others. In vernacular terms, morality became known as *doing the right thing, especially when no one is watching*. It is *one's own thinking* about living humbly and respectfully, avoiding violence and egoism, anger, greed, or envy. One should also note that while many people pretend they are moral (for example, the Sophists of Athens and the Pharisees we met in Chapter 1), these need not be emulated—they should either be reschooled or estranged from the community. Accordingly, falsely calling oneself ethical without being moral is contradictory, a behavior that can lead to disastrous results.

3. *Civility* is an overt act, meeting, or decision intended to create (or enhance) the right environment to motivate people to submit to the common good. It is "a virtue expressed in action to recruit communities and individuals into the service of the common good." Another definition can be "a collective set of practices that highlights a consensus among people to serve each other, help the needy, maintain order, and promote the human quest" (Shils, 1997:4). Shils also defined civility as a "virtue expressed in action on behalf of the good of all members of society." In some orthodox communities, civility was akin to chivalry or "secular worship."

> McClellen (2000:78) proposed three requirements of civility: (1) "the recognition of the full humanity of both one's self and the others"; (2) the awareness of one's interdependence with the other; and (3) the desire to make common cause with one or more others. The British refer to civility as the practice of the "dones" and the "undones" that has been observed meticulously for several centuries. Maybe for that reason civility has been transmitted from one generation to another and from one continent to another with adequate ease. Another definition of civility is "a collective human sentiment that directs individuals and communities to promote harmony, cohesion, peacefulness, and beauty, and to abhor injustice, inequality, cruelty, and the absence of compassion."

Civil people are normally enlightened, optimistic, entrepreneurial, congenial, philanthropic, and sensitive, regardless of their economic status. They stand out among communities, sacrifice for others (not for themselves), and offer support to those who are in need. Seligman (2000) argues that a main characteristic of the modern era is to "overcome local territories and primordial ties and to destroy the bonds of local attachment to kith and kin." In an abstract sense, the *overriding habit of civility* is "sacrificing to help others to achieve the common good, to be seriously concerned for order, beauty, and good housekeeping" (for instance, in Germany many people decorate their balconies with fresh or artificial flowers). Civility is also concerned with keeping cities clean, buses and trains running on time, public parks well maintained, drivers complying with traffic lights, taxi drivers not overcharging passengers, complying with traffic laws, and people conversing in decent low voices, using no profanity or bad language. Moreover, civil cities also subsidize musical festivals, create statues for their heroes, organize national and state parades, and promote philanthropy and the arts. Not unlike Rawls (Chapter 4), McClellan concludes by offering three basic qualifications for civility: (1) a recognition of the full humanity of both oneself and the other; (2) an awareness of one's interdependence with others; and (3) a desire to make common cause with one other.

More pivotal, perhaps, among civil nations is upholding democracy, abiding with the constitution, enhancing justice, and establishing peace and sensibility—all of that to create harmony, sensibility, mutual respect, and concern for the common good. Civil society allows dissent by those who disagree and wish to demonstrate their disagreement publicly and peacefully. On the other hand, uncivil societies are mostly unkempt, noisy, poor, uneducated, disunited, and normally controlled by tyrannical leaders and despots. Uncivil societies are more commonly found in third-world countries such as some African countries, Latin American countries, Middle Eastern countries, and the former Eastern European countries (*Transparency International Annual Report*,

2008). Ironically, many of these so-called democracies are *false democ-racies*. They forcibly remove legally elected presidents, persecute politi-cal dissenters, imprison political rivals, and, almost always, defraud elections by stuffing ballot boxes that favor their candidates. Ironically, these countries also blame their misery on poverty, diseases, illiteracy, civil wars, and the lack of international aid. While most of these may be true, the original causes are more likely corruption, mishandling of foreign aid, and supporting drug traffic, as well as nurturing a violent culture that debases the value of human life.

Having said all that, it might be safe to consider three basic *phenome-nological* hypotheses closely associated with democracy and civility: First, like air and water, uncivil countries and institutions must educate their masses in order to understand the values of democracy; safeguard and organize their cities to attract foreigners; encourage civic brotherhood, religious traditions, and compliance with the conventions of the Human Rights Rules and sanctions, lest they turn back into medieval hoplites (for example, Bosnia, Rwanda, Liberia, and the Guantanamo prison). Second, the civility of nations is measured by the civility of their criminal justice systems, especially the conduct of police. This can be explained as follows: The more civil the police, the less desirous would be criminals to disobey rules and regulations. The police must look and act profession-ally, speak to residents with respect and dignity, and be penalized severely for accepting corruption. Third, true democracies are the highest level of self-governance (although some Greek philosophers disagreed, labeling it governance by the uninformed). As a rule, however, history shows that true democracies cannot be forced on residents until they learn how to apply it. In summary, not until a civil community is in place will democ-racy have the chance to emerge (for example, the reader should note the shameful distinction between Scandinavian democracy and those in the Congo, Somalia, or Rwanda).

Civility Defined

The concept of *civility* is closely associated with the works of Aristo-tle (384–322 B.C.), who defined it as "a partnership for a better living." As mentioned earlier, he was intellectually devoted to the idea of the polis, without which the civil city perishes. He condemned the life-style of Spartans and Persians who ranked far below Athenians on the scale of civility. He taught that human beings are "social animals," and if they are to survive, they must live in close cooperative associa-tion with each other. Thus, there would be an earnest collaboration to enrich and upgrade the polis. Toward this end, the civil polis should be actively involved in promoting happiness (eudemonia), education, the arts, sports, and, of course, in avoiding violence, physical harm, and unjust wars.

This would allow more citizens to perform more functions, more cohesively and more peacefully, than functioning individually. In Aristotle's thought, the polis was the highest social institution. It was designed to be anthropocentric (that is, conceiving of everything in terms of human values) and shaped, but not determined by, the gods, tradition, or the physical world surrounding it (Rouner, 2000:42). Aristotle argued that the more peacefulness the polis emits, the more industrious and happy its members would be. In Book II of *Nicomachean Ethics*, he emphasized that the virtue of a human being is closely associated with the virtue of the polis and, as such, can make "human beings perform their functions well" (Rouner, 2000:20). In the same source, when Aristotle was pressed for a clarification for what civility is worth, he responded,

> [civility] causes its predecessors to be in a good state and to perform their functions well; the virtue of the eyes, makes the eyes and its functioning excellent because it makes them see well. And similarly, the virtues of a horse make the horse excellent, and good at galloping, at carrying its rider, and at standing steady in the face of the enemy.
>
> Rouner, 2000:20

To further clarify the concept of civility, it is necessary to examine its antonym, *incivility*. The word is used to mean "barbarity, vulgarity, backwardness, or crudeness." In modern times, incivility has caused many vicissitudes, including urban decay, social disorganization, unhealthy communities, and, of course, the Holocaust. On the micro side, Rouner (2000:25) described an example of incivility during a visit by a visitor from France who was invited to dinner in a Virginian's house. The French visitor later recorded his experience by stating,

> Virginians do not use Napkins, but they wear silk cravats, and instead of carrying white handkerchiefs they blow their noses either with their fingers (I have seen the best-bred Americans do this) or with a silk handkerchief which also serves as a cravat.
>
> Rouner, 2000:25

During the sixteenth and seventeenth centuries, the scope of the word *civility* expanded to include the practice of *curteisie* (French for "courtesy"). The word denoted acting in one's best behavior in the presence of a king, queen, prince, or dignitary. Courtesy continues, as in modern-day monarchical systems, to be a sign of a heightened self-restraint, an alert sense of consciousness, and an ability to abstain from distasteful bodily functions as a matter of respect. These characteristics were popularized by the obligation to courtesy to noble persons, a behavior still common in many European and Asian societies (Rouner,

2000:42). Yet while the practices of *civilité* and *civilization* were the hallmarks of the French nobility, they were viewed differently by other European societies, most notably German and American cultures. In the next section, five true stories associated with civility will be presented.

Creating a Climate Conducive to Civility

Having been familiarized with the role of civility, we'll now examine the ways and means by which it can be established (or upgraded) in modern societies and institutions. The following perspectives should be considered in this order:

1. Developing an enlightened mind

2. Creating a climate conducive to civility

3. Preserving justice above all

4. Strengthening civility and democracy

5. Promoting the common good

6. Reinforcing integrated knowledge

7. What the theorists say

8. Five stories to remember

I: Developing an Enlightened Mind

As a future criminal justice practitioner, you must have learned the mechanics of criminal justice (for example, the U.S. Constitution, the Penal Code, the Code of Criminal Procedures); police systems and practices (for example, patrolling streets, preventing crime); criminal investigation (for example, searching crime scenes and interrogating suspects); court procedures (for example, the adversarial relationship between district attorneys and defense attorneys); and the role of probation/parole agents (for example, community-based supervision and community-based parole); as well as the correctional debate (incarceration versus rehabilitation, and capital punishment versus life sentences). This knowledge is not only essential to understand criminal justice, but is vital to broadening the intellectual universe within the student's mind. At this level you should also have learned the arts of gyrations (for example, theory building and theory testing), among other heuristics of crime and justice. You will also be versed in statistical analysis and logical conclusions (for example, if A equals B, and B equals C, then A must equal C). Yet this knowledge alone is insufficient because it would be compartmentalized in the human brain as disjointed clusters rather than adjoined and stirred up in a "soup" of brewing wisdom. The glue that creates this bond is the factor of *civility*: the willingness not to use force, not to turn someone away when one can help, not to move to the top of the line when others are ahead, not to act in a Bohemian manner, and not to cross the street except at the designated areas. Without observing such acts (and words), peacefulness, serenity, trust, and happiness cannot be genuinely achieved. Only civility can bring out the deepest and the most natural and renewable motivation into the criminal justice enterprise and between the enterprise and its customers and users.

Yet to say that one is competent does not mean that one is an *enlightened* person. Enlightened persons are a different breed of learners—they are genuinely dedicated to saving the world (literally!). They possess a special curiosity and utilize it to enhance the conditions of life. These individuals are gifted with *digital minds,* the kind that can figure out the turning of the world around them, the renewable essence of humanity, and the gentleness of sensible morality. They are highly educated and enjoy playing the Socratic *contrarian schema* (for example, good and evil, crime and justice, true and the untrue). According to this schema, and assuming that the former is the opposite of the latter, one must conclude that if the former doesn't matter, the latter can't exist.

Enlightened criminal justice practitioners and students embrace *integrated loyalty* (remember the dangers of misguided loyalty, Chapter 9). They are not satisfied with the dogma of labels such as *liberal* and *conservative* or *foreign* and *domestic*, because the spirit of the human judgment is rather global and interconnected (for example, American astronauts now fly in Russian spacecraft). Enlightened practitioners and students are more comfortable with their inner and outer selves. They realize that their loyalty is not only to country and giant statues, but also to the abstracts of technology, fairness, justice, and truth, among other principles. They are also humble enough to admit that they do not know when they are intrigued by the metaphysical or the sacred as well as how gravity works.

Enlightened criminal justice practitioners and students are of a higher level of reasoning because they think at a higher level than others. They understand the minute cultural differences that can cause communities to be civil and those who are sterile in matters of political institutions, social ideologies, and economic enterprises. They ask thoughtful questions because they possess enough intellectual curiosity to figure out why phenomena occur. They continue to distill information in their minds until the *truth* finally emerges. In essence, enlightened criminal justice practitioners and students are directed by two irreplaceable forces: *the power of reasoning,* without which nothing makes any sense, and *moral courage,* the only principle that can make all other virtues possible. As a result, they can celebrate the mutuality of ideas, the joy of discovery, and the dexterity of logic. Enlightened criminal justice practitioners and students are also by definition *existentially noble* with no grudge, bias, or contempt. They basically wish everybody well. They receive people as they come and treat them as they should. They come into the presence of their fellow citizens with a sense of awe and respect and express themselves in ways that might be too simple yet consequential. They are intellectually modest to the extent of listening to others with the knowledge of the possibility that they (others) might be right and they (students and practitioners) are wrong. They accept criticism and often provoke it as long as it is stated logically and delivered respectfully. They listen to others regardless of whether they like them or don't. Needless to say, with these characteristics, their judgment must transcend race, gender, ethnicity, age, and national origin, as if none of these really matter. They value freedom, creativity, and beauty above all other virtues, and condone civil disobedience if it supports a justifiable good.

With this generous overview, you may now begin to grasp the concept of civility. Yet the following comments are worth remembering: First, do not subscribe to the defeatist view that crime is a human destiny because criminological scientists, despite all their successes, failed to find a gene of criminality. Nor should you think that criminal justice is simply criminology in a sheep's skin and therefore alien to human nature. Such fallacies can excite you, but should not alter your enlightened mind. Second, civil societies produce less crime than others because citizens would be more peaceful, more just, and more sensible—characteristics that leave little or no incentive to act illegitimately. Third, humanity shapes the laws rather than the other way around because it (humanity) emanated before all laws, and may well survive after man ceases to exist. Furthermore, laws can only deter people from committing bad acts, while civility propels people to do good acts (a concern for those who advocate building more and more prisons). Fourth, criminal justice failures are not destined "in our lucky stars, they are in ourselves" because we are responsible for our thoughts, acts, and destinies. Fifth, criminality is environmentally learned, therefore it can be environmentally unlearned. One may wonder why this is not happening. It is possibly so because, as poet Maya Angelou stated, "we don't put our minds to it." Consequently, as a human rule, no human being is too good to be blameless or too bad to be unsalvageable. Sixth, compliance with a just law is a virtuous duty, but compliance with an unjust law is either cowardice or ignorance, or both, (for example, Nazism, communism, and terrorism). Therefore, attempts to abolish unjust laws should be hailed as an expression of true democracy.

Finally, if these assumptions are acceptable, then you will be able to understand the relationship between crime and civility, and only then would it be a *categorical imperative* (remember Kant, Chapter 4) to require criminal justice students and practitioners to embrace and promote civility.

II: Creating a Climate Conducive to Civility

Learning civility is a hard and long task. In some cases, it might take an entire lifetime. Learning civility requires a profound understanding of the broader dimensions of humanities as well as the art of building a civil environment. The latter hinges on several institutional interpretations we already learned, primarily Aristotle's idea of the *polis;* Plato's idea of *reasoning;* Kant's idea of *duty;* Epictetus's *moral courage;* and Rawls's theory of *justice;* and to unify all of this subknowledge through the medium of *verstehen* (German for "profound thinking with a commitment to serve").

These original works are essential for developing a culture of civility. As such, criminal justice institutions should reflect on the *original conditions of its components:* policing must police fairly and equitably; prosecutors must apply positive and natural laws; judges must rule honorably; correctional institutions must authentically correct; and probation and parole agencies must genuinely rehabilitate. This is consistent with the civility assumption: If nations are devoted to the virtues of liberty, justice, and the pursuit of happiness, its citizens must appreciate the virtues of freedom, decency, dignity, and the phenomenology of the human spirit.

Yet for all of these tasks to work, the workplace itself should be managed in a civil fashion and superiors should act as role models to their juniors; otherwise, the chances for success will be dismal. In a sense, the workplace is the institutional cradle from which all civility emanates. It is difficult to believe that junior practitioners can act with civility if they are not schooled into it or if the department's superiors act uncivilly. This behooves criminal justice superiors to act super-civilly and demand that their employees do the same. The supervisors should be above little things; they should not use stealthy or childish methods such as hidden listening devices, hidden agendas, favoritism, or retaliation, because—unless earnestly justified—these techniques are intrinsically illegal, deceptive, and demeaning. Moreover, from a humanistic perspective, if such techniques were allowed to be conducted by superiors, the organization would be displaying its ugliest image of incivility. Such acts can kill the moral fortitude of the practitioners and exacerbate their resentment to productivity. Included in this restriction, the institution should have already transcended all sentiments of *racism, sexism, discrimination, or oppression* because such practices are humanly offensive, let alone illegal. Promotions and demotions (the barometer of the agency) must be consistent and fair because inconsistency and unfairness in this context are considered *naturalistic fallacies* (wrong in themselves). Finally (and rather more importantly), every practitioner (including the lowest janitor in the building) should be addressed with respect and dignity.

Yet because this might be the most important chapter in this book, fairness requires that it also address the opposing view of the argument. For example, what can criminal justice institutions gain if all the practitioners are civil—a subject that ranges on idealism and liberalism? The answer to this question is that society will rise, brotherhood will reign, economy may increase (due to no corruption), and citizens will realize that *civility* is not a mark of weakness or submissiveness (as many criminal justice practitioners mistakenly believe) but a mark of transcendence that cleanses the soul of the agency, celebrates its tradition of the truth, and sustains its human spirit. In particular, police officers will note that civility will create a negative correlation between the *exercise of civility* and the *incidence of crime: The more civil the society, the fewer crime rates accrue.* Although it is rather difficult to test this issue empirically, it is not impossible to cognitively anticipate it.

Transparency International compares crime rates in the world—both civil and uncivil. In a global study of 145 countries conducted between 1993 and 2003 (2003:1), and assuming—as operational definition—that an act of corruption equals an act of incivility, this relationship is alarming. This inquiry compared crime rates in the top 30 countries on the civility scale (Finland was first) and the lowest 30 countries on the same scale (Haiti was last). The survey showed that the high–low range of serious crimes in Finland was 10.0 to 9.2, while in Haiti it was 2.4 to 0.8. Given this data, a strong negative correlation existed between the *existence of civility* and the *rates of crime* in both countries. Yet analytically it seemed apparent that civility, more than religion, perhaps, reduces the *human urge to act criminally* when other avenues for conflict resolutions are open and managed by fair means. In such an equation, promoting civility would be the independent variable and accomplishing the required task would be the dependent variable. As a result, Haiti would have 93.4% less crime if it were as civil as Finland.

III: Preserving Justice Above All

St. Augustine (fourth century) wrote in *Confessions*, "when there is no Justice, what then would be the role of the State, but a band of Robbers Disbanded" (Souryal, 2007). St. Augustine's dictum confirms two Aristotelian doctrines: (1) It is on justice that the ordering of society is centered; and (2) all virtue is summed up in dealing justly. Aristotle's dicta suggest that justice is the highest moral principle without which the universe might dysfunction. Muggeridge states, "Either justice is always and in all circumstances sacred, or it is intrinsically of no account, It is inconceivable that it should be in some cases the one and in some the other" (Souryal, 2007:359). Consequently, civil communities would apply strict standards of justice if they want to regulate their relationships with others peacefully and fairly; engage socially with one another; uphold partnerships; and honor other obligations without the need for a template of assumed legality.

The need for justice is not a novel idea. It has existed since *homo sapiens* began to stabilize and organize their lives. The early Egyptians, Assyrians, and Mayans formalized justice measures with even more severe punishments. They realized that peaceful coexistence requires as much *horizontal tribalism* as it does *vertical hierarchy*. It shouldn't be surprising, then, that far back in history, judges were appointed from members of the priesthood. In this context, one may recall that Jesus Christ was judged by priests, not by Roman governors, and when the latter offered to set him free, the former rebelled and wanted ultimate cruelty. This point may show that the priests who clamored to crucify an innocent man never really knew what civility is nor cared for it. Later in the nineteenth century, it took the famous French Dreyfus affair (for treason) and the subsequent Napoleonic reforms in France to realize that without civility, there can't be justice. This, in itself, might have led to the evolution of the three components of civility: *liberté*, *egalité*, and *fraternité* (liberty, equality, fraternity), without which societies would lose a major dimension of what makes them legitimate.

Daniel Quinn in *Beyond Civilization* (1999) argued that the study of civility is more essential to understanding justice than the study of bureaucracy, because justice is the essence of civility, while bureaucracy is a mere license to practice authority, whether just or unjust. Indeed, tyrannical societies can exercise power without civility but never can they apply justice without civility. If that were true, the quality of civility today must be much too relevant to the conduct of criminal justice and ignoring it may be an invitation to violence, hatred, or indifference.

Maslow produced his profile of the civil person in Chapter 1. According to that profile, highly civilized individuals and nations delight in bringing about justice (for example, the reader may appreciate that the first clause in the Preamble to the U.S. Constitution was establishing justice); in stopping cruelty and exploitation; and in enjoying peace, quiet, and pleasantness. Civil persons do not knowingly do unkind things to one another, nor do they respond with anger when others do unkind things to them. Their fighting is not an excuse for hostility, paranoia, grandiosity, authority, or rebellion, but for the sake of settings things right. They manage somehow to love the world as it is, and to try to improve it. However, civil communities cannot be thought of as naive or gullible. They are also good punishers of evil and correctors of human behavior. For instance, 35 of the American states still support capital punishment on the condition of it being carried out fairly and civilly. They (communities) hate evil to be rewarded, and hate people to get away with it (Maslow, 1971).

Yet the subject of *civility* is more than simple politeness. If it were not, it would not be worth writing about. Reiterating apologies such as "excuse me, Sir or Madam," while—figuratively speaking—stabbing one another in the back exacerbates deception, even betrayal. Yet civil society does not shrink from discussing tough issues because they are difficult or inconvenient. There is more to civility than mere adherence to laws; there is the imperative of sacrifice without which civility would be merely obedience. The practice of civility cannot be any more reinforced than when people intelligently debate social and moral issues. For that reason alone, perhaps, instituting a debate society of the kind common in Oxford and Cambridge Universities might be beneficial to establish in American universities. Nevertheless, debating civility should be performed in a solemn, serene, and respectful manner. Indeed, it would be a mark of true enlightenment if an agonist were able to defend an argument that one does not personally accept, because to perceive is to suffer.

IV: Strengthening Civility and Democracy

While learning civility is thought to begin with the family, the school, or the church, learning democracy is not. It takes a long time to grow before one can decide to be democratic rather than any other kind of government. Furthermore, the integrity of democracies is usually guarded by the power of the people, while the integrity of all other forms of government are by the army or the police forces. In addition, because people are not born democratic, fascist, socialist, or communist, they identify themselves on the basis of belief or convenience. Democracy is also a very complicated theory because of its multilevel governments, wide decentralization, and conflict among its branches, as well as the term in office. Democracy is also a controversial practice because of the "unlimited" freedom people mistakenly assume they possess. Democracy can be particularly puzzling when people realize they have "good" democracies or "bad" democracies, while fascism, socialism, or communism are assumed to be equally bad and their articles of government are in the hands of one person who cannot be legitimately removed.

While civility is an informal social system and democracy is an informal political system, the two systems are more compatible with each other than with another ruling system. Foremost among them is a social contract (either written or unwritten) that is primarily based on the inevitability of liberty, fairness, and choice. There are several reasons the role of civility is paramount. First, because ethics is only theoretical and cannot be physically applied, then ethics cannot be a method of government. Second, because morality is ostensibly personal and cannot be codified to fit everyone's whim, this cannot work either. This leaves only civility as a model of freedom, maturity, and compassion. In this context, civility can adapt to fit the democratic needs for flexibility, compassion, and transcendence. Among the joint features of both civility and democracy are the following:

- Recognize that the sovereignty of life is in the hands of the people.

- Recognize that agonists are equal and can solve their disputes peacefully.

- Reject any restrictions on the right of man to think, reason, or debate.

- Allow disagreements among the agonists without fear, and fight oppression.

- Disallow governments "to violate their own rules" to preserve legitimacy.

- Abhor brutality whether by excessive bail, excessive fines, or cruel treatment.

- Seek and encourage consensus and good faith among the parties and citizens.

- Replace governments when they fail to preserve tranquility and common good.

From the previous analysis, it appears plausible that civility is the most appropriate tool to measure the moral individualism of each party (public or government). By *moral individualism* we mean one's freedom to express dismay to the highest level of government when justified. No traditional methods such as custom, habit, or religion could constrain one: "whatever I owe others, I owe them by virtue of my willing to sacrifice" (Sandel, 2009:213). Because civility is the only visible component of ethics (while morality and the theory of ethics are not), then civility should be the only measure of what it means to be free or to debate political and administrative issues that shape government and regulate social issues. And because "all politics are local," it becomes the obligation of all citizens, rich or poor, to participate in affairs of government; to accept what one can and to correct what one cannot.

The previous discussion seems more closely associated with the practice of the criminal justice community since the practitioners engage most of the time with diverse populaces—the old and the young, the powerful and the powerless, the innocent and the guilty. One should also note that while people, especially in democratic societies, are free to do good or not, criminal justice practitioners, unless justified, must act honorably, considering the legal and moral consequences, as well as the attributes of a civil society. While some may disagree, the reason for this assertion is two-pronged. (1) Criminal justice practitioners are a special community. They are well selected, well trained, well supervised, well led, and, at times, well paid. They are also ubiquitous and almost always in touch with their communities. In the final analysis it would be safe to state that the police are the most likely to promote democracy, not doctors, lawyers, teachers, priests, or the armed forces. As such, creating a civil police force must be the front line against incivility, corruption, and mischief. (2) Criminal justice practitioners, especially the police, should always act civilly if they truly want to promote a civil society; otherwise, it would simply be a costly charade. Indeed, the civility of nations is measured by the civility of its police. As evidence, one can easily compare the civility of the British Bobbies or the Canadian Mounties to the police in Mexico, Nigeria, or various Latin American countries.

V: Promoting the Common Good

More than anything else, enlightened criminal justice practitioners and students are expected to engage and accomplish civil actions because that is their life mission. They spend most of their careers in fighting crime, maintaining peace, upholding the rule of law, and promoting justice (for example, the first commandment in the Preamble to the U.S. Constitution), as well as in interacting with men and women from all walks of life.

Yet the ultimate value of life action is clearly developing and promoting the *common good*. If that were not the case, then Socrates (469–399 B.C.) was misguided when he stated that "a life unexamined is not worth living." He advocated this dictum to provoke—as some may say—the Athenians into avoiding war with Sparta (which the Athenians lost and then blamed their loss on Socrates), caring for the poor and the needy, pursuing justice, and *promoting the common good* for all Athenians. In Socratic thought, thinking was the function of the *civil person* while living was the destiny of all others. That is why, perhaps, the word *good* is now used universally as to mean "popular." In the pursuit of the common good, enlightened criminal justice practitioners and students have the best opportunity to always think deeply and act honorably, because each of these activities has the capacity to reinforce the other. Through this continuing process, enlightened criminal justice practitioners and students learn to think profoundly, reason logically, and develop a strong aptitude to achieve the common good—the result of all thought and the eventual purpose of all action.

Yet while the ideal of the common good has been broadly assumed, it has rarely been articulated, let alone defined (Miller & Browning, 2004). Part of this difficulty is the metaphysical origin of the word *goodness*, which some argue is a derivation of the word *God*, which, in turn, is mysterious to most people. Subsequently, the most likely meaning of the word is "acting in a god-like manner." Yet because the idea of the gods is strongly metaphysical and thinking about it is a product of personal belief, one would be at a loss when articulating the characteristics and intentions of being good. As a result, the ideal of the common good is basically left to the interpretation of the gifted philosophers. For example, Rouner (2000:27) quotes Leonardo Bruni (1438) defining common good as "a term used by political theorists to describe that form of association which is conventionally called *polis* or *civitas*." For the time being, this definition might be satisfactory until it is sharpened later in this chapter.

Many enlightened theorists offered their own interpretations of the common good, each in a broad and naturalistic paradigm. One common paradigm is "serving the public interest in whatever way one can" (Miller & Browning, 2004:7). Among the most famous supporters of this paradigm was John Locke, who advocated that the "common good is not good unless liberties are protected," come what may. James Mill advocated that good is the "greatest good for the greatest number." The younger Mill (John Stuart) focused on promoting public welfare and, of course, John Rawls advocated the "state's obligation to distribute justice among the consumers with the proviso of rewarding the poor and the needy." More recently, Hale (1994:368) observed in his discussion of enlightened manners, that civility is "all about taming." For example, within the classical republican tradition, civic virtues aim at taming individual avarice and binding individuals into a republican concern; if such concern does not emanate, such virtues cease to be virtuous. In 1948, civility between nations and states were collectively articulated in the United Nations Universal Declaration of Human Rights.

What makes the ideal of common good rather easier for enlightened criminal justice practitioners and students is the relatively humanistic nature of the discipline, especially its focus on the *lawful society* and the *primacy of justice*. While many other concepts were not fully clear (for example, probable cause, equal protection, jury of one's peers, or even social control), the remarkable advancement in the criminal justice subdiscipline today and the higher standards for hiring criminal justice scholars and practitioners are indicative of the discipline's resolve to better serve the common good. Having said that, the intellectual sophistication of modern-day criminal justice students and practitioners should be the most redeeming means to embrace the essence of civility by incorporating it into their continuous and immutable pursuit of the common good.

VI: Reinforcing Integrated Knowledge

The theory of civility goes far back in the history of the human race. Simply stated, it is "an insight into the complex relationship between what a society believes and how it behaves." Driven by envy, idolatry, greed, racism, megalomania, or lust, there is no end to the creeping harm by sinners and no greater challenge than understanding what is meant by a civil society (Thompson, 1993:cover page). Enlightened criminal justice practitioners and students can enhance their enlightenment, and that of others, by understanding Figure 14.1. I call it the Square of Sensibility. The purpose of this square is to expose criminal justice practitioners and students to the broader knowledge of three important questions: (1) Who are they, really, and whom do they think they are? (2) Whom do they serve, and whom do they think they should serve? (3) What are their professional duties, and how do they interpret these duties to be? Figure 14.1 and the brief discussion should enlighten what the answers to these questions are more likely to be.

Figure 14.1 is self-explanatory. It emphasizes four specific virtues: examination, investigation, offering justice, and understanding the mysteries of the world. If enlightened criminal justice personnel are able to clearly, deeply, and faithfully understand and embrace each of these four "points of light," they will certainly be on the threshold of entering the shrine of civility.

Figure 14.1
The Square of Sensibility

The Square of Sensibility

Socrates	Newton
• A life unexamined is not worth living. • Know thyself.	• All people saw apples falling from trees. Only Isaac Newton asked why.
St. Augustine	Schopenhauer
• When there is no justice, what then, is the role of the state? But a band of robbers expanded.	• I can conquer the world because I can understand it!

VII: What the Theorists Say

In the following segment is an overview of what several authors and ethicists wrote about the subject of civility. Although they may differ in particular issues, they collectivity present a holistic portfolio of what civility is or should be.

Civility by George Washington

The father of our country exhibited notable manners throughout his life. Diligence in social matters was common practice in society the world over during his lifetime. At the age of 14, George Washington wrote down 110 rules under the title *Rules of Civility & Decent Behavior in Company and Conversation* (Washington, Applewood Books 1988:8). These rules, drawn from the English translation of a French book of maxims, were to polish manners, keep alive the best affections of the heart, impress the obligations of moral virtues, teach how to treat others in social relations and, above all, inculcate the practice of self-control. In Figure 14.2, 16 of the more important rules and their optimal virtue are presented. A glance at Washington's list suggests that civility in his time was concerned with so many different principles that they were difficult to specify in their range or their applicability (Rouner, 2000:22). The 16 selected items from Washington's book are stated with the moral value each represents.

Civility by James Q. Wilson

James Q. Wilson, one of the true luminaries of modern-day criminal justice ethics in the United States, discussed the subject of civility in *The Moral Sense* (1993:240–241). Although he has written several distinguished books on crime and its causes, he laments the fact that he and most other American criminologists ignored the role of morality and civility in crime. He identified civil persons as "nice persons" who are "dedicated to the virtues of sympathy, fairness, duty, and self-control," among other higher-level habits. In his profile of civil persons, Wilson characterized such individuals using the term *ladies* and *gentlemen*. He described their behavior as follows:

> They take into account the feelings of others and sympathize with the joys and sorrows of those with whom they deal to the extent that those joys and sorrows are justifiable and proportional to the circumstances. Even when not expressing sympathy, they do not inflict unjustified harm on innocent parties.

> They are fair in dealing with others and do not attempt to be a judge in their own cases. They have prudent self-control; they are not in the grip of extravagant passions that compel others to deal with them only on

Figure 14.2
Washington's Rules of Civility

1. If any one far surpasses others, either in age, estate, or merit, yet would give place to one mean than himself in his own lodging, the one ought not accept it; so he, on the other hand, should not use such earnestness nor offer it above it above once or twice.	Respect
2. When you sit down, keep your feet firm and even, without putting one on the other or crossing them.	Reverence
3. Read no letters, books, or papers in company, but when there is a necessity for the doing of it, you must ask leave. Come not near the books or writings of another so as to read them or give your opinion of them unasked; also look not nigh when another is writing a letter.	Keeping privacy
4. Show not yourself glad at the misfortune of another, though he were your enemy.	Empathy
5. When you see a crime punished, you may be inwardly pleased; but always show pity to the suffering offender.	Mercy
6. If any one comes to speak to you while you are sitting, stand up, though he be your inferior, and when you present seats, let it be to everyone according to his degree.	Equality
7. In writing or speaking, give every person his due title according to his degree and the custom of the place.	Politeness
8. Strive not with your superiors in argument, but always submit your argument to others with modesty.	Modesty
9. Do not express joy before one is sick or in pain, for that contrary passion will aggravate his misery.	Sympathy
10. Being to advise or reprehend any one, consider whether it ought to be in public or in private, presently or at some other time; in what terms to do it; and in reproving show no sign of choler, but do it with all sweetness and mildness.	Tenderness
11. Mock not nor jest at any thing of importance; break no jests that are sharp, biting, and if you deliver any thing witty and pleasant, abstain from laughing thereat yourself.	Self control
12. Use no reproachful language against any one; neither curse nor revile.	Politeness
13. Be not hasty to believe flying reports to the disparagement of any.	Reasoning
14. Associate yourself with men of good quality if you esteem your own reputation; for it is better to be alone than in bad company.	Keeping company
15. Let your conversation be without malice or envy, for it is a sign of a tractable and commendable nature, and in all causes of passion admit reason to govern.	Transparency
16. Never express anything unbecoming, nor act against the rules moral before your inferiors.	Confidence

their terms, but that self-control does not prevent them from taking strong actions or expressing justified anger when important matters are at stake.

They try to take the long view when the more distant goal is clearly superior to the immediate one (being human, they will not always succeed in doing so). When this is difficult they look for ways to force themselves to do the right thing.

Among these such habits are practicing routine ways of acting, each rather unimportant in itself, but, taken together, producing action on behalf of quite important sensibilities. For example: the habit of courtesy (which over the long run alerts us to the feelings of others), the habit of punctuality (which disposes us to be dutiful in the exercise of our responsibilities and confirms to others that we have a sense of duty), and the habit of practice (by which we master skills and proclaim to others that they are capable of excellence). They are capable of seeing themselves as others see them and, even more important, as they wish the *noblest* others to see them.

Civility by Tom Morris

Tom Morris, in *If Aristotle Ran General Motors* (Morris, 1997), advocated the cause of civility in general and in business institutions, in particular. He identified civility as the quest for the truth, goodness, beauty, and unity. He pointed out the civil obligations of management, as well as the ethical obligations of workers. He lamented the vanishing dream (he called it the "pursuit of happiness") in business situations, the nature of business excellence, and the imperative of business values as well as personal commitments.

Morris conceptualized four dimensions of civility. He thought together they constituted a square of an elevated state of human sensibility. These include the following (pp. 25–127):

> *First*, an intellectual ability that aims at acting honestly. In this dimension, civil business people should have an accurate map of what it is they steer. Such a map guides them in discerning the needs of their clients, the moves of competitors, benefiting from the experience of associates, and serving all others well. Civil business people cultivate an environment in which people are not afraid to be honest with each other, frontline workers and managers are not reluctant to pass on a hard truth to their superiors without offending them, and everyone is pleased to ask (and be asked) what one would think of this commodity and to respond truthfully.

> *Second*, an aesthetic ability that aims at *beauty*. In this dimension, Morris examines the power of beauty in liberating the human spirit of workers. He describes the civility of beauty as the "bread of happiness,"

and civil workplaces as locations where nature may heal and cheer the body and the soul alike. Morris explains that beautiful buildings express the philosophical beliefs about what human beings are and aspire to, and what they cherish in order to experience the highest levels of happiness and excellence at work.

Third, a stern intent to achieve goodness. In this dimension, Morris defines goodness as "true nobility, a special mixture of truth and beauty." It 's special because the elements of truth and beauty are found in it. Morris describes goodness as the "soil within which the soul can grow and flourish." Without it, human beings wither and harden and spiritually die. As such, goodness is a necessary condition for healthy relationships and for thriving communities.

Fourth, a spiritual ability to accomplish unity. In this dimension, Morris defines the spiritual ability as the aspect of our nature that strives for unity and connectedness. He added that most people seem to spend the majority of their waking hours at work. The workplace therefore may be thought of as the new neighborhood, and the workers as one's extended family. Having stated that, Morris expected that civil workers should interact with each other in an environment of friendship, fairness, openness, and appreciation. Neglecting this kind of genuine sentiment, Morris points out, is the major reason why so many people in American business feel more victimized than helped by the latest management techniques and companywide processes for improvement.

Civility by James O'Toole

James O'Toole, in *Leading Change: Overcoming the Ideology of Comfort and the Tyranny of Custom* (1997), discussed principles of civility in the private sector. His prescriptions are equally suitable to public enterprises, including criminal justice institutions. He suggested that every chief executive officer should at least possess and exercise four main characteristics of civility:

1. *Integrity*, the capacity to overcome any obstacle without compromising the main rules of fairness. For example, he mentioned Abraham Lincoln's unwavering belief in the immorality of slavery.

2. *Trust*, the capacity to keep promises and to deliver fully on each promise as originally contracted. For example, he cited Washington's ability to diffuse his courage and optimism among his troops, and later the nation, as a by-product of the trust he earned by serving them.

3. *Listening*, the will and capacity to understand the needs of those whom one serves or anyone who asks for assistance if such assistance is available to offer. For example, he cited Lincoln's will

and capacity to benefit from the strong and antagonistic views of two unfriendly members of his cabinet even during the times when the American Civil War was not going in the Union's favor.

4. *Respect for followers*, the ability to act civilly toward all subordinates (whether one likes them or not) and to support them whenever possible to achieve higher positions if they are qualified to achieve. For example, O'Toole again cited Jefferson, who believed that "too much leadership—particularly of the wrong kind—is tyranny."

O'Toole called individuals who possess and exercise these four virtues *Rushmoreans*, after the famous Mount Rushmore. The title is indicative of the four most revered presidents in American history: Washington, the father of the nation; Jefferson, the prophet and protector of democracy; Lincoln, the unifier of the Union and the emancipator of the slaves; and Theodore Roosevelt, the expander of the nation— from the Atlantic to the Pacific.

VIII: Five Stories to Remember

The following five stories are presented to illustrate the practice of civility as the human foundation of character, one that many enlightened thinkers consider even higher than intellect. The reason for this assertion was justifiable because intelligent persons can commit intelligent crimes, but civil persons are capable of preventing such thoughts before they materialize.

1 Rudeness at the Houston Airport

It was about 10:15 P.M. at the George Bush International Airport in Houston, Texas, when a criminal justice professor from Huntsville, Texas, arrived from Albuquerque. The professor had lectured the day before at the International Police Academy in Roswell on issues of police ethics and integrity. To get back to Huntsville (65 miles north of the airport), he first had to take the shuttle bus that connects the airport with the city's parking lot.

After picking up his luggage from the airport carousel, the professor exited the airport gate and waited in line with the other passengers who were awaiting the next shuttle bus. A few minutes later, a young couple who appeared to be husband and wife arrived and "elbowed" their way in line ahead of the waiting professor. The professor politely called that to their attention and asked them to be more considerate of the civility principle "first come, first served." The couple did not respond and ignored the professor's remark. When the professor repeated his request the husband became hostile, accusing the professor of being rude.

The professor kept quiet to avoid creating an unnecessary scene, especially when the waiting passengers were visibly tired and the time was getting late. When the shuttle bus finally arrived, everyone got onboard and remained silent. Upon reaching his parked car, the professor packed his luggage in the car's trunk and drove off toward the parking lot's exit, which was about 200 yards away. Halfway through that distance, the professor noticed two persons in the foggy night flagging down passing cars as if they needed immediate assistance. Upon looking closely, the professor was surprised to find that these two persons were indeed the same couple who had insulted him earlier while waiting for the shuttle bus outside the airport. The professor wondered whether, in light of their previous rudeness, he should offer them assistance or simply drive off as a way of getting even with their previous act of rudeness. He nevertheless stopped and inquired what kind of assistance they needed. When the couple identified who the driver was, they were taken by surprise. They looked embarrassed and could not look straight into the professor's eyes. The husband ashamedly asked whether the professor had a jumper cable because their car's battery was dead. The professor hesitated for a moment and then decided to offer them the jumper cable they needed. It took the husband about 10 minutes to start up his car. During that period of time, the couple stood silently and "stonelike." Before the professor drove off, the husband looked up at the professor's face and said "thank you." But the wife followed by adding the words "we are sorry." The professor involved in this case has his name on the cover of your book. This story is a graphic testament to the true essence of what civility ought to be: sacrifice.

2 The Finnish Minister

It was lunchtime in Helsinki, Finland, several years ago. The same criminal justice professor had finished a series of lectures at the University of Turku and had a couple of days for sightseeing in the capital city of Helsinki. The day was Wednesday, a special day for Rotarians (members of the Rotary club worldwide) to eat lunch together. The weekly lunch has been an old tradition designed to strengthen brotherhood among the members, to listen to a humanitarian speaker, and to enjoy each other's company. Rotarians who cannot keep this tradition in their hometowns are expected to make up for it by performing the same ritual at the town or country they are at, at the time.

The professor entered the hotel restaurant where the Finnish Rotarians were eating. There were about 300 of them. The professor noted an available table labeled "foreign guests only." Being a guest and a foreigner, he sat alone at that table. As he was eating, he noticed from some distance a tall, well-dressed Rotarian stand up from his seat and walk toward the professor's table. The man did not introduce himself but just asked if he could sit down to keep the professor company. He spoke fluent English and talked about his numerous visits to the United States. They spoke about many subjects, including sports, sociology, psychology, the environment, and, of course, politics and criminal justice. After they finished their lunch, the Finnish man—who still did not introduce himself to the professor—offered to give him a ride to his hotel. The professor politely declined in the beginning as he was hesitant to bother a stranger he had never met before. The Finnish man insisted, and finally the professor accepted. As both of them exited the hotel, the professor noticed a big black limousine that looked like an official vehicle with a driver waiting for the mysterious man. The Finnish man motioned to the driver to step out of the car and then sat in the driver's seat and motioned the professor to sit in the front passenger's seat. As they were both seated, the Finnish man put his seat belt on and alerted the professor to do the same saying, "I signed the law."

As they reached the professor's hotel, and before the professor exited the vehicle, he was curious to know who that mysterious man was, and why he paid so much attention to a foreigner he just met. The professor politely, but persistently, asked the Finnish man who he was. The man paused, lowered his head, and softly replied, "I am the vice president of Finland." The professor was dumbfounded and impressed by the behavior of such a high official who acted so civilly. Not only did the vice president not reveal who he was for fear of intimidating his guest, but he also took the time from his busy schedule to give a ride to a fellow Rotarian for no reason than that it was the civil thing to do for a fellow Rotarian in a foreign country. To make his virtue even more original, he offered the car ride knowing he would never meet the professor again. This story is a graphic testament to the true essence of civility.

3 Is There Crime in New Zealand?

It was a few years ago when this professor was invited to lecture at the University of Canterbury in Christchurch, New Zealand. The university was impressive, the students respectful, and the academic environment comforting. After the time of his visit, the professor—trying to kill some idle time—walked the streets of the city as well as an adjacent city trying to take pictures of police activities, police officers, or police equipment. For two days he tried but failed. There were no visible police cars, patrol officers, or even cameras hanging on traffic signs. Notwithstanding, the professor was unable to witness any criminal acts, traffic violations, disputes, or even hear loud voices. There were also no homeless persons, drunks, or loiterers. The people walked the streets calmly and pleasantly, crossed the streets at the designated intersections, and demonstrated a high level of respect to one another's rights. Furthermore, taxicabs were clean and parked in an orderly manner. People awaiting buses stood patiently in a queue and engaged in what seemed like a nice party.

At the end of the trip, the professor visited with the city's police chief and raised the issue of why no police officers were visible on the streets. Casually, the professor asked "Chief, where are the police?" The chief was not amused. He paused for a short time and answered authoritatively, "Professor, where is the crime?" The police chief, who turned out to be a graduate of the FBI Academy, and the professor engaged in a professional discussion about the role of civility in reducing crime in New Zealand, as well as the role of thousands of Japanese families whom the police chief accredited with raising the level of civility in New Zealand because of their gentle nature, high educational level, and willingness to work hard, yet silently and honorably. Given this level of civility, the police preferred to promote civility by reducing their presence on the streets lest the residents feel the police did not trust them. This story is graphic testament to the essence of civility: the presence of an enlightened populace.

4 Civility among Enemies

The first person in this story is Admiral Chester Nimitz, commander of the American Navy in the Pacific during World War II. The other is German Grand Admiral Karl Dönitz, head of the German Navy in the Atlantic. Both were also the heads of their submarine divisions in their respective navies. Throughout the years of war, they came to know a great deal about each other: their strategies, styles of attack, behavior on the seas, and how they rescue and treat their enemies sailors when fallen—consistent with the rules of war. During the war, Dönitz's submarines were lethal in the Atlantic and scored many more hits on the American ships than vice versa. Indeed, Dönitz wrote to Hitler requesting 300 more submarines so that he single-handedly would win the war. Before Hitler's suicide, he appointed Dönitz to fill his place as Führer of Germany. Dönitz only lasted 8 days in this capacity before Germany surrendered. Soon after, Dönitz was arrested by the American forces and brought to Nuremberg to be tried as a war criminal.

Unlike other German defendants, Dönitz was not charged with crimes against humanity nor was he involved with the Holocaust affair. He was charged only with committing crimes against the laws of war. Dönitz believed he would certainly be hung with the rest of his comrades. But an extraordinary event of civility occurred. Nimitz—who still had never met his counterpart—appeared in court to testify in favor of his most famous rival. He defended him as a professional mariner, a decent man who saved enemy sailors, an officer who never tortured or humiliated his enemy sailors, and a leader who kept his sailors from humiliating American prisoners of war. Nimitz concluded his defense by stating that "nothing Admiral Dönitz did which he himself [Nimitz] did not do." As a result, Dönitz's life was spared. He was sentenced to 10 years in Spandau prison. This sentence was later reduced to 5 years, during which he devoted himself to writing his memoirs, titled *Ten Years and Twenty Days*. Dönitz dedicated his book to Admiral Nimitz. It was most noteworthy that during the trial, numerous Allied Naval officers sent letters to Admiral Dönitz expressing their dismay over the verdict of his trial. Dönitz died of natural causes in December 1980. Thus ended the most civil relationship between two giant mariners who had some years back taken an oath to destroy each other. This story is another graphic testament to the essence of civility: good-faith service.

5 The Pope Who Made Civility a Religion

Pope John Paul II (Karol Jozef Wojtyla) was elected to the papacy in October 1978. Upon graduation from Marcin Wadowice, he enrolled in Krakow's Jagiellonian University. When the Nazi forces closed the university in 1939, he worked in a quarry to earn his living. In 1942, aware of his call to the priesthood, he began courses in a clandestine seminary of Krakow. He was ordained to the priesthood in 1946. After several quick promotions, he served 30 years as professor of moral theology and social ethics in the Faculty of Theology of Lublin. He also became the chaplain for the university students. Later he was appointed archbishop of Kracow by Pope Paul VI and became a cardinal in 1967. In 1978, the cardinals elected him pope. He took the name of John Paul II and devoted himself to upgrading the 2000-year-old papacy into a new culture of true humility, service, and religiosity. As such, Pope John Paul II had more meetings with the peoples of God and the leaders of nations than any of his predecessors. He presented the world with a different kind of leadership based on love, dignity, and sacrifice. More than 17 million people participated in the General Audiences he held every Wednesday, and millions of the people of the faith met him during pastoral visits in Italy and around the world. He reformed the Eastern and Western Codes of canon law, created new institutions, and reorganized the Roman Curia. Throughout his service at the Vatican and his travels around the world he never forgot his years of teaching ethics at Lublin.

Although hundreds of books were written about Pope John Paul II, he treated civility as an integral part of religiosity. He made them one and the same—one cannot be religious without being civil nor civil without being spiritual. He visited the poorest of the poor as well as wealthy nations, whether they were Muslim, Jewish, Christian, or atheist.

Throughout his papacy, John Paul II had three moral trademarks. Each of them changed the ancient protocols of the Vatican. These were (1) kneeling and kissing the land of each country he visited the moment he came down from his plane as a mark of blessing, redemption, and hope; (2) visiting Mehmet Ali Agca, the man who would have been his assassin at the Basilica Square, in his prison cell and pardoning him; and (3) changing the bureaucracy of the Vatican in a manner that assures humility and equality throughout the human race.

Kissing the Ground of the Tarmac: John Paul II held his pontificate for 27 years (1978–2005). He traveled extensively. He made 104 pastoral visits outside Italy and 146 within Italy. He had more meetings than any of his predecessors with the people of God and the leaders of nations. He met with 738 heads of state. His 2000 jubilee was attended by 8 million pilgrims. His love for young people brought him to establish the World Youth Days, when millions of young people came to hear him and embrace him. He created 231 new cardinals. More important, he spent most of his life denouncing fascist and communist regimes and freeing the oppressed countries under Soviet domination. At the end of his life, he was diagnosed with Parkinson's disease. He died in April 2005.

He left behind one of the most civil gestures symbolizing love, reverence, humility, equality, and hope that no other pope ever attempted before him. Each time his plane landed on foreign land (other than Italy), he climbed down the plane's stairs and, before meeting with any waiting head of a state, prime minister, or dignitary on the receiving line, he took a couple of minutes to kneel down and kiss the earth of the country he was visiting, including saying a prayer for the people he was about to meet.

Pardoning His Would-Be Assassin Face to Face: Mehmet Ali Agca was the Turkish would-be assassin of Pope John Paul II in Saint Peter's Square on May 13, 1981. He shot him four times. The Pope was seriously wounded and underwent several surgeries.

Mehmet Ali Agca was a professional assassin, trained by the Russian secret service in Yemen. He reportedly was instructed to travel to Italy and kill the pope during his weekly ride around the Vatican Square blessing the multitudes of worshipers. The conspirators were eager to kill the pope because he was against communism and encouraged the small Soviet republics to secede from the Soviet Union. Mr. Mehmet, a member of the Grey Wolves far-right militant group, was tried in Rome and sentenced to 20 years in prison before his sentence was commuted to 10 years.

When the pope recovered, one of his first acts was to visit his would-be assassin in the Italian prison of Rebibbia. When they met in Mehmet's cell, the pope touched him and talked with him for a long time, and then the pope prayed with Mehmet and wished him well. The pope's rationale, in addition to "loving one's enemies" was his belief that because Mehmet was a professional assassin, he was not the initiative behind the killing attempt, but merely a tool that might not have known what he was doing. The pope later met with Mr. Mehmet's mother.

He embraced her and prayed with her. When the pope much later was sick in the hospital with another illness, Mr. Acga reportedly sent him a personal get-well card.

The act of the pope to go to the prison and grant pardon to the man who would have been his killer demonstrates an unheard of act of civility and one of the world's greatest and most courageous gestures.

Changing the Elitist Practices of the Church: When Cardinal Wojtyla was elected pope, he obviously was not fully aware of the inner procedures and bureaucracies of the Roman Basilica. Originally, Catholic procedures required that when the pope holds an audience for the cardinals, the bishops, and the priests, the pope would sit on a large throne-like golden chair elevated about 3 feet from the floor. He was not supposed to stand up during the audience. The groups of cardinals, bishops, and priests were to line up to approach the pope's seat, and each would climb up three steps and then bend down and kiss the pope's ring (or hand). This procedure was standard procedure in the Vatican for several centuries, if not since the Catholic church was born. No Pope ever before attempted to change this protocol.

But when Pope John Paul II was first ushered to his golden throne to meet his cardinals and bishops, he angrily refused the protocol of having to sit down, loudly declaring "I receive my brothers standing up!" By these words, the pope abolished an ancient symbol of dominion, hubris, and undue pride and ushered in one of the greatest symbols of ecclesial civility.

Conclusions

This might be the most important chapter in this book. Our journey started in 1829 when Robert Peel was looking for an optimal method to make a country safe to govern itself. Our journey was tedious until we discovered the moderate, faithful, and honest way to govern each other. But you will never forget that civility—if applied faithfully—can increase the safety, security, and happiness of citizens and save nations billions of dollars in return. The world was not supposed to be so complicated, but it is the people who make it this way. Also keep in mind that philosopher Arthur Schopenhauer assured us that "we can conquer the world because we can understand it." If so, then the role of criminal justice (except in the most violent crimes) must be civil, fair, reasonable, and conducive to the common good. Correctional officers must be even more patient because society has charged them with transforming a generation of human beings who were not born with crime but inherited it from us, the parents, the priests, the merchants, as well as police officers, correctional officers, and probation/parole officers.

This book has been divided into three topical sections. First, what is the philosophical method and how it can be used, including moral principles (Chapters 1–5). Second, a thematic section of four universal vices. These vices are epidemic to the human race and will continue to happen because it is the nature of institutions where workers have their agendas of hedonism, secrecy, and selfishness (Chapters 6–9). Third, this book focuses specifically on the trademark subjects of police, corrections, and probation and parole within the criminal justice discipline. The rest of the book warns against acquiring bad habits among leaders and practitioners and how we can purge these habits from our hearts and minds. Finally, remember that the civility of criminal justice is now in your hands. Unless it is there, nothing is there!

Review Questions

1. Discuss and explain the phrase "all nations have crime but only a civil nation can offer justice."

2. Discuss and explain Aristotle's phrase "excellence is not an act, it is a habit." How can this assist in the conduct of criminal justice today?

3. Why does a higher level of civility lead to a lower crime rate?

4. Discuss and explain the natural relationship between ethics, morality, and civility. Give examples.

5. Give your own definition of *civility*. Be precise.

6. Discuss and explain the characteristics of Aristotle's polis. Why is it so important to the idea of civility?

7. Define *logic* and present a sample of a logical assumption that each student should know and apply.

8. Why in the study of civility is preserving justice above all virtues?

9. Define and discuss the principle of the "common good."

10. How does civility according to James Wilson differ from civility according to Tom Morris?

11. Why does James O'Toole emphasize civility in the workplace?

12. Why was the pope's refusal to sit while the cardinals filed by him such a great ethical change?

References

Carter, S. L. (1998). *Civility: Manners, Morals, and the Etiquette of Democracy.* New York: Basic Books.

Hale, J. (1994). *The Civilization of Europe in the Renaissance.* New York: Touchstone.

Maslow, A. (1971). *The Farther Reaches of Human Nature.* New York: Viking Penguin.

Miller, R., & Browning, S. L. (2004). *For the Common Good: A Critical Examination of Law and Social Control.* Durham, NC: Carolina Academic Press.

Morris, T. (1997). *If Aristotle Ran General Motors.* New York: Henry Holt and Company.

O'Toole, J. (1995). *Leading Change.* San Francisco: Jossey-Bass Publishers.

Quinn, D. (1999). *Beyond Civilization.* New York: Three Rivers Press.

Rouner, L. (2000). *Civility.* South Bend, IN: University of Notre Dame Press.

Sandel, M. (2009). *Justice: What Is the Right Thing to Do?* New York: Farrar, Straus, and Giroux.

Shils, E. (1997). *The Virtue of Civility.* Indianapolis, IN: Liberty Fund, Inc.

Souryal, S. (2007). *Ethics in Criminal Justice: In Search of the Truth.* Newark, NJ: Lexis Nexis.

Teske, R. (1995). *Crime and Justice in Texas.* Huntsville, TX: Criminal Justice Center, Sam Houston State University.

Thompson, O. (1993). *A History of Sin.* New York: Barnes & Noble Books.

Transparency International (2003). *Transparency International Corruption Perceptions Index.* Berlin: Author.

Transparency International (2008). *Annual Report.* Berlin: Author.

Washington, G. (1988). *Rules of Civility & Decent Behaviour in Company and Conversation.* Bedford, MA: Applewood Books.

Wilson, J. Q. (1993). *The Moral Sense.* New York: The Free Press.

15
What Can Be Done to Restore Ethics?
Concluding Comments

A man's mind, once stretched by a new idea, can never go back to its original dimensions.

Oliver Wendell Holmes Jr.

Speech was given to man, not that men might therewith deceive one another, but that one might make known his thoughts to another.

Saint Augustine

He is not wise to me who is wise in words only, but he who is wise in deeds.

Saint Gregory

To make no mistakes is not in the power of man; but from their errors and mistakes the wise and good learn wisdom for the future.

Plutarch

Reflections and Ethical Lessons to Teach

We have come a long way together since our initial tour of the Ethics Hall of Fame. We have learned the philosophy of ethics, the history of ethics, the origins of ethics, the categories of ethics, and how ethical judgments can be made. We have also studied the sources of criminal justice ethics and the root sins that criminal justice practitioners should avoid. Finally we spent a longer time examining the ethics of policing, corrections, and probation and parole.

In discussing what can be done to restore, or reinforce, ethics in criminal justice agencies, I shall be brief. The worth of what follows will depend on your understanding and appreciation of what has already been said. It is now time for your knowledge, reasoning, and conscience to work for you toward the achievement of justice—the essence and *summum bonum* of this book. What can be done to restore ethics at your agency, in your classroom, in your home, or simply in your day-to-day life, will depend on you.

As a parting note, I will propose to you some recommendations that I consider essential. I have reached these conclusions from many years of reading, reflection, and experience in the field of criminal justice. In presenting these recommendations, I believe no further narrative is necessary, because by now we clearly understand.

1. **Talk about ethics.** Make it a household term. The power of ethics is the power of the truth. It will make you stronger as a person, as a criminal justice practitioner, and as an agent of change.

2. **If you search for the truth, you will find it.** Stick with principles, because anything that is not grounded in principle is meaningless. Transcend opinions, beliefs, desires, conveniences, and, most certainly, political correctness. Half-truths or convenient compromises do not suffice.

3. **Demand ethical solutions to common problems.** Do not succumb to social, legal, or organizational clichés. In addition to laws and regulations, seek out what is right and avoid what is wrong.

4. **Create an environment conducive to civility everywhere you are.** Set the tone for civil thoughts, talks, and interactions. These can exhilarate your mind and soul. Be optimistic—it is better to light a candle than to curse the darkness.

5. **Do not laugh at unethical statements, stories, slurs, or jokes.** They are not funny anymore. Remember that little people laugh at little things, and the civilization of people is also measured by what they do *not* laugh at.

6. **Reinforce ethical principles by rewarding those who practice them,** regardless of how minute the practice or how symbolic the reward.

7. **Read philosophical literature and enjoy good books.** They can reinforce your ethical stamina. Refer them to your subordinates, colleagues, and superiors, so that they might grow along with you.

8. **Monitor your commitment to justice, the *summum bonum* of all virtues.** Test your sense of justice by regularly examining your decisions—whom they favored and whom they did not, and why.

9. **Keep your soul active, clean, alert, and rejuvenated.** Develop a passion for defending right causes and denouncing wrong ones—especially if they do not involve you. It is more ethically rewarding to defend others than to defend yourself.

10. **Ethics must be rendered first and foremost by you.** Others should account for their own.

An Ethical Lesson to Teach Criminal Justice Practitioners

1. America is great because America is good ... If it ceases to be good, it will cease to be great (Thomas Jefferson).

2. In a free society, the solutions to human problems can be reached only through reasoning and goodwill.

3. If you hate violence and disagree with politics, the only alternative left is education (George Orwell).

4. The demise of any person diminishes us all, because we are involved in mankind.

5. Criminal justice without justice is a farce.

6. The foundation of all ethics is honesty, fidelity, and obligation.

7. Legal ethics is a misnomer; laws can only deter us from doing wrong deeds, they cannot make us do good and honorable deeds.

8. The civility of societies can also be measured by how few prisoners they keep.

9. All the constitutions of the world cannot protect an African American, a Jew, or a foreigner from hatred and prejudice.

10. All the rules and regulations of government cannot force excellence on workers. They offer excellence only voluntarily, and in return for fair treatment.

11. Professionalism without goodness is empty and often dangerous.

12. Every policy, act, or decision not based on principle is questionable and often injurious.

13. At the workplace, loyalty to principles is more worthy than loyalty to persons, regardless of who they are.

14. A leader must be virtuous to represent a virtuous organization (George Washington).

NAME INDEX

SUBJECT INDEX

A FAREWELL NOTE

This is the first time I include a farewell note in my book. Yet because this book is unique in its objectives, context, style, and passion, I felt it would be incomplete without it. Throughout this book we have been searching for the truth of the conduct of criminal justice and the public at large, especially in the United States. We used reasoning and logic to capture the objective truth. Also, while this book could be easily applied universally, the readers may have reasoning and ambitions that are different from the assumptions of this book. For that reason, perhaps, I kept a wide separation between the legal, social, practical, and cultural aspects of life and the sacred, evangelistic, theological, or religious—for obvious reasons. Also remember that this book had to be written from a philosophical perspective because any other perspective is bound to be either anecdotal or authoritative: The rich and powerful can impose their views on the poor and the powerless who cannot understand the difference between power and truth.

Sam S. Souryal
icc_sss@shsu.edu